THE LIFE AND TIMES
OF
WILLIAM HOWARD TAFT

Books by Henry F. Pringle

ALFRED E. SMITH: *A Critical Study.*

BIG FROGS.

THEODORE ROOSEVELT: *A Biography.*

THE LIFE AND TIMES OF
WILLIAM HOWARD TAFT: *A Biography.*

Photo by J. Knowles Bishop

THE PRESIDENT—BEFORE THE WINDS OF ADVERSITY BEGAN TO BLOW

William Howard Taft

The Life and Times

By

HENRY PRINGLE

A Biography in Two Volumes
★ Volume One ★

Published by American Political Biography Press

Newtown, CT

Published by
AMERICAN POLITICAL BIOGRAPHY PRESS

Library of Congress Catalog Card Number 97-74247
ISBN Number 978-0-945707-19-6

AMERICAN POLITICAL BIOGRAPHY PRESS
39 Boggs Hill
Newtown, Connecticut
06470-1971
Tel: (203) 270-9777 ✧ Fax: (203) 270-0091
E-Mail: APBPress@EarthLink.Net

WWW.APBPRESS.COM

This is the third printing of the first edition.

All publications of
AMERICAN POLITICAL BIOGRAPHY PRESS
Are dedicated to my wife
Ellen and our two children
Katherine and William II

This particular book is
Dedicated to:

Stuart Benedict, Bruce Ipe & Richard Wolstoncroft

Henry Pringle
Dedicated his work
To
Dr. I.C. Rubin
WHO HAS SUPERVISED THE
PUBLICATION OF TWO
FAR MORE IMPORTANT EDITIONS
With Love and Gratitude

FOREWORD

<hr>

IT IS not improbable that William Howard Taft would disapprove of certain parts of this biography. Outwardly, he was the soul of decorum; too much so, perhaps, for his own good. Beneath the decorum, however, was a man with very pronounced views. He had emphatic opinions about people as well as issues and these opinions were often set forth in his private letters. "Confidential and personal" was the warning on many of his communications. Taft would have been scandalized had they been published while he was alive.

This life of Taft is authorized but not official. The distinction is vital. The author was given unrestricted access to all the hundreds of thousands of letters in the Taft collection at the Library of Congress and to all other available material. This was due entirely to the very unusual position taken by Robert, Charles and Helen Taft (now Mrs. Frederick J. Manning). They are the owners of their father's papers and are his literary executors. They permitted the author to wander at will through the enormous treasure house which the collection is. He could quote as he pleased. He could draw what judgments he liked. The sole restriction was the logical one against involving the Taft estate in a libel suit. This book, then, has no trace of official, family endorsement. The literary executors did not even read the manuscript in its present, final, revised form.

Needless to say, then, the executors are in no way responsible for any statement I have made concerning their father or anybody else or for any conclusions I have drawn.

But to their unfailing aid, assistance and patience I must pay full tribute. More than to any other single person, on the other hand, I am indebted to Professor Manning of the History Department, Swarthmore College. Without his help and learning, particularly with respect to the chapters on the Supreme Court, the book could not have been written. Yet he, too, is hereby absolved from all responsibility.

It should be noted, perhaps, that this is not a legalistic account of a lawyer who became President and then Chief Justice. The writer has had no training in the law. I hope that it is an objective account of a man whom the public sometimes regarded as too large and too jolly but whose soul was, in fact, often tortured.

H. F. P.

New York, July 21, 1939

CONTENTS

FOREWORD   vii

I.   SO FAT, SO CHERUBIC   3

II.   BIG LUB   20

III.   AND FOR YALE   31

IV.   RELUCTANT FEET   47

V.   THE LOVER, SIGHING   69

VI.   CRUSADER FOR A TIME   83

VII.   THE FIRST HARBOR   93

VIII.   AMONG THE BIGWIGS   108

IX.   THE SECOND HARBOR   121

X.   THE WORLD OUTSIDE   148

XI.   HALF DEVIL AND HALF CHILD   163

XII.   HEAT AND WORK   181

XIII.   NO TAWDRY RULE OF KINGS   200

XIV.   THE WICKED PRIESTS   220

XV.   I NEED YOU; COME HOME   237

XVI.   WAR LORD   256

XVII.   TROUBLE-SHOOTER AT HOME   272

XVIII. TROUBLE-SHOOTER ABROAD   291

XIX.   SURRENDER   311

XX.   GOOD OLD BILL   334

x CONTENTS

XXI.   VICTORY, PERHAPS   358

XXII.   A NEW KING RIDES   371

XXIII.   THE LONELY HOUSE   399

XXIV.   LEGACY OF DOOM   418

XXV.   DARKENING SKIES   442

XXVI.   THE INEVITABLE VILLAIN   470

XXVII.   MY DEAR GIFFORD . . .   491

XXVIII.   FORGOTTEN CREDITS   515

XXIX.   THE HUNTER RETURNS   538

LIST OF ILLUSTRATIONS

———

THE PRESIDENT—BEFORE THE WINDS OF ADVERSITY BEGAN TO BLOW

Frontispiece

OPPOSITE PAGE

ALPHONSO TAFT—SOON AFTER HIS ARRIVAL IN CINCINNATI   20

TAFT WITH HIS MOTHER   21

WILLIAM H. TAFT, AGE 10   52

TAFT'S BOYHOOD HOME ON MT. AUBURN, CINCINNATI   53

WILLIAM HOWARD TAFT AND HIGH SCHOOL CLASSMATES   84

TAFT IN HIS TWENTIES   85

ALPHONSO TAFT   116

MRS. ALPHONSO TAFT   117

MR. AND MRS. JOHN HERRON   148

FASCINATING NELLIE HERRON   149

TOM CAMPBELL, TAFT'S FIRST ADVERSARY   180

BOSS JAMES B. COX OF CINCINNATI   180

EN ROUTE TO THE PHILIPPINES   181

THE CIVIL GOVERNOR OF THE PHILIPPINES   212

THE CIVIL GOVERNOR'S AMPLE BATHTUB   212

TAFT AS CIVIL GOVERNOR OF THE PHILIPPINES   213

"HOW IS THE HORSE?"   244

"I HAVE NO APTITUDE FOR MANAGING AN ARMY"   245

CARTOON FROM THE WASHINGTON POST   276

xi

OPPOSITE PAGE

CARTOON FROM COLLIER'S   277

THE BASEBALL FAN. WASHINGTON, 1908-1909   308

SECRETARY OF WAR TAFT INSPECTING PANAMA   309

NOT "IMMEDIATE" FOR THE SECRETARY OF WAR   340

AWAKE AND ASLEEP   341

CARTOON FROM THE WASHINGTON POST   372

FROM A CONTEMPORARY CARTOON   373

THE TAFT SMILE   404

THE AGE OF PHOTOGRAPHY IN POLITICS   405

CARTOON FROM THE NEW YORK WORLD   436

THE CHUCKLE BEGINS—THE CHUCKLE EXPLODES   437

LETTERS ATTACKING TAFT AS A UNITARIAN   468

SILK HAT—SOFT HAT   469

SENATOR HENRY CABOT LODGE AND PRESIDENT TAFT   500

THE FIRST LADY   501

MRS. TAFT AND THE PRESIDENT   532

TAFT THE SPORTSMAN   533

THE LIFE AND TIMES
OF
WILLIAM HOWARD TAFT

CHAPTER I

SO FAT, SO CHERUBIC

THE INFANT was immediately called Willie, of course; no other name was possible for so round, so fat, so cherubic a child. "He is very large of his age and grows fat every day. . . . He has such a large waist, that he cannot wear any of the dresses that are made with belts," wrote his mother when Willie was seven weeks old.[1] "He spreads his hands to anyone who will take him and his face is wreathed in smiles at the slightest provocation," she added.[2] At five and a half months, he had "a solitary dimple in one cheek which contributes much to his beauty."[3] And in the remote, imponderable stretches of the future— when a not too-friendly fate had forced him into the highest office in the land— it was to be cruelly said of him that he was "a large, good-natured body, entirely surrounded by people who know exactly what they want."[4]

But fat men are not necessarily jolly. Corpulence may cushion the bones but it does not cushion nerves. Fat men, although they must struggle against lethargy, are not necessarily weak. It should be noted, in any event, that the diminutive, Willie, was abandoned before many years had passed. He became Bill Taft of the class of 1878 at Yale. To his intimates, in the later years, he was always known as Will and he so signed himself in letters.

By the time he was eight years old his mother was admitting that she was "prouder of him" than of the three younger children who had followed in rapid succession.[5] His father agreed, when the boy was fifteen, that Will was "the foremost and I am inclined to think he will always be so."[6] Yet fat, the sheer, physical handicap of being far too heavy, was a thing he had to contend with as long as he lived.

[1] Louise Taft to Delia Torrey, Nov. 8, 1857. [2] *Idem*, Feb. 12, 1858. [3] Louise Taft to Susan H. Torrey, Feb. 28, 1858. [4] Hapgood, Norman, *The Changing Years*, p. 183. [5] Louise Taft to S. D. Torrey, June 6, 1866. [6] Alphonso Taft to S. D. Torrey, Oct. 16, 1872.

3

Cincinnati was his birthplace. The meandering Ohio River, so lovely a stream— even if muddy— that the French had once musically called it "La Belle Rivière," lay beneath the city. The emerald slopes of Kentucky were beyond. But the hillside house where William Howard Taft was born on September 15, 1857, a Tuesday, was a New England home. Alphonso Taft, his father, had pushed westward from Vermont two decades before. His mother, who was Alphonso's second wife, was a native of Millbury, Massachusetts. The Taft home on Mt. Auburn, then an outlying section of the city, was not, however, a New England house in the sense that it had a graceful Colonial doorway or old furniture that was beautiful because it was simple. The New England émigrés somewhere lost, as they moved across the Alleghenies, their innate and unconscious gift for architecture. Their devotion to hard work remained. So did their Puritanical traits.

"I suppose," wrote Delia Torrey, Mrs. Taft's sister, "we might almost as well ask for a train of cars to go out of its course . . . as to expect Mr. Taft to turn aside from business for the pursuit of pleasure." [7]

The home of Alphonso Taft reflected his substantial standing in Cincinnati as an attorney and a future judge. Louise Torrey had been married to him some four years when Willie was born. She had found the house "most capacious," that a fine view of the countryside was to be had from a back window.[8] It was a large, rather ugly house from the outside with too many cornices and bay windows. It was furnished in the fussy mode of the day. Louise had spent $300 for furniture upon her arrival; the new pieces included a parlor table with a black marble top, which cost $65, a Gothic chair covered with "fiegurell plush," at $15, a whatnot costing $25. Mrs. Taft reported that prospects for a pleasant life in Cincinnati were excellent. Fifty families, most of them from New England, dwelt on Mt. Auburn. Although "none among them are remarkably intellectual or highly cultivated," there would be plenty of social life, if the Tafts wanted it.[9] But young Mrs. Alphonso Taft learned, if she was not aware of it before her marriage, that there was to be little social life. Indeed, there is nothing to indi-

[7] Delia Torrey to Louise Taft, Jan. 15, 1859. [8] Louise Taft to Delia Torrey, Jan. 4, 1854. [9] *Idem,* Jan. 12, 1854.

cate that she desired it any more than did her husband. The Tafts were substantial, not fashionable as compared with another family, the Longworths, who would also rise to distinction in Ohio and the nation. Alphonso Taft, already successful at the bar, was far too serious-minded. He never used liquor and rarely wine. He abhorred smoking as a filthy, wasteful habit.

—2—

So the Tafts played small, if any, part in the more glittering aspects of Cincinnati life. The Queen City of the West, as Longfellow was to christen it, was already dropping behind in the fevered race for supremacy and size among the cities of the United States. In 1840 it had been the sixth largest city, but now the railroad had come and commerce was shifting to St. Louis and Chicago. Cincinnati was still the gateway to the South, however. The Civil War had not yet blasted the markets which lay in Dixie. The Queen City had distinction. It basked in the smiles, all too rare as far as America was concerned, of Charles Dickens. It had survived the scorn of the querulous Mrs. Trollope. In 1860, three years after the birth of Willie Taft, it would be honored by a visit from the Prince of Wales; a ball was to be given for him at Pike's Opera House.[10]

The figures of Alphonso and Louise Taft are not discernible in the tapestry. But there was color to spare, along the streets of Cincinnati, on that September day of 1857 when little Willie Taft was born. The yellowing files of the Cincinnati *Daily Enquirer* bear witness to the importance of the city as a center of commerce, industry and entertainment. The summer droughts had caused low water in the Ohio. There was a scant four feet in the channel between Cincinnati and Louisville. The waterfront was busy, none the less. Thirty vessels were in port. Negroes were loading cotton. On September 15 the magnificent passenger packet, *William M. Morrison,* would leave for New Orleans. At four o'clock on the same day the *Tennessee Belle* would cast forth and thump-thump toward St. Louis. Ten vessels had arrived and four-

[10] Chambrun, Clara Longworth de, *The Making of Nicholas Longworth,* p. 97.

teen had departed, despite the difficulties of shoal water. The river might be dying, but death was still some years away. And along the waterfront, at intervals of every few feet, were saloons for the thirsty.

Yet death was certain for the river. In those same newspaper editions were advertisements of the new, brash railroads. The Little Miami Railroad, of which Alphonso Taft was a director, boasted of rapid service to the East; its "Lightning Express" left at six o'clock each evening for Pittsburgh. The Cincinnati, Hamilton & Dayton Railroad had six trains daily to the Northwest; by its lines, alone, could you reach Chicago with but a single change of cars. The Marietta & Cincinnati Railroad was the best route to Baltimore, Maryland. The smart shippers of Cincinnati were already patronizing these carriers and the riverboats sailed with smaller cargoes. But not one of the railroads except the Pennsylvania—among all the ones which advertised their merits in 1857—survives today under its original name.

The streets of Cincinnati were gay in September, 1857. At Melodeon Hall, where twenty years later Will Taft was to study law in a converted building, a Madame McAllister was to entertain with magic on the night of September 15. At Wood's Theatre, at Sixth and Vine streets, Mrs. Sidney F. Bateman was presenting a comedy, *The Golden Calf, or Marriage à la Mode*. At Baker's New National Theatre, the most luxurious in town, Mrs. Alexino Fisher Baker would be seen for the first time in Cincinnati. The management announced that a New York expert had designed the interior of the playhouse, that even the papier-mâché gilding and carved work in the ceiling had been executed by artists from the eastern metropolis. There were additional sources of entertainment: Madame Blanche, "the world-renowned planet-reader and physician," was seeing clients at her establishment at Fifth Street, near Elm. She could cure, in two hours, nearly every known ailment, and also foretell the future.

It is safe to assume that none of this touched the home on Mt. Auburn where, in due time, young Willie Taft was to play with his older half brothers and his younger brothers and sister. Their father worked very hard; scarcely a night would pass that he was not bent over a table deep in papers or books he had brought from his office. Life had been serious indeed for Alphonso Taft when he had set out from Vermont to make, if he could, a living at the bar in the West. He had been very poor.

"I have not," he assured his father in 1839, "spent one dollar, not a farthing, for any amusement or for anything which was not of immediate and necessary use." [11]

Alphonso Taft achieved success, although never wealth. He was a member of President Grant's Cabinet; also minister to Vienna and to St. Petersburg. He lived to be eighty years old; long enough to have the fires of his pride replenished by the achievements of his sons, particularly by those of Will. Alphonso Taft is entitled to a biographical note in his own right. He was a first citizen of Cincinnati, loved and respected. Men referred, when they spoke of him, to his honesty most of all. Twenty years after Alphonso Taft died his son, in the White House, was informed that political enemies in Cincinnati were spreading rumors that the Tafts were not simple, average Americans, after all. Even his father had been regarded "as a cold, blue-blooded aristocrat." [12] The President turned from the heartaches and perplexities of the 1912 campaign to answer, half in amusement and half in chagrin:

"It is pretty hard to bring poor old father in—who was as little like an aristocrat as anybody I know." [13]

The son was right. Alphonso Taft, although often a leader, had no apparent desire to rise very far above his fellow men. For that matter, William Howard Taft was never seized by a lust for leadership or supremacy, either, unless in the law. The elder Taft was born on November 5, 1810, on a farm near Townshend in the Vermont uplands. Peter Rawson Taft, his father, was largely self-educated but he had won distinction, as a lawyer, by serving as judge of the probate and county courts. Alphonso's mother was Sylvia Howard, in whose veins also flowed New England blood. Alphonso was their only child. He attended the near-by country schools and helped with the chores on the farm. His parents ex-

---

[11] Alphonso Taft to Peter Rawson Taft, March 30, 1839. [12] A. H. Bode to Taft, July 19, 1912. [13] Taft to C. P. Taft, July 22, 1912.

horted him regarding three aspects of life: the virtue of economy, the need for an education, the importance of religion. He took the first two to heart, but he was not, after he left home, very religious.

Alphonso Taft was impatient to leave home; he did not like the farm. "As to Vermont," he wrote four years after he had graduated from Yale College in 1833, "we may say of it as Jeremiah Mason said of New Hampshire, 'It is a noble state to emigrate from.'"[14] First, however, Alphonso had to get his law degree, which he accomplished in 1838 after a period of schoolteaching in Connecticut. Alphonso Taft was no pioneer. He had no desire for the adventure or hardship or suffering which might still have been found in the frontier beyond the Mississippi River. He had no taste, either, for the frontier wheel of chance by which fortunes are sometimes made and often lost. He wanted to leave New England, but he wanted to go to a safe place. He intended to practice law. He was able. He was tall and rugged and healthy, but he was cautious. Where should he settle down?

Pennsylvania, he confided to his father, was "a fine state to settle in."[15] He decided, however, to look further. In October, 1838, he set forth on a journey in which mediocrity was to be the standard by which he judged his future home. New York, obviously, was not the place for him. "At New York," he wrote back, "I made myself acquainted with several lawyers . . . for the purpose of learning what would be the prospect if I were to cast my lot in New York.

"I feel well assured that I might make a living in that city, but I don't think it is the place for me. . . . I dislike the character of the New York Bar exceedingly. The notorious selfishness and dishonesty of the great mass of the men you find in New York is in my mind a serious objection to settling there. You find selfishness elsewhere, I know, but it is a leading and most prominent characteristic of New York. . . . Money is the all in all."

These evils were less pronounced, he found, in Philadelphia: ". . . the scene is entirely different. . . . Men of business are not, as in New York, generally adventurers. . . . The Bar of Philadelphia is a perfect contrast to that of New York."[16]

[14] Alphonso Taft to P. R. Taft, July 22, 1837. [15] *Idem.* [16] Alphonso Taft to Fanny Phelps, Oct. 9, 1938.

He moved on toward Cincinnati and was much impressed with the town. It had 40,000 residents, compared with 14,000 in 1814. "At least," Alphonso added cautiously, "it is said by those who live there." More important was the fact that it was a middle-class town. The profits, Alphonso felt, were not potentially as great as in New York. But they were good enough. "I believe," he said, "they have but very few men at this Bar of much talent . . . while there is an immense amount of business." "It ought to be possible," he added, "to earn from $3,000 to $5,000 a year." [17] So he settled on the banks of the beautiful river, labored industriously at the law, walked on the hills for exercise and lived abstemiously in all things. For a time he received an allowance from home, and his letters reassured his father and mother that he was living as a young man should. He was delighted, he told his mother on April 1, 1839, that a drive was under way in Cincinnati to close up the "coffee shops" and other "haunts of vice" where liquor was sold.

"You caution me against strong drink," he wrote his father on April 7 of the same year. "Now I assure you that I do not drink any strong drink, that is to say, I have drunk but one glass of wine since coming to Cincinnati and that was at Mr. Wright's and he is a temperance man."

The emotions of Alphonso Taft were under similarly rigid control. He had decided, before leaving Townshend, Vermont, that marriage was the only proper estate for a young barrister. He would become engaged before he left home; in due time he would send for his bride. But what lady should be favor? He worried about it while still at Yale. Should it be Elisa Phelps, the older daughter of Judge Phelps of his home village? Alphonso was quite cold-blooded about his affairs of the heart; and very practical. The wisest course, he confided to his father, was "first to take means of ascertaining more perfectly the character and worth of Elisa." Perhaps she was "more deserving than I have supposed in point of energy and talents."

"If Elisa won't do," he concluded, "I had better cast an eye around for another . . . I would rather someone would do it for me. I have enough else to do. Besides my opportunities are not good."

[17] Alphonso Taft to Fanny Phelps, Oct. 27, Nov. 12, 1838.

Also, there was Fanny Phelps, the judge's younger daughter. Fanny "is so young and her character so little formed," wrote Alphonso, "I don't think it is worth while to take any trouble about her. If I should make no bargain until she becomes of age, then it will be in season to think of her." [18]

Fanny, it would seem, was worth far more trouble than Alphonso complacently supposed. Born on March 28, 1823, she was hardly more than fourteen when thus dismissed as a possible mate. By the time he had settled in Cincinnati two years later, however, they were engaged. Their correspondence was steady. Fanny, who was attending the Misses Edwards' School at New Haven, confided to her fiancé that she had done well in algebra and geometry, but that logic was puzzling. [19] Alphonso was affectionate in a superior, masculine way. In her letters, he said, she had used the phrase "I must say" too often. At best, it was "generally superfluous" and he advised against it. [20]

"I know nothing of domestic duties," lamented Fanny the following June; ". . . how mortified should I be to have my husband come home to dinner and have to sit down to a piece of meat either not half done or burnt to a crisp (as the saying is) and all because his *wife did not know how to do any better . . . now, my Dear,* you may think that Fanny is getting to be quite old womanish about such things, but it is no more than what I am determined to know." [21]

They were married on August 29, 1841, when Fanny had just passed her eighteenth birthday. Five years later she told her old teacher that "we ever have and continue to live happily together and . . . I have never regretted the choice that I made." [22] They had known sorrow, of course; two children died in infancy—Mary at five days and Alphonso Jr. at ten months. Three survived: Charles Phelps, Peter Rawson, and a second boy christened Alphonso. On June 2, 1852— her health had been bad for almost a year— Fanny died from what appears, in the light of current medical knowledge, to have been tuberculosis. And Alphonso, following

[18] Alphonso Taft to Peter Rawson Taft, no date. [19] Fanny Phelps to Alphonso Taft, Nov. 8, 1839. [20] Alphonso Taft to Fanny Phelps, May 15, 1840. [21] Fanny Phelps to Alphonso Taft, June 13, 1840. [22] Fanny Phelps Taft to Miss Edwards, Aug. 25, 1846.

the custom of composing a memorial to her, unconsciously set forth his ideas on women.

They were not as conservative as might be imagined. True, Fanny was "much too devoted to the duties of wife, daughter, and friend, to go into the theories of Woman's Rights, was too happy with things just as they were, to interest herself extensively in that line of philanthropy." But Taft also emphasized "for the especial benefit of our children," that she had been an "excellent scholar," that she carried out many financial details of the household and her "calculations always came out right." [23] He preferred women with brains. He may have had no faint doubts regarding the basic superiority of his own sex, but he did not shrink, as so many men of his day did, from releasing women from unhappy marriages through divorce.[24] In fact, probably without his knowing it, the first early signs of feminism influenced Alphonso Taft's taste in women. He seems to have been fond of a remote cousin, Cynthia Buck, who was teaching school in Tennessee. Alphonso had picked up a knowledge of shorthand; Cynthia was also familiar with the art. So they wrote to each other at frequent intervals in that cabalistic medium.[25] He became devoted, too, to the charming Delia Torrey, certainly a lady of rare mental gifts, the sister of his second wife. Alphonso Taft remained unmarried for only eighteen months. His courtship of Louise Torrey was almost as unromantic as his courtship of little Fanny Phelps.

—4—

Precisely how they met is not clear. None of Alphonso's sons recalled hearing their father mention it.[26] His parents had moved to Cincinnati and were living with him during his widowerhood. His mother managed the house after Fanny died. Alphonso appears to have visited New England not long afterward, possibly to see the Phelps family. But he had a more vital objective. He wanted to get married again. He preferred to find another girl from New England. Sometime during 1852, probably in the fall, he was taken

[23] *Memorial.* [24] Alphonso Taft to Susan H. Taft, May 17, 1840. [25] Cynthia Buck to Alphonso Taft, March 4, 1860. [26] Horace Taft to author, Dec. 2, 1933.

to Millbury, Massachusetts, by a cousin. There he was entertained at the home of Samuel D. Torrey and met that gentleman's second daughter, Louisa Maria. (She was so christened, but always called herself Louise.) The solemn Alphonso concluded that Louise might —he was careful not to commit himself hastily— make a fit wife. On returning to Cincinnati he wrote a Mr. Dutton that he was giving due consideration to her merits as a future Mrs. Taft. Dutton was vastly amused. Louise must have been amused, too. She preserved through all the years a letter, dated merely 1852, and signed with the initials H.W.D. This was from Mr. Dutton's wife to Louise and it told her of the inquiries made by Alphonso Taft. First, were her affections directed elsewhere? Mrs. Dutton continued:

The second difficulty is respecting your character and this arises from the energetic manner in which you decried yourself to him, and he wishes to know of Mr. D. or rather of me if all you say is true. In substance, if you are as profuse and extravagant, as romantic, as undomestic, as willful as you represent yourself. He wants to know if you have been badly crossed in love matters! Isn't it funny?

In conclusion he says "I need not be told that Louise is a splendid woman— one of whom a man might be proud. I sincerely believe that it will turn out that she is just the companion I want and I hope it would be a fair match. Whether she may think so is more doubtful." But you know he says that "even a splendid woman without domestic qualities makes a sad wife, and though I believe she has them, my knowledge and belief is [sic] drawn from very slender observations." So he wants from me a "well-considered opinion" which I am going to give to him. . . . Till he receives this I suppose he will not venture to write to you, and you, when you write to him, must not let him know that you have heard of his communication to us.[27]

The ladies kept their little secret. The mother of William Howard Taft, it may be assumed, never showed this letter to his father. The widower of forty-three was married on December 26, 1853, to this girl of twenty-six and she, like Fanny, moved into the relatively unknown and uncertain West. Meanwhile little

[27] H. W. D (utton). to Louise Torrey, 1852.

Alphonso II had also died; a fact which must have heightened his father's desire to find a second mother for the other two boys. If Mr. Taft had any lingering doubts regarding Louise's character, they were quickly dispelled. Louise faced an assignment far from easy. She had to live amicably with her parents-in-law. Second, she had to win the affections of small Charles Phelps, aged ten, and Peter Rawson, called "Rossy," who was seven. She promptly succeeded in doing both. The first task cannot have been too hard. Alphonso's mother, she wrote, was "thoroughly kind and good; [she] seems anxious to do everything in her power for me and yet wishes me to feel that things are to be as I want them." As for her father-in-law, he was "a pleasant, cheerful old gentleman whose whole object is to make people happy."

"They seem to have opened their hearts to receive me," she added, "and I shall try not to disappoint them." [28]

Louise was equally successful with the small boys, for she had a warm and loving heart. In the summer of 1854, the first after her marriage, she went back to Millbury and took Charley with her. Rossy was left behind with his father and she worried when she heard that the terrific heat of Cincinnati was sapping the boy's vitality.

"I must go to Rossy or have him come to me if he does not get better," she told her husband. "I cannot feel easy away from him." [29]

"I do feel under the greatest obligation to you, my dear Louise," wrote Alphonso, in a letter which crossed hers in the mail, "for the great care and attention you have given to the lads to improve their education and teach them propriety and manners." [30]

She wanted children of her own, of course. "I delight in large families," she told her sister, "and if my health is spared to me I intend to make it the business of my life for the next few years." [31] Her first child, Samuel, was born in February, 1855, but he died from whooping cough on April 8, 1856. She was pregnant again before many months had passed and both she and her husband confessed that they preferred a girl.[32] But the child who came on

[28] Louise Taft to Delia Torrey, Jan. 4, 1854. [29] Louise Taft to Alphonso Taft, July 30, 1854. [30] Alphonso Taft to Louise Taft, July 31, 1854. [31] Louise Taft to Delia Torrey, Dec. 13, 1858. [32] Susan Holman Torrey to Louise Taft, undated (1857?).

September 15, 1857, was the large and smiling Willie and Louise was glad that he was "well and hearty . . . a great contrast to Sammie." [33] She continued to hope for a daughter, but a second son, to be christened Henry Waters, was born on May 27, 1859. Now there were four boys in the Mt. Auburn house. A fifth arrived, Horace Dutton, on December 28, 1861.

The household on Mt. Auburn and the distant one of the Torreys in Millbury were disgusted with the deluge of male infants. Louise reproached her mother that two weeks had passed without a word of congratulation. Delia, she said, "has been a long time smoothing her face and clearing her throat to make him [Horace] welcome, but never a word from you or father." Even young Charley had been disappointed; he had announced that he was "very mad" that a sister had not arrived.[34] Willie shared the gloom, too. He insisted, his father reported, "that Old Santa Claus brought Horace here because nobody else wanted him." [35] Louise persisted. On July 18, 1865, a girl, Frances Louise, was born.

Louise Torrey, for all of Alphonso's misgivings when he first weighed her merits as a wife, was a stronger character than Fanny Phelps. On the other hand, she was less artistic. She lived to be very old, to have the exquisite pleasure of seeing her son rise to high office. She died before he became president, however, and she was spared watching the days of his disappointment and grief when the man who had placed him in the White House, whom he had believed his close friend, turned against him. When seventy-nine years old, Mrs. Taft was seized with an attack of appendicitis and was told by the doctors that an operation was necessary. She was well aware that it might, at her age, be fatal.

"When do you want to operate?" she asked. "I'm ready now." [36]

—5—

The marriage of Alphonso and Louise was successful, in the Victorian manner. She was never heard to refer to her husband

[33] Alphonso Taft to ———— Tarbox, Sept. 21, 1857. [34] Louise Taft to Susan H. Torrey, Jan. 12, 1862. [35] Alphonso Taft to S. D. Torrey, Dec. 28, 1861. [36] Horace Taft to author, Dec. 2, 1933.

except as Mr. Taft; she so addressed him, always. And he, at least in the early years of their marriage, could not restrain a desire to admonish and improve his weaker partner. He told Louise that she must read good books, cultivate her mind, pay less attention to the vanities of life. She answered that the letter had brought "tears to my eyes and sleep away from them." She received "in all humility what you say of my need of application to some course of readings and the danger of letting my mind run to waste from want of systematic culture." But it was not dress, she said, which absorbed her attention nor the reading of frivolous books. She had been dismayed to find that household matters wearied her so that "even when you found time to read to me I found it difficult to listen with unbridled attention."[37] And why not? Louise had already given birth to two sons and would bear three more children. Alphonso's own two sons roared through the house. Business conditions, at the moment, were not good. Louise was overburdened with work.

"I hope," she told her sister, Delia, "you will not have so many dresses when you are married that you are known by them as I am by mine. But money is so scarce I am glad I have nothing to get this year."[38]

Such was the master, and such the mistress, of the home on Mt. Auburn. Alphonso Taft occasionally indulged in homilies on the virtues of industry, thrift and integrity or held forth on the necessity for filial obedience. It was, he said, not half so important how this was obtained "as the great question whether it is *done at all.*" The rod might be necessary, he said.[39] But there is no record that his own sons were ever thus punished; it was not necessary, for they were good boys. The austerity of Alphonso Taft masked a gentleness and sweetness far more familiar to the children than the austerity itself.

"I miss the little boys who always made so much mischief," he wrote when Willie was not quite three and they were away for the summer. "I find that everything about the house is just as I leave it. There is no noise and no mischief . . . and on the whole it is not satisfactory to have no mischief about the house."[40]

[37] Louise Taft to Alphonso Taft, Aug. 22, 1858. [38] Louise Taft to Delia Torrey, Nov. 8, 1857. [39] Address, "Cincinnati House of Refuge," Oct. 7, 1850. [40] Alphonso Taft to Louise Taft, no date (1860?).

The decades passed. In May of 1891 Alphonso Taft was lingering close to death. The son of whom he was most proud—he was solicitor general of the United States, by then, and distinguished in the law—sat by the bed and tried to penetrate through to his father's failing consciousness. He sent away the nurse and administered a stimulant.

". . . he looked up at me in the sweetest way imaginable," wrote William Howard Taft to his wife, "and said to me 'Will, I love you beyond expression.' "

"I am not superstitious as you know, my darling," Taft added, "but I have a kind of presentment that Father has been a kind of guardian angel to me in that his wishes for my success have been so strong and intense as to bring it, and that as his life ebbs away and ends I shall cease to have the luck which has followed me thus far. I have a feeling that I shall not be appointed circuit judge and I shall settle down to humdrum commonplace practice in Cincinnati, managing to eke out only enough to support us." [41]

The grief of the full-grown man was a throwback, of course, to the years in the house on Mt. Auburn. Love dwelt there. From it the children derived security. Alphonso Taft never made a fortune, but he supported his family well. They had the good things of life; assurance of an education, assurance of loyalty and affection. In the summer of 1882, when the boys were grown men, Alphonso Taft asked his eldest son, Charles, about the welfare of the others. He described an occasion in his own early days when he had met with severe financial losses and had told his father about the disaster.

"He could not contain himself, but burst out crying like a child," he wrote. "So it is, we are bound up in the honor and prosperity of our children." [42]

—6—

For whatever it may have been worth, the Taft children possessed, too, a luxuriant family tree. Its branches were numerous

[41] Taft to Helen H. Taft, May 16, 1891. [42] Alphonso Taft to C. P. Taft, July 15, 1882.

rather than distinguished. On August 12, 1874, as Will Taft was preparing to go east to Yale, his father was the principal speaker at a gathering of the vast Taft clan at Uxbridge, Massachusetts. Almost a thousand members of the family, from all parts of the country, came together in the small village which was their ancestral home.

"The American branches of our family tree," said Judge Taft at this genealogical mass meeting, "do not flatter our vanity with many brilliant public careers, but they have proved a vigorous and prolific stock, of which we have no occasion to be ashamed."

Later in the day Judge Taft was called upon to respond to a toast: "Though often called to the bench, this family is never required to answer at the bar." It was true, he answered: "The Tafts have needed no advocate at the bar of any criminal court in our country. They have wasted none of the time, or the money of the public, by offenses requiring judicial investigations." [43]

Most of the Taft forebears, in short, would have felt comfortably at home in the house on Mt. Auburn, Cincinnati. Most of them would heartily have echoed the moralistic aphorisms of Alphonso Taft. They had done their duty. They had bred with enthusiastic fecundity. Occasionally they had been leaders, but more often they had rested serenely in the comfortable anonymity of being average Americans. They had bothered little about their ancestry until Peter Rawson Taft, the father of Alphonso, had amused himself by research during the long winter evenings at Mt. Auburn. Alphonso Taft had added a few facts. [44]

The first member of the family in America was Robert Taft who settled at Braintree, Massachusetts, in 1678; the same Braintree which more than two hundred years later was to figure in the Sacco-Vanzetti case. Robert, a carpenter and farmer, emigrated from England, but the date is not known. Neither is there any information regarding his forebears. The name, originally, was probably Toft or Taffe, which may be either a Scotch or an Irish name. Had William Howard Taft, whose eminence was to be the greatest of any Taft by far, been truly a politician he would have capitalized this foggy nativity. Theodore Roosevelt, whose own

---

[43] *Proceedings at the Meeting of the Taft Family, Aug. 12, 1874.* Spencer Brothers, Book and Job Printers, 1874, pp. 14, 66. [44] *Ibid.,* p. 13.

blood was mixed, often boasted of his Dutch, Scotch, English, Huguenot and Welsh ancestors and warmed the hearts of possible constituents. But Taft never claimed that he was an Irishman or a Scotsman and therefore entitled to votes.

Robert Taft of Braintree moved to Mendon, which had first been part of the larger village. There he achieved mild distinction. He served on the board of selectmen. He acquired property. Some crumbling records show that he died, a very old man, on February 8, 1725, and it is thought that he was born in about 1640. Of his wife, save that her first name was Sarah and that she died soon after Robert, there is no trace at all. Next in the line was Joseph Taft, fourth son of this couple, who was born in 1680. Mendon was a frontier settlement; it had been destroyed in King Philip's War five years before and hostile Indians still lurked in the forests. Joseph Taft was a captain in the militia and also a farmer. He moved to Uxbridge, and he married a girl named Elizabeth Emerson in 1708. From this family was indirectly descended Ralph Waldo Emerson.[45]

"I believe," wrote Secretary of War Taft in 1904, "my father did succeed in establishing a relationship between . . . Emerson and our family, but I fear that it was so distant that the influence of the philosopher upon us must be through his books and not through his blood."[46]

So the line continues. Joseph and Elizabeth had nine children; Peter, the second child, was also a military man and may have fought at Bunker Hill. Peter's third son was Aaron Taft, the grandfather of Alphonso. Aaron went to Princeton College for a brief time. In 1799 he set out from Uxbridge and crossed the granite hills to Townshend, Windham County, Vermont. Aaron was married to Rhoda Rawson and their eighth child— the flair for propagation was not yet fading— was Peter Rawson Taft, the father of Alphonso and the grandfather of William Howard Taft. Peter Taft and Sylvia Howard, his wife, must have been mortified; Alphonso was their only child.[47]

On his father's side, then, William Howard Taft came from a line of estimable Yankees who managed to acquire substance. They

[45] Washburn, Mabel T. R., *Ancestry of William Howard Taft*, pp. 13, 49. [46] Taft to M. D. Conway, March 12, 1904. [47] Washburn, Mabel T. R., *op. cit.*, pp. 14-17.

respected education, in the New England tradition, and obtained as much of it as they could. Never, until Alphonso set forth, did they join the march of empire westward.

The distaff branches of the tree, infinitely less important by any standard of the day, show no marked differences from the masculine boughs. Appropriately, too, they have been the subject of less research. Sylvia Howard, Alphonso's mother, was also Scotch-Irish. Her first ancestor, then probably named Hayward, settled near Braintree in 1642.[48] Louise Maria Torrey, William Howard's mother, was descended from a William Torrey of Somersetshire, England. Captain William Torrey came to the New World in 1640 and settled in Weymouth, Massachusetts. Samuel Davenport Torrey was the tenth of the Torrey line. He was married a second time—his first wife died in 1821— to Susan Holman Waters. Louise was their second daughter.[49] So none save New England blood, in so far as America was concerned, flowed in the veins of William Howard Taft.

". . . brilliant political careers have not been characteristic of the Tafts, in the past," admitted Alphonso Taft at the family gathering in August, 1874. He added: "It is not safe to say what may yet be in store for them. 'There is a tide in the affairs of men' and so of families." [50]

The tide was to catch up William Howard Taft and bear him, not always willing, to far places of the earth, to ports he had not dreamed of. It was to run at flood, for a few years, and to bring him political distinction but not, as it did so, happiness. It was to bear him, at last, into a lovely harbor: the chief justiceship. This, for decades, had been his heart's desire.

[48] *Taft Family Proceedings,* p. 53. [49] Washburn, Mabel T. R., *op. cit.,* pp. 26-27. [50] *Taft Family Proceedings,* p. 39.

CHAPTER II

BIG LUB

ALTHOUGH the city had, by 1870, a population of over 200,000, the Cincinnati of Will Taft's adolescence was a series of villages rather than a midwestern metropolis. The low-lying Basin, along the river, was congested enough. But the seven hills above the town— Mt. Auburn where the Tafts lived was one of these— were still sparsely settled communities. Walnut Hills, Clifton, Evanston, Mt. Adams and the others were distinct from each other. Green fields and open lots lay between them. The business and professional men who lived there met daily in the city proper, of course, but the sections were rather complete entities socially.

Thus Will Taft's formative years were those of a village rather than a city boy. He seems to have lived a normal small-boy existence. One feature of it, long remembered, consisted of bitter feuds between the boys of Mt. Auburn and the youths of the other hills. The Mt. Auburnites would venture down from their fortress to Reading Road, which divided it from near-by Walnut Hills, and would immediately become involved in a pitched battle with the Walnut Hills warriors. Stones were the ammunition. No one knew what the hostilities were about except that, vaguely, they were supposed to determine the superiority of the various sections. One time Mrs. Alphonso Taft lost patience; Will came home badly cut from a stone. What were they fighting about?

"It started when Charley and Rossy were small," he answered. "We haven't got it settled yet." [1]

The two older brothers— Will Taft never regarded them as half brothers— had abandoned the war by this time. So Will and Harry, and little brother Horace, as soon as he was able, carried it on. Will, being very tall and stout, was called Big Lub. Harry, tall but less heavy, was merely Lub. Horace was Little Lub. Will,

[1] Horace D. Taft to author, Dec. 2, 1933.

20

ALPHONSO TAFT—SOON AFTER HIS ARRIVAL IN CINCINNATI

See page 8]

TAFT WITH HIS MOTHER

[*See page 14*

as the oldest and most powerful, was usually the leader and accomplished the most carnage.

Not far from the battlefield at Reading Road lay, in the late sixties, an abandoned quarry with a broad, level floor. This was used as a ball field by the Mt. Auburn boys. Several times each year they would be ambushed, while playing, by a gang from Vine Street, down in the Basin, who insisted that they were the conceited sons of rich men and should therefore be exterminated.

Until he was almost through high school, Will Taft was an enthusiastic baseball player. He covered second base and was unusually accurate in throwing the ball to first. His strong arms made him a fairly good batter. But he could not run very fast. Will was also fond of swimming in the old canal, since transformed into one of Cincinnati's main streets. In winter, the boys skated on the canal's frozen surface.

". . . we would swim there all day," Taft recalled as an old man. "I remember one occasion . . . when the sun was very hot and . . . the next day my back was so burned that I had to have a doctor and remain in bed. . . . I am sure that an examination of my back will still show the freckles that were the result of that day's excursion." [2]

Decidedly, he was popular among his fellows. He was good nature personified. On the baseball diamond he accepted adverse decisions amiably.[3] Tranquillity marked those years. It was assumed from an early date that Will Taft would ultimately go to Yale, that he would become a lawyer.

—2—

Taft was bright, if sometimes inclined toward procrastination. A year after he had graduated from Yale his father rebuked him for wasting his time and recalled that W. H. Pabodie, a teacher at the high school, "hit your case when he said that you had the best head of any of my boys and if you was [sic] not too lazy you would have great success." [4]

[2] Taft to Charles Ludwig, Feb. 16, 1929. [3] James A. Green of Cincinnati to author, March 9, 1935. [4] Alphonso Taft to Taft, July 3, 1879.

At first Louise worried, like nearly all mothers, and felt that he was backward about talking.[5] But at six years, beginning school, Willie was reading and spelling although he was less able in arithmetic and writing.[6] All the Taft boys attended the Sixteenth District School on Mt. Auburn; Cincinnati had one or two excellent private schools for boys, but Alphonso Taft seems to have had pronounced ideas on the virtues of public education. When Willie was twelve years old his father reported, with satisfaction, how well he and his brothers were doing at the school:

. . . the boys ought to be in good humor. They have all been examined this week. . . . The trustees offered silver medals to each class. The classes are large, say, thirty to forty in each, and there are supposed to be a good many bright scholars in each class. Willie and Horace won medals. Harry came within one of it. . . . Willie took the first in his class handsomely. His average was 95 and the nearest to him averaged 85. This . . . makes us all very happy. . . . The problems were difficult and he lost thirty on them; that is, his examination in what is called practical arithmetic was marked at 70. But in mental arithmetic, history, grammar, geography, composition and spelling, he was perfect and received 100 in each. . . . Willie is certainly distinguishing himself for scholarship and intelligence. I am delighted with his writing, and his expression of his thoughts. . . . I hold myself debtor to Willie and Horace five dollars each on account of the examinations.[7]

It was well for their happiness that the Taft boys were above the average in intelligence. Otherwise, in all likelihood, their lives would have been wretched because their father was exceedingly intolerant about stupidity. Will once stood fifth in a large class. This was far from good enough.

"Mediocrity," said Alphonso Taft, "will not do for Will."

The boy was fortunate. He combined a good mind, although not an astonishingly precocious one, with an ability to concentrate. While still in the grammar grades he lingered one night in the

[5] Louise Taft to Delia Torrey, May 15, 1859. [6] Louise Taft to Anna Torrey, May 14, 1864. [7] Alphonso Taft to Delia Torrey, Dec. 24, 1869.

living room where his parents were entertaining callers. His mother asked whether it was not time to go upstairs and get at his lessons.

"It isn't time yet," he answered, "and, besides, I don't have to go upstairs." He brought down his books and studied while conversation continued all around him.[8]

The boy was almost too perfect; he would surely have been an obnoxious youth had it not been for his placid good nature and the fact that he took few things, particularly his own gifts, very seriously. An influence toward normalcy was present, too, in the person of Grandfather Torrey. The three Taft youngsters were terrified of their septuagenarian grandfather to whose house at Millbury, Massachusetts, they were sometimes sent in the summer. At home in Cincinnati they were required to work a little in the orchards behind the house, but there was ample time for swimming and other sports. Mr. Torrey, however, believed in a stern hand and no nonsense. A Boston merchant, he had retired with a small competence at forty because he thought that his health was failing. Then he had proceeded to live to be over eighty. The Puritanical strain, no doubt somewhat diluted for Alphonso Taft by Ohio tolerance, was undefiled in Grandfather Torrey. The first of the seven deadly sins, in his mind, was extravagance. Each morning he went to market himself and drove shrewd bargains with the Millbury tradesmen. He owned the town woodlot and here, during their supposed summer vacations, the small Taft boys were forced to saw wood. He was an extremely religious man, so that Sunday was devoted to church. He believed in such fundamental verities as reward for virtue and punishment for wickedness, and whatever spankings were experienced by Will, Harry or Horace came from his vigorous, if elderly, arm.[9]

Such, at least, was the picture of Grandpa Torrey which lasted, for the boys, throughout the years. Again, however, the harsh outlines are softened by documents which have survived. In the early spring of 1868 (Will was ten years old, Harry was eight and Horace was six) Mr. Torrey addressed a letter to Harry Taft.

"I rec'd your letter," he wrote, "and your talk about school brings to mind a proposition from your Grandpa (don't mean dancing school, any boy can dance and save his money) I mean I

---

[8] Horace D. Taft to author, July 12, 1933. [9] H. W. Taft to author, Jan. 24, 1935.

will give 75 cts. to the boy who stands at the head of his class the most times at the end of this term and 50 cts. to the next, and 25 cts. to the next . . . no cheat, but report to your mother daily on your arrival home, the money will be enclosed in an envelope forthwith. . . ."

Their grandfather added that he was equally concerned about penmanship and instructed them to submit samples of their handwriting. "I tell you Harry I begin to be stirred up about these things, folks are asking me all the time if my boys are going to be as smart as Charles and Peter all I have to say is I will lick them if they don't do it."

The letter reveals that the old gentleman's bark was deceptively ferocious. When were his grandsons coming to visit him again? He told Harry that he had a good horse, ready for "boys to ride and drive any time." He reported new chickens in the barnyard. "Why only think," he concluded, "I have never seen that little beauty Fanny [the small Taft daughter]. Aunt Anna says she is as handsome as any of you boys!!!" [10]

—3—

Will's health continued to be good. He was, if too plump, an attractive, fair-haired boy with blue eyes. The only major crisis of his childhood seems to have been when a carriage in which he was being driven down the steep slopes of Sycamore Street in Cincinnati was suddenly and inexplicably run away with by the family horses. Will's head was badly cut and he suffered a slight fracture of his skull. He was nine years old at the time. [11]

Meanwhile, his father's law business was prospering. In March, 1865, Mr. Taft was offered the nomination for judge of the Cincinnati Superior Court with a salary of $3,000 a year. He declined because this was smaller than his law income. [12] In December of the same year he accepted an interim appointment to this bench, however; he had made some careful investments and his private

---

[10] S. D. Torrey to Henry W. Taft, April 21, 1869. [11] Louise Taft to Delia Torrey, June 6, 1866. [12] Louise Taft to Anna Torrey, March 7, 1865.

income had grown.[13] Four years later he was nominated by both Republicans and Democrats for the Superior Court— the same bench, incidentally, was to mark the start of Will Taft's judicial career— at an increased salary of $5,000.

"We shall think ourselves well off," wrote Louise Taft. ". . . Aside from the pecuniary advantages, I am not a little proud of the popularity of my husband which this double nomination indicates."[14]

In 1869, as Will was approaching twelve, his father and mother took Charley and Rossy abroad and left him in Cincinnati where, as always, it was hot. The boy's letter told of earning twenty-five cents in the garden "which makes my money that I have with you $8.95."

"I want to know if you will give me your gold pen with a short handle for one or two dollars," he asked his father. "I do not suppose you will sell it to me, but it will do no harm to ask you about it."[15]

Nothing disturbed the routine of life; neither death nor financial upheaval nor illness nor sudden fortune. Will Taft went, at about this time, to a dancing school run by a Professor and Mrs. Ernst in the Mercantile Library Building. The school was held twice a week, and one or two white-haired ladies of Cincinnati still remember that the boy danced very well indeed.[16] In fact, even during the years of his extreme corpulency, Taft was an excellent dancer. He was, despite his bulk, light on his feet. When they were quite small, the Taft boys attended Sunday school at the Western Unitarian Conference Church.[17] In contrast to the Torrey household at Millbury, however, the Taft home was not a religious one. Alphonso Taft had revolted from the Baptist tradition of his childhood and had become a Unitarian. Will followed in his footsteps.

Religion, to William Howard Taft, was a matter of relatively slight importance. But it disgusted him, when he was caught in the turbulence of politics, to receive scores upon scores of letters branding him a Unitarian atheist and demanding that he be barred forever from the White House.

[13] Louise Taft to Susan H. Torrey, Dec. 10, 1865. [14] Louise Taft to S. D. Torrey, April 2, 1869. [15] Taft to Alphonso Taft, ? 16, 1869. [16] Mrs. Frank Jamison of Cincinnati to author, Feb. 27, 1935. [17] Louise Taft to Susan H. Torrey, June 24, 1863.

—4—

Not even the Civil War could shatter the somnolent peace of Mt. Auburn. Charley Taft was almost eighteen as Fort Sumter was fired upon; he was old enough to enlist for the preservation of the Union. But he continued his studies at Yale while the battle raged and received his M.A. in 1864. The other boys, thank Heaven, were too young. Willie was but four when the war started. To sharp-tongued Delia Torrey, still back in abolitionist Massachusetts, the war was real and vivid, clearly a struggle between Christ and the Devil. She expressed gratification, in a letter on May 5, 1862, to Louise Taft, over Confederate reverses.

"They run well, do they not?" she asked. "Will there be much credit in beating them?"

The issue was far less clearly drawn in Cincinnati than in Millbury. The people, it is true, had no taste for slavery, and Levi Coffin, sometimes called the "President of the Underground Railroad," had a home in town where runaway blacks were certain to find protection. But sympathies, in war or peace, are never wholly divorced from practical considerations. The city's trade was with the South. Southerners drifted across the river from Louisville. They came north from Memphis and Mobile. They were pleasant gentlemen and they spent their money freely. Cincinnati, even in 1861, was taking form as an industrial city. Commerce was still her life-blood, but her wise men knew that manufacturing would enrich the stream. And the South, the rich and fertile South, was to be her market. So Cincinnati had small use for the hotheads who talked about freeing the slaves with the sword. One abolitionist was declined a hearing. And Dr. Lyman Beecher of Boston, always sensitive to public opinion, softened his diatribe when he spoke in Cincinnati.

Ohio was not yet the birthplace of presidents. That day was coming soon. Before sixty years had passed six native sons had entered the White House. They did their best; such must be the collective epitaph for the presidents from Ohio. They were, if another generalization is permissible, earnest and sometimes hard-working, and they were never wholly qualified for the job. Ohio became a birthplace of presidents for the simple reason that her loyalties were divided between the North and the South. Besides, she had a number of generals who made excellent candidates; over their military exploits could be waved the Bloody Shirt. The G.A.R., which had saved the Union, would rally to the generals and to the Republican party, which boasted that it had won the war. The exquisite Nathaniel Hawthorne saw it coming while the struggle still went on. He drifted to Washington to write some essays for the *Atlantic Monthly* and watched the soldiers milling through the hotel lobbies.

". . . one bullet headed general will succeed another in the Presidential chair," he wrote, "and veterans will hold the offices, at home and abroad, and sit in Congress and the state legislatures, and fill all the avenues of public life." [18]

It was well that Will Taft was not born until 1857 and missed all this. The Bloody Shirt had become frayed in its shame by the time public office confronted him. Its color guard— James G. Blaine and Roscoe Conkling and the rest— were vanishing from the national scene. In the White House, Taft was vainly to dream, as all Republican presidents do, that the North and the South would unite again under the beneficent rule of the Grand Old Party. But he gave more than lip service to the dream. He appointed a Confederate veteran chief justice of the United States.

The Civil War brought prosperity, of a sort, to Cincinnati; at least until the panic of 1873 set in and the breadlines began to form. But Mrs. Alphonso Taft worried from time to time, as a good mother should, about the start in life her boys would receive. Charley and Rossy were fortunate, compared with Louise's own children. They had received an inheritance, probably $100,000 between them, from their grandfather Phelps. [19] Nor was Mrs. Taft wholly innocent of social yearnings, a weakness which did not touch her husband at all. During the summer of 1864 the Tafts made several excursions to near-by watering places. In August Mr. Taft accompanied Charley and Rossy— they were now young men of twenty-one and eighteen, to Yellow Springs, Ohio, where Cincinnati's rising middle class often congregated. When they returned home, Louise told her sister, Anna, about it.

[18] Beer, Thomas, *Hanna,* pp. 49-50. [19] Louise Taft to Delia Torrey, Dec. 11, 1854.

The boys, she related, had been captivated by a "Miss Winslow and a Miss Tillotson" who had at first been so aloof and "so exclusive as not to be easily accessible." They were Cincinnati young ladies, but they had been to school at a Mrs. Ogden Hoffman's in New York: "They speak French with great fluency, are elegant and stylish in appearance, animated and yet perfectly refined and lady-like." The father of Miss Winslow, she continued, was "a wealthy iron merchant, and is building an elegant home on the corner of Fourth and Vine." [20] But if Mrs. Taft, in her heart, was guilty of matchmaking, the attempt failed. Neither of these alluring and lucrative ladies is mentioned again.

—5—

In the fall of 1870, Will Taft entered Woodward High School which was located downtown. Each day he had to walk more than a mile to the school; in the afternoon the climb up the steep hill was excellent exercise. High school in the seventies was strictly a business matter. Such institutions had not yet imitated the colleges with football teams and fraternities. Classes started at 8:30 in the morning and lasted until 1:30 in the afternoon. A reward for merit was dismissal at 12:30.

Will Taft must often have climbed the Sycamore Street hill at the earlier hour, for he again distinguished himself for scholarship. He took the routine classical course: Latin, Greek, mathematics, history, literature and elocution, which led to college entrance. His average the first year was 93.73. The second year it was 94.28. The third he slumped, for some unknown reason, and his average dropped to 86.84. But in his senior year it was 91, and he stood second highest in the class. Will continued to be a model youth. His mark for deportment never dropped below 92 and it was usually above that.[21]

The people of Cincinnati, undoubtedly with reason, were exceedingly proud of Woodward High School. It was one of the first public schools to offer adequate preparation for college. Taft was proud of it, too. He was president of the Woodward Alumnal Asso-

[20] Louise Taft to Anna Torrey, Aug. 27, 1864   [21] *Records,* Woodward High School.

ciation from 1883 to 1884. On November 4, 1908, the day following his election to the presidency, he spoke at the laying of a new building's cornerstone. He had been talking steadily for forty days on the stump, the President-elect said; only a sense of obligation for Woodward, a consciousness of "the thoroughness of the education I received at her hands," had persuaded him to be present. In his day it had been "the most thorough training school in the country" despite its ancient building. He went on:

"Well, a modern building is all right for utility, but it will never have for me . . . gathered about it the sweetness of memory of that old school. I presume . . . there will be a volume of air, without microbes, sufficient to support one and a half of every student that you have, and that is as it should be; but somehow or other one is perverse in looking back to one's own youth and thinks that the privations which he underwent were necessary to form character, and therefore that the good old smell that used to pervade the halls and rooms of old Woodward were necessary really to make up a thoroughgoing man."

At this point, perhaps, the President-elect saw a disapproving frown on the face of some loyal Woodward alumnus. "That doubtless is not true," he said hastily, "and I withdraw the remark if it is to be construed in any serious way." [22]

The orderly years moved past, and Will Taft made ready to become Bill Taft of Yale, the lasting pride of that institution. His father continued to work at night until midnight or after. There was little light reading at home and not much discussion of books except, it is recalled, the novels of George Eliot which were read and, on the whole, approved.[23] Will Taft, although universally liked, seems to have had no inseparable boon companions. As a grown man, in fact, he had a host of friends but few or no intimates. His closest companion was Rufus B. Smith who lived near by. He was fond, too, of Rufus's charming sister Sallie.

"I spent a large part of my boyhood in your house," Taft wrote her in 1909, "either playing with you or the boys, or reading *Harper's Weekly* in those great volumes of which I was so fond. It is

[22] *The Woodward Manual,* Cincinnati, 1910, pp. 23-25. [23] H. W. Taft to author, Jan. 24, 1935.

sad to look back and see how closely associated we all were in those days and how time and circumstances have set us apart now." [24]

The boy liked intelligent girls, particularly when they were attractive too. He married one who was both charming and intelligent. A Miss Woolley was another of that youthful group; she was the belle of the neighborhood and he took her to many dances.[25] Times were changing; woman was emerging from her role of corseted, pretty, foolish, protected chattel of man. The feminist leanings of Alphonso Taft, for the most part so sternly suppressed, were more outspoken in the son. While at Woodward, the exact date is not clear, Will Taft wrote an essay on woman suffrage and looked back in superiority at "the barbarous ages when [it was agreed] that the stronger sex should rule, when influence was measured by muscular strength."

"However different man and woman may be intellectually" he wrote, "coeducation . . . shows clearly that there is no mental inferiority on the part of the girls. . . . Give the woman the ballot, and you will make her more important in the eyes of the world. This will strengthen her character. . . . Every woman would then be given an opportunity to earn a livelihood. She would suffer no decrease in compensation for her labor, on account of her sex. . . . In the natural course of events, universal suffrage must prevail throughout the world." [26]

Such serious, and visionary, expositions did not often flow from the pen of young Will Taft. Life was easy. It was not difficult to excel. Friendships were sweet. It was pleasant to play ball and swim. It was pleasant to visit among the boys and girls of Mt. Auburn on long, fragrant summer evenings. Sometimes a craving for adventure moved them. Then they would march stealthily toward a beer garden called Inwood Park—the girls as daring as the boys—and would squeeze through the fence until the excitable German proprietor discovered and ejected them. The breathless conspirators would compare notes on somebody's front porch, and lemonade would be served. Nice boys and girls did not visit beer gardens.[27]

---

[24] Taft to Mrs. Sallie Shaffer, Jan. 7, 1909. [25] Mrs. Frank Jamison to author, Feb. 27, 1935. [26] Autograph Mss., Taft papers, Library of Congress. [27] Ibid.

CHAPTER III

AND FOR YALE

IT WAS March 18, 1909. He had been president of the United States for a scant two weeks and the nation, as it always does while the pages of an administration record are still white, was resounding with praise of William Howard Taft. Now, for the day, he was back at Yale where, thirty years before, Bill Taft '78 had been as popular as he had been big and friendly. Life had been simple then, devoid of responsibility, devoid of the burdens and the complications which make men tired and often irritable. Remembering all that, he now smiled.

"Great things have happened and luck came my way," said the President to a group of Yale undergraduates at Woodbridge Hall, "and I want to say that whatever credit is due of a personal character in the honor that came to me, I believe is due to Yale." [1]

In many ways the future must have seemed bright as the President walked the familiar paths under the remembered elms. Had not the country overwhelmingly elected him and rejected, as it seemed for all time, the radical and unsound doctrines of William Jennings Bryan? Were not both houses of Congress comfortably Republican? Could he not lean on his great and good friend, Theodore Roosevelt, whose word had been the voice of destiny— Theodore, who had an uncanny and envied knack for getting along with politicians, for knowing what the people wanted, for telling the people what to want? Surely, he could always turn to Theodore.

And yet the President, even though fortified by being a son of Yale, had inner doubts. He may well have wished, for a fleeting moment as the students cheered him, that time could be halted in its fatalistic rush. The start of a journey is nearly always brighter than its end. Wherein lay his talents for this appalling role of president? He had been a lawyer, a judge. Perhaps he should have

[1] *Addresses,* Vol. XIV, p. 10.

remained so. Taft may have recalled a letter written some twenty-five years before by his wise old father.

"I am glad that Will is going to work at the law with all his might. That is his destiny, and he should be in it." [2]

On the night after he spoke at New Haven, the President again addressed some Yale men, this time an alumni gathering in New York. As on the previous day, there were compliments; too many of them and too many florid predictions of a successful administration.

"It is a great deal better to leave office with the plaudits of your countrymen than to enter it with them," President Taft warned. "The opportunity for mistakes, the opportunity for failures . . . the opportunity for a kind of dead level of doing nothing are so many that I look forward with great hesitation and with reluctance to the result of the next four years."

"Eight years!" shouted some Eli enthusiast. The President shook his head. "If I attend to the next four years," he answered, "I will be doing all that is in the contract; and the next four years can take care of themselves." [3]

The four years went by. It was April 1, 1913, and spring was beginning to whisper through the elms of New Haven. A train slipped into the station and a former president of the United States stepped off. Some minutes later he was surrounded by jostling, cheering undergraduates.

"Men of Yale," said Taft, and the hush grew profound. "I am greatly touched. . . . With the opportunity of . . . assisting in . . . the Law School I am here again to become an active Yale man. And as I hear your cheers and your songs, and feel the energy of your spirit, it seems to me as if I were young again and had shed some of the flesh that evidences advancement in years."

Clearly, Taft was thinking about the bitter campaign which had ended in defeat. The personal attacks of Roosevelt had wounded him deeply. The onslaughts of Roosevelt against, as Taft saw it, the Constitution and the law, had alarmed him. He went on: ". . . it is hard to avoid the personal. One of the opportunities that I now cherish here is to bring what little help I can to the young men now going out into life to become the leaders of

[2] Alphonso Taft to C. P. Taft, Feb. 1, 1883. [3] *Addresses,* Vol. XIV, pp. 30-31.

thought in the nation . . . what little help I can bring to them to preserve to the nation and our people that of our present government which is worth preserving, and without which the government cannot remain permanent. . . . I shall thank God for the opportunity." [4]

—2—

As far back as he could remember, there had always been a Yale for William Howard Taft. He was fond of relating how "traditions of the old college" had been described to him when he was a boy of six. His father, he liked to recall, had gone on foot from Townshend, Vermont, to Amherst Academy to prepare for college. ". . . there he heard that there was a larger college in New Haven, Connecticut, and so he walked on from Amherst to New Haven. He walked back in the summer to help his father farm in Vermont, and he walked back again in the fall. He did not have a dress suit until the senior commencement when he hired a Baptist minister . . . to make it for him. . . . I tell you these stories to show you the influences that prevailed in our home, and they were Yale all through." [5]

Mother Eli grew less severe, less rigid in the forty years between the arrival of Freshman Alphonso Taft in the fall of 1829 and the arrival of Freshman Will Taft in 1874. In 1829 Yale was not yet trifling with the liberal and dangerous notions of Harvard College. In the summer classes began at the ghastly hour of five o'clock; at six o'clock in the winter months. Compulsory religious services were held daily. Life was as simple as it was austere. The annual tuition fee was $33; the total yearly expenses of a student would not exceed $110. Parents were warned by the college authorities that it was dangerous to supply money in excess of that needed for bare necessities because to do so would "expose the student to numerous temptations, and . . . not contribute either to his respectability or happiness." [6]

Yale was expanding when Will Taft '78 matriculated. President

[4] *Ibid.*, Vol. XXXI, p. 17. [5] *Ibid.*, Vol. XIV, pp. 28-29. [6] *Yale College Catalogue*, 1832.

Noah Porter had come into office in 1871. Not many years before, the Sheffield Scientific School, the School of Fine Arts and a graduate school had been established. The financial resources of the university had been greatly augmented. President Porter had instituted the elective system of studies so that the undergraduates had a degree of choice among the courses in the catalogue.

Some strong men were on the faculty. The ones that Taft remembered, in later years, were Professor Cyrus Northrup, who taught rhetoric and was afterward president of the University of Minnesota; Professor Thomas A. Thacher, of the Latin Department; Henry A. Beers, literature; and William Graham Sumner. Best of all, he remembered the vigorous Sumner. "I have felt," Taft wrote fifty years later, "that he had more to do with stimulating my mental activities than anyone under whom I studied during my entire course."

Sumner actually shook, although not to its foundations, the placid Republicanism which the boy had brought to New Haven from his Ohio home. He debated with Northrup the burning issue of free trade versus protection, and Taft, for a little while, wondered whether Sumner might not be right. By and large, the undergraduate of Taft's years at Yale was a serious young man with a deep respect for scholarship. Taft, at least, so believed. He deprecated, again after fifty years, the change whereby the valedictorian and the salutatorian were no longer the most honored men in a class. The athlete, in 1874 to 1878, was far less important on the campus.[7]

—3—

Nearly all the classmates of Will Taft are gone now and are attending, it may be hoped, celestial reunions where "Eli Yale" is sung with far more harmony than on this earth. Most of the ones who remain are prone to say that Taft—he was being called Bill Taft by then—was easily the most brilliant youth who ever entered the college, that from the start they knew he was destined to be president of the United States. One or two were more ob-

[7] *Yale News,* Jan. 28, 1928.

jective. Herbert W. Bowen believed that as a scholar Taft "stood high; but that was because he was a plodder and not because he was particularly bright." [8]

Yet Taft became, by far, the most prominent man in the class. He was not quite eighteen when college opened. He was big and heavy with fair skin, blue eyes and light hair. He was good-natured, but authority marked his bigness and integrity his personality.

". . . he towered above us all as a moral force," Bowen also believed, "and, consequently, was the most admired and respected man not only in my class but in all Yale." [9]

Taft's admirable qualities were the heritage of his home. It is not to be wondered that he studied hard and thus excelled. The rebukes from his father would have been prompt and stern had he failed to do so. Alphonso Taft, in fact, was not too pleased with early reports that his son had unusual talent for making friends.

"I doubt that such popularity is consistent with high scholarship," he complained to brothers Harry and Horace one night.[10]

The boy's letters home must have reassured his father. "I begin to see," he wrote as his freshman year started, "how a fellow can work all the time and still not have perfect [marks]." [11] He reported his daily schedule: "Rise at half past six, generally look over my lesson before breakfast, breakfast, prayers, recitation, grubbing until half-past eleven, recitation, dinner, grubbing until 3 o'clock, gymnasium half an hour, study until five, recitation, supper. Here I sometimes go down to the P.O. Then I work till ten, sometimes till eleven. . . .

"You expect great things of me," the boy added, "but you mustn't be disappointed if I don't come up to your expectations."

He was doing creditably, however. The class had been divided into sections according to merit and he had been placed in the first division along with Harry Coe and Howard Hollister, also of Cincinnati.

"But the way that first division recites is astonishing," he told

[8] Bowen, Herbert W., *Recollections Diplomatic and Undiplomatic*, p. 52. [9] *Ibid.*, p. 53. [10] Horace Taft to author, Dec. 2, 1933. [11] Taft to Alphonso Taft, Sept. 13, 1874.

his father; ". . . it seems as though a fellow would have to make a rush every day to keep in the front. Every one watches the reciter with fervent wishes that he may miss. . . . There is a fellow from Andover named Ripley [Alfred L. Ripley, ultimately the Boston banker] whom they say will take the valedictory."

The letter concluded with some aloof, elder-brotherly advice. "Harry and Horace," he wrote, "are putting in their best licks at study, I suppose. I advise Harry to do so for he may expect nothing but grind when he comes to college." [12] A month later Will was still protesting about his arduous labors.

"The lessons take just as much time as ever," he protested, "for as it gets easier for us, they pile on longer lessons." [13]

In his freshman year he roomed in Farnham Hall with George Edwards of Kentucky, a classmate. Later, he shared a room with his younger brother, Harry, who entered Yale in the fall of 1876. Will was scrupulously careful about his expenses. Among detailed reports sent home was one late in September, 1874. On leaving Cincinnati he had received a total of $35. It had been spent as follows:

Sept. 6th	Meals	$2.25	
	Novel	.35	$2.60
Sept. 7th	Meals	1.65	
	Fee to the Porter	.50	
	Transfer	.75	
	N. Y. to N. H.	2.00	
	Express	.25	
	Loomis' *Algebra*	.85	
	Todhunter's *Euclid*	.45	
	Wick	.03	6.63
Sept. 8th	Meal	1.00	
	Post O. Box	2.00	
	Student's Lamp	6.30	
	Kerosene oil with can	.95	
	Matches	.20	10.45

[12] Taft to Alphonso Taft, Oct. 1, 1874. [13] *Idem*, Nov. 8, 1874.

Sept. 9th	Repairing of watch	$ .25	
	Scissors	1.15	
	German Edition of		
	Homer's Odyssey	.50	
	Hair cut	.50	$2.40

Sept. 11th	Packard's notes on B. 1 & 2 *Homer's Odyssey*	.60
	Note Book	.20
		.80
Sept. 14th	Class Atlas	3.00
	Postage Stamps	.99
		3.99
Sept. 16th	10 Bath tickets	1.50
	1 Candle	.10
	3 wicks	.10
		1.70
Sept. 19th	Blue shirt	1.75
	Washing for two weeks	1.20
		2.95

Sept.	6th	$ 2.60
	7th	6.63
	8th	10.45
	9th	2.40
	11th	.80
	14th	3.99
	16th	1.70
	19th	2.95
Subscription to the		
Freshman Boating Club		1.00
		32.52
Received		30.00
Borrowed		5.00
		35.00
		35.00
		32.52
		2.48

I forgot the subscription to the *Record* $2.60
   Also one copy before I subscribed   .10
                                                                         ————

                                                                       2.70

                           $2.48
                           2.70

                           ————

                       —$ .22
I have subscribed for the *Yale Lit.* but have not paid   — $3.00

"I am therefore $5.22 behind," he explained. ". . . If you find any mistakes in the account please write me of it. . . . I have spent no money for candy or fruit as you see. I don't think I have been extravagant but I leave you to judge. I bought what I thought necessary. The blue shirt was for the rush. It is good yet and went through the rush well. A good many fellows were stripped to the waist after they got through the tussle. You may perhaps think that I have devoted too much attention to the *rush* and the athletic sports in this letter, but it is the day after the rush and . . . there are gentle reminders in the joints, every now and then, as though they needed oiling, so that I can't help but have my mind upon it." [14]

The "rush" referred to was the annual freshman-sophomore contest and Bill Taft, with his bulk, pulled and wallowed in the mud nobly for his classmates. In 1874, however, the Yale faculty was viewing the rush with disfavor and suggestions were being made that it be abandoned. Some of the freshmen, who invariably got the worst of it, were inclined to agree until Taft started to make pleas and to ask whether the glorious class of '78 would be the first to run away from the wicked sophomores. So it was held, as before.[15] The big freshman from Cincinnati distinguished himself again when he was selected as the representative of his class to engage in a wrestling bout against E. C. Cook, a sophomore. Young Mr. Cook promptly found himself pinned to the floor under 220 pounds. Otherwise, Taft was not athletic. He was not on the crew. He played neither baseball nor football.[16] This

[14] Taft to Louise and Alphonso Taft, September (?), 1874. [15] Boston *Herald*, Aug. 16, 1903. [16] G. W. Burton to author, Oct. 18, 1933.

was because his father condemned such activities as a waste of time.

"I was urged to offer myself for the crew," Taft recalled, "but my father had other ideas which I induced him to modify with respect to my brother, who came after me, and who made the crew." [17]

He had to work fairly hard at Yale. He was facing competition far more keen than he had known at the Woodward High School in Cincinnati. "I have not done so well this term as I did last," he confessed in his junior year. "I don't know why. Perhaps it is because I do not like what we have read this term as well as I did last. I find nothing so interesting and thrilling in these prosy Greek tragedies as I did in the sentences of Demosthenes." [18]

The class of 1878 learned, as other men were to discover in time, that their first impression of Bill Taft—a big, jovial, happy-go-lucky blunderbuss who never lost his temper—was not quite accurate. He had a temper. He sometimes lost it.

In his senior year Taft lived in Old South College. One night, when he was studying, two frivolous youths from across the corridor insisted on interrupting him. They lounged in his room, smoked and told stories until finally he exploded. He told them, in language which would have shocked his mother, to get out of the room without delay. When they still lingered, he seized books, pillows, bric-a-brac and everything else he could lay his hands on and hurled them at their rapidly departing figures.[19]

—4—

Life was not too different from that in Cincinnati. Bill Taft continued to be a model young man. He did not smoke. He drank, if at all, only an occasional glass of beer. He did not join the rowdy youths who broke loose, from time to time, and cavorted through the streets of New Haven. He was little interested in college dances or other social affairs. As far as girls were concerned, he seems to have been loyal to the maidens of Cincinnati. He suggested, on

[17] *American Physical Education Review,* April, 1916. [18] Taft to Alphonso Taft, March 19, 1876. [19] W. V. Dorner to author, Nov. 14, 1933.

the eve of his first Christmas recess, that they "shake up a dance for us" during the vacation.[20] One feature of Yale life, the chapel services, definitely bored him. He complained, particularly, of the hard seats. He reported that "the Fickle Goddess sleep wouldn't come worth a cent and so I was doomed to listen to one of the dryest sermons I ever heard."[21]

"Why don't they try to make religion a little more attractive?" he demanded.[22]

He was tapped for Skull and Bones, an honor by no means due to the fact that his father was one of its founders or to the prominence at Yale of the Taft name. The senior society pays the tribute of election not merely to athletes or college intellectuals. It seeks men of outstanding personality and great force in undergraduate life and Taft was such. Throughout his life the memory of Skull and Bones was precious. He was certain that it represented the very best among all the excellent phases of Yale life. He returned to its meetings when he could.

In his junior year he won a mathematics prize. In his final year he was awarded prizes for composition. Taft's only excursion into college politics occurred when he was a junior.

He wanted to be class orator, an honor conferred by vote of its members, but as the day for the balloting drew near some other '78 man was pressing him hard. When the class gathered for the voting, Taft made a rapid count of his supporters and discovered that he needed one more in order to win. So he dashed out of the room and located a young Japanese, Tanika Tajiri, with whom he was on very good terms. Tajiri returned with him, voted according to instructions and brought about the election of Taft as class orator.[23]

Hardly a first-class speaker as an undergraduate— ". . . he labored somewhat," said a contemporary critic, "was never fluent, facile and ready."[24]—Taft had, nevertheless, great respect for oratory, and ultimately deplored its passing:

In my day [at Yale] the DeForest prize for speaking was regarded as the greatest prize in college, perhaps being even more

---

[20] Taft to Alphonso Taft, Nov. 15, 1874. [21] *Idem*, Nov. 8, 1874. [22] *Idem*, Nov. 15, 1874. [23] Judson Starr to author, May 15, 1933. [24] G. W. Burton to author, Oct. 17, 1933.

important than valedictorian. But today there seems to be a slumping off of interest. The DeForest men and the Townsend men used to have prominence. One of the greatest needs of men in the professional and business worlds is the ability to express their views in clear and good English. . . . In Oxford they have the Oxford Union. . . . In Oxford those who shine in the Union are the coming premiers, the coming men of England, who succeed to the government control and politics in that kingdom.[25]

—5—

The lives of men, until they cross, often move in parallel lines. In the fall of 1876, over at Harvard College, young Theodore Roosevelt was looking with eager if nearsighted eyes at the unfolding collegiate world. Born on October 27, 1858, he was more than a year younger than Taft. His health had been bad, however, and he was not as far along in his studies. He was only a freshman in 1876. Roosevelt, too, was a model young man. He neither smoked nor drank. But he did not conform to the Harvard pattern as Taft conformed to Yale. He was eager, hurried and nervous when it was the Harvard manner to be indifferent and composed. He bristled with ideas. He kept interrupting his instructors by asking questions. He rushed about the Harvard Yard at a half trot and was, to his classmates, a rather alien figure.

Roosevelt, like Taft, was little interested in the world beyond the academic gates. He wrote a paper on "The Machine Age in Politics," it is true.[26] Bill Taft, at about the same time, made a speech on "The Vitality of the Democratic Party, Its Causes"; the influence of Sumner therein may be assumed. Impulses toward political leadership were to rise much more rapidly in Theodore than in William; within ten years he was to find himself in the center of the reform movement in New York. If either youth, as an undergraduate, looked seriously at the turbulent currents outside, however, he failed to give much indication of it. The currents were turbulent indeed. Hayes had been declared elected over Tilden, to the outraged indignation of Marse Henry Watter-

[25] *Addresses*, Vol. XXXI, p. 66. [26] Pringle, Henry F., *Theodore Roosevelt, a Biography*, pp. 26-39, 57.

son of the Louisville *Courier-Journal*. Marse Henry had indiscreetly demanded that the swindled Democrats "rise in their might . . . send a hundred thousand petitioners to Washington" to end the conspiracy. This alarmed the Republicans, who said that the Kentucky editor was calling for civil war.

The closeness of the 1876 election was proof of the friction in the nation. The Democratic party, impotent since the Civil War, was returning to power because it was the party of protest. The first of the Ohio presidents, Grant, had bungled his job. The second, Hayes, was soon to do a little better but not much. The third, Garfield, was to be assassinated before he had a real opportunity to show whether the White House, as the White House sometimes does, would inspire him to rise from previous mediocrity. The Republican party had saved the Union, even a Democrat was likely to admit that. But how, asked too many voters, about saving our jobs and our farms? How about enough to eat? The depression of 1873 was still a cloud on the land. Smart men in the East had made their fortunes by pushing railroads across the plains. But the men who lived on those plains were wondering how they could pay their debts. They resented the movement toward retirement of the Civil War greenbacks. They talked of controlling these railroad octopi which once had not seemed octopi at all. William Jennings Bryan was still winning oratorical contests at Illinois College. Grover Cleveland was practicing law in Buffalo; he would have snorted with indignation, as he drank his daily lager, had anyone suggested that he was to sit up, for many a weary night in Washington, and apply his slow and thorough mind to these perplexities.

Of the two Taft, rather than Roosevelt, was the more aware of the world outside. He commented briefly on Massachusetts politics in the fall of 1874. This was the year which marked the turning of the tide: the Democratic party gained control of the House.

"I think that when Massachusetts politics goes Democratic," wrote the freshman at Yale, "the Republican party better give up the ghost. . . . Well, I don't know but a change in power is good for the country." [27] In the spring of 1876 the sophomore had small

[27] Taft to Louise Taft, Nov. 8, 1874.

use for James G. Blaine or Roscoe Conkling as possible Republican presidential nominees, because they "all [*sic*] smell too much of rings." [28] It was later in that year that Taft delivered his oration on the vitality of the Democratic party. Fortunately for his success in the campaign of 1908, the oration remained buried in the oblivion which is the normal destiny of undergraduate efforts.

". . . now," he said, "seventy-six years after its [the Democratic party's] first victory and only twelve after a Civil War . . . which was its apparent destruction, it comes before the country and makes such a fight as to *create doubt in many an honest mind as to whether the decision against it was according to equity and justice.*"

Taft traced the history of Democracy from Jefferson's day, its defeats and its victories. What, he demanded, undoubtedly with appropriate oratorical gestures, "has given the Democratic party such remarkable vitality?" He answered his own question:

In a Republic like ours where the powers are so nicely adjusted, because the resources of the general government are so much greater than those of any single state, there is always danger that the former may gain preponderance. A close watch, therefore, must always be kept over the encroachments of the general government. In other words, the states' rights principle is a constant quantity in the politics of the country so long as the Republic continues to exist as it ought. The party, therefore, which takes this as its fundamental principle has an everlasting foundation on which to base its party faith.

Such a foundation has the Democratic party. From the time that Jefferson penned the Kentucky resolutions of '98 down to the beginnings of the war for the Union the Democratic party has been the exponent of states' rights.

This principle, he went on, had led the party into the fatal error of the Civil War. But he paid tribute to Andrew Jackson who had "that hard common sense which is only acquired by knocking about among the masses." Jackson, he said, "sympathized with that class from the bottom of his heart and they knew it. . . . They . . . admired the bulldog pluck which characterized him in

[28] Taft to Alphonso Taft, March 19, 1876.

every emergency. His empire, his whole success, lay in the hearts of men." [29]

Clearly, even as a young man, Will Taft was judicial beyond the comprehensions of a Theodore Roosevelt. The youthful Roosevelt, in contrast, would soon write that Thomas Jefferson was guilty of criminal folly in not preparing for the War of 1812, that Jackson was a spoilsman before anything else, that Jefferson Davis of the Confederacy was an unhanged traitor.

In his senior oration on June 25, 1878, Taft continued the objective note. He called his speech "The Professional and Political Prospects of the College Graduate." It was not a distinguished effort, even for a young man not yet twenty-one. The content had little to do with the title. The senior orator traced the evils which afflicted the country: political corruption, the growth of unsound radical thought, the too-great centralization of government. The Republican party, he said, "has lost its grip on the affections of the people." But, as he ended, Taft tossed out encouragement to his audience. The only hope of the nation was in "the educated citizen." Individuals in every community would affect government, he said, instead of being dependent upon it.

"It is to be an age," he prophesied blithely, "when there are no political giants because of the absence of emergencies to create them." [30]

Commencement was held on June 27, 1878. Taft just missed leading his class. He was salutatorian, while Clarence Hill Kelsey of Connecticut, who was to be his close friend through life, gave the valedictory. Taft stood second in a class of 132. His father must have been amply satisfied.

—6—

The link with Yale was never broken. In January, 1899, he received from his brother, Henry Taft, word that the "liberal element" of the Yale Corporation desired that he accept the presidency of the institution. The salary would be $10,000. Would he

29 Taft papers, Library of Congress. (Italics mine.) 30 *Valedictory, Poem and Oration,* June 25, 1878. New Haven, Morehouse & Taylor, Printers, 1878.

accept?[31] Taft delayed for almost a week before he answered. Then he told his brother that "two insuperable objections" stood in the way.

"The first," he said, "is my religious views. The second is that I am not qualified to discharge the most important duties of that office."

Yale's strongest support, he continued, came from "among those who believe in the creed of the orthodox evangelical churches." It was unwise to deprive Yale of that aid. Taft did not mean, he said, that the next president should be "an ordained minister of the gospel." It would "be a wise departure from a narrowing tradition if a layman should be chosen." He added:

But it would shock the large conservative element of those who give Yale her power and influence in the country to see one chosen to the Presidency who could not subscribe to the creed of the orthodox Congregational Church of New England. If the election of such a one were possible, it would provoke a bitterness of feeling and a suspicion of his every act among those with whom he would have to cooperate in the discharge of his duties that would deprive him of all usefulness and would be seriously detrimental to the university.

Thereupon Taft set forth the gospel of his faith; it was the faith which had been handed to him by his father. Again it was well that political enemies did not have access to his private files. A single sentence in this letter— "I do not believe in the Divinity of Christ"— would have been more than enough to send Bryan to the White House in 1908. Taft wrote:

I am a Unitarian. I believe in God. *I do not believe in the Divinity of Christ,* and there are many other of the postulates of the orthodox creed to which I cannot subscribe. I am not, however, a scoffer at religion but on the contrary recognize, in the fullest manner, the elevating influence that it has had and always will have in the history of mankind.

However, this would not be enough to satisfy most of the friends of Yale, he continued. He would be an object of suspicion

---

[31] H. W. Taft to Taft, Jan. 14, 1899.

and would face "the unconscious distrust of those whose cooperation would be indispensable— a distrust due wholly to the fact
that I am not a believer in the orthodox Christian faith."

Taft was attracted, he admitted, by the influential position
held by the president of Yale, by the power of the office as an
influence for good "in the discussion of public affairs and the
guiding of public thought." But was there not too great a tendency
to pick a college president who was a power in the world rather
than an educator? Taft was beginning to ponder the virtues of
true, wide, sound scholarship.

So for that reason, too, he rejected the presidency of Yale;
possibly with regret but with no doubts whatever. This time no
one persuaded him to alter his judgment; people were to do so
when a far greater presidency was offered to him. Within a brief
time his life was to be changed completely, as governor general
of the Philippine Islands. Even in torrid Manila his thoughts often
turned to his beloved Eli; he wished that he could return for some
reunion. Next he became secretary of war and, when possible,
called upon classmates or other Yale men as assistants. He also got
jobs for them on the federal payroll. This greatly entertained President Roosevelt, whose own weakness, in so far as appointments
were concerned, was not Harvard '80 but the Rough Riders of 1898.
In 1906 Secretary Taft asked for the nomination of a Yale classmate
to some post in the Southwest. The President wrote:

I guess Yale '78 has the call, as there seems to be no Rough
Rider available and every individual in the Southern District of
the Indian Territory (including every Rough Rider) appears to be
either under indictment, convicted, or in a position that renders
it imperatively necessary that he should be indicted. Let us, therefore, appoint George Walker, '78, charge to Taft, and see if the
Senate (God bless them!) will confirm him.[32]

[32] Pringle, H. F., *op. cit.,* p. 198.

CHAPTER IV

RELUCTANT FEET

DIRECT evidence is lacking, but it is a safe assumption that Taft might have studied law at Yale, Columbia University or any other institution had he been anxious to do so. His father had taken an LL.B. at Yale. Charles P. Taft went to Columbia. So did Harry. But Will, greatly as he loved New Haven, entered the Cincinnati Law School in the fall of 1878. Perhaps he was drawn by the friends and acquaintances of his boyhood. His interest in the minutiae of Cincinnati social life— the activities of the people of Mt. Auburn and Walnut Hills— never faded. When he was chief justice of the United States, and old age had settled upon him, it delighted him to hear the latest gossip. He would sit on his cottage porch at Murray Bay, Quebec, and watch the colors of the changing river. Nothing pleased him more, at such hours, than telling and hearing stories about the men and women who had been the boys and girls of his youth, whether such stories were new, old or even scandalous.

The choice of a law school may not have mattered much in the seventies. To an extent, the degree was superfluous anyway. In many states a man became a lawyer by hanging out a shingle: "Attorney-at-law. Wills. Deeds. Notary Public." The pursuit of a legal education was a leisurely affair and the work, particularly for a college graduate, was less than arduous.

"What I really know of the law," Taft was fond of declaring, "I learned at the expense of Hamilton County, Ohio, as assistant prosecuting attorney, and judge of the Superior Court." [1]

The pace of life, fairly fast at Yale, slowed down during the summer of 1878 and for some years the particular devil assigned to William Howard Taft, the devil of lethargy, got in its work. On his twenty-first birthday he congratulated himself that he was "able to vote, to make a will or do anything which becomes a man. It hardly seems possible that I have arrived at manhood for I feel

[1] Horace D. Taft to author, Dec. 2, 1933.

like a boy yet. Manhood doesn't properly come, I think, until one is thirty years of age." [2]

Clearly he was in no hurry to plunge into life. The heat of Cincinnati—a curious fate decreed that Taft was ever to be tormented by heat—had something to do with his reluctance. During the summer he started reading law in his father's office.

"It isn't," he confessed to his aunt Delia, "as pleasant as one's fancy might paint it. The heat has been so overpowering as to prevent any hard study. However, the fact of being in the office and in the midst of business has the effect of making me absorb some of the practical workings of the law." [3]

Other things were far more attractive. He was a grown man now and therefore, it seems, less strictly held down by the New England codes of Alphonso Taft. The girls of Mt. Auburn, for instance, had emerged from scrawny, giggling adolescence and now were charming, inscrutable young ladies. Picnics were held on the green, if mosquito-infested, banks of the Ohio River. The thongs of boyhood were broken. Taft and his friends actually dined down in the city; with wine and a theater performance afterward. They were, of course, careful never to drink too much.

It was all very pleasant indeed; much too pleasant in the eyes of a parent who had not, himself, relaxed at all. Within a year, Will's head was being bludgeoned with rebukes. In July, 1879, he was off at a boat race, probably at New Haven, when he should have been helping with a minor lawsuit.

"You ought to be at home for the business you have to attend to . . ." Alphonso Taft wrote. "Telegraph me when you get this whether you will be home and when." [4]

On the following day his father wrote that the case had been settled, "a thing which you could have done if you had been here, and earned a nice little fee for yourself. . . . I can imagine that you are pretty busy, but you will get a scolding when you reach home for not writing more and for going off after pleasure instead of attending to business. This gratifying your fondness for society is fruitless or nearly so. I like to have you enjoy yourself, so far as it can be consistent with your success in life. But you will

---

[2] Taft to Delia Torrey, Sept. 14, 1878. [3] *Idem.* [4] Alphonso Taft to Taft, July 1, 1879.

have to be on the alert for *business,* and for influence among *men,* if you would hope to accomplish success." [5]

Another chastisement was mailed almost immediately: "I do not think you have accomplished this past year as much as you ought with your opportunities. You must not feel that you have time enough to while away with every friend who comes." But Alphonso Taft could not maintain unbroken his severity. He noted that Yale, alas, had lost the boat race. He added:

"The Harvard boys, like the Democrats, don't care how they win, so they win." [6]

—2—

The trouble, no doubt, was that the Cincinnati Law School consumed little of Will Taft's time. It was by no means, however, a second-rate institution. It had been founded in 1833 when but three or four other law schools were in existence. Ultimately it was combined with the University of Cincinnati, a city institution of learning, but when Taft was a student it was still independent. Some distinguished attorneys were on the staff. The dean was Rufus King, who also taught real property and evidence. Among the others were George Hoadley, professor of the law of civil procedure; Henry A. Morrill, professor of torts and contracts; Manning F. Force, professor of equity jurisprudence and criminal law. In 1878 the school was housed in the old Mercantile Library Building in the heart of the city. The lectures for the first-year students were held on the third floor in a large, barnlike room heated only by an iron stove.[7]

"The law school which I attended," Taft told the young men at Yale, to whom the days of 1878 must have sounded prehistoric, "was one of the old style." [8] That is, the case system, whereby the wisdom and mistakes of dead lawyers became familiar to embryo ones, had not been adopted. The manner and quality of the instruction depended wholly upon the professor in charge. The pedagogical theory, if a theory existed, was that the students listened to the broad, sweeping philosophies of the law—and received their

---

[5] *Idem,* July 2, 1879. [6] *Idem,* July 3, 1879. [7] Robert C. Pugh to author, Feb. 21, 1933. [8] *Addresses,* Vol. XXXI, p. 44.

practical training later, either in some law office or at the expense of clients. It was the same theory, although less perilous to the customers, which prevailed in many a medical school at that time.

The hours of work at the school were adjusted to this conception. The average required was two hours per day. Classes were held in the morning, the late afternoon or, less frequently, in the evening. Thus, if they chose, the students had ample time to earn their way through college by holding jobs. Most of the class, consisting of sixty-six young men, did so. In this respect, Taft did very well. He obtained a post as reporter on Murat Halstead's newspaper, the Cincinnati *Commercial*. The work further made up for the deficiencies of the current legal education, for he was assigned to the courts and had an opportunity to watch the wheels of the law as they actually turned or, what was more probable, failed to turn.

Even these duties, if the complaints of his father constitute reliable evidence, allowed too much time for leisure and the pursuit of wicked pleasure. Faint traces of the man about town are discernible in the youth who had just turned twenty-one. Will Taft was tasting the sweetness of universal popularity. He was tall and fair. He still carried his weight well; he was comfortably plump rather than fat. He was deliciously strong, and his blue eyes twinkled merrily. The young ladies of Cincinnati, decorously, of course, and from behind the shutters of their fastidious upbringing, may have sighed as he walked in the evening along the streets of Mt. Auburn and had a pleasant word for all. He was not to succumb to any one of them for some years, however; then he was to fall utterly. His nonchalance irritated his mother.

"I thought," she wrote from abroad, "you would be engaged and out of Horace's way before this time . . . you treat serious subjects with levity. A *real* heart trouble would sober you and perhaps it will some someday." [9]

[9] Louise Taft to Taft, Sept. 22, 1884.

—3—

He was, by now, a young man of assured position. Alphonso Taft had been secretary of war and attorney general in the Cabinet of President Grant. In 1879 he had been defeated for the Republican nomination for governor of Ohio. What need was there, Will may have reflected, for undue haste; either in affairs of Blackstone or affairs of the heart? Cincinnati had ceased to be a series of villages and had become a city with 250,000 people. Some of them were wealthy and had built fine homes, the more turrets the finer, on the hills which once had been so nearly deserted. Sophistication had come, too. Culture was being enthroned, particularly by Cincinnati wives. A music hall had been built. There was an art school in the town and an excellent library. Good plays came to the theaters. If only Mrs. Trollope could visit Cincinnati now! Through all of this Will Taft moved, as became a young man of his position.

Amiable companions were at hand. Howard Hollister, with whom he had set forth to Yale, was now in the law school, too. William S. Turner, slightly older, was already practicing law. Others in the small group were Frank Shaffer and Cyrus Turner, William's older brother. All these young men were gentlemen. New England was in their blood. They relaxed from time to time, but many of the restraints remained. They did not slink off to furtive resorts, of which there were many in Cincinnati. But they went to the beer gardens which abounded in the section called "Over the Rhine," across the canal. There they would have dinner with beer or wine and enjoy the music. One night, during the 1880 campaign, some politicians began to argue vociferously. Taft reached for the check and suggested to his companions that they leave before beer bottles started to fly.

Taft and his friends often went to the theater. The Grand Opera House and Pike's Opera House were both doing good business. In the early eighties Sarah Bernhardt was among the distinguished artists who visited Cincinnati. The young men— none of them had too much pocket money— had a stroke of luck when their friend, Will Turner, did some legal work for the theatrical owners and managers. Passes for most of the attractions thus became available to Taft and the rest of them, and it was rare that they missed a performance. Will Taft's taste, it seems, ran to the lighter musical comedies. He had a weakness, too, for soubrettes who added sparkle to these productions. In the winter of 1880 Fay Templeton, then almost unknown, had a leading part in a production which they witnessed. On the following night the young men dined at the St. Nicholas Hotel and Taft came to the table humming a song. Miss Templeton, dressed as a telegraph messenger, had sung it on the previous evening; the chorus was substantially: "I am just a Western Union boy, but I bring you lots of fun and joy."

Will Taft ceased his humming and picked up the menu. "That little girl rather caught me," he remarked.

Meanwhile Turner left the table and went to another where two young actresses were dining. In a moment he returned with them. "This is Miss Templeton," he said to Will. Taft blushed to the roots of his hair as he arose. But the two girls joined their party. After dinner the boys escorted them to the theater and climbed the long hill to Mt. Auburn. It had been quite an adventure.[10]

These plunges into the world of pleasure did not, needless to say, cause Taft to neglect his work entirely; it would have been wholly out of character for him to lose himself in gay abandon. He had no cause for apprehension about admission to the bar. For one thing, only obvious idiots or persons of demonstrable depravity were denied a certificate of fitness for the Ohio bar. True, admission was no longer automatic. Four or five weeks before journeying to Columbus, the state capital, for his examinations, Will breezed into his father's office and started to pull lawbooks off the shelves. He announced that he would not be seen in public again until after the tests; he was going to cram as much law as possible into his head. The amount was ample. Taft did not wait for his degree from the Cincinnati Law School, but went to Columbus on May 5, 1880, with a group of fellow students. A committee of judges had been appointed to examine the candidates. So confident of success was the Cincinnati delegation that its members spent part of the

[10] W. S. Turner to author, March 2, 1935.

Photo by Underwood & Underwood

WILLIAM H. TAFT, AGE 10

See page 24]

TAFT'S BOYHOOD HOME ON MT. AUBURN, CINCINNATI. ON THE LAWN ARE HIS MOTHER, HIS SISTER, HIS BROTHERS AND TAFT

See page 26]

previous night at the Neil House singing Yale songs and drinking beer. All of them were admitted.[11]

—4—

No post as partner or even as junior associate was waiting for Will Taft in Cincinnati. His father was withdrawing, to an extent, from private practice to devote himself to politics and public affairs; his diplomatic career was soon to start. Charles and Peter Rawson, the sons of Fanny Phelps Taft, had been in partnership for several years. But Charles, now approaching forty, had been in the state legislature and had opened an office of his own. Peter was proving to be the final tragedy in Alphonso's life. He, too, had been a member of the firm, "Alphonso Taft & Sons," so proudly organized when the boys had been admitted to the bar. Now Peter's mind was giving way and with it his health.[12]

Will Taft did not enter private practice in the summer of 1880. He continued his work as reporter for Halstead's newspaper. A weakness for permitting time or circumstances or other people to make the decisions he should have made himself was already setting in. He might have started a partnership of his own. His popularity and position in Cincinnati would have brought in the clients. But he did not do so. And journalism, even though he covered only the law courts, was a curious profession for Taft.

"Don't worry over what the newspapers say," he was to declare from the White House. "I don't; why should anyone else? . . . I told the truth to the newspaper correspondents . . . but when you tell the truth to them they are at sea." [13]

It was unfortunate that Taft could forget so completely the journalistic associations and experiences of his more flexible years. Had he made use of them as president he might have been treated less unfairly. He did quite well as a court reporter. He made the rounds of the county and federal courts in the daytime and wrote his stories, often as many as five or six, before going home to dinner. Halstead was impressed with his work and offered him

---

11 Simeon Jones to author, Feb. 26, 1935. 12 Taft to Delia Torrey, Sept. 14, 1878. 13 Taft to Marion DeVries, Aug. 12, 1909; Taft to W. C. Brown, Jan. 5, 1910.

$1,500 a year, more than an average newspaper man's salary in 1880, if he would permanently desert the law for journalism.[14] This he had no desire to do. He told his friends that he continued the work because of the legal knowledge he gained by daily attendance in the courts.

There were other advantages. He was able to repay his friend, Will Turner, for the many theater passes by writing a laudatory account of his defense of an alleged burglar.[15] Journalism was also to place in his path the first of the many public offices he was to hold, and to postpone the fateful plunge into the chilly competition of private practice. On October 25, 1880, it was announced that William H. Taft had been appointed assistant prosecutor of Hamilton County.[16]

He was to be on some public payroll, with very rare exceptions, until March 4, 1913.

"I was a law reporter about the time I came to the bar," Taft said, when asked to explain his appointment as assistant prosecutor. "I fell in with Miller Outcault, who was assistant prosecuting attorney. He had a row with his chief, Samuel Drew, and charged Drew with being corrupt and with being in connivance with Tom Campbell [the defense lawyer] in attempting to acquit Cy Hoffman, a Democratic auditor [of Cincinnati] of embezzlement. I was then reporting for the Cincinnati Commercial, and my reports were of assistance to Outcault. He was a young man, only two or three years older than I was." [17]

The peculations of this Cy Hoffman had aroused widespread interest in Cincinnati. Some time in October, 1880, he was accused of having stolen about $12,000 of city market license fees. An item in the Commercial, undoubtedly written by Taft although news stories were not signed in that day, stated that he had denied his guilt and had been admitted to bail.[18] Thomas C. Campbell, Hoffman's attorney, was a noted criminal lawyer of the town. His reputation was not too good; four years later disbarment proceedings were to be instituted against him, with Taft as one of his accusers and prosecutors. Whether County Prosecutor Drew was

[14] Horace D. Taft to author, Dec. 21, 1933. [15] W. S. Turner to author, March 2, 1935. [16] Cincinnati Commercial, Oct. 26, 1880. [17] Taft to W. A. White, Feb. 26, 1908. [18] Cincinnati Commercial, Oct. 5, 1880.

actually in league with Campbell to free Hoffman was not proved. Outcault clearly thought so. He said that the jury in the Hoffman case had been tampered with, and he threatened to resign unless an investigation was made. A few days later the court suspended Drew from connection with the trial; in any event, he was soon going out of office. Outcault had been elected prosecutor in the county balloting two months earlier. He had named Taft as his assistant.[19]

Taft took office on January 3, 1881, at $1,200 a year. The first objective of himself and Prosecutor Outcault was, of course, to put Hoffman behind bars and, incidentally, revenge themselves on the astute Tom Campbell. Hoffman had now escaped once, through a hung jury. On April 21, 1881, Taft spoke for an entire afternoon as he opened the prosecution's argument at the second trial. Again, however, the villain eluded justice and Campbell, still the defense attorney, gloated. Five ballots by the jury resulted in another disagreement.[20]

A Theodore Roosevelt might have won renown, glory and headlines in this post of assistant district attorney. He could have conducted elaborate and sensational raids and "cleaned up the city" in the manner of politically ambitious prosecutors since the office was created. Within a year of this time, in fact, young Theodore was to achieve election to the New York State legislature and to attract attention to himself immediately by charging a justice of the New York Supreme Court with corruption.[21] Will Taft, however, was no showman nor was he, to the same extent, personally or politically ambitious. He accepted life as it unrolled. As assistant prosecutor in Cincinnati in 1881 he did his work well, but without trumpetings. After all, he had accepted the post largely to supplement his law school training; this was really only a postgraduate course. A procession of dreary swindlers and petty thieves passed through the criminal courts and Taft convicted them when he could. His first case was that of a scrubwoman, Mary Finckler, who had taken $35 from her employer. She admitted guilt and Taft joined in the defense attorney's plea for mercy.[22] Cincinnati, with its waterfront and river population, had a due share of crimes

19 *Ibid.*, Dec. 3-17, 1880. 20 *Ibid.*, April 22-26, 1881. 21 Pringle, H. F., *Theodore Roosevelt, a Biography*, p. 70. 22 Cincinnati *Commercial*, Jan. 21, 1881.

of violence. Taft prosecuted murderers and cutthroats along with
the petty thieves. He does not, though, appear to have been successful in sending anybody to the gallows. He had at least one
sensational murder case in which Nellie Stickley— who, from Taft's
description, was a lovely but unfortunate prostitute— had been slain
by her one-time lover, a wretch called Joseph J. Payton. In asking
that the jury send the murderer to eternity, the young prosecutor
grew very eloquent. Nellie had been only sixteen, he said, when
Joe had lured her from Madison, Indiana, to Cincinnati.

Unfortunately, the reporter who covered the story did not
use quotation marks and so Taft's language cannot be set forth
exactly. He told the jury that Joe's interest in Nellie had been im-
pure—mere animal passion; that they had quarreled, that then
she had been murdered. The young prosecutor must have been
quite effective, for the ubiquitous Tom Campbell, again attorney
for the defense, arose with a pained expression and said that the
district attorney had attempted to awaken prejudice against his
boy, that he had been guilty of gross impropriety. Campbell tri-
umphed again. The jury said that Payton was not guilty, by virtue
of insanity.[23]

Taft had one direct encounter with crime in the raw. In the
fall of 1881 some young toughs decided to demonstrate their virility
by throwing bricks through windows. A patrolman arrested one of
them and started toward the jail with his prisoner. The other
hoodlums were massing to effect a rescue when Taft, on his way
to court, came by and joined two additional patrolmen in arresting
four of them. The others ran away.[24]

—5—

Undoubtedly, Taft augmented his knowledge of the law during 1881. More important perhaps, he gained excellent practice
in trial and courtroom work. That he was not particularly interested in the work was indicated by his prompt acceptance, in
January, 1882, of an offer from President Arthur to become collector of internal revenue for the first district, with headquarters

[23] Cincinnati *Commercial*, Feb. 17-27, 1881. [24] *Ibid.*, Sept. 12, 1881.

in Cincinnati. Precisely what this post had to do with the law is impossible to fathom. But taking it was, at least, a further postponement of private practice.

A quarter of a century later Editor William Allen White of the Emporia *Gazette* promised to write a magazine sketch; Taft was fairly certain, in February, 1908, to receive the Republican presidential nomination and his writing friends were doing what they could to help his cause. Mr. White wrote Taft on February 24, 1908, that he was puzzled. He had delved into the records. Yet he could not understand why it was that Taft, in those early Cincinnati years, had been rapidly pushed from office to office with so little effort on his own part. Had he been a faithful worker in the Republican vineyards? Had he taken part in county and state conventions? Or had he been a fighter against the machine?

"I went out to see your brother [probably Henry Taft] this evening," wrote Mr. White, "in the hope that he might tell me how you got these jobs at so young an age. . . . I find in conversation with your brother that you were given these appointments chiefly because you were an angel of light, and the offices were chasing you around in your youth without reference to the rules of the political game as it was played in the world at that time. . . .

"I admire greatly your brother's fraternal admiration for you, and doubt not that he is perfectly sincere in believing that in those young days you were a Lovely Character to whom offices were drawn as to a magnet, but someway politics as I know it makes me think that you were active, forceful and not entirely a negligible force in Cincinnati politics, or that you had powerful friends who pushed you. . . .

"Will you therefore tell me frankly (and kindly) where you got your political pull?"

Taft replied at some length and with charming candor on February 26 and described his experiences as assistant county prosecutor and collector of internal revenue. He denied that offices had pursued him because he had been a Lovely Character.

"Like every well-trained Ohio man," Taft wrote, "I always had my plate the right side up when offices were falling. . . . Looking back to your letter, you ask me this—'Will you therefore tell me . . . where you get your political pull?' I got my political pull, first, through father's prominence; then through the fact that I was hail-fellow-well-met with all of the political people of the city convention-going type. I also worked in my ward . . ."

As a Yale senior in 1878, Taft had declared that "discontent in France makes a riot, in America a political party." The political corruption of the postwar years had been due, he also told his classmates, to "the irresponsible position of power to which the Republican party was elevated by the war." But no discontent troubled Will Taft, the Yale alumnus. And the kindly sentiments he had expressed toward Democracy were only the theoretical ideal-isms of a college senior. Reality was different. Taft rarely worried when the Republican party was in power; he was nearly always uneasy when it was not. He rarely fought the Republican bosses, however corrupt. After an occasion when he had launched a vig-orous attack on one of them, George B. Cox, of Ohio, he modified it. In February, 1924, Chief Justice Taft watched with unbelieving indignation as the trail of oil began to lead down Pennsylvania Avenue. He wrote:

I think the anti-Daugherty Republicans and the Democrats are not helping themselves in their unfairness to [Harry] Daugh-erty. . . . They are charging Daugherty with all sorts of things, and then they propose to set up a committee which has convicted him in advance.[25]

That, of course, was in the dim decades of the future, and in due time he was convinced of Daugherty's guilt. Taft's political faith, like his faith in the Unitarian Church, came from his father. So it is with nearly all men; Alphonso Taft had inherited his own Republicanism. "I know not what could lead you to suppose me anything else than a Whig," he had written to Fanny Phelps soon after moving to Cincinnati from Vermont. His fiancée replied that she had no doubts of his orthodoxy; "You are a true and firm hearted Whig," she agreed.[26]

[25] Taft to R. A. Taft, Feb. 24, 1924. [26] Alphonso Taft to Fanny Phelps, April 3, 1841; Fanny Phelps to Alphonso Taft, April 25, 1841.

—6—

For Will Taft to have been anything except a Republican was clearly impossible. His father, already one of the elder statesmen of the party, was being considered for governor of Ohio. The campaign for the nomination took place in the summer of 1879. The opposing candidate was Charles Foster.

"I went out in the city of Cincinnati to secure delegates to the state convention in his [Alphonso Taft's] interest," Taft said, in describing his own entry into politics. "The convention was a very large one—some 800 delegates—and Foster with superior political experience, finesse and the use of money got away what was a majority for my father." [27]

The defeat of his father was hardly an auspicious start in politics. On the other hand, the political situation in Ohio and Cincinnati was turbulent. The Mugwump movement, which so profoundly shook Massachusetts and New York in the 1884 campaign, was not felt as much beyond the Allegheny Mountains, and Ohio was to remain faithful to the party. But Cincinnati was a madhouse. The best people, in general, were Republicans; it was the party of the respectables. Few citizens had illusions, though, regarding the virtues of either Republican or Democratic bosses in Cincinnati. Their political platforms had but two planks and they were identical: stay in office if possible; get all the graft available while in office.

On the Republican side a few of the respectables, who would have indignantly rejected illicit profits for themselves, perpetuated the machine. They were called "Royalists." They met at the Lincoln Club, sipped port after dinner in what they conceived to be the British manner and decided what should be done. Their power was, though, beginning to fade. The rank and file of the party resented the superiority of the Royalists. Out of their resentment arose a new group called "Mudsills"—save that it was a term of derision, the meaning of this has been lost—and their leader was a rough, tough, bootblack-bartender whose name was George B.

[27] Taft to W. A. White, Feb. 26, 1908.

Cox. Will Taft, in the early eighties, swam amiably amid these conflicting currents.

"I worked in my ward and sometimes succeeded in defeating the regular gang candidate by hustling around among good people to get them out," he told Will White. "I didn't hesitate to attack the gang methods, but I always kept on good terms with all of them so far as was consistent in attacking them. . . . I had frequently to fight Cox in conventions, and did not hesitate to do so, but personally he and I have always been on speaking terms, although I never had any intimate association with him. In my early political days the organization was by no means as powerful as it is today." [28]

No record of antiorganization onslaughts in the eighties is discoverable. Taft campaigned, it is true, for Miller Outcault in the summer of 1880.[29] That fall he made several excursions into the hinterlands to speak for the state and national Republican tickets.[30] One scrap of evidence survives to indicate that Taft did not always stand for righteousness. In March, 1885, some voters in Cincinnati's Eighteenth Ward rebelled against Boss Cox's selection of delegates to a city convention at which a municipal ticket would be chosen. So they named, instead, delegates of their own. Cox was defiant. "The Credentials Committee of the convention will take good care of the matter," he said. It was an excellent prophecy. The machine delegates were seated next day—and William H. Taft was chairman of the Credentials Committee.[31] In justice, no evidence survives to show they had been illegally named.

But these were trivialities and doubtless it would have been foolish for Taft to make an issue of them. He may, in general, have been willing to forgive the irregularities of his political associates. But when he was asked to commit irregularities himself, he drew back in stubborn disgust. The distinction is vital; it marked his entire political life. He found it impossible to remain collector of internal revenue for longer than a year.

"I did not like the office," he told Editor White.[32]

No wonder he did not like it. The work, in the first place, was dull. How could Taft be interested in the fact that it was one of

[28] Taft to W. A. White, Feb. 26, 1908. [29] Cincinnati *Commercial,* Aug. 7, 1880. [30] *Ibid.,* Sept. 6, 1880. [31] *Ibid.,* March 18, 19, 1885. [32] Taft to W. A. White, March 31, 1908.

the largest internal revenue districts in the country, owing to the large number of whisky distilleries in Ohio and Kentucky? Certainly he was entirely unmoved by the fact that William Henry Harrison, who became president of the United States, had once been collector for the same district. Taft, in 1881, would have agreed that a future as trapeze artist in a circus was more probable than a future in which the presidency figured. His appointment, and Taft must have known it, was another indication that the inner wheels of the party were grinding badly. His selection was a blow aimed by President Arthur at Senator John Sherman of Ohio, who was not consulted. The senator announced that he would, none the less, vote to confirm Taft. However, he was doubtful that "so inexperienced a person" would be able to handle the job.[33]

The only possible explanation of why Taft took the office is that thereby he might repay some of the political debts incurred by his father who was, very shortly, to sail for Vienna as American minister by appointment of President Arthur. As he assumed office as collector in March, 1881, Taft was hailed by Bonfort's *Wine and Spirit Circular,* the organ of the liquor trade, as a precocious young man of twenty-four, "the personal choice of the President and the youngest collector in the United States." The editor added, perhaps too optimistically: "Personally, Mr. Taft is large, handsome and fair, with the build of a Hercules and the sunny disposition of an innocent child." [34]

The sunny disposition was not so sunny that the job did not cast shadows on it. Taft may have looked innocent, but he soon knew why he had been appointed. The internal revenue service in 1882 was, like most government agencies, a refuge for politically deserving veterans of the G.A.R. and other hacks. A few trusted employees did the actual work and Taft was promptly informed that these should be replaced by still more hacks. Former Congressman Thomas L. Young of Ohio first told him to put on the payroll, as storekeeper, "an old and tried Republican of the right sort." The congressman, who belonged to President Arthur's wing of the party, was again seeking the nomination. Certain of Taft's men, he next said, were hostile to his candidacy and should be removed at once.

[33] Cincinnati *Commercial*, Feb. 4, 1882. [34] *Ibid.*, Feb. 12, 1882.

"Unless they are removed," Young wrote, "I shall have a squabble for the nomination which ought not to be and the President so thinks . . . he thinks you are shrewd enough and have sufficient knowledge of the politics of Hamilton County to know who these men are. . . . He depends on you as his friend."[35]

It was not pleasant for Taft to refuse a favor to a president who had sent his father abroad on a mission of honor. It was not easy to turn down the organization in its hour of need. He reported the situation in detail to Alphonso Taft. It was true that the party was slipping. But the four or five men whose removal was being demanded, he said, "are perhaps the best men in the service so far as reliability, knowledge of duty and energy is [sic] concerned.

". . . if they are removed for this cause, it will cause a very big stink in this district and I do not want to have any hand in it. I would much rather resign and let someone else do Tom Young's service and dirty work. . . . I think he misrepresents the President."[36]

Taft learned that Young had been accurate enough. He declined to bow to the demands, however, and was criticized for disloyalty to the organization.[37] By Election Day in November he had made up his mind to quit. He announced his intention in December, giving the conventional assurance that no friction whatever existed between himself and the White House. He had called on President Arthur and had pointed out that he wished to begin the active practice of law. The President "very kindly consented to accept my resignation inasmuch as it was made on personal grounds, alone." He held office until his successor took over in March, 1883.

It was a burden lifted. Taft had been harassed and bothered by running an office about which he knew little and cared less. The work was complicated and he had been at his desk too many hours each day. A Cincinnati newspaper reporter noticed him seated, one afternoon, in his office overlooking Fountain Square. A new building for the federal offices was being erected across the street. "His face," said the reporter, "wore a tired expression

[35] L. Young to Taft, April 17, May 7, June 29, 1882. [36] Taft to Alphonso Taft, July 24, 1882. [37] Cincinnati *Commercial*, Oct. 13, 1882.

and he watched the big Government Custom House with the air of a man who cared very little whether the internal revenue service ever occupied a place within its walls or not." [38]

Alphonso Taft, in Vienna, was a shade apprehensive; he hoped that Will could resign, if resign he must, "without censure and without loss of popularity." [39]

The youngest of the Taft boys, Horace, was delighted, however, and wrote his brother to that effect.[40] Horace was ever to be the least hidebound of them all, ever to be vastly pleased when Will was independent. Meanwhile the famine years for young men with Republican leanings were beginning. The G.O.P. lost the House of Representatives in 1882. Among other victories, the Democrats gained heavily in Hamilton County.[41] Taft decided to make his long-delayed plunge and formed a partnership with Major Harlan Page Lloyd, who had been associated with his father.

—7—

Lloyd was some twenty years older than Will Taft. He had graduated from Hamilton College in New York in 1859 and had fought in the Civil War. Taft testified that "he was a man of high character and very great ability . . . who always did his duty." He was the only law partner with whom Taft ever was associated.[42] Taft made no sensational success in his law practice. In less than two years he was to be back on a public payroll. The only case important enough to attract public notice was a libel action, which Lloyd & Taft defended, against the Cincinnati *Volksblatt,* a German newspaper. A lady named Dora Hershel asked for $20,000 damages because the *Volksblatt* had published a news story stating that one Moritz Wehrle had been found, when sought for burglary, in bed with her. The lady's husband, Charles Hershel, had already been arrested for his part in the burglary; he had been caught in the act of pilfering a grocery.

Taft stated the case for the defense and must have found it

---

[38] *Ibid.,* Dec. 14, 1882. [39] Alphonso Taft to C. P. Taft, Dec. 28, 1882. [40] Horace Taft to Taft, Nov. 2, 1882. [41] Cincinnati *Commercial,* Oct. 13, Nov. 11, 1882. [42] *Addresses,* Vol. XXXI, p. 69.

hard to maintain the serious countenance required of a young barrister. He admitted publication of the item. But he insisted that
there had been no malicious intent on the part of the newspaper.
The facts, Taft said, were that Hershel and another man were
discovered in the grocery. The companion escaped, was pursued
to the Hershel home and, when discovered in Mrs. Hershel's bed
with all his clothes on, turned out to be Wehrle. The *Volksblatt*
had printed only the details furnished by the police. Moreover, the
reporter who wrote the story had been careful to say that Wehrle
was in "der" bed in Mrs. Hershel's room and had avoided any
insinuating "mit." A rascally or careless printer had, however, substituted "mit." In the room, incidentally, were numerous packages
from the grocery store. The jury decided that newspapers must
pay for the mistakes or pranks of compositors and returned a verdict that Mrs. Hershel's good name had been damaged to the
extent of $800.[43]

That summer Will went abroad and visited his mother and
father at the American legation in Vienna. It was his first journey.
He saw Ireland first, then Scotland and England. He stayed in
Vienna for about three weeks, and went on a walking trip through
Switzerland with his boyhood friend, Rufus Smith. In October he
sailed for home on the S.S. *Germanic,* and prepared to take part
in the Ohio campaign.[44] The son must have been cheered by the
obvious delight of his mother and father in Viennese life. While
the "Austrian nobility are very haughty and exclusive," his mother
reported, the members of the diplomatic corps were friendly and
charming. They saw many Americans, for Vienna was quite a thor-
oughfare to the East: "A lightning train called 'The Orient' is established, making quick time to Constantinople from London and
Paris and people are going every day." The minister and Mrs. Taft
had done some traveling, themselves: "Our official rank was recognized everywhere and we were sufficiently lionized." Mrs. Taft
added:

Mr. Taft enjoys the situation perhaps more than I do. The rest
and leisure for study are delightful to him, the duties of the official
position being light. He is not worried about entertaining as I am,

[43] Cincinnati *Commercial,* April 20, 22, 1883. [44] Taft to C. P. Taft, July 24, Aug. 12,
1883; Alphonso Taft to Taft, Oct. 1, 1883.

and looks on coolly at the ceremonies with American self-posses-
sion.[45]

Happiness in full measure had come to the elder Tafts as the
shadows of their lives lengthened. Their children were doing well.
Will and Harry, said Alphonso, were busy and fairly certain to
make a mark in the world.[46] The daughter for whose birth they
had waited so long was now a girl of eighteen. Her mother, on
the occasion of Fanny's visit to Vienna, commented that the girl
was "not a beauty by any means. But she has style—quite dis-
tingué indeed, and good taste in dress. . . . She is not as worldly
as her mother. . . . She will, of course, be presented at court." [47]
A year later, Louise Taft was worrying about a husband for Fanny.
Only half jokingly, she asked why Will and Horace did not find
one for their sister.[48]

The post in Vienna did not diminish Alphonso Taft's interest
in politics at home. Will, whether he so desired or not, had to
take part. Minister Taft worried over the Republican party's advocacy of prohibition in Ohio—neither the first nor the last time
that this mortal error brought defeat to the G.O.P. Despite his
own stern views on drinking, he knew that the Germans in Cincinnati would revolt, and he called it "coercive and officious legislation." [49] Will told his father that the party had learned its lesson
and would fight the Demon Rum, by legislation, no more. The
minister answered that he hoped so; "not only because it is the
only way in which the party can hope to survive, but because it
is absolutely right." [50]

The father worried, also, over the possibility that President
Arthur might be aggrieved that Will had gone abroad when Joseph B. Foraker was the Republican candidate for governor of
Ohio.[51] It would have made no difference had Will slaved for
Foraker through all the Cincinnati heat that summer. The Democratic nominee, George Hoadley, who had been Taft's professor
at the law school, was elected. Taft's disappointment cannot have
been great. He must have known that Hoadley was the better

[45] Louise Taft to Mrs. F. C. Caldwell, Oct. 20, 1883. [46] Alphonso Taft to C. P. Taft,
Dec. 18, 1882. [47] Louise Taft to Mrs. Caldwell. [48] Louise Taft to Taft, Sept. 22, 1884.
[49] Alphonso Taft to C. P. Taft, Oct. 14, 1882. [50] Alphonso Taft to Taft, Nov. 4, 1883.
[51] Alphonso Taft to Taft, June 17, 1883.

man; for thirty years Joe Foraker was to be his friend at times and more often his bitter enemy.

—8—

In New York State, as that winter of 1883-1884 passed, young Theodore Roosevelt, although ultimately brought into line by the more practical Cabot Lodge, was raging against the probable nomination of—as marching Democrats were to sing—"Blaine, Blaine, James G. Blaine; the continental liar from the state of Maine." Other Republicans were listening to the thunderings of Lawrence Godkin of the *Post,* to the measured orations of Carl Schurz. The drawings of Thomas Nast, those bitter cartoons of a "Plumed Knight" soiled with mud, were biting deeply into the public consciousness. Soggy defeatism gripped the Grand Old Party. Now, at last, it faced retribution for the frauds which the railroad men, the land speculators and all the other rascals who had been "opening up the country" had perpetrated with its connivance. No candidate actively sought the Republican nomination that summer. President Arthur was weary of the White House. Roscoe Conkling of New York was sulking. Even Blaine hesitated. Stained by the universal dishonor, himself, he was far less guilty than many a fellow Republican. He hesitated, but he took the nomination.

The righteous tumult of 1884 reached neither Alphonso nor William Howard Taft. In May, it is true, the son preferred President Arthur and was told by his realistic mother that he was "leading a forlorn hope." [52] Alphonso agreed, from Vienna, that the selection of Blaine was a disappointment. He feared that the canvass would be doubtful. He said nothing whatever, however, about the dishonesty of Blaine. He told his son to take the stump.

"We have but one course," he said, "and that is to support the ticket." [53]

Will answered that the Republican masses had received Blaine with the "greatest enthusiasm" although the independents were disappointed.[54] A good son, he did his duty and spoke for the

[52] Louise Taft to Taft, May 19, 1884. [53] Alphonso Taft to Taft, June 10, 1884. [54] Taft to Alphonso Taft, June 16, 1884.

Republican ticket as often as he could. He had an official connection with the balloting in Cincinnati when he was appointed chief supervisor of the election. In this capacity he was supposed to prevent fraud at the polls. But fraud prevention, in Cincinnati in 1884, was an utter impossibility. So Taft contented himself with preventing as many Democratic frauds as he could.

Under the Ohio system at the time, the election for county offices was held on October 14. Taft appointed more than sixty assistants and told them they were "clothed with all the powers of special deputy United States marshals." They were to take their posts at the polling places and keep the peace. Taft hoped, he said in his official announcement, that they would "encounter no opposition . . . especially from the municipal or county authorities." This was a hint that the police, controlled by the Democratic city administration, might get tough. If opposition came, however, Taft's marshals were to "treat them as you would any other citizens committing crimes against the United States and have them arrested."

The inevitable result was bloodshed. A Negro was slain, apparently without reason, by one federal marshal. There is no evidence, however, that the killer was one of Taft's men. The Republicans captured the city. Boss Cox hailed the "glorious victory" and congratulated Cincinnati that its best citizens had repulsed the "desperate mob" which had sought to steal the election.[55] It is quite impossible for the historian to make distinction between Republican and Democratic conduct on that day. When it was all over, the House of Representatives sent a committee to investigate the election. A majority of the committee— Democratic, of course— found that United States Marshal Lot Wright had imported Negro deputies and then had armed them. He had been guilty of high crimes.

Taft was a witness before the committee. He had no knowledge that voters had been intimidated by the deputies, he said, until late in the day. His own deputies had been of no use whatever. He quoted an assistant who had come to headquarters and informed him that "they are not worth three rows in hell." [56]

[55] Cincinnati *Commercial,* Oct. 14, 15, 1884. [56] Cincinnati *Enquirer,* Jan. 16, Feb. 26, 1885.

Alphonso Taft, now transferred to St. Petersburg, congratulated his sons for the "risk and labor" they had taken in the 1884 campaign. It could not all be lost, he said, despite Grover Cleveland's victory over Blaine.[57] Even Horace Taft, the liberal of the family, was cast down by the result and was saddened that "the country must suffer the disgrace of having a Democrat for president again."[58] Clearly, Will Taft was glad when it was all over. He had never been much interested, really. They were getting ready to disbar his old adversary, Tom Campbell, a proceeding which had "robbed politics of any interest for me. . . .

"If I can assist to get rid of Campbell I think I shall have accomplished a much greater good than by yelling myself hoarse for Blaine."[59]

His life was being touched, however, by still another interest; beside it even the Campbell case was insignificant. He was falling in love with a girl named Nellie; the most intelligent, the most charming— and sometimes the most critical— girl he had ever known. The adolescence which still marked him was soon to vanish.

[57] Alphonso Taft to Taft, Nov. 7, 1884. [58] Horace D. Taft to Alphonso Taft, Nov. 9, 1884. [59] Taft to Alphonso Taft, June 16, 1884.

CHAPTER V

THE LOVER, SIGHING

O H, NELLIE . . . I believe you could be happy with me," he wrote, "and could have a lifelong pleasure in the thought that the influence of your character and society and (I hope) love has made a good and just member of society out of one whom indifference and lassitude was [*sic*] likely to make only a poor stick among his fellows. Oh, Nellie, it is an awful question for you to solve whether you will put yourself in the keeping of a man for life . . . I ask you for everything, Nellie, and offer but little. . . . I know it is not enough for what I ask." [1]

So he sighed in May of 1885; partly, no doubt, because it was spring and even smoky Cincinnati seemed washed and fresh and new. Will Taft was almost twenty-eight now, and the days when he had been wholly lighthearted, when no emotion had touched him deeply, were gone forever. Life was real. Life was stern. The mere thought of the fascinating Nellie Herron shook the portly frame of Will Taft with a mixture of ambition, humility and the solemn desire to be more worthy. This courtship by the son bore no possible resemblance to the calmly superior attitude of Alphonso Taft toward women and matrimony.

"Oh, Nellie," he pleaded, "do say that you will try to love me. Oh, how I will work and strive to be better and do better, how I will labor for our joint advancement if you will only let me." [2]

She was the daughter of John Williamson Herron, a Cincinnati attorney, and Harriet Collins Herron, and her family was one of substance and intelligence. Mr. Herron, a graduate of near-by Miami University at Oxford, Ohio, had been a United States attorney and could have held judicial posts had he been able to afford judicial salaries. There had been eleven children, however, of whom eight survived. Nellie was fourth in the line. The Herrons

[1] Taft to Helen Herron, May 1, 1885. [2] *Idem*, May 10, 1885.

69

lived on Pike Street, which was in the city itself rather than on Mt. Auburn.

Helen Herron— she was always called Nellie— was a young lady of unusual intelligence. She did not hide it. She did not pretend, as many an intelligent girl of the eighties felt it necessary to do, that she was merely a pretty little thing with soft brown hair and brown eyes. She said what she thought and she thought with conviction on many subjects. If people referred to Nellie's brains rather than to her beauty, it was because she was ahead of her day. Will Taft may have lacked his father's restraint as a lover. But, like his father, he was attracted by brains in women.

On the surface, Miss Herron must have been just a little formidable; she had a firm way of taking charge at literary discussions. She maintained a salon where culture permeated the atmosphere. She was very musical. She was to be a spur to Will Taft throughout his life; to find fault with him at times, to praise him at others. She was always to insist that he must not retire, when infinite possibilities lay ahead, to the monastery of judicial life, and she saw the ultimate consummation of her ambition in March, 1909. Not long afterward she was stricken with a serious illness. But by midsummer of the same year she was on the road to recovery.

"She is quite disposed to sit as a pope and direct me as of yore which is an indication of the restoration of normal conditions,"[3] Taft, relieved and delighted, informed his brother.

—2—

The Cincinnati girl who in 1882 or soon afterward tumbled Will Taft from his pedestal of complacency was not, however, quite as confident and secure as some of her friends supposed. In 1879, when she was nineteen years old, she started to jot down her inner reactions in a diary. The scattered notes reveal that she suffered from maidenly vapors. "I am as blue as indigo and I have got the indigestion," she scribbled on a July night that year. ". . . I am sick and tired of myself. I would rather be anyone else. . . . I have

[3] Taft to Horace D. Taft, Aug. 11, 1909.

cried myself to sleep half the time." Self-deprecation surged through her: "I have discovered positively that I can never be a success in society, and it is against my nature to try." Her miasmal state of mind was partly due to the fact that she had just finished school: "To one who feels, as I do, that I will probably never marry, this leaving school seems like settling down in life."

Nellie Herron was, however, popular among the young people of Cincinnati. The diary is filled with references to drives through the countryside, to evenings spent at whist or in dancing. The front steps of the Herron house were crowded with young men calling on Nellie and on Maria, her younger sister. There were times when the indigo fogs were dispelled entirely. Miss Herron was quite capable of having a good time. Chaperons may have weighted the lives of young girls in Boston and New York, but they do not seem to have been oppressive in Cincinnati in 1880. Nellie confided to her dear diary that she relished a touch of the unconventional now and then. In September, 1880, she had been invited to a reception at the Highland House, a Cincinnati hotel: "I agreed, well pleased, there being something Bohemian about it, which delighted me. . . . We drank beer and ate Wieneg Wurst [sic] which would have greatly horrified probably some of my friends." It was even possible for young girls to visit, unescorted, resorts where beer was served! In the summer of 1880, Nellie Herron was about to go on a trip to Cleveland. On July 2, she noted:

This morning Sallie [probably Sallie Woolley] sallied forth nominally to do some errands but mostly to pay a farewell visit to our favorite place of entertainment, a beer saloon opposite the Music Hall. The proprietor who knows us well met us at the door and asked us if we would not like to go upstairs as there were men in the room. Though that was really no drawback as there are always men, still we accepted the offer and went upstairs onto a porch which overlooks the park. There we sat and drank our beer and ate our cheese sandwiches . . . with our feet on the railing in front.[4]

Variety marked the pleasures of Cincinnati's upper middle class. There was a tennis club at which both the girls and the

[4] Helen Herron diaries; Taft papers, Library of Congress.

boys played. Another form of diversion was to charter a small steam launch and sail up the river to some point where the banks sloped gently down. A picnic supper would be spread under the trees and then, in the moonlight, the party would float back toward the lights of the city and would lift their voices in what seemed, under the circumstances, to be melodious song. It was on one of these excursions that the astute Horace Taft first suspected that Will and Nellie were beginning to be gently agitated about each other.

"I just heard Nellie say that you didn't sing so badly," he teased when they got home. "She must be in love with you."[5]

They were nice young people, these boys and girls of the eighties and they conducted themselves with decorum. The girls may have occasionally gone so far as to take wine and beer, but the age of the cocktail had not arrived. And yet we have evidence that certain pleasures, to be proclaimed a new evil when the flapper of 1922 first rolled her stockings, were not unknown. Will Taft described an entertainment he had attended:

Last night Edith Harrison gave what has come to be known as a haycock party. The grass had just been cut and dried and stacked in cocks, distributed at judicious intervals over their beautiful place. There were thirty people at the party and fifteen haycocks on the grounds. A little mental arithmetic will enable you to determine how many people were intended to sit on each haycock.[6]

Nellie Herron liked the company of men; among others, she saw a great deal of Howard Hollister, Will Taft's classmate, a youth named John Holmes, and a somewhat older man, Tom Mack. Too often, she complained, men grew sentimental and talked of love. "Why is it so very rare in a man and woman to be simply intimate friends?" she asked her diary in the fall of 1880. "Such a friendship is infinitely higher than what is usually called love, for in it there is a realization of each other's defects,

[5] Horace D. Taft to author, Dec. 2, 1933. [6] Taft to Louise T. Taft, June 28, 1885.

and a proper appreciation of their good points without that fatal idealization which is so blind and, to me, so contemptible. . . . From my point of view a love which is worthy of the name should always have a beginning in the other. . . . To have a man love you in any other way is no compliment."

Will Taft fitted this specification at first; he was a companion before he talked of marriage. It may be doubted, though, that he gazed upon the lovely Nellie for very long with the objectivity she affected to prefer. As late as April, 1884, he was still addressing her as "My dear Miss Herron." For some reason they had not been acquainted as children. They first met when she was eighteen at a winter night's coasting party.[7] The diary indicates that he went out with her about a year later, in February, 1880. Will's brother, Charles, was giving a reception. "I was surprised immensely a week before," Nellie jotted down, "by receiving an invitation from Will Taft. Why he asked me I have wondered ever since [as] I know him very slightly though I like him very much. Then, though attentive enough, he was not in the least devoted, but appeared very distrait. He sent me a lovely bouquet, too, which one appreciates more from a person who is not accustomed to sending them though I have had one almost everywhere I have been this winter." [8]

Young Will Taft of Cincinnati was definitely an eligible prospect for matrimony. He was the son of a distinguished father. He was not wealthy, but he was fairly certain to do well in the law. Other young men may have had more ambition; Taft, however, had a fine reputation for intelligence and he had no vices whatever. He was absolutely trustworthy. Many a Cincinnati mother must have wondered hopefully whether he would cast his large blue eyes upon her daughter. Besides all this, Will Taft was tall and muscular. He was brave. Had he not proved his valor when a rascally editor had printed some attack on his father? This occurred while he was a student in the law school. In the years that have intervened the story has been embroidered and amplified and it is now difficult to separate legend from truth.

The accurate version is probably that one Rose, who published

---

[7] Taft, Mrs. W. H., *Recollections of Full Years*, p. 7. [8] Helen Herron diaries, Taft papers, Library of Congress.

a cheap and sensational little newspaper, referred maliciously in his columns to Alphonso Taft. The item, reflecting on Taft's integrity, was false. Will Taft happened to be in his father's law office when Charles Taft came in and showed him the newspaper. Will put on his hat and went to Rose's newspaper shop. He asked whether he assumed responsibility for the item. Rose admitted it. Taft thereupon jerked the editor to his feet, told him to put up his hands and administered a drubbing.[9]

Will Taft had social graces, also. He danced well. He was a good conversationalist. He belonged to the Literary Club of Cincinnati, which his father had helped to organize. The club is still in existence and its files show that he prepared a paper on "Crime and Education" and others on legal and political subjects. At about the same time he joined the Unity Club, which was affiliated with the Unitarian Church. In 1879 or 1880 a burlesqued version of *The Sleeping Beauty* was given by the young people of the Unity Club. With rare judgment, the casting director chose Will Taft to play the title role. His portrayal of the beautiful maiden so convulsed the audience that his nickname of Big Lub was changed, by the girls of Cincinnati at least, to Angel.[10] It was a term of endearment seasoned with a touch of derision. When St. Valentine's Day rolled around in 1885 he found in the morning mail poetic tributes to his chubby build.

Taft kept the valentines. They repose among his private papers along with account books and check stubs and letters. They were unsigned, of course, and the handwriting of all eludes identification. None was in the hand of Nellie Herron. One of the epistles ran, in part:

> Fond Will, the fairest, gallant gay
>   Immensity is thine
> Fair, fat and only twenty-eight,
>   But still a friend of mine.
>
> Popular in every sense,
>   And with the ladies fair
> An Adonis, while the golden tinge
>   Gleams in your sunny hair.

[9] Adolph Richter to author, Feb. 26, 1935. [10] Mrs. Frank Jamison to author, Feb. 27, 1935.

He had been busy with the Thomas Campbell disbarment until late January. One of the valentines was based entirely on this legal proceeding through which Taft had won local fame. Another poetess teased him because "T.C.," that is, Campbell, won the case:

> William, William,
>   Light and airy,
> William, William,
>   Sylphlike fairy,
> Tell me, Tell me why you pine!
>   Is it because your Valentine
>   Is not true?
>   Or are you
>   In troubled spirit wrought
>   That T. C. has not been caught?
>   Never mind, Never mind
> If the troubled world does seem unkind.
>   Love will show you ways of bliss
>   And seal your life with a loving kiss.

Will Taft had his rivals with the ladies, though. One of these, it appears, was Horace, the young brother who was so tall and thin and who in 1885 was twenty-four years old. A valentine referred to this, too:

> Oh! William Taft; I love thee well,
>   Ah! me; how much, 'tis hard to tell.
> But— if the truth must be confessed
>   I love your little brother best.

—4—

Until he was overwhelmed by Nellie Herron, Taft distributed his favors with impartiality. His mother kept insisting that marriage would be good for him. The income from his law practice, she pointed out, was adequate.

"... your father's fancy turns to the tallest girl he knows," Mrs. Taft wrote from Vienna, partly as a joke. "... He is thinking of the governor's [Governor Hoadley of Ohio] daughter as eligible. I know your dutiful disposition and feel sure that you need only a hint. A tall wife would be so becoming to you, showing off your broad proportions to full advantage." [11]

Will did not, however, take this advice; there is nothing to show that he called on the lady. The diary kept by Nellie Herron even discloses that he did not follow up whatever advantage he may have gained by taking her to his brother's reception in February, 1880. His name appears only once or twice in the volume. On August 29 she recorded the fact that she had met Will Taft on the street; that this was the first time she had seen him that summer. Still in the law school and covering the courts for the Cincinnati *Commercial,* Taft was undoubtedly fairly busy. Possibly he preferred associating with men; he was attending the theater with his fellow law students. Then Nellie Herron organized her salon and Taft became a member. Weekly meetings were held at the Herron home on Pike Street. In time, literature and love were blended in happy union. Taft began to escort Nellie to social functions, also.

On April 19, 1882, he asked whether she would accompany him to a "German" at Clifton, one of the outlying suburban districts. "The pleasure of a dance in that beautiful Clifton Hall we ought not to forgo," he suggested. Germans flourished in Cincinnati in the eighties. When the dance was held at Clifton or elsewhere some distance from the city it was necessary to engage a rig for the evening at $10. Usually two of the men did this together. Sometimes the girls shared in the cost. When possible, the young people walked and saved their money.[12]

"Do you think, if it does not rain, that it will be possible to get from your house to the Pendletons' in a party dress without a carriage?" Will asked on another occasion. "Such frankness . . . is the awful result of our salon relations, but you will understand it and pardon it I know." [13]

By the winter of 1884, Taft was seeing Nellie constantly. Their relationship was on a high, intellectual plane and he never minimized the intelligence of Miss Herron. He was, in fact, quick to apologize when it might have appeared that he had done so. There had been a brisk discussion on slavery one night.

[11] Louise Taft to Taft, May 18, 1884. [12] Maria Herron to author, Feb. 28, 1935. [13] Taft to Helen Herron, April (?), 1885.

"I deeply regret," he wrote, "that my manner was such as to leave the impression on your mind that I held your suggestions or arguments lightly or regarded them with contempt. I was not conscious of such feeling and if my manner indicated it, I can only explain it by the heat of the argument. In the discussion I forgot myself and that was inexcusable. I beg your pardon. . . . So far from holding your opinions lightly, I know no one who attaches more weight to them or who more admires your powers of reasoning than the now humbled subscriber." [14]

Taft told his sister, Fanny, who was abroad with their parents during the winter of 1884, that the sessions of the salon had been most successful, that he had "profited greatly by the reading which I have done for it . . . I value the friendships which have grown out of it *very highly*." But there was no indication that he had fallen in love. He expressed some amusement to his sister, in fact, over the plight of some friend who had just been married and was settling down into the faintly absurd status of husband.[15] Taft continued, though, to see a great deal of Nellie. He willingly gratified her craving for occasional indulgence in Bohemian pleasures.

"We are prepared to test your unconventionality and Bohemianism," he wrote. "Rufus [Smith] and I have developed a plan. We want to take a view of blooded canines. We hope that you and Maria [Herron] can go with us tomorrow evening to the dog show." They would have dinner, he said, at Hoffman's, an excellent German restaurant.

We would call for you at about six o'clock. If you would like it, we can make the bill of fare beefsteak and onions. If this plan involves any impropriety, I know you will not hesitate to say so. . . . If we finish the dogs at an early hour, the roller skating rink offers attractions for spectators. . . . The memories of yesterday's walk and refreshment are so delightful that I long to try some similar experience. . . . Will you kindly let me know whether our plan is feasible and you can make us happy by going with us? [16]

[14] *Idem*, April 29, 1884. [15] Taft to Fanny Taft, Feb. 24, 1884. [16] Taft to Helen Herron, April (?), 1885.

—5—

Sometime in April, 1885, Will Taft asked Nellie to become his wife and was, of course, rejected; it was the invariable custom for well-bred young women to refuse the first two or three proposals. The intensity of the lover's sighs increased. Always conciliatory in his treatment of her, he now fairly groveled at her feet. "I was a brute to weaken and exhaust you as I did tonight with the long walk and importuning conversation I had with you," he wrote. ". . . Do not coldly reason away every vestige of feeling you may have for me. . . . I have walked the streets this morning with the hope of seeing you and with little other excuse. . . . You reflected a light, the light of your pure and noble mind over my whole life. . . . With your . . . sweet sympathetic nature . . . you would strengthen me where I falter and make my family life a deep well from which I could draw the holier aspirations for a life of rectitude." [17]

The lover was dramatizing his own unworthiness. He dramatized, too, the supposed hardships and sufferings which would wilt so fragile a flower if she became Mrs. William Howard Taft. He cited the Campbell disbarment case to prove this. Because he had dared to prosecute this notorious wretch, Taft told Nellie, he was already being subjected to slanderous attacks.

"I hated," he wrote, "to think of your linking your fortunes with one who has at so early a period in his life called down on his head the bitter enmity of such a devilish and powerful combination as that headed by Campbell. I felt as if it were too much to involve you in a life of such heartburning and sorrow as may result from a war thus begun."

Noble resolution, it seems, had swelled in Taft's breast as a result of his love. Where once he had been quite calm in the face of knowledge that the world was evil, he was now a crusader for righteousness. ". . . if you were to become my wife," he warned, "you must share with me the life which I propose and shall have to lead in a war of self-defense and offense against evil. And yet,

17 Taft to Helen Herron, May 1, 10; July 1, 1885.

Nellie, such a prospect only makes me yearn for you the more." [18]

Miss Herron surrendered to the bombardment some time in May, but she specified that their engagement must be kept secret for the present. His parents, of course, could be informed.[19] Sanity returned and Will was able to write a more or less coherent letter to his father, who was at St. Petersburg. He recited the facts of his courtship.

"She could not have been unconscious of my feeling for some time before I spoke," he wrote, "but . . . she persists in thinking that I was precipitate . . . for nearly a month she held me in suspense and then with some hesitation consented to our engagement. I know that you will love her when you come to know her."

The future Mrs. Taft, he said, was quite exceptional. He pointed out that she had been teaching school in Cincinnati for three years—at Miss Nourse's, a preparatory school for girls. She had "been no expense at all to her father" during that time:

She has done this without encouragement by her family, who thought the work too hard for her, because she chafed under the conventionalities of society which would keep a young lady for evening entertainments. She wanted to do something in life and not be a burden. Her eagerness for knowledge of all kinds puts me to shame. Her capacity for work is just wonderful.[20]

In early July, Nellie accompanied her parents to the Adirondacks and Taft was left alone in a city from which all the enchantment had vanished. "I find great difficulty in enjoying my evenings now that the steps at 69 Pike Street offer no attractions to me," he told his mother.[21] At least, he could do some work and wait for letters from his beloved.

"I am sitting in my office this evening where I find more of a draft than at my room," he told her on a hot night in July. "It is two weeks tonight since you left. It seems much longer than that to me. . . . I find no pleasure in going anywhere. . . . The only real pleasure I take is in writing to you and the hope, so often vain, that the mail carrier's appearance inspires in me. When I don't get a letter I read all the old ones over again. I did this tonight." [22]

[18] *Idem*, May 1, 1885. [19] *Idem*, July 5, 1885. [20] Taft to Alphonso Taft, July 12, 1885. [21] Taft to Louise Taft, July 5, 1885. [22] Taft to Helen Herron, July 16, 1885.

The gloom was lifted for a fortnight when he journeyed to the Adirondacks to see Nellie. Will told his mother about the ecstasies of the visit. "Each day found Nellie and me on the lake and in the woods," he wrote. "She sews or sketches while I read aloud to her." Among the books they had sampled was *The Mill on the Floss*. There had also been delightful picnics on the banks of some mountain stream. Love, not ants, had seasoned these pastoral feasts: "The fried potatoes, although they had fallen once or twice into the fire and been nearly destroyed, were as fine as anything Delmonico could serve. . . . History fails to record a meal more enjoyable. . . . It was a little touch of housekeeping which gave the excursion an additional charm." [23] Relative sanity was, indeed, returning to the sighing lover; now he could actually laugh at his sighings.

—6—

Taft was kept waiting a long time, again according to the custom of the day, before the happy hour when he became the husband of Nellie. The date chosen was June 19, 1886, more than a year after she had consented to a formal engagement. He had many things to keep him busy, however. The solemn estate of being a prospective husband made Taft ponder seriously the earnings from his law partnership with Major Lloyd. The agreement was that he received a one-third share, while the older and more experienced lawyer was paid two-thirds of the profits.[24] They would have to economize, as young married couples should according to sound New England tradition. The first year, he resolved, they would live on $2,500.[25]

He was, however, doing distinctly well. In 1885 he had earned $5,000, which included a salary of $2,500 as assistant county solicitor. He had paid the premiums on a $10,000 life insurance policy. He had bought the engagement ring for Nellie and still had been able to save $2,500. This, he admitted, was the first money he had ever been able to accumulate; the happy-go-lucky days of bachelorhood had not been conducive to economy. In February, 1886, he decided

[23] Taft to Louise Taft, Aug. 13, 1885. [24] Taft to Helen Herron. [25] *Idem*, Jan. 25, 1886.

to borrow $1,000 or $1,500 and build a house on Walnut Hills. His future father-in-law, Mr. Herron, had given them a lot overlooking the river. His father would endorse the notes,[26] and they would spend about $6,000 for the house.[27]

Taft went on occasional trips in connection with his law practice. He told Nellie, from New York, that he had been interviewing witnesses in a case. In March, 1886, Miss Herron went to Washington, D. C., for a few days.

"I hope you will think of me when you take your Sunday walk along the beautiful streets of Washington," her fiancé wrote. "I wonder, Nellie dear, if you and I will ever be there in any official capacity? Oh, yes, I forgot; of course we shall when you become secretary of the treasury." [28]

The marriage took place at five o'clock on the scheduled afternoon at the Herron house on Pike Street. The Reverend D. N. A. Hoge of Zanesville, Ohio, who had officiated at the marriage of Mr. and Mrs. Herron, performed the ceremony. The society reporter for the Cincinnati *Enquirer* was on hand and wrote:

The bride on this occasion was attired in a superbly-fashioned satin robe with embroidered front, and veil caught with sprays of white lilacs. A bouquet of sweet peas and lilies of the valley rested lightly in her gloved hand. Misses Maria Herron and Fanny Taft, all in white as bridesmaids, and Mr. Horace Taft as best man completed the bridal party. The handsome home with its burden of floral decorations was the scene of a brilliant reception from 5 until 8 o'clock. The bride and groom . . . soon will sail via City of Chester for Europe. A handsome house on East Walnut Hills awaits their return.[29]

They stopped at Seabright, New Jersey, for a few days before sailing. At the Albemarle Hotel, Mrs. Taft was as nonchalant as possible under the circumstances.

"I am afraid we are marked here as a 'b. and g.,' " she wrote regretfully, "but in New York I think we escaped detection, though Will laughs at the idea." [30]

They toured France, England and Scotland during the sum-

---

[26] Taft to Delia Torrey, Feb. 23, 1886. [27] Taft papers, Library of Congress. [28] Taft to Helen Herron, March 6, 1886. [29] Cincinnati *Enquirer,* June 20, 1886. [30] Helen Taft to Harriet C. Herron, June 22, 1886.

mer. By fall they were back in Cincinnati and were living in the new house. In many of its aspects, life had not changed a great deal. They saw the same friends, the neighbors of Mt. Auburn and Walnut Hills whom they had always known. They entertained rather more than Mr. and Mrs. Alphonso Taft had done. Nellie continued her interest in music; she became one of the organizers of the symphony orchestra.

It was sometimes remarked, after a dinner party, that Mrs. Taft had a sharp tongue. It was not unusual for her to rebuke her husband. On the other hand, it was conceded that Will Taft had some annoying habits. He would get so interested in the conversation, for example, that he would pay no attention to his duty of carving. He would pile two-thirds of a tenderloin steak on one plate and then have little left for the other guests. This was true even after he had become a judge of the Superior Court; finally, Mrs. Taft often carved the meat herself.

But underneath the occasional criticism, everyone agreed, was a deep, sincere, warm love which promised well for the success of the marriage.[31] Taft knew that it existed; the sharp tongue of his wife never bothered him.

"I know that I am very cross to you," she told him in a letter "but I love you just the same." [32]

[31] Maria Herron to author, Feb. 28, 1935. [32] Helen H. Taft to Taft, June 9, 1890.

CHAPTER VI

CRUSADER FOR A TIME

WILLIAM H. KIRK, who owned and operated a livery stable in Cincinnati, did not know on the afternoon of December 24, 1883, that he was about to become a cog in the wheels of destiny geared to the life of William Howard Taft. Had Mr. Kirk known, he would certainly have rejected the distinction. For he was, on this Christmas Eve, to be murdered. One of his murderers was to escape the gallows through the eloquence and persuasive legal talents of Thomas C. Campbell, the noted criminal lawyer with whom Will Taft had already exchanged epithets. The miscarriage of justice caused an extraordinary uproar. Rioting followed. The courthouse was burned to the ground. Men beat each other to death in the streets. And in due time the respectable people of Cincinnati decided that responsibility could logically be placed at the feet of Tom Campbell. So disbarment proceedings were started and Will Taft was the particular star of the case.

Otherwise Mr. Kirk of the livery stable was of no importance whatever. He was a good-natured nonentity whose only vice was a tendency to display bills of large denomination and to boast about his shrewdness in horse trades. In his employ, in December, 1883, were two boys named William Berner and Joseph Palmer; the former of German extraction and the latter a mulatto. Liveryman Kirk, during the week before Christmas, had flashed a roll which, he said, totaled $600. The stableboys conspired to get it, and they pounced on Kirk on Christmas Eve. One or both of them struck him with a blunt instrument and choked him with a horse halter. Together, they dumped the unfortunate Kirk into a wagon and left the body in a gully on the outskirts of the city. They were somewhat disappointed when they learned that their booty was only $245, but they made the best of the situation by spending money as freely as possible; in saloons and other resorts. They were immediate objects of suspicion when the police found Kirk's body and, when arrested, they both confessed participation in the crime. Each said he had been led into it by the other.[1]

Berner and Palmer erred seriously in killing Kirk during a crime wave in Cincinnati. They were indicted for murder and their outlook was black. But when the case of Berner, who was to be tried first, was called the usual delays of the law began to operate in his behalf. Jurors pleaded for exemption because they had already formed an opinion. Technicalities were interposed. Tom Campbell was engaged, at considerable expense to the family, as Berner's attorney and did his job so well that the public grew indignant. The Cincinnati *Commercial-Gazette* remarked editorially that forty-two individuals charged with murder— among them Berner and Palmer— were now in the Hamilton County jail; four of them had confessed their crimes.

"Comments now," said the editor, "in view of the excited state of the public mind, may be said to be in the nature of a warning. If the courts cannot enforce laws and protect society, there is imminent danger that other ways will be sought and found."[2]

—2—

Will Taft played no part in the trial of Berner which started, at last, in March. He must have regretted that he was no longer assistant prosecutor of Hamilton County, that he was only a private lawyer. As assistant prosecutor, Taft had tasted the bitterness of defeat by Tom Campbell when the facts clearly showed his clients guilty. He must have fervently hoped that County Prosecutor Pugh, now in charge for the state, would be more successful. It appeared, at first, that he would. Berner's confession was placed in evidence, although Campbell protested that it had been obtained by duress. Berner, on the stand, admitted the day and hour of Kirk's murder and also that he was present when, as he claimed, Palmer struck the fatal blows. But on March 24 the jury ruled that Berner was guilty only of manslaughter. That night, in murderers' row at the county jail, the spirits of the inmates soared. Only one, "Red" McHugh, who was accused of wife murder, was displeased. He said, sourly, that a lynching might be expected at any moment.

[1] Cincinnati *Commercial-Gazette*, Dec. 28-30, 1883. [2] *Ibid.*, March 9, 1884.

WILLIAM HOWARD TAFT (SEATED CENTER) AND CLASSMATES AT THE WOODWARD
HIGH SCHOOL

See page 28]

Photo by Adèle

TAFT IN HIS TWENTIES

[*See page 47*

Cincinnati's newspapers had given columns daily to the Berner case. Nearly all the reports were biased. No reader was allowed to doubt that Berner was guilty of murder in the first degree. "Nobody," remembered Nellie Herron, "could see how an honest jury could have rendered any other verdict." [3] And so, when the finding of manslaughter came in, the reports of the proceedings were virtually hysterical.

"Our citizens have, in this verdict, the estimate which such a jury as can be secured for trying a murderer places on their lives," thundered one editor. "Women and children have in this a jury's measure of the offense of killing husbands and fathers to get money for sensual indulgence. . . . The brutalized criminal class can see in this that they can trust with safety to a jury of their peers— eminently of their peers— if they get, by their crimes, the means to fee criminal lawyers.

"The people of Cincinnati are abundantly warned that the law furnishes no protection to life. Trials of murderers are made mockeries of law and justice. . . . The county jail is a hotel for murderers. . . . Soon there will be no legal or social or moral distinction between murderers and other citizens." [4]

The jury, even more than Tom Campbell, was held up to vitriolic scorn. One by one, after the verdict, its members "rose from their seats and slunk over to the clerk's desk to get the warrants for their fees." A. F. Shaw, the foreman, was greeted with hisses when he reached the street; he walked away at a rapid pace when one or two hotheads hurled "Hang him!" in his direction. Another juror, Henry Bohne, hurried back to the cigar store which he operated not far distant. He passed through excited groups on the street corners, who looked at him sullenly and said that he should be exiled from the city. No accusations of bribery were made, though. Berner was a poor youth. His father had scraped together $2,500 for Campbell's fee.

If cooler heads existed in Cincinnati in March, 1884, there is no evidence to indicate that they did anything. Prosecutor Pugh said that among all the murderers in the jail none was so clearly guilty as Berner. An inquiring reporter questioned citizens at random

[3] Taft, Mrs. W. H., *Recollections of Full Years*, p. 11. [4] Cincinnati *Commercial-Gazette*, March 16, 18, 23, 25, 1884.

and their inflammatory statements were published at length. One of these proclaimed the necessity for a vigilance committee of the San Francisco type; the only remedy for the situation was "to visit summary justice on the crowd of murderers in the county jail." [5]

A mass meeting was arranged at the Music Hall for the night of March 28. Will Taft did not attend because Miss Herron's salon was in session that night; its members gave all their attention to the Berner case, however.[6] The hall was packed and cries of "Hang him!" were frequent during an inflammatory speech which opened the meeting. Judge A. G. W. Carter was the only important individual present who saw that moderation was necessary and even he berated the "cunning and adroitness" of criminal lawyers who allowed miscreants to escape the gallows. Judge Carter ignored repeated cries for a lynching and offered, somewhat lamely, a resolution calling for the expulsion of the Berner jurors from the city; he did not, however, explain how this could legally be accomplished.

"If Tom Campbell is the dishonest man you believe he is, let him go too," he said.

—3—

Soon the sober and respectable people of Cincinnati were trying desperately and in vain to extinguish the fires of violence which they had so carelessly ignited. Immediately after the meeting a mob surged toward the jail. At 9:55 o'clock fire bells proclaimed a riot. Bricks crashed through the jail windows. Men brought up large poles and started to batter at the gates. But Sheriff Hawkins of Hamilton County and Chief of Police Reilly of Cincinnati showed exceptional courage. They massed their men and defied the mob. Fighting continued all that night— utterly senseless street fighting between men who were mainly intoxicated— and just before dawn the state militia arrived. With daylight came relative quiet. But the hysteria mounted again toward evening and the night of March 29 was sheer horror. The militia had been concentrated around the jail, which was behind the Hamilton County courthouse. Repeated

[5] Cincinnati *Commercial-Gazette*, March 25, 1884. [6] Taft, Mrs. W. H., *op. cit.*, p. 11.

forays by the mob were hurled back. At last, blind with fury and liquor, the crowd hurled itself, instead, at the courthouse and soon this was in flames. By next morning it was a crumbled heap of charred stone. The casualty list revealed that forty-five men had been killed in the rioting and one hundred and twenty-five wounded.

The respectable people were appalled. Charles P. Taft was one of a committee which sought to restore order. The saloons were closed. Berner, to add the final sardonic touch, had not been in the jail at any time during the rioting. He had been hastily taken to Columbus by alarmed deputies.[7] Meanwhile Tom Campbell, for whose head the mob had cried, had been quietly waiting at his house. The man had unquestioned courage, whatever his faults. He recalled that night when, the following year, he was called upon to defend his integrity and when Will Taft spoke for hour after hour on his delinquencies.

"The clients who have come to me," he said, "have not come to me because they were friends. . . . And yet I would not disparage the steadfastness of friends. . . . Some of them offered, when my life was in peril, to arm themselves for my protection. But I walked these streets with no one at my side to protect me but my brother. They said there were soldiers and squads of police guarding my house from destruction. This was not true. No one but my servants, my brother and one other, assisted me in protecting my property."[8]

—4—

Almost a year intervened between the murder of Kirk and the start of Campbell's disbarment trial. During it— in addition to seeing as much as he could of Nellie Herron— Will Taft had been qualifying for his part. He had campaigned more or less energetically for the Republican party. He had been, it will be recalled, an official in the Cincinnati elections that year. He was adding to his standing at the bar; partly by working more diligently and partly by identifying himself with that minority among the members of

[7] Cincinnati *Commercial-Gazette*, March 29, 30, 31, 1884. [8] *Ibid.*, Jan. 8, 1885.

the legal profession who viewed themselves as something more than fee collectors and courtroom spellbinders. Thus in April, 1884, he went to the state capital with a bill to amend the criminal law in some technical detail.[9] Consequently Will Taft was in every way eligible for appointment to the legal staff which would present the evidence against Campbell. The position would pay nothing. It required a vast amount of labor. As a junior counsel, Taft had small prospect of being more than a minor figure in the case. He was deeply in earnest, however. He was holding aloft, for the first time, the banner of righteousness. He found satisfaction in being a crusader and he wrote his father about the wickedness of Tom Campbell. The diplomat viewed the Campbell case, from Vienna, with characteristic caution.

"I expect you will be disappointed and lose all your labor," he warned. "I have an idea you will find that while his ways are not such as you would approve, he is not as bad as you have taken him to be." [10]

Taft rejected discouragement. Campbell was indicted in the spring of 1884 for having attempted to bribe one of the Berner jurors, but escaped conviction when the jury failed to agree. This did not dismay the young crusader. Taft traveled widely through Ohio investigating cases which Campbell had tried, examining witnesses, attempting to find enough evidence to expel his enemy from the legal profession. He turned his material over to E. W. Kittredge and William M. Ramsey, senior attorneys in the case.[11]

Under the Ohio statutes an attorney could be removed by the Supreme Court, the District Court or the Court of Common Pleas for "misconduct in office, conviction of crime involving moral turpitude or unprofessional conduct involving moral turpitude." Suspension applied to all the courts in the state. The prosecution of Campbell (it was not, technically, a prosecution since he was not being tried under criminal law) began in the District Court on November 20, 1884. Mr. Kittredge opened with general allegations that Campbell was guilty "of general and notoriously bad reputation as an attorney . . . of corruptly obtaining jurors, and of corruptly and

---

[9] Taft to Alphonso Taft, April 27, 1884. [10] Alphonso Taft to Taft, June 26, 1884. [11] Taft, Mrs. W. H., op. cit., p. 13.

improperly influencing their verdicts." [12] Taft sat at the counsel table for almost a week and supplied Mr. Kittredge with specific facts on these alleged corrupt practices. The trials of Cy Hoffman, the county auditor whom Taft, as assistant prosecutor, had attempted to convict for embezzlement in 1881, were reviewed. Campbell had been Hoffman's attorney in those cases and had obtained acquittals. In gathering evidence for the Campbell disbarment, Taft had located a saloonkeeper named Henry Kline. He was produced before the District Court on November 25, 1884, and swore that Campbell had approached him four years before and had asked him to get on the Hoffman jury. Kline said Campbell promised to "make it right" if he did so.

January 5, 1885, was Taft's lucky day. Mr. Ramsey, his senior, had been scheduled to sum up for the prosecution. But he had been taken ill and Taft, like an understudy suddenly emerging from obscurity to play the part of a leading actor, took his place. He spoke for four hours without stopping and his admiring younger brother, Horace, reported to their father that he had been "complete master of the situation," that during the long and involved summation of the case, "the life, the interest, the logic, the facts and the eloquence did not fail for one minute." [13]

"I spoke three or four hours and won very considerable credit for that speech," was Taft's own happy recollection of his first big moment.[14]

Opening his argument, he told of one case in which Campbell was supposed to have obtained a client's release from the penitentiary by means of fraud. He went exhaustively into the Hoffman case. He said that in the trial of young Berner, Campbell had managed to smuggle a former client on the panel which rescued the slayer from the gallows; he did not, however, describe the riotings and killings which had followed that verdict. They had nothing to do, legally, with the disbarment proceedings. Actually, of course, the disbarment would never have been attempted had it not been for those tragic nights in March, 1884. Taft's closing remark to the three judges of the District Court, who would decide Campbell's fate, were eloquent:

[12] Cincinnati *Commercial-Gazette*, Nov. 21, 1884. [13] Horace D. Taft to Alphonso Taft, Jan. 11, 1885. [14] Taft to W. A. White, Feb. 26, 1908.

We have sat here, your Honors, for a month trying what? We have sat here, may it please your Honors, deciding whether or not success at the Bar is to be attended by such practices as have been proven before this court. . . . We admit the ability, the energy, the shrewdness of the respondent and his power in the community. It is no small reason that would lead to the prosecution of this case with the lifelong hostility that it must engender and the danger that there is in incurring the undying enmity of a man as powerful as the respondent has grown to be. . . . We have presented the case which we think calls for the action of your Honors in saying that the profession must be kept pure. We deny nothing to Mr. Campbell except integrity, and we say that that is the essential, the indispensable quality of a member of the Bar.[15]

William Howard Taft, a young attorney of twenty-eight, was a fathom or two beyond his depth. First, his own conception of legal ethics was then, and always would be, far more rigid than that of the majority of his profession. He had proved that Tom Campbell had been a shrewd, clever, shady attorney. But he had not proved guilt beyond a reasonable doubt and lawyers— ever resentful of restrictions on legal conduct— require more than even reasonable proof. Secondly, Taft was handicapped, as he always would be, by using intellect to combat emotion. On January 7 Campbell arose to plead in his own behalf. He was an impressive figure; he had flowing brown hair and a magnificent beard. A watch chain curved across his ample stomach. He portrayed himself as the defender of the poor, the rescuer of the oppressed. His own emotions overcame him from time to time and his large frame shook with sobs. Yet otherwise he was restrained and calm. He did not abuse his detractors. He did not ask for leniency.

"There is a homely maxim," he began, "that where there is so much smoke there must be some fire. Two, at least, of this court must know enough of my career to know why so much smoke or suspicion attaches to what I have done. I have had many cases in which there was much public interest and feeling. There has not been a single contested election since 1876 in which I have not taken a prominent part. The bitterness which was excited in that contest did not die in many bosoms."

[15] Cincinnati *Commercial-Gazette*, Jan. 6, 1885.

Hoffman, charged with stealing, had been an honest man, Campbell continued. Berner, the killer of Kirk, was a victim of wild public passion. The address was extremely effective because it played upon the loyalty of lawyers for their own, because Campbell offered himself as a victim of political prejudice. He concluded:

Mr. Taft, in his argument, said that I had become wealthy, powerful and dictatorial. If Mr. Taft will give me considerably less than $50,000 he may have all the property I have in the world. I have no power. I have no influential relatives. . . . My father has been an invalid for twenty-five years. . . .

Mr. Taft has said that the relators deny me nothing save integrity. That is like saying, let me wound you just once with a rapier, and I will be merciful and thrust you not through the arm or the leg, but through the heart. Integrity is to a man what chastity is to a woman. When that is gone, all is gone. . . .

Enemies, like plants, well watered, grow in profusion. There is but one of the relators for whose position in this matter I could not account. That one is Mr. Taft. . . . I am glad a man of so much energy as Mr. Taft has given months of time in collecting the evidence to be used against me. . . . I only ask that justice shall be done. And if your judgment be adverse, let it be with me as with the soldier who has proved to be a traitor. I shall cherish no revenge. The case is in your hands and I shall be content.[16]

The court deliberated until February 3 and then absolved Campbell of all the charges except a minor one; that when prosecutor in a police court many years before he had used his official position to collect a debt for a private client. The penalty was ten days' suspension from the bar and the costs of the trial. But on the following day the court decided that this constituted cruel and unusual punishment; so the suspension was lifted and the costs remitted.[17]

—5—

It cannot have been a very bitter blow to Taft. He would have gained little more in reputation had Campbell been found guilty. Vindictiveness was rare with Taft. On January 1, 1885, he had been

16 *Ibid.*, Jan. 8, 1885. 17 *Ibid.*, Feb. 4, 5, 1885.

appointed assistant county solicitor under his close friend, Rufus B. Smith. As such, he tried civil cases for Hamilton County, but the office did not require much work. His partnership with Major Lloyd was not affected.

"My fixed salary as assistant county solicitor is not unpleasant just now," he wrote his mother in May.[18]

Otherwise, the year was important only because of the courtship and final winning of Nellie Herron. His ardor for crusading appears to have been cooling somewhat. He continued to take part in city and county politics, but he was beginning to believe that it was a dirty trade. There had been another Republican primary convention in September.

"Hol [Howard Hollister] and I were discussing our feelings today . . ." he told Nellie, "and we both said that such a convention as that almost cured us of any desire to take part in politics."

It had been a rough gathering. Taft described a brawl into which he had, himself, been forced. A delegate had been overheard remarking that Will Taft had paid money for illegal voting. They had called each other liars and Taft had slapped the man in the face.

"I didn't want to hit him because he was not my size," Taft explained. "It was in a crowd in a narrow hall . . . and two or three persons interfered. He was in the act of drawing a pistol, but his arms were pinned to his side by a man who told me afterwards of the pistol which he felt in his pocket. . . . I was near enough to have prevented his using it on me if he had drawn it. This will serve to show you the men we have to deal with. I am too quick-tempered and like to talk too much. I shouldn't have engaged in any talk with him at all." [19]

Taft's opinion of the political arena never grew much better. And yet, by 1885, prospects were brighter for eligible young men of true Republican faith. Taft's own reward for services rendered was to be the first of three judicial harbors where the waves of political turbulence beat with diminished force. Very soon, still remarkably young for the progress he had somehow achieved, he was to be appointed to the Superior Court of Cincinnati.

[18] Taft to Louise Taft, May 16, 1885. [19] Taft to Helen Herron, Sept. 2, 1885.

CHAPTER VII

THE FIRST HARBOR

JOSEPH BENSON FORAKER, whose political career would one day slide down the slippery path of Standard Oil money to oblivion, was an important figure in Ohio politics in 1887.

In September, 1908, when Taft was campaigning for the presidency, Theodore Roosevelt telegraphed that "if I were running . . . I should . . . decline to appear upon the same platform with Foraker." Taft answered that he had not the slightest intention of doing so.[1] Even a political debt of the first magnitude had been liquidated in twenty-odd years, however. Candidate Taft was no longer, in 1908, under obligation for the fact that Foraker gave him his first judicial post in March, 1887. Besides, he had never really trusted or liked the Ohio politician.

In 1884, for instance, Foraker had been defense counsel for the nefarious Campbell when that attorney had been tried for attempting to bribe a juror. He had, Will Taft told his father, "conducted the defense in a most shystering and ungentlemanly way.

"Everybody is indignant and Foraker has sunk in public estimation so suddenly that he himself has no idea of the feeling of the people about it."[2]

A year later, Taft was dismayed by the probability that Foraker would again, after being defeated in 1883, receive the Republican nomination for governor of Ohio. "He is not a great man in any sense," Taft said, "and many people are beginning to realize it . . . [his] relations to Campbell have been close, too close for him to retain the friends he once had."[3]

The animosity between Taft and Foraker was deeply personal. At about this time they were on opposite sides in some private litigation. Taft asked for a continuance in the suit, a routine request granted as a matter of courtesy by attorneys. But when the

[1] Pringle, H. F., *Theodore Roosevelt, a Biography*, p. 505. [2] Taft to Alphonso Taft, June 16, 1884. [3] Taft to Louise Taft, May 24, 1885.

Taft & Lloyd clerk appeared with the papers, Foraker declined to
consent and made disparaging remarks which the clerk repeated
when he returned to his own office. Taft telephoned and suggested
that such aspersions might well, in future, be made in his presence.

"You're a bully," said Foraker, in substance. "If you come
around to my office, I'll slap you in the face."[4]

Taft kept his temper and declined to accommodate his foe.
He recalled the incident in a letter, some time afterward, to Nellie
Herron:

> You remember, do you not, Nellie, my telling you of a row
> I had with Foraker in which he threatened among other things
> over the telephone to slap my mouth . . .? It was a display of
> boyish temper on his part of which he might well have been
> ashamed. . . . You may infer from this account that I do not
> like Foraker. Your inference is correct. He is a double-faced Camp-
> bell man and when a man bears such a brand, I'll have none of
> him.[5]

—2—

Taft found it inexpedient, though, to adhere to this resolution.
Foraker's defeat in 1883 had been a temporary setback. Foraker had
perfected an alliance with Boss Cox. He was building a state
machine of his own and his dream of future greatness included
the presidency itself. He was elected governor in 1885 and re-
elected in 1887. On his part, Foraker also quietly forgot his impulses toward fisticuffs. He reacted amiably when a suggestion was
made that Will Taft, who had done so admirably in the Campbell
case, should be appointed to an unfinished term on the Superior
Court. The governor was suave. He had known Will Taft favorably
for some years, he said. As judge of the Superior Court, himself,
he had been impressed by Taft's intelligence, by his bright and
agreeable manners when he was a reporter for the *Commercial*.
Governor Foraker had no doubts regarding Taft's "strong intellectual endowment . . . keen, logical, analytical mind." There was

---

[4] Horace D. Taft to author, Dec. 2, 1933. [5] Taft to Nellie Herron, July 10, 1885.

no question of his fitness for the post.[6] The governor was careful, though, not to commit himself.

A vacancy existed on the Superior Court— which was actually a lower court of first instance— because Judge Judson Harmon desired to resume private practice. The post was really elective, but the law stated that a vacancy must be filled through appointment by the governor if it occurred within thirty days of the election. Just why Will Taft was considered at all is one of those problems which defy the biographer. He was very young to be a judge. His legal career, aside from the Campbell case, had amounted to little. When, in 1908, Editor White asked whether he had actually risen to eminence simply by being a "Lovely Character," Taft gave his own explanation:

I . . . became junior counsel in the prosecution of Campbell. . . . This was subsequently reported to Foraker, and . . . he appointed me without any solicitation on my part. . . . Foraker appointed me on the recommendation of Judge Harmon, who was my predecessor in office, and who had been a colleague of Foraker on the same bench. The appointment was a temporary one for fourteen months, to be succeeded by election for a full term.[7]

The explanation is not entirely satisfactory because it does not go far enough. Foraker was a shrewd and practical politician and elevations to any bench, even of lower jurisdiction, can be used by a politician to advantage. Possibly Governor Foraker had two motives. The appointment of Taft would redound to the credit of his administration; he could point to it, in campaign speeches, as evidence of his high regard for the judiciary and his devotion to a nonpartisan bench, for the Superior Court was a highly respected tribunal. On the other hand, he may have been confident that Taft had a bright political future. In that event, his support would be important. In April, 1888, Taft was easily elected for a full term in his own right. The governor, possibly thinking of that support, warned him that he must "quit the bench at the end of the term for which you have been elected.

"You will then be of mature age and experience," he pointed

[6] Foraker, J. B., *Notes on a Busy Life*, Vol. I, p. 237. [7] Taft to W. A. White, March 31, 1908.

out, "and so established in the confidence of the people that all other things will come naturally." [8]

Governor Foraker did not specify what he meant by "all other things." Fairly soon, however, Taft was wondering—all the while repeating to himself that it was utterly out of the question—whether he might not, still in his early thirties, be chosen by President Harrison as associate justice of the Supreme Court. For the moment, he assured Foraker that "my debt to you is very great" because of the opportunity which the Superior Court offered "to a man of my age and circumstances." [9]

Taft was twenty-nine when appointed to the Superior Court; what type of man was this who, so inexplicably, was pushed from office to office without, as it appears, doing much about it himself? What was the state of the nation in 1887? It needed no profound discernment to see that the currents of revolt, which would run at millrace speed by 1896, were already moving swiftly. Some of the problems— economic, labor, social— which caused the currents would be passed upon by Judge Taft of the Cincinnati Superior Court. First as to Taft. He was, for instance, an ardent Republican and therefore conservative in his political and social views. He noted that a friend of the family, Guy Mallon of Cincinnati, was active in Democratic politics and proposed to reform his party in Hamilton County and Ohio.

"The housecleaning that Hercules attempted in the Augean stables is as nothing," Taft remarked, "compared with the work Guy has assigned himself." [10]

Not long after, his brother, Charles, who had acquired a large interest in the Cincinnati *Times-Star,* was considering the advisability of political independence for his paper; he might support certain of the Democratic candidates in Cincinnati and Ohio. Will Taft was indignant.

"He cannot be blind to the fact," he complained to his father, "that no matter how bad the Republican legislative ticket, the Democratic members will work much more mischief." [11]

Thus the political independence, so proudly proclaimed at

[8] J. B. Foraker to Taft, April 3, 1888. [9] Foraker, Julia B., *I Would Live It Again,* p. 305. [10] Taft to Alphonso Taft, July 10, 1889. [11] *Idem,* Sept. 18, 1889.

New Haven in June, 1878, had faded still further. Taft had changed in other ways. He was a married man and responsibility had sobered him. Until two years before he had been inclined to postpone work until the last possible moment. This had worried his younger brother, Horace. On one occasion Will had promised to prepare a paper for the Unity Club on "Pontifical Rome." Horace complained that, "as usual," Will had "put the thing off until he had only two or three hours to prepare in and then he had to work like a slave. . . . He has a wonderful power of work when he once gets started and the only danger is his trusting to it too much."[12] But now, as he prepared to mount the bench in March, 1887, Taft was better able to get started, and his "wonderful power of work" remained the same. The talent was to be useful, for he still knew little about the law.

The state of the nation had certainly not improved in the nine years since Will Taft had graduated from Yale. It was at last clear, as the men of the western plains had begun to suspect a decade before, that scarcely any frontier remained toward which men could push. In 1887 farm mortgages in Kansas, Nebraska and other parts of the valley between the Mississippi River and the Rockies were mounting at an appalling rate. It was hard to pay the interest because tight money had arrived after the United States returned to gold in 1879. The voice of Bryan was not yet heard, but hundreds of thousands in the Middle West were already demanding that the nation must not be crucified on a cross of gold. The revolt had its spokesmen; far too many of them to please the comfortable people of Cincinnati among whom Will Taft moved. There was, for instance, Robert M. LaFollette of Wisconsin— he was to oppose many a cherished project of President Taft between 1909 and 1913. There was Samuel Gompers— he was to fight against the election of Taft in 1908. There was John P. Altgeld of Illinois— who was no better than a socialist in the minds of conservatively intelligent people. There was Henry Demarest Lloyd

[12] Horace D. Taft to Louise Taft, April 19, 1885.

of Chicago, who had once been a harmless literary man, but now was viciously and wantonly attacking the Standard Oil Company and the railroads.

Economically, during 1886 and 1887, conditions were a degree better; that is, the large corporations were earning bigger profits. But the workingman felt that he was not getting a proper share of these profits. He resented the fortunes which, so his leaders proclaimed, had been built by his sweat and toil; had not Commodore Cornelius Vanderbilt died with over $100,000,000? What chance had labor in Congress when the Senate was dominated, more or less, by such millionaires as James G. Fair of Nevada, Leland Stanford of California, and Don Cameron of Pennsylvania? The gentlemen of the upper house may have come from the several states and may, technically, have represented their residents. But everyone spoke of "railroad" or "oil" or "silver" or "coal" senators; these industries were their real constituencies.[13] The House of Representatives, supposedly more democratic, was not much better. Its members, so common talk ran, were bought and sold at will by the millionaires. Occasionally, it is true, some state legislature would decree that working conditions must be improved. Usually, then, the courts stepped in and invalidated the reform. Labor saw slight basis for hope in politics. Its members had learned a little about organization in the past decade and early in 1886 the country was swept by a series of violent strikes. By spring, the respectable people throughout the country were very much frightened. They had no doubt whatever that the Haymarket Square bombing in Chicago was the work of anarchistic labor leaders. In Washington Grover Cleveland labored on, although he would soon be defeated. His place would be taken by Benjamin Harrison, another of the Ohio presidents, who had been a general in the Civil War. He, too, tried hard to make a success.

Such were a few of the national currents as Taft entered his first harbor of judicial life in March, 1887. He wrote nothing, at the time, to show that he was aware of them. His viewpoint toward labor and unrest was to be made amply clear a few years later, though, when in private letters he expressed deep hostility toward the workers involved in the Pullman strike. In this attitude, Taft

13 Nevins, Allan, *Grover Cleveland, A Study in Courage.* pp. 340-345.

accurately reflected the ingrained opinions of his class. Many years later, in drafting his memoirs, Theodore Roosevelt described with indignation a decision by the New York Court of Appeals which invalidated regulation of cigar manufacturing in unsanitary tenements. The judges, he wrote, "knew legalism, but not life." [14] This, however, was written decades after the decision. In 1884 Roosevelt was opposing as "purely socialistic" measures limiting the daily toil of streetcar employees and increasing the wages of New York City firemen. In 1886 he was candidate for mayor of New York in a three-cornered fight with Abram S. Hewitt and Henry George. The author of *Progress and Poverty,* according to Roosevelt's final verdict, was "an utterly cheap reformer." [15] Beyond any doubt, Roosevelt and Taft agreed completely on the menace of labor and watched askance the slowly rising liberalism of the eighties.

—4—

It was, although of lower jurisdiction, a distinguished bench which Taft ascended in March, 1887, and on which he sat for almost three years. Appropriately enough, Alphonso Taft had graced it. Taft's colleagues, at first, were Judges Hiram Peck and Frederick W. Moore, both much older than he; later Judge Peck resigned and his place was taken by Judge Edward F. Noyes. No official record of the Superior Court was kept, either in transcript or printed. Almost the only source for the decisions written by Judge Taft is a private publication, the *Weekly Law Bulletin and Ohio Law Journal.* In this are some two score of Taft's opinions and they are, all in all, decidedly dull reading. Their significance, with one or two exceptions, lies in the degree to which they show the early development of traits which later became pronounced.

Taft was not, in any sense, a literary craftsman and this, curiously, was despite the fact that he enjoyed writing. Whenever, during all his life, he was on journeys he would refresh himself by frequent letters to his wife. Sometimes he would write twice in one day and would describe in detail what he had done, what he had

[14] Roosevelt, Theodore, *An Autobiography,* p. 81. [15] Pringle, H. F., *op. cit.,* pp. 78, 111-112.

said, what he had seen. His official and personal files during the White House period were crammed with letters in which he explained his views on the tariff, on currency reform, on all the innumerable problems which plagued him. His letters lacked style or grace, however. They were too verbose and rarely had charm. He had no flair whatever for the turning of a phrase, for brief analysis of a technical subject. The same faults are to be found in his messages as president and in other official documents. They are discernible in the first judicial opinions which he wrote on the Superior Court of Cincinnati. They marked, although to a lesser degree, his decisions as chief justice of the United States.

Taft had a thorough mind rather than a facile or brilliant one. Thus his opinions as an Ohio judge were fortified by countless citations from early decisions. Yet by sheer application he was often able to penetrate through an involved situation and present the facts logically and, save for the excess verbiage, clearly. As chief justice he had the right to reserve for himself any cases that he preferred and he often took extremely complicated patent cases. He did this not so much because he enjoyed wrestling with their technicalities as because the associate justices begged to be excused from doing so. The majority of the cases which confronted him when his judicial career began were, of course, on such routine matters as the wording of contracts, wills and statutes. Examination of Ohio court records discloses that he was upheld by the State Supreme Court to a gratifying extent. He was sometimes overruled in cases which involved the Cincinnati municipal government. Taft had small respect for Cincinnati's machine; it is difficult to avoid suspicion that he strained the law to find against it.

A few highlights in the files of the *Weekly Law Bulletin* are of interest. In November, 1887, a case with the appalling title, *Societe Anonyme de la Distillerie de la Benedictine* v. *Micalovitch, Fletcher & Co.* came before the Superior Court. This concerned the use by the defendants of a trade-mark owned by the plaintiffs. Taft's opinion bristled with erudition. The young judge dug back into his recollections of French and discussed the meaning of obscure words. He wrote a little essay on the history of the French liquor industry. He granted a perpetual injunction, and then threw a judicial fee into the lap of his boyhood friend, Rufus B. Smith, by naming him special master to assess the damages.[16] Such bright spots are infrequent. In January of the following year a fourteen-year-old boy asked for damages because, while playing in a cigar factory, he had been caught in an elevator and had lost a leg. His attorneys contended that the foreman in the plant should have warned him. Judge Taft thought otherwise. A boy of fourteen should have sufficient discretion, he wrote, "to prevent his placing himself without any reason in the only place of danger in the elevator." [17]

Taft was by no means a procorporation judge, however. At the same session of the Superior Court the estate of a deceased inebriate asked for damages against the Cincinnati, Hamilton & Dayton Railroad Company. The intoxicated man had walked through a train and had tumbled to the tracks from the rear platform where he was killed by a following train. The point of the action lay in the fact that another passenger had informed the brakeman of the drunkard's condition, but he did nothing, and in the further fact that no guard rails or lights protected the rear platform. In this litigation, which refuted the theory that a divine providence protects inebriates, Judge Taft held that the railroad company was liable.[18]

In May, 1889, he was required to decide against the newspaper on which he had once been employed, the Cincinnati *Commercial-Gazette*. A reporter for that journal had written a minor news item about the alleged misconduct of one Annie Grooms. The lady in question was declared to have been caught in an adulterous episode at the firehouse. She denied the accuracy of the report. Judge Taft ruled that a newspaper was liable "in exemplary damages for the malice or wanton recklessness of its reporter." [19] Unfortunately, the *Weekly Law Bulletin* did not give further details regarding the reported, but denied, romance between Mrs. Grooms and the fire fighter.

[16] *Weekly Law Bulletin and Ohio Law Journal*, Nov. 21, 1888. [17] *Ibid.*, Jan. 9, 1889. [18] *Ibid.* [19] *Ibid.*, May 11, 1889.

—5—

By far the most important decision of Taft, J. on the Superior Court was in *Moores & Co.* v. *Bricklayers' Union No. 1, W. H. Stephenson, P. H. McElroy et al* in January, 1890. Cincinnati, like the rest of the country, was being torn by labor troubles during this decade. The suit grew out of one of the strikes. Taft's decision was his first important one concerning labor and it was to return to plague him sorely when, in 1907 and 1908, he began his active campaign for the Republican presidential nomination.

Serious discussion of Taft for president had started before then—far back in his Philippine Island days and consistently, for years, he sincerely objected. He declared that his ambition remained the Supreme Court. He cited with obvious relief his record of anti-labor decisions while on the state and the federal bench and said that it was preposterous to suppose that any political party would burden itself with so handicapped a candidate. To friends who suggested it in 1903, he wrote:

Don't sit up nights thinking about making me President for that will never come and I have no ambition in that direction. Any party which would nominate me would make a great mistake. . . . I appreciate highly the compliment, but I must tell you that the suggestion to me only affects my risibles. I was a federal judge for ten years and I enforced injunctions against labor organizations as I did against others, and it so happened that more injunctions of this kind fell to me than almost any other judge of the United States. I have nothing to apologize for in what I did at that time, but it needs no politician to understand that a candidate who has that kind of a record would only be a burden to the party which undertakes to carry him.[20]

His decision in *Moores & Co.* v. *Bricklayers' Union* was not an injunction case although Democratic orators were frequently to call it such. Republican spellbinders were just as erroneously to insist that Taft's ruling was in no way a blow at labor organizations or the workingman. The facts in the case were simple. The Bricklayers' Union of Cincinnati was engaged in a dispute with a local

[20] Taft to Judson Sparr, Oct. 27, 1903; Taft to J. K. Ohl, Nov. 3, 1903.

contracting firm, Parker Brothers. This involved, among minor points, the reinstatement of a dismissed apprentice bricklayer and the employment of another. Rebuffed, the bricklayers announced to all the Cincinnati firms dealing in building materials that no supplies should be sold to the offending Parker Brothers.

If any firm did so, the union warned, bricklayers all over Cincinnati might refuse to work with the materials it sold. This meant two things: first, that Parker Brothers could get no supplies and, second, that a supply house which attempted to sell to Parker Brothers might find all its other markets cut off. Moores & Company, plaintiffs in the action on which Judge Taft passed, were dealers in lime and Parker Brothers were among their customers. Upon receipt of a circular warning them to sell no more lime to Parker Brothers, the house did halt deliveries. When, however, Parker Brothers sent a teamster and truck to their yards they made a sale for cash. The union thereupon notified all of Moores & Company's customers that lime from this house would not be worked by Cincinnati bricklayers. Naturally, the contractors bought from other dealers. Moores & Company thereupon sued the union and its agents for loss of business caused by a malicious conspiracy. The case was heard in special term by one of the judges of the Superior Court and damages of $2,250 were assessed by a jury against the bricklayers.

The case reached Judges Taft, Moore and Noyes on a motion for a new trial. Taft wrote the opinion, his colleagues concurring, that the award of $2,250 against the union was proper, and a new trial was denied. His opinion was detailed and exhaustive. The issue, he said, was really not complicated. Had the bricklayers engaged in an illegal conspiracy to injure the business of Moores & Company? Before he gave his views, Judge Taft set forth the common-law rights of the employer and his employee; it was these sentences which, taken out of their context, were used by Republican propagandists in 1908 to prove that Taft had really ruled on behalf of the downtrodden workingman.

"Every man, be he capitalist, merchant, employer, laborer or professional man," Taft wrote, "is entitled to invest his capital, to carry on his business, to bestow his labor, or to exercise his calling, if within the law, according to his pleasure. Generally speaking, if, in the exercise of such a right by one, another suffers a loss, he has no ground of action. . . . Again, if a workingman is called upon to work with the material of a certain dealer, and it is of such a character as either to make his labor greater than that sold by another, or is hurtful to the person using it, or for any other reason is not satisfactory to the workman, he may lawfully notify his employers of his objection and refuse to work it. The loss of the material man in his sales caused by such action of the workingman is not a legal injury, and not the subject of action. And so it may be said that in these respects, what one workman may do, many may do, and many may combine to do without giving the sufferer any right of action against those who cause his loss."

Then, however, Judge Taft added that "there are losses willfully caused to one by another in the exercise of what otherwise would be a lawful right, from simple motives of malice."

Such words as "malice," "intent," "purport," it may be noted in passing, are the ones which learned jurists write volumes about, which have caused unending litigation. Who can state accurately whether an act was malicious and therefore illegal? "We are not sure that we can," the jurists have answered, "but we do." So Taft, in *Moores & Co.* v. *Bricklayers' Union* reached back into the annals of English law and brought forth precedents to show that the Cincinnati bricklayers had maliciously damaged the business of Moores & Company. The sturdy bricklayers, assuming the improbability that they read the decision of Judge Taft in January, 1890, must have pondered anew the mysteries of the law. Some of the precedents cited were remote.

There was, for example, the ill-mannered Englishman who fired a gun in the air so that his neighbor, guarding a wild-fowl decoy, would be cheated out of his bag of game. That, said the English courts, was wrong; it would have been legal, however, had he fired his gun for some purpose other than mere malice. Judge Taft cited, too, another English precedent, *Gregory* v. *The Duke of Brunswick,* 6 Man. & Or., 953, wherein an actor had sued because he had been hissed off the stage. Naturally, said the courts, it was wholly proper for any person to hiss an actor to his heart's content. But to combine with others and hiss the Thespian was malicious conspiracy. Such had been the case in this instance;

therefore, the actor could sue the hissers. Whether he did so, whether he recovered anything, was not mentioned by Judge Taft.

"Malice, then," said Judge Taft, after the precedents, "is really intent to injure another without cause or excuse."

He cited other cases, among them the famous Mogul Steamship Company case in which six companies engaged in the China tea trade combined to drive a rate-cutting rival out of business. The English courts held this to be proper, but Taft doubted whether another view might not have been adopted in the United States. The germ of his reasoning against the Cincinnati bricklayers is to be found in his definition of malice. That he was leaning toward conservatism is clear. Not very many years before, as history is counted, any combination of workingmen whatever was "without cause or excuse." In this instance, Judge Taft pointed out that Moores & Company had a right to sell their lime where they chose. True, the bricklayers could dispose of their labor as they pleased. But when the bricklayers used Moores & Company as a means of injuring Parker Brothers, they stepped beyond the law.

"The immediate motive of the defendants here was to show the building world what punishment and disaster necessarily followed a defiance of their demands," he wrote. "The remote motive of wishing to better their condition by the power so acquired will not, we think we have shown, make any legal justification for defendants' acts."

Taft's reasoning is hard to follow. Because the motive—of self-improvement— was "remote," the action was without just cause. The bricklayers had forced one party, Moores & Company, to injure a third, Parker Brothers, and this was malicious and illegal.[21] In other words, the "secondary boycott" had no standing in law. Taft always held firmly to this decision, reached so early in his judicial career. In 1914 he quoted long extracts from it in a series of essays. He insisted, again, that the secondary boycott was illegal. He cited many of the same cases.[22] It was good law. Other jurists have held the same way. The decision of Judge Taft in *Moores & Co.* v. *Bricklayers' Union* did much to befog the labor issue.

21 *Weekly Law Bulletin*, Jan. 20, 1890. 22 Taft, W. H., *The Anti-Trust Act and the Supreme Court*, pp. 12-27.

—6—

The Superior Court was a pleasant harbor. But by July, 1889, Taft had his eye on a far more attractive one: the Supreme Court of the United States. To say that Taft was conceited or had an exaggerated conception of his talents would be to deny basic characteristics. Too often he was overly modest. Too often he was insecure and apprehensive. None the less, although he reiterated that the possibility of appointment was fantastic, Taft pulled all available wires. A vacancy existed. President Harrison had offered the appointment to Thomas McDougall of Cincinnati, who had declined. Now various jurists, Taft told his father, were engaged "in the innocent amusement of pushing me." [23] Judge Peck, his former associate on the Superior Court, was working on his behalf.

"He says," Taft wrote, "that he thinks the President is very much in doubt from all he can learn and that the chances are excellent. This is a very roseate view to take, but of course it doesn't disturb my equanimity for I know the chance is only one in a million, but still the chance is something at so great a prize." [24]

Governor Foraker, who once had been that "double-faced Campbell man," was Taft's chief advocate. In late August, 1889, Foraker was running for his third term and Taft assured him that, this time, he was an ardent supporter. If he was elected, he told the governor, the presidency loomed in the immediate future.

"Well," answered Foraker, "if I get there, you would have a show for the Supreme Bench sure enough."

Taft described these tantalizing possibilities in a letter to his father. The occasion had been a visit of President Harrison to Cincinnati:

I went about as a member of the committee in the presidential train and came in contact with Foraker again. F. said he had put in some good work for me with the President. He said it came about this way. He was curious to see whether the President had taken in who I was. So when he got the opportunity, he asked

[23] Taft to Alphonso Taft, July 20, 1889. [24] *Idem*, Aug. 10, 1889.

him whether he noticed me. To which the President replied, "Oh, yes, what a fine-looking man he is. What a fine physique he has." Whereupon Foraker says he proceeded to give me a first-class recommendation without mentioning the place to the President. Of course F. is after votes and how much this story is to be discounted each one must judge.[25]

". . . all this is very good fun and that is all," he continued. "My chances of going to the moon and of donning a silk gown at the hands of President Harrison are about equal. I am quite sure if I were he I would not appoint a man of my age and position to that bench." [26]

It would, in fact, have been an unusual appointment. Taft would not have been the youngest associate justice in history. Justice Joseph Story was only thirty-two when he was elevated. But Taft had, as yet, hardly the legal background to justify the promotion. He continued to hope until the end of September. Foraker went so far as to write to the President, and sent a copy to Taft.

"He is a man of strong physique," said Foraker, "of positive convictions, fine address and in every way well adapted to fill the place with credit to yourself and to your administration. *His appointment would be satisfactory to an unusually high degree to the Republicans of this state, and no Democrat could justly criticize it.*" [27]

"I am very grateful," acknowledged Taft, "for the handsome and much too complimentary words of your letter." [28]

The President concluded that it was not necessary to award so high a post in order to please the Ohio Republicans. As a consolation prize, he offered Taft appointment as solicitor general. Taft accepted. He subsequently assured William Allen White it had come "without the slightest solicitation on my part or knowledge that there was a vacancy in that office." [29] The fates were, as always, pushing Taft higher and higher. Perhaps he was the only man in American political history who can, with complete accuracy, be described as a creature of destiny.

[25] *Idem,* August (?), 1889. [26] *Idem,* Aug. 24, 1889. [27] Foraker to Taft, Sept. 23, 1889. (Italics mine.) [28] Foraker, Julia B., *op. cit.,* p. 307. [29] Taft to White, March 31, 1908.

CHAPTER VIII

AMONG THE BIGWIGS

THE solicitor general of the United States is, in a sense, counsel to the attorney general. He is called upon to advise that Cabinet officer. He may be asked to draft legal opinions for the President. He appears for the government in most of its cases in the Supreme Court. Taft was, as usual, apprehensive that he was not qualified. He was sworn in on February 14, 1890, and promptly told his father that the prospect was "rather overwhelming." He felt "entirely unfamiliar with the rules of practice. . . . I have very little familiarity with the decisions of the court and [with] the federal statutes." From California, where he was making a vain fight to regain his health, Alphonso Taft was as reassuring as he was proud of his son. It was a "Herculean task," he conceded. But "go ahead and fear not." [1]

Taft had resigned from the Superior Court with regret and misgivings. Perhaps he would not have done so had it not been for the ambitious Pike Street girl who had become his wife. Nellie Taft never considered it a virtue to suffer in silence or to refrain from expression of dislikes or grievances. She had been frank in admitting that she had been bored by too much association with learned jurists while her husband was on the Superior Court. Too often, at dinner parties, the conversation was limited to *Moores & Co. v. Bricklayers' Union* and other profundities of the law. Young Mrs. Taft preferred— as her sister long recalled— music, books, or merely light and gay gossip about life in Cincinnati.[2] Besides, she had more than a suspicion that she could mold this marital clay into a really important public figure. Shortly after she became engaged in 1885, Nellie discussed the future with her mother.

"You know," she said quietly, "a lot of people think a great deal of Will. Some people even say that he may obtain some very important position in Washington." [3]

[1] Alphonso Taft to Taft, Feb. 1, 1890. [2] Maria Herron to author, Feb. 28, 1935. [3] *Idem.*

After all, had not Will Taft, himself, gladly admitted her to the role of sculptor?[4] The possibilities for making something out of Will Taft were infinitely greater in Washington than in Cincinnati. His talents would be appreciated there. The solicitor general was only one step removed from the Cabinet of President Harrison and he would meet all the major politicians of the day. But Mrs. Taft was constantly forced to struggle against her husband's judicial tastes. He had been solicitor general for hardly more than a year and a half when a chance came for appointment to the Circuit Court, the highest federal bench except the Supreme Court. He said that he would accept the appointment if it came. Mrs. Taft was dismayed. Her husband had just been on some journey.

"Think of your going off on a trip with two Cabinet officers!" she wrote. "If you get your heart's desire, my darling, it will put an end to all the opportunities you now have of being thrown with the bigwigs."[5]

Taft could never regard the bigwigs with quite the pleasure they afforded his wife. He saw, however, obvious advantages in the post of solicitor general. Governor Foraker, by now his guide and mentor, had been instrumental in obtaining the appointment for Taft. He said that the importance of the post lay "in the other position to which I can clearly see that it leads . . . the bench of the Supreme Court."[6]

—2—

The morning of Taft's arrival in Washington in February, 1890, was gloomy. He came in on the sleeper from Cincinnati and tumbled out of his berth in the gray dawn of six o'clock. He was weary and bedraggled, because no berth could accommodate his large body so that anything more than fitful sleep was possible. This was long before the new Union Station had been built; trains from Cincinnati came into the ancient, dirty terminal. Taft looked in vain for a porter. Finally he trudged, bag in hand, up to the old Ebbitt House. Mrs. Taft had decided to remain in Cincinnati until

[4] Taft to Helen Herron, May 1, 1885. [5] Helen H. Taft to Taft, July 18, 1891. [6] Foraker, Julia B., I Would Live It Again, pp. 307-308.

notified that some kind of accommodations had been secured. Their first son, Robert, was only six months old. Travel with a baby was an ordeal.

The new solicitor general ate a lonely breakfast at the hotel and then walked over to the Department of Justice where he paid his respects to Attorney General W. H. H. Miller. The roseate conception of solicitor general, as offered by Foraker and others, began to fade. His office consisted of a single shabby room up three flights of stairs. The only stenographer was a telegrapher officially detailed to the chief clerk's office. When the honorable, the solicitor general, wished to write a letter he bellowed for this versatile functionary. If the wires were quiet, a few moments of dictation were possible. A mass of work lay piled on the old-fashioned desk. Ordow W. Chapman, Taft's predecessor, had died in January. Virtually nothing had been done in the meanwhile and the Supreme Court was, of course, in session. Taft learned that he would have to digest ten complicated cases, prepare briefs and argue them before the court adjourned in June. For a few minutes on that first day, February 15, 1890, Taft sat and thumbed through legal papers in utter discouragement. Why had he left the quiet harbor of the Superior Court? [7]

His melancholy meditations— Taft told Nellie all about them later— were interrupted by a department messenger who announced that United States Senator William M. Evarts of New York was calling. The solicitor general was astonished. Evarts was a distinguished attorney as well as a member of the awe-inspiring upper house and he had been secretary of state. They had never met.

"Judge Taft," said the senator as he came in, "I knew your father. I was in the class of 'thirty-seven at Yale and your father was tutoring there then. I valued his friendship."

The solicitor general beamed with pleasure. Then his visitor said that he was giving a dinner that night for Mr. and Mrs. Joseph Choate and that they needed another man. Would Judge Taft— purely in consideration of the friendship between his father and Mr. Evarts— waive the formality customary in Washington and attend? Taft knew nothing about Washington formalities. He was lonely. He accepted with celerity. On his right and left at the dinner table, that night, were Mrs. Henry Cabot Lodge and Mrs. John Hay. The capital, after that, was lonely no longer.

"I am gradually getting acquainted with the prominent people here," he told his father in April, "and I have no doubt that after one year I shall have a pretty general knowledge of the persons who run things." [8]

—3—

After two weeks, Mrs. Taft came on with Robert and they took a house at 5 Du Pont Circle. It was small and the rent was $100 a month; a major item since the post of solicitor general paid only $7,000 a year and Taft had no private income. The house was, however, "very pleasantly situated with an outlook on a delightful little park and is very convenient to the streetcars." A library had been established on the second floor; here Taft had lined the walls with shelves so that there was room for all his law volumes as well as for Mrs. Taft's books.[9] "This changing of a family and home from one city to another and furnishing the house is not by any means a cheap matter," Taft complained, "and it makes my salary look a little sick to pay the bills." [10] No serious financial embarrassment arose, owing to the readiness of Brother Charles to advance any necessary funds. Charles P. Taft was always to do so whether Will, of whom he was so proud, was secretary of war or president. In May, 1890, Will Taft asked whether "it will be entirely convenient for you to let me have $250 more," that his bills had been higher than he had expected.[11]

Despite apprehensions about his qualifications as solicitor general, Taft was contented in the house on Du Pont Circle. He was tasting the prideful joys of fatherhood. Robert Alphonso Taft, his first son, had been born on September 8, 1889. "There is something charming about Bobbie that I don't see in any other baby," he admitted. "Of course I look at every baby I see, but it is not satisfactory. I need not argue with you to establish the fact that our boy is different from other babies in many most desirable ways." [12]

[8] Taft to Alphonso Taft, April ?, 1890. [9] Taft to H. D. Peck, April 26, 1890. [10] *Idem*. [11] Taft to C. P. Taft, May 2, 1890. [12] Taft to Helen H. Taft, May 16, 1891.

There was little pretension in the small house. In the summer ot 1890, Mrs. Taft fled from the heat of the capital to the Massachusetts seashore. Taft stayed behind, and found that Negro servants were temperamental and unreliable. Sometimes he had none at all.

"How I would have laughed to see you making your bed," wrote his wife.[13]

Washington, itself, was an unpretentious city in 1890. "The United States are the only great country in the world which has no capital," James Bryce had written two years before. ". . . By a capital I mean a city which is not only the seat of political government, but is also by the size, wealth and character of its population the head and centre of the country, a leading seat of commerce and industry, a reservoir of financial resources, the favoured residence of the great and powerful, the spot in which the chiefs of the learned professions are to be found, where the most potent and widely-read journals are published, whither men of literary and scientific capacity are drawn." This, of course, was an accurate tabulation of precisely the characteristics which Washington did not have. Bryce added that its population was only 150,000, and that a third of these people were Negroes. Society consisted largely of congressmen, government officials, the diplomatic corps "and some rich and leisured people who come to spend the winter." [14] True, Washington was changing somewhat by 1890. Huge fortunes had been made in the United States. The "oil" and "silver" and other commodity-nurtured members of the Senate were beginning to build themselves colossal houses and to entertain elaborately. But the United States was still, in the minds of most Europeans, an outpost beyond the border of civilization. After the Spanish-American War it was to be different. Through that comic struggle, by the simple expedient of defeating a decrepit nation in an unnecessary war, Uncle Sam was to be accorded almost complete equality in the family of nations.

A few amusing, intelligent, and vivid people did dwell in Washington in the nineties, however. Cecil Spring Rice was beginning his diplomatic career at the British embassy. Theodore Roosevelt was a member of the Civil Service Commission and was

[13] Helen H. Taft to Taft, Aug. 10, 1890. [14] Bryce, James, *The American Commonwealth* (1888 ed.), Vol. III, pp. 585-589.

alarming, by his crusades, the Republican leaders who had given him the post. Thomas B. Reed, the "Czar" Reed who shone brilliantly as speaker of the House but who was too sardonic to be seriously considered for president by the G.O.P., was on hand to tell his savage stories. John Hay had erred in supporting Senator John Sherman in 1888 and was, therefore, out of favor with the administration. He was a literary man, again, instead of a publicist. "I am a worthless creature, destitute of initiative," he wrote.[15] This meant little; Hay was constantly uttering premature obituaries about himself. Even gloom did not dim the sparkle of his conversation. Mrs. Lodge, Mrs. Hay, and Mrs. Don Cameron (wife of the Pennsylvania senator) were the arbiters of Washington society; they were gracious, charming, beautiful women. And at 1603 H Street, across Lafayette Square from the White House, Henry Adams brooded and opened his doors to amusing people.

Roosevelt, Hay, Adams, Spring Rice and Lodge saw each other almost daily. They knew— and in their superior wisdom had small use for— all the great figures of Washington. "Springy" went to the White House with his friend, Theodore, in April, 1890, and described President and Mrs. Harrison. "They are small and fat," he wrote. "They said they were glad to see us, but they neither looked it." [16] During the summer of 1891, when Mrs. Roosevelt was away, Spring Rice and Roosevelt kept joint bachelor hall. Sometimes Rudyard Kipling would drop in. The romantic and theatrical Richard Harding Davis was often there. Always Roosevelt would be talking; talking and gesticulating and shooting out ideas like sparks.

Solicitor General Taft must have met all these people, or most of them. But he was not admitted to their inner circle. Perhaps he was not quite effervescent enough for their tastes. Perhaps his interests, and therefore his conversation, were too closely linked to the law. Roosevelt and Spring Rice had only the vaguest interest, if any, in legal abstractions. That Taft met Roosevelt, for the first time, not long after coming to Washington as solicitor general is certain. But there is no record of when or where the meeting took place.

"I saw Mr. and Mrs. Roosevelt in the reserved gallery and

[15] Dennett, Tyler, *John Hay*, p. 150. [16] Gwynn, Stephen, *The Letters and Friendship of Sir Cecil Spring Rice*, Vol. I, p. 104.

called them over," he told Mrs. Taft in March, 1892, referring to a visit to the House of Representatives. "We sat and heard Reed make a capital five-minute speech in which he roasted the Democrats." [17]

Spring Rice, fascinated by all the prominent figures in this strange, new land to which he had been assigned by his government, does not mention Taft at all during this period. There is no reference to him in Roosevelt's own voluminous letters to Lodge. Yet Taft was fairly close to the seats of the mighty. He had called on the attorney general and had there seen President Harrison in April, 1890.[18] But his tastes were more legal than political; Attorney General Miller and the justices of the Supreme Court were, it seems, the men whom Taft saw the most.[19] Mrs. Taft must have been a degree chagrined.

Ample opportunity for social contacts existed, however. In May, 1890, they attended a dance at the Country Club where "all the swells"— among others, the British, Turkish and Danish ministers— were present.[20] At about this time, Mrs. Taft came out victorious in one of those minor altercations which typify a happy and spirited marriage. Her husband had asked her to call on Mrs. Horace Gray, the wife of Associate Justice Gray of the Supreme Court as soon as possible. Mrs. Taft was delayed, owing to the pressure of getting settled, and when she did so she apologized. Mrs. Gray was amused.

"I should have waived ceremony and come myself to welcome you to Washington," she said, "except for one thing which I could not very well overlook, and that is— that Mr. Taft has not yet called on Mr. Justice Gray." Mrs. Taft, delighted, hurried home to report this to her spouse and to gloat over his confusion.[21]

—4—

In addition to being apprehensive that his knowledge of federal law was inadequate, Taft worried over the possibility that he was

---

[17] Taft to Helen H. Taft, March 9, 1892. [18] Taft to Alphonso Taft, April ?, 1890. [19] Taft, Mrs. W. H., *op. cit.,* p. 28. [20] Taft to Alphonso Taft, May 6, 1890. [21] Taft, Mrs. W. H., *op. cit.,* pp. 28-29.

a mediocre speaker and would, in presenting cases for the government, make a bad impression on the Supreme Court. "I do not think I acquitted myself with credit and went home from the court a great deal discouraged," he wrote after his maiden appearance. ". . . I do not find myself at all easy or fluent on my feet. I am afraid I never shall be." He wrote his father that his second speech had been a little better, "but I seemed to manifest the same soporific power with reference to the court that had been present in my first attempt." He added:

I have difficulty in holding the attention of the court. They seem to think when I begin to talk that that is a good chance to read all the letters that have been waiting for some time, to eat lunch, and to devote their attention to correcting proof, and other matters that have been delayed until my speech. However, I expect to gain a good deal of practice in addressing a lot of mummies and experience in not being overcome by circumstances.[22]

The amount of work harassed Taft, too, and so did the climate of Washington as summer approached; he was to find the heat even worse than that of Cincinnati. In May, 1890, Attorney General Miller fell ill and Taft became acting attorney general. "The novelty of it wore off in just about a day," he reported, "and no man will be happier than I shall be when he returns to his desk. What with appointments, dilatory officials throughout the country and cranks, one's time is all occupied and nothing is accomplished." [23] Depression weighed heavily, at times, that first summer. President Harrison had consulted him on judicial appointments in Texas and in the Oklahoma Territory, but "I find it somewhat difficult to be of any assistance . . . because I have yet to learn his views and just what facts he wishes to be dwelt upon." [24] Besides, "The President is not popular with the members of either house. His manner of treating them is not at all fortunate, and when they have an interview with him they generally come away mad. . . . I think this is exceedingly unfortunate, because I am sure we have never had a man in the White House who was more conscientiously seeking to do his duty." [25]

[22] Taft to H. D. Peck, April 26, 1890; Taft to M. W. Myers, April 26, 1890; Taft to Alphonso Taft, April ?, May 6, 1890. [23] Taft to C. P. Taft, May 2, 1890. [24] Taft to Alphonso Taft, May 6, 1890. [25] Taft to Alphonso Taft, June 16, 1890.

As for the weather, its effect on a stout man was far worse than on men of average weight. He commiserated with a corpulent Cincinnati acquaintance: "I hope you are getting along as well as could be expected in this very hot weather. You and I have a sympathy on that subject that men with less dignity of stomach and rotundity of form can hardly appreciate." [26] That year Taft began a more or less consistent, and nearly always futile, battle against weight. Doctors had warned that "if my fat continues to increase it may be deposited in the muscles of my heart and seriously interfere with its healthy action."

"Nothing will do for me . . . but regular and hearty exercise," he told his wife. "This is my fate and is the essential to my living to a good old age. You must, therefore, make yourself a thorn in my side to that end, my darling." [27]

The chief attraction to the work of solicitor general during the first year was its variety. Taft acquired detailed knowledge of federal procedure. He was required to dig out precedents. In June, 1890, the attorney general requested an opinion on whether Congress could, by legislation, annul the findings of an army court-martial. Taft was clear that the legislative branch had no such power. That same month, also, Taft came into contact for the first time with a phase of the conservation problem; he was to worry about this a great deal in the years ahead. Congress had ceded to Alabama certain federal lands which were to be used to encourage the construction of a railroad within twenty-five years. The time had elapsed, the railroad had not been finished, and now timber on the land was being ruthlessly cut. Could the attorney general of the United States intervene to stop this? Taft expressed hope that the federal government had the power; he intended to look thoroughly into the matter.[28]

On the whole, the problems were less interesting than the ones which had come before Judge Taft of the Ohio Superior Court until, in January, 1891, the solicitor general was confronted with the Bering Sea case. This was an ancient controversy with Great Britain and Taft's own connection with it concerned only an ill-

[26] Taft to J. Schaufert, June 24, 1890.   [27] Taft to Helen H. Taft, May 20, 1891.
[28] Taft to Alphonso Taft, June 16, 1890.

ALPHONSO TAFT, FATHER OF WILLIAM H. TAFT

See page 64]

MRS. ALPHONSO TAFT

[*See page 64*

judged lawsuit instigated by the English in the United States Supreme Court. The quarrel over seal hunting off Alaska was one of a long series of incidents which caused friction between the United States and Great Britain. The basic source of the disharmony was, of course, memory of the war for the independence of the colonies. The hard feeling had been heightened by the influx of Irish immigrants into the United States. They became politically important. Twisting the lion's tail grew to be as important in every campaign as kissing babies. Added to all this was the sense of inferiority felt, but never admitted, by many Americans in the presence of the English. Even so intelligent an American as Theodore Roosevelt would thunder, during the unfortunate Venezuela episode in 1894, that Great Britain never permitted "a consideration of abstract right or morality [to] interfere with the chance for her national aggrandizement or mercantile gain." [29]

—5—

In retrospect, the United States clearly seems to have been highhanded in the Bering Sea matter. Soon after the acquisition of Alaska from Russia in 1867 the United States claimed control over seal fishing in the entire Bering Sea; not merely in the immediately adjacent waters. Its reason was the fact that seals were being indiscriminately slaughtered beyond the three-mile limit; there was danger that the vast, rich herds might be exterminated. So the United States started, through its revenue cutters, to confiscate sealing vessels caught in the Bering Sea. Sometimes these were as far as sixty miles from land. The protests from Great Britain, during 1886 and 1887, had been vigorous and prompt. Meanwhile, by diplomatic representations, the United States tried to persuade Great Britain, Russia and Japan— all of them interested in the question— to sign an agreement which would protect the seals. The matter dragged. Distrust increased in England and the United States. Spring Rice, normally so sensible and friendly, suggested in 1890 in a private letter that some member of President Harrison's

[29] Pringle, H. F., *Theodore Roosevelt, a Biography*, p. 167.

Cabinet might have been "given an interest in the Bering Sea Company." [30]

From time to time the owners of vessels seized by the United States had brought suit for damages in American courts. They met with small satisfaction. Then the *W. P. Sayward*, a Canadian sailing vessel, was forfeited and condemned after capture by a revenue cutter. The British government formally appealed to the United States Supreme Court for a writ of prohibition which would halt the Federal District Court of Alaska, charged with sale of the vessel, from taking action. Taft, as solicitor general, drafted the answer to the application. Although he said nothing to indicate that he shared the general hostility toward England, he expressed indignation to his father that the application had been made suddenly and without due notice. A stay of two weeks had been obtained while the attorney general and he were "working like beavers" preparing their brief.

"On Monday," Taft reported, "we shall be in court prepared to argue. The case has aroused great public attention . . . and . . . I look forward with considerable trepidation to making an argument orally before the court in a case which will be so conspicuous. . . . I think Great Britain has departed from diplomatic courtesy in going by the executive and state department to the courts, and I shall not be surprsied if they go out of the court with a flea in their ear on this point." [31]

The flea was successfully implanted in John Bull's ear. The Supreme Court declined to enjoin the sale of the *W. P. Sayward;* it concurred in Taft's argument that a foreign power could not, while diplomatic negotiations were in progress, ask for review of conduct by a branch of the government. The Bering Sea case was returned to the diplomats, who continued to write notes to one another. Spring Rice hoped that it would not lead to war. Great Britain, he warned with one of his penetrating glances into the future, could not afford war with America for "we get an enormous proportion of our food from the United States." [32] The dispute over the seals was finally settled by international arbitration. American contention that the whole of Bering Sea constituted territorial

[30] Nevins, Allan, *Henry White*, pp. 61-67; Gwynn, Stephen, *op. cit.,* Vol. I, p. 105. [31] Taft to Alphonso Taft, Jan. 23, 1891. [32] Gwynn, Stephen, *op. cit.,* Vol. I, p. 113.

waters was rejected, but steps were taken to protect the seals from extermination.[33]

A personal matter was soon to make Taft's work as solicitor general still more difficult. Early in 1891 he began writing almost daily letters to his father, for Alphonso Taft, now past eighty, was growing weaker and weaker in San Diego, California. The son sent on all news which he knew would cheer his beloved sire. He had personally written most of the Bering Sea case brief, he said, and had revised all of it. Up to February, 1891, he had argued a total of eighteen cases; one was still to be decided, but of the others, Taft wrote, he had won fifteen and lost only two. The year as solicitor general had been pleasant and replete with valuable legal experience.[34] The old gentleman was unquestionably gratified. He did not like being in California where he had been sent for his health.

"Think of . . ." he had written, "the fate of an old man who has to be across the continent from the best children in the world." [35]

The children had been greatly alarmed by their father's health since the summer of 1889. Typhoid pneumonia while in St. Petersburg had weakened him. The doctors found that cardiac asthma had developed. The humid heat of Cincinnati, when he returned from abroad, aggravated the condition.[36] So he was sent to San Diego with his daughter, Fanny, who ultimately married Dr. William Edwards, his physician. In May, 1891, discouraging reports reached Washington and Taft hurried west. He found his father unconscious most of the time. One morning the father asked for his son and was told he had not yet come down to breakfast. "He's a noble boy," said the old man.[37] There were occasional moments when the fogs lifted. He asked Will how, as solicitor general, he had liked "those old fellows" on the Supreme Court. Will Taft was amused and touched. His father was eighty; none of the jurists was as old. But he always referred to them as old men.[38]

Alphonso Taft died on May 21, 1891. Will Taft was greatly

[33] Gwynn, Stephen, op. cit., Vol. I, pp. 153-155. [34] Taft to Alphonso Taft, Feb. 9, 10, 14, 1891. [35] Alphonso Taft to Taft, July 10, 1890. [36] Taft to Horace Taft, June 17, 1889. [37] Taft to Helen H. Taft, May 20, 1891. [38] Idem, May 16, 1891.

depressed. The inevitable sorrow had come at a time when his own life was plagued with uncertainty. Six years had passed since he had become engaged to Nellie Herron and had throbbed with new ambitions. In that time he had tasted the placid contentment of judicial life. He had been solicitor general of the United States. His advance had been spectacular and, to Taft himself, puzzling. Had it been caused by the intense desire of the "guardian angel" who now was dead? Taft dismissed the superstitious idea.

Two paths faced him in 1891. One led away from Washington, away from the Roosevelts and the Tom Reeds and the Cabot Lodges— all of whom had dedicated themselves to the active arena of politics and waited hopefully for the lightning which would hurl them into high office. It led back to a second judicial harbor. Even this, Taft felt as his father lay dying, was an improbable consummation. Only mediocrity was ahead. To this he was reconciled.

". . . if I am limited in good fortune," he told his wife, "it is some satisfaction to have had it come at a time when it added to father's happiness. . . . In any event, my darling, we can be happy as long as we live, if only we love each other and the children that come to us." [39]

The other path pointed to public office and fame. Alas, for Nellie Taft, she was to watch her dreams of importance disappear for a time. Alas, for the bigwigs. Alas, for the excitement of life in Washington. She was pregnant that summer of 1891. Mrs. Theodore Roosevelt, whose own husband rarely doubted destiny, was also to have a child. Mrs. Taft derived fractional satisfaction when her daughter, Helen Herron, was born on August 1.

"I see that I got ahead of Mrs. Roosevelt and feel quite proud," she wrote.[40] In most other ways the Roosevelts were to get ahead of the Tafts.

[39] Taft to Helen H. Taft, May 16, 1891. [40] Helen H. Taft to Taft, Aug. 22, 1891.

CHAPTER IX

THE SECOND HARBOR

THE SECOND judicial harbor, where Taft was to rest for eight years, already lay ahead in March, 1891. If he would avoid the harbor, Taft was told, he might enter far more sparkling waters. Alphonso Taft, before he died, described a conversation with his son-in-law, Dr. Edwards of San Diego. "The doctor . . . says there will always be something good for you in your line," he wrote. "He says the presidency will be for assignment and that there will be no especial trouble in your being prepared for it." [1] But Taft did not take the visions seriously at all. They did not allure him particularly. His one ambition, and he had few illusions regarding even this, was the Supreme Court.

Yet the might-have-beens of history are as absorbing as they are harmless. A number of rising young statesmen were being assured, between 1890 and 1896, that the White House was more than an iridescent fancy. "I am no dreamer . . ." insisted, for example, Cabot Lodge to Theodore Roosevelt in 1895. "I do not say you are to be president tomorrow. I do not say it will be— I am sure it may and can be." [2] Taft, had he remained in public office instead of returning to judicial life, might well have received the vice-presidential nomination in 1900. But this would have been possible of course only if William McKinley, also from Ohio, had been rejected for the head of the ticket.

Litigation in the federal courts had been increasing for a number of years. In March, 1891, Congress acted to relieve the situation by creating an appeals court in each of the nine circuits in the nation. The new court would consist of the existing circuit judge, the existing circuit justice and a new judge to be named in each district. ". . . the number of candidates is legion," Taft pointed out,[3] but he pulled all the wires he could reach. He was recommended by a

[1] Alphonso Taft to Taft, March 18, 1891. [2] Lodge, Henry Cabot, *Selections from the Correspondence of Theodore Roosevelt and Henry Cabot Lodge*, Vol. I, p. 179. [3] Taft to Helen H. Taft, March 7, 1891.

committee of Cincinnati lawyers. Senator Sherman of Ohio spoke
to the President in behalf of his selection. But months elapsed before
the appointment came through. On March 21, 1892, he resigned as
solicitor general to become United States circuit judge for the Sixth
Judicial Circuit and ex-officio member of the Circuit Court of
Appeals of the Sixth Circuit.

Taft would again live in Cincinnati, but the jurisdiction of the
Circuit Court covered all of Kentucky, Michigan and Tennessee in
addition to Ohio so that he would be required to travel a great deal.
Mrs. Taft, worrying about finances on a salary of $6,000, went on
ahead in February to prepare a home. Taft was frankly delighted.
He ordered a silk judicial robe for himself, his first robe because
the Superior Court of Ohio had not required this ornament of
office. Taft said he would wear it only when the Court of Appeals
met. "Harlan [Associate Supreme Court Justice Harlan] wants me
to wear it as a circuit judge," he explained. "They do this in Massachusetts, but I don't feel equal to introducing an innovation in our
circuit." [4]

For eight years life moved in an orderly fashion, on the whole,
undisturbed by the tumultuous improbabilities of politics. Taft
would have been as astounded as he would have been unbelieving
had anyone parted the curtains of the future and informed him
that in 1900 he would sail far into the east and find his destiny—
find that and the work which may have been the most valuable in
his long career— on remote islands of which he had barely heard.
In February, 1892, the Taft house on Walnut Hills was under lease
to tenants, so Mrs. Taft had to find some other place for the family
to live. They stayed temporarily at the Burnet House, but the
cost— $300 a month— was prohibitive. In May they moved into the
home of Mary Hanna, a friend, at Third and Lawrence streets; the
rent was $60 a month. Mrs. Taft, by no means reconciled to inter-
ment on the bench, found it difficult to manage on her husband's
salary. In January, 1894, she reported that paying the household
bills had been "as close a squeeze as usual." [5]

Taft did not worry much; money was never important to him.
There was always enough to eat; eating was among the very

important things of life. Federal Judge Taft, for all his talk about the happiness of poverty, was not a bad provider. In the summer of 1892 they went to Murray Bay on the St. Lawrence River for the first time. Except during the presidency, when Taft bowed to the precedent against leaving American soil, the family returned to Murray Bay almost every summer. Taft grew to love the place; when he was away he yearned for the cold air sweeping up the St. Lawrence from the forests which lined the banks of the Saguenay.

By June, 1909, although he had been in the White House for only three months, discouragement had already started to mount.

". . . there is no place like Murray Bay," the President wrote. "If I only have one term, as seems likely in view of the complications that will be presented during that term, one of the great consolations will be that I can go to Murray Bay in the summers thereafter." [6]

Taft longed for the quiet days in the cottage which he had rented. They began with an ample breakfast of meat, eggs and innumerable cups of coffee. Then came golf and then lunch, with as many guests as the table would seat. The afternoons were tranquil. The great St. Lawrence flowed below the cottage. Sometimes it was gray and sometimes flecked with sunset colors, like the varied bits of glass in a child's kaleidoscope. There was always so much to see from the porch at Murray Bay, and Taft did not have to move his large body from the most comfortable chair. To his immediate left, as he looked out, rose the green heights of Cap à l'Aigle; to his right, a distance up the stream, were the slopes of Les Eboulements. Often white "whales" would blow and play immediately in front; sometimes a seal would come from the colder waters of the Saguenay and stay for a little while. And where did the sea gulls go at six o'clock? They came at dawn and did their hunting on a bar below the Taft cottage when the tide was out. But every night they flew away and no one, in all the years, had found the river haven which was their noisy dormitory.

Taft was always a great man in Murray Bay. Tragedy and frustration never touched him there. The habitants— the more literate among them— spat when they heard of the Roosevelt who had, by the great God, betrayed their beloved "petit juge" in 1912.

[6] Taft to C. P. Taft, June 28, 1909.

So they called Taft, in their native blend of amused affection and respect. They raised their caps, as to a seigneur, when he drove down the steep roads. But in the winter, it was authentically reported, the habitants occasionally staged burlesqued versions of life among the summer folk. Then the largest, most massive, among them would play the role of le petit juge. When he died they burned a candle for his Protestant soul.

—2—

Mounting the bench in March, 1892, Taft found that the work was to have a large measure of variety. As a federal circuit judge he would hear motions, write decisions, and preside at civil and criminal trials. As a member of the Sixth Circuit Court of Appeals he held court in Cincinnati, Cleveland, Toledo, Detroit and Nashville. The variety attracted him. He enjoyed the social contacts, in particular the dinners which were given by his legal associates in the cities which he visited. The work, if arduous, was interesting. In less than two months, during one session, he had written twenty opinions.[7] Mrs. Taft, too, appears to have found life fairly satisfactory. Her devotion to music was finding outlet in the organization and management of the Cincinnati Orchestra Association and she taxed her strength raising funds and selling tickets.[8] She was, however, "dreadfully upset" when her too, too honest husband became quixotic about the matter of traveling expenses.

The judge, it appeared, had returned to the federal treasury a sum of money which he had not actually used in going from city to city. Mrs. Taft told him acidly that the allowance had never been intended simply to cover expenses "as judges on a judicial salary do not ordinarily live at the rate of ten dollars a day or five either."

"You would not," she observed accurately, "be very popular with the Supreme Court any more than your own bench if your views were known and I advise you to keep them to yourself." [9]

[7] Taft to Louise Taft, Jan. 5, 1893. [8] Taft, Mrs. W. H., *Recollections of Full Years*, pp. 30-31. [9] Helen H. Taft to Taft, July 4, 1893.

It is to be hoped, although no reply to this letter is available, that Judge Taft learned the art of padding an expense account.

The reference to possible unpopularity with the members of the Supreme Court was shrewd on Mrs. Taft's part. During his eight years as a federal judge, Taft never ceased to hope for elevation to that august bench. He greatly valued the respect and friendship of the current justices. In December, 1893, he journeyed to Washington to attend a session of the Supreme Court.

"I held quite a levee in the courtroom," he reported in mild elation regarding the greetings from attachés and attendants. ". . . Then the court came in and I got a bow from them all and then the notes began to come down, first from [Associate Justice] Harlan and then from [Associate Justice] Jackson." On the following night— obviously this was of much less importance— he would visit "Teddy" Roosevelt.[10] Taft's stature, even in nonlegal circles, grew larger during his period of service on the Circuit Court. In March, 1896, he was in Washington again and called on President Cleveland. "We found his Royal Nibs in excellent humor," Taft wrote home, "and we had a very pleasant interview of some fifteen or twenty minutes."[11]

In 1896, also, Taft became dean and professor of property at his legal alma mater, the Cincinnati Law School. He did this, of course, because of his devotion to the institution and because of his deep interest in legal education. He taught two hours a week, lecturing to the first-year class on Mondays and to the second-year group on Saturdays. The textbook was Gray's *Cases on Property*.

"We reorganized the law school for the purpose of introducing the case system," he recalled. "As a teacher I had a hard time trying to keep ahead of the class and trying to teach Gray's cases."[12]

Taft's students remembered that he was filled with energy. He combined his lecture with recitations during the hour. He rarely failed to ask some question of each member of the class and he was stern enough when some dullard failed. Taft took his duties and the law school itself very seriously. The school was not generally so regarded. Cincinnatians did not view it as a beehive of industry. On one occasion a local newspaper published a drawing of students

[10] Taft to Helen H. Taft, Dec. 4, 1893. [11] *Idem*, March 22, 1896. [12] *Addresses*, Vol. XXXI, p. 44.

playing poker on the top of professors' desks. Dean Taft was furious when he arrived for his lecture. He said he would expel any youths found guilty of playing poker during working hours. But when five or six of them confessed shortly afterward, he merely gave them a stiff scolding in class. The dean grew very excited as he spoke. He banged the desk until the room trembled, and frightened the culprits half out of their wits.[13]

But Taft was kindly too. There was a distressing incident when a student at the school, an older man who had been in business for some years, was indicted in some swindle which was a violation of federal statutes. Federal Judge Taft presided at his trial and the man was found guilty. A delegation of students called to ask for mercy. Taft listened, distress plain on his broad face. He said he was glad they had come to him. But the man was guilty, he pointed out unhappily. He would be sentenced to eighteen months in the penitentiary.

The Cincinnati law students found a warm welcome when they visited a courtroom where Taft presided. When they did so, they watched a human rather than a stern judge. One of the students remembered Taft's annoyance when the prosecuting attorney continued to badger a witness who had already admitted the shame of being unable to read or write.

"Stop that!" he ordered. "You have brought out that this man cannot read; that is enough. I will not have you humiliate this witness any further, because it has no relation to the case."[14]

—3—

On many occasions, in the minds of gloomy and apprehensive reactionaries, the United States has been on the verge of collapse. The years which followed hard upon 1890 constituted one of these periods. Memory of the bombing in Haymarket Square, Chicago, was still all too vivid. Prosperous gentlemen stirred from their sleep in the best clubs in New York, Philadelphia, Chicago and San Francisco and cursed the labor leader-anarchists who, so they still insisted, had been responsible. In 1893 Governor Altgeld of Illinois

---

[13] Stanley Matthews; John Schindel to author, March 1, 1935. [14] John Schindel to author, March 1, 1935.

alarmed them even more when he dared to pardon two men who had first been sentenced to death and then to life imprisonment for the Haymarket outrage. The evidence against them had been flimsy in the extreme. Other worries troubled the respectables. In May, 1892, Henry Clay Frick of the Carnegie Steel Company had announced some wage reductions. In July came the clash between the Pinkertons and the strikers at the Homestead plant near Pittsburgh. On July 23, the gentlemen in the best clubs read of the attempted assassination of Mr. Frick by Alexander Berkman, the self-admitted anarchist. This made the issue alarmingly personal; they began to hire bodyguards. Things grew worse, not better. Breadlines started to form during the depression in 1893. Next year came the Pullman strike in Chicago— imagine a strike against George M. Pullman, the model employer who had done so much for his men! Labor, said the conservatives, was being led astray by radical leaders. One of these was Eugene V. Debs, who ought to be deported or hanged or something. Other subversive influences were undermining the contentment of the honest and, until now, humble American workman. Bryan was talking. Senator Ben Tillman of South Carolina was talking. That curious figure, Jacob Coxey of Massillon, Ohio, was doing more. He had started a march on Washington to demand $500,000,000 in paper money. And what would good securities be worth if these greenbacks spewed from the presses? By 1896, with Bryan calling for free silver, and with William McKinley vehemently but belatedly proclaiming that he had always stood for gold, the respectables had no doubt that the United States stood on the brink of populist ruin.

"Messrs. Bryan, Altgeld, Tillman, Debs, Coxey and the rest," shouted Theodore Roosevelt in a speech for McKinley, "have not the power to rival the deeds of Marat, Barrère and Robespierre, but they are strikingly like the leaders of the Terror of France in mental and moral attitude." [15]

No such nonsense was publicly uttered, of course, by Federal Judge Taft. But he was alarmed, deeply alarmed, by the Pullman strike of 1894 and was almost ferocious in his reaction toward the strikers. Mark Hanna was less than a flaming liberal, but even he had exclaimed in wrath against George Pullman when someone

[15] Pringle, H. F., *Theodore Roosevelt, a Biography*, pp. 152-153.

had praised the model town of Pullman, Illinois, its model streets and homes and had damned its striking workers who were model no longer.

"Oh Hell," Hanna said. "Go and live in Pullman and find out how much Pullman gets selling city water and gas ten per cent higher to those poor fools. A man who won't meet his men half-way is a God-damn fool!" [16]

The American Railway Union, of which Debs was the leader, had announced in June, 1894, that it would handle no Pullman car on any railroad in the United States. By July the roads were paralyzed. Cleveland sent troops to move the mails. Destruction, bloodshed and rioting followed. Judge Taft was in extremely close touch with the situation; he had already ruled in one major labor dispute involving the Brotherhood of Locomotive Engineers. His private letters reveal a shocking hostility toward the strikers:

July 4, 1894: The strike is still on and the railroads are pretty hard hit. . . . They talk about compromising the strike with Debs. If they do, I shall be much disappointed because it will only mean the postponement of the fight which must be fought out to the bitter end. . . . It is the most outrageous strike in the history of this country and ought to fail miserably. . . . The presence of the federal troops at Chicago will have a wholesome effect, I hope.[17]

July 6, 1894: Affairs in Chicago seem to be much disturbed. It will be necessary for the military to kill some of the mob before the trouble can be stayed.[18]

July 7, 1894: The situation in Chicago is very alarming and distressing and until they have had much bloodletting, it will not be better. The situation is complicated by the demagogues and populists . . . who are continually encouraging resistance to federal authority. Word comes tonight that thirty men have been killed by the federal troops. Though it is bloody business, everybody hopes that it is true.[19]

July 8, 1894: The Chicago situation is not much improved. They have only killed six of the mob as yet. This is hardly enough to make an impression.[20]

July 9, 1894: The strike situation is very bad. The workingmen seem to be in the hands of the most demagogic and insane leaders

[16] Beer, Thomas, *Hanna*, pp. 132-133. [17] Taft to Helen H. Taft, July 4, 1894. [18] *Idem,* July 6, 1894. [19] *Idem,* July 7, 1894. [20] *Idem,* July 8, 1894.

and they are determined to provoke a civil war. It is announced that all trades unions have been called out in Chicago for next Wednesday and this will only add to the mobs who are now holding that city by the throat. . . . The lunatics, and they are numerous, think this is a fight between labor and capital and that something is to be gained by destroying capital. Then there are a lot of sentimentalists who . . . allow themselves to sympathize with the wild cries of socialists and labor agitators.[21]

Such were the views of many well-to-do Americans in 1894. Such were the views of Federal Judge Taft, expressed at the very time that he was presiding at the trial of Frank M. Phelan, a Debs lieutenant, for contempt of court, a trial which was to end with the imposition of six months' imprisonment. Does the fact that Taft held such opinions mean that he was disqualified and should have withdrawn from the case? The question is not easy to answer. Any answer must take into account his stubborn conviction that the judicial mind could rise above prejudices of the individual. His violent disapproval of the Pullman strike really goes back to his decision, as judge of the Ohio Superior Court, in *Moores & Co. v. Bricklayers' Union*. The American Railway Union was using an illegal weapon, the secondary boycott. The bloodshed and violence grew out of that illegality. It is safe to say that Taft would never have voiced such lust for suppression in Chicago had this been an ordinary strike. He usually agreed when labor sought better wages.

Taft worshiped the law; no understanding of him is possible without appreciation of that fact. The fallacy in his philosophy lies, of course, in the fact that there is no such thing as "the law." It is a mass of opinion, formulated by men throughout the centuries, and is constantly being altered. What Taft really did was to revere the law, as he understood it, himself, or as judges with whom he agreed had interpreted it. Yet even in 1893 and 1894 he was no hard and fast foe of organized labor. He had made this clear on the Superior Court. Prior to the 1894 Pullman strike he did so again. This was the decision, to be cited so many times in the campaign of 1908, in which Taft was supposed to have ruled against the right to strike. The fact that Judge Taft made no ruling

[21] *Idem*, July 9, 1894.

whatever against the right to strike was soon lost in labor's growing hatred of government by injunction.

A detail in the labor unrest of 1893 was a grievance of the locomotive engineers against the Toledo, Ann Arbor & North Michigan Railway Company. In March of that year the engineers had asked for wage increases and had been refused. On March 7 the men went on strike. Thereupon P. M. Arthur, chief of the Brotherhood of Locomotive Engineers, sent instructions to subordinate leaders on eleven different railway systems in Ohio and neighboring states to the effect that a strike had been declared on the Toledo & Ann Arbor and that all the rules of the brotherhood were to be obeyed. Among these was by-law No. 12 which specified that locomotive engineers could not handle property belonging to a road toward which the brotherhood had an unsettled grievance. Arthur told his leaders to notify the general managers of the various railroads that Rule 12 would be enforced. Thereupon several of these general managers, facing a strike of their own engineers, told the Toledo & Ann Arbor that it might be necessary to refuse to handle freight from that line. This would have meant, obviously, such severe losses to the Toledo & Ann Arbor that the wage demands of the engineers would be granted.

The Toledo and Ann Arbor brought a bill in equity against the various railroads to force them to handle its freight. An injunction to that end had been granted in the Federal Court. Judge Taft, himself, on April 3, 1893, handed down a lengthy decision allowing an injunction. Taft declared that the brotherhood's action was in violation of the Interstate Commerce Act which specified that all common carriers "afford all reasonable, proper and equal facilities for the interchange of traffic between their respective lines." He pointed out that a penalty of $5,000 was provided for any railroad, "or any receiver, trustee, or lessee, agent, or person acting for or employed by" the railroad responsible for willful violation of the free interchange of traffic.

"As every locomotive engineer . . . is a 'person employed by' a common carrier corporation subject to the provision of the interstate commerce law," Judge Taft ruled, "he is guilty of the offense prescribed. . . . Arthur and all the members of the brotherhood engaged in enforcing Rule 12 . . . are equally guilty with him as principals . . . and they are thereby also guilty of conspiring to commit an offense against the United States."

In *Moores & Co.* v. *Bricklayers' Union,* decided in the Ohio Superior Court in January, 1890, Taft had said that "every man is entitled . . . to bestow his labor . . . according to his pleasure." But this lawful right, he had then added, might be invalidated by motives of malice. Taft wrote:

. . . it is said that it cannot be unlawful for an employee either to threaten to quit or actually to quit the service when not in violation of his contract, because a man has the inalienable right to bestow his labor where he will, and to withhold his labor as he will. *Generally speaking this is true, but not absolutely.* If he uses the benefit which his labor is or will be to another, by threatening to withhold it or agreeing to bestow it, for the purpose of inducing, procuring or compelling that other to commit an unlawful or criminal act, the withholding or bestowing of his labor for such purpose is itself an unlawful and criminal act.

This paragraph is a fairly typical example of the involved manner in which Taft often wrote. The complexity of his phraseology was partly caused by his desire to be exact. With reluctant apologies to the legal mind, a simple translation may be offered:

It is said that any workman can legally quit his job as long as he does not break his contract when he does so. But this is not always true. The workman cannot force his employer to break the law by threatening to walk out. The locomotive engineers did just that. They said they would not work if their railroads handled the freight of the Toledo & Ann Arbor. But it was against the Interstate Commerce Act for the railroads to refuse to handle that freight.

Taft labored to make clear to, as he said, "the intelligent and generally law-abiding men who compose the Brotherhood of Locomotive Engineers" the difference between a strike and a boycott. The engineers of the Toledo & Ann Arbor, he said, were entitled to walk out because they had a wage dispute. But the engineers of the other railroads were "not dissatisfied with the terms of their employment." Their threatened strike was only to club into line the Toledo & Ann Arbor.

"Neither law nor morals," said Taft, "can give a man the right to labor or withhold his labor for such a purpose."

Judge Taft then cited his own decision in *Moores & Co.* v. *Bricklayers' Union* and added that the engineers were guilty, like the bricklayers in that litigation, of malice. They were also guilty of a combination to bring about a violation of the federal law.

"The temporary injunction will be allowed, as prayed for," he concluded.[22] And thereby was added another count to the indictment, by no means fair, which was to be found by organized labor against Presidential Candidate Taft in 1908. Thirty-four years later, when chief justice of the United States, Taft referred to both these cases and upheld their validity.[23]

Taft was consistent. The third case in which he outlawed the boycott was *Thomas* v. *Cincinnati, N.O.T.P. Co.,* or the phase of that litigation which is known to lawyers as "In re Phelan." In sending Frank Phelan, the lieutenant of Debs, to jail for six months, Judge Taft was merely applying the law he had voiced in the bricklayers' strike and in the attempt of the locomotive engineers to aid their brothers by applying Rule 12.

Mark Hanna, whom history has sadly maligned, was correct in his profane disgust for George Pullman's labor policies. During the depression-deadened winter of 1893-1894, the Pullman Palace Car Company had cut wages by about one-fourth. In addition, many men had been dismissed. The issue was relatively new in 1894, but to the men of the Pullman Company it was very clear. Could a vast corporation ruthlessly cut wages and reduce employment in a time of depression or was there an obligation to maintain both, as far as possible, out of treasury reserves? The respectables of 1894 were unanimous, of course, in declaring that no such obligation existed.

The Pullman Company was very wealthy in 1894. An impartial commission subsequently reported that its surplus profits came to about $25,000,000 and that, in the previous year, it had paid out $2,500,000 in dividends on a capital of only $36,000,000. Would it not have been wise, Mr. Pullman was asked, to divide just a little

---

[22] 45 *Federal Reporter*, pp. 730-745. (Italics mine.) [23] Taft to S. C. Justice Sanford, Jan. 25, 1927.

of this with his workers, just enough so that the men could have had an adequate wage? He did not think so.

"It would have amounted to a gift of money to these men," he answered. In brief, socialism.

Mark Hanna was right, too, when he said that the "model" homes of Pullman, Illinois, were a burden on the workers. Rents charged by the company were, so the commission of inquiry found, from one-fifth to one-fourth higher than in similar suburbs. One expert testified that a typical Pullman family, having paid the company's bills for rent and light and water, had seventy-six cents a day left for food and clothing. In May a group of employees called on their benevolent employer and asked for either wage increases or rent reductions. Mr. Pullman bristled at their presumption and three members of the delegation were promptly removed from the payroll. Revolt spread through the model streets of Pullman and five-sixths of the workers struck. The loyal remainder was dismissed. The shops were closed. Mr. Pullman could well afford to wait. Business was bad, anyway, and his reserves would carry the company for a long time. But the workers had no reserves and hunger would not wait.

So they appealed to gentle, sad-faced Eugene Debs, who hated bloodshed and yet did not shrink from it. He heard their plea. In fact, four thousand of the Pullman workers were members of the newly organized American Railway Union of which Debs was president. In June, 1894, the American Railway Union asked the Pullman Company to arbitrate the dispute; the company declined. Thereupon a boycott against all Pullman cars was declared for June 26, 1894. On July 2, in Chicago, Federal Judges Peter S. Grosscup and William A. Woods issued a sweeping injunction against Debs and the strikers. It went much further than any decision by Judge Taft. It said that interference with railroad traffic in any manner would be punished by summons for contempt and sentence without trial. Elated, the General Managers Association, leading the strike for the railroads, called the injunction "a Gatling gun on paper." It was at least that. But violence flared, first in the small town of Blue Island down toward Joliet, when federal marshals tried to enforce the order. Grossly exaggerated statements were telegraphed to President Cleveland and on the following day federal troops were sent to Chicago so that the mails would be moved. Now the mob violence was real. Debs, his nerves frayed and his delicate body exhausted by the strain, lost his normal common sense and said that civil war would follow any shots fired by the troops. The shots were fired. Blood seeped through the coal dust and grime of Chicago's labyrinth of railroad yards, and the respectables watched, in terror, a sky crimson with the flames of burning freight and passenger cars.[24] The glare did not reach Cincinnati, but Taft shuddered too. His indignation lasted for years.

". . . why should the right of labor be used to coerce third persons and thus bring about a result to terrorize a community, as it did in the Debs case?" he asked, after two decades had passed. ". . . the combination of the American Railway Union took the public by the throat and said, 'We will starve your babies, we will prevent your food coming to you by stopping these railroads unless you intervene between Pullman and his employees and compel Pullman to pay higher wages than he is now willing to pay them?' "[25]

Meanwhile, a relatively unimportant labor leader, Frank Phelan, had packed a grip and set out for Cincinnati to convince the railway workers of Ohio and the Middle West that they must stand, shoulder to shoulder, with their embattled brothers in Chicago. He arrived on a Sunday, June 24, 1894. His purpose, wrote Taft, was "to enforce and carry out the contemplated boycott and paralysis of business on all railway lines running into Cincinnati which used Pullman cars until they should cease to use them." Two nights later a meeting was held by switchmen employed in the Cincinnati yards. On June 27, three switchmen on the Cincinnati, Hamilton & Dayton Railroad were discharged when they declined to route Pullman cars. Immediately a general strike of all Cincinnati railroad workers was called: this was precisely how paralysis had settled over railroads throughout the country. First had come the embargo on Pullman cars only. Men had been dismissed because of this; then all the workers had walked out.

Among the lines affected in Cincinnati was the Cincinnati, New Orleans & Texas Pacific Railway, commonly called the Cin-

---

[24] Nevins, Allan, *Grover Cleveland, A Study in Courage*, pp. 611-623. [25] Taft, W. H., *The Anti-Trust Act and the Supreme Court*, p. 26.

cinnati Southern. This had gone into receivership a year earlier; thus the Federal Court and Judge Taft had a direct interest in its operation. Phelan, when tried for contempt, denied that he had urged a walkout on the Cincinnati Southern, but Taft declared in court that he placed no credence whatever in his denial. Phelan had been arrested on July 3 and enjoined, as Taft stated the case, from "inciting, encouraging, ordering or in any other manner causing the employees of the receiver to leave his employ with intent to obstruct the operation of his road, and thereby to compel him not to fulfill his contract and carry Pullman cars." Phelan was admitted to bail. Judge Taft insisted that he had continued his agitation and therefore was guilty of contempt of court. His trial was set for July 5; a week would be necessary to hear all the evidence.[26]

It was a harassed young federal judge who presided during these troubled days in Cincinnati. Nellie was at Murray Bay and he suffered, alone, in the heat. "I sleep in the customhouse, but strange to say I find it quite noisy and not very cool," he wrote. "It is a bit lonely . . . I still feel as if I were leading a solitary life. I am homesick for you and the children.

". . . what has worried me more than anything else is this railway boycott. I have a force of fifty deputy marshals on one side of the river and of seventy-five on the other. Men are constantly being arrested and brought before me and I am conducting a kind of police court. I issued a warrant for Phelan, the head strike man here and Debs's assistant, and he was brought in yesterday afternoon. All the labor men are engaged in holding meetings every night. Last night . . . I was the object of fiery denunciations in many meetings. I hate the publicity that this business brings me into. My days are spent in trying to say nothing to reporters, or in issuing injunctions, or in examining authorities to be certain about my jurisdiction."

On the eve of Phelan's trial, Judge Taft was troubled by no doubts as to the man's guilt. "I do not know," he told his wife, "just what the evidence . . . will show, but I am pretty sure he will have to be found guilty from his own published utterances. I am a good deal in doubt as to what I ought to do with him. I do

[26] 62 *Federal Reporter*, pp. 802-823.

not wish to make a martyr of him nor do I wish to be so easy with him as to encourage him or his fellow conspirators to think that they have nothing to fear from the court." [27] Certainly Taft was, privately, less than impartial as the trial got under way. He called Phelan's attorney a "shrewd, unscrupulous criminal lawyer with outrageous grammar and little or no knowledge of legal principles. . . . I do not expect to be much enlightened by what may fall from him." He told Mrs. Taft that the courtroom had been crowded with strikers and other spectators: ". . . Phelan says in an interview he expects me to send him to jail because I have the power. If I find the case strong against him he will not be disappointed." [28] Next day, "Woodward of the *Commercial* came to see me. . . . He had been in consultation with Mayor Caldwell and the chief of police and they were afraid I was going to send Phelan to jail at once and that it might . . . produce a riot." [29] After the evidence had been taken, Taft reported:

As I now think, I shall find Phelan guilty of contempt of court and send him to jail for six months. I shall not find him guilty of counseling violence but of conspiring unlawfully to tie up the road by a boycott. This decision will enrage his followers, I doubt not, but I cannot see my duty any other way. He and his associates have wrought such havoc that this will be a very small penalty to inflict upon him. Debs and his lieutenants have been arrested in Chicago. I do not know whether they can be convicted, but I think so.[30]

The decision was handed down on July 13, 1894, and Taft read his opinion for more than an hour. He reviewed the activities of Phelan. He analyzed the testimony of the witnesses; including that of a gentleman named E. W. Dormer, a detective in the employ of a St. Louis agency who had disguised himself as a brakeman and had testified regarding Phelan's threats of violence. Judge Taft said that he would not have credited the statements of Dormer had they been flatly denied by Phelan; the defendant had, however, evaded doing so. Taft read an extract from his own decision in *Moores & Co.* v. *Bricklayers' Union* in support of his contention

[27] Taft to Helen H. Taft, July 4, 1894. [28] *Idem*, July 6, 1894. [29] *Idem*, July 7, 1894. [30] *Idem*, July 11, 1894.

that the boycott against Pullman cars was illegal and that Phelan, continuing to advocate a boycott after his first arrest, was in contempt.

In his earlier important labor decisions, Judge Taft had taken pains to differentiate between a legal strike and an illegal boycott. This time he was far more specific and his defense of the right to strike was the first clear, emphatic judicial expression on that subject. He pointed out, first, that the employees of a railroad under receivership had all the rights of employees for a company not under jurisdiction of the court. He added:

Now it may be conceded in the outset that the employees of the receiver had the right to organize into or join a labor union which should take joint action as to their terms of employment. *It is of benefit to them and to the public that laborers should unite* *in their common interest and for lawful purposes. They have labor* *to sell. If they stand together, they are often able, all of them, to* *command better prices for their labor than when dealing singly* *with rich employers, because the necessities of the single employee* *may compel him to accept any terms offered him.* The accumulation of a fund for the support of those who feel that wages offered are below market prices is one of the legitimate objects of such an organization. They have the right to appoint officers who shall advise them as to the course to be taken by them in their relations with their employer. They may unite with other unions. The officers they appoint, or any other person to whom they choose to listen, may advise them as to the proper course to be taken by them in regard to their employment, or, if they choose to repose such authority in any one, may order them, on pain of expulsion from their union, peaceably to leave the employ of their employer because any of the terms of their employment are unsatisfactory. It follows, therefore (to give an illustration which will be understood), that if Phelan had come to this city when the receiver of the Cincinnati Southern reduced the wages of his employees by 10 per cent, and had urged a peaceable strike, and had succeeded in maintaining one, the loss to the business of the receiver would not be ground for recovering damages, and Phelan would not have been liable to contempt even if the strike much impeded the operation of the road under order of the court. His action in giving the advice, or issuing an order based on unsatisfactory terms of employment, would have been entirely lawful.

Phelan had, on the contrary, come to Cincinnati to carry out the purposes of a combination of men whose object, the Pullman boycott, was illegal.

"His purpose," said Judge Taft, drawing toward the close of his opinion, ". . . was unlawful by the law of Ohio and the laws of the United States. . . . It follows that the contemner is guilty as charged, and it only remains to impose the sentence of the court. . . . The punishment for a contempt is the most disagreeable duty a court has to perform, but it is one from which the court cannot shrink. If the orders of the court are not obeyed, the next step is unto anarchy. . . . After much consideration, I do not think I should be doing my duty without imposing . . . the penalty of imprisonment. The sentence of the court is that Frank M. Phelan be confined in the county jail of Warren County, Ohio, for a term of six months. The marshal will take the prisoner into custody, and safely convey him to the place of imprisonment." [31]

Taft arose. He had been wearing his silk judicial robe for this solemn occasion. If any political ambitions still remained, he must have abandoned them now. His wife wrote in hope that he would not "be attacked as much as you fear." [32]

Taft was certain, however, that the blight extended even to his brother, Charles. In September, 1894, Charles P. Taft was offered a Congressional nomination by Boss Cox of Cincinnati. Will Taft hoped that he would decline.

"The fact that I am his brother will solidify the labor vote against him," he wrote. [33]

Taft's years as circuit judge were not, on the other hand, barren of rulings which specifically and permanently benefited labor in its slow, heartbreaking fight against the abuses of entrenched wealth. In October, 1908, when the leaders of organized labor were calling for the defeat of Presidential Candidate Taft and urging the election of Bryan, President Roosevelt grew apprehensive that his personal selection for the White House might be defeated. He hastened to offer reassurance regarding Taft's profound love for the workingmen of the nation.

"I do not believe the wage workers of this country," he in-

[31] 62 *Federal Reporter*, pp. 802-823. (Italics mine.) [32] Helen H. Taft to Taft, July 21, 1894. [33] Taft to Helen H. Taft, Sept. 22, 1894.

sisted, "have ever had a better friend in the White House than Mr. Taft will prove to be."

President Roosevelt cited, in proof, the Narramore case as one in which Federal Judge Taft "rendered a service to labor so great that it can hardly be overestimated." [34] The President might also have mentioned the litigation instituted by an obscure express company employee named William Voight. Voight sought employment with the United States Express Company and was informed that he could not have work unless he first released the company, and any railroad upon which he might be required to travel, from all liability in the event of injury or death. Desperate for work, Voight signed the waiver of culpability. The company then made an agreement with Baltimore & Ohio Southwestern Railway whereby the railroad, in turn, was absolved from damage suits in the event of injuries to Voight. This was, of course, the express company's practice with all its employees.

Voight was seriously injured in an accident and his attorney brought suit against the railroad on the ground that it could not relieve itself from gross negligence by such an agreement with the express company. Taft heard the case and awarded $6,000 damages to Voight. He said that such contracts were oppressive, unreasonable, unjust and against the public policy. The railroad's liability to the express messenger was just as great as to any other passenger.[35] The case was appealed to the United States Supreme Court which reversed Judge Taft on the time-honored theory that the sanctity of contractual freedom must be preserved.[36] But the plight of the unfortunate Voight was not forgotten. President Roosevelt asked Congress to legislate against such unfair contracts and on April 22, 1908, he signed a law which declared void "any contract . . . the purpose or intent of which shall be to enable any common carrier to exempt itself from liability." [37]

The Narramore case was an even stronger blow against the abuses which had flourished under the old laissez-faire doctrines. Small progress had been made, when Taft became a federal judge in 1892, toward the enactment of either safety or workmen's com-

---

[34] Theodore Roosevelt to P. H. Grace, Oct. 19, 1908, Roosevelt papers. [35] 79 *Federal Reporter*, p. 561. [36] 176 U. S. 498. [37] Kansas City *Star*, Oct. 7, 1908.

pensation laws. They were still widely condemned as socialistic. But Taft soon learned, if he was not already aware of it, that grave wrongs were being inflicted on wage earners by industrialists and factory owners. Day after day and year after year he presided over suits brought by workers for injuries they had sustained. He saw justice thwarted by legal technicalities and by lawyers extorting huge fees when damages were awarded. A major influence against the award of damages was the legal theory of "assumed risk." This had been affirmed by the Supreme Court of Ohio in *Krause* v. *Morgan* in 1895. Some years earlier the Ohio legislature had required that coal mines must be kept free of fire-damp, a frequent cause of explosions. Morgan, a coal miner, was badly injured in a blast due to fire-damp and sued the coal company. He was awarded damages, but the coal operator appealed on the ground that the miner was fully aware that fire-damp was present. He should have left his job. This contention was upheld by the state Supreme Court which said: "One who voluntarily assumes a risk, thereby waives the provisions of a statute made for his protection." [38] It was a legal invitation for all mines, factories and railroads to violate safety provisions required by law.

Among these provisions was one which specified that railroads must block frogs and switches so that employees would not be caught in them. Organized labor, slowly awakening to this aspect of its program, attempted to force the Ohio legislature to abolish the doctrine of assumed risk. A powerful lobby killed their bill at Columbus. In 1899 Narramore, a brakeman employed by the Cleveland, Cincinnati, Chicago & St. Louis Railway Company was at work with a switching crew. His foot became wedged in an unprotected frog just as some cars came along. He was so badly injured that one leg was amputated. Narramore sued in the Federal Court. The railroad admitted that the tracks were not properly protected, as required by statute, but introduced evidence, as in the case of Morgan, to show that Narramore was aware of that fact. So damages were refused him. The case was, however, carried to the Circuit Court of Appeals where Taft was sitting. Taft's decision was a magnificent stroke on behalf of the abused workingmen of America. He dared to turn his back— part way, at least— on the ruling of

[38] 53 *Ohio State Report*, p. 26.

the Supreme Court of his own state and on the vast majority of the
precedents. He saw the issue clearly: to continue the doctrine of
assumed risk was to nullify all of the statutes which provided safety
measures or appliances. He said, in part:

Will the courts enforce or recognize against a workman an
agreement, expressed or implied on his part, to waive the performance of a statutory duty of the master, imposed for the protection of the servant, and in the interests of the public? *We do
not think they will.* . . . The manifest legislative purpose was to
protect the servant by positive law because he had not previously
shown himself capable of protecting himself by contract, and it
would entirely defeat this purpose thus to permit the servant "to
contract himself out of the statute." . . .

The sole question in this case is whether the statute requiring
the railroad company in penalty of a fine to block its guard rails
and frogs, changes the rule of liability of the company and relieves
the injured man from the effect of the assumption of risk which
would otherwise be implied against him.

To confine the remedy to a criminal proceeding in which
the fine to be imposed on a conviction was *not even payable to the
injured employee or to one complaining, would be to make the
law not much more than a dead letter.*

The intention of the legislature of Ohio was to protect the
employees of railways from injury from a very frequent source
of danger by compelling the railway companies to adopt a well
known safety device. And although the employee impliedly waives
a compliance with the statute and agrees to assume the risk from
unblocked frogs and switches by continuing in the service without
complaint *this court will not recognize or enforce such an agreement.* . . . The imposition of a penalty for the violation of a statute
does not exclude other means of enforcement and to permit the
company to avail itself of such an assumption of risk by its employees *is in effect to enable it to nullify a penal statute and is against
public policy.*

Federal Judge Taft did not wholly repudiate the ruling of the
Ohio Supreme Court in the earlier case of Coal Miner Morgan. In
that instance, he said, Morgan had been specifically warned of the
danger of fire-damp by his superiors and had continued to expose
himself to almost certain injury. Thus Morgan was guilty of con-

tributory negligence and not entitled to damages. Taft drew a line between assumption of risk and contributory negligence. The latter applied to cases "where the danger is so obvious and imminent that no ordinarily prudent man would assume the risk of injury therefrom.

". . . but where the danger . . . is one which many men are in the habit of assuming," Judge Taft continued, "and which prudent men who must earn a living are willing to assume . . . then one who assumes the risk cannot be said to be guilty of contributory negligence if . . . he uses care reasonably commensurate with the risk." [39]

The Narramore decision had remarkably wide influence on future rulings in negligence cases. The following year, when a second brakeman was similarly injured, Judge Neff of the Common Pleas Court in Cleveland set aside a verdict for damages. The weight of legal authority in Ohio, Massachusetts, New York and other states "is against Judge Taft," he said. But he admitted that "the reasoning of Judge Taft is very forcible and very clear." [40] In 1902 a comparable case was decided in Cincinnati and damages were again denied. The court suggested, however, the possibility that "Judge Taft and some other courts are only a little in advance of those courts" which held to the assumption of risk doctrine. The Supreme Court, it was suggested, might well reverse itself.[41] That high tribunal did not have the courage to do so. But the Ohio legislature ultimately killed the doctrine of assumed risk; similar action was taken in other states.

The New York State Court of Appeals had taken a position similar to the Ohio ruling. Early in 1900, George W. Alger, a New York attorney, appeared before a committee of the New York legislature to urge the adoption of an Employers' Liability act which, among other things, would provide that corporations be prohibited from availing themselves of the defense of assumed risk where violations of a statute enacted to provide for the safety of workers were involved.

New York's own leading case, *Knisley* v. *Pratt,* decided in 1896, required, as a matter of law, that these risks be assumed by the

[39] 96 *Federal Reporter*, p. 928. (Italics mine.)   [40] Vol. 10, *Ohio Decisions*, p. 348.
[41] 12 *Ohio State Reports*, p. 597.

worker. A member of the committee asked Mr. Alger whether he could refer to any court decision upholding his view, which the railroad lawyers, who appeared in opposition, considered entirely radical and unsound. He replied that he would do his best to find some such decision and returned to a subsequent hearing with Taft's Narramore case. "Do you know this case?" asked Senator Brackett, the committee's chairman. "Yes," said Lewis E. Carr, general counsel for the Delaware & Hudson Railroad Company, "it is written by one of those Western labor judges."

The Knisley decision was subsequently reversed by the New York Court of Appeals on its own initiative in 1912 and the Narramore case was cited as an authority for doing so.[42]

The charge that Taft was radical was, at the least, exaggerated. But another of his decisions as circuit judge, in the Addystone Pipe case, illustrates again the impossibility of classifying as either liberal or conservative the honest judicial mind. This was handed down on February 8, 1898, and it was probably the most important ruling of Taft's eight years on the Circuit Court. Judge Taft's decision definitely and specifically revived the Sherman Antitrust Act.

"The case went to the Supreme Court," wrote Taft, not without pride, in referring to the Addystone Pipe litigation long afterward, "and the Supreme Court unanimously affirmed the judgment of the court below." [43]

Popular distrust of large corporations had been increasing during the eighties. The Sherman act, passed in 1890 during the administration of President Harrison, was another of those dreams of reform which fade under the light of judicial interpretation. The terms of the act had seemed simple enough. Congress, under the Constitution, had power over interstate commerce. The Sherman act said that contracts or combinations in restraint of trade among the states were illegal. But within two years the process of judicial invalidation had started. The Federal Circuit Court for Massachusetts said that a whisky distilling company could acquire some seventy distilleries throughout the country and could control prices. Surely, said the court, Congress had not intended to limit the acquisition of property "which might become the subject of interstate commerce." What was ultimately done with the property was irrelevant.

A death-blow to enforcement of the Sherman act was delivered by the Supreme Court in January, 1895. This was in a suit against the American Sugar Refining Company in which the government, through Attorney General Richard Olney of the Cleveland administration, charged that a monopoly of ninety-eight per cent of the sugar refineries in the United States had been achieved, that the American Sugar Refining Company controlled the sale and price of sugar. The government's petition asked for dissolution of this sugar trust. But Chief Justice Fuller, delivering the opinion of the Supreme Court, said that the agreements and contracts in question related only to the acquisition of refineries in Philadelphia and bore no relation to interstate commerce.

"The court," wrote Taft in 1914, "could not apparently look beyond the acquisition of property in one state to its ultimate purpose, which certainly was the control of the sale of refined sugar in the country-wide trade." [44]

Profound discouragement overcame those who had hoped to control the octopi of American business. President Cleveland decided that it could come only through the states. During the McKinley administration not a single indictment was found under the Sherman act. Enforcement virtually ceased until, in February, 1902, President Roosevelt ordered a suit against the Northern Securities Company, the first important holding company, which sought control of trunk railroad lines in the Northwest.

Looking back, it is clear that the federal authorities, had they chosen, might have placed greater confidence in the ruling of Circuit Judge Taft in the Addystone Pipe case. The lower court had dismissed the federal government's suit against six corporations engaged in the manufacture and sale of cast-iron pipe. Taft wrote the decision, on the appeal to the Circuit Court, which reversed the dismissal and ordered dissolution of the combination. The defendants included the Addystone Pipe and Steel Company of Cincinnati. The government declared that all the iron-pipe companies in the Ohio and Mississippi valleys had agreed to maintain prices and

[44] Taft, W. H., *op. cit.*, pp. 53-57.

share profits and were thereby effectively throttling competition.

"Two questions are presented in this case for our consideration," wrote Judge Taft. "First, was the association of the defendants a contract, combination or conspiracy in restraint of trade, as
the terms are to be understood in the act? Second, was the trade
thus restrained trade between the states?"

Taft went back to basic fundamentals of the law in his opinion.
He denied a contention that such a monopoly would have been
legal under common law. He refuted the argument of the defendant
companies that the combination of pipe manufacturers did not
create a monopoly because their aggregate tonnage did not exceed
thirty per cent of the total tonnage in the country. The Addystone
Company and its associates had power to control prices, Judge
Taft insisted. He explained how they had done so:

> The most cogent evidence that they had this power is the
> fact, everywhere apparent in the record, that they exercised it. . . .
> The defendants were, by their combination . . . able to deprive
> the public in a large territory of the advantages otherwise accruing
> to them from the proximity of defendants' pipe factories, and, by
> keeping prices just low enough to prevent competition by eastern
> manufacturers, to compel the public to pay an increase over what
> the price would have been, if fixed by competition between de-
> fendants. . . . The defendants acquired this power by voluntarily
> agreeing to sell at prices fixed by their committee, and by allowing
> the highest bidder at the secret 'auction pool' to become the lowest
> bidder . . . at the public letting.

Judge Taft said that the legal question was not greatly affected
by whether, as contended, pipe had been sold at reasonable rates
since the tendency of the combination "was certainly to give defendants the power to charge unreasonable prices." As a matter of
fact, the rates in the area controlled by the combination had been
high. Nor was there any doubt whatever, the judge said, that the
business of the pipe companies had constituted interstate trade.
Then Taft struck directly at the allegation that the Supreme Court
had, in the sugar trust case, affirmed the legality of such combinations. The government's suit had been dismissed in the lower court

on the basis of that decision. Judge Taft denied its application to this case. In the sugar trust decision, he said, the monopoly did not fall within the prohibitions of the Sherman act because the agreement on which it was based "related only to the manufacture of refined sugar, and not to its sale throughout the country." The Supreme Court had said, declared Taft in his own words, that "manufacture preceded commerce, and though the manufacture under a monopoly might and doubtless would indirectly affect both internal and interstate commerce, it was not within the power of Congress to regulate manufacture within a state on that ground. . . .

"The goods are not within the control of Congress," Judge Taft said, "until they are in actual transit from one state to another. But the negotiations and making of sales which necessarily involve in their execution the delivery of merchandise across state lines are interstate commerce, and so within the regulating power of Congress *even before the transit of the goods in performance of the contract has begun.*" This was, obviously, diplomacy on the part of a younger and inferior judge who was in disagreement with the great minds of the Supreme Court. Nobody supposed, including those great minds, that the manufacturing combination of the American Sugar Refining Company had been for any other purpose than to control prices. Circuit Judge Taft, in another genuflection toward the Supreme Court, quoted its opinion that there was "nothing in the proofs [regarding the sugar trust] to indicate any intention to put a restraint upon trade or commerce."

There being "nothing in the proofs," the Supreme Court had followed the traditional legal custom of evading the issue— although Circuit Judge Taft, needless to say, did not point this out. He did say that the pipe combination was clearly "a direct restraint upon interstate commerce." It was "on its face an extensive scheme to control the whole commerce among thirty-six states in cast-iron pipe." Thus it was illegal. Taft entered a decree "perpetually enjoining the defendants" from continuing the combination and doing any business under it.

More than a hint of Taft's views regarding corporations and restraint of trade, as well as his disapproval of courts which supported monopolistic tendencies, is to be found in this decision;

certainly the clearest and most forthright he had yet uttered. He could discern, he said, no general tendency on the part of the courts to greater liberality in supporting combinations. But he added, at that point, a sentence which has a faint, faint flavor of heresy.

"It is true," he said, "that there are some cases in which the courts, mistaking, as we conceive, the proper limits of the relaxation of the rules for determining the unreasonableness of the restraints of trade, have set sail on a sea of doubt . . . and have assumed the power to say . . . how much restraint of competition is in the public interest and how much is not."

Hastily— if the adverb may be permitted in discussing a judicial opinion— Taft added that he had not, himself, set forth on any new seas, doubtful or otherwise. Lawyers for the Addystone Pipe and Steel Company and for its partners in sin had voiced solemn warning during the hearings of the peril which lay in enlarging the federal powers regarding trade and industry.

"We do not announce any new doctrine in holding either that contracts and negotiations for the sale of merchandise to be delivered across state lines are interstate commerce," he said, "or what burdens or restraints upon such commerce Congress may pass appropriate legislation to prevent, and courts of the United States may in proper proceedings enjoin. . . . If this extends federal jurisdiction into fields not before occupied by the general government, it is not because such jurisdiction is not within the limits allowed by the Constitution of the United States." [45]

Combinations . . . monopolies . . . Northern Securities . . . Standard Oil . . . International Harvester . . . the rule of reason. These were words, names and phrases to become familiar, all too familiar, during the new century about to dawn. As president, seeking to control the trusts, Taft was to make speeches about them and order prosecutions. As chief justice of the United States he would write decisions concerning them.

[45] 85 *Federal Reporter*, pp. 271-273, 278-302. (Italics mine.)

CHAPTER X

THE WORLD OUTSIDE

P ERHAPS," Taft wrote in January, 1900, "it is the comfort and
dignity and power without worry I like." [1]
    Undoubtedly they were among the attractions of the
bench, but the fascination of judicial life was even more important
to him. By 1896 Taft was confident that he would remain a judge
for the rest of his life. If he was elevated to the United States Supreme Court, so much the better—and he had reasons for optimism.
No other jurist in the country was contributing so much to judicial
thought as was William Howard Taft between 1894 and 1898. Had
he been an older man, his appointment to the highest bench would
have been certain. His relative youth meant merely that he would
be forced to wait. Taft was constantly being encouraged in his
ambition. When Associate Justice H. E. Jackson died in August,
1895, his widow addressed a letter to President Cleveland. Her
husband, she told the President, had remarked that Circuit Judge
Taft was best qualified to take his place.[2]

    In March, 1896—as the Cleveland administration was ending—
Taft went to Washington for a few days and again was encouraged
by the widespread belief that he would soon be on the Supreme
Court. "Almost every person I met spoke of my coming there as
a certainty," he reported to Mrs. Taft. "I only allude to what is
said to me on this subject to indicate the friendly feeling at Washington for me and the expectation would suggest my name to any
president who was not prejudiced against me. . . . Most of the
supreme judges [sic] seem to regard it as very probable." [3]

    These were years of contentment. Taft was happy in his
work, happy with his wife and children. "How does the ball dress
come on?" he asked Nellie, from Grand Rapids where he was
holding court. "I look forward with much pleasure to see you

---

[1] Taft to H. W. and Horace D. Taft, Jan. 28, 1900. [2] Mrs. H. E. Jackson to Cleveland,
Aug. 10, 1895; copy to Taft. [3] Taft to Helen H. Taft, March 25, 1896.

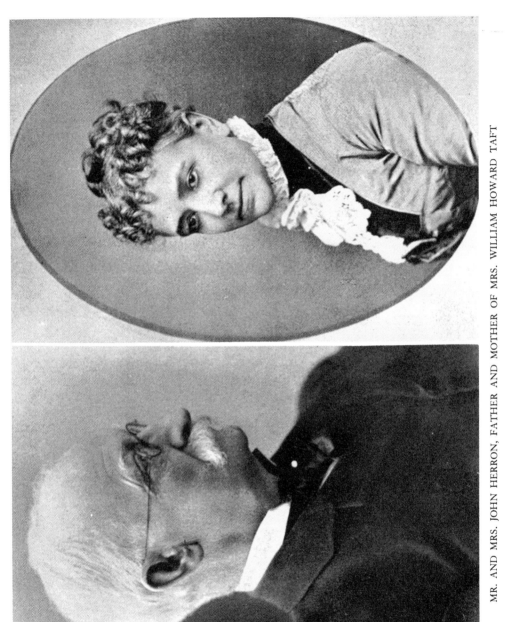

MR. AND MRS. JOHN HERRON, FATHER AND MOTHER OF MRS. WILLIAM HOWARD TAFT

See page 69]

FASCINATING NELLIE HERRON

[*See page 78*

properly arrayed for the dance. . . . I propose to dance a great deal with you that night, so be sure you are in training for it." [4] In June, 1897, he recalled that eleven years had passed since his marriage.

". . . never for one moment have I regretted the step I took that day," he said, "but each year has only made me happier in the result. Can you say the same, my dear?" [5]

Taft's original conviction that an intelligent, candid woman made the best wife did not alter with the years. "Thought of you," he wrote, "has so much intellectual flavor and sweet sentiment, too. I am so glad that you don't flatter me and sit at my feet with honey. You are my dearest and best critic and are worth much to me in stirring me up to best endeavor." [6] He was, of course, an affectionate parent. "Tell Robbie," he asked, "that I send him as many kisses as there are squares between Third and Lawrence [streets in Cincinnati] and Freeman and Liberty, and as many to Helen as there are squares between Freeman and Liberty and Third and Lawrence." [7] Their third child, Charles Phelps Taft 2nd, was born on September 20, 1897. The family was now complete.

As a judge, Taft was barred from active political life and he was scrupulous in observing the limitation. He was, however, deeply interested in the momentous issues which were presenting themselves. Always a Republican and a conservative, he continued to be alarmed by the state of the nation as 1896 approached. He was not, though, as frightened as he had been during the Pullman strike in 1894 and he was, on the whole, both cynical and pessimistic concerning both the major parties. Like Theodore Roosevelt, who was to declare that McKinley had "no more backbone than a chocolate éclair," Taft had a low opinion of the future nominee. Hanna was very busy on behalf of his candidate in 1894, but Taft did not believe that such a "timid statesman" would be chosen. "I cannot find that anybody in Washington wants him." [8] By March, 1896, however, he had changed his mind regarding McKinley's prospects. The Ohio delegation would probably vote for this native son; Foraker was on the bandwagon.

[4] *Idem,* March 25, 1896. [5] *Idem,* Nov. 27, 1894. [6] *Idem,* July 8, 1895. [7] *Idem,* July 6, 1896. [8] *Idem,* Nov. 21, 1894.

"I do not think . . . that anything can prevent the nomination of McKinley," he wrote. "He seems to have a popular ground swell in his favor and he will ride to a great victory only to demonstrate his incapacity. It is a case of 'fooling the people.'" [9]

Charles P. Taft, who had been elected to Congress despite his brother's labor decisions, was also behind McKinley. He had contributed $1,000 to the fund of $100,000 whereby certain embarrassing debts of the next president had been paid.[10] Tom Reed, speaker of the House, would have been a much more satisfactory candidate to Circuit Judge Taft. But Reed— whom Spring Rice had referred to as "that fat, sarcastic man"— had tossed away his chances in 1891 when he had spoken in Ohio and had impressed Hanna as too sardonic and too sophisticated to win the hearts of simple, honest, rugged American voters. By 1896 Speaker Reed had withdrawn from the race and was assuring his friend, Roosevelt, that politics was a "farce," that he intended to retire to private life so that he might be certain "that my debts won't have to be paid by a syndicate." [11] This, of course, was an acid reference to McKinley.

The Democrats, in Taft's view, were definitely more reprehensible than the Republicans. They were the party of discontent and Taft was never able to endorse discontent. The people of the West were discontented because they could not pay their debts. Grover Cleveland, for whom they had voted in 1892, had betrayed them by approving repeal of the Sherman Silver Purchase act which provided almost unrestricted coinage of silver and which was draining the country of gold. The farmer could not sell his crops. The city man could not sell his labor. The issue of 1896 was translated into Gold versus Silver, but it was, more basically, a fight of the privileged few against the impoverished many. Even the courts seemed to be on the side of wealth. The laboring man brooded over the injunctions which had been issued against him. In 1894 the Supreme Court had ruled that a federal income tax, surely a fair device for taxation of the wealthy, was unconstitutional.

[9] Taft to Helen H. Taft, March 18, 1896. [10] *Idem,* March 24, 1896. [11] Pringle, H. F., *Theodore Roosevelt, a Biography,* pp. 158-159.

—2—

Warnings reached Taft's ears that the conservatives had gone
too far. His friend, William Hallett Phillips, who was a member of
the Henry Adams circle in Washington, wrote in scathing denun-
ciation of the Supreme Court's decision. Phillips said that "an old
dotard" like Associate Justice Stephen J. Field, who had been on
the court since 1863, had been able, by his vote in this five to four
ruling, to cast "aspersion on the validity of the . . . law and make
it a subject of confusion and doubt." Phillips added that Associate
Justice John M. Harlan, whom Taft knew well and respected, was
"divided between rage and mortification and thinks the time not
far distant when the present parties will be dissolved and the issue
directly made between the forces of capital and the forces which
are opposed to capital. . . . His views are shared by a great multitude of our people." Phillips concluded:

The Supreme Court at the present time will make a record
for itself. It has determined that trusts may continue to flourish . . .
They [*sic*] have determined that the wealthiest classes cannot be
taxed on their income. They are yet to determine that Mr. Debs is
to go to jail as a result of his protest against aggrandized capital.
Do I not talk like a Populist, Socialist, anarchist or any other
kind of "ist" that future times may develop?[12]

"You certainly do," might well have been the substance of
Taft's answer although no letter to Hallett Phillips remains in his
papers.
    On July 2, 1896, just a week before Bryan was to make his
famous speech to the Democratic National Convention in Chicago
and find himself, amazingly, the presidential nominee of his party,
Taft predicted that the convention would be a "wild affair." It
would "be anarchistic, Socialistic, free silverite, and everything
pleasing to the Populists." After Bryan's selection, he said that "the
Democrats are crazy and the crazier they are the surer their defeat."
    "If only McKinley would speak out!" he added.[13]
    Taft's sole part in the actual campaign was to worry about it.

[12] W. H. Phillips to Taft, April 15, 1895. [13] Taft to Helen H. Taft, July 9, 1896.

The general ignorance on the currency question bothered him. The silver men, he assured Nellie, who was in Murray Bay again, "are magnificent liars." But Taft confessed that he was not, himself, too well informed on bimetallism and on the reasons for the superiority of gold as a standard.

"I think we ought to take a course ourselves on the question," he said as he prepared to join Mrs. Taft on the St. Lawrence. "I shall . . . get a volume or two to read aloud this summer in the summer house or kiosk." [14]

Taft's apprehensions increased. He was afraid that hoarding of gold would start as a result of the noisy marchings of Bryan and his silver battalions, that the government reserves would dwindle, that a panic was inevitable:

. . . it will be impossible to keep gold from going to a premium and the depreciation of the currency will have begun even before the election and just because of the hideous threat of repudiation contained in the Chicago platform.[15]

At that, Taft was far less violent in his expressions than countless others of his class. Roosevelt was threatening that he might have to march in actual combat against Candidate Bryan and "meet the man sword to sword upon the field of battle." The clergy did their bit by intimating that Bryan was the foe of Christianity. The New York *Tribune* summed it up on the day after election; McKinley had won because "right is right and God is God." [16]

Taft must have sighed with relief too. But the election of McKinley was, if anything, a blow to his ambitions for the Supreme Court. So, in any event, Taft had felt earlier in the year. McKinley, he thought, "would be likely to be" prejudiced and to refuse the appointment.[17] Taft's reasons for thinking so are as obscure as they were inaccurate. His friend, Foraker, was a McKinley man. Taft had said nothing, publicly, in opposition. The hostility was imagined rather than actual and it had vanished entirely by the time John Addison Porter, a classmate at Yale, became secretary to the President. In November, 1897, Porter asked Taft whether he would consider the post of attorney general in McKinley's

[14] Taft to Helen H. Taft, July 14, 1896. [15] *Idem,* July 15, 1896. [16] Pringle, H. F., *op. cit.,* pp. 162-164. [17] Taft to Helen H. Taft, March 25, 1896.

Cabinet. The offer was informal and nothing came of it.[18] But Taft was, at the least, *persona grata* at the White House. Ohio politicians seeking patronage asked for his intercession with the President. So did Theodore Roosevelt, with whom Taft was becoming increasingly friendly. Roosevelt had grown tired of his post as police commissioner of New York; besides, things were not going too well in his campaign to make the town spotless. He had labored hard and effectively in the campaign of 1896 and was, so he felt, due for reward at McKinley's hands. The Bellamy Storers of Cincinnati, who had tossed $10,000 into the McKinley debt redemption pot, also urged Theodore's cause. Promptly after the inauguration, Taft joined the pro-Roosevelt chorus.

"Judge Taft, one of the best fellows going, plunged in last week—got Herrick, a close friend of the President, to take hold which he did most cordially," reported Cabot Lodge.[19]

Myron T. Herrick, also an Ohio politician, had helped Hanna in raising campaign funds. At about this time Taft personally called on the President on behalf of the yearning Theodore. McKinley was receptive but apprehensive.

"The truth is, Will," he replied, "Roosevelt is always in such a state of mind." [20]

A decade of judicial training may have enabled Taft to avoid a chuckle. ". . . we got Theodore into the Navy Department," he remembered, "and . . . when he . . . demanded war with Spain and [was] almost attacking the administration for not declaring it, I think McKinley wished he had been anywhere else." So Roosevelt became assistant secretary of the navy and won glamour and renown by making ready for war. But Taft did not get his heart's desire. In 1898 McKinley selected Joseph McKenna for the Supreme Court. Taft remained a circuit judge.

[18] J. A. Porter to Taft, Nov. 20, 1897. [19] Lodge, H. C., *Selections from the Correspondence of Theodore Roosevelt and Henry Cabot Lodge,* Vol. I, p. 253. [20] Butt, Archie, *Taft and Roosevelt,* Vol. II, p. 441.

—3—

President McKinley was a man of peace; so was Circuit Judge Taft. But the truculence of Roosevelt, who desired war at any price, was far more typical of the popular will as the administration started. The belligerent stand taken by President Cleveland in the Venezuela boundary dispute in 1895, applauded by Roosevelt and the nation, met no echo of approval in Taft's mind. The President's message was "phrased in such a way as to make it difficult for the country to avoid a war with England without a backdown that will be humiliating.

"It might have accomplished the same purpose," Taft felt, "had it assumed a more conciliatory tone and still recommended an investigation into the boundary question in order to determine whether England's course has been in fact an attempt to steal by force a large territory under the guise of a contention over a mere boundary dispute." [21]

Taft ultimately decided that McKinley could not have avoided the war with Spain, although this was not wholly in accord with the facts.[22] But he was entirely unsympathetic to the clamor for war,[23] and its prosecution, either in the Pacific or in Cuba, interested him hardly at all. His comments were few. He was visiting his mother in Millbury, Massachusetts, on the morning of July 3, when the ramshackle Spanish fleet steamed out of Santiago harbor to certain destruction. On July 5, Taft was back in Cincinnati and reported the celebration inspired by the naval victory. "The sky was full of balloons," he told Nellie, "and everyone was in a good humor over the news." [24] Taft noted, too, the heroic exploits of Roosevelt, at San Juan. He wrote:

"Teddy Roosevelt, although in the thick of the fight, has thus far escaped unhurt. The loss among the officers has been proportionately very much greater than among the men." [25]

It never entered Taft's mind to go to war himself. This may be additional evidence that Taft had a nonpolitical mind. Even William Jennings Bryan had drawn his sword and had organized

[21] Taft to Helen H. Taft, Dec. 18, 1895. [22] Butt, Archie, *op. cit.,* Vol. II, p. 441. [23] Horace D. Taft to author, Dec. 2, 1933. [24] Taft to Helen H. Taft, July 5, 1898. [25] *Idem,* July 8, 1898.

a "Silver Battalion" to fight for the oppressed Cubans. Unfortunately, a Republican administration had sidetracked Colonel Bryan
and his men on the flea-infested sands of Florida. Taft did not go
to war because he was the antithesis of the Rooseveltian doctrine
of strenuosity. He was growing more stout year by year. Exertion,
to Taft, had but one purpose; the reduction of flesh. And he did
not like to kill anything, even animals. In October, 1909, President
Taft visited the ranch of Charles P. Taft in Texas and was invited
to go hunting by Mrs. Taft.

"It has turned out in a singular way," he wrote, "that the only
member of our family that is a really good shot is Fanny [Mrs.
William Edwards, his sister]. She hunts on their Mexican ranch,
and Bill says that she is as good a shot as he knows. I hate to kill
things anyhow, and I am content to be a tenderfoot." [26]

The foolish war with Spain was soon over. Its effect upon
America was to be in reverse proportion to its importance among
the wars of history. Its indirect effect upon the life of William
Howard Taft was to be just as profound. He was to abandon, for
more than twenty years, any active desire to sit in the pleasant,
historic room which had once been the Senate Chamber and had
become the abode of the Supreme Court. The American people
had made war to free the people of Cuba. The strategy of war
caused Admiral Dewey to seize Manila in the remote Philippine
Islands. Somewhat to their surprise, the American people learned
that another race, also oppressed by Spain, dwelt on that far-off
archipelago. What was to be done with the Philippine Islands? By
all means, said a large segment of American opinion, let us keep
them. Are we not a world power now? Have we not survived the
sneers of England and the contempt of Germany? Did we not
knock the stuffing out of Spain? Manifest destiny— in the saloons
men phrased it as "We won 'em and we'll keep 'em"— demanded
sovereignty in the Philippines. Besides, so the experts said, American goods could be sold there.

". . . the pacification of the Philippines," cried the oratorical
Chauncey Depew, "gives a market of ten millions of people. It
will grow every year as they come into more civilized conditions
and their wants increase." [27]

[26] *Idem*, Oct. 24, 1909. [27] New York *Times*, Sept. 9, 1900.

—4—

It was not so simple as that. McKinley, in the White House, knew that it was not. He may not have wholly grasped the forces which were shaping the future of the United States in 1898, but he knew more about their complexities than did most of the imperialists who shouted for dominion over palm and pine. He knew more than did the businessmen who saw riches and wealth in an expanded export trade. So did John Hay, who became secretary of state in September, 1898. For the interests of America no longer stopped at her boundaries to the north and south and east and west. She had become, in fact as well as in Independence Day orations, a world power. There was heartache as well as grandeur in the role. Only a little while before, the conduct of foreign affairs had been easy. It had been a process, first, of pushing other powers from the lands which were to be the continental United States and, second, of making certain that they did not acquire new territory in either North or South America.

But now there was a Far Eastern problem. The Hawaiian Islands had been annexed in July, 1898. The United States discovered, tardily, that the nations of Europe had been busily engaged in cutting for themselves large slices of the rich cake which China constituted. Russia, France, Germany, England and Japan were all vitally interested. Thereupon John Hay voiced his open-door policy, which meant that all nations should trade alike in China. The Far Eastern problem was to alarm Theodore Roosevelt in the years ahead and was to worry Taft as well. It lay behind, although it was not the entire cause of, our decision to hold the Philippine Islands.

President McKinley had not appreciated the situation, at first. In April, 1898, while the war was in progress, word was dispatched to Hay, then United States ambassador to England, that the islands would remain with Spain save for a port to be used by the navy.[28] The protocol for peace, signed by Spain in August, specified freedom for Cuba, and it was ultimately agreed that the peace commissioners of the two nations, who would meet in Paris, would

[28] Dennett, Tyler, *John Hay*, p. 190.

decide the disposition of the Philippines. McKinley was greatly disturbed.

"I walked the floor of the White House night after night until midnight . . . I went down on my knees and prayed Almighty God for light and guidance," he remembered.

The Lord, it appears, was familiar with our foreign problem. If the Philippines were turned over to France or Germany, American trade in the Far East would suffer. They were unfit for self-government. Nothing remained but for the United States to assume control, civilize, Christianize and trade with the little brown men. So the United States paid $20,000,000 for the islands.[29] The treaty of peace was signed on December 10, 1898. And to all this Taft gave, if anything, no more than a passing thought. Nothing could be more remote to a federal circuit judge than the future of the Philippine Islands. In so far as he expressed any opinion, it was opposed to annexation.[30]

In short, Taft knew as much—and as little— about the Philippine Islands as the average American. It may be doubted that he had any knowledge of the grave questions of Far Eastern policy which forced the hand of President McKinley. It is equally certain that he knew little about the history of the Filipino people, to whom he was to become so greatly devoted, or their struggle for freedom.

The first major revolt on the archipelago took place in 1872 and was suppressed by Spain without great difficulty. But resentment continued to grow. In 1892 this found a leader in José Rizal, one of those astonishing figures in the eternal struggle of man against the oppressor. Rizal, who was born on the island of Luzon in 1861, had been educated in Europe where he distinguished himself for scholarship. He had studied medicine, law and philosophy. He was proficient in most of the European languages and could read Greek, Latin, Sanskrit, Arabic and Japanese. He could converse in a number of the Philippine dialects. And he became, on his return from Europe, a profound student of the affairs of his native land.

Rizal was an extraordinary propagandist. He wrote well. He

[29] Rhodes, J. F., *The McKinley and Roosevelt Administrations, 1897-1909*. pp. 106-107. [30] Taft, Mrs. W. H., *Recollections of Full Years*, p. 32.

called attention to the abuses of the Spanish authorities in the islands and to the even greater ones perpetrated by the Spanish priests. But Rizal believed in peace. He did not advocate revolution or independence. He asked that reforms be instituted gradually; from within. He organized the younger intellectuals and also the less literate classes into an organization called the "Liga Filipina." To the Spanish rulers he was, of course, an object of suspicion, and finally he was deported to Dapitan, a remote village on Mindanao Island. Spain learned, however, as the oppressor always learns, that ideas are difficult to suppress by force. A group of young leaders gathered around the exiled Rizal and received an education in freedom at his hands. On the morning of December 30, 1896, after a grotesquely unfair trial, Rizal was executed. Thereby Spain played into the hands of a more radical group which called themselves the "Katipunan." This demanded sweeping reforms and expulsion of the hated Spanish friars from the archipelago. Torture and scores of executions followed. New leaders arose, among them Emilio Aguinaldo, and independence was proclaimed. Such was the situation when Admiral Dewey destroyed the Spanish squadron in Manila Bay.[31]

Aguinaldo assisted the American forces in seizing the city of Manila. He always contended, but on unsubstantial proof, that he had been promised independence in return for this aid. By December, 1898, the Filipino leaders learned that this was to be denied them. They concluded that the Spanish tyrant had merely been replaced by an American one. Aguinaldo had already declared himself president of the Philippine Republic and on February 4, 1899, American troops fired on some Filipino soldiers. On February 22 an uprising took place in Manila with the avowed purpose of killing all American and European residents in the city. The troubled McKinley rushed additional troops to the islands and soon war— a war of raids and small engagements and frequent casualties— was on in earnest. The white man's burden was beginning to bear down heavily.[32]

President McKinley appointed a commission of five, with President Jacob Gould Schurman of Cornell University as chair-

[31] Forbes, W. Cameron, *The Philippine Islands*, Vol. I, pp. 52-60. [32] *Ibid.*, Vol. I, pp. 82-95.

man, to visit the Philippine Islands, explain the American program and convince the majority of the Filipinos, if possible, that control by the United States was not comparable to control by Spain. The commission arrived in Manila, unfortunately, in March, 1899; a month after hostilities had started. It was forced to talk peace amid the rattle of rifles. The authority of the military was supreme. Yet Dr. Schurman and his associates accomplished a great deal. A proclamation was issued which pledged justice and a marked degree of self-government under American supervision. The members of the commission concluded that the insurrectionary leaders represented, after all, but a small proportion of the native people. In a four-volume report, the commission offered many suggestions which ultimately were adopted when a civil government was formed. The Schurman commission wound up its work in January, 1900, with the submission of this report. Dr. Schurman's duties at Cornell did not permit his return to carry the plan into execution.[33]

—5—

Meanwhile Circuit Judge Taft continued to hear arguments as a member of the Circuit Court of Appeals, continued to wonder whether another associate justice of the Supreme Court would resign or die and whether he would be appointed to that bench. On a Monday afternoon, late in January, 1900, he was startled to receive a telegram from the President of the United States. On Wednesday night he took a train for Washington. Taft had no idea what was wanted. No vacancy existed on the Supreme Court at the time, so it could not be that the elevation was to come at last. When he got off the train he hurried to the White House and was received at once. Secretary of War Elihu Root was present and so was Secretary of the Navy John D. Long. The astonished circuit judge heard the President say that he was going to name a new commission to the Philippine Islands and that he wanted him to be a member. It was intimated that he might be its president.[34]

[33] Schurman, Jacob Gould, *Philippine Affairs*, pp. 1-50. [34] Taft to W. H. and Horace D. Taft, Jan. 28, 1900.

"He might as well have told me," said Taft, in describing his surprise, "that he wanted me to take a flying machine." [35]

The President went on to say that Dr. Schurman could not return to the islands and asked for Taft's views on the Philippine problem:

> I told him I was very much opposed to taking them, that I did not favor expansion but that now that we were there we were under the most sacred duty to give them a good form of government, that I did not agree with Senator Hoar [Senator George F. Hoar of Massachusetts] and his followers, that the Philippines were capable of self-government or that we were violating any principles of our government or the Declaration of Independence so far as they were concerned, that I thought we were doing them great good, but that I deprecated our taking the Philippines because of the assumption of a burden by us contrary to our traditions and at a time when we had quite enough to do at home; but being there, we must exert ourselves to construct a government which should be adapted to the needs of the people so that they might be developed into a self-governing people.

Judge Taft at first deprecated, too, the unexpected proposal that he was the man to go as head of the commission. He pointed out that he was not familiar with even the Spanish language, that others could serve better. But the President "said that he had selected me, that Hay, Root and Long had all said I must go when my name was suggested." [36] Taft was still dubious; he was doubtful that it was wise to abandon his judicial career. Two arguments convinced him that he must accept. The first was that it was his duty. The second was that the Philippine Commission was only temporary and would, in the long run, advance his judicial career. Secretary of War Root, whom Taft had encountered in his years as solicitor general, argued the first point; for many years the conversation lingered in Taft's mind.

"You have had an easy time of it holding office since you were twenty-one," Root said severely. "Now your country needs you. This is a task worthy any man. This is the parting of the ways. You may go on holding the job you have in a humdrum, mediocre way. But here is something that will test you; something in the way

[35] *Addresses,* Vol. XXXI, p. 70. [36] Taft to H. W. and Horace D. Taft, Jan. 28, 1900.

of effort and struggle, and the question is, will you take the harder or the easier task?" [37]

Taft was impressed. But did this mean, he asked, an end of his judicial career? President McKinley said it did not. "All I can say to you," he answered, "is that if you give up this judicial office at my request you shall not suffer. If I last and the opportunity comes, I shall appoint you."

"Yes," echoed Secretary of the Navy Long, "it means judicial promotion to you."

"Yes," said the President, "if I am here, you will be here."

Root put in a final word: "This will make you a great deal broader judge on your return."

Taft requested and was granted a week in which to make up his mind.[38] He returned to Cincinnati to ask advice of his wife and to be urged by that adventurous lady, of course, to take the post immediately. But Taft did not enjoy making decisions, unless from the bench regarding the affairs of others. He was assailed by doubts, as he had been when the post of solicitor general had been tendered him. He asked brothers Henry and Horace to tell him what to do:

The question, of course, is am I willing and ought I to give up my present position for what is offered in *praesenti* and in *futuro*. The opportunity to do good and help along in a critical stage in the country's history is very great. Root especially urges this view. I am still young as men go and I am not afraid to go back to the [law] practice though I confess that I love my present position. Ought I to allow this to deter me from accepting an opportunity thrust on me to accomplish more important and more venturesome tasks with a possible greater reward? Write me what you think.[39]

A few days later he decided that he should go, if at all, only as the head of the commission. He wanted to be in a position "in which I shall be really responsible for success or failure," he told Root. He added that this was no reflection on the other commissioners. The reason Taft gave was that the problem of the Philippines was now principally that of reframing the government and this was a lawyer's job.[40]

[37] *Addresses,* Vol. XXXI, p. 70. [38] Taft to H. W. and Horace D. Taft, Jan. 28, 1900. [39] *Idem.* [40] Taft to Elihu Root, Feb. 2, 1900.

Horace Taft urged acceptance. He was amused. "You can do more good in that position in a year than you could on the bench in a dozen," he wrote. "They can't get a better man than you. . . . As for your future, it is too bad about that. If you get stuck I can give you a place in the school [the Taft School which Horace had recently started]. I can give you . . . the chair of Christian manhood." [41] So Taft sent his acceptance to the President. After all, the job would take only six months; nine at the most— so he had been assured at the White House. [42]

But it was to be February, 1904, before Taft, finally and by then reluctantly, gave up his post as guardian of the small brown men of the distant isles. By that time it had become the most important work in the world to him. Even President Roosevelt's repeated offers of the Supreme Court could not tempt him home. That January day in 1900 on which the post in the Philippines was tendered was another of those vital milestones at which men hesitate and ponder, decide to go forward or remain behind. Taft always remembered the exhortation of Elihu Root on that occasion:

"I followed his advice. He didn't know he was getting me into such a job as would land me in the White House, but he did. It's a long way round." [43]

Mrs. Taft wondered throughout the years "how our lot happened to be so cast." [44] The biographer must share her bewilderment. It is known that President McKinley consulted Foraker of Ohio before making the appointment. Taft expressed appreciation for the cordial endorsement given by the senator from Ohio. [45] But Foraker cannot have supposed that Taft could gain a reputation which would make him obvious presidential material by 1903; this was not in the Foraker program at all. Only one explanation is logical. Taft was named to the Philippine Commission because a man of high integrity was needed and because he was eligible for favors from a Republican administration. At that, it was not a major favor. The appointment was to have been brief. It was far more likely to lead to disillusionment and grief than to honor and renown; such had been the story of the Philippine Islands.

[41] Horace D. Taft to Taft, Jan. 31, 1900. [42] Taft, Mrs. W. H., *op. cit.*, p. 34. [43] *Addresses*, Vol. XXXI, p. 70. [44] Taft, Mrs. H. W., *op. cit.*, p. 31. [45] Foraker, Julia B., *I Would Live It Again*, p. 308.

CHAPTER XI

HALF DEVIL AND HALF CHILD

O N MAY 21, 1900, the United States Transport *Hancock* paused in the harbor of Nagasaki for the coal which would carry her on to Manila. William Howard Taft, president of the Philippine Commission, leaned over the side and watched the antlike gangs of Japanese transfer fuel into the ship's cavernous bunkers. He wondered, idly, how they could work from dawn to dusk and not get weary in the heat. He marveled that they seemed so cheerful for a wage, so he was informed, of twenty cents a day.[1] But this, he was learning, was the incredible East. It was the East where any generalization was unsound, where any conclusion was unreliable. Very soon he would dwell among other small men who did not emulate the ants at all, who considered them silly insects and believed that the only purpose of labor was to gain time for doing nothing.

Mail and newspapers were put aboard the *Hancock* at Naga- saki; among the items was a two-week-old issue of the Manila *Times,* a journal written in English. Taft unwrapped his copy. He cut out a lengthy poem and mailed it to Mrs. Taft, who had re- mained in Yokohama to escape the heat of the Philippines that summer. The poem was anonymous. It was called "Greeting" and was addressed to the head of the arriving Philippine Commission. The poet, well-drenched in the lyrics of Kipling, described the work which awaited the members. He gave warning of the fate of other administrators, who had labored too hard in the equatorial heat. He spoke, indeed, as one of those who had done so:

> But don't you do it, Judge, it doesn't pay.
>   It is a foolish game; I was a fool
> To tear my health to pieces day by day,
>   Doing too much to leave me time to rule.

[1] Taft to C. P. Taft, May 27, 1900.

Construct! Construct! That is the simple plan.
  Destruction has been reigning here for years.
A doctor must build up an ailing man
  Rather than pour in drugs up to his ears.

One thing I ask of you: I beg, I pray,
  I conjure you to treat my children well.
I am my master's slave, and this the day
  When I must bid his babes, my charge, farewell.

They thought me harsh, as children always do
  When they are petulant and want the moon.
They know a little better now; and you
  Will hear them singing to a softer tune.[2]

The verses, Taft admitted, contained "some very good advice" [3] and he followed it, to an extent. But eighteen months later his own health gave way and he prepared to sail back to the United States for treatment. A meeting of the Philippine Commission was held and its President sent for champagne to mark the occasion. Taft charged his fellow members to carry on during his absence; he would return as soon as possible. At the close of his informal address he picked up a small piece of paper and quoted Kipling:

Now it is not good for the Christian
  To hustle the Aryan brown
For the Christian riles and the Aryan smiles,
  And he weareth the Christian down;
And the end of the fight is a tombstone white
  With the name of the late deceased,
And the epitaph drear "A fool lies here
  Who tried to hustle the East." [4]

The first American viceroy escaped the tombstone. In many ways Taft was ideally suited to the arduous duties which lay ahead of him when on April 17, 1900, he boarded the *Hancock* at San Francisco and began the journey to the Philippines. He was as patient as he was large in frame. He was tolerant. He could be stubborn when stubbornness was a virtue. Above all, he had a vast capacity for affection and before very long he had become very fond, indeed, of the little men who had become, sometimes gladly and sometimes resentfully, the wards of Uncle Sam. It was to be said, when Taft became a candidate for president of the United States, that his experience in the Philippine Islands qualified him for the White House. Great executive responsibilities, it is true, had been placed upon him. He had been forced to master tariffs, currencies, public improvements, governmental finance. But the analogy between ruling the Philippines and being president of the United States was false. Taft was, to a marked degree, a dictator in the archipelago of the far Pacific. No Senate Progressives plagued him there. No Gifford Pinchot quarreled about the forests. No Democrats abused and attacked him. No Theodore Roosevelt turned against him. The politicos of the Philippines disagreed with his policies, of course, but in the last analysis Taft could impose his own will. His voice was the law. He was, again, a judge. And so the petulance of the presidential years did not arise. Nor did the torments and the anxieties of probable defeat.

—2—

Taft was well-satisfied with the other four appointments made by President McKinley to the Philippine Commission. General Luke E. Wright, second in command, was a resident of Tennessee, a lawyer and a veteran of the Confederate Army. He was a gracious gentleman of the old school; deliberate, tranquil in nature and really learned in the law. Henry C. Ide was also a lawyer, a New Englander. He brought to the commission a degree of experience in colonial government because he had been chief justice of Samoa. Dean C. Worcester had been a member of the first Philippine Commission and was the only one of the five who had been in the islands. A zoologist, he was on the faculty of the University of Michigan and had been on several scientific expeditions to the Far East. Bernard Moses was also a professor. He was affiliated with the history department at the University of California. Taft, as president of the commission, leaned on Moses for economic and sociological information. He felt that the commission was an excellent one because of the diversified talents of its members.[5]

The voyage to Manila was colorful and interesting rather than eventful. The *Hancock* touched at Honolulu where Taft was taken surf riding in native canoes and reported that he had never enjoyed "more exhilarating sport." The party went sightseeing in Yokohama, for all the world like any American round-the-world tourists. At Tokyo the men of the party were received by the Emperor of Japan and the women by the Empress. Taft was not greatly impressed:

The Emperor is by no means a beauty. I have rarely seen a homelier man. He looks like a dark mulatto, who has been "soaking" for a good many years, and that, I am afraid, is the fact. He is said to be intensely fond of sake, a distilled liquor which is made from rice in this country. . . . He has five or six wives and ten or twelve concubines, and the present Prince Imperial . . . was the son of a concubine. He was at once adopted by the Empress. . . . The son . . . is permitted but one wife, which seems rather hard when his father has been so liberally treated in this matter.

In short, to Taft's too-simple Ohio mind, these were outlandish foreigners as well as heathens. At a reception later that day, he again met his Japanese classmate, now Baron Tajirijnajiro and vice-minister of finance, whose vote, far back in 1878, had won for Taft the post of class orator at Yale.[6] During the long days at sea the commission had pored over the volumes of the Schurman report and discussed the problems soon to be faced. Taft, worried about his bulk, exercised by tramping around the deck.[7] His weight both amused and annoyed him when he rode, for the first time, in the jinrikishas on shore. The party had visited the temples at Nikko, high in the mountains:

The road was steep and got steeper. I had one "pusher" in addition to the jinrikisha man when I began, another joined when we were halfway up, and it seemed to me that [when] we struck the last hill the whole village was engaged in the push. The Japanese seemed to look upon me with great amusement; at the

[5] Taft, Mrs. W. H., *Recollections of Full Years,* pp. 40-45. [6] Taft to C. P. Taft, May 8, 18, 1900. [7] Taft, Mrs. W. H., *op. cit.,* p. 46.

various places where we changed cars there were a great number of people clattering along on their wooden platforms which they use as shoes, and they gathered in crowds about me, smiling and enjoying the prospect of so much flesh and size.[8]

A house for Mrs. Taft and the children had to be found in Yokohama. Servants had to be hired for Manila and supplies purchased. The day came when the *Hancock* steamed on and Taft left Japan with the members of the commission. The presence of Mrs. Taft and her sister, Maria, he wrote home, had until then given the journey the "air of a tourist jaunt." But leaving them had brought "home . . . the seriousness of our mission with emphasis." Life had changed appallingly since the peaceful days when he was a respected judge of the Federal Circuit Court of Appeals, and he began, again, to worry. The work ahead would "be slow and discouraging at times and full of difficulty." [9] At Nagasaki he received reports of "an uprising in Manila on the arrival of the commission to convince us of the hopelessness of our mission," but discounted the probability of it.[10] He wondered, instead, about his fitness for the work at hand.

As we get nearer and nearer . . . my thoughts are much occupied with the question how well I am adapted to succeed . . . I feel woefully deficient . . . My ignorance of Spanish . . . will put me at a disadvantage. I cannot get close to many men with whom it is important I should converse intimately. . . . I do not know how much executive ability I have. I have never been really tried. I very much doubt my having a great deal.[11]

On the morning of June 3, 1900, a Sunday, the *Hancock* slipped through the last oily waters of the China Sea and pointed her bow toward the island of Luzon, the largest in the Philippine group. It was hot. The thermometer hovered above the ninety mark. The air seemed to have come pouring from some damp infernal furnace. Taft had known heat before; the smoke-laden heat of

[8] Taft to C. P. Taft, May 18, 1900. [9] *Idem*. [10] Taft to Helen H. Taft, May 21, 1900. [11] *Idem*, May 21, 1900.

Cincinnati and the humid, muggy vapors of the Potomac basin. But this heat had a new and menacing quality. As you looked across the water the air shimmered and yet lay still, too still. This was not the friendly heat of the Middle West which covered the valleys of the Ohio, Missouri and Mississippi rivers and caused the corn to grow with soft rustlings in the night. It was tropic heat; its embrace carried cholera, malaria. It beat down upon inland lakes until they lay stagnant under the sun. Instead of corn, it caused vines with grasping tendrils to flourish. Insects that crawled or flew and snakes with the sting of death were its offspring. It was a heat which banished sleep by night. By day it made men drink too much in hope that they might forget it. Instead, as Taft of the Philippine Commission would learn, they forgot family and home and honor. They betrayed their government and became thieves.

Taft must have looked out on that morning with mixed emotions. To the north— that is, on the port side of the *Hancock* as the vessel came in— was a mountainous country. There, he knew, dwelt some of the little brown men who had sworn eternal war on manifest destiny and the United States and were causing no small inconvenience to their benefactors. Ahead lay Corregidor past which the valorous Dewey had steamed and had humbled the Spanish dons. The *Hancock* went on, now at reduced speed. Native boats with their crazy, colored sails dotted the bay. Off the starboard bow was Cavite and straight ahead the city of Manila. Beauty was there too. Red roofs gleamed in the sunlight above their white walls. Church spires pointed toward the cloudless sky. But the city seemed to have been built on a pestilential stretch of lowland. Everything was flat. Down in the bowels of the *Hancock* bells sounded and her screws stopped turning. The anchor dropped and a tender came alongside. It had grown still warmer since the early morning.

Taft, with his fellow commissioners, did not go ashore at once and Professor Worcester, who had been in the Philippines before, noted a "certain frigidity" in the air despite the heat. He knew what this meant, and so did Taft. It was the resentment of General Arthur MacArthur who had been in the Philippines since the summer of 1898 and who had been appointed military governor just a month before.[12] The general was a military man and so, of course, were the members of his staff. They were utterly cynical regarding their brown brothers— cynical and convinced that civilization could be brought to the Philippines by the Krag and the bayonet alone. The general brooded at his desk in the city and did not come to the *Hancock* to extend a greeting to the commission. The arrival of these civilians would upset all his plans. They would interfere with his subjugation of the Filipinos.

Taft was to fight MacArthur long and stubbornly. He was to send innumerable letters of complaint to Secretary of War Root. The lawyer was, in the end, to strip the military governor of most of his powers; the bayonets were to be sheathed and the Krags stacked in the armories.

It was discouraging to the commission, though, to learn thus at the start that friction was inescapable. Taft convened his associates in the *Hancock's* cabin and waited for General MacArthur to pay his respects. But the general did not appear. Instead, Colonel Enoch H. Crowder came aboard; he was the general's aide and a far more diplomatic officer. He did his best in a difficult situation. Shortly afterward a large number of Filipino leaders came over the side; these were the *Americanistas* who were friendly to the United States and hostile to Aguinaldo's struggle for independence. Taft talked with them through an interpreter. He concluded to remain on the *Hancock* that night and to land on Monday, June 4.[13]

The landing was made with appropriate ceremonies. Perspiring and hot, feeling faintly foolish in the white suit which seemed to increase his elephantine size,[14] Taft led his commission through a line of artillerymen to carriages which bore them to the palace of the Ayuntamiento which was the headquarters of the military governor.

"The populace that we expected to welcome us was not there," Taft recalled, "and I cannot describe the coldness of the army officers and army men who received us any better than by saying that it somewhat exceeded the coldness of the populace."[15]

Icicles dripped from the hand of General MacArthur as he

[12] Worcester, Dean C., *The Philippines, Past and Present*, pp. 330-331. [13] Forbes, W. C., *The Philippine Islands*, Vol. I, p. 125; Taft, Mrs. W. H., *op. cit.*, pp. 80-81. [14] Taft to C. P. Taft, May 12, 1900. [15] Forbes, W. C., *op. cit.*, Vol I, p. 125.

arose to greet Taft, Wright, Worcester, Moses and Ide. In describing the visit to Mrs. Taft, the president of the commission said that the frigidity had made his perspiration stop.[16] The civilian commission, said the general, was "an injection into an otherwise normal situation." He said with military candor that the Filipinos would need bayonet treatment for at least a decade.[17] Taft attempted to smooth the ruffled eagle feathers. After all, he pointed out, the general would still be in supreme command of the military and would have great power.

"That would be all right," MacArthur answered, "if I had not been exercising so much more power before you came."[18]

At the least, it was confusing to Taft and his colleagues. They were halfway across the world from Washington. They had no very specific guarantee that the President and his secretary of war might not, in this altercation, support the military rather than the civilian arm. The general was not above an occasional mean gesture. Later, on the day of their landing, the commission found that they had been assigned to one small room in the palace; they could hardly walk about without climbing over desks and chairs.[19] But MacArthur was not yet aware, apparently, that the President had given to the commission full power over appropriations. Taft controlled the purse strings.[20] On the whole, even at the beginning, he was optimistic:

The situation in Manila is perplexing. You meet men who are completely discouraged at it; you meet men who are conservative but very hopeful of good results; and you meet men who have roseate views of the situation. My own impression is that the back of the rebellion is broken, and that the state of robbery and anarchy which exists in the islands where the soldiers are not in control has induced a number of leading generals, quite a number of whom have been captured, to take the view that surrender is the best course. This is perhaps an optimistic view, but I am told that for two years there have been constant threats of surrender, and I believe there is more reason to believe in it this time than any time before. I am very anxious that civil government shall be established. . . . However . . . we must be patient and amiable in this climate.[21]

[16] Taft, Mrs. W. H., *op. cit.*, p. 81. [17] Worcester, D. C., *op. cit.*, p. 331. [18] Taft, Mrs. W. H., *op. cit*, p. 82. [19] Worcester, D. C., *op. cit.*, p. 331. [20] Forbes, W. C., *op. cit.*, Vol. I, p. 125. [21] Taft to C. P. Taft, June 12, 1900.

—4—

The first necessity, obviously, was to learn as much as possible regarding actual conditions in the island. Taft began, at once, to interview as many of the residents of the islands as he could. He had already acquired, as a judge, a gift for sifting the truth from prejudiced statements. Now a stream of witnesses began to pass before the president of the Philippine Commission. They argued for immediate independence and against it. They praised the fugitive Aguinaldo and damned him. They declared that the archipelago was a land of gold and honey, or said that it was a worthless jungle. They accused the military of outrageous cruelties or said that but for the army chaos would have ruled. The witnesses spoke in Spanish or English or a mixture of both and learned, rather promptly, that the large and amiable gentleman who presided was very much interested in facts and not at all in arguments. His blue eyes could be cold as well as merry. He shut witnesses off ruthlessly when they started to make speeches. Before very long, Taft had accumulated a mass of fact. And on the basis of it he was not afraid to enunciate a policy. He recalled it in a speech some years later.

"We hold the Philippines for the benefit of the Filipinos," Taft said, "and we are not entitled to pass a single act or to approve a single measure that has not that as its chief purpose." [22]

And just what measures, actually, would benefit the Filipinos? Working ten or twelve hours a day in July and August, 1900, Taft found that it was not easy to decide. On one point he was certain: independence could not be granted for decades. Beyond that, it was impossible to generalize about the Philippine Islands or the Filipinos. Magellan, searching the East for spices, had discovered the islands early in the sixteenth century; they had become a colony of Spain in 1565 in the reign of Philip II. Spain was to be disappointed in her new possession, for few spices and little gold were found. And yet this was virtually an empire; its area was 114,000 square miles, larger than any of the United States save Texas, Cali-

[22] *Addresses*, Vol. I., p. 154.

fornia, Montana or New Mexico. The Philippine Islands were three-quarters the size of insular Japan. But nobody knew, or knows even now for that matter, the exact number of the islands. In 1918 the total was placed at 7,083, but it was explained that some of the smaller ones had not been included. They were mere dots on the sea, too small for any map. Of the 7,083, this survey stated, 1,095 were large enough to be inhabited and had water. But only 463 had an area greater than a square mile. On the other hand, eleven of the islands were more than a thousand square miles each in size.

Almost 95 per cent of the total area is on these eleven islands. Two-thirds of this 95 per cent is represented by the islands of Luzon to the north and Mindanao in the south. The former has 41,000 square miles and the latter about 37,000. These vast territories are crossed by rivers. Water power is available. Timber is to be found in the forests and the fertile valleys seem ideal for agriculture. Fish abound in the rivers and in the waters off the coast.[23] But these sparse statistics were of slight interest to ardent enthusiasts of the Philippines, whose ranks Taft soon joined. They pointed out that beauty dwelt amidst the heat, that the waters of the sea were blue, that nowhere else in the world were such sunsets seen, that nowhere were floral colors so varied or floral odors so sweet. Ordinarily, Taft was not quickly stimulated by the aesthetic things of life. Music bored although it sometimes soothed him. He cared almost as little for art. But he was moved by the beauty of the Philippines on a morning soon after his arrival. He had arisen at 5:30 and the air, washed by showers in the night, was still cool. He sat on the porch and scribbled a note to his wife:

The mountains on the other side of the bay are touched at their summits with pink, a beautiful rainbow reaches from sea surface to sea surface and the many graceful oceangoing steamers that lie two miles from shore are outlined clearly by the morning sun against the foot of the mountains beyond. Far over at Cavite, too, the white war vessels of the United States show themselves in the morning light.[24]

[23] Forbes, W. C., op. cit., Vol. I, pp. 5-6. Worcester, D. C., op. cit., pp. 792-793.
[24] Taft to Helen H. Taft, June 14, 1900.

Taft was more interested in the faults and virtues of the Filipino people than in the economic and geographic aspects of the islands. On board the *Hancock* he had learned that the Filipino was of Malay origin and that his blood had been mixed with Mongolian, with other Asiatic and Polynesian races.[25] Some of the people were pronouncedly Malayan while in others the Mongoloid strain predominated. At least seven main languages were spoken and innumerable dialects. The aristocrats were the ones who had some Spanish blood;[26] these were the professional men and the politicians. In many instances they had studied abroad and were well-educated. But nobody knew in the summer of 1900 precisely how many Filipinos existed. No census had been taken. The most authoritative estimate was that the population was 6,700,000. Of these, 90 per cent professed devotion to Christianity; the Spaniard, in his eternal quest for salvation, had done his missionary work thoroughly. Most of the rest were Mohammedans; they were the wild Moro tribes of Mindanao and the Sulu archipelago and they were hated, feared and despised by the more orderly Filipinos who had embraced Catholicism.[27]

—5—

By the middle of July, Taft had arrived at conclusions of his own regarding the people he had come to rule. He described them to Secretary of War Root and to his wife:

The population of the islands is made up of a vast mass of ignorant, superstitious people, well-intentioned, lighthearted, temperate, somewhat cruel, domestic and fond of their families, and deeply wedded to the Catholic Church. They are easily influenced by speeches from a small class of educated meztizos [those with Spanish blood], who have acquired a good deal of superficial knowledge of the general principles of free government, who are able to mouth sentences supposed to embody constitutional law, and who like to give the appearance of profound analytical knowledge of the science of government. They are generally lacking in

[25] Forbes, W. C., *op. cit.*, Vol. I, p. 14. [26] Roosevelt, Nicholas, *The Philippines, a Treasure and a Problem*, pp. 8-9. [27] Forbes, W. C., *op. cit.*, Vol. I, pp. 15-16.

moral character; are with some notable exceptions prone to yield to any pecuniary consideration, and are difficult persons out of whom to make an honest government. We shall have to do the best we can with them. They are born politicians; are as ambitious as Satan, and as jealous as possible of each other's preferment. . . .

All the people are small and they are not very muscular. They are lighthearted, musical and good-tempered. They are also light-fingered and the greatest liars in the world. One of the greatest difficulties in getting a coachman is to secure one who will not steal your horse's fodder. They are careless and cruel to animals. They are respectful and polite. . . .

One of the great evils in this community, the far reaching effect of which I did not realize until now, is the effect of the gambling spirit among these people and the absolute necessity of restraining the opportunities for gambling by rigid enforcement of the laws. . . . The mania is so great that men will gamble away the chastity of their daughters and their wives, and finally, beggared by their excesses in this vice, they have no other recourse than to robbery and preying on the public.[28]

"They have all the politeness and all the insincerity of the Spaniards, but they are a pleasant people to meet," he added.[29] Taft began almost immediately to grow fond of the Filipinos, who seemed by every possible standard to differ so widely from himself. His most important discovery— the one which may, in itself, have determined the success of his career as a colonial governor— was that the Filipinos were proud and sensitive and quick to resent any implication of being an inferior race. Even before the *Hancock* had entered Manila harbor, Taft had determined on a policy which was to reassure his wards on this point.

"We expect to do considerable entertaining . . ." he wrote, "and especially of Filipinos, both ladies and gentlemen. . . . We are advised that the army has alienated a good many of our Filipino friends . . . and given them the impression, which the ladies of the army certainly seem to have, that they regard the Filipino ladies and men as 'niggers' and as not fit to be associated with. We propose, so far as we are able, to banish this idea from their mind."[30]

[28] Taft to Elihu Root, July 14, Oct. 1, 1900; Taft to Helen H. Taft, July 22, 1900.
[29] Taft to C. P. Taft, July 7, 1900. [30] *Idem,* June 2, 1900. [31] Taft to Root, Aug. 18, 1900.

This was one of the principal reasons for Taft's resentment toward the army and its methods, a resentment which increased with the months. General MacArthur did not approve of the policy adopted by his subordinates toward the Filipinos. But he was not active enough, to suit Taft, in taking steps toward changing it.[31] The president of the commission appealed to Mrs. Taft, who was still in Yokohama:

One of the things we have to do here is to extend hospitality to Filipino families of wealth and position. The army circles definitely and distinctly decline to have anything to do with them . . . I need your assistance in taking a different course. . . . Its political effect will be very considerable. . . . These people are very polite and decorous and the fact that their fathers and mothers or their grandfathers and grandmothers may not have been willing to pay a heavy tax for a marriage ceremony ought not to make us hesitate to receive them and entertain them.[32]

With the cordial assistance of Mrs. Taft, the president of the commission took steps to mollify the islanders. The color line was never drawn at official or unofficial dinners or receptions.[33] Taft continually complained to Washington regarding the widespread idea, for which the army was in a measure to blame, that the United States would make an inferior race of the Filipinos as soon as pacification had been accomplished. He told of a conversation between a Filipino lawyer and a native driver:

. . . the cochero asked him whether it was true that the Americans proposed . . . to pass laws confining each Filipino to a mile square of ground, out of which he could not go without being imprisoned. He said further that he understood the Americans proposed to hitch the Filipinos to carriages as soon as American power was established here, and make them take the place of horses.[34]

Such stories, Taft knew, constituted valuable propaganda material for secret agents of the revolutionary leaders. He was aware that pacification would be long delayed if the lower classes con-

[32] Taft to Helen H. Taft, July 8, 1900. [33] Taft, Mrs. W. H., *op. cit.*, p. 125. [34] Taft to Root, Sept. 13, 1900.

tinued to give credence to such nonsense. So he strove with energy and intelligence to convince the Filipinos that America was sincere in its announced intention of governing for the benefit of the governed. He attended a cockfight during a visit of inspection in the interior in June.

"It was curious," he reported, "to watch the interest of these people in a cockfight. It is their national amusement and we have advised MacArthur that we think the order forbidding it is a mistake. It perhaps promotes gambling, but it is a venial offense and it is a capital mistake to give these people the impression that we are here to restrict their ordinary enjoyments." [35]

A direct path to the hearts of the people, Taft concluded, would be to encourage their taste for music. He suggested that a fund be raised for a conservatory, to be named in honor of the patriot, José Rizal. As for the effect:

. . . a thing of this sort which would strike the hearts of the people of Manila would produce a throb throughout the entire archipelago. . . . These people are emotional and sentimental, and such an act of generosity would touch them more and affect them more than administrative reforms of a much more important kind.[36]

Taft knew that subjugation of the insurrectionists would be far more rapid if, first, the confidence and respect of the masses were obtained. He may have been inclined to underestimate the sincerity and patriotism of Aguinaldo and other of the more patriotic insurgent leaders; he was careful, though, to refrain from any public utterance in disparagement. A single serious mistake during the first year would probably have been fatal to the commission. Additional troops would have been detailed to General MacArthur. The bloodshed of guerrilla warfare would have continued for a decade at least. But Taft walked with a firm yet wary step. Vociferous critics waited hopefully. Some years later Taft described the opposing viewpoints:

The English student of colonial government is fixed in his view that we have pursued a wrong course in the Philippine Islands

[35] Taft to Helen H. Taft, June 26, 1900. [36] Taft to Root, Aug. 31, 1900.

by conferring upon the people much more popular control than was wise and by attempting to give them an education, which instead of tending to improve matters will tend to create popular agitation and discontent and constant conspiracy and plotting against the government. On the other hand, our American critics, who like to describe themselves as anti-imperialists, condemn the course of the United States . . . on the ground that sufficient self-government has not been extended to the Filipinos and that immediate preparation is not being made to abandon the islands to an independent government. Now it sometimes happens that the concurrence in condemnation . . . of people having the exactly opposite views is a fairly good indication that the course taken is somewhat near that golden mean— that line of average good— which should be the object of all practical legislators and governors. I venture to think it is so in the present case.[37]

Part of the credit must go to Dr. Schurman and the First Philippine Commission on whose recommendations President Mc-Kinley, Secretary of War Root and Taft leaned heavily. The achievement of the "golden mean" was, even more, due to Taft's innate impartiality and judicial mind. He was also clever. He had, for example, thoroughly mastered the complicated problem, carefully outlined by Dr. Schurman, of the Spanish friars, so bitterly hated by the native Filipinos. The insurgents told their followers that, unless they wished a return of the hated and autocratic friars, they must unite against the imperialist demons from the North American continent.[38] Taft was to wrestle with the friars' lands for many months to come. He was finally to journey to Rome and present the facts to the Pope. The issue faced him even before he landed at Manila in June, 1900. Word came from the Most Reverend P. L. Chapelle, archbishop of New Orleans and chargé d'affaires on behalf of the Vatican in the Philippine Islands, that he desired a conference with the Philippine Commission. Taft was suspicious of his Grace:

I fear that he has not a great deal of common sense . . . [and] seems to think it possible to send the Spanish friars back to their charges in these islands. If there is one fact that is settled by

[37] *Addresses*, Vol. I, pp. 201-202. [38] Schurman, J. G., *Philippine Affairs*, pp. 76-80.

all the evidence it is that these friars will be killed if they go back and some other provision must be made for the spiritual control of the inhabitants.[39]

He conferred with the archbishop, of course. The *Hancock* still lay in the harbor and Chapelle was invited on board. Champagne was decorously sipped and polite nothings were exchanged. Taft saw a decorative old churchman whose accent was still slightly French, "with a fine eye and a ruby nose and cheek, which indicate his appreciation of a good dinner." The archbishop was genial, if a shade pompous. He expressed the greatest sympathy with the American problem. He asked only for a judicial attitude toward the involved situation. The commissioners bowed him into the tender which took him ashore. A few days later they returned the call. This time the archbishop was more specific; he berated the Filipinos who, although loyal to the United States, were hostile to the exiled friars.

Archbishop Chapelle was most cordial. He suggested that the commissioners attend a dinner which he would give in their honor. Taft and General Luke Wright exchanged glances as the invitation was given and said something to the effect that they would come if the pressure of business permitted; a definite decision would be given in a day or two. But as soon as they left the archbishop's house they decided not to go. Taft knew that every step, during these first critical days, was being watched. To accept formal hospitality from a friend of the friars ". . . it would give the impression," he remarked, "that we had already decided the question in favor of the friars." So he called on the archbishop again, explained the situation and asked that the invitation be withdrawn. Monsignor Chapelle did not permit his amiability to crack. There would be no dinner, he said. Indeed, in the same position as the commission, he would have done the same thing.[40]

[39] Taft to Helen H. Taft, June 10, 1900. [40] Taft to C. P. Taft, June 15, 1900.

—6—

Other pitfalls yawned. Taft neatly evaded one which had been dug by an insurgent leader, Señor Don Pedro A. Paterno. The señor, if Taft correctly judged him, was a somewhat uncertain gentleman. Early in July, after taking an oath of allegiance to the United States, he had made a speech on behalf of independence under an American protectorate. Punished by the traditional military method of jail, he had recanted and had sworn fealty again. Taft called him a "turncoat of long experience." But Taft had learned, even by July, not to be too squeamish about the varying colors of Filipino coats. When the don señor announced that he was organizing a three-day fiesta on behalf of peace, the president promised to attend with the other members of the commission. Taft reported to Secretary Root: "If there is one thing more than another that a Filipino likes it is a fiesta . . . it will be quite an important event, in that it brings home to the people the fact that peace is near." [41]

The celebration was scheduled to begin on July 28, a Saturday. In the morning, Taft heard that Paterno and others among the leaders had written speeches advocating independence. He decided that it was, all in all, a seditious affair, so he dispatched a letter stating that the commissioners would not attend. Then he went home to dinner. At nine o'clock he was sitting on the porch of his house with General Wright when a very agitated Filipino appeared:

Paterno begged like a whipped boy that I should go with him to the banquet, where the guests were all assembled and waiting. He said that it would be regarded as a great discourtesy to the persons who had gotten up the banquet and to the Filipino people generally, if it were to be suspended. . . . I told him the difficulty was that he had attempted to deceive many of the insurgents into the view that we would grant a protectorate, that he had violated his instructions in this respect, and that he had put himself in the position where he was. He said that no speeches were to be delivered at all.

So Taft and Wright went to the banquet where the audience cheered enthusiastically, perhaps with relief that an embarrassing situation had ended. "Paterno and I walked out of the hall arm in

[41] Taft to Root, July 26, 1900.

arm," said Taft. ". . . the real friends of the Americans here are laughing in their sleeves at the result." [42] Again, as in the case of the dinner with Archbishop Chapelle, word of the incident was rapidly spread by the gossipy Filipinos. The prestige of the commission was augmented.

Taft also made friends in less negative ways. In June, 1900, a series of public hearings was started at which Filipino leaders, politicians and churchmen were asked for their views. Nearly all the testimony was in Spanish and was interpreted for the benefit of the commissioners. At a session in August a native cleric was describing the characteristics of the wild and untamed Tagalog tribes. The churchman said that they were savage and unlettered, but very fond of music. Taft, who was presiding, offered the suggestion that their musical taste might have developed from their knowledge of Spanish, which many of the tribesmen had learned.

"What your Grace is now saying," he said smoothly, "sounds like a melody." [43]

Nor did Taft limit personal association with the Filipinos to the relatively few and prosperous meztizos of Manila. Throughout his administration he went on frequent journeys into the interior. He attended elaborate banquets given by local officials. He went to their fiestas and danced, his vast bulk dominating the hall, with their wives. On one of the first of these journeys, into the hills above Baguio, he was considerably surprised to have the Igorot children bow very low as he approached and say, "Good morning, Mrs. Kelly."

The Igorots were a Malay mountain people whom civilization had barely touched. Taft was puzzled, as well as amused, at the greeting. The explanation was simple. Some years before Mrs. Alice McK. Kelly, whose husband was investigating a near-by gold mine, had started a school among the children. She had taught them to greet her in English. So now, seeing another white face, they chirped, "Good morning, Mrs. Kelly."

Taft was delighted. His roar of laughter convinced the young Igorots that they had said something very clever. They told their parents that this large, fat stranger was a very nice man.[44]

[42] Taft to Root, July 30, 1900. [43] *Message of the President,* 56th Congress, 2nd Session, Sen. Doc. 190; pp. 98-99. [44] Fred W. Carpenter to author, Feb. 13, 1935; Forbes, W. C., *op. cit.,* Vol. I, p. 600.

BOSS JAMES B. COX OF CINCINNATI

Photo by Lawrence J. Neumann, Courtesy The Cincinnati Enquirer

TOM CAMPBELL, TAFT'S FIRST ADVERSARY

See page 90]

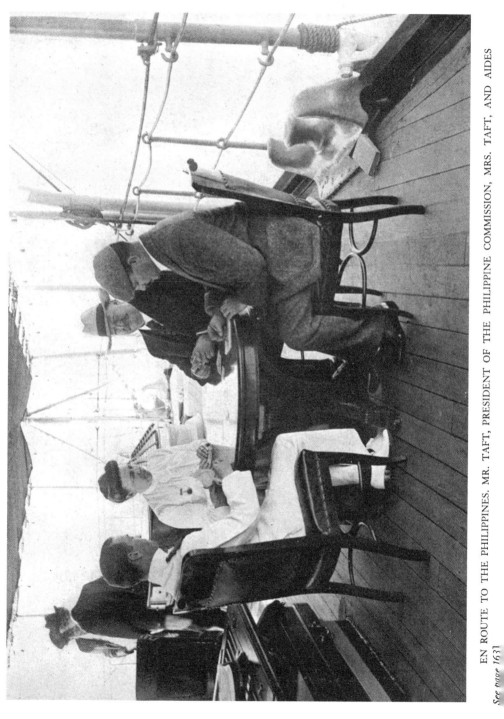

EN ROUTE TO THE PHILIPPINES. MR. TAFT, PRESIDENT OF THE PHILIPPINE COMMISSION, MRS. TAFT, AND AIDES

See page 163]

CHAPTER XII

HEAT AND WORK

ENERAL MAC ARTHUR, as military governor, still occupied Malacanan Palace, the home of the Spanish governors general before Spain was stripped of her glory in the East. So the army authorities arranged for Taft to rent a house on the Calle Real in Malate, a suburb adjoining Manila. He was to pay $150 a month rent and it was described, in advance, in glowing terms. But the president of the Philippine Commission was discouraged when he saw it. The house was in bad repair. The yards had been used to pasture army horses. When Taft first visited the place, on the morning of June 4, 1900, he found that the furniture was stacked in corners and that the building had not, apparently, been cleaned for months. It needed new decorations and new plumbing; the gardens had to be planted.

It was, however, the best house available in Manila at a rental Taft could afford; a hurried inspection of other places convinced him that he would have to get along on the Calle Real. There was, at least, enough room. The ceilings were high, an important detail in the tropics. The house was immediately on Manila Bay; the sea came to within a few feet of a broad back porch where, should there be any breeze at all, some relief from the heat might be found. Taft concluded to make the best of it. He ordered fairly extensive repairs; by the time Mrs. Taft arrived from Yokohama in the fall it would, he hoped, be habitable. At Hong Kong, on advice of those who knew Manila, Taft had acquired Chinese servants who had boarded the *Hancock*. They were Ah See, a wrinkled old cook, two houseboys and a laundryman.[1] Taft, who enjoyed material comforts and particularly good food, found the superfluity of servants pleasant.

"The truth is," he told his half brother, "that I have lived a

[1] Taft to Helen H. Taft, June 5, 1900; to C. P. Taft, June 12, Aug. 11, 1900; Taft, Mrs. W. H., *Recollections of Full Years*, pp. 103-104.

181

good deal better here than I did at home. I have a better cook . . .
and the method of living with a good many servants . . . leads
one to considerable luxury." [2]

But there was an enormous amount of work to be done. Taft
rose to the emergency; he did not even follow the custom, universal in Manila, of taking a siesta in the middle of the day.[3] The
instructions given to the Philippine Commission by President Mc-
Kinley were specific and detailed and Taft, more than any other
member, was familiar with them. This was because he had helped
to draft the document during the weeks which followed his acceptance of the appointment in February, 1900. Secretary Root
wrote the first draft.

"Mr. Root . . . initiated our Philippine policy, and is responsible for its success from the standpoint of statesmanship and far-
sightedness," explained Taft more than a decade later.[4]

The secretary of war asked Judge Taft to read the original
draft during one of his visits to Washington. It was then submitted to the other members of the commission. Judge Ide was
the one who had the happy idea that the commission should have
charge of appropriations; this power was vital in thwarting the
militaristic desires of the army authorities in the islands. But the
plan for control of the islands was mainly the work of Root and
Taft; they conceived it. President McKinley accepted their views,
apparently without question. Thus the "Instructions of the President to the Second Philippine Commission"— the formal title of
the document— might more accurately be called "Instructions of
Elihu Root and William Howard Taft to the Second Philippine
Commission." [5] Taft made formal reports to the President, of
course. Actually, the secretary of war was, throughout four years,
Taft's guide, superior officer and friend. McKinley, after all, had
many other worries; for one thing, as the work started, he was
facing a campaign for re-election.

Taft always remained proud of the document he had helped
to write. It offered no promise of independence. The United States,
in the last analysis, was the arbiter over the Filipinos. But Taft
pointed out that it "secured to the Philippine people all the guar-

[2] Taft to C. P. Taft, Aug. 11, 1900. [3] Fred W. Carpenter to author, Aug. 12, 1933.
[4] Addresses, Vol. XXXI, p. 375. [5] Forbes, W. C., The Philippine Islands, Vol. I, p. 130.

anties of our Bill of Rights except trial by jury and the right to bear arms." The authority of the President lay in his power as commander in chief of the army and navy. Complete subjugation, in the British manner of colonial government, might as easily have been decreed. Instead, the basic philosophy of the document was that the Filipinos were to be given the greatest possible degree of influence in their own affairs. They were to hold all the offices for which they were qualified. They were to have, at least, advisory rights in the matter of legislation.[6] And for these democratic principles Taft, even more than Root, was responsible. It was his idea also that, as conditions in the islands improved, a popular Assembly should be established.[7]

The President's letter of instructions was to be attacked by ardent believers in freedom for the Filipinos. It is difficult to avoid the conclusion that they did not read it. Its phrases stand up well, very well indeed, even though forty years have passed since it was drafted. And Taft transformed the phrases, by and large, into facts. General MacArthur was to remain in charge of military operations. Taft's powers, as president of the Philippine Commission, included that of approving or rejecting recommendations by the other four members. The secretary of war would be the final authority over both the military and the civil branches so that the "most perfect cooperation" between them could be achieved. The instructions provided that in creating a government the commission must bear in mind that it was "designed not for our satisfaction, or for the expression of our theoretical views, but for the happiness, peace and prosperity of the people of the Philippine Islands, and the measures adopted should be made to conform to their customs, their habits, and even to their prejudices, to the fullest extent consistent with the accomplishment of the indispensable requisites of just and effective government." At the same time, the Filipinos must be warned that their experience in government was meager and that, under the American system, "certain great principles of government" existed which "we deem essential to the rule of law and the maintenance of individual freedom." Where these principles conflicted with local customs, the local customs must give way.

[6] *Addresses*, Vol. XXXI, p. 375. [7] Forbes, W. C., *op. cit.*, Vol. I, p. 130.

Thereupon the letter of instructions quoted, in substance, the American Bill of Rights and its strictures against deprivation of life, liberty or property without due process. In criminal cases the accused was to be granted a speedy, public (but not a jury) trial. He was to be allowed reasonable bail and, if convicted, protected against cruel or unusual punishments. He was to be provided with counsel. He could not twice be placed in jeopardy for the same offense or forced to testify against himself. Slavery was to be barred. Laws limiting freedom of speech and the press or peaceful assembly were prohibited. Religious freedom was guaranteed. Not all these ideals, it must be said, were achieved. Slavery continued among the Moro tribes. Taft found it necessary, at times, to forbid expressions regarding independence and the publication of journals which urged it. But in the main they were put into effect.

"It will be necessary," stated President McKinley's letter of instructions, "to fill some offices with Americans which after a time may well be filled by natives of the islands." As soon as possible, however, a civil service system was to be established. The first duty of the commission was rapidly to establish municipal governments "in which natives of the islands, both in the cities and in the rural communities, shall be afforded the opportunity to manage their own local affairs . . . subject to the least degree of supervision." Speedily, also, were to be appointed judicial, educational and civil officers in the larger administrative divisions of the islands. A system of education was to be organized. This must be free to all. In view of the innumerable dialects and languages (Spanish was spoken by only a small minority), the official medium would be English and special efforts must be made to see that opportunity to learn English was everywhere available.

—2—

On September 1, 1900— a little more than two months after its work got under way— the commission would be clothed with full legislative powers, now held by the military governor. It could then raise taxes, appropriate funds, specify tariff rates and establish courts. As president of the commission, Taft would have veto power over these legislative acts. The military governor would remain the chief executive, however, and therein— as Taft soon learned— lay the one flaw in the plan which had been drafted by Root and himself.[8] The boundary between the executive and the legislative was not very clear in a wild country still torn by insurrectionist activities. Since the secretary of war was the court of final jurisdiction on both legislative and executive powers, it was necessary for Taft to turn, in many matters, to Washington. Soon his appeals were flowing in a steady, verbose stream.

Taft had two grievances against the military from the start. The first was the extremely chilly reception which had been accorded the commission. The second was the attitude of the army toward the Filipinos. His irritation increased during the first week in Manila. "The army is a necessary evil," he said, "but it is not an agent to encourage the establishment of a well-ordered civil government, and the Filipinos are anxious to be rid of policing by shoulder straps. . . . the army is not well-adapted to the administration of civil government, and . . . the sooner it be made auxiliary the better. We shall not be in control for sixty or ninety days, but we shall be in control when the time comes, and the army will be auxiliary." [9] General MacArthur, as military governor, soon became the specific object of Taft's wrath.

The general was an excellent soldier and Taft granted that the "situation is distinctly better than it was six months ago." [10] The president of the Philippine Commission began to draw, however, a series of pen portraits of General MacArthur for the benefit of Secretary Root and none of these was particularly flattering. He was a "very courtly, kindly man; lacking somewhat in a sense of humor; rather fond of profound generalizations on the psychological conditions of the people; politely incredulous, and politely lacking in any great consideration for the views of anyone, as to the real situation, who is a civilian and who has been here only a comparatively short time, and firmly convinced of the necessity for maintaining military etiquette in civil matters and civil government." [11] Taft said that MacArthur was far too pessimistic on pacification

[8] Worcester, D. C., *The Philippines, Past and Present*, pp. 980-988. [9] Taft to C. P. Taft, June 12, 1900; Taft to E. G. Rathbone, June 16, 1900. [10] Taft to Rathbone, June 16, 1900. [11] Taft to Root, Aug. 18, 1900.

and "regards all the people as opposed to the American forces and looks at his task as one of conquering eight millions of recalcitrant, treacherous and sullen people."[12] By November, Taft said, the commission had concluded that MacArthur "lacked any vigorous initiative; that with him almost everything new was premature; that he was naturally timid and that . . . he is very set in his opinion."[13] The president of the commission even found it necessary to tell Root that he would, with his colleagues, resign unless some degree of cooperation with the military governor could be achieved:

It would seem as if he were as sensitive about maintaining the exact line of jurisdiction between the commission and himself as about winning a battle or suppressing the insurrection. I sincerely hope . . . that he may cease to fume— for no other expression suits his present condition— over the injustice done him and the situation in sending out the commission and giving them the powers which they have. . . . But if his attitude continues unchanged and the commission finds— as it is likely to find if that be the case— that his attitude seriously interferes . . . with the attainment of our common purposes under tremendous difficulties, we may have to submit the situation to you *and invite action either in respect to ourselves or in respect to him.*[14]

Taft offered repeated bills of particulars in his controversy with the general. MacArthur, he told Mrs. Taft, had cabled to Washington to ask that no appointments be made without his approval. The secretary of war had, however, upheld the civil arm and its specific powers. The military governor, Taft feared, might convince Washington "of some fancied danger of an uprising which is always held up by military men as a bogey"; if Washington gave credence to such rumors, the commission would go home.[15] The general, he reported to Root, had been negligent with regard to the fiesta organized by the insurgent, Don Señor Paterno, in July. He ought to have known that speeches urging independence were to be made. He ought to have supervised the affair from the start.[16] Taft's patience gave way when, in August, MacArthur's

[12] Taft to Root, Aug. 18, 1900. [13] *Idem*, Nov. 14, 1900. [14] *Idem*, Oct. 10, 1900. (Italics mine.) [15] Taft to Helen H. Taft, July 18, 1900. [16] Taft to Root, July 30, 1900.

military superintendent of education ordered fifty thousand histories for the schools from a publishing house about which no educational authority knew very much. The book was still unpublished and had not been seen by anyone in the islands. The civil commission's own superintendent of education was to take office in a week.

". . . as the history is probably worthless," Taft commented, "you see how admirably adapted to a harmonious adjustment of co-ordinate branches the military arm is." [17]

—3—

No open break between Taft and MacArthur occurred, however. The president of the Philippine Commission could afford to be magnanimous. On September 1, 1900, he pointed out, the commission would assume its legislative functions and MacArthur's "power will be cut down to almost nothing, for we shall have the filling of all the civil offices and the passing of all the laws." [18] The following July, MacArthur was replaced by Major General A. R. Chaffee.[19]

Taft had other matters to think about and the chief of these was the presidential campaign in the United States. He convinced himself that a victory for Bryan, again the Democratic nominee, would mean disaster in the Philippines. Bryan appears to have forgotten that he had, in the war with Spain, unsheathed a sword on behalf of manifest destiny and imperialism. He calmly ignored the fact that he had used his influence with Democratic senators for ratification of the Treaty of Paris whereby the Philippine Islands had been retained by the United States. Perhaps his motive— history is not clear— was to provide an issue for the 1900 campaign. In any event, he became an ardent anti-imperialist as soon as the Democratic National Convention had adjourned; he continued to ask for free silver but he subordinated this issue to attacking McKinley's policy in the East.

[17] Taft to C. P. Taft, Aug. 23, 1900. [18] *Idem*, Aug. 11, 1900. [19] Forbes, W. C., *op. cit.*, Vol. I, p. 109.

On his way to the Philippines, in April, 1900, Taft had a con-ference with Bryan and reported that "my respect for him was measurably decreased by the exhibition he gave of himself." The respect had never been very profound. While on the Pacific coast, preparatory to sailing on the *Hancock,* Taft had gone to San Diego to visit his sister, Mrs. Edwards. Bryan had been on the train and had requested an interview with the president of the Philippine Commission. Taft was puzzled and cautious:

He seemed to be desirous of catching me in some statement which he could use on the stump. I finally asked him why he had come to me and asked me to talk with him; whether he thought he could convince me, or whether he thought I might convince him. He said no, neither, but that he wished to get my views.

If Taft's version of the conversation is accurate it was, in truth, nonsensical. Bryan expressed the thought that "the divine right of kings was still the moving force in the British form of govern-ment, and that there were a great many people in this country who wished we had a king." Then he added, irrelevantly, that the Eng-lish were robbing India by means of the gold standard. Taft denied, quite specifically, any devotion to divine right. He pointed out that the English monarch no longer interfered with government and had no authority. Yes, agreed Bryan, but interference might come at any time. Taft then asked whether Bryan was implying "that I believed in the divine right of kings. He said he thought it was the equivalent of that."

I told him that I had expressly stated that I preferred our form of government . . . but that I was not unfamiliar with the form of argument in which the contestant stated the position of his adversary to suit himself, and then knocked it over. He sought the interview and pressed it on me, and I confess quite irritated me with his catchpenny statements and that spirit which seems to actuate the small pattern of a man in making an argument on the floor of the House of Representatives. . . . His knowledge of his-tory is defective; his style is that of the veriest demagogue, and, while he is a handsome fellow, and has a good voice, I should be sorry to think of him as president of the United States, even if I agreed with his peculiar views.[20]

Just before Bryan's nomination in Kansas City, Taft grew much alarmed and predicted that if he came into power "and attempts to carry out his announced views, chaos will follow here and the interests of civilization, of individual liberty, and of religion will certainly suffer."[21] Taft's apprehensions were sound. Bryan declared in August that the Filipinos had as much right to freedom as the people of Cuba. If elected, he would convene a special session of Congress to grant independence, under a protectorate, to the archipelago. In contrast, McKinley said that American authority must continue supreme, that it was out of the question to desert, at this stage, the 7,000,000 inhabitants of the islands.[22] To Taft, the Democratic pledge of independence had a very practical significance. Publication of Bryan's promise in the islands, he predicted, "will have considerable effect in stiffening the hopes of those insurrectos who remain in arms. . . . The only thing that keeps up these insurrectos who are in the mountains and in the retired parts of the islands," Taft added, "is the hope that by Mr. Bryan's election they may secure that independence of which they say so much and know so little. Should by any chance Mr. Bryan be elected to the presidency and attempt to put into operation his announced policy, two years would demonstrate the necessity for . . . taking the country again with a firm hold, and the work of the last two years would then have to be done all over again."[23] Some weeks later Taft told of reports that Aguinaldo had been on the verge of surrender, but had withdrawn into his mountain retreat upon hearing of Bryan's promise.[24]

Taft was certain that the insurgents were "making strenuous efforts to influence the presidential campaign by an appearance of strength" and pointed to the attack on American troops in Bahia, in September, in which a score were killed. Another successful insurgent foray occurred in Marinduque later that month and a third toward the middle of October.

[20] Taft to Annie G. Roelker, April 16, 1900. [21] Taft to Maria Storer, June 22, 1900. [22] Rhodes, J. F., *The McKinley and Roosevelt Administrations, 1897-1909*, pp. 137-138. [23] Taft to Root, Aug. 11, 1900. [24] *Idem*, Sept. 13, 1900.

"We are very confident," he said, "that the election will clear matters and that the dry season will bring about a state of affairs which will properly inaugurate the policy of greater severity." [25]

Taft's apprehensions increased further as Election Day drew near. He said that he would resign by January or February if the Democrats won.[26] On November 6, 1900, he waited uneasily for word from Washington. He was elated when a cable from the War Department told of a second victory for righteousness.[27] A fortnight later he told Charles P. Taft that no attacks or ambushes had occurred since McKinley's re-election, that the insurgents were stunned.[28]

Meanwhile Theodore Roosevelt, maneuvered into accepting the vice-presidential nomination, had been doing valiant campaigning. He wrote mournfully to his friend, Taft, regarding the predicament in which he found himself. He would have preferred to continue as governor of New York. But the "feeling for my nomination was practically unanimous and I could not refuse without giving the ticket a black eye."

"I had a great deal rather," he wrote, "be your assistant in the Philippines or even Root's assistant in the War Department than be vice-president. The kaleidoscope will be shaken, however, before 1904 and some new men will come to the front." [29]

Again, the might-have-beens of history intrigue. Roosevelt might easily have been appointed to the Philippines had he declined to run for vice-president. Then he would not have become president of the United States in September, 1901. Then, in all probability, the friendship of Taft and Roosevelt would have terminated abruptly. For Roosevelt would surely have disagreed on minor and major policies had he traveled to the East as assistant to the president of the Philippine Commission. He did not believe in patience or in amiability, whether the climate was hot or cold. He did not believe in peaceful methods. As it was, although gloomy in the vice-presidential chair, Roosevelt continued to look toward the White House.

[25] Taft to Root, Sept. 18, Oct. 1, Oct. 13, 1900. [26] Taft to Louise Taft, Oct. 30, 1900. [27] Taft to Root, Nov. 14, 1900. [28] Taft to C. P. Taft, Nov. 30, 1900. [29] Roosevelt to Taft, Aug. 6, 1900.

"I have no doubt," soothed Taft in January, 1901, "that you will be the nominee in 1904."[30]

Meanwhile, despite the uncertainties caused by the election at home and the friction existing between the military and the Taft commission, work went on steadily in Manila. As president, Taft assigned specific problems such as public improvements, education, currency and taxation to the other commissioners. He reserved for himself the most difficult subject, that of the friars' lands. An oath of allegiance was drafted whereby former insurgents swore renunciation of "all so-called revolutionary governments" and obedience to the "supreme authority of the United States." Upon taking the oath in June, 1900, the rebels were declared spotless and white; the commission and the military governor sensibly concluded not to inquire into their past sins of murder and rapine. About five thousand Filipinos who had been active in the insurrection took the amnesty oath.[31] But Aguinaldo continued to lurk in his mountain retreats.

Taft had given attention to an educational system even before leaving the United States. He needed a good man to take charge in the islands. His brother, Henry, suggested in March, 1900, that a youthful professor of philosophy and education at Columbia University, Nicholas Murray Butler, might "consent himself to go . . . for a limited stay." Henry Taft said that Professor Butler was an organizer of talent and an educator of wide reputation. Also: "Butler is extremely ambitious. He is strongly Republican in his political views, and I think is convinced that he has a great future."[32] Apparently Butler was not interested. In two years he was to be president of Columbia University and the post went to Frederick W. Atkinson. In tendering to Atkinson the position of general superintendent of education, Taft said that a large number of men and women teachers, to be paid from $600 to $1,500 a year, would be needed and asked that he comb the colleges of the country for candidates.[33]

The young people who came, and scores of them did, were

[30] Pringle, H. F., *Theodore Roosevelt, a Biography*, p. 229. [31] Forbes, W. C., *op. cit.*, Vol. I, p. 126. [32] H. W. Taft to C. P. Taft, Aug. 11, 1900. [33] Taft to F. W. Atkinson, May 8, 1900.

real pioneers of the blackboard. To the native Filipino it was a mark of superiority to speak what he fondly imagined to be English. "Presidents of towns," reported Taft, "come to the commission and write to the commission asking for the assignment of teachers."[34] The Filipinos came flocking to the schoolhouses. Their quick, imitative minds, peculiarly sensitive to sound, enabled them to acquire large English vocabularies in short order. But they repeated whole sentences like parrots. The teachers often discovered that they did this without the slightest idea of what they were talking about. So the benefits of the educational program were, for a while, indirect. A large amount of friendly sentiment for the American authorities was created.

—4—

September 1, 1900, was the day for which Taft waited eagerly; then would the commission be vested with legislative powers and assume a position superior to that of the military governor. A fund of $2,500,000, accumulated by MacArthur from customs and other sources, would be turned over.[35] When the happy day arrived a proclamation would be issued setting forth the new powers of the Philippine Commission and stating that criticisms of any policy would be welcomed. All proposed legislation would be preceded by public hearings at which anyone with a grievance would be heard.[36] As September approached, Taft was inclined toward optimism regarding civil government and wise disposition of the $2,500,000 surplus:

My own impression is that part of it, at least, ought to be devoted to increasing the harbor accommodations, which are so very defective now, and to increasing facilities for landing goods at the customhouse. Another very good job would be to construct in Manila five or six good, well-built schoolhouses. . . . The Filipino people are a people upon whom outward show makes a great effect.[37]

[34] Taft to C. P. Taft, Aug. 11, 1900. [35] Idem, July 30, 1900. [36] Forbes, W. C., op. cit., Vol. I, p. 126. [37] Taft to Root, July 26, 1900.

Taft was cheerful, also, regarding the organization, as specified in the McKinley instructions, of municipal governments in Manila and other cities. The Filipinos were to be given a voice in them.

"We get reports from many districts," Taft told Root, "that the people are just awaiting the establishment of municipal governments . . . and we are not at all sure that it ought not to be done in Manila at an early date. . . . The good effect of a change from a provost marshal government to that of a popular civil government cannot, I believe, be exaggerated."

The responsibilities and labor of the commission were, naturally, greatly augmented by assumption of legislative authority. A tariff law had to be drafted. Internal revenue taxes had to be established. Schools, a system of courts and public works had to be inaugurated.[38] Taft labored zealously in the heat and prayed that his health would continue to be good.

"The amount of work which we have to do I shudder to think of," he wrote, "but I suppose that in time . . . things will fall into their places in a way which we hardly expect them to do now. . . . So many things are to be done that it would need twenty-four hours a day to do the work. . . . I cannot work here as I could at home . . . such work would break me down here. . . . I try to get along without night work. I get to the office from eight to half past eight in the morning, leave at one, get back between three and half past three, taking a Spanish lesson of an hour after lunch. . . . I am not a good linguist and Spanish is not easy for me; still I must learn it."[39]

On August 21, on the eve of assuming civil powers, the commission spent $4,000 to send a lengthy confidential cable to Secretary of War Root. It was signed by all the members and summarized the situation in detail. Taft expressed confidence that the analysis was correct although "General MacArthur would think that our statement was too favorable."[40] The cable dispatch pointed to seventy-five days of "diligent inquiry into conditions" on the part of the commission. Among its conclusions were that:

[38] *Idem.* [39] Taft to C. P. Taft, Aug. 11, 1900; to Louise Taft, Nov. 30, 1900. [40] Taft to Root, Aug. 23, 1900.

The mass of the people had an aptitude for education, but were credulous and superstitious. Their hostility toward America was inspired by unscrupulous leaders. A large majority longed for peace.

All prominent generals except Aguinaldo had surrendered and remaining insurgent forces were small, scattered bands.

Most of northern Luzon had been cleared of insurgents.

Danger to Americans still existed in remote sections due to four years of war.

A native constabulary and militia should at once be organized to end terrorism where it still existed.

Business conditions would improve with peace.

The cultivation of rice had in some provinces been retarded by loss of draft cattle through disease and war.

Customs collections for the last quarter had been fifty per cent greater than ever in Spanish history and August collections showed further increase.

Manila, with proper tariff and facilities, would become the great port of the Orient.

The balance of the dispatch described the measures which, in Taft's judgment, should be enacted in order to advance the peace and prosperity of "these wonderfully rich, beautiful, and healthful tropical islands." The current tax laws needed drastic revision; now they were "throwing burden of taxation on poor [and] giving wealthy comparative immunity." The currency required stabilization and the gold standard should be resumed, the cable said. Railroad franchises should be granted. Business should be encouraged to invest capital. Above all, there should be a stable, central government "like that of Porto Rico under which substantially all rights secured in Bill of Rights in [the] Federal Constitution are to be secured to people of Philippines [and] will bring to them contentment, prosperity, education and political enlightment." [41]

As the months passed Taft was to learn that the people of the United States cared very little about his brown brethren. He was to find it exceedingly difficult to obtain from Congress the authority to carry on his reforms. A less robust, or a less optimistic, viceroy might have grown discouraged; he might have resigned, or spent

[41] Cable: Taft, Worcester et al. to Root, Aug. 21, 1900.

his days amid the amiable relaxations of social life, whisky and soda. Taft's buoyancy faded little, however. As soon as the Philippine Commission was granted legislative powers on September 1, 1900, he began the passage of necessary laws. By the end of the year he was able to report tax revision, establishment of municipal government in many communities, harbor and other public improvements, increased educational facilities and additional surrenders on the part of the insurgents. Civil service had been instituted. Natives were being appointed to such posts as they could handle.[42]

Affairs moved rapidly after January 1, 1901, but in the United States there was considerable dissatisfaction over dispatches from the islands which indicated that bloodshed and war continued. Taft protested to the secretary of war that these were inaccurate. He said that the engagements, magnified into battles by bored correspondents, actually were insignificant and invariably resulted in the capture of insurgents and a new flood of natives eager to swear fealty to the United States.[43] One by one, the native generals found that the struggle was hopeless. It was increasingly difficult for them to live off the land or to recruit soldiers by the time-honored method of intimidation and cruelty. It is hard for the impartial observer to subscribe to the theory that the Filipinos were engaged in a desperate battle for freedom against the imperialist forces of the United States. The Filipino's conception of freedom was that it allowed him, if he could get the power, to prey upon his countrymen and live in easy comfort from the proceeds.

Toward early spring, 1901, word was brought to the military authorities that Aguinaldo was hiding in the mountains of northeastern Luzon. A diary kept by Simeon A. Villa, the rebel leader's chief of staff, was ultimately captured and its pages are a convincing record of the futility of the insurgent resistance. Aguinaldo had but a handful of men. They were badly equipped and sparingly provisioned. The little Filipino must have known on January 6,

[42] *Report, Taft Philippine Commission*, 56th Congress, 2nd Session, Sen. Doc., 112, pp. 18-121. [43] Taft to Root, Jan. 29, 1901.

1901, that hope was dead; on that day, so slowly did news penetrate into the hills, he heard that McKinley had been elected and his defender, Bryan, defeated in the presidential campaign. Aguinaldo had, at the least, stubborn courage. On March 7, 1901, he was informed that amnesty would again be granted if the rebel leaders would surrender. But Aguinaldo answered that he would fight until independence was promised. On March 22, 1901, the "honorable dictator," as he was addressed by his men, celebrated his thirty-second birthday and received congratulations. He did not know that General Funston was within a few leagues of his camp.[44] On the following day he was captured. He was conducted to Manila with appropriate ceremonies as an honored prisoner of war; General MacArthur entertained him at Malacanan Palace. On April 19, 1901, he swallowed his pride and took the oath of allegiance.[45]

Surprisingly, in view of his normally kindly nature, Taft considered deporting Aguinaldo to Guam. "He is a natural conspirator . . ." Taft told Root, "and I should doubt the sincerity of any acquiescence in the sovereignty of the United States by him. If he is to remain in politics here, he will form the nucleus for agitation in the United States by the fools whom the Philippine problem has brought into prominence. . . . I do not share the opinion of some as to the disinterestedness or the ability of Aguinaldo. . . . He is an intriguer, not of sufficient mental stature to attract the jealousy of able men."[46] Taft was wrong. Aguinaldo inspired no new hostilities. He devoted himself largely to economic matters, conducted himself with intelligence and dignity.

The Philippine Commission was not above one or two rather shabby devices in its efforts, prior to Aguinaldo's capture, to break the insurrection. It decreed that the property and funds of all insurgents still in arms would be confiscated after April 1, 1901. Taft noted that one Aguinaldo lieutenant had "about $60,000 in Manila which we shall get at and take."[47] Even more effective— could this idea have been derived from Taft's brief contact with Ohio machine politics?— was a ruling that anyone still fighting on April 1, 1901, would be disenfranchised and therefore ineligible for

[44] *Hearings, Senate Committee on the Philippines,* 57th Congress, 1st Session, Sen. Doc. 331, pp. 2058-2067. [45] Bount, James H., *The American Occupation of the Philippines,* pp. 338-339. [46] Taft to Root, April 3, 1901. [47] Taft to C. P. Taft, Jan. 23, 1901.

political appointments. General MacArthur informed Taft that this fearful threat of *"no* peace—*no* jobs" was proving very effective.

". . . the insurrectos . . ." commented Taft, "see that their game is up and . . . hope for political preferment under the American government."[48]

The most important work of early 1901 was the organization of municipal governments under authority granted by the commission. Wisely, Taft decided that this democratic innovation should be given prestige by visits of the commission to the localities where municipal governments were established. The first of these journeys started in February and was along the route of the Manila-Dagupan railroad; it included the provinces of Bulacan, Pampanga, Tarlac and Pangasinan. Native officers were appointed after consultation with the military authorities. Taft or his fellow commissioners made speeches, translated for the benefit of their audiences, explaining the new system. On one occasion, the president of the commission got into difficulties when he was emphasizing the standards of honesty which would be enforced. He said that any thieving functionary would be removed at once; he used the phrase: "he will have his official head cut off." The Filipinos applauded, but exhibited surprise, too, when this was translated. It was a penalty, they said, to fit the crime. But had they not been told that Americans were humane people and did not follow the Filipino custom of beheading adversaries? Taft found it difficult to explain that he had used a figure of speech.[49]

"The people . . . manifested great interest in the proceedings," Taft said, describing the trip, "and received us with much enthusiasm."[50]

On March 10, 1901, a much longer journey, for the same purpose, was started. The commission and a party of about sixty boarded the U.S.S. *Sumner,* an army transport, and began a tour of the southern provinces. The wives and children of the commissioners were on board. So were prominent Filipinos and some newspaper correspondents. The party visited eighteen provinces and did not return to Manila until May 3. It was the hot season. The incessant

[48] Taft to Root, March 17, 1901. [49] Worcester, D. C., *op. cit.,* pp. 335-336. [50] Taft to Root, Feb. 15, 1901.

round of banquets and fiestas proved a severe strain on the stamina of the commissioners. Taft complained whimsically to Root:

I am obliged to say that while the salaries paid to us by the government are large, they are not more than commensurate with the burdens imposed upon the commission of eating the Filipino dinners, which, in order to maintain peaceable relations with the people, we are obliged to eat. The Filipino idea of a meal is an extravagant number of courses with meats of various kinds served in most mysterious forms, with a flavor of garlic and Spanish oil that need the strongest American stomach to be able to take and digest. I suppose we may get used to it, but it is really a basis for a claim of self-sacrifice to the accomplishment of our purpose in coming here that I should desire to have noted. . . . The sense of hospitality of the Filipino host, however, is so fine and delicate that he feels hurt if a single one of his courses is declined, and the difficulty which eating any of the meals presents is thus greatly increased by having to eat it all.[51]

"The trip is anything but a junket," he later said. "It is the hardest work I have had to do since I have been out here." [52]

The tour added to Taft's knowledge of the islands. Among other things, it confirmed his existing belief that the time had come to terminate the authority which still remained in the office of military governor. "Things are certainly coming our way," he had declared even in January, 1901, "and if we could only have a civil government supreme here with an efficient police force . . . the situation of the islands would change marvelously." [53] A few days later he suggested that conditions would be ripe for the change in two or three months.[54] The secretary of war agreed. He expressed, on behalf of the President and himself, the utmost gratification at the manner in which the Philippine problem had been handled. He asked that Taft draw up a general plan for the new civil administration.

"In all probability," Mr. Root said, "you will be appointed civil governor." [55]

"Of course one likes to be at the top," wrote Taft, after the

[51] Taft to Root, Feb. 14, 1901. [52] Taft to Horace D. Taft, April 11, 1901. [53] Taft to C. P. Taft, Jan. 9, 1901. [54] Taft to Root, Jan. 13, 1901. [55] Root to Taft, Jan. 21, 1901.

letter from the secretary of war had been received, "but I doubt if my life at the palace of Malacanan, to which I suppose I shall move, will be near so pleasant as that . . . out on the seashore at Malate. . . . The responsibilities will be very great." [56]

At about this time, in far-off Oyster Bay, a very bored Vicepresident Roosevelt was turning, again, to literary pursuits. He was confident that his own public career had ended. But his friend, Will Taft, had a dazzling future. Theodore Roosevelt was delighted to hear that Taft had been promoted to civil governor of the Philippines and gladly consented when Lyman Abbott of the *Outlook* asked him to write an appreciation of his friend. The opening paragraph was:

A year ago a man of wide acquaintance both with American public life and American public men remarked that the first Governor of the Philippines ought to combine the qualities which would make a first-class President of the United States with the qualities which would make a first-class Chief Justice of the United States, and that the only man he knew who possessed all these qualities was Judge William H. Taft, of Ohio. The statement was entirely correct.[57]

[56] Taft to C. P. Taft, March 17, 1901. [57] *Outlook,* Sept. 17, 1901.

CHAPTER XIII

NO TAWDRY RULE OF KINGS

RUMS punctured the shimmering heat on the morning of July 4, 1901. The Cathedral Plaza in Manila was festooned with flags; their stars and stripes gleamed in the white sunlight but their folds lay inert in the quiet tropical air. A covered pavilion had been built in the center of the square. Massed in front of the stand were thousands of Filipinos. Most of them were garbed in white, the civilian dress in equatorial countries. But many were native tribesmen from the hills. Signal fires had flashed across the mountains and had called the Negritos, the Igorots and the other strange people to watch the inaugural of their first civil governor. A Filipino band had for weeks been practicing the furious music of America. Now, as the hour for the inauguration approached, the musicians blew an occasional experimental note as though to be certain that the high reaches of "The Star-Spangled Banner" could actually be achieved.

At his home on the Calle Real, soon to be abandoned for the elaborate and yet dingy Malacanan Palace, William Howard Taft fingered a cable which had just arrived from the President of the United States.

"I extend to you my full confidence and best wishes for still greater success in the larger responsibilities now devolved upon you," Mr. McKinley said, "and the assurance not only for myself but for my countrymen of good will for the people of the islands and the hope that their participation in the government, which it is our purpose to develop among them, may lead to their highest advancement, happiness and prosperity. . . ."

Taft hastily inserted the message into the text of the speech he would soon make. He then drove to the Ayuntamiento, the building which contained the offices of the Philippine Commission and where Taft had now been laboring for more than a year. The Ayuntamiento faced Cathedral Plaza; from his office Taft could see the milling crowds and hear the premonitory tootings of the band. Then he left the building and walked across the square toward the pavilion. General MacArthur, retiring as military governor, walked with him. So did General Chaffee, who was taking over the military command of the archipelago. On the way over Taft walked on the right of the trio, with MacArthur in the middle. But on the return journey Taft was in the center, to symbolize the fact that the civil authority, instead of the military, was now supreme in the islands.

General MacArthur presented Taft to the waiting thousands. Cayetano Arellano, chief justice of the Supreme Court and by far the most distinguished and learned among all the Filipinos, opened a Bible and Taft took the oath as civil governor. The band played and the audience cheered. The civil governor stepped forward and began to read his inaugural address. Very few in the crowd understood English. By no means all of them understood Spanish. But this, they knew, was an auspicious occasion. They divined that the large man in white was uttering friendly sentiments. So they applauded when Taft read a paragraph in English. They applauded again when Arthur W. Fergusson, secretary of the commission and a lightning interpreter, translated the paragraph into Spanish. Within an hour the ceremonies were over. The crowd dispersed to prepare for the reception at Malacanan Palace that night.

Much of Taft's speech was given to a résumé of the accomplishments of the past twelve months. Part of it concerned the innumerable problems which remained. It was an honest speech. The creation of a civil governor, he said, was another step toward the day when government on the islands could be placed "on a more or less popular basis"— but he gave no hope that it would ever be more instead of less. The speech reveals a Taft who had acquired a marked degree of self-confidence during the past twelve months. He said, of course, that he assumed the governorship with humility, "with no exultant spirit of confidence." Yet the confidence existed. In the year since he had arrived in the Philippines Taft had tasted the sweet wine of popularity. He had won the trust of his wards. He had the inner satisfaction of knowing that he, more than any other man, was qualified to deal with their perplexities and yearnings.[1] Less than six months later Taft was a very sick man and a vacation in the United States was imperative. But he insisted on being allowed to return.

"I think I do not exaggerate and am not misled by flattery," he told the secretary of war, "when I say that generally the Filipino people regard me as having more sympathy with them than any other member of the commission and that they would regret anything which would make impossible or improbable my continuing as the civil governor. . . . Perhaps I ought not to say this much in regard to my standing . . . but I am anxious to possess you of the facts as I see them." [2]

Malacanan Palace, to which Taft moved on July 5, was palatial in name rather than in fact. Residence there was essential. Outward symbols were important to even the educated Filipinos; if the civil governor was really supreme, they argued, he must live in the house of the most high. So Mr. and Mrs. Taft, with a backward look of regret, left their smaller house on the shores of the sea which, so Taft felt, "is very much more homelike . . . and I rather think more healthful." Malacanan had been built on the Pasig River. It was "an old, irregular and somewhat dilapidated residence with very large and fine rooms for entertaining but with not very comfortable living rooms." It looked, in fact, far more like a large summer hotel than a palace. The architecture was Spanish, modified by sloping roofs. The windows opened their full length, so that such breezes as swept down the river might be enjoyed. On the second floor was a vast porch, uncovered so that it was of no use in the day time but cool and pleasant, save for the mosquitoes, at night. Mrs. Taft was delighted with the old Spanish portraits and the porcelains which she found in the structure. She was annoyed by the zeal of a Spanish predecessor who had covered with black paint some rather fine mahogany furniture, giving a mortuary air to the place.[3]

A salary of $20,000 had been granted Taft upon becoming civil governor, but he soon found that it was far from munificent.

[1] *Addresses*, Vol. I., p. 2; Taft, Mrs. W. H., *Recollections of Full Years*, pp. 206-209; Taft to Root, July 8, 1901; Taft to Louise Taft, July 19, 1901. [2] Taft to Root, Dec. 9, 1901. [3] Taft to C. P. Taft, June 23, 1901; Taft to Louise Taft, July 19, 1901; Taft, Mrs. W. H., *op. cit.*, pp. 212-214.

The palace was a costly structure in which to live, and much entertaining had to be done. The civil governor was alarmed when he found that General MacArthur's electric light bill—paid by the government in the case of that fortunate officer— had been $306 for a single month.

"I shall hope to . . . reduce the consumption somewhat," he told Root, "by more economy . . . by shutting it off after we go to bed."

Innumerable servants were needed; their cost was $2,750 a year. Horses cannot be worked hard in the tropics, so twelve or fourteen were in the stables; this item was $1,200 a year for feed alone. The rest of the $20,000 salary vanished incredibly fast. Receptions were given at least once a week. Dinners were nearly as frequent.

"I do not," mourned the governor, "expect to have a cent left out of the salary." [4]

—2—

Life was, however, distinctly pleasant. Being a viceroy had its compensations, despite the heat and the work; for one thing it was as different from Cincinnati as existence on the moon. Taft arose early. Always a large eater, he breakfasted at eight o'clock on mangoes or oranges, bacon and eggs, toast and coffee. The dining room was handsome in its dark, carved Spanish fashion. The servants were Chinese. Behind a screen a Filipino boy pulled the cord of a punkah over the heads of those at the table. Sometimes it moved so slowly that it almost stopped. Then one of the Chinese would go behind the screen, plant an accurate kick and awaken the drowsing boy. After breakfast, the governor went over the morning mail with Fred W. Carpenter, his secretary. At ten o'clock he would drive to his offices at the Ayuntamiento, some two miles distant.

Lunch came at one-thirty o'clock and consisted, as Taft remembered, of "crabs or small lobsters or shrimps, beefsteak, cheese and salad, banana fritters or griddle cakes and fruit." Ah See, the

---

[4] Taft to Root, July 14, 1901; Taft to H. C. Lodge, Oct. 22, 1901; Taft, Mrs. W. H., *op. cit.,* pp. 215-217.

cook, considered this a deplorably light meal; until ordered to cut down he had served at least one more course. Taft was gratified to find that heavy eating was necessary in the tropics.

"The truth is," he explained, "that in this climate one's vital forces are drawn upon by work so much that one's appetite is very strong and one's desire to sleep is also great."

Taft returned to his office at three o'clock. Toward six o'clock he closed his desk and started to walk back to Malacanan. This was his daily gesture to physical fitness, his rather futile attempt to keep down increasing weight. Dinner was formal. The men wore tuxedos and the ladies evening gowns whether guests were present or not. Sometimes after dinner there would be cards. Sometimes an hour or two were spent on the porch above the river. The Tafts usually retired early, to get what sleep they could in beds swathed with netting to keep off the myriad insects. At the first gray tints of dawn, soft noises would rise from the winding Pasig. Small boats with fruits and vegetables and chickens were being paddled toward the Manila markets and passed directly under the windows of Malacanan. The sleepers woke as the singsong voices of the native boatmen penetrated their slumbers. It was still cool; the Eastern day had started.[5]

But the work was unending. Taft's responsibility was great. He had repeatedly advised Secretary of War Root that the time had come to end military rule. He had insisted that the islands were, for the most part, peaceful. Now he had to provide a form of government which, without giving independence or too much native participation, would be satisfactory to the majority of the people. Otherwise there might be renewed outbreaks. His own career would then be ruined and civil government of dependent peoples would be discredited. The Philippine Commission continued in existence under the new plan. Taft, in addition to being civil governor, was its chairman. By September 1, 1901, he had appointed Commissioner Wright to the office of secretary of commerce and police. The other assignments were: Commissioner Ide, secretary of finance and justice; Commissioner Moses, secretary of public instruction; Commissioner Worcester, secretary of the interior. An important and in-

[5] Fred W. Carpenter to author, Aug. 12, 27, 1933; Taft to Mrs. John W. Herron, Jan. 19, 1901.

telligent step was the addition of three Filipinos to the commission. They were Benito Legarda, José R. de Luzuriaga and T. H. Pardo de Tavera. All three were men of education and moderate wealth. But none was an advocate of independence. None, indeed, was even an outspoken proponent of a greater degree of self-government. Taft remained unshaken in his conviction that the Filipinos would not for decades be capable of ruling themselves.[6]

Yet Taft was more liberal than his fellow commissioners regarding representation of the Filipino people on the board which would govern the islands under the new arrangement. He thought that five native leaders should be named. He even considered, but rejected, the advisability of offering one of the places to Aguinaldo. He was overruled by his colleagues, however, and the number of Filipinos was reduced to three.

"Some of us," Taft complained, "have not as much confidence in the Filipino as others." It was important, he added, to avoid the charge that a small group of Americans were running the islands without consulting their wards. There was no possible danger, he assured the secretary of war, that the Filipino members of the commission would be a radical influence.

"We can select the men who will be *as orthodox in matters of importance as we are,*" he wrote, "and by the vote of the Chief Executive, the majority will be American at any rate."[7]

Señores Legarda, de Luzuriaga and de Tavera proved to be orthodox enough. The meetings of the commission were nearly always harmonious. Disagreements were rarely based on racial differences and the view of the majority was accepted without rancor.[8] Governor Taft was not entirely astute, however, in dealing with political issues among the Filipinos; his lifelong ineptitude in the complicated art of politics created resentment among certain factions in the islands. Late in 1900 a group of Filipinos, Señores Legarda and de Tavera among them, had organized, with open American encouragement, the Federal party which called for peace, perpetual fealty to the United States and ultimate admission into the Union as a state. Taft supported it from the start.

"I really think that there is a great deal of hope to be placed

---

[6] Worcester, D. C., *The Philippines, Past and Present,* p. 345. [7] Taft to Root, April 3, 1901. (Italics mine.) [8] Forbes, W. C., *The Philippine Islands,* Vol. I, p. 171.

in the growth of this party," he wrote in January, 1901, "for people
are seizing it with avidity as a means of relieving themselves from
oppressive inaction." Shortly afterward he said that it had 25,000
members in Manila alone. The party, he said, was a definite force
for peace.[9]

That the leaders of the Federal party worked zealously to end
the insurrection is clear. It was natural and proper for Taft to give
its program his sanction. But Taft went a good deal further. In 1902
some distinguished Filipinos, men of standing and education, suggested the formation of a party which, while it called for law
and order, declined to admit eternal subservience to the United
States. The civil governor refused to give permission. He made
matters much worse by selecting most of his important officeholders from the ranks of the Federal party. In 1907, when the first
general elections were held, it was found that a large majority of
the voters believed in independence. It was necessary for all the
parties to insert a nationalistic plank into their platforms. Even W.
Cameron Forbes, who served as governor general of the Philippines
when Taft became president of the United States, wrote in his
history of the islands that a mistake had been made. Taft played
into the hands of the radicals who demanded immediate independence.[10]

—3—

An honest judiciary, an adequate revenue and the organization
of municipal governments were three of the major problems which
occupied Governor Taft during the last six months of 1901.

"The administration of justice through the native judges in
Manila stinks to Heaven," he had informed Root early that year.
He decided to substitute American judges for the Filipino, bribe-
loving jurists. A new Code of Civil Procedure was drafted. As soon
as he could get them, Taft summoned judges from the United States
and put them on the bench.[11]

Revenue for the islands depended largely on the right of the
commission to impose duties on imports from the United States.

[9] Taft to Root, Jan. 9, 13, 1901. [10] Forbes, W. C., op. cit., Vol. I, p. 146; Vol. II,
p. 102. [11] Taft to Root, Jan. 9, 1901; Taft to C. P. Taft, June 23, 1900.

Without these, the taxes on land and on individuals would have been far too heavy. Under the rule of a military governor, the import levies had been made. But the right of a civil government to continue them, now that peace had come, was under discussion in the Supreme Court of the United States during the three months before Taft assumed his new post. Taft was greatly agitated over the possibility that the decisions in these insular cases, which applied to Porto Rico as well as the Philippines, might invalidate much of the work already accomplished. The question, translated into nonlegal terms, was whether duties could be assessed and whether the Filipinos enjoyed all rights under the Constitution.

Taft had slight patience with those who contended that the inhabitants of island possessions had the full protection of the Constitution. Only "cranks, fanatics or men who do not desire to make the best of conditions that exist," he declared in March, 1901, would propose to injure the Philippines "by enforcing the application of principles to the government of the islands . . . that are utterly unadapted to their development." [12] The Supreme Court was due to make its views known in June. Taft addressed a letter to his friend, Associate Justice Harlan, setting forth his own ideas:

We are awaiting anxiously the decision of your Court on the Porto Rican and Philippine question. With deference to a great many people who know more about it than I do, it seems to me that the issue . . . is simply whether the tax uniformity clause [of the Constitution] applies by way of restriction to the clause conferring power upon Congress to pass . . . rules and regulations for the government of the territory of the United States, and that depends only upon what the meaning of the words "United States" is in the tax uniformity clause. . . .

That clause may or may not apply by way of restriction, but . . . it . . . does not involve the question whether the Constitution follows the flag. . . . Of course the Constitution follows the flag, for no authority could exist except under the Constitution for an officer of the United States to do anything. The only question is, what are the restrictions in that instrument which apply to the particular power which he is exercising. . . .

Before this reaches you, I suppose the case will be decided, and

[12] Taft to H. H. Hoyt, March 6, 1901.

therefore I may say that if you should decide that the Dingley law must extend to these islands, it will produce a confusion in the finances of the government here, for which at present I see no remedy, and it will subject these islands and their business to a tariff law framed only for the United States and inapplicable to islands so far removed from that country.[13]

It would be necessary either to continue the emergency military regime, Taft felt, or to assess such heavy internal revenue taxes as seriously to cripple industry in the Philippines.[14] But the Supreme Court, in a five-to-four decision, agreed with Taft and decided that the protection of the Constitution could be extended to new territories only by specific act of Congress. Governor Taft expressed irreverent amusement to Justice Harlan:

I do not know who it is that said so, but it amused me very much when I heard it, that the position of the court was in this wise: that four of the judges said the Constitution did follow the flag, that four of them said it did not . . . and one said, "It sometimes follows the flag and sometimes does not, and I will tell you when it does and when it does not." [15]

Such was the practical effect of the decision. The people of the United States still found imperialistic delight, in 1901, in control of the Philippines. They had endorsed McKinley and expansion at the polls in 1900. As Mr. Dooley said: "No matter whether the Constitution follows the flag or not, th' Supreme Court follows th' illiction returns." Governor Taft was authorized to levy duties on imports. He was soon asking for reduced rates, in the United States, on goods exported from the islands. But Congress was apathetic to the idea; delay followed delay. Enactment became increasingly difficult as the imperialistic ardors of the voters began to cool.

—4—

In August, 1901, Governor Taft went on another provincial tour to establish civil governments. This time the party penetrated the

[13] Taft to J. M. Harlan, May 19, 1901. [14] Taft to John Warrington, July 19, 1901. [15] Taft to J. M. Harlan, Oct. 21, 1901.

remote mountains of Luzon. At Vigan, on the northwestern coast, the civil governor and several other members of the official party were nearly drowned when light, native boats were used to make the crossing from the steamer to the shore. The boat in which Governor Taft and Commissioner Ide sat was pounded by the surf and they were drenched to the skin. The weather was excessively hot. After two weeks of it, Taft began to complain.

"I have suffered on this trip more than on the southern trip from the heat, which has brought out prickly heat all over my body, and this and the pimples from the heat have broken out into little fistulas, within which there seems to be a slight infection." [16]

Taft was not yet aware that his health had been seriously undermined by the Manila climate and by the unceasing labors of the past fifteen months. Soon after returning from the Luzon tour he was shocked by the news that President McKinley had been shot. Taft had completely revised his early derogatory opinion of William McKinley. The crime committed in Buffalo seemed an augury of disaster. Everything had, perhaps, been going too smoothly. Now, as though they were savage echoes of the insane shot fired in Buffalo, rifles were to rattle again in the mountain jungles of the Philippines. Frightened men, fearing an insurrection, were to walk, heavily armed, through the streets of Manila. And Taft, who more than any other man was trusted by the Filipinos, was to linger for hours at the point of death and finally to crawl aboard a transport and sail, at this critical stage, for surgical attention in the United States.

The civil governor had spent the morning, as usual, at the Ayuntamiento, and a guest or two had been invited for lunch at Malacanan Palace. It was September 7, 1901, because Manila lies across the date line. Usually prompt enough, Taft did not arrive when lunch was announced that day. Mrs. Taft waited for a time and then took her visitors in. Meanwhile telegraph wires had been carrying calamitous dots and dashes from Buffalo across the continental United States. Cables had picked them up and they had been relayed under the endless Pacific until at last they had reached the civil governor of the Philippine Islands. Mrs. Taft was greatly alarmed when he came into the dining room. His face was white.

[16] Taft to Root, Aug. 25, 1901.

Only a great disaster could have given that air of stunned disbelief. His shoulders sagged.

"The President has been shot," he said. Then he explained that McKinley was not yet dead; he still might live but his condition was grave in the extreme.[17]

He had not seen the President, of course, since sailing for the Philippines. Few, if any, letters passed between them. McKinley, however, had given unstinted support to the Philippine Commission and had, through the secretary of war, passed on and approved the suggestions offered from time to time by Taft. McKinley died of his wound on September 14. Although he knew Roosevelt and trusted him, on the whole, Taft felt that the Philippine program had lost its stanchest ally. He wrote, in sorrow, to Root:

The dreadful shock caused by President McKinley's death and the feeling that he who had instituted the Philippine policy, and was more interested than anyone else could be in its issue, was no more, have robbed our work since his death of the interest which it had before, and it is only now that we are again taking up the burden with vim to accomplish our purpose.[18]

It was, said Taft, "a very sad feature of his death" that the President had not been permitted to live and watch the consummation of the work which he had started in the Philippines.[19] What of Theodore Roosevelt, who now, after bewailing his sad plight as vice-president, found himself catapulted to Olympian heights? It was impossible for Taft to believe that Roosevelt had all the qualities or capacities necessary for the presidency. For Roosevelt was so young; younger, indeed, than Taft himself. He had been born on October 27, 1858, whereas Taft had been born on September 15, 1857. Yet Taft was already deeply fond of Roosevelt; they called each other by their first names. He reiterated his conviction that his friend would make an excellent president. He pointed out that Roosevelt had been his choice for the 1904 Republican nomination. He dismissed, one by one, doubts which lingered in his mind.

". . . the new President . . . coming into office under the shadow of a great tragedy like this must have a burden which it

[17] Taft, Mrs. W. H., *op. cit.*, pp. 223-224. [18] Taft to Root, Sept. 26, 1901. [19] Taft to J. B. Bishop, Sept. 20, 1901.

will need all of his rugged strength to bear," he told Root. "He has my deep sympathy. . . . I know that he has the courage, the intelligence and the valuable experience of dealing with men which will enable him to discharge his duties with satisfaction to all who desire a pure, honest and straightforward administration." [20] As for Roosevelt's "impulsiveness and lack of deliberation— traits which it was suggested might involve us in a foreign war or something of the kind . . ."

I think these criticisms are altogether unjust, and yet if there were anything in them as applied to him when a candidate elected by the people, the circumstances under which he enters upon his office, under the shadow of a national tragedy, would render a man much more impulsive than he conservative to the last degree. I sincerely hope and believe that his administration will be a great success. It does not necessarily follow that he will be nominated [in 1904]; such a thing has not occurred in the history of the country, though men of his talents and character have not generally been made vice-presidents.[21]

But Taft, alas for political prognostication, did not believe that Roosevelt possessed "the capacity for winning people to his support that McKinley had." [22] Nor was it "to be expected that he will be able to retain the control over Congress which McKinley by reason of his long Congressional experience had succeeded in obtaining." [23] Before a month had passed Taft had concluded that Roosevelt "does not use the same tact in dealing with his subordinates that McKinley did." [24] He was more than a little hurt when he received two curt cablegrams from the President. Taft explained the facts of the situation in a letter to his brother, Horace.

Under the civil code, recently adopted by the Philippine Commission, the right of habeas corpus was permitted and Taft contended that this applied to military as well as civil prisoners. General Chaffee, the new military governor, declined late in October, 1901, to produce a prisoner named in a writ. Thereupon an appeal was made to Washington for a ruling "and resulted in two tele-

[20] Taft to Root, Sept. 26, 1901. [21] Taft to J. B. Bishop, Sept. 20, 1901. [22] Taft to H. W. Taft, Oct. 21, 1901. [23] Taft to J. B. Bishop, Sept. 20, 1901. [24] Taft to Louise Taft, Oct. 21, 1901.

grams from the President— one to me and one to Chaffee— in
which the President expressed his deep chagrin at the disagreement
and . . . his great desire that we should come to an agreement and
that the matter should be settled in the Philippines:

> The tone of the dispatch was, to a man who was struggling
> with the situation, by no means satisfactory. He spoke as if Gen-
> eral Chaffee and I were in a two-foot ring and all we had to do
> was to shake hands. We are on excellent terms and we showed
> each other our telegrams, and he told me that there was no glory
> for him in the Philippines, that he did not care to be told that the
> President was chagrined at a course which he had taken, and that
> he expected to ask to be relieved as soon as this matter was settled.
> I doubt if he follows it out. But it indicates the difference between
> Roosevelt's and McKinley's method. I think we can reach an agree-
> ment and I think we might have reached an agreement by reason
> of a less peremptory and unpleasant dispatch than the one which
> was sent.[25]

—5—

September through October, 1901, constituted the low point in
Taft's career as viceroy. On September 29 word reached Manila
that Company C, 9th Infantry, stationed on the island of Samar,
had been ambushed in the early morning. Thirty men managed to
fight their way through the bolomen. But fifty were killed. Again,
Taft was appalled. "It comes like a clap of thunder out of a clear
sky, for the reason that everything has been going well in Samar,"
he wrote. ". . . This is the worst blow we have had since we have
been in the islands, so far as loss of men is concerned. It is . . . very
discouraging, but there will be no shadow of turning from the
course we have marked out because of it." [26] Days of panic followed.
The massacre, Taft reported, was being capitalized by the interests
which sought to exploit the Philippines:

> You know we have the rag, tag, and bobtail of Americans,
> who are not only vicious but stupid. . . . The Samar incident has
> furnished them material and I regret to say that they had found
> in army circles a great deal of sympathy with their position. The

[25] Taft to Horace Taft, Oct. 21, 1901. [26] Taft to Root, Sept. 30, 1901.

Above: THE CIVIL GOVERNOR OF THE PHILIPPINES WITH MR. LUKE E. WRIGHT (LEFT) AND JUDGE IDE (RIGHT). *Below:* THE CIVIL GOVERNOR'S AMPLE BATHTUB—AFTER HIS

See page 165] DEPARTURE

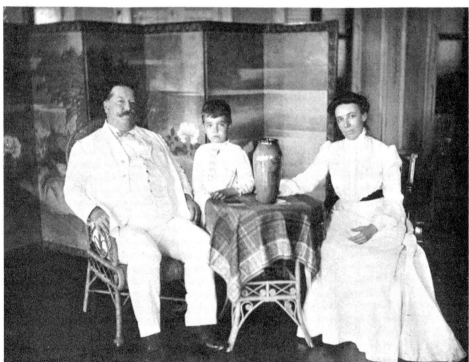

TAFT AS CIVIL GOVERNOR OF THE PHILIPPINES

[See page 200

army have been completely stampeded by the Samar affair. Chaffee has mounted patrols running about through Manila at night and he repeated to General Wright a number of times that we were standing on a volcano. This feeling seems to have been communicated to all of his subordinates and the Army and Navy Club is filled with rumors of insurrection in the most peaceful provinces.[27]

Taft's shoulders were broad. He had a stubborn faith and a vigorous belief in the Filipinos which made him hold out against General Chaffee and the others who insisted that they were treacherous. His innate sympathy for his wards, combined with his distrust of the military viewpoint, enabled him to see that the Filipinos had reason to hate the American soldiers who had ruled them for so long. Even in October, 1901, there were almost five hundred military posts in the islands. Taft described conditions in them:

The officers take the good houses in the town and the soldiers live in the church, the "convento" (which is the priest's house), the schoolhouse or the provincial building, and in many cases in all of them. The owners . . . are paid an arbitrarily fixed rent and are very fortunate if they get their rent. Nothing can so well show the wide difference between civil and military government as the indifference with which the military treat claims for the use of property by individuals.[28]

The civil governor, not General Chaffee, was right, as it turned out, regarding the dangers of insurrection. No further major outbreaks occurred. But Taft was discouraged. The death of McKinley, tactless cablegrams from the White House, the Samar disaster and, finally, increasing ill health combined to make "a hard and troublesome period in our life out here." Only Secretary of War Root remained steadfast. Taft felt that he could not go on if Root were to desert him.

"I fear from not seeing your name attached to any of the cablegrams that you have been ill," he wrote. "It seems to me sometimes as if all our woes have begun with the assassin's bullet, but I earnestly and anxiously hope that you will consent to remain at the War Office and keep the hold of the threads with which you

[27] *Idem.* [28] Taft to Horace D. Taft, Oct. 21, 1901.

are so familiar in Philippine matters. Without you, the commission would almost feel like giving up, for in you they feel that they have a tower of strength." [29]

By early October Taft was, although he declined to admit it, a distinctly sick man. He had returned in poor condition from the Luzon tour. Then he was attacked by dengue fever, a common tropical ailment. Mrs. Taft, with Mrs. Wright and Mrs. Moses, had departed for a China tour on October 1. It was on the following day that Taft fell ill. He remained in bed for about eight days. Then he began to suffer severe intestinal pains.[30] Cables carried the news to Mrs. Taft at the Hotel Astor, Shanghai:

Manila, October 25, 1901

Taft,
    Astor, Shanghai.
        Come dear am sick

Taft

Manila, October 26, 1901

Taft,
    Astor, Shanghai.
        Much better don't shorten trip

Will

Shanghai, October 28, 1901

Taft,
    Manila
        What is trouble love

Taft

Manila, October 29, 1901

Taft,
    Astor, Shanghai.
        Fistula operation First Reserve Hospital Sunday successful days or weeks needed complete recovery

Will

---

[29] Taft to Root, Sept. 30, 1901. [30] *Idem,* Oct. 14, 1901; Taft to Horace D. Taft, Oct. 21, 1901.

For a time the situation had been exceedingly grave. Mrs. Taft found that it was impossible to get a boat to Manila from Shanghai. The physicians in Manila had been puzzled by the condition of the civil governor. He had been in acute pain for several days. Then a rectal abscess broke and on Sunday afternoon, October 27, he was taken to the First Reserve Hospital on a stretcher for an immediate operation. The surgeons found an abscess in the perineum. A very extensive incision was necessary and until Tuesday morning the surgeons were apprehensive that gangrene might set in. Then, however, the wound began to heal. Taft was told that he must avoid all work for at least a month. He recalled with mild amusement his first experience under an anesthetic:

"I came to in the operating room and found myself in a condition in which I desired to hire a hall and make a speech. The drug seemed to make me tight. After an hour they gave me water and it seems to me that I must have drunk the entire Pasig River dry during the following night." [31]

Any immediate danger was over, but he was still far from well. In Washington, Secretary of War Root arranged to have General Wright made vice-governor so that Taft could get away at any time.[32] A second operation was performed on Thanksgiving Day, and Taft made ready to return to the United States for recuperation. He had an official as well as a personal reason for making the trip. In January, 1902, a committee of the Senate would begin a series of hearings on Philippine matters. Taft realized that many hostile witnesses would be heard. He desired to refute any statements that they might make.[33] Accommodations were reserved for the Tafts, including their three children, on the transport *Grant* and on Christmas Eve, 1901, the steamer slipped its moorings and turned out of Manila harbor. The civil governor was very weak. He lay in a steamer chair and watched the islands fall backward into the tropical haze. Almost nineteen months had passed since, in June, 1900, he had arrived in the Philippines as president of the Second Philippine Commission.

[31] Taft to C. P. Taft, Nov. 8, 1901. [32] Root to Taft, Oct. 30, 1901. [33] Taft to Root, Dec. 9, 1901.

—6—

Taft would have been inhuman if, as the *Grant* plowed through the China Sea, he failed to look back on the past year and half with satisfaction. He had demonstrated, among other things, that he was a good executive and not merely a jurist. He had no doubt, despite the Samar massacre, that the vast majority of the Filipinos desired peace. Civil government had been extended to a large part of the archipelago. The judicial system had been fumigated. Public works, including harbor improvements and roads, had been started. Primary and secondary schools were in operation. Measures had been taken to improve health conditions in the islands.[34] Most important of all, the military had been relegated to a subordinate position. The military men would certainly have continued a policy of bloodshed, and the American people were already growing weary of killings in the Philippines. It was not unlikely, had they continued, that Congress would have voted to wash its hands of manifest destiny, of the white man's burden, of dominion over palm and pine.

Taft cannot have been unaware, too, as his boat turned westward, that his own status had been incredibly enlarged by the work he had done. He was a modest man; too modest for his own good. Had he been otherwise the drums of glory would have been beating in his ears during these weeks at sea. He would have told himself that the campaign of 1904 was not far distant. No vice-president had ever been elected president in his own right after taking office owing to the death of a president. Had not Roosevelt, himself, been insisting in the spring and summer of 1901 that William Howard Taft, among all those available, was best fitted for the presidency? The envious Theodore, drying of slow rot in the vice-presidency had doubted, in March, 1901, "if in all the world there has been a much harder task set any one man during the past year than has been set you. . . . Yet in spite of all the difficulties you have done well, and more than well, a work of tremendous importance. You have made all decent people . . .

---

[34] Worcester, D. C., *op. cit.*, pp. 346-347.

your debtors, and . . . you . . . stand up well among those Americans, the sum total of whose work has made America's greatness. It has paid, after all, old man." [35]

In June, 1901— Taft was immediately informed of it by mail— Joseph Bucklin Bishop, who would one day be Theodore Roosevelt's biographer, had dined with the vice-president. The conversation shifted to Taft and the Philippines.

"By George!" exploded Roosevelt, "I wouldn't ask any higher privilege than to be allowed to nominate Taft for president in the next national convention. What a glorious candidate and President he would make!" They drank a toast to the prospect.

"This is not taffy, my dear judge," declared Bishop in describing the conversation.[36]

A few weeks later, from Oyster Bay, Roosevelt set forth his own views. "Of course I should like to be president," he said, "and I feel I could do the work well." But he believed, with the gloom which often overcame him when he discussed his political prospects, that he had no chance for the nomination. His enemies controlled the New York machine; ". . . looking at it dispassionately, I cannot see that there is any but the smallest chance of my getting enough hold even to make me seriously spoken of as a candidate." This being so, the colonel of the Rough Riders was willing to consider a substitute, if not a lesser, candidate. He added:

I should like to be president. But I want you to understand that I should throw up my hat for the chance of nominating one or two outside men for president. For instance, I believe Root would make a most admirable president. I am inclined to think that Spooner [Senator J. C. Spooner of Wisconsin] would. But if I had the naming either of President or Chief Justice, I should feel in honor bound to name you. Sometime I want to get a chance to say this in public.[37]

The exchange of salutations was Gallic in its politeness. It was also sincere. Roosevelt wanted the nomination, but concluded that it was beyond his reach. Taft did not want it at all. In June, 1901, as he had already done the previous January, Taft told T. R.

[35] Theodore Roosevelt to Taft, March 12, 1901. [36] J. B. Bishop to Taft, June 24, 1901. [37] Roosevelt to Taft, July 15, 1901.

that he "looked forward with confidence to your nomination for president at the next convention and I sincerely hope it may be brought about. . . . I look forward to voting for you." [38] From time to time letters reached Malacanan Palace in which old friends predicted the nomination of Taft. Such suggestions, he replied, constituted "one of those breezy indications that a man is getting more or less notoriety in the position he holds, rather than any serious indication on the part of the dear people to call him to the chief magistracy." His ambition, he said, "lies in a different direction, and I should like to occupy myself with something more attractive to me than a presidential campaign or the dodging of office seekers in the White House." He repeated, as he was to do so often, his conviction that the Republican party could "hardly take a weaker candidate than I should be, with my record as a federal judge in labor troubles." [39]

All this, of course, was prior to the assassination of McKinley. Taft gave not the slightest hint that he was in any way disappointed because the discussion for 1904 would now concentrate around Roosevelt rather than himself.

"Unless something unexpected happens," wrote his brother, Henry, "it seems to be thought that he [Roosevelt] will be a strong candidate for a renomination. It is fortunate that you are not of the temperament to be disappointed as to prospects on account of the sudden turn of affairs." [40]

The disappointment was limited to the loyal and ambitious members of the Taft family and, no doubt, to his wife. During the following year he was to refuse importunities from President Roosevelt that he return from the islands and accept appointment to the Supreme Court. He would not do this because he felt that his work was not finished. By the end of January, 1902, Taft was in Washington to testify before the Senate regarding the Philippines. He was warmly received by Roosevelt who "was just the same as ever and it is very difficult to realize that he is the President. He . . . shows not the slightest sign of worry or hard work in his looks or manner." [41] He added:

[38] Taft to Roosevelt, May 12, 1901. [39] Taft to A. P. Wilder and J. J. Cherry, May 20, 1901. [40] H. W. Taft to Taft, No. 8, 1901. [41] Taft to Helen H. Taft, Jan. 30, 1902.

Roosevelt blurts out everything and says a good deal that he ought to keep to himself. As we were standing in the hall . . . he said to me that he was praying that there would be no vacancy of the Supreme Court until after I had concluded matters in the Philippines. . . . I told him that if he were to offer me a vacancy now, I should decline it.[42]

The weeks in Washington were not entirely happy ones. Mrs. Taft's mother had died while she was en route from the Philippines. She was in a highly nervous condition and remained in Cincinnati. Taft's health was still bothering him; it soon appeared that another operation would be necessary. Most of all, he was irritated by the accusations made by the members of the Senate committee. He was on the stand for two hours daily and he talked for "as much time as the Democrats do not consume in asking fool questions." [43] He was questioned at great length on instances of cruelty to the Filipinos by the American army. He admitted that there had been cases of this, but said they were isolated.[44] Taft acquitted himself well, but the attacks depressed him.

"Sometimes I feel anxious to get out of the country to avoid them . . ." he admitted, "and yet it shows my unfitness for public life for me to dislike them so and be so sensitive about them. I suppose it indicates a thin-skinned vanity." [45]

[42] *Idem,* Feb. 24, 1901. [43] *Idem,* Feb. 6, 1902. [44] *Hearings,* Senate Committee on the Philippines, 57th Congress, 1st Session, Sen. Doc. 331, Part 2; pp. 854-859; Taft to Horace D. Taft, Jan. 30, 1902. [45] Taft to Helen H. Taft, April 18, 1902.

CHAPTER XIV

THE WICKED PRIESTS

IN OCTOBER, 1900, Señor Don Felipe Calderón, a Filipino lawyer, appeared before the Second Philippine Commission at Manila and gave testimony which was decidedly unpleasant. The commission was seeking evidence on the troublesome question of what should be done with the rich and fertile lands owned by the Spanish friars under the old regime. What, moreover, should be its policy toward the discredited men of God themselves? Their lands had been declared forfeited by Aguinaldo, and the priests, gathering their robes about them, had fled the islands. Señor Calderón spoke from firsthand knowledge. His mother, he admitted, was the daughter of a Franciscan friar. What would happen, asked Chairman Taft, if the friars returned to the native villages and pueblos?

"I will answer that," said Calderón, "by stating what a countryman told me: he says that all the friars have to do is to go back to their parishes and sleep one night, and the chances are they would never awaken. I do not mean to say by this that every pueblo in all the provinces would cut the throats of the returning parish priests. . . ."

Chairman Taft and his fellow commissioners stirred uneasily at this sanguinary prophecy. The next witness was José Roderiques Infante, a graduate of the University of Santo Tomás. He described the extent to which the friars had abandoned the things of God to mingle in the affairs of Caesar. They had wielded great political power and had removed from office the officials of whom they did not approve. Señor Infante may have been a shade prejudiced, but he told a convincing story. He said: that many of the priests were sadists and had derived enjoyment from watching floggings and other tortures at the jails; that they had extorted blackmail payments through secrets whispered by their parishioners in the confessional; that they had aided the tyrannous Spaniards in the collection of taxes. A few days later a Filipino physician gave further points for the bill of indictment. He told of an ingenious method whereby the clerics had raised funds for their churches and themselves. They had attended the bedside of many a dying Filipino— the doctor said he knew, personally, of scores of such cases— and had painted vivid pictures of the horrors of hell and damnation. These could be escaped, the friars promised, if the expiring man would donate his wealth or his lands to the church.[1]

Taft was inclined to believe the testimony. "On the issue whether the friars were immoral or not," he wrote, "the bright Filipino lawyer, Calderón, who is himself the grandson of a friar, has given me a list of the friars in the Philippines who have children. He has not finished . . . yet, but he has given us a detailed statement of seventy-four of them with their names and the number of their children. . . . This shows the kind of men who were engaged in teaching religion and in carrying on the government of these islands. The priests were, in fact, the governors here."[2]

The immorality of the churchmen was, however, only a detail; Taft was more shocked by it than were the Filipinos. The problem was an exceedingly difficult one and its reverberations were to sound, during the next few years, from the far Pacific to Washington, to the grandeur of the Vatican at Rome and back again. Its political aspects were grave in the extreme; President McKinley and then President Roosevelt were to worry over the possibility that the Catholic voters in the United States had been alienated by their treatment of the Spanish friars. But Taft did not evade the issue.

". . . in the assignment of subjects," he reported, as work in the Philippines started, "the most delicate matter of the whole lot— the friar question— has fallen to me. I made the assignment myself so that I have no reason to complain of it."[3]

His mother, who was watching the career of her son with an eagle eye, was amused "that you should be the one to identify yourself with the religious contests of the people . . . not being

[1] *Message of the President on Ecclesiastical Lands*, Philippine Islands, 56th Congress, 2nd Session, Sen. Doc. 190, pp. 133-156. [2] Taft to C. P. Taft, Dec. 13, 1900. [3] Taft to Horace Taft, Sept. 8, 1900.

theological in your tastes, or fitted for it by education." Mrs. Taft was not optimistic about the outcome.

"You will have the whole Catholic world down on you," she warned. "They quarrel among themselves, but like the Democratic party, they stand together against outsiders." [4]

—2—

The friars had been in the Philippines from the start of Spanish rule. Andrés de Urdaneta, an Augustinian, had accompanied the conqueror, Legaspi, when the islands had been seized in February, 1565. Four other Augustinian friars came with him and they proceeded at once to convert the Filipinos to the Catholic faith. Shortly afterward the Jesuit, Franciscan, Dominican and Recollect orders sent missionaries to aid in the work. The natives were easily converted.[5]

"The imagery and forms of the Roman Catholic Church appeal to the religious emotions of the Filipino," explained Taft, "and are, in my judgment, better adapted to his needs than those of any other religion. The church has wielded a powerful influence with the people for centuries and it only shows the depth of the feeling against the friars that it should find such open and violent expression among a people who are still profoundly attracted to the church whose sacraments these friars have administered." [6]

For a good many years the friars limited themselves to religion and education. The Schurman commission, which had made the first thorough study of the Philippines, found, however, that they had greatly extended their activities by the nineteenth century. The parish priest attended meetings of his municipal council and aided in its deliberations. He supervised elections. He decided whether public works were to be built and where. Very often he was in direct charge of public health and charities. He supervised the police force. He was censor of the provincial theater. He regulated the municipal budget. He had charge of the prison.[7]

[4] Louise Taft to Taft, Jan. 30, 1901. [5] Forbes, W. C., *The Philippine Islands*, Vol. I, pp. 50-51. [6] Taft to Mrs. Bellamy Storer, June 22, 1900. [7] Forbes, W. C., *op. cit.*, Vol. I, pp. 54-55.

"The truth is," wrote Taft in December, 1900, "that the friars ceased to be religious ministers altogether and became political bosses, losing sight of the beneficent purpose of their organizations. They unfrocked themselves in maintaining their political control of this beautiful country. Distance from Rome and freedom from supervision made them an independent quantity and enabled them to gratify their earthly desires for money and power and other things and they cut themselves off from any right to consideration by the church, by those who are in the church, or by those, who being out of it, respect it. It is said that all the civilization these islands have is due to the friars. In the first place, the civilization is not a great deal, and in the second place the obligation was contracted many years ago and the condition of things was much better in the early days of the islands than it has been during the present and last generation." [8]

Almost ninety per cent of the Filipinos were at least nominal communicants of the Catholic Church. It was the cruelty and greed of the friars which caused their downfall. A major grievance of the agrarian Filipinos was that by the late nineties the friars had acquired more than 400,000 acres of the best farm lands. They rented these to over 60,000 tenants who felt, justly or not, that the rates were excessive.[9] The insurgent movement prior to 1896 was partly due to hatred of the friars. Then came the declaration of Aguinaldo that their lands were confiscated. Fifty of the priests were slain; several hundred were imprisoned and many of them were tortured. No rents had been paid since that time. Under the Treaty of Paris, whereby the United States acquired the Philippines from Spain, all property rights were guaranteed, however. Taft and his colleagues were faced with the problem of restoring the lands without incurring bitter resistance from the natives. The Philippine Commission quickly reached two conclusions. The first was that the lands should be purchased from the friars, whose legal title was clear. The second was that the Catholic Church must send other priests in place of the Spanish friars. American priests were favored by Chairman Taft.

[8] Taft to Mrs. Bellamy Storer, Dec. 4, 1900. [9] Forbes W. C., *op. cit.*, Vol. II, pp. 56-57.

"These Philippine people," he wrote, "are yearning for the church to send them ministers whom they can respect and love, and the influence of the church can be restored and increased beyond what it ever was, if only an effort is made to send enlightened priests here." [10]

Delay followed delay. Archbishop Chapelle, who continued to represent the church at Manila, proved to be a most difficult prelate. Taft complained that his evidence on either side of the friar question was "altogether worthless, and the sooner Rome finds out how utterly useless he is for bringing about a solution of these difficulties here . . . the better." [11] For his part, the archbishop declared that the Philippine Commission "has taken, unconsciously perhaps, indirectly surely, a hostile attitude towards the Catholic Church and her interests." [12] The charge was baseless. So were the rumors that the opposition to the friars was an opening wedge in a drive to substitute Protestant missionaries for the Catholics who had been in the island for so long.

"As to the schools," Taft assured Mrs. Bellamy Storer who was, if anything, a shade too active in the situation, "I can assure you that we do not expect or wish to make them proselyting instruments." [13]

Taft erred, perhaps, in using the Storers as an avenue by which the situation could be presented to Pope Leo XIII and the other Vatican authorities. Mrs. Storer was an ardent Catholic and she possessed more energy than discretion. A native of Cincinnati, her daughter was married to the Marquis de Chambrun and her nephew, Nicholas Longworth, would soon be married to the bewitching Alice Roosevelt. In 1900 her husband was American minister to Spain and she was beginning a campaign for the elevation of Archbishop John Ireland, an American prelate, to the rank of cardinal. It was this campaign which was to end so disastrously in March, 1906, when President Roosevelt, charging that his name had been improperly used on behalf of Ireland, peremptorily dismissed Storer from the diplomatic service.[14]

[10] Taft to Mrs. Bellamy Storer, June 22, Dec. 4, 1900. [11] Taft to Root, June 23, 1901. [12] P. L. Chapelle to Taft, April 13, 1901. [13] Taft to Mrs. Bellamy Storer, June 22, 1900. [14] Pringle, H. F., *Theodore Roosevelt, a Biography*, pp. 454-458.

In October, 1900, Mrs. Storer suggested from Rome that Taft use his influence with McKinley and persuade the President to endorse, in a letter, the promotion of Ireland. It would, she said, greatly advance the solution of the Philippine question.[15] But Taft had far too much common sense to recommend that the President involve himself in a church matter; he declined to appeal to McKinley.[16] He did suggest, though, that the friar problem be explained to Archbishop Ireland so that he could, in turn, appeal to the Vatican.[17] This was done. Mrs. Storer also presented the facts personally to Cardinal Rampolla, the papal secretary of state.[18]

"The Vatican," wrote Mrs. Storer triumphantly in March, 1901, "has *almost* promised to make Archbishop Ireland a cardinal either in April or June." [19]

It did not do so, however; Mrs. Storer continued to agitate in vain. It is not unlikely that the friar question became, in the minds of Vatican authorities, confused with the crusade being conducted for the American archbishop. Meanwhile, in Manila, Taft was finding it very difficult to fix a price at which the lands could be bought and then resold to the natives.

"The promoters whom the friars have employed . . ." he reported, "desire to hold up the price as much as possible." [20] Such was the situation as Taft, in the late fall of 1901, prepared to return to the United States to regain his health. Before leaving Manila he suggested that it would be wise to send a representative directly to Rome.

"It would need, of course, a very clearheaded man to carry on the negotiations," he said. ". . . Now have we a man competent to do this business?" [21]

—3—

Late in February, 1902, a conference was held at the White House at which Roosevelt, Root, Archbishop Ireland and Taft discussed the situation.

[15] Mrs. Bellamy Storer to Taft, Oct. 9, 1900. [16] Taft to Mrs. Bellamy Storer, Dec. 4, 1900. [17] *Idem,* July 12, 1900. [18] Mrs. Bellamy Storer to Taft, Oct. 9, 1900. [19] *Idem,* March 21, 1901. [20] Taft to Carmi Thompson, April 12, 1902. [21] Taft to Root, Sept. 26, Oct. 14, 1901.

"You'll have to go to Rome yourself," was the resulting presidential order. Taft went to Cincinnati for the third abscess operation and then prepared for his first assignment as the troubleshooter of the Roosevelt administration.[22] He was to receive many more such assignments before Roosevelt went out of office. They were to take him to Japan, to the Philippines, to Cuba and to Panama. They were to convince the public that Taft had extraordinary talents for bringing order out of chaos. His achievements persuaded the voters that Taft, more than any other man, was qualified for the presidency in 1908.

The mission to the Vatican was delicate. In the instructions handed to Taft, Secretary of War Root specified that the journey "will not be in any sense or degree diplomatic in its nature, but will be purely a business matter of negotiation by you as governor of the Philippines for the purchase of property from the owners thereof, and the settlement of land titles, in such a manner as to contribute to the best interests of the people of the islands."[23] This was vital. If the United States were to send a diplomatic mission to the Vatican it would mean, in the eyes of anti-Catholic voters, recognition of the Pope as a sovereign. And this, in turn, would spell defeat for Roosevelt or any other Republican candidate in 1904. But the Vatican, in contrast, greatly desired that a diplomatic flavor be given to the American mission; this would increase its prestige in the courts of Europe. A battle of wits was forthcoming among the hills of Imperial Rome.

Mrs. Taft was to have gone with her husband on the S.S. *Trave* in the middle of May, 1902. But shortly before the date of sailing young Robert Taft came down with scarlet fever, so Taft's mother, by now a vigorous old lady of seventy-four, decided to accompany the official party and protect her boy, if she could, from the machinations of the papists.[24] Taft sailed with his mother and the members of the commission who were to assist him in the negotiations. These were James F. Smith, associate justice of the Supreme Court of the Philippines, and Major John Biddle Porter, Judge Advocate Department, U.S.A. A third commissioner, the Right Reverend Thomas O'Gorman, bishop of Sioux Falls, had

[22] Taft to Helen H. Taft, Feb. 24, 1902. [23] Root to Taft, May 9, 1902. [24] Taft, Mrs. W. H., *Recollections of Full Years,* pp. 236-237.

taken an earlier boat in order to prepare the way. Bishop O'Gorman was, perhaps, the most valuable aide. He was an Irish-American with an innate distrust of Italians, even when they were high prelates of his own church. He had "a keen sense of humor and . . . an imperturbability under attacks which it is pleasant to see," reported Taft.[25] A sense of humor was to be needed. Taft's experiences at the Vatican were not greatly different from those Theodore Roosevelt would have in 1910. Roosevelt, on that occasion, told Cabot Lodge that he had an "elegant row" in the Holy City, that a representative of the Pope had "made a proposition that a Tammany Boodle alderman would have been ashamed to make." [26]

Root's official instructions to Taft summarized the friars' land situation in the Philippines. The civil governor was directed to learn which church authorities had power to negotiate the sale of the lands so that Congress could act in the matter. The secretary of war pointed out that the monastic orders which had incurred the hostility of the Filipinos could not remain at their posts. Other spiritual leaders should be sent in their places.

"It is the wish of our government . . ." wrote Root, "that the titles of the religious orders to the large tracts of agricultural lands which they now hold shall be extinguished, but that full and fair compensation should be made therefor." [27]

So the Rome expedition had two main objectives: consent of the Vatican to recall the friars and sale of their holdings at a fair price. Prior to leaving for Rome, Taft thought that $5,000,000 in gold would probably be an acceptable figure, although he was apparently willing to bid up to $8,000,000.[28] The negotiations did not progress to the point of bidding, however.

"The Vatican," warned Lyman Abbott of the *Outlook* from Florence where he was touring, "appears to me to be ruled by politicians who are not overscrupulous, and whose ideals of diplomacy like their ideals of theology belong to the age of Machiavelli." [29]

[25] Taft to Root, July 5, 1902. [26] Pringle H. F., *op. cit.*, p. 513. [27] Root to Taft, May 9, 1902. [28] Taft to H. C. Lodge, March 26, 1902. [29] Lyman Abbott to Taft, June 1, 1902.

—4—

At first, though, the outlook was encouraging. The *Trave* arrived at Naples on May 29, 1901, and two days later Taft and his colleagues reached Rome. On June 2 they called on Cardinal Rampolla. It was all done in the best manner. Letters were presented from the President and from Secretary of State Hay. As a present to the Pope, Roosevelt sent eight volumes of his own writings; what better gift could a literary chief executive make? On June 5 at twelve-thirty, garbed in full evening dress, the Americans were received at the Vatican. Taft was impressed by the pomp and color. But he was also entertained. Pope Leo, by now extremely old, was as friendly as possible.

"The old boy is quite bubbling with humor," Taft wrote. "He was as lively as a cricket."

We were ushered through I know not how many rooms between guards of all uniforms including the Swiss and the Noble Guards and were finally met by the master of ceremonies. We waited not more than two minutes when we were taken to a small audience chamber where we found the Pope seated on a little throne and saying something in French in the way of welcome. He told us to be seated, but I stood up and fired a speech at him which Major Porter read in French. The Pope followed closely and when something was said he liked he bowed and waved his hand at me. He surprised me very much by his vigor and the resonance of his voice. . . . After that he sat down and we had fifteen minutes' conversation. . . . He said that he had heard of my illness but that my appearance didn't justify any such inference. . . . He expressed the most emphatic interest in my success and my good health. When the audience was at an end, he got up, gave the bell rope behind him a jerk, asked me to give him the pleasure of shaking hands with him and then escorted us to the door. . . . I understand from persons coming from the Vatican that the old gentleman was very much pleased with the interview and spoke of it a number of times. I have no doubt that it will attract some criticism from our Methodist and supersensitive Protestant friends, but if we can succeed in our purpose, that will, I believe, pass away in the excellence of the result.[30]

Taft's address to the Pope outlined the changes necessitated by the transfer of the Philippines from Spain, a nation closely allied to the Catholic Church, to the United States where no church alliance of any kind was possible. The "justice or injustice" of the hatreds incurred by the monastic orders, he said, had no relation to the problem of their lands and their recall. The Philippine government, he said further, proposed to purchase their property and to bring about, thereby, the substitution of priests "whose presence would not be dangerous to public order." The price should be fixed by arbitration. Taft closed by reiterating that the United States was in every way friendly to the Catholic Church; that it treated all churches and all creeds alike.[31] The nonagenarian prelate bobbed and bowed his approval as Major Porter read the French translation of this speech. He said that he could not go into the details of the proposals made by the United States. A commission of cardinals would be appointed and would have charge of the matter.[32]

Even Bishop O'Gorman was hopeful during the next few days that an agreement would be reached. He kept a day-to-day record of the proceedings and noted that "the United States government is giving the Holy Father the chance of his life and he is going to use it to the fullest extent. The religious orders, so recalcitrant to his policies most everywhere, are to be brought under his thumb. Washington asks him to exercise his supreme power over them." [33] O'Gorman assured Taft that success would crown the visit. Any delay would be due only to anxiety on the part of the Pope to appoint cardinals who would do as they were told. The archbishop of Sioux City fell back on a phrase of the American politician to describe what was going on in the Vatican.

"Boys," he said, "the Pope had already declared to the cardinals, 'this thing goes through.' " [34]

It did not, however, go through. A week after the audience with the Pope, Taft was beginning to have misgivings. "These

[30] Taft to Helen H. Taft, June 7, 1902. [31] Taft to Horace Taft, June 10, 1902. [32] Memorandum, Bishop O'Gorman, June, 1910, Taft papers, Library of Congress. [33] Ibid. [34] Taft to Helen H. Taft, June 11, 1902.

Italians are such liars," he wrote, "that I do not wish to express confidence until my ground is black and white."[35] On June 21, 1902, the answer came from the cardinals; the church agreed to the sale of the lands but it would not promise to withdraw the Spanish friars. There the matter rested. Secretary of War Root cabled Taft to stand by the original instructions. Further delays were caused by further debates. Finally Root ordered Taft to end the negotiations as well as to cancel the proposals made by the United States. The matter would have to be settled at some later date in the Philippine Islands.

"I wonder," noted Bishop O'Gorman in his diary, "if the Vatican realizes what it has lost in material profits and in diplomatic prestige."[36]

Outward harmony was preserved. On July 21 the Americans were received by the Pope again and he was "full of honeyed expressions," Taft said.[37] He felt that the Pope, himself, had been anxious to accede to the American demands but "the influence of the monastic orders at Rome is now all-powerful. The Pope does not dare antagonize them and they have beaten us."[38] Taft thought, however, that the visit had been valuable even if the main objective had not been gained.

"We have told the Vatican the plain truth, and while it is not disposed to make written admission of it," he wrote, "we shall have considerably less difficulty hereafter in making Rome understand the situation."[39]

The venerable Leo XIII was to die, though, before the troublesome question of the friars and their lands had been settled. The matter assumed all the aspects of a New England horse trade. Archbishop Guidi, a far more reasonable man than Chapelle in Taft's mind, became the Philippine representative of the church in the summer of 1902. In September, 1903, he informed the civil governor that $10,700,000 in gold was the lowest possible figure; this had, he said, been approved in Rome.[40] But $10,700,000 was far more than the Philippine Commission was willing to pay. Taft

[35] Taft to Helen H. Taft, June 12, 1902. [36] O'Gorman memorandum. [37] Taft to Delia Torrey, July 27, 1902. [38] Taft to Horace D. Taft, July 10, 1902. [39] Idem, July 15, 1902. [40] Memorandum, by Taft, Sept. ?, 1903.

employed experts who again told him that $5,000,000 was a fair price.

"For the sake of peace and to accomplish our purposes," Taft reported to Washington, "I should be willing to increase the estimate of our surveyor by fifty per cent, making the offer seven and one half millions. I think this is too great probably by a million or a million and a half, but I am willing to recommend the offer with a view of closing the matter up."

The real difficulty lay in the fact that the monastic orders knew that the Pope intended to assign the funds to general church work in the Philippines and that they would not, themselves, benefit. As the months passed, Taft grew impatient and wondered whether it would not be better to let the "owners of the friars' lands, whoever they are, 'stew in their own juice.'"[41]

"We are still very far apart and the attitude . . . of my colleagues on the commission is that of hostility to the purchase of the lands," he told Root in September, 1903. "They think that the time is past and that it would be assuming a great burden. Still, if we can buy the lands anywhere near my figure, I think it will be a good thing. . . . I should judge from what I hear that the new Pope is quite as liberally inclined toward a settlement as was Leo."[42]

An agreement was finally reached in November, 1903. About 10,000 out of the 400,000 acres owned by the friars were withdrawn from the sale, and for the balance $7,543,000 was paid.[43] Under authorization by Congress, the insular government raised the cash through the issue of bonds. Then the lands were gradually sold, in small parcels and on easy terms, to the natives. By 1912, some 50,000 new landowners were a stabilizing force in the archipelago. Meanwhile, although Rome never formally recalled the Spanish clerics, their influence waned. American and Filipino bishops were appointed in their places. Only two hundred remained in the islands by the end of 1903 and they had no political power whatever.[44]

[41] Taft to Root, April 26, 1903. [42] Taft to C. P. Taft, Sept. 24, 1903. [43] *Report, Philippine Commission*, 1903, 58th Congress, 2nd Session, House Doc. 2, pp. 38-44. [44] Forbes, W. C., *op. cit.*, Vol. II, pp. 58-60.

—5—

But the "beautiful islands" toward which Taft sailed from Rome in July, 1902, were burdened with woes during the balance of that year and most of 1903. Disease and famine had come. Business conditions were bad. Bands of outlaws were roaming the mountain districts and were preying upon the natives. The arrival of the U.S.S. *General Alava* on the morning of August 22 was, at the least, a good omen. On the bridge, as the vessel dropped anchor, could be seen the broad, white bulk of the civil governor. The viceroy had returned to his wards and they needed him more than ever before. Rumors had been current for months that he would not come. He had been due in May. His enemies had been active in spreading word that Taft's pledge to return, given as he sailed on Christmas Eve, 1901, had meant nothing.[45] Now he had actually come, to confound his critics and to keep the faith. Guns from Fort Santiago boomed a salute. Word of his arrival spread through Manila. Soon there was a vast crowd at the wharf, and it followed the official party to the Ayuntamiento. The civil governor spoke. His words, as always, were quickly translated into Spanish by Arthur Fergusson.

"I am glad to be in Manila again and to look into your familiar faces and to find there a heartfelt welcome," Taft began. ". . . During my absence has come the awful scourge of cholera and though abating in severity it has not yet disappeared. How much the poor suffering people of the Philippine Islands have had to bear of late years! War that stops agriculture, that destroys peace of mind, that brings sorrow and loss to many a household and poverty to nearly all, this they have had since 1896. Then came the rinderpest, a disease that carried off seventy-five per cent of the faithful beasts of burden upon which depended so much of the prosperity of the islands; and now the cholera that brings in its train not only cruel suffering and much loss of life, but also those severe restrictions necessary to prevent its spread which to a people unused to them and unable to understand their necessity are almost a greater burden than the cholera itself."

[45] Taft to Root, Oct. 25, 1902.

A brighter side of the picture existed and "all is not woe," Taft went on. He said that peace had come to the islands and the military regime had ended. Congress had enacted a tariff bill which admitted Philippine products to the United States at a rate twenty-five per cent lower than the products of other countries. Congress had further authorized the exclusion of Chinese labor. Finally, Congress had enacted the Philippine Government Bill which gave augmented powers to the local government. It provided that a popular Assembly would be created within two years after a census had been taken.

"The present year, I believe," said Taft, "marks the beginning of an era of prosperity and happiness for the Filipino people. . . . I have a deep affection for the Filipino people. . . . I mean to do everything that in me lies for their benefit and I invoke their sincere and earnest co-operation in the great work of teaching a capable people the art of wise self-government." [46]

—6—

Yet 1902 and 1903 were far from happy or prosperous years. More than 100,000 Filipinos were to die of cholera before the plague had been controlled.[47] It was almost impossible, at first, to enforce quarantine or health restrictions. Taft must have remembered, as he labored too hard during these eighteen months, the poem which had been handed him— could it actually have been only two years before?— when first he had drawn near to the unfortunate isles. He knew all too well, by now, that his charges had been children who often cried for the moon. They were still superstitious and gullible. One outbreak of cholera near Manila had been traced to a spring supposed to have been holy water. Rumors had spread that an infant Jesus had been found there, so the natives had flocked to it and had taken the water home in bottles. The health officers, puzzled by a sudden increase in cholera cases, discovered that a sewer drained into the spring.[48]

By November, 1902, Taft found that the rice crop would be

[46] *Addresses*, Vol. I, pp. 38-43. [47] *Report, Philippine Commission*, 1903, pp. 16-17.
[48] Taft to D. C. Worcester, Sept. 14, 1903.

only twenty per cent of normal and the danger of famine arose. Nearly nine-tenths of the carabao, used as pack animals by the natives, had died of rinderpest. The fall in the price of silver had cost the insular government $1,000,000.[49] Taft successfully appealed to President Roosevelt for a Congressional grant of from $2,000,000 to $3,000,000 for relief work in the islands.[50] There were other troubles. Unemployed and starving natives, made desperate by the situation, were organizing into outlaw bands and were robbing their neighbors. Commissioners Ide and Worcester were incapacitated by overwork and ill-health, so that Taft's own burdens were doubled. In March, 1903, an undercurrent of dishonesty among minor American officeholders was discovered. This, Taft said, was "due to the temptations to dishonesty that beset young Americans removed from the restraints of home life, without their families and with a disposition to gamble or drink or lead a lewd life. . . . Two disbursing officers have defaulted. . . . I now learn . . . that they both married prostitutes; enough to explain anything in their lives."[51] Nearly a score of officials, it developed, had stolen funds entrusted to their care and Taft deplored the demoralizing effect their thefts would have on Filipinos to whom similar positions of trust had been given. He was relentless in his prosecutions. All but two were sent to the penitentiary.[52]

"We are passing through a period of discouragement now," he wrote. "The long-continued stagnation in agricultural production is beginning to bear the fruit I feared. The people are beginning to feel discontent and hardship and they naturally make the government and the Americans responsible for the rinderpest, the cholera, the locusts, the fall in silver and the decline in business."[53]

Surely vengeful gods brooded over the archipelago as Roosevelt's first administration drew to a close. Taft was further exasperated by many of the Americans who had flocked to the islands to make their fortunes. They were disgruntled by the withdrawal of United States troops, who had been their best customers. They growled that Taft had favored the natives instead of the Americans. Of course, he had done so:

[49] Taft to H. C. Lodge, Nov. 27, 1902. [50] Taft to Roosevelt, Nov. 9, 1902. [51] Taft to Root, March 2, 1903. [52] *Report, Philippine Commission,* 1903, pp. 63-71. [53] Taft to Louise Taft, March 7, 1903.

We have in these islands possibly eight thousand Americans
and we have about eight millions of Christian Filipinos. If business is to succeed here, it must be in the sale of American goods to
the eight millions of Filipinos. One would think that a child in
business might understand that the worst possible policy in attempting to sell goods is to abuse, berate and vilify your only possible customers.[54]

Somehow Taft managed to preserve his sanity, even his sense
of humor. Early in 1903 a drought killed additional crops. In June,
1903, a storm swept over one part of the Philippines and unroofed
most of the houses.

"You remember the man in Mark Twain," the civil governor
suggested, "who was a patient man, but when his house fell down
from a landslide and the material fell on him, struggled from under
it with the remark 'This thing is becoming monotonous.' However,
it is a long lane that has no turning, and I will not allow these
things to discourage me." [55]

Nor was Taft's health any too good. The abscess which had
brought him perilously close to death seemed to have healed. But
in January, 1903, he attended a Filipino christening during a journey into the hills and came down with indigestion.[56] In March he
was suffering from amoebic dysentery, a stubborn and sometimes
fatal disease in the tropics.[57] By the end of the month the members
of his family in the United States were seriously alarmed; so were
President Roosevelt and Secretary of War Root. Taft declined to
give in. He went to Baguio, the mountain resort, in April and made
the last part of the journey, under a broiling sun, on horseback.
He sent a cable to the secretary of war:

Stood trip well. Rode horseback twenty-five miles to five thousand feet elevation.

The secretary of war, reassured and with a picture of the 300-
pound civil governor flashing through his mind, called a stenographer and dictated a reply:

[54] Taft to H. C. Hollister, Sept. 21, 1903. [55] Taft to Edward Colston, June 7, 1903.
[56] Taft to Root, Jan. 25, 1903. [57] Taft to C. P. Taft, March 27, 1903.

Referring to your telegram . . . how is the horse? [58]

The witticism became famous. It was told and retold during the campaign of 1908. The exchange of cables has been reprinted again and again. It has never been known, however, that the *mot* of the secretary of war first became public through Taft himself. The civil governor had the ability to laugh at himself. He told Root:

Your cable inquiry about the condition of the horse that brought me up the mountain was too good to keep, so I published the dispatch and have been made the subject of jokes in the local newspapers ever since. The horse which I did ride was the horse which General Chaffee used to ride, and is a magnificent animal 17½ hands high, a singlefooter, gentle and intelligent and of great power. He stood the trip without difficulty.[59]

Meanwhile a new series of crises had arisen to plague Taft. On two occasions, beginning in October, 1902, President Roosevelt offered him the kingly crown of appointment to the Supreme Court. Twice Taft refused this, his heart's desire, because he would not desert the people of the Philippines. Then came a virtual order to report to Washington and accept the portfolio of secretary of war. Taft did not want the post. As always, he doubted his qualifications. As always, he shrank from an assignment which led, inevitably, into the confused and swirling waters of active politics. But this time he could not decline.

"It seems strange," he wrote, "that with an effort to keep out of politics and with my real dislike for it, I should thus be pitched into the middle of it." [60]

[58] Taft, Mrs. W. H., *op. cit.*, p. 135. [59] Taft to Root, May 13, 1903. [60] Taft to H. C. Hollister, Sept. 21, 1903.

CHAPTER XV

I NEED YOU; COME HOME

Early in January, 1903, the Taft clan gathered in family conclave in New York City to consider an absorbing question: What decision should our famous kinsman make at this critical stage of his career? Will Taft was not present himself, of course. He was in Manila replying to cablegrams and letters from the White House. Theodore Roosevelt persisted in demanding that he accept appointment to the Supreme Court.

Mrs. Louise Torrey Taft, his mother, was at the meeting. So was Aunt Delia Torrey who, like his mother, continued to have emphatic and intelligent opinions despite her advanced age. Mr. and Mrs. Charles P. Taft had come to town from Cincinnati. Henry W. Taft lived in New York and therefore took a prominent part in the deliberations. He drafted a report for Brother Will describing them.

The clan did not share Will's conviction that he was, by reason of his labor decisions, disqualified for ultimate election as president of the United States. They did not have a comparable distaste for the horrors of a political campaign. On these points, the family were in agreement. They differed, however, on the best path to be followed to glory. Brother Charley, reported Brother Henry, "is in favor of your accepting the appointment [to the bench] upon the general ground that you had better take what happens to be in your reach." He saw no reason why, tradition to the contrary, Will could not resign should "some other branch of public life" become more attractive. Mother and Aunt Delia, Henry Taft continued, "are both quite strongly opposed to your going on the bench." But they, too, had visions of higher things. As for himself, Henry Taft agreed that the presidency was a definite probability:

Of course . . . I would not have you embitter your life by seeking to satisfy ambitions in politics and perhaps suffering dis-

237

appointments. I am quite sure that you would not be subject to that sort of unhappiness. What you might attain would probably come with little effort on your part. . . . Without belittling . . . your ability to be a great judge, I really think you have the capacity to be a greater politician (or statesman, if you please), or lawyer, and that you will be of greater use to a greater number of people and have a broader influence and leave a deeper impress upon the history of the country if you do not limit the scope of your activities by taking a position on the bench.[1]

Year by year, as his reputation continued to grow, Taft was increasingly besieged by these petitions from the people who loved and were proud of him and to whom he was more closely bound than to any others on earth. His ambitious wife had, of course, joined the affectionate cabal long before. In the end, to his lasting sorrow, Taft would give in and would walk, with slow, hesitating and uncertain steps, into the political arena. But as 1903 began he was still adamant in his determination to go on the bench or to practice law as soon as he had terminated his work in the Philippines. His mother, too, had written a letter of advice.

"Nellie was especially pleased," Taft answered, "to see that you and Harry and Horace agreed with her that I ought not to go on the bench. Still, I venture to differ with you and her." [2]

The crisis— that is, the necessity for making a decision between the Philippines and the Supreme Court— confronted Taft in October, 1902, because Theodore Roosevelt was in a disturbed state of mind concerning the highest court. Among the presidential powers which Roosevelt relished, took very seriously— and augmented when possible— there was none more vital than his duty of naming the distinguished jurists of the Supreme Court. Among the doctrines of government which he viewed lightly, and undermined when possible, was the theory that the executive, the legislative and the judicial branches are co-ordinate and equal.

"The President and the Congress," he was to declare in 1906, "are all very well in their way. They can say what they think they think, but it rests with the Supreme Court to decide what they have really thought." [3]

[1] H. W. Taft to Taft, Jan. 10, 1903. [2] Taft to Louise Taft, March 7, 1903. [3] Pringle, H. F., *Theodore Roosevelt, a Biography*, p. 259.

Inevitably, then, it was essential for President Roosevelt to mold, in so far as his power of appointment enabled him to do so, a Supreme Court which agreed with his own views; in short, to have "men of my type" on the highest tribunal. Only thereby could potential nullification of the executive will be halted. His first opportunity came during July, 1902, when Associate Justice Horace Gray, a member of the court for twenty years, decided to resign. The President asked Cabot Lodge whether Oliver Wendell Holmes, chief justice of Massachusetts, was a man who met the Rooseveltian specifications.

"In the ordinary and low sense which we attach to the words 'partisan' and 'politician,'" Roosevelt wrote, "a judge of the Supreme Court should be neither. But in the higher sense, in the proper sense, he is not in my judgment fitted for the position unless he is a party man, a constructive statesman . . . and . . . [keeps] . . . in mind also his relations with his fellow statesmen who in other branches of the government are striving in co-operation with him to advance the ends of government." [4]

Mr. Justice Holmes succeeded in passing the tests and was appointed. The President ultimately made his judicial philosophy even more clear. In 1906 he was debating the selection of Horace H. Lurton for the Supreme Court. It did not matter, Roosevelt said, that Lurton was a Democrat. He was, none the less, "right on the Negro question . . . right on the power of the federal government . . . right on the insular business . . . right about corporations . . . right about labor." [5]

But presidents are frequently deceived in the jurists they name; the judicial mind has a deplorable habit of deciding cases on the law and declining to indulge in statesmanlike co-operation. Justice Holmes, in March, 1904, was one of the four justices who refused to hold with the majority of the court that the Northern Securities Company was in violation of the Sherman act. The attack on the merger, which sought control of railroad transportation in the Northwest, was Roosevelt's first onslaught against the trusts. It was being argued in the lower courts during the summer of 1902 and would ultimately be passed upon by the Supreme Court. The

[4] Lodge, H. C., *Selections from the Correspondence of Theodore Roosevelt and Henry Cabot Lodge*, Vol. I, p. 518. [5] *Ibid.*, Vol. II, p. 228.

Northern Securities case— rather, a victory for the government in the case— was very close to Roosevelt's heart. It was among the reasons which led him to summon a stenographer on October 26, 1902, and dictate a cablegram to Civil Governor Taft of the Philippines. Associate Justice George Shiras, Jr., had signified his intention of leaving the bench by the first of the year and, again, the President had to find a suitable successor.

"It is in my judgment of the utmost importance to get our strongest men on the court at very earliest opportunity," Roosevelt told Taft. ". . . You can at this juncture do far better service on the Supreme Court than any other man. I feel that your duty is on the court unless you have decided not to adopt a judicial career. I greatly hope you will accept. Would appreciate early reply." [6]

The message reached Taft at the governor's offices in the Ayuntamiento in Manila. With it had come a message from Secretary of War Root deploring the loss of his services in the Philippines but admitting that he might do well to accept. Mr. Root expressed concern over Taft's health. Would it not be wiser to go on the bench and avoid danger of another collapse? [7] The civil governor was puzzled. As recently as February, in Washington, he had discussed with Roosevelt the subject of appointment to the Supreme Court. Taft had insisted that he would not accept until his work in the East was finished. What did this cable really mean? Was the President embarrassed by his administration of the Philippines? Were fanatical Catholics threatening political reprisals because of the campaign against the Spanish friars? Taft was wounded as well as puzzled when he reached Malacanan Palace that night. Next morning he dispatched a cable to Brother Henry:

See Root immediately . . . tell him my withdrawal now great political mistake Philippine standpoint. Unless administration embarrassed somehow by my continuance as governor emergency in court should otherwise be met.[8]

At the same time he sent a firm message of declination to the President.

[6] Roosevelt to Taft, Oct. 26, 1902. [7] Root to Taft, Oct. 26, 1902. [8] Taft to H. W. Taft, Oct. 27, 1902.

Great honor deeply appreciated but must decline. Situation here most critical from economic standpoint. Change proposed would create much disappointment and lack of confidence. . . . These are sentiments of my colleagues and of two or three leading Filipinos consulted confidentially. Look forward to time when I can accept such an offer but even if it is certain that it can never be repeated I must now decline. Would not assume to answer in such positive terms in view of words of your dispatch if gravity of situation here was not necessarily known to me better than it can be known in Washington.[9]

Taft continued to worry over the possibility that the President was attempting politely to recall him from the Philippines. He informed Root that his health was as good as when he had first reached the islands in 1900 and that he would be careful.[10] He elaborated this in a letter. If it were really true that the President desired him to leave, Taft said, he would resign at once.

"Of course, under such circumstances . . . I could not accept a position on the Supreme bench. I shouldn't enjoy being kicked upstairs." [11]

Taft was partially reassured a fortnight later when the President, by implication, bowed to his refusal and asked by cable whether Lloyd Bowers, an intimate Yale friend, was qualified for the court. Taft's answer was an enthusiastic affirmative.

"One of your kind of men," he assured Roosevelt.[12]

Letters from the President were, at this time, making their slow passage across the Pacific; had Taft seen them before the cables arrived, his alarm and resentment would have vanished. A week prior to his first cable, the President had written that Justice Shiras was resigning, that no one could really take Taft's place in the Philippines but "we do need you on the court." Whatever decision Taft might make, however, would be accepted at once.[13] Three days later the impetuous Roosevelt wrote a second letter. It was "of the very highest importance" that he mount the bench.

"I am not at all satisfied with its condition— let us speak this only with bated breath between you and me," he said. "I think we

[9] Taft to Roosevelt, Oct. 27, 1902. [10] Taft to Root, Oct. 27, 1902. [11] *Idem,* Oct. 29, 1902. [12] Roosevelt to Taft; Taft to Roosevelt, Nov. 9, 1902. [13] Roosevelt to Taft, Oct. 18, 1902.

need you there greatly. I may have to cable you before you get this." [14]

—2—

Meanwhile Henry Taft, as the advance agent for Taft Presidential Prospects, Inc., had been conferring in Washington with Roosevelt and with Root. He, too, was reassuring. He found no evidence whatever that Roosevelt was attempting to get rid of Taft in the Philippines. The President made it clear, moreover, that in his judgment Taft would be the probable Republican nominee in 1908. The conversation with the President, Henry Taft added, had convinced him of his sincerity. Further, it had been made clear that Roosevelt desired to have Brother Will in Washington for a dual role; in addition to being on the Supreme Court, he would be a personal counselor and adviser to the President.

"Of course you know Roosevelt," said Henry Taft, in commenting on this unique amplification of the duties of a Supreme Court justice, "and know that he will not expect you to do anything except act on your own judgment— I mean, that you will not yield your judgment to his."

Henry Taft was neither facetious nor satirical when he dictated that paragraph; a great many changes were to take place and the Taft clan was to suffer many a troubled heartache before Roosevelt cut away his conservative moorings and drifted on the sea of progressivism and judicial recall. In December, 1902, and January, 1903, when the conversations with Henry Taft were held, Roosevelt was conscientiously seeking advice from Root, Hanna, United States Senator Aldrich and other right-wing leaders. He desired similar advice from Will Taft. Henry Taft wrote:

He said he wanted you to consider him and his difficulties and that he needed your counsel here. Evidently he contemplates seeking your advice upon questions of policy from time to time, outside of your judicial duties, but he is chiefly solicitous to secure your presence on the bench, not only to deal with all the insular questions, but, also, those affecting labor and the trusts. He evi-

[14] Roosevelt to Taft, Oct. 21, 1902.

dently thinks he has secured the right man in Holmes and now seeks you, because, as he remarked to me, you will approach all the industrial questions without fear of the effect upon yourself, of either the J. P. Morgans or of the labor leaders. He thinks you have pretty well solved the chief Philippine questions, and it only needs someone else like General Wright to go on and build on the foundations you have laid. . . . I think he has been brought face to face with the labor and trust questions since he had his talk with you [in February, 1902], and he does not deem it of so much importance as he did then that you should stay in the Philippines.

Henry Taft had also conferred with Secretary Root, who had declared that, in his personal view, Will Taft should not go on the bench at all but should "reserve yourself for another career." Loyalty to the President, however, had made it impossible for him to emphasize this at a time when Roosevelt was seeking to put him on the court. Brother Henry told of this conversation too:

. . . he said that you had a personality which made you nothing but friends and, finally, that you came from Ohio, the home of presidents. He could not see why you should not be the surest candidate as Roosevelt's successor, at the end of his second term.[15]

Roosevelt and Taft were drawn very much closer to each other by this troublesome matter of elevation to the Supreme Court. It was the real beginning of an extraordinary friendship based on mutual respect, admiration, even love.

"I have never in my life felt like criticizing anything that Will did, but, upon my word, I do feel like criticizing this mental attitude of his!" Roosevelt indignantly wrote when informed of Taft's suspicion that Catholic antagonisms were behind the whole matter. "It would never have entered my head so much as to deny . . . that I would have given half a second's thought to any such consideration. I should have brushed it aside so contemptuously as to forget it immediately afterwards." [16]

So the air was cleared of suspicion. Entirely satisfied, Taft apologized for his unworthy apprehensions. "I feel ashamed . . ." he wrote to Roosevelt, "but when one is ten thousand miles away

[15] H. W. Taft to Taft, Jan. 10, 1903. [16] Roosevelt to H. W. Taft, Jan. 19, 1903.

from home he has a very indefinite knowledge of how his course really strikes people. I heard . . . that the Catholics wanted my head and . . . the Presbyterians and Evangelicals had been abusing me for not going to church and for favoring the Catholics. I feared a man doubly damned might be heavy for you to carry. . . . With my respectful compliments to Mrs. Roosevelt, believe, respectfully, gratefully and affectionately . . ."[17]

The President decided, for reasons which are not clear, that he would not select Bowers and that Taft was essential on the Supreme Court. On January 6, 1903, another letter arrived at the governor's office in Manila; it was half apologetic and completely affectionate:

I am awfully sorry, old man, but after faithful effort for a month to try to arrange matters on the basis you wanted I find that I shall have to bring you home and put you on the Supreme Court. I am very sorry. I have the greatest confidence in your judgment; but after all, old fellow, if you will permit me to say so, I am President and see the whole field. The responsibility for any error must ultimately come upon me, and therefore I cannot shirk this responsibility or in the last resort yield to anyone else's decision if my judgment is against it. . . . I am very sorry if what I am doing displeases you, but as I said, old man, this is one of the cases where the President, if he is fit for his position, must take the responsibility and put the men on whom he most relies in the particular positions in which he himself thinks they can render the greatest public good.

The President added that he would nominate General Wright for the position of civil governor. Associate Justice Shiras had agreed to withhold his resignation until the middle of February. It would not be necessary for Taft to reach Washington until August, 1903; thus he would have nine additional months in the archipelago.[18] This was, of course, a royal command, disobeyed only at great peril. But Taft, too, was stubborn. Brother Henry had warned the President of this during the conversations at the White House.

"I told him . . . you sat down hard when you did sit— to

[17] Taft to Roosevelt, March 4, 1903. [18] Roosevelt to Taft, Nov. 26, 1902.

"HOW IS THE HORSE?" TAFT AND HIS SON, CHARLIE. SUMMER OF 1903

See page 236]

See page 256]

"I HAVE NO APTITUDE FOR MANAGING AN ARMY"

which he responded, with a laugh, that he had a habit of doing so too," he wrote to Manila.[19]

So this became a contest between equals. The civil governor of the Philippines was not ready, even now, to desert his charges. A cable sped to Washington:

Recognize soldier's duty to obey orders. Before orders irrevocable by action, however, I presume on our personal friendship even in the face of letter to make one more appeal, in which I lay aside wholly my strong personal disinclination to leave work of intense interest half done. No man is indispensable, my death would little interfere with progress, but my withdrawal more serious. Circumstances last three years have convinced me these people controlled largely by personal feeling that I am their friend and stand for a policy of confidence in them and belief in their future and for extension self-government as they show themselves worthy. Visit to Rome and proposals urged there assure them of my sympathy in regard to friars in respect of whose far-reaching influence they are morbidly suspicious. Announcement of withdrawal pending settlement of church questions, economic crises and formative period when opinions of all parties are being slowly molded for the better will, I fear, give impression that change of policy is intended because other reasons for action will not be understood. My successor's task thus made much heavier because any loss people's confidence distinctly retards our work here. I feel it is my duty to say this. If your judgment is unshaken I bow to it and shall earnestly and enthusiastically labor to settle question friars' lands before I leave and to convince the people that no change of policy is at hand.[20]

—3—

Taft did not believe that his plea would be effective. He felt that "the President has made up his mind."[21] But the morning of January 10, 1903, was to be one of the proudest and happiest of his life; the elation which surged through him was not greater even on that March day, in 1909, when he swore to defend, as president,

[19] H. W. Taft to Taft, Jan. 10, 1903. [20] Taft to Roosevelt, Jan. 8, 1903. [21] Taft to C. P. Taft, Jan. 7, 1903.

the Constitution and the laws of the United States. For on the
morning of January 10 the murmur of many voices, outside the
gates of Malacanan Palace, rose above the sound of boatmen on the
Pasig River. The military guards at the gates— for long years they
had been ready to shut them against advancing mobs— smiled,
now, and swung them open. In marched the advance guard of a
column of Filipinos. To the civil governor and Mrs. Taft, watching
from the windows, it seemed that the line was endless. Flags waved
in the morning air. Bands blared. Every third or fourth Filipino,
strutting with pride over the distinction, carried a banner or trans-
parency with, in Spanish, "Queremos Taft!" or, in English, "We
Want Taft!" lettered upon it.

There were, of course, to be speeches; florid speeches in Spanish
praising the beloved Taft. Soon some six thousand Filipinos were
massed in front of the palace waiting for the feast of oratory from
the leaders who had entered Malacanan and were standing, with
the civil governor and Mrs. Taft, on a balcony. Dr. Dominador
Gomez, a labor leader of suspiciously radical views, began it by
saying that Governor Taft was a "saint with the power to perform
the great miracle" of uniting all of the factions in the islands. Dr.
Xeres Burgos, who had been prominent in the insurgency, cried
that no calamity— earthquakes or typhoons or plagues— could be
so fearful as the departure from the islands of Taft. Tomaso G. de
Rosario chose the neat figure of comparing Mr. Taft to a ship's
rudder which avoided the shoals and the rocks. Pedro A. Paterno—
the identical Paterno whom Taft had been forced to chastise for his
revolutionary activities some two years before— was easily the
winner when he said that "as Christ had converted the cross into a
symbol of glory and triumph, so had Governor Taft turned a dying
people to the light and life of modern liberties." [22]

It was all very moving. Meanwhile less colorful but more
important influences were at work to retain Taft. Commissioners
Worcester, Ide and Smith cabled the President stating that grave
risk would attend his going.[23] A group of distinguished Filipino
leaders added a plea of their own. They notified Roosevelt that
their fellow countrymen "have absolute confidence in Taft." He

---

[22] Taft, Mrs. W. H., *Recollections of Full Years*, pp. 267-269; *Literary Digest*, Jan.
24, 1903. [23] Worcester, Ide and Smith to Roosevelt, Jan. 7, 1903.

was the only man "able to count upon the co-operation of all the political parties."

"We solemnly affirm that feelings Philippine people would be deeply hurt by the departure of Taft," concluded the cable. It was signed by the native members of the Philippine Commission— Señores de Tavera, Legarda and Luzuriaga. Also by Chief Justice Arellano of the Supreme Court and others of equal standing.[24]

The telegraph room at the White House clicked with the receipt of these messages. Roosevelt read them and wrote, somewhat plaintively, to Henry Taft that "Will sprung a surprise on me. He must have given the contents . . . of my letter to a number of the natives and I received the most fervid telegrams from them. . . .

"I suppose Will could not help letting the natives know before he came to a conclusion; but in any event I think he has carried his point . . . as long as this is the tack on which the native mind is working it would be inadvisable to take him away." [25]

"All right, you shall stay where you are," the President cabled to Malacanan.[26]

—4—

So life settled calmly into its accustomed groove again and none but familiar worries, infinitely less bothersome to William Howard Taft than new and unfamiliar ones, remained. Conditions in the islands continued to be bad as the days of 1903 became weeks and the weeks turned into months. But it was possible to do something about famine, plague and murderous bands of robbers in the hills; Taft did not doubt his competence in dealing with them. Even the case of Padre Gregorio Aglipai, an Ilokano priest, was not too troublesome. Padre Aglipai had been stirring up considerable excitement since October, 1902, by starting an independent church movement which, although professing to be Roman Catholic, did not accept the authority of the Pope. He had won many followers because of Rome's refusal to withdraw the Spanish friars. He came into conflict with the Philippine Commission when he began to seize churches and other property which allegedly belonged to the

[24] Tavera et al., to Roosevelt, Jan. 7, 1903. [25] Roosevelt to H. W. Taft, Jan. 12, 1903. [26] Roosevelt to Taft, Jan. 13, 1903.

old regime. Taft handled the situation smoothly. He said that the government had no interest in church schisms. But the laws against the seizure of property would be enforced.[27]

Taft's health was not good during the first part of 1903. But he was, on the whole, contented. He would continue as civil governor for about two years more. He would settle the friars' lands quarrel, carry out a public works program, stabilize the currency, conduct the census, prepare the Filipinos for the election of the Assembly which would give them further privileges in self-government although not independence. Then he would return to the United States to practice law or, if the fates were kind, to mount the Supreme Court. But these placid expectations were soon shattered; even while he enjoyed them, although Taft did not know it, still another letter from the President was en route to the Philippines. Not only that; the currents of the outside world had found their way to the shores of the happy isles. No matter how fast he swam, no matter how agile his divings and twistings, Taft could not escape those currents. He might well and truthfully have protested, when finally they swirled him into troubled waters, that the fault was not in himself but in his stars.

The campaign of 1904 kept intruding, for example, on the peace of the Philippines. Henry Taft warned that there "has been some talk in the newspapers about the opponents of Roosevelt taking you up as their candidate for the nomination in 1904." Behind the gossip, he added, was the hostility of the large business interests to the President's trust-control program. Roosevelt did not have the wholehearted support of the Republican machine. His friendly attitude toward the Negro had alienated many southern Republican leaders.

"The condition of affairs here is such," Henry said, "that it is not at all improbable that the opponents of Roosevelt may wish to use your name in connection with the nomination for the presidency." [28]

Taft was, of course, disgusted. ". . . the moneyed interests of Wall Street . . . cannot use my name for the reason that I would not be a candidate," he answered. "I think his nomination is inevitable and I think it ought to be. If they were to succeed in

<hr/>

[27] Taft to Roosevelt, Nov. 9, 1903. [28] H. W. Taft to Taft, Feb. 24, March 2, 1903.

beating Roosevelt, they would beat the Republican party. . . . I do
not think they have any serious idea of using my name and I find it
difficult to treat the matter in a sober way." [29] A few weeks later he
wrote his brother again:

> You seem to have some fear . . . that if you did not warn
> me . . . I should have the presidential bee buzzing in my bon-
> net . . . I beg to assure you . . . that there is not the slightest dan-
> ger of my being afflicted with any such defect in my hearing
> organs.[30]

"You know it, and I know it, and Dick ought to know it. I am
not running for president either in 1904 or 1908," he wrote
vehemently when Charles P. Taft relayed a suggestion from Charles
Dick, a Hanna lieutenant, that Taft should stand for governor of
Ohio in 1903 as a curtain raiser for the presidency in 1908.[31]

In short, like General William T. Sherman in the campaign of
1884, Taft had no desire for the nomination, no yearning for the
White House, no qualifications— in his own judgment— for the
post. He might have quoted, had he known it, the violent answer
of the Union general that he would be "a fool, a madman, an ass"
to embark on any such career.[32] But Taft did not have the flinty
character of that warrior and his resolution was, in the end, to be
broken down. In the spring of 1903, as these appeals continued, he
wanted only to finish his work in the Philippines. And then, to add
a touch of the ludicrous, the Bellamy Storers began to write from
Vienna that he must go to Washington at whatever cost to save
mad Theodore Roosevelt from himself, to save the world from a
war of mad Theodore's making. At this, Taft could chuckle.

Among the other problems which confronted President Roosevelt were the persistent refusal of Venezuela to pay certain legitimate debts to foreign countries and the danger that Germany and
England might collect their money by force of arms. Roosevelt did
not object to this form of collection, in itself, but he was apprehensive that in applying it the nations of Europe might follow their
time-honored policy of acquiring some land. This, of course, would

---

[29] Taft to H. W. Taft, April 16, 1903. [30] Idem, June 7, 1903. [31] Taft to C. P. Taft,
Feb. 24, 1903. [32] North American Review, December, 1888.

be in violation of the Monroe Doctrine. In December, 1902, British gunboats hurled a few shells at a Venezuelan port. During the next few months there were alarming rumors that Roosevelt had threatened the German Kaiser, William II, with war unless he desisted from further imperialistic gestures. Undoubtedly Roosevelt helped to spread the rumors. It is also true that the United States was, in fact, far from war with Germany.[33]

In Europe, however, a war was considered not improbable— reported Mrs. Bellamy Storer in February, 1903— because of the "strenuous hotheadedness of two men; the Kaiser and Theodore Roosevelt." They were, she said, very much alike. She told horrific stories of the changes which had swept over Roosevelt upon entering the White House. She was present when a report had reached him that Civil Governor Taft and Military Governor Chaffee were having their dispute over the powers of the courts in the Philippines.

"They've got to agree!" she heard the President say. "By Jove, I'll make them agree!"

She cited, in addition, a distressing incident which occurred when the French ambassador to the United States had called on the President, with all due formality, to ask his presence at the Rochambeau celebration. Roosevelt, Mrs. Storer wrote, had received his excellency "reclining on a couch, with his riding boots on." He did not arise. He said that he and his daughter, Alice, would attend the gathering. Then he jumped up suddenly and cried out, 'Alice and I are toughs, that is what we are, toughs!' . . .

"Imagine," implored Mrs. Storer in her appeal to Taft, "the feelings of the French ambassador! Now all this would be of little moment anywhere else, but where it is, it is dangerous and what may not another year bring forth?"[34]

Bellamy Storer, now American ambassador to Austria, echoed the words of his wife. "William," he wrote, "I almost think I'd feel safe if you were at home. . . . We want men who keep their heads cool . . . who do not need to jump around to show that they are alive."[35] But Taft declined to be alarmed, and he tried to soothe his friends:

[33] Pringle, H. F., *op. cit.*, pp. 281-289. [34] Mrs. Bellamy Storer to Taft, Feb. 1, 1903. [35] Bellamy Storer to Taft, Feb. 3, 1903.

I understand something of the condition of mind, or rather the condition of nerves, in which Theodore Roosevelt finds himself, though we have very different dispositions in the matter of talking. His mind is exceedingly active, and when he is worried he talks about the matters that worry him, indeed he cannot help talking about them, and he is not especially careful, as he ought to be, with respect to the persons to whom he talks. Nervousness and worry loosen his tongue, but it would be quite a mistake and quite an injustice to him to suppose that his action will follow his words where he is merely thinking aloud. . . . With me it is somewhat different. The more I worry the less I talk. I do not think this is as safe a condition for a person as that which relieves itself by the use of the tongue, but the nervousness is present in both of us, and if I were to express or follow the impulses that come to me in a condition of worry it would lead to disastrous results. Now I think that Theodore Roosevelt is no more likely to follow out his nervously spoken impulses and extreme statements . . . than I am those thoughts caused in the same way.[36]

Taft mentioned the alarmist Storer communications in a letter to a Cincinnati friend: ". . . they seemed greatly troubled about the President's attitude toward Germany . . . and were very strenuous in the argument that I ought to be in Washington to hold 'Teddy' down. . . . I wrote . . . that their fears . . . had but slight, if any, foundation." [37]

On March 27, 1903, Taft's hopes that he would be allowed to stay in the Philippines were blasted again, this time permanently. The letter which President Roosevelt had written the middle of February arrived on that day. "You will think I am a variety of the horse leech's daughter," apologized the President:

The worst calamity that could happen to me . . . is impending because Root tells me that he will have to leave me next fall. I wish to heaven that I did *not* feel as strongly as I do about two or three men in public life. But I *do*. I want to ask you whether if I can

[36] Taft to Mrs. Bellamy Storer, March 23, 1903. [37] Taft to Annie G. Roelker, April 26, 1903.

persuade Root to stay until a year hence, you cannot come back and take his place.

The President pointed out— and this was one of the arguments which persuaded Taft to become secretary of war— that he would still have charge of the Philippine Islands inasmuch as the archipelago was administered in Washington by the War Department. Thus, "from the standpoint of the interests of the islands alone you could well afford to take the place." Nor was the President, on this occasion, taking any chance that Taft's impending departure might start another bombardment of protest from the Filipinos.

"I do not want you to mention this to a soul, American or Filipino," he ordered, "for I desire your decision on your own thought and on the proposition's merit by itself."

He added, warmly, that as president he needed "the aid and comfort you would be to me not merely as secretary of war, not merely as director of the affairs in the Philippines, but as my counselor and adviser in all the great questions that come up." And then he scribbled as a postscript one of those Rooseveltian touches which so enchanted the men with whom he worked.

If only there were three of you! Then I would have put one of you on the Supreme Court, as the Ohio member, in place of good Day [Associate Justice William R. Day, appointed instead of Taft]; one of you in Root's place as secretary of war, when he goes out; and one of you permanently governor of the Philippines. No one can quite take your place as governor; but no one of whom I can now think save only you can at all take Root's place as secretary.[38]

Taft obeyed that part of the President's order which said that the matter was not to be mentioned to any of the Filipino leaders. It was, however, quite impossible for him to reach so important a decision without again conferring with the members of his family. This time it was not necessary to use the cables. He copied the President's letter and dispatched it toward Cincinnati.

"Please circulate this letter as quickly as possible to the family so that I may get their judgment," Will Taft asked Charles. He

[38] Roosevelt to Taft, Feb. 14, 1903.

specified that it should go to Henry, Horace and his mother. The civil governor was not without natural reactions of pride that the President of the United States had summoned him for a third time: "Roosevelt's attitude seems to be expressed by the method in which Root paraphrased . . . the attitude of the Filipino people toward me, as 'I want you, my honey, yes, I do.' . . ."

Taft added that the post of secretary of war "would not be particularly congenial" except to the extent that it still related to the Philippine Islands. He was, however, inclined to accept, and this was for the additional reason that amoebic dysentery had been discovered in his system. It was, he said, "a disease which sometimes defies the efforts of the physicians in the tropics." [39]

Root, in a letter urging Taft to become his successor in the War Department, had already pointed out that the civil governor was working too hard, that nature "doesn't mean men to work that way in the tropics and she punishes them for it in time." [40] At about this time Taft was forced to his bed by the disease and so cabled to Washington. [41]

"Seriously concerned for your health," telegraphed the President. "Conscientiously believe this attack emphasizes advice in my letter and Root's which you should receive at about this time." [42]

But there was, in Taft's mind, a further obstacle to life in Washington; the low salary of a Cabinet member. He told the President that he had not been able to save a single dollar out of his generous compensation in the Philippines. The premiums on his life insurance, alone, came to $2,000 a year:

You know by experience the cost of living in Washington. You know, too, the obligations that are usually felt by cabinet officers in the matter of entertainment, and you know the kind of a dog's life, not that a cabinet officer, but that his wife, has to live in trying to keep up appearances on an insufficient salary. [43]

He accepted, however, and the President wrote that the cost of Washington life was not so excessive as might be supposed:

[39] Taft to C. P. Taft, March 27, 1903. [40] Root to Taft, Feb. 20, 1903. [41] Taft to Root, March 27, 1903. [42] Roosevelt to Taft, March 28, 1903. [43] Taft to Roosevelt, April 3, 1903.

I hope you will live just exactly as you and I did when you were solicitor general and I civil service commissioner. Mrs. Roosevelt comes a great deal nearer my ideal than I do myself, and she never minded our not having champagne at our dinners, for instance. At first I did, but I got over it; and moreover I found out that we could do most of our entertaining at Sunday evening high tea. I should feel that you added dignity to my administration if you lived in the simplest way as cabinet member. . . . Thank Heaven you are to be with me! [44]

Taft was not deceived by this bright picture of poverty combined with dignity. He was aware that his wife would not at all enjoy economizing, particularly now that her husband was dwelling amidst the bigwigs once again. To Howard Hollister, his boyhood friend, Taft expressed his misgivings:

The President said he hoped I would live quietly and modestly. . . . You should see Nellie's lip curl at the suggestion of Sunday high teas and dinner parties without champagne. [45]

Before this, however, Taft's generous brother had cabled that the entire Taft family was heartily in favor of his going to Washington. Charles P. Taft offered, as he was invariably to do, to make up any deficit: ". . . rely on me for $6,000 annually, more if necessary," he cabled. [46] So Secretary of War Taft would have, with his salary of $8,000, a total of at least $14,000 a year. Mrs. Taft was very much pleased that the graveyard of the Supreme Court had been escaped once more.

"This . . ." she remembered, "was in line with the kind of work I wanted my husband to do, the kind of career I wanted for him and expected him to have." [47]

So at last the viceroy was to leave his charges. He had about six months in which to settle, in so far as he could, the perplexities which remained and to convince his wards that General Wright, who would be the new civil governor, loved them as much as he did himself. Taft was filled with forebodings, as always, about his ability to do the new work well. Even a friendly letter from Root—

[44] Roosevelt to Taft, June 9, 1903. [45] Taft to H. C. Hollister, Sept. 21, 1903. [46] C. P. Taft to Taft, May 6, 1903. [47] Taft, Mrs. W. H., op. cit., pp. 269-270.

"I consider you one of the most valuable assets of the United States"— could not dispel the apprehensions with which he viewed the future.

"The confidential relation with the President . . . will, of course, be most pleasant, instructive and interesting," Taft wrote. "Following Secretary Root . . . leaves me no opportunity to distinction as secretary of war. All I can do is merely to follow . . . his footsteps." [48]

Taft announced that he would leave Manila on December 23, 1903, on the S.S. *Korea*. He was given a reception by the English Club a fortnight before he sailed and he recounted, in a brief address, the previous occasions when his recall to Washington had seemed inevitable:

In accepting your farewell I am conscious of a feeling on your part that these farewells are somewhat long drawn out. I am reminded of that passage in the operetta of *The Pirates of Penzance* where the king of the pirates is about to depart and sings a number of verses in a song which ends, "We go! We go!" and the refrain of the chorus is, in response, "But you don't go!" [49]

This time he really left.

[48] Taft to Mrs. Bellamy Storer, Oct. 26, 1903. [49] MS. copy of speech, Dec. 10, 1903, Taft papers.

CHAPTER XVI

WAR LORD

THEODORE ROOSEVELT might have been a degree disturbed, as he waited with anticipation for the arrival of his new secretary of war, had he been permitted to read certain private letters of William Howard Taft. For Taft in 1903, as throughout his life, was a stubborn advocate of peace.

"I find it hard, myself, to subscribe to the Monroe Doctrine," he had written nine months before, "and to deem it of sufficient importance to warrant, as Bismarck said with respect to the Turkish question, 'the loss of the bones of one Pomeranian grenadier.' . . ."[1]

"I have no particular aptitude for managing an army," he wrote on a second occasion, "nor do I know anything about it."[2]

But these views, if heretical, were actually not a basic disqualification. Taft was to change his mind, no doubt largely through conversion at Roosevelt's hands, regarding the Monroe Doctrine. And as far as the army was concerned, the President would run it himself. Taft was being brought home for an entirely different purpose. He had won a wide measure of public confidence during his two and a half years in the Philippines. His presence in the Cabinet would strengthen the administration. He would be a useful and effective spellbinder in the fast-approaching campaign of 1904. His legal knowledge was essential, now that Elihu Root had retired, to a chief executive who knew very little about the law.

War clouds covered the Far East as Taft, on the S.S. *Korea,* returned to the United States. President Roosevelt, in Washington, was anxiously watching the growing friction between Russia and Japan. He was aware that the peace of Europe was closely linked, all too closely, with peace in the Orient. He believed that the safety of American interests— that is to say, trade— depended upon a

[1] Taft to Bellamy Storer, March 23, 1903. [2] Taft to Mrs. Bellamy Storer, Oct. 26, 1903.

balance of power between Russia and Japan. Roosevelt was to play a very important part, perhaps a more important one than he realized, in the affairs of the East. It is enough to point out, for the moment, that he was suspicious of both Japan and Russia. But he feared Russia the more. His sympathies, as yet unspoken, were with Japan in her desire to control Korea.[3] The President had no intention, however, at the close of 1903, of taking any overt action.

A year and a half later, in July, 1905, Secretary of War Taft would visit Japan as the official emissary of the President and would have an extraordinary conversation with Count Katsura, the Japanese premier. By then, fortunately, he had already been received by the highest officials of that nation on two occasions. The first time was en route to the Philippines in the spring of 1900. He stopped again on his return to Washington in January, 1904. No evidence exists to indicate that this visit was at the suggestion of the White House. On November 23, 1903, Taft was informed by Lloyd C. Griscom, the American minister at Tokyo, that the Japanese Emperor would be "gratified" if he would call. Taft promptly agreed to do so.[4] He was received by the Emperor on January 6 and was used by that monarch as an avenue for a communication to Roosevelt. The cable which Taft sent after the interview confirmed the probability of war between Russia and Japan:

Had audience and luncheon with the Emperor yesterday in the course of which he said:
"In view of the most friendly relations existing between Japan and the United States we feel special pleasure in extending to you our cordial welcome. It is our sincere desire to promote the further development and consolidation of those friendly relations. You are no doubt aware of the gravity of the actual situation in the Far East. It has been our earnest endeavor to bring about a pacific solution of the question and we will still continue to exert our efforts in the interest of peace. We wish you will upon your return home convey this message to the President of the United States."

Taft also saw Marquis Ito, who was a statesman with conciliatory views and an advocate of peace. Ito, too, agreed that war was

---

[3] Pringle, H. F., *Theodore Roosevelt, a Biography*, pp. 376-380. [4] Lloyd C. Griscom to Taft; Taft to Lloyd C. Griscom, Nov. 23, 1903.

inevitable. So did Minister Griscom. So did all other Japanese authorities whom Taft had seen.[5]

The brief pause in Japan had its lighter side. The Japanese government was aware that Taft was going home to become secretary of war, and General Terauchi, the Japanese minister of war, naturally assumed that his guest was an expert in military matters. So a regimental review was arranged in his honor. The conversation at this and other functions was replete with the jargon, as incomprehensible to Taft as Sanskrit, of the professional soldier. One of the warriors in attendance was General Kodama, ultimately chief of staff, who had been military governor of Formosa. The general felt that a bond existed between himself and this large American. Had not they both been in supreme command of subject peoples?

"We had to kill a good many before they would be good," confided General Kodama. "But then, of course, you understand— you know, you know!"

Heroically, the former civil governor of the Philippines suppressed his laughter. No, he confessed, he had not personally killed a single Filipino nor even ordered the death of one.[6]

—2—

Mrs. Taft decided to remain in Santa Barbara for the rest of the winter. The new secretary of war, arriving in Washington the end of January, 1904, promptly discovered— if he was not aware of it before— that the administration of the War Department was to be an insignificant part of his work. Nor did he find the sessions of Roosevelt's Cabinet either interesting or important. He told of the first meeting with the President's advisers: "It was largely devoted to politics. I suppose it is natural, but it seems to me . . . undignified for us to devote so much time to mere political discussion. Perhaps I'll get over this after I become saturated with the politics of the nation." [7]

Yet Taft's relations with the President were, from the start, charming. He tried to reassure Mrs. Taft, who never quite sur-

[5] Taft to Root, Jan. 7, 1904. [6] Taft, Mrs. W. H., *Recollections of Full Years*, pp. 275-276. [7] Taft to Helen H. Taft, Feb. 2, 1904.

rendered to Rooseveltian wiles: "The President seems really to take much comfort that I am in his Cabinet. He tells me so and then he tells people who tell me. He is a very sweet-natured man and a very trusting man when he believes in one. I am growing to be very fond of him. I hope you will agree with me when you have fuller opportunities of observation." [8]

"The President is very sympathetic and renders every assistance he can," Taft reported after further contacts. "He takes suggestions easily and is very amenable to change when reasoned with." [9]

The new boy enjoyed a minor triumph, too, during the first weeks. He advised, on technical grounds, against making a $4,000,-000 payment with respect to the Panama Canal. Roosevelt, however, was anxious to accelerate the work of starting the canal. Attorney General Philander C. Knox had given the opinion that it was legal.

"All the rest of the Cabinet agreed with the President . . ." Taft said. "I warned the President . . . of the mistake he was making. . . . Today I observe they have taken a back track and decided to delay the payment of the money until the time I said it should be delayed to." [10]

As presidential cabinets go, the official family of Theodore Roosevelt was no better or worse than the average. It was adorned by the sparkling John Hay who, if he was too completely dominated by the President in the conduct of foreign affairs, was a gentleman of intelligence, wit and culture. Knox, the head of the law department, was an excellent lawyer. The secretary of the navy, John D. Long, was a courteous gentleman of the old school; his courtesy was sometimes strained, though, by the fact that he had been secretary of the navy when Theodore Roosevelt had been merely an upstart of an assistant secretary. Mr. Long found the reversal of positions very confusing; indeed, everything had been confusing since McKinley was slain. The other members were even less colorful. Leslie M. Shaw was secretary of the treasury. James Wilson, who was apparently striving for an endurance record and would fill the same post for Taft as under McKinley and Roosevelt, was secretary of agriculture. George B. Cortelyou was secretary of the newly created Department of Commerce and Labor. Ethan A. Hitchcock was secretary of the interior and Robert J. Wynne was

[8] Idem, March 18, 1904. [9] Idem, March 30, 1904. [10] Idem, March 4, 1904.

postmaster general. John Hay was getting old and would live hardly more than a year. Knox had political ambitions. No wonder that Roosevelt leaned more and more, as the weeks passed, on his friend, Will Taft.

For the President, facing the campaign of 1904, was in a jumpy mood. About a year earlier, defending his program in the West, Roosevelt had mourned that he would never be elected president in his own right. The roars of the crowd meant nothing, he said. Mark Hanna was opposed to his nomination. The New York Republican machine was conspiring to defeat him.

"I have no faction, no money," said the lachrymose Theodore. "I will become a subject for elimination." [11]

He was a little less blue in March, 1904. But he was still apprehensive. It is extraordinary, but true, that Roosevelt seems to have quite forgotten the really unusual accomplishments of his brief administration. He had settled, amid frenzied public applause, a coal strike in the fall of 1902. He had inaugurated his corporation-control policy by the Northern Securities suit. He had begun regulation of the railroads through the passage of the Elkins act which forbade rebating. He had spanked the "Dagos," as he termed them, of Venezuela. He had obtained a victory for the United States in the Alaska boundary dispute. Above all, he had seized Panama. Soon the dirt would fly. The voters knew little and cared less about the injustice done to the republic of Colombia. The Colombians, in the public mind, were dirty little Dagos too.

Instead of remembering these victories, Roosevelt fretted over the fact that nothing had been done about the tariff. He had backed away from currency reform because he could not understand finance— and now concluded that the voters would punish him for his negligence. He was afraid that greedy old men of the G.A.R., who again were asking for pension increases, might throw their strength against him. So, in March, 1904, he reached into the treasury and awarded them $5,000,000 additional a year.[12] Then he continued to worry. Taft was much more optimistic. He assured the President that Ohio was safe.[13]

"The fight may be close in New York," Taft concluded, "but I

[11] Denison, Lindsey, "Seven Years of Roosevelt," *Circle*, March, 1909. [12] Pringle, *op. cit.*, pp. 342-343. [13] Taft to Roosevelt, Feb. 8, 1904.

cannot think that there is the slightest danger in the country of Democratic victory." [14]

The day was not very far distant when Taft, quailing before the voters himself, would be far more sympathetic to the pre-election weaknesses of a president. During the 1904 campaign, however, he was a shade impatient with Roosevelt.

Certain interests are using the present critical situation to frighten him into some promises. I shall be much disappointed in him if he yields. He ought to stand "pat." His election is, in my judgment, sure and at any rate, he ought not to sacrifice his principles already announced by Secretary Root, by McKinley and by myself.

"I would not run for president if you guaranteed the office," Taft added virtuously. "It is awful to be made afraid of one's shadow."

Thus critical, the secretary of war had in mind an issue close to his heart. Ever since returning from the Philippines he had continued to work for free trade or, at least, lower tariffs between the United States and the islands. The commodities principally affected were sugar and tobacco and protests began to flow in from the sugar interests of the West and from the tobacco growers of the Connecticut valley. Taft was inconsiderate enough to work his demands for tariff cuts into pro-Roosevelt campaign speeches and the President, it appears, protested.

"I wrote . . . that of course he would not expect me to retract my position, but that if my presence in the Cabinet embarrassed him I would retire at once," Taft explained.[15]

"Fiddledeedee!" was Roosevelt's prompt answer. "I shall never send you another letter of complaint if it produces such awful results. . . . As for your retiring from the Cabinet, upon my word, Will, I think you have nerves, or something." [16]

In every other respect, Taft's speeches were to be as orthodox as they were partisan, although he did not enjoy himself on the stump.

[14] Taft to Helen H. Taft, March 31, 1904. [15] *Idem,* Oct. 12, 1904. [16] Roosevelt to Taft, Oct. 11, 1904.

"The next ten days," he wrote, "I must devote myself to the preparation of a political speech. . . . I don't know whether I shall make a failure . . . or not. The bench disqualifies one in this respect." [17]

—3—

But Taft was signally successful— he was, of course, a confirmed Republican— in suppressing any judicial liabilities incurred during his services on the bench. He had a low opinion of Alton B. Parker, who had been a distinguished jurist, himself, and was now the Democratic presidential candidate. The trouble with Parker, Taft said, "is that no one knows what he thinks about anything . . . he is not in favor of anything and is not opposed to anything." [18] In other words, he had a judicial mind. As for the political organization which presumed to oppose the G.O.P.:

The great trouble about the Democratic party is that it is not a party at all, in the proper sense of that term. It is a conglomeration of irreconcilable elements that have no solidarity so far as carrying through any policy affirmatively is concerned. Even in the matter of the tariff, with respect to which Cleveland at one time seemed to have made them more or less solid, they now differ so widely that were they to come into power the only effect would be to frighten everybody without really accomplishing anything.[19]

This was accurate enough. The nomination of Judge Parker had been a Democratic gesture toward the moneyed East and a repudiation of Bryan and western liberalism. It was a disastrous surrender of principle, certain to end in defeat. In one or two of his major speeches, however, Taft went a great deal further. He defended, literally, every controversial aspect of the Roosevelt administration. He said that the President had been wholly right even in the Panama rape and in the pension grab.

"I have not looked into the Panama question because it all took place while I was away," he admitted before the campaign. "I suppose I shall have to examine the papers with a view to discussing the matter on the stump." [20]

[17] Taft to Helen H. Taft, Aug. 15, 1904. [18] *Idem,* March 31, April 15, 1904. [19] Taft to Horace D. Taft, Aug. 4, 1904. [20] *Idem,* Feb. 6, 1904.

Perhaps he did study the mass of documents and the compli-cated issues of international law. But he did so, if at all, with the mind of a counsel for the defense rather than that of a judge; such was his role in the spring and summer of 1904. His speeches might have been dictated by the President, so closely did they echo the insistence ultimately voiced by Roosevelt that every step "was taken with the utmost care . . . was carried out with the highest, finest, and nicest standards of public and governmental ethics." [21] Taft did not mention the parts played by M. Philippe Bunau-Varilla, of France, and William Nelson Cromwell, the New York attorney, in inciting the revolt of Panama from the republic of Colombia. He did not mention— possibly he had not studied the documents carefully enough and did not know it— that the conspiracy on the isthmus was a clever and successful scheme to make money for unidentified stockholders. In an address at Montpelier, Ver-mont, in August, the secretary of war reviewed the issues at length. He was just as inaccurate in his language as Roosevelt. He used all the familiar phrases, such as "a Colombian attempt to black-mail the United States" into paying more money for the right to build a canal. He portrayed the Panamanians as liberty-loving patriots who tore themselves loose from the tyrant's chains on their own volition.

"Our course of dealing with Colombia," said Mr. Taft, "has been characterized by the greatest patience and honor and probity. Colombia's course has been vacillating and dishonorable." [22]

Nor did the disqualifying fairness of his judicial years deter Taft from attributing all virtues to the G.O.P. and all vices to Democracy. He said:

Since the birth of the Republican party it has stood for the affirmative of every proposition . . . which involved doing some-thing for the country. The Democratic party has generally stood for negation. . . . The Republican party dates back to 1854, when it was organized to resist the encroachments of the slave power and ultimately to save the Union and to eradicate the cancer of slavery from the body politic. It carried on a four years' war of proportions never before and never since exceeded. It fought the way of the government back to the resumption of specie payments from the

21 *Outlook*, Oct. 7, 1911. 22 *Addresses*, Vol. I, pp. 251-252.

sea of . . . depreciated paper currency. It built the Pacific railroads, which united the East and the West and brought into close contact with the markets of the world the vast expanse of territory between the Mississippi and the Rocky Mountains. A hundred other great governmental policies it has carried out since 1861 . . . policies in all of which it has been opposed by the Democratic party.[23]

Alas, for the brief reach of human memory! Taft could not have remembered, as he thus hurled anathema, his own undergraduate oration at Yale: "The Vitality of the Democratic Party, Its Causes." Then, he had expressed the thought that the election of 1876 had probably been stolen by the G.O.P. Then, he had praised the Jeffersonian conception of states' rights. And two years later, under the elms of New Haven, Senior Orator Taft had declared that the Republican party had lost its grip on the affections of the people.[24] Taft had forgotten these early utterances, as men always do. He was pleased, but not surprised, when victory came in November, 1904.

"The victory is very complete," he said, "and shows . . . that the American people are not to be misled by humbug, for that was all that the present campaign on the part of the Democrats had as capital." [25]

Taft was glad when it was all over—"A national campaign for the presidency is to me a nightmare"— was his summation of the weeks just ended. He continued to spurn suggestions, more frequent now because of the Republican victory and the added prominence which had come to him in the campaign, that he was the inevitable candidate for 1908.[26] Despite the appointment of Justice Day, who was also from Ohio, Taft persisted in hoping that the Supreme Court was a possibility. Everyone told him that he would be the next chief justice, that Roosevelt could make no other appointment. But would Chief Justice Fuller resign or die? Was Attorney General Knox a more probable candidate?[27] Taft was a little ghoulish as he pondered the unreasonable longevity of Chief Justice Fuller. He told Mrs. Taft of a conversation with Associate Justice Henry B. Brown "who became quite confidential . . . he said he wished to see me Chief Justice."

[23] *Addresses*, Vol. I, pp. 157, 242-243. [24] See page 44. [25] Taft to Seth Low, Nov. 9, 1904. [26] Taft to M. A. McRae, Nov. 12, 1904. [27] Taft to Helen H. Taft, March 14, 1904.

"The Chief Justice is getting old and he'll have to go soon," Justice Brown had said optimistically, "but I don't think he'll ever resign."

But Taft was not confident. "The Chief Justice," he mourned, "is as tough as a knot so that if he does not go by resignation, I shall have to whistle for his place." [28] He was properly sympathetic, in August, when Mrs. Fuller died, and sent a message of condolence. But he could not avoid looking at the practical aspect of the jurist's bereavement.

"It leaves the poor Chief Justice a stricken man . . ." he commented. "I don't know whether it will hasten his retirement or not. He told me he was getting very tired of cases." [29] On the other hand:

"You must not be too confident of Teddy's giving me the chief justiceship," he told his wife. "He likes Knox and Knox has fought his trust fight and he feels under deep obligation because Knox has won. . . . I think Knox would like to be chief justice. Should an issue come, I could put up a pretty good fight for it . . . Root would help me and Root is a power with Teddy and no mistake." [30]

This hazard of the presidency, although not the continued health of Chief Justice Fuller, was momentarily overcome before the summer of 1904 closed. Taft had a conversation at the White House during which Roosevelt said that Root would in all likelihood be the Republican presidential candidate.

"He said that so far as I was concerned," Taft reported, "I was out of it because my ambition was to be chief justice, as he knew." [31]

The worst apprehensions of Taft proved to be correct. It was 1910 before a successor had to be named for the Chief Justice and then, by a strange quirk of fate, Taft was president of the United States and did the naming himself. In the interim, a post as associate justice had become vacant once more and Roosevelt tendered it to Taft. But by then the presidential bee was really buzzing. He declined.

[28] *Idem,* April 12, 1904. [29] *Idem,* Aug. 15, 1904. [30] *Idem,* March 31, 1904. [31] *Idem,* Aug. 3, 1904.

—4—

It was during 1905 that Taft, because of his absorbed interest in the Philippine Islands, reacted with wrath and indignation toward the Supreme Court for which, in general, he had such reverence. Under an order by President McKinley issued on July 12, 1898, the military governor and then the Philippine Commission had levied duties on imports. From time to time the original executive order had been amended and amplified. The funds collected had been used for the archipelago. Some doubt had existed as to the legality of these levies, particularly during the period after the termination of military rule. So Congress had been asked to enact a blanket ratification and this, with the aid of Secretary of War Root, had been done on July 1, 1902. But certain of the business houses from which the imposts had been collected started litigation to recover. Among others, Warner, Barnes & Company sued for $7,000,000 which it had paid. The case reached the Supreme Court and to Taft's astonishment that normally wise, but now idiotic, tribunal handed down a unanimous decision ordering that the $7,000,000 be paid back to Warner, Barnes & Company. It was, in substance, a reversal of the 1901 ruling. Other claims would, inevitably, follow. Taft was scandalized.

"I told Brewer [Associate Justice David J. Brewer] last night that I thought the court had made a break," wrote Taft, "and did not understand that it was involving this government in the payment of $7,000,000 to a lot of Englishmen who had been at the bottom of the insurrection. He replied that he and his colleagues who differed on the insular question had paid no attention to the case at all and let the other five run it. Certainly the other five ran it into the ground."

Just why Englishmen, even Englishmen who sympathized with the insurrection, had less right to recover was not made clear by Taft. The case was complicated. The court had ruled that the Congressional action by which the duties had been approved applied only to levies made under President McKinley's first order. This, it said, had been terminated by the Treaty of Peace with Spain on April 11, 1899. The court declined to admit that Congress had ratified the amendments to the presidential order by which the collections had been continued. Taft suggested to Solicitor General Harry M. Hoyt that Elihu Root be called in as special counsel in an attempt to have the court reopen the case. Root, he pointed out, had drafted the statute now declared invalid. He was familiar with all aspects of the question.[32]

At the same time the secretary of war appealed to Root. The letter was typical of many that passed between the two men. Usually, Taft was a pedestrian and verbose correspondent. But Elihu Root inspired him, as he did other men, to a sharp, gay brilliance of expression.

"There was a time I cherish fondly in our friendship," he began, "when we had a bond of peculiar strength uniting us in that we were liable, jointly and severally, for indictment as embezzlers of funds collected without authority in the Philippine Islands, which we disbursed for the benefit of the citizens of those islands.

"There was another period that I recollect with great distinctness, too, when we congratulated ourselves that by the ratification of Congress, the prospect of the possible wearing of penitentiary stripes had been taken away."

By this decision of the Supreme Court, however, "we can . . . assure ourselves that we have been returned to the condition of joint embezzlers or highway robbers." Taft said he had supposed "in my simplicity . . . that when you wanted to ratify something you knew how to draw an instrument which would accomplish the ratification:

But I commend to you the reading of the last paragraph of Mr. Justice Holmes's opinion, and if it does not start you into that profanity which at times is as relieving as a safety valve, I shall miss my guess. If there ever was a fool decision, this is it, and turned off as flippantly, though it involves $7,000,000, and the legality of transactions of the government extending over two years, as if it involved a bill at the corner grocer's. . . .

Now we propose to move on the court again and see if we can't hammer a little sense into some of them, for it was a unanimous opinion. . . . I think the rest of the court have merely passed it off without fully examining the foolishness of Holmes. . . .

[32] Taft to H. H. Hoyt, April 5, 1905.

Shouldn't you like, as *amicus curiae,* to tell the court what damn fools you think they are? [33]

Pending a possible reversal, Taft drafted legislation which would, he hoped, accomplish the same purpose and halt restitution of the $7,000,000 to Warner, Barnes & Company. He even went so far as to request Attorney General Knox to defy the Supreme Court and "advise the secretary of the treasury not to pay any claims made on the basis of the decision." [34] In the end, Congress again ratified the customs collections and this time the Supreme Court upheld the legislation.[35]

The year moved on. President Roosevelt, becoming more and more confident of Taft's qualities, placed more and more burdens on him. Taft had the Philippines to supervise. He was in charge of the Panama Canal. John Hay fell ill, and he was made acting secretary of state. When Roosevelt was away, Taft was actually a pro tem president of the United States. These arduous assignments did not worry him unduly. But he could not escape, try as he might, from the involved labyrinths of the political issues which constantly arose. In October, 1905, for example, Governor Herrick of Ohio was a candidate for re-election. It was a turbulent campaign, marked by ugly evidences of interparty strife. Herrick was charged with having bowed to the yoke of Cox, the Republican boss of Cincinnati and Hamilton County. A revolt against Cox was in progress. There was danger that many Republicans would vote against Herrick for his supposed subservience. So Taft, who believed utterly in the independence and integrity of Herrick, confided that he would go to Ohio and make a speech on his behalf.

Taft's earlier tendencies toward political independence had, obviously, faded by now. They were to disappear completely before long. This was his swan song; this was the last gesture of a man who was pushing into the background of his desires the emphatic

[33] Taft to Root, April 7, 1905. [34] Taft to P. C. Knox, April 26, 1905. [35] Taft to J. C. Spooner, May 28, 1907.

belief that he was to carve his real career in the granite of legal knowledge. It was a forceful, courageous and convincing song, even if the last. He spoke at Akron on the evening of October 21, 1905. The main portion of the address was devoted to a defense of the Roosevelt administration, particularly with respect to its railroad-regulation program. The election of Governor Herrick, Taft said, was essential from the standpoint of national politics. Toward the close of the speech he took up "Herrick's alleged subserviency to the Republican machine of Hamilton County . . . a grave charge." Taft denied its truth. He described the situation under the rule of Cox as "one of absolute helplessness on the part of any independent Republican seeking to take part in politics and to act independently of the machine." Taft continued:

It is a condition of affairs— a local despotism— much to be deplored. . . . But the truth is that this machine, if it is to be broken up, must be broken up by the voters of Cincinnati and Hamilton County themselves. *This is an end devoutly to be wished,* but it will take the hardest kind of work in the city itself. . . . If I were able, as I fear I shall not be, because public duty calls me elsewhere, to cast my vote in Cincinnati in the coming election, *I should vote against the municipal ticket nominated by the Republican organization, and for the state ticket.*[36]

Applause echoed back to Washington. Howard Hollister, Taft's schoolmate, telegraphed that twenty thousand Republicans of Hamilton County joined in congratulations.[37] The Cleveland *Leader* proclaimed the courage of William Howard Taft, who "of all the conspicuous Republicans in Ohio . . . had the courage to call corruption by its right name and to repudiate the archcorrupter of Republican politics in the state."[38] But Taft had not the faintest intention of becoming a reform leader in Ohio. Herrick was defeated. The net result of Taft's swan song to independence— he was soon to accept the support of Cox himself— was further complication of an already tangled political situation.

In twenty-two months, from February of 1904 to the close of 1905, Secretary of War Taft had been able to give hardly more

[36] *Addresses,* Vol. III, pp. 70-73. (Italics mine.) [37] H. C. Hollister *et al* to Taft, Nov. 8, 1904. [38] Cleveland *Leader,* Nov. 10, 1905.

than a passing thought to the affairs of the department over which, in theory, he presided. The War Department is barely mentioned in his letters. During his first weeks he was called upon to review a court-martial which had dismissed a philandering lieutenant. The unfortunate officer had debased the army by making overtures to the wife, not of a fellow officer and gentleman, but of a company sergeant. Taft approved the sentence although he expressed some doubt as to its severity. But the lieutenant "seems to have been a very great fool . . . and I suppose the service will be better off without . . . such an ass." [39] In December, 1905, Taft replied to a protest that the young men of Annapolis and West Point indulged in fights which endangered their lives; in fact, one Annapolis midshipman had just died after such a brawl. Taft's answer was robust; the voice was the voice of Roosevelt:

. . . everybody knows that knows anything about either West Point or Annapolis, that this fighting has gone on for years, and that many commandants have thought that if it was carried on in a square way, it was the best way of settling disputes. . . . The fact that a poor fellow in the course of it was injured so that he died has nothing whatever to do with the case. He might have died from a fall down the steps. I feel very much about his death as the man did who was convicted of manslaughter for killing a fellow in Tipperary County in Ireland, for striking him with a blackthorn stick. The evidence was that death ensued from the blow because it broke the skull, but that the skull was known to medicine as a "paper skull" because it was so thin. When brought up, the court asked what he had to say. He said he had only one question to ask, and that was, "What the divil a man wid a skull like that was doin' in Tipperary?" So with respect to the boys in Annapolis. They have to be put through strenuous exercise to stand the risk of blows and all sorts of dangers, and if one is structurally weak, he must expect that there is a very great danger of that weakness being shown and leading to severe injury.[40]

In 1906, Taft hoped, he would be able "to take a little more part in the administration of the War Department than heretofore." He intended to change the regulations so that additional de-

[39] Taft to Roosevelt, March 31, 1904. [40] Taft to A. P. Humphrey, Dec. 7, 1905.

tails would come before him. Until now he had "so much outside work to do that I was entirely willing to turn the control over to the chief of staff." [41] But 1906 would see Taft laboring, as usual, at his varied tasks for Roosevelt. Besides, he had virtually made up his mind to surrender to his wife and family and accept, if it came his way, the Republican presidential nomination.

[41] Taft to C. P. Taft, Dec. 3, 1905.

CHAPTER XVII

TROUBLE-SHOOTER AT HOME

PRESIDENT ROOSEVELT was in high spirits in the spring of 1905. He had been inaugurated in his own right. Great plans for the approaching four years seethed in his active mind. He would settle, if he could, the war between Japan and Russia. He would further control the malefactors of great wealth and their wicked allies, the railroad magnates. He might even have a try at tariff reform and currency revision.

Business conditions were good. Even the farmers were happy. But more personal reasons were also behind the presidential radiance. The people loved him and he loved the people. He was a young man, not yet forty-eight years old. Best of all, he was about to start on a well-deserved vacation. On April 3, he described the anticipated joys of a hunting journey in the Rockies. All would go well in Washington, the President said, because he had "left Taft sitting on the lid." [1]

The phrase, like so many of Roosevelt's, caught the public imagination. It referred, specifically, to potential uprisings in Central and South America and Taft's ability to suppress them. Actually, Taft was so busy as secretary of war that he did no sitting at all. Between 1905 and the end of 1907, Taft was an able executive assistant rather than an adviser to Roosevelt. He no longer viewed the President objectively and weighed his virtues and faults. He agreed without question on nearly every policy, large or small. It was less than a perfect method for training the man who would one day sit in lonely splendor, himself, and ponder how in the world he could escape disaster now that Theodore would no longer tell him what to do.

One searches in vain for a major issue on which Taft took a stand, even in private, against Roosevelt. He agreed with the President on foreign affairs, railroad regulation, antitrust legislation and

[1] New York *Times*, April 4, 1905.

on the possible menace of labor unions; on the growth of radicalism and on pure-food reform. Roosevelt's sudden crusade for simplified spelling in the summer of 1906 appears, it is true, to have caused vague inner annoyance.

"I am glad the new spelling is dead," Taft wrote when, at last, Roosevelt admitted that his utopian gesture was premature, "for it 'grated on me rite thru.' " [2]

On the somewhat more important matter of the Monroe Doctrine, however, Taft quickly revised his earlier theories. Indeed, he was in active charge of the incident whereby Roosevelt, through his Corollary of 1904, very greatly extended the meaning of the doctrine. This was the Santo Domingo affair. It was, of course, another case of a Latin-American power unable to pay its foreign obligations. Until after the similar Venezuela episode in 1902, the United States had been willing enough to have such obligations collected by the powers to which they were owed; provided only that permanent acquisition of territory was forbidden. Apprehension that acquisition would, in fact, follow led to the enunciation of Roosevelt's augmented doctrine that the United States, alone, would be the policeman of the Caribbean.

Germany, Spain and Italy were seeking, in the summer of 1904, to collect from Santo Domingo about $22,000,000 due their nationals. Agreements had already been made which, in effect, mortgaged the customs receipts of the revolution-tossed little republic and which permitted foreign governments to take over the customhouses if payments were not made. The agent of one creditor corporation, a New York concern, was finally installed at Puerto Plata as a collecting agent. But this so annoyed the poor but proud Santo Domingans that President Carlos F. Morales was confronted by revolution. So he offered, wisely enough, to turn over his customhouses to the United States. Roosevelt was willing. It was ultimately agreed that forty-five per cent of the revenues would go to the Dominican government while the balance would be assigned to her creditors by the agents of the United States. [3]

The United States Senate, whose participation in foreign affairs is specified by the Constitution, was not consulted regarding this

---

[2] Taft to Mrs. M. C. Audenreid, Jan. 12, 1907. [3] Hill, Howard C., *Roosevelt and the Caribbean*, pp. 153-160.

agreement. Taft appears, for a fleeting moment in March, 1905, to have protested against the extension of presidential authority.[4] But he cheerfully took charge of the situation when Roosevelt left for the West. The arrangement meant, obviously, that the United States must protect the Morales government against further insurrection. American warships were on hand for that purpose.[5]

Colonel George R. Colton, who had done similar work in the Philippines, was assigned to the task of collecting the money. The secretary of war reminded him that he was "acting as an agent of the Dominican government . . . and not as a subordinate of either the State or War Department, or of the President of the United States." And yet it would be well, Taft added, for him to send regular reports to the War Department.[6]

During all this the Senate voiced its protest and declined to ratify the agreement with Santo Domingo. Roosevelt continued to exercise what was, in effect, a protectorate. It was Elihu Root, not Taft, who took issue with the illegalities. He became secretary of state on July 1, 1905. He saw the situation clearly. When the inevitable revolution came and Morales was driven from office the United States, very properly, refused to take sides. But the customs collection continued despite Root's protests. In November, 1905, the secretary of state wrote:

I strongly disapprove of the proposition. If the Senate refuses to give the President the legal right to act officially in regard to Dominican finances, I do not think that we should go on as we are now. The result sooner or later would be an uprising against the existing Dominican government to which the customs officers supposed to represent the United States, although not legally doing so, would have to yield, to the great injury of our prestige and credit, or which would be suppressed by a use of force on the part of our government difficult to justify on constitutional grounds.[7]

[4] Bishop, J. B., *Theodore Roosevelt and His Time*, Vol. I, p. 433. [5] Taft to Roosevelt, April 5, 1905. [6] Taft to G. R. Colton, April 8, 1905. [7] Root to Taft, Nov. 16, 1909.

—2—

Roosevelt, Root and Taft were an unusual combination; fortunate, indeed, was the nation which had such a trio on the bridge of its ship of state. They admired each other extravagantly; indeed, they regarded each other with a deep affection. They had humor as well as keen intelligence. They sometimes referred to themselves— Taft and Root more than Roosevelt— by the names of the swashbuckling "Three Musketeers" created by Dumas. The President, of course, was D'Artagnan. Root was Athos. Taft was Porthos. Thus, they often signed their letters. So their relationship might have continued had not the tragic days of 1912 come finally upon them and had not a bitter D'Artagnan set forth alone to wage a war of his own. Roosevelt forgave Taft, at least partially, for the harsh words of the campaign of 1912; it is easier to pardon a subordinate who has erred and Roosevelt, in his heart, ever regarded Taft as less capable than himself.

But Roosevelt never forgave Root. He never forgot that Root presided at the Republican convention which, so he charged and perhaps believed, stole the 1912 nomination from him. It is more difficult to forget the wrongs perpetrated by an equal. And Root was, at the very least, an equal. He had a first-class mind. He was a first-class executive. He was a first-class wit. His eyes would gleam from beneath his shaggy brows and from his lips would issue some remark, always devastating and occasionally malicious, which would rout hypocrisy or adolescence or shoddy thinking. No one, not even the President of the United States, was immune. Roosevelt rarely felt resentment; he had a flair for objectivity surprising in view of his egocentric qualities.

But Mrs. Roosevelt— so Taft heard from Alice Roosevelt and repeated with relish to Mrs. Taft— had objected when her husband had revealed his intention of asking Elihu Root to become secretary of state. The First Lady had preferred to have Taft in that high post. Taft wrote:

Her [Mrs. Roosevelt's] reason for disliking Mr. Root is a funny one. The President and Mr. Root, as you remember, used to go out on long walks and the President insisted on climbing precipices. He carried poor old Root through the same places until Root got out of patience. One day when Root was not along, the President in his wild career had a severe fall which lamed him, and when Mrs. Roosevelt told Root about it, he laughed and said he was very glad. Mrs. Roosevelt was very indignant on the subject and did not see why he should express himself in such a brutal manner.[8]

Taft, although less forthright than Root, had other qualities of infinite value to a busy president. He was a great conciliator. He was an excellent channel through which Roosevelt's opinions and desires could be passed on to others. He was a useful clearing-house for the opinions and desires of others. A confidence reposed in him was as safe as one murmured to a priest in a confessional.

". . . when it is really necessary to keep a secret," Roosevelt said, "you and I keep it absolutely, as we kept the secret of the Algeciras negotiations with Germany, for instance." [9]

This was a reference to the Moroccan crisis of 1905 whence had issued ominous rumblings of a European war. President Roosevelt often referred to the part he played in averting it. He was never wholly aware that the issue had been postponed rather than settled. Among all the countries of the world, the United States had a minimum interest in Morocco. True, we had signed an agreement in 1880 whereby all nations had been guaranteed equal trade rights. But the United States had done nothing, in the years which followed, while France went into Algeria, while Great Britain strengthened her position at Gibraltar, and while France, Italy and Germany developed large commercial interests in the shabby little dominion of the Sultan. Nor did the United States take action— in fact, there is no sign that Roosevelt knew of its existence— when England and France signed a treaty in April, 1901, which provided that France could have a free hand in Morocco if England were allowed to rule Egypt.[10] Certainly Taft knew nothing about it. He was, at the moment, exceedingly busy in the Philippines.

But William II, Kaiser of all the Germanies, was keenly aware

[8] Taft to Helen H. Taft, Sept. 24, 1905. [9] Roosevelt to Taft, Aug. 1, 1906. [10] Fay, Sidney B., *The Origins of the World War*, Vol. I, pp. 160-164.

SENT TO THE BENCH.

Cartoon by G. K. Berryman, Courtesy The Washington Post

Drawn by "C.I.R.," Courtesy Collier's, April 13, 1907

of the Moroccan question and saw in it, with accuracy, a plan by France, England and Spain to rob the Fatherland of its rights. Being ignorant, Roosevelt was amused and incredulous when the Kaiser, in March, 1905, ordered Ambassador Speck von Sternberg to call at the White House. He was fond of von Sternberg, who was a tennis player of skill. But Specky submitted ridiculous, so it seemed to Roosevelt, reports of a European attempt to divide up Morocco. He even said that France and England had an alliance to that end. Would the United States join with Germany to guarantee the open door in Morocco? The President answered that this was out of the question. The United States had no concern with Morocco.[11] Then he left, lightheartedly, on his hunting trip and Taft, as acting secretary of state in the absence of John Hay, took over the negotiations.

Taft's part in the affair is historically important only to the degree that his letters reveal the underlying bitterness between England and Germany. He fully shared Roosevelt's theory that the Kaiser was having hallucinations.

"Your friend Speck came in with a letter conveying the thoughts of his imperial master, which he desired to have communicated to you," Taft reported on April 5, 1905. "I have read them in his presence and find that they most concern Morocco and the French relations to Morocco and the 'open door' in Morocco. . . . It seems that Germany has substantial interests in Morocco. . . . I do not remember that we have, and in any event they are not so valuable as to call upon us, I presume, to range ourselves on the side of Germany in this matter." [12]

"I wish to Heaven our excellent friend, the Kaiser, was not so jumpy and did not have so many pipe dreams," answered the President, as he moved across Texas toward Colorado.[13]

Soon afterward, the German ambassador again visited Taft and said that his government was desirous of learning the true attitude of England toward Germany and the Moroccan question. Taft told the President that he had consented to sound out Sir Mortimer Durand, his Britannic Majesty's ambassador in Washington:

11 Bishop, J. B., *op. cit.,* Vol. I, p. 468. 12 Taft to Roosevelt, April 5, 1905. 13 Roosevelt to Taft, April 8, 1905.

I stated to him that I came at your direction because you had had direct communication with the German government . . . which made you somewhat anxious; that the United States had no particular interest in Morocco . . . and was not inclined to take sides as between Germany and England . . . that your action in the matter grew out of a real concern lest the two countries to whom [*sic*] we stood near, to wit, England and Germany, and always desired to stand near, should through sheer misunderstanding of each other's motives, be brought into a feeling of hostility which could not but be of great misfortune to the world.

The secretary of war found, of course, that the British ambassador was excessively polite and excessively dubious concerning Germany's motives:

He said that his government did distrust Germany because it had good reason to; that the German government had played tricks with the English for many years, and that it was very difficult to induce Englishmen to believe Germany was sincere in her expressed desire to retain the friendship of England. This, he said, was especially the case with respect to the Boer War, in which the British government, the royal family and the English people were made the subjects of the most virulent attack, so extreme that the English people could not forget it. He said that the English government did not fear that Germany would attack England because it was not in a position to do so with its inferior navy. He said, however, that for years Germany, although the traditional friend of England since Waterloo, had, ever since Bismarck's time, frankly and unblushingly declined to co-operate with England, merely on the ground that it wished to cultivate the good will of Russia. He said that his government with respect to Morocco had advised him that Germany had desired England, Italy and other European states to join in a conference with respect to France's relation to Morocco, and that England had declined to do so. He says he is unable to account for the enmity which the German government and people seem to cherish toward the English government and people. Whether it is jealousy because of the extent of the English colonial possessions he is unable to say, but that it exists England knows. . . . He said that it is quite possible that Germany fears England and her attack because of a guilty conscience.[14]

[14] Taft to Roosevelt, April 26, 1905.

It was an explanation replete with virtue and more than a little ridiculous in view of the treaty for the partition of Morocco into which Great Britain had already entered with France. Taft knew as little as Roosevelt did about the forces— far beneath the surface— which were at play. On May 11, 1905, the President returned from his hunt and again became his own secretary of state. In January, 1906, a conference of the powers opened in the Andalusian city, Algeciras. The attitude of the United States at this gathering— an attitude dictated, of course, by Theodore Roosevelt— was pro-English, pro-French and anti-German. The President felt that the outcome was entirely happy and that he had averted a possible war. But the drums were merely muted. They continued to beat and their tempo heightened as the years slipped by toward 1914.[15]

—3—

The Panama Canal and Philippine Island affairs consumed more of the time and energy of Secretary of War Taft than any other matters. The President had seized the necessary land on the isthmus; now it was necessary to dig a canal across the strip. The sooner it was done the better. But what kind of canal would it be: a sea-level ditch or a complicated affair with locks? And who would build it? Congress had given wide powers to the President. It specified that the work was to be in the hands of the Isthmian Canal Commission, with seven members. They were appointed by the President and responsible only to him. Rear Admiral John G. Walker, a retired naval officer who had already served on two similar commissions, was made the first chairman. As soon as Taft became secretary of war, however, Roosevelt determined that he should be in general command.

"I lunched today with the President and the Isthmian Canal Commission," reported Taft as he entered the Cabinet. "The President announced to the commission that they were to be under me as secretary of war whether the law so provided or not. Admiral Walker has been very anxious to avoid my supervision, but he will have to have it."[16]

[15] Pringle, H. F., *Theodore Roosevelt, a Biography*, pp. 393-397. [16] Taft to Helen H. Taft, March 22, 1904.

Roosevelt and Taft were equally ignorant regarding the technical engineering aspects of the work. The canal commission was instructed, therefore, to convene a body of American and European engineers who would make a thorough study. Meanwhile, in the United States, editorial writers discovered a topic which invariably brought response from their readers: "Make the Dirt Fly!" was the heading on many a leader during 1904 and 1905. But nobody knew how or in what direction it was to fly. Supervision of the Panama Canal, Taft soon learned, was really enough to occupy the whole time of any average executive. Friction developed among the members of the commission. Sanitation, sound currency for the new and feeble republic of Panama, labor for the actual digging: such were merely a few of the matters which had to be solved.

Most of Taft's labors on the canal were to be performed at his desk in Washington. These were preceded, however, by a journey to the isthmus late in 1904. The President had learned that it was easy enough to be forthright, daring and imperialistic. The canal strip now belonged to the United States and would unquestionably retain that status, for all the snarlings of Democratic senators. But Roosevelt's virile policies had brought resentment which failed to subside. The people of Panama, for example, were apprehensive that the United States intended to impose subjection upon them. So the President called upon Taft to exercise again those qualities which dispelled suspicion and put trust and confidence in its place. He must visit the isthmus at once and make clear that Uncle Sam was "about to confer . . . a very great benefit by the expenditure of millions of dollars in the construction of the canal." The President continued:

. . . this fact must not blind us to the importance of so exercising the authority given us under the treaty with Panama as to avoid creating any suspicion, however, unfounded, of our intentions as to the future. We have not the slightest intention of establishing an independent colony in the middle of the state of Panama, or of exercising any greater governmental functions than are necessary to enable us conveniently and safely to construct, maintain and operate the canal. . . . Least of all do we desire to interfere with the business and prosperity of the people of Panama. However far a just construction of the treaty might enable us to go, did the exigencies of the case require it, in asserting the equivalent of sovereignty over the canal strip, it is our full intention that the rights which we exercise shall be exercised with all *proper care* for the honor and interests of the people of Panama. The exercise of such powers as are given us by the treaty within the geographical boundaries of the republic of Panama may easily, if a real sympathy for both the present and future welfare of the people of Panama is not shown, create distrust of the American government. This would seriously interfere with the success of our great project in that country.[17]

So Taft was to put a cloak over the wolfish head of Uncle Sam and assure the Panamanians that the teeth in the Hay-Bunau-Varilla treaty were not, for the moment at any rate, to be used for purposes of mastication. Taft disclosed that he had been the one to suggest the high sentiments of friendship set forth in the letter of instruction. They were, he said, "founded on a sense of justice to Panama and prompted by no other motive."[18] Taft shared fully Roosevelt's contemptuous view of Panama.

"It is a kind of opera bouffe republic and nation," he said as he prepared to leave for the isthmus. "Its army is not much larger than the army on an opera stage. We have four hundred marines and a fleet on one side and three naval vessels on the other."[19]

Taft permitted no such derogatory opinions to escape from his lips when he reached the Canal Zone on November 27, 1904. He was received with outward cordiality. Dr. Manuel Amador, the President, was called upon in the afternoon. The secretary of war, in a confidential report to Roosevelt, remarked that Amador was an elderly man whose wife "is much younger . . . has the courage and snap and President Amador's prominent part in leading the movement for independence . . . is largely attributed to the influence of his wife." In fact, another of the heroes of that struggle, General Huertas, had already attempted to evict Amador from the presidential chair.

"The threat of the use of United States forces," remarked Taft, "ended the power of Huertas. His army . . . disbanded a few days before I reached Panama."

[17] Roosevelt to Taft, Oct. 18, 1904. (Italics mine.) [18] Taft to Cromwell, Oct. 21, 1904. [19] Taft to C. P. Taft, Nov. 17, 1904.

Honeyed words of friendship from Secretary Taft can hardly have deceived the Panamanians. But they were practical men. Taft held forth promises of practical benefits. Machinery and other supplies for the building of the canal were to be admitted free of duty, he suggested. But all dutiable imports were to enter through the Panamanian ports of Panama and Colon, instead of at ports under the jurisdiction of the United States; thus large revenues would pour into the treasury. The Panama postal system, instead of a new American one, was to be used. A nice profit would come from that too. Food and clothing for the laborers in the zone would be purchased from the local merchants. The only flaw in the prospect was a warning that extreme profiteering, if attempted, would result in the establishment of a commissary by which, Taft told Roosevelt, the United States would "undersell and drive out of competition the merchants of the zone and the republic." There was, however, gravy enough. Taft received a popular demonstration of approval when he left the isthmus.

During his visit Taft learned something, although not a great deal, about the engineering angles. He conferred with John F. Wallace, the chief engineer. He concluded that no insuperable obstacles existed.

"The problem of the canal," Taft told Roosevelt, "is a problem of the excavation of a mass greater than ever before made in the history of the world." [20]

He refrained from an official opinion. Inwardly, however, Taft was convinced that the "only canal to build . . . is a sea-level canal." He agreed that it would cost more and take a longer time to build, "but when it is done it will be done for good." [21] A majority of the consulting engineers, at work for almost a year, were to agree that locks were dangerous and impracticable. Long before then, however, the President had taken matters into his own hands. He had concluded prior to May, 1905, that a lock canal would cost only half as much, that it could be built in half the time, that it would serve larger vessels.[22] Taft thereupon agreed with his chief. He submitted the reports of the experts and said he favored the minority plan for a lock canal. The estimate for

[20] Taft to Roosevelt, Dec. 19, 1904. [21] Taft to C. P. Taft, Dec. 15, 1904. [22] Bishop, J. B., op. cit., Vol. I, p. 451.

a sea-level project was $247,021,000 and for the lock canal $139,-705,200. The former would take from twelve to twenty years to construct and the latter only eight and one-half years.[23] It was so ordered. Roosevelt obtained the approval of Congress in June, 1906, by a large margin in the House and by five votes in the Senate.[24]

In the interim, Taft had a multitude of other canal questions to settle. The Isthmian Canal Commission had proved unwieldy, so active management was turned over to an executive committee of three members. Chief Engineer Wallace resigned on June 28, 1905, and was succeeded by John F. Stevens, a distinguished railroad construction engineer. But Stevens, too, grew discouraged.

"There are three diseases in Panama," he said savagely. "They are yellow fever, malaria and cold feet; and the greatest of these is cold feet."[25]

The work dragged. Dr. William C. Gorgas, who had been assigned to the prodigious task of ending yellow fever, was resentful that complete co-operation was not being given him. Other sanitary experts laughed at his theory that the mosquito was responsible for spreading the plague and that the first step was to destroy the swamps and pools where the insect bred. Even Taft, although he stood behind Colonel Gorgas, considered that he had "no executive ability at all."[26] In February, 1907, Chief Engineer Stevens told the President that he desired to resign. The secretary of war was not, it would appear, greatly surprised. He had been prepared for this possibility.

"There is a very able army engineer— Major George W. Goethals," he had informed the President in June, 1905. "I feel very certain that after he has studied the situation and given his heart and mind to it, as he will, that were Stevens to desert us or fall by the wayside, Goethals would be in a position to take his place."[27]

Taft had been impressed with the talents of Goethals when, in November, 1904, the major had been one of the army engineers who had accompanied the official party on the visit to the isthmus. When Stevens resigned, Taft told the President that Goethals was

[23] Taft to Roosevelt, Feb. 18, 1906. [24] Bishop, J. B., *op. cit.*, Vol. I, p. 451; *War Secretary Diaries*, pp. 368, 379. [25] Bishop, J. B., and Bishop, F., *Goethals, Genius of Panama*, pp. 128-133. [26] Taft to C. A. L. Reed, Dec. 23, 1904. [27] Taft to Roosevelt, June 30, 1905.

best qualified to carry on the work. He had the unanimous backing of his superiors.[28] The troubles of the secretary of war, in so far as actual construction of the canal was concerned, ended with the arrival of Goethals in the zone.

An embarrassing detail— Taft assured himself that it was not more— was the almost constant presence of Cromwell, the New York attorney who had conspired with Bunau-Varilla, who had earned thereby a legal fee of $800,000— and possibly additional benefits— and who had been counsel to the Panama Railroad Company. Taft invited Cromwell to accompany him on the November, 1904, visit.

"I have been warned against him," Taft told the President, "as a man not always nice in his methods and as one usually having some ulterior motive. . . . Thus far . . . I have discovered no such traits. Certainly he has sufficient knowledge with respect to the canal and the isthmus to be of great usefulness." [29]

Taft expressed his appreciation in a warm and friendly letter to Cromwell.[30] He must have been a degree surprised to receive a note from the President six months later in which Roosevelt pointed out that "Cromwell's reputation is very unfortunate. Do minimize his connection with Panama as far as possible." [31] Even Roosevelt softened this verdict, though. Additional details regarding Cromwell's role in the Panama affair came to light during the next few years. Taft was, in 1908, faintly dubious about accepting a campaign contribution of $50,000 from the attorney.

"If I were in your place," said Roosevelt, who had, after all, taken $5,000 from Cromwell in 1904, "I would accept that . . . contribution with real gratitude." [32]

—4—

These were crowded years. "I have never been quite so busy with various things," he told his brother in January, 1906.[33] "I am overwhelmed with work," he repeated some months later. "Philip-

[28] Bishop, J. B., and Bishop, F., *op. cit.*, p. 138. [29] Taft to Roosevelt, Dec. 19, 1904. [30] Taft to W. N. Cromwell, Dec. 12, 1904. [31] Roosevelt to Taft, June 29, 1904. [32] *Idem,* Aug. 7, 1908. [33] Taft to Horace D. Taft, Jan. 22, 1906.

pine matters, Panama Canal matters, army matters, the disaster at San Francisco, which has to be looked after by the army and this department, together with the session of Congress, where I have to appear before many committees, have all thrown a heavy burden on me." [34] The earthquake on the Pacific coast had been scarcely more than an added detail. The secretary of war received news of it by telephone from the White House after midnight on the morning of April 16. He promptly ordered that tents and other supplies be rushed to San Francisco. He supervised the expenditure of $2,500,000. He brushed aside the law, an anarchistic gesture which must have brought an inner qualm, and shipped army property worth $1,000,000. Congress promptly legalized his action. [35]

A splendid efficiency marked the crowded years. It was partly due, no doubt, to the fact that Taft was a happy man. Not a few inner doubts had faded. He no longer was apprehensive that he was a bad executive. He knew, if any man in public life ever knew it, that the people held him in high esteem. It was pleasant to be admired. Applause was sweet. "We want Taft!" . . . "Taft for President!" . . . "Taft in 1908!"— these cries were musical even to a man who still declared, although now less positively, that he preferred to go back into the quiet harbors of judicial life. Life in Washington was pleasant too. These were the imperial hours of his friend, Theodore, and victory was in the air. The Tafts knew all the great people of the capital. They knew them intimately, now, instead of only casually as in the solicitor general days. The great people were frequently at the home of the secretary at 1603 K Street. Nor was Mrs. Taft forced to entertain at high tea instead of at dinner. There was money enough for champagne. Taft's generous brother was remitting $8,000 a year. Later, Charles gave even more.

"The truth is . . . that we could not live here at all, we couldn't have come into the Cabinet, if it had not been for you . . ." Taft wrote in gratitude. "This is a commentary on the salaries that are paid by the government, and also a commentary on the good fortune that I have in such a brother as you are, for you are in a

[34] Taft to Benito Legarda, May 15, 1906. [35] *War Secretary Diaries,* p. 233; Taft to J. D. Phelan, May 1, 1906.

class by yourself." [36] In March, 1907, by Congressional action, all Cabinet salaries were raised to $12,000 and Taft insisted that Charles P. Taft reduce the monthly payments to fit the new figure.[37]

They were, all in all, happy years. Taft's chuckle enchanted nearly every visitor to the War Department. Sometimes his merriment sent laughter rolling down the dingy corridors. Life was entertaining. The secretary of war even found time to tease his venerable mother when that lady, in May of 1906, cajoled him into appointing a New England acquaintance to a post as master on an army transport.

"I hope the man is equal to the position," Mrs. Louise Taft later wrote. "We cannot be responsible for his fitness."

Her son pretended to be scandalized. "Of course," he wrote with mock severity, "we relied on your knowledge of his ability to manage a large steamship. Of course, we should never have appointed him if we did not know that you knew that he was a very good navigator. . . . I felt certain that such civil service reformers as you and Aunt Delia would never have recommended a man for a place . . . where he will have hundreds of thousands of dollars of the property of the government in charge, unless you knew . . . that he was a competent mariner, navigator and sailor of the seas! However, it is only another instance of how reformers, when they seek to be spoilsmen, lose all their principles . . . so that their friends may be put at the public crib." [38]

Taft's new efficiency included zealous attention to physical fitness. "I will make a conscientious effort to lose flesh," he promised. "I am convinced that this undue drowsiness is due to the accumulation of flesh . . . were I appointed to the bench I fear I could not keep awake in my present condition." [39] He rode horseback almost daily. In December, 1905, he began a diet under the supervision of Dr. N. E. Yorke-Davis of London, and the results were as astonishing as they were beneficial. On the S.S. *Korea,* returning from his visit to the Philippines that year, he had weighed 326 pounds. The secretary of war submitted daily reports on his vanishing weight. It was a gallant record:

[36] Taft to C. P. Taft, Oct. 19, 1906. [37] *Idem,* March 8, 1907. [38] Louise Taft to Taft, May 3, 1906; Taft to Louise Taft, June 14, 1906. [39] Taft to Helen H. Taft, Oct. 9, 1905.

1905			
Dec.	1st	Dressed 7 P.M.	320–3/4
1905		Stripped	
Dec.	2	7 A.M.	314–3/4
"	3	9:30 A.M.	313
"	4	8:30 A.M.	312–1/2
"	5	8:30 A.M.	312–1/8
"	6	8:30 A.M.	311
"	7	8:30 A.M.	312–3/4
"	8	8:30 A.M.	312
"	9	8:30 A.M.	310
"	10	Absent from home	
"	11	8:30 A.M.	309–1/8
"	12	"	308–1/2
"	13	"	308[1/4
"	14	"	307–3/4
"	15	"	305–7/8
"	16	"	305–15/16
"	17	"	304–3/4
"	18	"	303–15/16
1906			
Feby.	3	8:45	284
"	4	9:30	283–9/16
"	5	9:00	282–7/8
"	6	8:45	282–9/16
"	7	8:45	282–1/16
"	8	8:45	282–1/16
"	9	8:15	281–7/8
"	10	8:30	281–7/8
"	11	In New York	
"	12	Before 9:00	281–3/4
"	13	" "	281–5/8
"	14	" "	281–3/4
"	15	" "	280–3/4
"	16	" "	282
"	17	" "	281
"	18	9 A.M.	279–1/2
March	12	9:15	267–1/4
"	13	9:15	266–11/16
"	14	In New York	

March 15	In New York	
" 16	9:00	266–5/8
" 17	9:15	266–15/16
" 18	9:30	266–5/16
" 19	9:00	267–1/2
" 20	9:00	266–5/8
" 21	9:10	265–13/16
" 22	9:00	264–15/16
" 23	8:45	265–3/4

By the middle of April, 1906, he was down to 255¾ pounds. That summer he weighed only 250 pounds, by no means too much for a man of Taft's height and build. His health, of course, was infinitely improved. His digestion was better. At no time, despite the rather drastic reduction, had he experienced the slightest discomfort.[40] But his pocketbook felt it.

"I have had to pay . . . $400 for clothes alterations, etc., so you see that considering my bills for medical advice and my tailor's bill, a reduction of seventy pounds is not an inexpensive luxury," he told Mrs. Taft.[41]

—5—

The only serious flaw in the perfection of life was the Congressional campaign in 1906. It was essential to Roosevelt's program to have a Republican Congress returned and he was, as always, worried over the possibility of defeat. He could not, as president, properly take the stump. So Taft and other Cabinet members set forth with their valises of ideas to sell Rooseveltism to the nation. The secretary of war was the star salesman. He went on a tour which took him through Ohio, Illinois, Nebraska, Wyoming and Idaho and then back through Kansas, Oklahoma, Texas and Louisiana. But he had, he insisted, nothing to ask, for himself, of politicians anywhere.[42]

Reluctantly, because he was resting at Murray Bay and viewed the approaching weeks with distaste, Taft went to Bath, Maine, on September 5, 1906, and made an address which Roosevelt praised

[40] Taft to N. E. Yorke-Davis, Dec. 9, 18, 1905, March 23, 1906; Taft to W. M. Laffan, June 19, 1906. [41] Taft to Helen H. Taft, July 13, 1906. [42] Taft to Albert Douglas, July 29, 1906.

as the "great speech of the campaign." [43] It is to be regretted that
Roosevelt, in the days of his hostility, did not take time to thumb
through the Taft speeches of the 1906 campaign. They would have
revealed an honest sincerity and an utter belief in the principles
for which Roosevelt was fighting. They might have persuaded
Roosevelt that the man he had placed in the White House was
entitled to sympathy instead of criticism, to support instead of antagonism. The Bath speech was a calm presentation of Roosevelt's
case rather than a political oration. But it was forthright and direct. A chief issue in the Congressional campaign, Taft began, lay
in the "evils arising from the misuse and abuse of the powerful
instrumentalities which the free opportunity to organize and combine capital has placed in the hands of the comparatively few."
The secretary of war described the varied methods by which competition was being restricted. He recited the history of antitrust
legislation and the court decisions, including his own ruling in the
Addystone Pipe case, upholding the warfare against the trusts. Taft
then took up the railroad rate question and told of the step forward
represented by the Hepburn act which gave augmented powers to
the Interstate Commerce Commission. He praised other administration victories: the pure-food laws, the Panama Canal, the admission of Oklahoma to statehood, the consular act whereby the consular service was made more efficient. Taft was on less certain
ground when he turned to tariff revision. It was a complicated
matter, he pointed out, on which party members too often disagreed. He added:

> Speaking my individual opinion and for no one else, I believe
> that since the passage of the Dingley Bill, there has been a change in
> the business conditions of the country making it wise and just to
> revise the schedules of the existing tariff. The sentiment in favor
> of a revision . . . is growing in the Republican party. . . . How
> soon the feeling in favor of revision shall crystallize into action
> cannot be foretold. [44]

It was not to be soon enough for the political safety of William
Howard Taft. The tariff confronted him as an immediate per-

[43] Roosevelt to Taft, Sept. 6, 1906. [44] *Addresses*, Vol. IV, pp. 145-168.

plexity when he entered the White House two and a half years later.

Taft's swing around the circle started late in October. He spoke several times each day and was gratified by the response received from his audiences. The routine was interrupted at Fort Leavenworth in Kansas when he shifted from his role of spellbinder back to secretary of war and reviewed the troops.

"They gave me a trotting horse," he told Mrs. Taft. "The horse was large enough to carry my weight, so that it did not seem to be embarrassed, and I got through without mishap, although the horse stumbled once and I thought I was going down . . . You would have enjoyed the fuss and feathers." [45]

The result on Election Day was victory, and Roosevelt congratulated Taft for the "great part you have played in the contest." [46] Some weeks later, back in Washington, Taft gave a brief interview on the political events of the past year. The Congressional elections, he said, portended Republican success in 1908. During the past year the Roosevelt administration had pacified Cuba, had done much to benefit the Philippines, had pushed construction on the Panama Canal, had brought greater prosperity to the country.[47] Taft might have added, had he been a less modest man, that he had been a major factor in nearly all the negotiations or battles which had led to these accomplishments. More than any other Cabinet member— more, indeed, than any other man in the country save the President alone— he left his mark on the legislation of 1906. But he had not— he insisted— changed his mind about active participation in public affairs.

"Politics, when I am in it," he had written to Nellie during the campaign, "makes me sick." [48]

[45] Taft to Helen H. Taft, Nov. 12, 1906. [46] Roosevelt to Taft, Nov. 8, 1906. [47] *War Secretary Diaries*, p. 978. [48] Taft to Helen H. Taft, Oct. 31, 1906.

CHAPTER XVIII

TROUBLE-SHOOTER ABROAD

TAFT was to be criticized, during his administration as president of the United States, for the extent to which he traveled. His excursions up and down the land exhausted the allowances granted for that purpose by Congress. Hostile editors said that he spent far too much time on the road.

The President might have retorted, but did not, that he had contracted the habit as governor of the Philippine Islands and secretary of war. Voyages to Manila, to Rome, to Panama, to Cuba and tours in the United States itself had totaled, between 1900 and 1908, over 100,000 miles.[1]

"The beauty . . . of Secretary Taft's trips," commented the Washington *Evening Star,* "is that they produce results. He is no junketer, but a man of affairs, with business in hand and a knowledge of how to transact it." [2]

"Incidentally," wrote Frederick Palmer in a friendly appraisal, "Taft is a cabinet officer. Primarily, he is the proconsul of good faith to fractious islands; an ambassador to stubborn tasks at far corners of the earth." [3]

It was an accurate analysis and the American people, who would so soon sneer and criticize, applauded with unanimity. The first journey had been to Panama. The second, which interested Taft even more, was to the Philippine Islands in the summer and fall of 1905. He had been true to his pledge that the welfare of the Filipinos would be his paramount concern as secretary of war. He continued to deprecate any suggestion that they were ready for independence.

"We have," he protested when petitions demanding independence were circulated in the United States, "a definite, practical problem in the Philippines, and it serves no useful purpose to hinder

---

[1] Fred W. Carpenter to Frederick Palmer, March 4, 1907. [2] Washington *Evening Star,* March 23, 1907. [3] *Collier's Weekly,* April 13, 1907.

its solution by discussing what we are going to do fifty or a hundred or one hundred fifty years hence, or by binding ourselves to a fixed course so far in advance. . . . When we shall have made a successful government; when we shall have created an independent public opinion—then the question of what shall be done may well be left to both countries; for if America . . . follows her duty . . . I do not think that the Filipinos will desire to sever the bonds between us and them." [4]

The movement for independence continued to grow, however, until finally, after Taft's death, independence of a limited kind was granted. Taft's contention would surely have been, had he lived, that the United States had failed in its duty to the archipelago. At no time was he satisfied that the pledges, actual or implied, were met. He worried about the failure constantly while he was secretary of war. He continued to lobby for the Philippines in Congress, particularly with respect to tariff slashes. He desired to effect currency reform and to encourage the development of railroads. [5] He was constantly thwarted by the sugar, tobacco and other lobbies but he kept doggedly at his task.

"Please don't misunderstand me to think that I am indispensable or that the world could not run on much the same, if I were to disappear in the St. Lawrence River," he begged the President from Murray Bay when, for a third time elevation to the Supreme Court was offered and declined in July, 1906, "but circumstances seem to me to have imposed something . . . of a trust on me personally." [6]

—2—

All this while troubled voices crossed the interminable Pacific and reached the sympathetic ears of the secretary of war. Señores de Tavera and Legarda of the Philippine Commission both protested that they no longer had much authority in the affairs of the islands.

"I fear very much that since I left attention is not paid as it

[4] Taft to William Lawrence, Feb. 16, 1904. [5] Taft to L. E. Wright, April 23, 1904, Jan. 21, 1905; to S. E. Payne, Jan. 20, 1905. [6] Taft to Roosevelt, July 30, 1906.

should be to the Filipino members," Taft wrote. "Of course, they are unreasonable and childish in many ways. . . . It may be essential for me to visit the islands . . . to straighten matters out." [7]

By the end of 1904 he had concluded that the journey was inescapable. The man-who-was-not-a-politician, and who never mastered the black mysteries of politics on his own behalf, could be politically minded enough on behalf of his beloved brown children. He decided to take a party of congressmen on the visit in the summer of 1905.

"I doubt if so formidable a Congressional representation ever went so far," he observed complacently. "The great advantage to the islands . . . is that hereafter the members of the delegation will always have an interest in the legislation which will come up in respect to the Philippines and . . . I am hopeful that they will support measures of benefit to the archipelago." [8]

About thirty influential members agreed to go on; influential Democrats as well as Republicans. A particularly thrilling goodwill ambassador would be Alice Roosevelt, who was at the height of her public renown. The President, Taft said, hoped that the visit of Alice "might show to the people of the islands his interest in them and his confidence in their hospitality and cordial reception of his daughter." [9]

The S.S. Manchuria, steaming westward in July, was a Congressional ark with Taft as its Noah. The party would, on the round trip, spend more than two months at sea. A Noah with lesser harmonizing talents might easily have brought back to shore a cargo of snarling, discordant men and women and might have further jeopardized, thereby, the success of his Philippine program. On the contrary, the tour was devoid of friction.

"We took eighty people with us and came back so harmonious that everyone was able to speak to everyone else," Taft reported with justifiable pride.[10]

He found time, during the quiet days at sea, to observe with interest the charms or peculiarities of his fellow voyagers. Representative Nicholas Longworth of Ohio was on board and Taft, quite naturally, shared in the universal speculations regarding the

[7] Taft to Helen H. Taft, Aug. 9, 1904. [8] Taft to H. C. Corbin, March 14, 1905.
[9] Taft to L. E. Wright, March 17, 1905. [10] Taft to Sir John Rodger, Nov. 16, 1905.

possibility that he was to be married to Miss Roosevelt. Taft wrote a few thumbnail sketches of the notables on board:

Senator and Mrs. Nathan B. Scott. Senator Scott is from West Virginia. . . . He is a loud-mouthed, porcine, coarse, somewhat purse-proud man, who made his money himself and brought himself up from a very humble condition to that of a millionaire and a senator. He is good-natured, he is generous with his money, though somewhat hoggish in his desire for accommodations . . . Mrs. Scott . . . is a lady of saturnine expression when unaroused. She has a deep voice . . . and is disposed to complain especially on the sea, which does not appeal to her. . . . The senator took me around the ship the other day and said he would say I was a liar if I ever told this to anyone, but that he intended to carry the West Virginia delegation for me and to contribute $5,000 to my preliminary presidential campaign. I thanked him and told him that I did not intend to organize a preliminary campaign. . . .

Representative and Mrs. William A. Jones from Virginia. A Democratic member and bitter opponent of our policy. His wife is a lovely Virginian, somewhat younger than he, though she must be thirty-six or seven. She uses some rouge, but she has a very shapely form, is very active, dances well, is greatly interested in everything she sees and has the sort of beauty that some women think attracts men. Her husband is one of those amiable men, stubborn beyond expression. . . .

Representative Charles Curtis of Kansas wishes to be a senator. He is part Indian, and while I do not think he would adorn the Senate Chamber, he would do as well as many. . . .

Representative W. Bourke Cochran . . . is a very curious individual. . . . He was born of Irish parentage and received an education with his brother who was sent to France to become a priest, so that he speaks French as he speaks English. . . . He has the air in discussion of a pseudo philosopher and reduces everything to a syllogism, but like many pseudo philosophers he reaches his conclusions from very different motives than from pursuing general principles. . . . He affected great interest in Alice Roosevelt. She hates him because he attacked her father in the last campaign . . . and so when he laid himself open she attacked him in a way that I cautioned her against later on. She called him a man who posed as an Anglophobe and was an Anglophile in private; as a stage orator, a man who was always playing to the galleries with no principles. . . . His good nature, for he must have some, prevented him from getting angry.[11]

The weeks in the Philippines were filled with the usual receptions, banquets and oratorical orgies. To the rest of the official party it must have all seemed a degree wearisome. But to Taft, making the first formal address at Malacanan Palace on August 5, 1905, it was deeply moving. He looked at the crowds massed before him.

". . . every face," he said, "suggests something of crisis or something of interest that filled four years of the life that I spent on these islands."

A week later, perspiring and mopping his face in the hot sunshine, Taft mentioned that many problems had come before him as secretary of war "but always in my heart the Philippine Islands have had the first place." He again looked at the earnest men who hung on his every word.

"I love the noble Filipino people," he said. "I respect to the full their many virtues. I acknowledge their kindness, their hospitality, their love of home and friends. I admire their courage as a warlike people and least of all do I underestimate their aspirations to become a self-governing people and a nation." [12]

But the time had not come for independence, the former civil governor frankly said. He did not add that it would be a long and weary time before prosperity arrived, either. His visit buoyed the courage of the Filipinos immeasurably. But Congress was to remain deaf to many of Taft's pleas on their behalf. He could not longer stay in the islands. Other problems were calling him away. Indeed, on the journey itself, matters of greater importance had occupied much of his time. Among these were Japanese-American relations.

—3—

In 1886, Theodore Roosevelt had hoped for war with Mexico. In 1896, he considered the possibility of sanguinary combat against William Jennings Bryan and his fellow Populists. In 1898, he

[11] Taft to Helen H. Taft, Sept. 24, 1905. (Italics mine.) [12] *Addresses,* Vol. III, pp. 5, 27.

agitated for war with Spain. In 1911, he volunteered to fight against Mexico. In October, 1914, he said that the United States should uphold the neutrality of Belgium.[13] It will be noted, however, that not a single one of all these belligerent expressions was voiced between September, 1901, and March, 1909. It was one thing to urge that some other president involve the nation in blood. It was a far different thing to face the responsibility himself. Theodore Roosevelt, as president or private citizen, was a mixture of many emotions. As president he was the victim of apprehensions, alarms and worries. He was, all in all, a passionate advocate of peace. What would Woodrow Wilson not have given, during the campaign of 1916, to have seen certain confidential letters written by Theodore Roosevelt in 1905 to 1909? But the letters remained hidden, for years and years, in the files which were removed from the White House after March, 1909.

Secretary of War Taft, even more than Elihu Root, was Roosevelt's personal ambassador for peace. Taft's part in the Moroccan crisis of 1905 was, as we have seen, largely limited to the transmission of reports to the President from the German, English and French ambassadors at Washington. In 1905 and 1907, however, he was to be very active indeed in the Far East. There were many things that Roosevelt did not know about foreign affairs; one thing he did know was that Morocco and the East were potential centers of an European conflagration. It was for this reason that he intervened to terminate the Russo-Japanese War. A similar desire for peace lay behind Roosevelt's apprehensions regarding the increasing anti-Japanese sentiment in California. This alarmed him, first, in June, 1905. The situation steadily grew worse.

The Russo-Japanese War came first. As between Russia and Japan, the President admired and favored Japan. In Taft, who also sympathized with the smaller nation, Roosevelt had an emissary who agreed with his views.

"The truth is," the secretary of war wrote in March, 1905, "that the governing classes of the Japanese have elevated the people, and it is the aim of the governing classes that is important. I have no fear of a yellow peril through them. Their purpose is to stand high among the nations of the earth. . . . I think they are more

[13] Pringle, H. F., *Theodore Roosevelt, a Biography,* p. 583.

sincerely friendly to us than they are to any of the other nations, though of course a Jap is first of all a Jap. . . . Still I do not look for any movement of Japan toward the Philippines . . . for I am quite confident that she will look toward the United States as her friend in any negotiations that may be the result of the war. She will have her hands full peopling Korea and the Li Tung [sic] peninsula, and she will be quite content to let the tropical end be on Formosa alone." [14]

This is worth a brief analysis. It may be assumed that Taft had discussed the situation with Roosevelt. It will be noted that even this early the Roosevelt administration conceded that Japan should have Korea. Even more remarkable is the implication that the whole of Liaotung peninsula instead of only Port Arthur at its southern tip was to be restored to Japan; this had been captured by Japan in 1895 but had been handed back to China on demand of Germany, France and Austria. [15] Roosevelt and Taft were to be excessively partial to Japan in the years between 1905 and 1908. They were even to view with complacency the probable domination of China by the Nipponese. Taft's part in the preliminary peace negotiations was, at first, similar to the one he played with respect to Morocco. The President was, in April, 1905, away from Washington and Taft was serving as secretary of state. He reported a visit of Baron Kogoro Takahira, Japanese minister to the United States, who said that an indemnity would be demanded from Russia as well as the cession of the entire island of Sakhalin, to the north of Japan and adjacent to Siberia. Japan would also take Port Arthur. [16]

"The Japs are evidently quite anxious for peace," remarked Taft three weeks later, "but they are also determined . . . not to lose the fruits of a successful war, and in this they are entirely right." [17]

When Taft sailed in July, 1905, ostensibly only to acquaint his Congressional delegation with the wonders of the Philippines, both Russia and Japan had agreed to a peace conference to be held in the United States; Roosevelt, almost singlehanded, had forced them to this decision. Many details remained to be settled, however.

[14] Taft to Martin Egan, March 25, 1905. [15] Dennett, Tyler, *Roosevelt and the Russo-Japanese War*, p. 26. [16] Taft to Roosevelt, April 5, 1905. [17] Taft to L. C. Griscom, April 25, 1905.

The President had instructed Taft to stop at Tokyo and pay his compliments to the Japanese. But the visit was destined to be much more important than that. Roosevelt gave no written instructions to his secretary of war, nor is there any memorandum of verbal orders. It is a plausible assumption, however, that the President imparted his views regarding the Far East. The Russian ambassador at Washington, he wrote in May, was "having a fit" over word that Taft would land in Japan.[18] The result, in any event, was an astonishing conversation between Taft and Count Taro Katsura, the Japanese premier. Its effect was virtually a secret treaty whereby Roosevelt agreed that Japan was to absorb Korea.

The secretary of war conferred with the Japanese premier on July 27, 1905. Two days later he dispatched a lengthy cablegram to Secretary of State Root which was, he said, the "agreed memorandum of conversation between prime minister and myself." No actual quotations were given. The substance of the conversation was as follows:

Taft: Certain pro-Russian influences in the United States are spreading the theory that Japanese victory would be a certain prelude to her aggression in the direction of the Philippine Islands. But Japan's only real interest in the Philippines would be to have them governed by a strong and friendly power such as the United States. Japan did not desire to have the islands governed either by natives, unfit for the task, or by some unfriendly European power.

Katsura: This is absolutely correct. Japan had no aggressive designs whatever on the Philippines and the insinuation of a "Yellow Peril" was only a malicious and clumsy slander circulated to damage Japan. The fundamental principle of Japan's international policy was the maintenance of peace in the Far East. The best and, in fact, the only means for accomplishing this was the drafting of an understanding among Japan, the United States and Great Britain which would uphold the open-door principle. The prime minister well understood the traditional policy of the United States in this respect and knew that a formal alliance was out of the question. But could not an understanding or alliance, in practice, if not in name, be arrived at? Such an understanding would benefit all the powers concerned and would preserve the peace.

18 Pringle, H. F., *op. cit.*, p. 383.

Taft: It is difficult, indeed impossible, for the President of the United States to enter even an informal understanding without the consent of the Senate. But without any agreement at all, the people of the United States were so fully in accord with the policy of Japan and Great Britain in the maintenance of Far Eastern peace that appropriate action by the United States could be counted upon, wherever occasion arose, just as confidently as if a treaty had been signed.

Katsura: As to the Korean question, Korea was the direct cause of the war with Russia, so a complete solution was a logical consequence. If left to herself after the war, Korea would certainly drift back to her former habit of entering into agreements with other powers and thus would be renewed the international complications which existed before the war. Therefore, Japan felt compelled to take some definite step to end the possibility of Korea lapsing into her former condition. This would mean another war.

Taft: The observations of the prime minister seem wholly reasonable. The personal view of the secretary of war was that Japan should establish a suzerainty over Korea. This would require that Korea enter upon no treaties without the consent of Japan. President Roosevelt would probably concur in this, although the secretary of war had no mandate from him. Since he had left the United States, Elihu Root had been appointed secretary of state.

In a postscript to the cable, Taft said that the prime minister had been "quite anxious for the interview." It appears further that Taft, not Roosevelt, took the initiative in suggesting that the United States would view Japanese domination of Korea with approval.

"If I have spoken too freely or inaccurately or unwisely," he concluded in the cable to Root, "I know you can and will correct it. Do not want to butt in, but under the circumstances difficult to avoid statement and so told the truth as I believe it." [19]

Approval from the White House was prompt. "Your conversation with Count Katsura absolutely correct in every respect," telegraphed Roosevelt. "Wish you would state to Katsura that I confirm every word you have said." [20]

Upon receiving this endorsement, Taft moved on toward Manila. The peace conference assembled at Portsmouth, New

[19] Taft to Root, July 29, 1905. [20] Roosevelt to Taft, July 31, 1905.

Hampshire, on August 9, 1905, and Japan, although permitted domination of Korea, was to be very much chagrined at the outcome. Russia paid no indemnity. During September rioting broke out in Tokyo and some of the agitators berated the United States and its president for marring the completeness of Japan's victory. The sons of Japan were learning that evil also lurked in the Occidental civilization which they had so recently adopted. They were discovering that no nation ever actually wins in modern warfare. The finances of Japan had been depleted and its man power drained. The fruits of victory had a bitter flavor.

—4—

Roosevelt was alarmed. He became more so in October, 1906, when the school authorities of San Francisco ruled that Japanese were to be excluded from classes attended by white children. Japan protested that this was in violation of the Treaty of 1894. The excitement increased during the rest of that year and in 1907. In California, of course, rumors persisted that the Japanese were secretly planning to capture the state, and make slaves of its Iowa residents. Hearst's curious newspapers published interviews in confirmation, with travelers returning from the East. Even more horrendous reports reached Roosevelt. Specky von Sternberg, the German ambassador, told the President that England was behind the belligerent attitude of Japan. Charlemagne Tower, the American ambassador at Berlin, said that the Japanese were arming to the teeth. The climax came in January, 1908, when the German Emperor summoned Ambassador Tower and told him, for transmission to Washington, that Mexico was filled with Japanese reservists.

"I say this only for the President's ear," whispered the All Highest; ". . . there are in Mexico at present ten thousand Japanese soldiers."

A less volatile president than Roosevelt might easily have been frightened by these movie-thriller reports. "Thank Heaven we have the navy in good shape," he breathed. But Roosevelt was as angry with California as with Japan. By February, 1907, he had forced the San Franciscans to withdraw their drastic school exclusion order and had effected the "gentlemen's agreement" whereby Japan promised to restrict the emigration of cheap labor. For a little while there was quiet. Then came outbreaks against Japanese in San Francisco.[21] So Roosevelt decided to dispatch the fleet around the world, as a vivid proof of Uncle Sam's power. He decided to have Taft again visit Tokyo as proof of Uncle Sam's amiability.

The secretary of war was going to the Philippines; this time to open the Assembly which was to provide a measure of self-government for the Filipinos. Taft was inclined to minimize the reports that Japan was on the war path.

"Personally," he told the President, "I never have been able to believe that Japan is serious about a war with us in the next three or four years. . . . I cannot think that in their present financial condition they desire to measure swords with us." [22]

That was in July, 1907. Roosevelt declined to be comforted. He had already sent Major General Leonard Wood, in command on the archipelago, detailed plans for holding the Philippines against an attack by Japan. He worried over immigration statistics which indicated that the gentlemen's agreement was being violated.[23] In August, the President dictated a panic-stricken letter to his good-will ambassador. He said that it might be well to grant independence to the Filipinos because the United States could not, in any event, hold the islands against an attack:

The Philippines form our heel of Achilles. They are all that makes the present situation with Japan dangerous. I think that in some way and with some phraseology that you think wise you should state to them if they handle themselves wisely in their legislative assembly we shall at the earliest possible moment give them a nearly complete independence. . . . Personally I should be glad to see the islands made independent, with perhaps some kind of international guarantee for the preservation of order, or with some warning on our part that if they did not keep order we would have to interfere again; this among other reasons because I would rather see this nation fight all her life than to see her give them up to Japan or any other nation under duress. . . .

[21] Pringle, H. F., op. cit., pp. 398-407. [22] Taft to Roosevelt, July 26, 1907. [23] Pringle, H. F., op. cit., p. 408.

The President pointed out, truthfully enough, that the public was rather weary of the Philippines. "In the excitement of the Spanish War people wanted to take the islands," he wrote. "They had an idea they would be a valuable possession. Now they think they are of no value . . . it is very difficult to awaken any public interest in providing any adequate defense of the islands." [24]

The secretary of war did not propose to promise independence if it could be avoided. He felt that this would do unmitigated harm:

I appreciate the difficulties that you present, but I sincerely hope that you will make no public declaration on the subject until I return from the Philippines. I shall then present in separate form my report on the islands, and it seems to me that at that time we can formulate an expression of opinion . . . which will be safer than anything that can be said now. It is not necessary for me to make definite statements to the Filipinos themselves. Indeed, I think it would be unwise to do so. All I expect to do is to point out to them that they now have before them the greatest opportunity possible to show such evidence for self-government as they claim to have, and that the American people are not anxious to retain control of the islands except as it may be necessary to do so in order to protect the Filipino people themselves. [25]

Thus it was doubly important, if his wards were to be protected, to convince Roosevelt that war between the United States and Japan was unlikely. The S.S. *Minnesota,* sailing from Seattle on September 13, 1907, reached Japan on September 28. Two days later, the secretary of war was given a dinner at the Imperial Hotel at Tokyo and he poured verbal oil on the waters of Japanese-American relations. He praised the heroism of the Japanese armies in the late war. He insisted that the peace treaty had established the nation in the family of great world powers. True, "for a moment only, a little cloud has come over the sunshine of a fast friendship of fifty years," the secretary said, referring to the agitation regarding California. And why was that? His explanation was, to say the least, ingenious:

". . . it took a tremendous manifestation of nature to bring it about. Only the greatest earthquake of the century could have caused the slightest tremor between such friends . . . there is nothing in these events of injustice that cannot be honorably and fully arranged by ordinary diplomatic methods between the two governments conducted as they are by statesmen of honor, sanity and justice. . . . War between Japan and the United States would be a crime against modern civilization. It would be as wicked as it would be insane."

Taft was clever. He referred to Korea and said that the American people were confident that Japan pursued there "a policy that will make for justice and civilization and the welfare of a backward people. . . . Why should Japan wish a war that must stop or seriously delay her plans of reform in Korea?" Taft was clever because he exuded honey and at the same time gave warning.

"Why should the United States wish war?" he asked. "War would change her in a year or more into a military nation . . . and tempt her into warlike policies. In the last decade she has shown a material progress greater than the world has ever seen before. . . . It has been suggested that we might relieve ourselves . . . by a sale of the [Philippine] Islands to Japan or some other country. The suggestion is absurd. Japan does not wish the Philippines. . . . But, more than this, the United States could not sell the islands to another power without the grossest violation of its obligations to the Philippine people." [26]

Taft summarized his findings in Japan in a long cablegram which was finally dispatched on October 14, 1907, from Manila. He was optimistic over the probability of peace. Count Hayashi, the Japanese minister of foreign affairs, had reiterated that his country had no lust for the Philippines and would feel concern if the islands were to be sold by the United States. Taft had given assurance that the outbreaks in California were the result of sensational journalism and did not represent American sentiment accurately. On his part, Count Hayashi replied that only a small part of the Japanese public had any interest whatever in the subject of emigration to the United States. He agreed, however, that the Japanese objected violently to any treaty which restricted Japanese and admitted Europeans. Taft reported to the President:

[26] *War Secretary Diaries*, pp. 2008-2015.

I said they seemed willing to restrict Japanese immigration provided it did not involve the open concession in a treaty; he [Hayashi] said that was true. I said it would be wise to cut off further immigration [*sic*] to Honolulu; that if they increased the number of Japanese workmen beyond the 65,000 who were now there it would probably result in an attempted reduction of wages and labor troubles. . . . Hayashi . . . repeated that it was impossible to put in treaty form such exclusion; said Japanese government would be most discreet in issuing passports.

Similar amicable expressions marked an audience with the Emperor. By far the most significant part of Taft's cable was his conclusion that the "Japanese government is most anxious to avoid war . . . they are in no financial condition to undertake it" and Taft's obvious complacency when he learned that Japan intended to dominate China. Regarding this, he said:

They have their hands full in the settlement of Korea which is more difficult than anticipated. Their attention is centered on China. *Their army has been increased by one division, not to fight with us but because of China;* they are determined to secure a predominance in China's affairs and to obtain every commercial concession possible and believe it essential to retain their armament to meet contingencies there.

The only chance of war with the United States, Taft concluded, lay in the fact that the "people are conceited, as Count Hayashi says, and would resent bitterly a concession by their own government supposed to involve an admission of inequality with other races." The wise course, therefore, was to maintain the *status quo* and secure a settlement by another informal agreement rather than a treaty.

"I hope this statement may assist you," Taft said, "in . . . making plain to California congressmen necessity for stopping agitation and accepting the present satisfactory *status quo.*" [27]

But this was to be very difficult. California congressmen could always win votes by howling about the "Yellow Peril." The friction continued through Taft's own administration as president. It was to be among the problems faced by Woodrow Wilson.

[27] *War Secretary Diaries*, pp. 2023-2033.

—5—

Meanwhile, during the fall of 1906, the peripatetic secretary of war had been dispatched to Cuba where smoldering fires of revolt seemed ready to flame. This, among all his assignments, worried Taft the most. Perhaps he was a degree out of breath. Undoubtedly, knowing nothing about Cuba, he had small confidence in his ability to deal with the situation. The weeks in Havana, he declared when it was all over, had been the most trying in his career.[28] At times his gloom was almost comical.

"It is in the midst of a great thunderstorm. I am looking out on Havana harbor and were it not for you and the children and others near and dear," he assured Mrs. Taft, "I should not regret it if one of the bolts now flashing and resounding struck me." [29]

Cuba was not, of course, really an independent nation. There were political as well as economic reasons behind this. Safety of the United States in the event of war depended on military control of so near-by a territory. Following pacification of Cuba, American capital began to flow in.

"The great trouble is," wrote Taft when he arrived in Havana, "that unless we can secure peace, some $200,000,000 of American property may go up in smoke in less than ten days." [30]

In April, 1898, when Congress authorized the war with Spain, a pledge was given that the United States would free, pacify Cuba and then "leave the government in control of the island to its people." But this lofty conception gave way to more practical considerations. The result was the Platt Amendment— so called because it was drafted by United States Senator Orville H. Platt of Connecticut and, in the mysterious fashion of Congress, added to the Army Appropriation Act in March, 1901. The Platt Amendment marked the end of Cuban self-government. It provided that Cuba could sign no treaties giving foreign nations control. Cuba's rights in contracting debts were limited. The nation agreed that the United States might intervene "for the preservation of Cuban independence, the maintenance of a government adequate for the protection of

[28] *Collier's Weekly,* April 13, 1907. [29] Taft to Helen H. Taft, Sept. 27, 1906. [30] *Idem,* Sept. 20, 1906.

life, *property* and individual liberty." Further, the United States was to be granted lands needed for coaling and naval stations. Naturally enough, the Cuban patriots who had objected to the yoke of Spain did not welcome this new yoke, even though it was a far lighter one. Protests were unavailing, however. The more fair-minded Cubans appreciated that the United States could take no other course. On May 2, 1902, Tomás Estrada Palma was sworn into office as the first president of the republic of Cuba and the United States withdrew. But it did not withdraw very far.[31]

The secretary of war was enjoying the breezes of Murray Bay and worrying, if at all, only about the 1906 Congressional campaign when the troubles of Cuba intruded upon him. It might be necessary, he informed Brigadier General J. F. Bell, chief of staff, to send troops to the Caribbean.

"Hurry the matter on . . ." he ordered, "and let me know . . . the situation . . . in respect to concentrating a force at a point where they could land in Cuba promptly and efficiently." [32]

For President Palma of Cuba, Taft had been informed, was in trouble. The Cuban President was a sincere and idealistic chief executive, if less wise and able than the crisis demanded. At first his administration had been nonpartisan and his Cabinet had numbered members of the Liberal as well as the Moderate party. But at the start of 1905, Palma concluded that his legislative program could best be accomplished through the Moderates. This meant an abrupt termination of government salaries and other lucrative revenues for the Liberals. Indignant at the deprivation, they began to talk of revolution. An even more serious grievance developed during the elections in 1905. The laws supervising them were faulty. General Freyre Andrade, secretary of the government, explained subsequently that a Cuban election without a degree of fraud was impossible. The degree in this instance was the addition of about 150,000 names to the registration lists, an overwhelming show of strength by the Moderates and the withdrawal of the Liberals from any participation whatever in the balloting. Their leaders said, frankly, that revolution was their only remedy. Palma was inaugurated in March, 1906, and Havana boiled with reports of impending strife.[33] These were immediately communicated to President Roosevelt. They increased through the spring and summer of 1906 and Roosevelt, as always, sent a hurry call for Taft. This time, in contrast to his Panama policy, the President had slight sympathy with the revolutionists. To his credit, he did not wish to interfere.

"I am doing my best," he said when a degree of quiet had been achieved, "to persuade the Cubans that if only they will be good they will be happy; I am seeking the very minimum of interference necessary to make them good." [34]

Taft's assignment was to make them good. On September 8, 1906, President Palma admitted that he could not guard life or property and requested protection by American naval vessels. Two days later he asked for American troops. On September 13 the Cuban President threw up his hands and confided that he would resign from office. He would gladly turn over the government to such representatives as the United States might send. Thereupon Roosevelt announced that Taft and Acting Secretary of State Robert Bacon would visit Cuba. He demanded that hostilities cease. The only alternative was intervention.[35]

So the secretary of war regretfully left the shores of the St. Lawrence, stopped off in Washington for a conference with army officials, and took a train for Florida whence he would be transported to Havana with all speed. The patience which had marked the attitude of Taft toward the equally volatile Filipinos was now absent. He wished that Secretary of State Root were going in his place.

"You know the Cuban situation . . . ," he said to Root, "and I am so lacking in knowledge of it, that it is quite embarrassing for me to go, but the truth is that the Cuban government has proven to be nothing but a house of cards." [36]

While in Washington, Taft also took time to answer an argument offered by William Jennings Bryan that the President could not intervene without the consent of Congress. The law, he wrote Roosevelt, was clearly on his side. On the other hand, might it

[33] Hill, H. C. *op. cit.*, pp. 86-90. [34] Pringle, H. F., *op. cit.*, p. 299. [35] Hill, H. C., *op. cit.*, pp. 90-96. [36] Taft to Root, Sept 15, 1906.

not be wise to refer the matter to Attorney General W. H. Moody and obtain an official ruling on the treaty with Cuba?[37]

"I shall not submit it to Moody . . ." the President answered. "I should not dream of asking the permission of Congress. . . . You know as well as I do that it is for the enormous interest of this government to strengthen and give independence to the executive in dealing with foreign powers. . . . Therefore the important thing to do is for a president who is willing to accept responsibility to establish precedents which successors may follow even if they are unwilling to take the initiative themselves."[38]

Taft and Bacon reached Havana on September 19. Taft cabled the President that the government controlled only the coast and the provincial capitals and that anarchy was prevalent everywhere else. A truce between the insurgents and the federal forces was thus far in force, but the situation was very serious.[39] He added that the Palma government lacked support of the large majority of the Cubans and that it could not be maintained except by "forcible intervention against substantial weight of public opinion in island." No doubt whatever existed that the Palma government "flagrantly and openly used and abused its power to carry the elections. . . . Quite probable that Liberals would have done same thing as Moderates had the power been theirs, but I cannot think they would have done it in such a brutal and open way entirely unnecessary to accomplish purpose." The best solution, Taft concluded, was to permit the resignation of Palma and select some impartial Cuban for a temporary chief executive. Then the election laws should be revised.[40]

On his arrival, clearly, the secretary of war was inclined to sympathize with the Liberals. He found, as he confided to Mrs. Taft, that Palma was "a good deal of an old ass," who was "quite obstinate . . . and difficult . . . and doesn't take in the situation at all."[41] Taft did not, however, adhere to these early conclusions. He had innumerable conferences with the federal and the insurgent leaders. By September 22, 1906, he had reached the conclusion that it would be better to continue Palma in office because "it gives

[37] Taft to Roosevelt, Sept. 15, 1906. [38] Roosevelt to Taft, Sept. 19, 1906. [39] Taft to Roosevelt, Sept. 20, 1906. [40] Idem, Sept. 21, 1906. [41] Taft to Helen H. Taft, Sept. 23, 1906.

THE BASEBALL FAN. WASHINGTON, 1908-1909

TAFT, AS SECRETARY OF WAR, INSPECTING PANAMA

continuity to the government and diminishes in some respect the evil of the present situation and of the compromises that must be effected." He felt that Palma, however, incompetent, was "honest and patriotic." There was, he told the President, "nobody in the Liberal party fit to be President." [42]

But Palma had already had more than enough of the presidency and continued to insist that he would resign; Taft told Roosevelt that intervention under the Platt Amendment was the only solution.

"In their characteristic Spanish way," he added, "Palma and the Moderates will now take away their dolls and not play." [43]

It was all very trying. Taft, on the scene, soon discovered that intervention would be inescapable. Roosevelt, in Washington, was learning once more that the American people had grown weary of imperialism and its obligations. The President always had a sensitive, not to say apprehensive, finger on the public pulse. Its sensitiveness increased during an election, and this was the 1906 campaign. So Taft was deluged with messages from the President ordering him to avoid intervention, or if not that, to "avoid the use of the word 'intervention' in any proclamation," to "do anything that is necessary . . . but to try to do it in as gentle way as possible." [44]

"Some of his telegrams have been a little extreme," Taft complained to his wife, "but on the whole he has been supporting me well."

The secretary of war was conscious, too, of the political potentialities of intervention. He no longer deluded himself that the 1908 presidential nomination was repugnant. A crucial day just prior to intervention was, as he described it, "the most unpleasant of my life. . . . I am in a condition of mind where I can hardly do anything with sequence. . . . I wake up in the morning at three and four o'clock and do not sleep any more. My appetite ceases to be sharp." In short: "I don't know what they are saying in the United States, but I feel as if I was going to have a great fall from the height to which the compliments of the press raised me." [45]

The picture Taft painted was far too gloomy. He became pro-

[42] Taft to Roosevelt, Sept. 22, 1906. [43] Idem, Sept. 24, 25, 26, 1906. [44] Hill, H. C., op. cit., pp. 99-100. [45] Taft to Helen H. Taft, Sept. 27, 18, 1906.

visional governor of Cuba on September 29, 1906, and described his position to Roosevelt:

My theory in respect to our government here, which I have attempted to carry out in every way, is that we are simply carrying on the Republic of Cuba under the Platt Amendment, as a receiver carries on the business of a corporation, or a trustee the business of his ward; that this in its nature suspends the functions of the legislature and of the elected executive, but that it leaves them in such a situation that their functions will at once revive when the receivership . . . is at an end, so all the documents that I sign are headed "Republic of Cuba under the Provisional Administration of the United States" and I have signed a decree continuing all the diplomatic functions of the government. . . . All this effort is apparently exceedingly gratifying to the Cuban people and softens much the humiliation that they have suffered from the intervention.[46]

It was the wisest of gestures. The insurgents, on appeals from the provisional governor, began to turn in their arms. The Cubans, generally, succumbed to the earnestness and patent sincerity of the large man who had arrived from the United States. They concluded that the United States did not, after all, propose to annex their country. On October 13, 1906, Charles E. Magoon succeeded Taft in Cuba. A census was taken. The election laws were revised. On January 28, 1909, the American troops were withdrawn and the Liberals took control of Cuba.

By then, Taft had been elected president. He had departed from Cuba as rapidly as he could. Before leaving, he described his anxiety "to get away from this fetid atmosphere and go even into one of Hearstism as a preference." [47] For Taft had turned his back on a life of judicial contentment and had become a politician; it was the most important decision of his life and the one, in all probability, which he regretted most.

[46] Taft to Roosevelt, Oct. 3, 1906. [47] Taft to C. P. Taft, Oct. 9, 1906.

CHAPTER XIX

SURRENDER

TWO FACTS regarding the presidential campaign of 1908 may now be set forth categorically. The first is that Taft had reluctantly become a candidate for the Republican nomination by the summer of 1905. The second is that he received, during 1905 and 1906, every possible assurance—everything short of a public announcement—that he could count on the active support of Theodore Roosevelt. The facts are important historically in view of the contradictory statements contained in memoirs and autobiographies published during the past twenty years. They are essential to any understanding of why Taft, loathing politics as he did, made the race.

On July 10, 1905, en route to the Philippine Islands on the S.S. *Manchuria,* he pondered the political situation at home. "It is evident that I am considered in the field," he wrote. He noted that Elihu Root had become secretary of state in President Roosevelt's Cabinet. He recalled a conversation with Roosevelt before leaving the United States.

"The President was particular to say to Root, so the President told me," Taft continued, "that he was committed to me for the presidency so far as his influence might properly go and I infer that Root has no definite intention of running for that office though 'you never can tell.' If the Chief Justice would retire, how simple everything would become." [1]

Unquestionably, Root did not want the nomination. He might have had it— by running for governor of New York in 1904. Heavy pressure had been brought for him to do so. Then he would, in all likelihood, have been reelected in 1906. He would have been the obvious presidential nominee in 1908. But Root pondered all the pros and cons in 1904 and decided that he "was not willing to pay the price." [2]

[1] Taft to Helen H. Taft, July 10, 1905. [2] Jessup, Philip C., *Elihu Root,* Vol. I, pp. 427-428.

So the tides swept Taft onward. He was wearied by them. "I am tired out with talking, and I do not see why I cannot be given some opportunity for a quiet enjoyment of a quiet life," he protested after returning to Washington that fall.[3] But the air hummed with political gossip. Only a dishonest man— or a man actively seeking the nomination and maneuvering to win it— could have evaded an admission that the prize would be accepted if it was offered. Taft was honest. He was a passive rather than an active contestant.

"My ambition . . . is to become a justice of the Supreme Court," he continued to insist. "I presume, however, there are very few men who would refuse to accept the nomination of the Republican party for the presidency, and I am not an exception. If it were to come to me with the full understanding by the party of the weaknesses that I should have as a candidate [by which he meant his labor decisions], I should not feel that I had any right to decline, and should make the best fight possible to secure my election. . . . No organization, formal or informal, exists. . . . If I am to be nominated (an hypothesis to me most improbable), it will be done without any organization with which I have any connection." [4]

These were the sentiments of a political amateur. An active organization for Taft would soon come into being. It would spend money, circulate propaganda, and would— in the end— appeal to President Roosevelt to make appointments from among the Republicans who had demonstrated their foresight by climbing aboard the Taft bandwagon at an early stage of its journey. Meanwhile, in the White House, President Roosevelt was considering his own responsibilities in the matter. Theodore Roosevelt, as a literary man and historian in 1887, had condemned the action of Andrew Jackson in selecting Martin Van Buren to succeed him in the presidency. Theodore Roosevelt, as President of the United States, was less condemnatory. After the election of 1904 he had announced, to his subsequent regret, that he would never again be a candidate for the presidential nomination. But Roosevelt was aware, by 1906, that the continuation of his policies would depend upon a successor who agreed with them.[5] Roosevelt was as sincere as he was high-minded.

[3] Taft to Horace D. Taft, Nov. 25, 1905. [4] Taft to Giles Taintor, Dec. 1, 1905.
[5] Pringle, H. F., *Theodore Roosevelt, a Biography*, p. 497.

He was wholly loyal to his friend. If Taft really wanted the Supreme Court, he should have that. If he desired the presidency, he would receive the administration's support.

A new crisis arose soon after New Year's Day, 1906. Another decision— life was so filled with the necessity for decisions!— had to be made. The secretary of war and Mrs. Taft had gone to Lakewood, New Jersey, for a visit at the home of their friends, Mr. and Mrs. John Hays Hammond. While they were there, a long-distance telephone call came from the President. Taft returned from the conversation to say that Roosevelt had again offered him a post on the Supreme Court; this time to take the place of Associate Justice Brown. He said that he was inclined to accept. Immediately an argument started. Mrs. Taft expressed her disapproval. So did Mr. Hammond. They both pointed out that he could have the presidential nomination in 1908. If the offer had been that of chief justice, both agreed, no objection would have been made.[6]

Some time later the secretary of war and Mrs. Taft were dinner guests at the White House. The President escorted them to the second floor library and threw himself into an easy chair. He closed his eyes.

"I am the seventh son of a seventh daughter and I have clairvoyant powers," he said in a sepulchral voice. "I see a man weighing three hundred and fifty pounds. There is something hanging over his head. I cannot make out what it is. . . . At one time it looks like the presidency, then again it looks like the chief justiceship."

"Make it the presidency," said Mrs. Taft.

"Make it the chief justiceship," said Mr. Taft.[7]

—2—

Taft did not commit himself. The matter dragged. On March 10, 1906, the secretary of war, aware that he moved in the stream of history, wrote down the developments of the past weeks:

The Supreme Court vacancy of Justice Brown I hoped I might escape, but the situation is veering around now to a position where

[6] Hammond, John Hays, *The Autobiography of John Hays Hammond*, pp. 532-533.
[7] Kohlsaat, H. H., *From McKinley to Harding*, pp. 161-162.

it may be impossible. I am very anxious to go on to the Supreme Bench. The President has promised me a number of times that he would appoint me chief justice if a vacancy occurred in that position and he knows that I much prefer a judicial future to a political future.

The secretary of war told, in this private memorandum, of a conference at the White House when the vacancy occurred in January, 1906. The President, Secretary of State Root, Attorney General Moody and Taft discussed the situation. Roosevelt said that Taft could have the appointment if he desired it. But the secretary of war declined on the ground that many matters relating to the Philippines remained to be settled. A few days later, Taft was invited to lunch with Root and Moody. Again, the Supreme Court was discussed:

Root was opposed to my taking it on the ground that I was a presidential quantity seriously, and that the President ought not to take me out of the running. Moody thought the same thing, but I did not agree upon that point. I said . . . that I did not want to take the appointment because I was in three jobs, the War Department, the Panama Canal and the Philippine business, and I thought these were critical times and I wanted to fight them out for a year or two longer.[8]

It is impossible to question Taft's sincerity as he thus continued to spurn the judicial post he really wanted. He had refused to leave the Philippine Islands in October, 1902, because his work was not finished. He repeated the declination two months later, on the same grounds. But it is not quite as easy to believe that Taft was entirely accurate in analyzing his inner, basic reasons for the persistent rejection of elevation to the Supreme Court.

"I know that few, even among my friends," he admitted, himself, "will credit me with anything but a desire, unconscious perhaps, to run for the presidency and that I must face and bear this misconstruction of what I do."[9]

Besides, Taft was confronted by energetic and potent opposition of his wife, who never faltered in her determination to keep him

[8] *War Secretary Diaries,* pp. 126-127. [9] Taft to Roosevelt, July 30, 1906.

from decay in judicial life. On March 9, 1906, following a Cabinet meeting, another session was held at which the President, Moody, Root and Postmaster General George B. Cortelyou debated Taft's presidential boom and decided "that I stood the best chance among the Republicans." Taft's version of the meeting was:

> The President, as is very frequent with him, began to compare Root, Moody and me, and . . . repeated the statement that I would become chief justice if the place became vacant. I left it in his hands, but asked him . . . not to decide the matter until after I had gone to New York to talk with my brothers. I also explained . . . that Nellie is bitterly opposed to my accepting the position and that she telephoned me this morning to say that if I did, I would make the great mistake of my life. The President has promised to see her and talk the matter over with her and explain the situation if he concludes to act.[10]

So Mrs. Taft called on the President and gave emphatic reasons, it may be assumed, why her husband should refuse the appointment as associate justice. The President outlined his reaction in a letter in which he mentioned "a half hour's talk with your dear wife." Roosevelt had supposed, he said, that his friend had desired the Supreme Court. Now he knew that this had been an error:

> My dear Will, it is pre-eminently a matter in which no other man can take the responsibility of deciding for you what is right and best for you to do. . . . As far as I am personally concerned I could not put myself in your place because I am not a lawyer and would under no circumstances, even if I had been trained for a lawyer, have any leaning toward the bench; so in your case I should as a matter of course accept the three years' of service in the War Department, dealing with the Panama and Philippine questions, and then abide the fall of the dice as to whether I became president, or continued in public life in some less conspicuous position, or went back to the practice of the law.

On the other hand, Roosevelt continued, the immense importance of the Supreme Court in the coming quarter century could not be minimized:

[10] *War Secretary Diaries*, p. 128.

I do not at all like the social conditions at present. The dull, purblind folly of the very rich men; their greed and arrogance, and the way in which they have unduly prospered by the help of the ablest lawyers, and too often through the weakness or shortsighted-ness of the judges . . . and the corruption in business and politics have tended to produce a very unhealthy condition of excitement and irritation in the popular mind, which shows itself in part in the enormous increase in the socialistic propaganda. . . .

Under such circumstances you would be the best popular leader, and with your leadership we could rest assured that only good methods would prevail. In such a contest you could do very much if you were on the bench; you could do very much if you were in active political life outside. I think you could do most as president; but you could do very much as chief justice; and you could do less, but still very much, either as senator or associate justice. . . .

As I see the situation it is this. There are strong arguments against your taking this justiceship. In the first place my belief is that of all the men that have appeared so far you are the man who is most likely to receive the Republican presidential nomination and who is, I think, the best man to receive it, and under whom we would have the most chance to succeed.

The President added that Elihu Root might "be at least as good a president as either you or I; but he does not touch the people at as many points as you and I touch them." Moreover, Root "would probably not be as good a candidate as I was, or as you would be."

It is not a light thing to cast aside the chance of the presidency, even though of course it is a chance, however a good one . . . it is well to remember that the shadow of the presidency falls on no man twice, save in the most exceptional circumstances. The good you could do in four or eight years as the head of the nation would be incalculable.

It was a wise, friendly and forthright letter. It concluded with the thought that Taft, if he now mounted the bench, would serve for twenty-five years, at least, on "the greatest court in Christendom (a court which now sadly needs great men)" and would pass on questions "which seem likely vitally and fundamentally to affect the social, industrial and political structure of our commonwealth."

The President made a specific pledge that he would move Taft to the center of the bench, as chief justice, if he now became an associate justice and the post became vacant prior to March, 1909. But if Taft declined, Roosevelt pointed out, this goal might be lost. For it was possible that he might persuade Knox or Root to become associate justice with the promise of the same elevation:

Now, my dear Will, there is the situation as I see it. It is a hard choice to make, and you yourself will have to make it . . . But whichever you take I know that you will render great and durable service to the nation for many years to come, and I feel that you should decide in accordance with the promptings of your own liking, of your own belief, as to where you can render the service which most appeals to you, as well as that which you feel is most beneficial to the nation. No one can with wisdom advise you.[11]

"No one can with wisdom advise you. . . . You must decide"; such phrases played a theme of warning throughout this remarkable letter. Was Theodore Roosevelt thinking, as he penned them, of the determined lady who had just called upon him and offered her own, pronounced views on the folly of judicial life? Taft read the letter, but did not heed these phrases. He did not decide for himself. The decision was, in any event, postponed. The President, at Taft's request, agreed to make no appointment to the Supreme Court until December, 1906. In the meanwhile, the President was shaken by occasional doubts as to the propriety of standing so squarely behind Taft in the presidential contest. He assured William Allen White that summer that "I am not going to take a hand in his nomination for it is none of my business."[12] But Roosevelt, too, had trouble in taking Roosevelt's advice. Taft told his wife in May:

I went to the White House for a long talk with the President. He was full of the presidency. . . . He wants to talk to you and me together. He thinks I am the one to take his mantle and that now I would be nominated. He said that Root had been out to talk the night before and had discussed me and my presidential chances with much detail.[13]

[11] Roosevelt to Taft, March 15, 1906. [12] Pringle, H. F., *op. cit.*, p. 499. [13] Taft to Helen H. Taft, May 4, 1906.

—3—

With the possible exception of Senator Foraker, the most reluctant person to believe that Taft was the best 1908 candidate was Taft himself. He wriggled and squirmed and suggested other men almost up to the day that the Republican National Convention assembled in June, 1908. In the fall of 1906 he said that Charles Evans Hughes of New York, who had achieved wide renown in an investigation of the insurance companies and had been nominated by the Republican party for governor, would make an excellent presidential contender. Taft also thought that Root should run instead of himself. Finally, he kept assuring Roosevelt that the people of the nation demanded a third term. Mrs. Taft, needless to say, did not share these views.

Mrs. Taft's distrust of the President— it was never to fade— was heightened by a conversation at this time in which Roosevelt discussed the excellent campaign being waged by Hughes in New York. He must have said something about the special qualifications of Hughes as a presidential nominee in 1908; Mrs. Taft so reported, in any event, to her husband who was campaigning for the Congressional ticket in the West. Taft wrote amiably that the nomination of Hughes was a sound idea:

Mrs. Taft said that you said that you might . . . have to support Hughes for the presidency. If you do you may be sure that you will awaken no feeling of disappointment on my part. While I very much appreciate your anxiety that I shall be nominated . . . as a most gratifying evidence of your good will, you know what my feeling has been in respect to the presidency, and can understand that it will not leave the slightest trace of disappointment should your views change and think it wise to make a start in any other direction.[14]

A prompt denial arrived from Roosevelt, who did not understand how Mrs. Taft could have conveyed such a sentiment. "What I said to her," Roosevelt told his friend, "was that you must not be too entirely aloof because if you were it might dishearten your

[14] Taft to Roosevelt, Oct. 31, 1906.

supporters and put us all in such shape that some man like Hughes
. . . would turn up with so much popular sentiment behind him
that there would be no course open but to support him." [15] Some
weeks prior to this exchange, Taft had been certain that Root
was the best man for 1908.

"I shall talk with the President about this . . ." he wrote. "The
prestige of his name is one which would sweep things." [16]

Meanwhile, Taft urged, why did not Roosevelt ignore his hasty
postelection pledge? He described the sentiment of the people, as
he saw it on his western trip that year, and said it called for the
renomination of the President. The voters ". . . if you will not
accept . . . flatter me by saying that I must come next," Taft wrote,
"but the second choice is so far from the first choice that I only
warn you that the ground swell . . . is beginning . . . and you are
going to have bad quarters of an hour during the next eighteen
months on this account." [17] A fortnight later, Taft told Root that
it would "be a great thing for the country to have another term of
Roosevelt." In all probability, Hearst would be the Democratic
nominee in 1908 and Roosevelt, Taft thought, was the only candidate certain to defeat "such a dealer in filth as this hideous prod-
uct of yellow journalism . . . [this] immoral monstrosity." [18] At
the same time Taft told his wife, who must have been immeasurably irritated by these reiterations, that he would be "personally
delighted" if, as he believed, Roosevelt could not escape the nomination.[19] Eleven months later, with campaign headquarters in
operation, Taft was still convinced that Roosevelt "does not know
his own strength with his own people." [20]

Taft's pleas fell on ears that would not hear. Only his aged
mother, now eighty years old and close to death, agreed— as she
had agreed before— that politics was not the forte of her son. She
was not surprised, Mrs. Alphonso Taft wrote in January, 1907, "that
public life looks less and less attractive to you:

So near the throne, you realize that "Uneasy lies the head that
wears a crown." Roosevelt is a good fighter and enjoys it, but the

[15] Roosevelt to Taft, Nov. 8, 1906. [16] Taft to Helen H. Taft, Sept. 14, 1906. [17] Taft
to Roosevelt, Oct. 31, 1906. [18] Taft to Root, Nov. 10, 1906. [19] Taft to Helen H. Taft,
Nov. 7, 1906. [20] Taft to C. P. Taft, Sept. 11, 1907.

malice of politics would make you miserable. They do not want you as their leader, but cannot find anyone more available.[21]

It was a prophetic statement from an old lady, soon to die. In April, 1907, she journeyed to California to visit her daughter and some reporter asked her, facetiously, to name her candidate for the presidency.

"Elihu Root," she answered, in all seriousness, while the reporter gasped.

Then she explained that her son belonged on the bench, not in the White House.[22] Mrs. Alphonso Taft did not live to see the accuracy of her prophecy or to say, as mothers sometimes do, "I told you so" when trouble followed trouble in the White House. She did not even live to watch her son in his day of unblemished triumph when he took his oath as president of the United States and the pages of his administration waited, clean and white, for the writings of wisdom, folly and destiny. She died on December 7, 1907, as her son sailed from Hamburg toward home. Taft did not get back in time for the funeral.

"She was a remarkable woman," he mourned, "and retained her mental and physical vigor for the full eighty years. . . . There was that sturdy element that she got from her Puritan ancestors that was seen in everything she did, everything she said. . . . I went out to Cincinnati simply for the purpose of putting a wreath on her grave." [23]

This year, 1907, was to be one of surrender. Taft knew perfectly well that a presidential nomination, Republican or Democratic, does not come from a mighty tidal wave of public endorsement. For all his dislike, he had been close enough to practical politics to know that some kind of organization was essential. He knew, too, that victory at the Republican National Convention in June, 1908, was possible only if delegates were pledged to his candidacy well before the convention assembled. And he knew, finally, that these delegates would consist, in the main, of state and county Republican leaders, of city and village bosses; in short, of the professional politicians who had, as officeholders, been happily

[21] Louise Torrey Taft to Taft, Jan. 21, 1907. [22] *Idem*, April 29, 1907. [23] Taft to Mrs. Samuel Carr, Dec. 24, 1907; to Delia Torrey, Dec. 26, 1907.

feeding at the public trough. Taft struggled to escape the corollary that only officeholders faithful to the Roosevelt-Taft cause should continue to find nutriment. But he accepted that necessity, too, before many months had passed. For him to have done otherwise would have been the height of folly. His chance of winning would have faded completely before the end of the year.

Charles P. Taft, loyal and vigorously active for his brother, was tossed by no such doubts. By March he had engaged A. I. Vorys to manage affairs in Ohio. Was it necessary to start so soon? asked Will. In one letter, suggesting delay, he spelled the name "Voris"; an indication, perhaps, of how remote it all seemed to him. In the same letter, he rejected a suggestion that the appointment of postmasters in Ohio be made on the basis of their pro-Taft sentiments.

"It would not do for me to be about that business anyhow . . . I would rather be out of it," he pleaded.[24]

By July, however, Taft was writing to William Loeb, Roosevelt's secretary and political strategist, for a list of southern Republican national committeemen which he wanted "for the purpose of sending to Vorys." He informed Loeb, also, that Charles Dewey Hilles, who had been active for McKinley in 1900, would take charge of the situation in New York.[25]

"I appointed no man *for the purpose* of creating Taft sentiment; but I have appointed men *in recognition* of the Taft sentiment already in existence," was Roosevelt's own ingenuous explanation of the events of these months.[26]

To that end, the President instructed Postmaster General George von L. Meyer to take personal charge of Ohio appointments and to follow the recommendations of Taft.[27] By August, the candidate had partially abandoned his earlier scruples. A postal employee in Ohio, it appeared, was not an entirely loyal supporter.

"I showed your letter to Postmaster General Meyer," Taft told Vorys. "From what you say . . . I doubt if he can remove Davis, if he has been a good postmaster. . . . I should not think he ought to." [28]

---

[24] Taft to C. P. Taft, March 23, 1907. [25] Taft to William Loeb, July 7, 1907. [26] Pringle, H. F., *op. cit.,* p. 497. [27] Roosevelt to Taft, July 15, 1907. [28] Taft to Vorys, Aug. 14, 1907.

Two collectors of internal revenue in Kentucky were, Taft complained to Loeb, behind the abortive presidential boom of Senator C. W. Fairbanks. "If those two men kept their hands out," he said, "there would not be the slightest difficulty in Kentucky." [29] Gradually Taft arrived at a doctrine of his own regarding the political activities of officeholders; they were either to work for him or maintain a peaceful silence.

"I am not asking," he explained, "that the federal officials shall help me, but I do not think it is unfair that they shall keep their fingers out. . . . It may be necessary to remove Capers [another internal revenue official in Ohio] at once." [30]

"Do you want any action about those federal officials?" volunteered Roosevelt as 1908, the crucial year, began. "I will cut off their necks with the utmost cheerfulness if you say the word!" [31]

On one point Taft was adamant. He declined to make any concessions to Foraker of Ohio, by this time a bitter opponent of Roosevelt particularly with respect to railroad regulation. The senator greatly desired the nomination, himself, and he must often have pondered his folly in starting Taft on the path to glory and to the status of powerful rival. He was now far too powerful. Foraker wisely concluded that the presidential nomination was beyond his reach. It was suggested, on his behalf, that he should endorse Taft for President in return for support of his senatorial candidacy.

"I have a right," Taft replied, "to ask those who honor me with their good opinion . . . not to do anything which shall, in its last analysis, be a bargain, for even the appearance of such a bargain would not make for the good of the Republican party of the state." [32]

A splendid forthrightness, as though to atone for the earlier instances when he had permitted Foraker to aid him, marked Taft's rejection of any deal. He told the President:

. . . rather than compromise with Foraker, I would give up all hope for the presidency. I must explain to you that the Ohio brand of politics the last twenty years has been harmony and concession on

[29] Taft to Loeb, Aug. 25, 1907. [30] Taft to C. P. Taft, to Vorys, Dec. 26, 1907. [31] Roosevelt to Taft, Jan. 6, 1908. [32] Taft to C. P. Taft, May 11, 1907.

the subject of principle to the last degree. Foraker has been the blackmailer in all Ohio politics. . . . He blackmailed McKinley and Hanna into allowing him to return to the Senate on condition of his support . . . and then he worked against and thwarted McKinley in all his desires whenever opportunity came. Now he may beat me, but he won't beat me through any concession or compromise of mine. If he beats me he will have to beat me in a stand-up fight. . . . I now feel as if were I defeated for the presidency I should go into the senatorial fight. . . . And if I didn't do anything more it would be greatly for the benefit of the country to remove from his powerful position in the Senate a man so reactionary, so unscrupulous, and so able as Foraker is.[33]

The fight was in the open. On July 29, 1907, Foraker announced that he was opposed to Taft's candidacy. On the following day the Ohio Republican State Central Committee met at Columbus and endorsed, by a vote of 15 to 6, that candidacy.[34] The incident marked the virtual elimination of Foraker from public life. His downfall was to be made utterly certain when Hearst, thirteen months later, revealed the connection between the Ohio senator and the Standard Oil Company.

—4—

The great legal abilities of Joseph Benson Foraker had been all too well impressed on Roosevelt and Taft. He had kept alive, whether for political reasons or because he sincerely believed that a great injustice had been done, that cause célèbre— the dismissal without honor of Companies B, C, and D of the 25th United States Infantry, Colored. This was a major embarrassment of Taft's preconvention campaign because, as secretary of war, he had approved and executed the President's orders. And now Taft faced the alarming possibility that the Negroes of the United States would visit punishment upon him. No Republican could be nominated for the presidency without the support of the Negro brethren from the

[33] Taft to Roosevelt, July 23, 1907. [34] Washington *Post*, July 30, 1907; New York *Tribune*, July 31, 1907.

southern states. Taft, at first, was really an innocent victim of Roosevelt's impetuosity.

On November 17, 1906, Secretary of War Taft returned from his campaign trip to find trouble awaiting him in Washington. On his desk were resolutions from various political clubs protesting against the discharge of the Negro soldiers which had followed a shooting affray at their post, on the outskirts of Brownsville, Texas, the night of August 13, 1906. A barkeeper had been killed; a police officer and another man were wounded. Bitter feeling against the Negro troops had been voiced by the white people of the dismal city on the Rio Grande River and they immediately placed the entire blame on the Negro soldiers. A preliminary investigation by the army authorities confirmed this contention. It was stated that certain members of B, C, and D companies must have done the shooting. All denied their guilt, however, and none would admit any knowledge of the outrage. So Roosevelt, on November 5, ordered that all the soldiers of the three suspected units be discharged. Among the 160 men were six Medal of Honor soldiers and a number of others with distinguished records. The order meant that they would receive no pensions and might, in their old age, be destitute. They were barred from admission to soldiers' homes. Having thus struck another blow for righteousness, Roosevelt left on a visit to Panama and permitted Taft to handle the vehement protests.[35]

The secretary of war was not familiar with the case. In view of the protests, he telegraphed Roosevelt suggesting that the dismissals be halted pending further inquiries into the probable guilt of the soldiers. But Roosevelt was in one of his pure action moods. He answered that he cared "nothing whatever for the yelling of either the politicians or sentimentalists. The offense was most heinous and the punishment I inflicted was imposed after due deliberation."[36] Unless additional information was available, the dismissals would continue.

"The President is worked up on the subject and does not propose to retreat from his position," remarked Taft to his wife. "I do not think he realizes quite the great feeling that has been

[35] Pringle, H. F., *op. cit.*, pp. 459-460. [36] Roosevelt to Taft, Nov. 21, 1907; *War Secretary Diaries*, pp. 664-665.

aroused on the subject. I assumed to delay the execution of the order till I could hear from him, and that has been heralded as an act of disobedience, but I do not think he will regard it as such. However, not hearing from him yesterday, I ordered the discharges to proceed." [37]

Taft was soon insisting that he regarded Roosevelt's order as "fully sustained by the facts." As in the case of the Panama revolution, he permitted temporary atrophy of the judicial lobes of his brain. "The truth is that there were about fifteen of them [the troops] who were engaged in murder," he said, "and the evidence seems to show that the rest of them destroyed, by agreement, every opportunity to detect who they were." [38] But there was no authentic evidence before Taft to show that ten or fifteen or fifty of the Negroes had done the shooting, and nothing whatever in proof of his assertion that a conspiracy of silence existed. These were merely Rooseveltian theories, accepted without question.

Thousands of pages of testimony were taken in the Brownsville case and an impartial examination of them leads to the conclusion that unknown Negroes of the 25th Infantry were, in all probability, guilty. But there are vital gaps in the evidence. An air of mystery still hangs, after thirty years, over the case. No individual soldier was ever successfully charged with participation in the crime. President Roosevelt was desperately anxious to have the responsibility fixed. Secretary of War Taft reverted to his old function, to the role he had played as prosecutor in Hamilton County, Ohio, and did his best to get evidence against the men. He failed to do so. At times, perhaps through proddings from the White House, he permitted his agents to step beyond the bounds of propriety.

"I am not responsible for the Brownsville order; but I think it entirely justified," he observed. "It would have been better, as I suggested to the President, to have a rehearing, as it always is where a decision is questioned. If a rehearing shows that the original conclusion was wrong, it presents a dignified way of recalling it; and if it does not, it enforces the original conclusion." [39]

The President, however, had stated all too definitely that he

[37] Taft to Helen H. Taft, Nov. 21, 1906. [38] Taft to R. H. Davis, D. E. Sickles, Nov. 24, 1906. [39] Taft to C. P. Taft, Jan. 1, 1907.

had been absolutely right in his order of dismissal. Now Taft
had to prove, if he could, that such had been the case. Assistant
Attorney General M. D. Purdy was delegated to Brownsville to
interview all possible witnesses. Taft took personal charge and gave
Purdy specific instruction regarding their examination.

"This is not an examination to support a particular side of the
case," he told Purdy, "but one to elicit the truth." [40]

But the truth never was uncovered. Weeks of investigation
brought out little more than the known facts: that a group of men
had shot up the town, that witnesses— not all of them reliable—
had sworn that they were Negro troops, that empty shells were
found in the streets and that these had come from army rifles, that
the troops had been abused and mistreated by the white people of
Brownsville and had every reason to hate them. Taft admitted
that there might be innocent men in the battalion. Some of the
troops might even know nothing whatever about their comrades'
guilt. But a battalion containing unidentified murderers could not
be allowed to remain in the army. If, in the future, any of the soldiers could prove his innocence, an application for reinstatement
would be heard. All of this was set forth in the secretary of war's
annual report on December 6, 1906. [41]

Roosevelt's error, for which Taft had to pay the penalty in
unjustified criticism, was that he was far too positive in his assertions of what had gone on on the night of August 13. The Senate,
egged on by Foraker, ordered an investigation on December 6. The
President answered with a pugnacious message filled with sweeping
generalizations from which, in due time, he was forced to withdraw. The senator from Ohio leaped joyously to point out the
contradictions in Roosevelt's message. On January 27, 1907, at the
Gridiron Dinner, both Roosevelt and Foraker shattered convention
by hurling anathema at each other. [42]

"Foraker is determined to make the President as uncomfortable
as possible, and incidentally eliminate me from the Ohio situation,"
said Taft, accurately enough. [43]

Roosevelt would have been wiser if he had limited his statements on Brownsville to Taft's reports. They were an honest sum-

[40] Taft to M. D. Purdy, Dec. 27, 28, 30, 1907. [41] *War Secretary Diaries*, pp. 767-792.
[42] Pringle, H. F., *op. cit.*, pp. 460-462. [43] Taft to C. P. Taft, Dec. 26, 1906.

mary of the evidence and left, as the secretary of war said, no "reasonable doubt that the men who committed this outrage were Negro soldiers from Fort Brown, and therefore of the battalion of the Twenty-fifth Infantry stationed there."[44] The investigations continued through 1907 and in March, 1908, a majority of the Senate committee upheld the President. But Foraker analyzed the minority opinion in a long and effective speech. He offered the theory that the shooting had been done by hostile residents of Brownsville so that the Negro troops would be blamed and transferred. His argument was shrewd and clever and it convinced the Negro voters, anew, that an injustice had been done.[45] Taft debated the wisdom of answering his adversary. He plowed through 3,000 pages of printed testimony during a brief rest at Murray Bay. He actually drafted a speech, running to some 25,000 words, but it was never delivered. Senator Lodge advised him not to do so.

"If I spoke, I should speak with candor," Taft explained to Roosevelt, "and I am not sure that I would win back any Negro votes, and I might drive some away."[46]

The President agreed. The important thing, Roosevelt answered, was not to allow an idea to get abroad that he was afraid of Foraker. But that, of course, was absurd.[47]

No valid criticism can be made against Taft, up to this point, regarding Brownsville. He was heir to a nasty situation. He could not take issue with the President. But wisdom would have dictated that nothing more be done after the Senate's report of March, 1908, had endorsed the administration. Instead, Taft engaged Herbert J. Browne, described as a journalist, and W. G. Baldwin, who was the head of a detective agency, to seek still further evidence.

"The Brownsville investigation before the Senate, while it established beyond any reasonable doubt the correctness of the conclusion reached by you . . ." he wrote Roosevelt, "has done nothing to identify the particular members of the battalion who did the shooting or were accessories before and after the fact."

Browne and Baldwin, with a "large force of detectives" were to interview all the former soldiers of the 25th Infantry who could

[44] *War Secretary Diaries*, p. 1047. [45] Foraker, J. B., *Notes of a Busy Life*, pp. 260-298. [46] Taft to Roosevelt, July 7, 1907. [47] Roosevelt to Taft, July 10, 1907.

be found; by now, back in civilian life, they were scattered through-out the country.[48] This was done. About $15,000 in government funds was spent in this final attempt to learn the identity of the murderers. But it resulted only in another Congressional message from Roosevelt and this was still another recession from his original accusations of guilt. The President said that the men who were innocent would be admitted back into the army. The investigation had determined "with tolerable definiteness" the ones who were guilty.[49]

It did nothing of the sort. No prosecutions were ordered. On January 12, 1909, Foraker again spoke on the Brownsville case and charged that Browne and Baldwin, as agents of Roosevelt and Taft, had used illegal and grossly unfair methods in attempting to obtain confessions. He said that Browne had reported falsely re-garding one alleged confession. The final speech by Foraker added to the peculiar odor which had hung over the Brownsville case from the start.[50] By now, however, Taft was president-elect and was less worried over the Negro vote. One of his first official acts in the White House was to recommend army courts of inquiry which would pass on readmission of the Negro infantrymen.[51]

The whole thing had worried the secretary of war for more than two years. But he had been able to laugh about it, too. He described a large dinner party at which Mrs. Taft had been unable to engage her usual head waiter. A new Negro proved incompetent and the function went off badly.

"I told Nellie . . . that it was simply the Twenty-fifth Infantry getting even with us," Taft reported.[52]

—5—

Other perplexities, although none so grave, marked emergence into active political life. In his speech at Bath, Maine, in the campaign of 1906, Taft had gone on record in favor of downward tariff revision. Now he was being urged to ignore the subject and

[48] Taft to Roosevelt, April 16, 1908. [49] Pringle, H. F., *op. cit.*, p. 463. [50] *Congressional Record*, Jan. 12, 1909, pp. 827-844. [51] Taft to Senator E. E. Warren, March 29, 1909. [52] Taft to C. P. Taft, Dec. 15, 1906.

imply, by his silence, that he was an unadulterated protectionist. Taft declined.

"I do not propose to be mealymouthed about the tariff," he said. "I have already taken a position . . . which is generally known and I don't know why I should run away from mentioning it." [53]

Wall Street was being shaken by tremors, which foretold the panic of 1907, and Taft was informed that the administration would be blamed for the disturbances. But Taft refused to become "greatly excited over the stock market" although he had "no doubt that there are a great many people who would conspire together to make it appear that the depression is due to the President, when in fact it is due to other causes. . . .

"The country is somewhat more independent of Wall Street than it used to be," he wrote, and revealed, thereby, that his knowledge of finance was less than thorough. "Accumulations of money in country banks and in other places have been so great in the past decade as to make the connection between New York banks and country banks less intimate than they were. Moreover, the financial solidity of the country has so increased in recent years that a mere slump in prices does not bring about failures and business disaster, that in times past attended these conditions." [54]

From time to time, during 1907, it was suggested that he should resign from the Cabinet and divorce himself from the possible handicap of Roosevelt. But Taft saw clearly the absurdity of this. If he were defeated "because I am close to Roosevelt, then . . . I ought to be defeated on that account. . . .

"I very much enjoy being in his Cabinet," he added, "and shall be quite content if the nomination goes elsewhere. He knows and I know . . . that if I am elected president, I will be president myself, and I don't have to convince either himself or myself by leaving. . . . From a political viewpoint . . . it would be a great mistake . . . my strength is largely as his friend." [55]

Suspicious Mrs. Taft did not agree. She had objected to the break with Foraker. Too close, perhaps, to the influences of the Atlantic seaboard, she believed that the President's strength was

[53] Taft to Vorys, Aug. 2, 1907. [54] Taft to Mabel Boardman, Sept. 11, 1907. [55] Taft to E. G. Lowry, Aug. 6, 1907.

ebbing fast. She did not trust Roosevelt's professions of support, either. She was certain, she wrote, "that this is all a part of his scheme to get himself nominated." [56]

"I do hope," said a subsequent letter, "that you are not going to make any more speeches on the Roosevelt policies as I think the matter should be left alone for the present— and you are simply aiding and abetting the President in keeping things stirred up. Let the corporations rest for a while. It is soon enough to talk about it when something needs to be done, and whatever the West may be, in the East it has an aggressive air." [57]

These wifely admonitions were not wholly wrong in so far as they concerned the political situation generally. Roosevelt was running head on into his final fight with Congress. It was true that the East was filled with hostile critics. But Mrs. Taft was utterly mistaken in her idea that the President was using Taft as a means for capturing the nomination himself. The mind of the President, Taft explained, "changes from time to time. . . . At one time he is very confident that I will be nominated . . . and at other times he thinks Hughes will be an obstacle to me, or that he may himself be forced in a position where he may be unable to decline, and so he writes me . . . long letters which I have to answer by saying that he need not be alarmed over my probable disappointment at not getting the nomination. . . . I think he is a good deal excited about the severe criticisms that he hears from his tribal enemies." [58]

Roosevelt, as always, had been airing aloud his inner doubts. He had declared to one White House visitor that the Taft boom was a disappointment in that it lacked spontaneity and resiliency.[59] Clearly, the President was leaving himself a bridge or two of escape in the event that the people did not, after all, want his secretary of war. He was perfectly frank about it. He told Taft, in September, 1907, that it still seemed probable that the party would unite on his candidacy. But there were other candidates with merit. Secretary of the Treasury Cortelyou, who would soon win renown in the 1907 panic, was more than receptive and Roosevelt had assured him that this was in no way disloyal to the administration. Senator Knox would make a good president. Amazingly,

[56] Helen H. Taft to Taft, "Easter Sunday," 1907. [57] *Idem*, Feb. 15, 1908. [58] Taft to Mabel Boardman, Sept. 11, 1907. [59] C. D. Hilles to Vorys, Nov. 13, 1907.

in view of his later criticism of Taft for working with Uncle Joe Cannon, Roosevelt wrote that even the speaker of the House would be "a good one except on one or two lines." But the strongest candidate of all was Governor Hughes of New York.[60]

Roosevelt and Taft shared a mutual dislike for Hughes. They conceded his ability. They conceded his integrity. They feared his political strength, and they did not like him personally.

"The politicians all dislike Hughes and so does the President," Taft wrote. "He has, however, the backing of the people of the state who have approved his policy. He is a man without magnetism and a conscientious man pursuing a plan of action which ultimately will throw him because it has no legitimate basis. He thinks he can command the support because it involves no obligation on him to look after the party or to recognize their interest."[61]

Thus Politician Taft recoiled from impartial, nonpartisan Hughes. He was, in the years ahead, to change his opinion radically. Part of Taft's dislike was based on the belief that the reactionaries of the G.O.P. planned to use Hughes as their candidate to beat Roosevelt.[62]

"Hughes is so cautious," Taft complained, "that he has not expressed himself on much of anything."[63]

Taft was not apprehensive about the other aspirants. He suggested, to Roosevelt, the possible wisdom of bringing the fight into the open by a statement, late in 1907 or early 1908, that the issue was really "between Hughes and me, with the distinct understanding that it is Roosevelt and anti-Roosevelt in that way. . . . I believe we could beat Hughes, for I think the Far West and a great part of the Middle West, some of the South, and some of New England, would be with us."[64] The President agreed that this might be wise. Hughes was their archenemy. Behind him stood the anti-imperialists, the big corporations, Wall Street, and those infamously anti-Roosevelt journals, the New York *Sun* and the New York *Evening Post*.[65] The alarm was, as it turned out, rather baseless, as baseless as the Taft-Roosevelt disparagements. Hughes

---

[60] Roosevelt to Taft, Sept. 11, 1907. [61] Taft to C. P. Taft, Aug. 18, 1907. [62] *Idem*, Sept. 11, 1907. [63] Taft to H. W. Taft, Sept. 12, 1907. [64] Taft to Roosevelt, Sept. 12, 1907. [65] Roosevelt to Taft, Sept. 19, 1907.

was elected governor for a second term. He promptly accepted when President Taft offered him a post on the Supreme Court.

It must have been with no small relief that Taft set sail for the Philippines in September, 1907. He made a number of speeches en route. One distressing incident occurred as he crossed the continent and he hastened to confess it to his chief:

A thing happened in the park [Yellowstone] which gave me a bad quarter of an hour of worry. We were traveling so fast in order to get through that I made a mistake as to the days of the week, and supposed that we were at the Old Faithful Inn on Saturday instead of Sunday, and so we played a game of whist in the lobby of the hotel Sunday night. I did not know it until Mrs. Taft came to me the next morning alarmed on the subject. The truth is that Mrs. Taft is quite particular about not playing cards on Sunday, inheriting that from her early training, and not deriving it from her marital association. It is quite probable that this will be published, and it is exasperating beyond words . . . but it was an entirely innocent breach of the Commandments. The difficulty is that . . . it may be as bad in the eyes of the Sabbatarians not to know when Sunday is as knowingly to desecrate the day. However, I wanted you to know the truth if the matter came out.[66]

The spies of the Democratic party appear to have been asleep, however, for no outburst of indignation followed this insult to Christianity. Taft left the Philippines in November and proceeded homeward by way of Vladivostok, the Trans-Siberian Railway and Europe. He did not call on the German Kaiser because of possible jealousy on the part of England and France.[67] He passed directly through Moscow, however, and could not avoid an audience with the Russian Czar. Taft complimented the Little Father on the rich, luxuriant topography of Siberia which he had supposed to be a barren, frozen land. Not very tactfully, Taft added that a good many Americans had been critical of the purchase of Alaska from Russia for the same reason; now, however, it had returned many times the purchase price.

"He said," pointed out Taft in his memorandum of the conversation, "that the criticism was not alone on our side; that there

[66] Taft to Roosevelt, Sept. 4, 1907. [67] Taft to Charlemagne Tower, Nov. 20, 1907.

were people who criticized the action of their government in having sold Alaska."

They shifted to the safer subject of armies, and Nicholas asked the secretary of war to tell him about the American military establishment. Taft remarked, in passing, that he regretted the briefness of his stay in Russia. He had pressing obligations at home.

"Yes," said the Czar, entirely unaware that humor touched his answer, "but after all, of course, you love the army as I do." [68]

The United States Army had nothing whatever to do with Taft's haste. He was boarding the S.S. *President Grant* out of Hamburg on December 7, 1907, so that he could return to run for president.

"We have heard little . . . from . . . home," Taft wrote as he was about to sail, "but such little as we have heard leads me to think that the so-called boom of your humble servant, unduly inflated at one time, is now having all the gas let out of the bag and that the references to the White House and other gratifying pipe dreams that were allowed to have their sway . . . will remain as nothing but a pleasant memory and will be like that light that never was on sea or land." [69]

Taft was rested by his long journey. He looked into the future with contentment. Even Mrs. Taft, he was aware, would soon get over her disappointment if Roosevelt found it wiser to nominate Hughes or Cortelyou or Uncle Joe Cannon. The previous summer, at Murray Bay, Mrs. Taft had answered consolingly when he had complained that he was not a facile and emotional public speaker.

"Never mind if you cannot get off fireworks," she said. "It must be known by this time that that is not your style. . . . If people don't want you as you are, they can leave you, and we shall both be able to survive it." [70]

[68] *War Secretary Diaries,* pp. 2200-2203. [69] Taft to Admiral Hemphill, Nov. 30, 1907. [70] Helen H. Taft to Taft, Aug. 18, 1907.

CHAPTER XX

GOOD OLD BILL

EVEN THE most astute strategists sometimes fail to distinguish political assets from political liabilities. Between 1904 and 1908 a legend was forming about William Howard Taft and he was, as long as he lived, never to escape entirely from its implications, good and bad. He was, said this legend, large and fat and always smiling. He was friendly and good-natured and sometimes lazy. He was too easily influenced. Good old Bill, the salt of the earth.

Many people contributed to the legend. Taft was responsible himself. He had encouraged publication of Elihu Root's witty inquiry, cabled to the Philippines, concerning the health of the horse which had borne his tonnage. Associate Justice Brewer of the Supreme Court added to it in an address at Yale.

"Secretary Taft is the politest man alive," he said. "I heard that recently he arose in a streetcar and gave his seat to three women." [1]

During the pre-convention campaign in the early spring of 1908, the New York *Sun* published a short item which sent waves of laughter, most of it affectionate and friendly, beating against the person of the leading contender for the Republican presidential nomination. On his Far Eastern trip the previous fall, it appeared, the secretary of war had paused in Hong Kong. On a former visit to Hong Kong his sedan chair, borne by coolies, had collapsed under his weight. So Consul General Wilder took pains to see that this did not occur again. He solemnly contracted with one Yu Wo, a chair builder of the city, to fashion a sedan which would be amply strong. The documents in the case were duly forwarded to the State Department at Washington and released for publication in New York.

[1] *War Secretary Diaries*, p. 421.

I, the undersigned, Yu Wo of 15B Wellington Street [stated the contract between Wilder and the chair builder] agree to make a sedan chair for the American consul general. . . . This chair is to be used to carry the American giant, the Honorable William Howard Taft. Said Taft being one of the most conspicuous orna- ments of the American Wai Wu Pai [Imperial Cabinet], it would obviously discredit this nation if the chair should disintegrate. . . . To avert international complications of this sort, I, Yu Wo, assert my skill as a chairmaker.

It shall be reinforced at all weak points. . . . The shafts shall be of double diameter. The body itself shall be of eventful width. . . . Red cloth shall adorn the seat of the chair and gleaming brass look defiantly out to a point that unconsciously, fokis, amahs and dealers in rice shall say: "Certainly this nation of the open door that has so long befriended the Middle Kingdom is a great power." . . .

The consul general may have the use of the chair October 11 and 12, 1907, after which the chair belongs to me, with the under- standing that if ex-President Cleveland, also reputed to be of heroic size, tours the world, the consul general shall direct his steps to my shop. . . . With such precautions do I safeguard the dignity of a friendly power and contribute an honest chairmaker's part in pre- serving the Peace of the East.[2]

Even Roosevelt, although he begged Taft to fight hard against the sinners who opposed his election and the administration's policies, urged his candidate to radiate good nature.

"Let the audience see you smile, *always,* because I feel that your nature shines out so transparently when you do smile— you big, generous, high-minded fellow," the President said. "Moreover, let them realize the truth, which is that for all your gentleness and kindliness and generous good nature, there never existed a man who was a better fighter when the need arose." [3]

Unfortunately, the two conceptions were mutually exclusive to a large segment of the public mind. The newspaper cartoonists added to the caricature, of course. So did various nauseating cam- paign jingles to which Taft, incredibly, seems to have offered no objection. At a banquet in February, 1908, the following lines, no worse than scores of others, were sung:

2 New York *Sun,* March 20, 1908. 3 Roosevelt to Taft, Sept. 11, 1908.

Billy Boy, we think you're awfully cunning,
Billy Boy, you're pretty round for running . . .
O, your smile is famed in story, Billy Boy,
        Broad and wide,
        Side to side—
It's a never-ending glory, Billy Boy,
And it wins a heap of delegates beside.[4]

It is possible, of course, that the portrait did actually win delegates although it may be stated as a political fact that the patronage power of the administration was far more effective. It is possible, too, that a rotund and chuckling Taft warmed the hearts of the voters. But grave peril as well as a large element of untruth lurked in the conception. In the years of trouble ahead, when Taft struggled against overwhelming odds in the White House, all other facets of his character faded. Men forgot the degree to which he had fought for his wards in the Philippines and the extent to which, in complete sincerity, he had upheld the Roosevelt program. All they could see was Taft's grin which hung, like the grin of the Cheshire cat, in a darkening political sky.

It is also possible, although this cannot be more than a theory, that Taft's advisers would have been wiser had they bent their efforts to show other sides of his character. They might, for example, have given wider circulation to a sketch written by Oscar King Davis of the New York *Times*. Mr. Davis spent a day in the war secretary's office in March, 1908, and described the arduous duties of the position and the incredible burden of work. An aide was helping the war secretary wade through documents relating to court-martial cases which had piled up. Taft had to approve or reject the findings. One of the more serious convictions related to a lieutenant who had been sentenced to dismissal.

"The man is a bad egg," said the aide. "The army is better off without him. If you will just read the judge advocate general's memorandum . . ."

Taft said, however, that he would go through the whole record. He did so rapidly. Silence fell over the room. At last Taft looked up as his eye reached a point in some typewritten page.

[4] *War Secretary Diaries*, p. 2737.

"The officer lied about the charges!" he said scornfully. "He tried to lie out of it. I think the sentence should be carried out." [5]

Another incident, if properly publicized, would have been useful, too, in dispelling the legend that Taft did little more than laugh. On March 3, 1908, he attended a banquet at Boston and a speaker who came before the secretary of war referred to President Roosevelt as a "political blue pill" which had, no doubt, been needed to cure the ills of the body politic, but which was necessary no longer. Taft's face grew crimson.

"When I love a chief," he said, when his turn to speak came, "and when I admire him from top to toe, I cannot be silent and permit such insinuations, although they may be hidden in a jest." [6]

—2—

The nomination of Taft for the presidency had been fairly certain, contrary to his gloomy expectations, when he returned from his world tour in December, 1907. Cortelyou had withdrawn from the race. The only rival was Governor Hughes of New York. Hughes had let it be known that he would accept if the honor came to him. But Hughes was less than zealous in pursuit of it. There is ample ground for the theory that the New York politicians were not actually behind him, but were using his name for strategical purposes. They proposed to switch the delegation to some other candidate at the convention. The New York governor did go as far as to deliver an address on January 31, 1908, at which he outlined, in a restrained and decorous way, the principles for which he stood. But Governor Hughes had slight knowledge of the cunning of the man who labored for Taft from the White House. The President selected that very day to send a bristling message to Congress. It was his most violent onslaught against corrupt business and voiced his most vehement plea for the "moral regeneration of the business world." The message monopolized the headlines and the judicious phrases of Hughes were swept into silent futility in the criticism and praise which followed the Rooseveltian utterance.

[5] New York *Times,* March 29, 1908. [6] Washington *Post,* March 4, 1908.

Delighted Washington correspondents flatly asked the President whether he had timed his outburst maliciously.

"If Hughes is going to play the game," he said, "he must learn the tricks." [7]

Some two months prior to this maneuver, Roosevelt had suppressed any lingering doubts as to the availability of Taft. On a morning in January his private secretary, Loeb, had suggested the necessity for making up his mind beyond change. Otherwise, he said, a chance still remained that he would be forced into the nomination himself. Roosevelt would not have objected to this had it not been for his firm conviction that he could not be elected. So he agreed with Loeb. He seems to have made one final gesture to Root— although Root, in later years, could not recall it— and was informed that this wise and able man would under no circumstances accept. Then he dispatched Loeb to Taft for final, emphatic instructions that he was the crown prince. No official statement would be made, of course. None was needed. But word would be allowed to get about. Friendly correspondents would circulate it. [8] So Taft, barring unforeseen improbabilities, would be the Republican nominee. What manner of man lay beneath the bulk and the smile? What did Taft really think on the issues of the day?

Taft was fifty-one years old in 1908; relatively, a young man for the presidency. He had been in public office, virtually without interruption, since 1880. For the first two decades he had been noted for his precocity. Taft had been a very youthful assistant prosecuting attorney of Hamilton County, Ohio, in 1881. He had been one of the youngest judges. So during these twenty years a great deal of praise had been heaped upon him; partly for the able work that he did and partly because he was so young to do it at all. Had life, until now, been too easy for William Howard Taft and the fates too kind? In March, 1900, he had been appointed president of the Second Philippine Commission and, again, success crowned his efforts. Four years later he joined Roosevelt's Cabinet as secretary of war. These last two posts were difficult in the extreme. But Taft mastered all the obstacles. A man who was more buoyant and more self-centered might have derived from them a deep, inner

[7] Sullivan, Mark, *Our Times*, Vol. IV, p. 304. [8] Pringle, H. F., *Theodore Roosevelt, a Biography*, pp. 500-501; Jessup, P. C., *Elihu Root*, Vol. II, p. 124.

security. Somehow Taft did not achieve this. There were elements of softness in his character, still. The difficulties which he was to face between 1909 and 1913 would have been well-nigh insuperable for any Republican president; such was the state of the nation. They were completely so for Taft because adversity had touched him so rarely, because he had not been hardened by misfortune or defeat.

He was to have more than his share of both in this approaching quadrennium. The fates had smiled upon him for twenty-eight years and now they were to frown. It was to be said that Taft betrayed the friend who put him in the White House. He was to be charged with having abandoned the principles of liberalism which had marked the Roosevelt years. I think it can be shown that the charge is untrue. It is important, then, to pause for a brief analysis of the social, economic and political views of Taft in 1908. He set forth the credo of his faith at the close of 1907 in a private letter:

I am a member of President Roosevelt's Cabinet. I agree heartily and earnestly in the policies which have come to be known as the Roosevelt policies. Those policies, stated succinctly, are that the guaranties of the Constitution shall be in favor of life, liberty and property and shall be sacredly maintained; that *the guaranty with respect to the right of property would be undermined by a movement toward socialism;* that this movement has gained force by the use of accumulated wealth and power in illegal ways and by duress to suppress competition and center financial control in a few hands; that these methods are contrary to statute law and that one of the commonest of them has been discrimination by the railroad corporations in favor of the great concerns that control enormous shipments of merchandise; that until Mr. Roosevelt came into control the laws adopted for the purpose of minimizing the evils of this misuse of aggregated wealth were almost a dead letter; that Mr. Roosevelt had the courage, energy and ability to rouse the people to the necessity of enforcing these laws, that he took the great corporations by the throat, so to speak, who had been increasing their profits by a violation of the law, and he put the fear of God into the hearts of their managers and he put an end to its being fashionable and conventional to ignore the existence of the statutes of the United States. . . .

He did not merely make speeches on this subject, but he did

the things which effected the purpose, and when he said that the laws must apply to the rich and the poor he made it so. Now I am in his Cabinet because I sympathize and believe in carrying out those principles, and because I do and say so I am to be called the subservient tool of the man with whose views I agree. If not, what is the alternative? It is that while I am in the Cabinet or having been in the Cabinet I shall come out and say that I don't agree with these policies with which I do agree. . . . Is it possible that a man shows lack of originality, shows slavish imitation, because he happens to concur in the views of another who has the power to enforce those views? *Mr. Roosevelt's views were mine long before I knew Mr. Roosevelt at all.* You will find them expressed in my opinions in so far as it was proper to express them in judicial opinions, and I am not to be driven from adherence to those views.[9]

It is vital to emphasize that Taft, speaking thus courageously, was talking about the Theodore Roosevelt who had, since September, 1901, been President of the United States. Another Theodore Roosevelt was to arise on Taft's political horizon and cause him heartache and bewilderment. The later Roosevelt cast loose from certain of the principles thus endorsed by Taft in December, 1907. The Roosevelt of 1901 to the end of 1908 (there were some indications that he was changing early in 1909) was not really a radical. His concern was the preservation of society in its existing form. On the one hand, labor must not be so powerful as to endanger capitalism. On the other, capitalism must be held within bounds so that socialism would not be encouraged. And how did Roosevelt work toward the ends he sought? In March, 1903, Taft had expressed anger and irritation over the conduct of Senator Aldrich regarding a reduction of the Philippine tariff. The President answered:

You are unjust to Senator Aldrich. My experience for the past year and a half, including the two sessions of the Senate which have just closed, has made me feel respect and regard for Aldrich as one of that group of senators, including Allison, Hanna, Spooner, Platt of Connecticut, Lodge and one or two others, who, together with men like the next speaker of the House, Joe Cannon, are the most powerful factors in Congress. With every one of these men I at times differ radically on important questions; but they are the

[9] Taft to C. M. Heald, Dec. 25, 1907. (Italics mine.)

THE RIGGS NATIONAL BANK.

FORMERLY RIGGS & CO.

Washington, D. C.,

Sepr. 8, 1906

Hon. Wm. H. Taft,

City,

Dear Sir:—

Your account appears to be overdrawn

$ 324 55

Please give it your ~~immediate~~ attention.

Very respectfully,

THE RIGGS NATIONAL BANK.

NOT "IMMEDIATE" FOR THE SECRETARY OF WAR

See page 285]

AWAKE AND ASLEEP

[*See page 286*

leaders, and their great intelligence and power *and their desire in the last resort to do what is best for the government,* make them not only essential to work with, but desirable to work with. Several of the leaders have special friends whom they desire to favor, or special interests with which they are connected and which they hope to serve. But, taken as a body, *they are broad-minded and patriotic, as well as sagacious, skillful and resolute.*[10]

Taft became too greatly influenced by these men. But no wonder he was confused, in 1911 and 1912, when emissaries who passed between Oyster Bay and the White House told him that Roosevelt was disappointed because he was working with these "sagacious, skillful resolute" men— as he had described them in 1903— who, despite their occasional conservatism, sought honestly to benefit their country. Taft was defending himself, in 1908 and 1909, against the charge of undue radicalism; not against being a reactionary.

"I believe myself to be as conservative as anyone within this company," he told a gathering of Boston manufacturers. "I believe that in connection with personal liberty, the right of personal property is the basis of all our material progress in the development of mankind and that any change in our social and political system which impairs the right of private property and materially diminishes the motive for the accumulation of capital by one individual is a blow at our whole civilization." [11] More specifically, these were Taft's views on the issues of the day:

Labor. Labor has a legal right to organize, to strike, to enforce its demands by any peaceful method. In some respects, the courts had abused their injunction powers to oppress labor. Labor leaders should have a right to be heard before being enjoined. It might be wise to have a second judge hear contempt proceedings following violation of an injunction. A jury trial would, however, weaken the power of the courts. The boycott in labor disputes is illegal. The closed shop was an influence against the right of every man to work for whom he pleased, without duress.[12]

Capital. It must be forced to obey the law. The trust magnates, the railroad leaders, the Wall Street financiers and other powerful

[10] Roosevelt to Taft, March 19, 1903. (Italics mine.) [11] *War Secretary Diaries,* p. 2268.
[12] Taft to Llewelyn Lewis, Jan. 6, 1908; *War Secretary Diaries,* p. 2423.

forces had worked to undermine the Roosevelt control program. The capitalist system is the best thus far devised, however, and should be preserved.[13]

Panic of 1907. The disturbance was caused, at least in part, by irregularities, breach of trust, stockjobbing, overissues of stock, violations of law "and lack of rigid state or national supervision in the management of some of the largest insurance companies, railroad companies, traction companies and financial corporations." The panic had followed an era of extravagance and inflated values. But the economic and financial condition of the nation was, on the whole, sound.[14]

Currency Reform. The existing currency system was defective in that it was "not so arranged as to permit its volume to be increased temporarily to counteract the sudden drain of money by hoarding in a panic."

Trusts. Legitimate enterprises, even with large capital, were to be encouraged. The fight of the Roosevelt administration had been on the combinations which violated the law providing free competition. The situation had been complicated because Congress, in drafting the Sherman Law, "didn't fully understand what the evil was that it was legislating against and, therefore, put the law in such general terms that the burden has been thrown on the courts of construing it." The time had come for a new, more specific statute.[15]

Railroad Regulation. The control gained by the Roosevelt administration had been justified by such abuses as rebating and other illegalities whereby the common carriers had combined with the large trusts to undermine free competition. The Interstate Commerce Commission should have power to fix maximum rates, but these should not be effective until after review by the courts.[16]

Government Ownership. The railroads should remain under private ownership. Government ownership meant "state socialism, an increase in the power of the central government . . . a long step away from the individualism which it is necessary to retain in order to make real progress." [17]

[13] *War Secretary Diaries,* pp. 2264-2265. [14] *Ibid.,* pp. 2258-2261. [15] *Ibid.,* pp. 2263-2264. [16] Taft to C. P. Taft, Dec. 3, 1905; *War Secretary Diaries,* p. 48. [17] *War Secretary Diaries,* pp. 2268-2269.

Socialism. The answer to the "very humane and kindly theories" which bore this name was that it was not possible "to carry on a business as economically and with the same production of profit by a government as it is under the motive of private gain." [18]

Tariff. Continued high rates constituted the only weakness of the Republican party. The exact reductions should be determined after careful study; in general, the rates should not be greater than the difference in the cost of production abroad and in the United States.[19]

Income Tax. The Supreme Court had ruled against the right of the federal government to pass such a tax. However, the Constitution could be amended. An income tax might be wise.[20]

So Taft stood, politically speaking, a little to the left of the center. He may have been fractionally closer to that center than Theodore Roosevelt, but that was all. He insisted that, with Root, he had "aided and abetted President Roosevelt in what were called his radical policies." He admitted, however, that he had not always approved of the methods used by the President to achieve his worthy ends.

"Roosevelt," he told Archie Butt in 1910, "believed in administrative justice, and as a rule he was seldom wrong; only he ought more often to have admitted the legal way of reaching the same ends." [21]

—3—

Strange and turbulent are the political currents as a presidential campaign draws near. Some of the currents run toward revolt. But they were not yet, in 1907 and 1908, very strong. LaFollette was more of a local than a national figure. Beveridge of Indiana had not yet made up his mind precisely where he stood. One thing was fairly certain; the die-hards of the Republican party were weary of rule by Roosevelt. A number of sincere, high-minded conservatives, among them Nicholas Murray Butler, recoiled from the Congressional message of January 31, 1908, in which the President moved

[18] *Ibid.*, p. 2471. [19] Taft to Roosevelt, Aug. 21, 1906; *War Secretary Diaries,* p. 2460; Baltimore *Sun,* Aug. 20, 1907. [20] *War Secretary Diaries,* p. 2470. [21] Butt, Archie, *Taft and Roosevelt,* Vol. I, pp. 128, 346-347.

farther to the left than ever before. He castigated the wealthy malefactors anew. He attacked Wall Street. He asked for physical
valuation of the railroads as a basis for fair rates. He said that
prosperity was secondary to honesty in finance and industry.[22] But
Taft insisted that even this diatribe marked no departure from
sound, liberal, conservatism.

"I have read the message with care," he said, "and I am bound
to say that the measures which he recommends . . . and the position he takes with respect to them, are all of a most conservative
character. . . . No man can find within the four corners of the
message anything to shake in the slightest the guaranties of life,
liberty and property secured by the Constitution. . . . Roosevelt
leads his party as Lincoln led his . . . to meet the new issues." [23]

The Republican party was not at all certain, however, that it
desired to meet those issues. Nor did the criticism come entirely
from G.O.P. conservatives. Frank I. Cobb, of the New York *World,*
wrote an editorial strangely prophetic of the dim future of twenty-
five years; of a day when another Roosevelt was to be in the White
House. Mr. Cobb, although the liberal editor of a liberal journal,
was watching the President with frightened disapproval:

> Always more law, more law, like the daughters of the horse-
> leech crying "Give! Give!" When will the President's clamor for
> new legislation end? When will be give the legitimate business
> interests of the country a breathing spell? The grave defect of Mr.
> Roosevelt's corporation policy is that he has no policy. . . . More
> legislation has been passed in a single year than the courts can
> dispose of in the next three years. . . . It is folly to invent new
> schemes of regulation and excite new unrest when acts already
> passed are yet to be worked out in the courts. . . .
> Nothing is settled. Nothing is certain. The demand for new
> experimental legislation goes on before the older experimental legis-
> lation has been tried and tested. Confidence is shaken, and con-
> fidence is the mother of credit. Credit is weakened, and without
> credit the business of the nation cannot be carried on. . . . It is time
> to call a halt. It is time to give legitimate business a breathing spell
> and to permit the restoration of confidence and credit. The country
> needs a rest from agitation.[24]

[22] Pringle, II. F., *op. cit.,* pp. 478-479. [23] *War Secretary Diaries,* p. 2748. [24] New York
World, Aug. 21, 1907.

The political currents ran against each other and the whirlpools they formed might easily have engulfed the candidacy of Taft and the Republican party itself. In general, this calamity did not occur because the Democratic party was in one of its frequent periods of impotence. It had been defeated in 1896, in 1900, and in 1904 and now it was devoid of intelligent leadership. Specifically, the G.O.P. continued to rule for another four years because William Jennings Bryan bungled, to an astonishing degree, what faint chance he had of becoming president in 1908.

Taft was not, at the time, aware of their import, but August 29 and August 30, 1907, were vastly significant days in his life. The first marked the arrival of Bryan in New York from Europe. The second was the date of Bryan's bid, in a speech at the Madison Square Garden, for the Democratic nomination. A great crowd was on hand. It seemed, for a little while, as though a militant Democracy might rise in its might. For all the varied factions of the quarrelsome party appeared to be united once again. Bryan arose to speak. His face was pale against the black of his coat and his lips were compressed into the straight, tense line which always preceded an important speech. He had not been speaking long when words came from those lips which marked his doom.

"I have already reached the conclusion," he said, "that the railroads partake so much of the nature of a monopoly that they must ultimately become public property and be managed by public officials . . . in accordance with the well-defined theory that public ownership is necessary where competition is impossible." [25]

This, of course, was rank, sulphurous socialism. For the past three years Roosevelt had been accused, with more than a shade of accuracy, of appropriating for his own use the doctrines conceived or publicized by Bryan. The Commoner had directly charged him with this larceny at a Gridiron Club Dinner in 1905. The President had conceded the theft of certain platform planks but had pointed out, also with accuracy, that they were of slight use to Mr. Bryan because he was unable to effect them into law.[26] The theory that Bryan and Roosevelt were political brothers was heightened during the railroad rate regulation fight when the Democrat openly

[25] *Ibid.*, Aug. 30, 31, 1907. [26] Dunn, A. W., *Gridiron Nights*, pp. 154-156.

pledged his support to the President.[27] All this was more than a little embarrassing at those times when Roosevelt was asserting his sound conservatism.

But Roosevelt had never succumbed, it could be proclaimed after Bryan's speech, to so scandalous a doctrine as government ownership. Taft, among others, hastened to assure the voters that there was, in reality, no similarity between the two. He was preparing a speech on this subject:

What I am most anxious to do is to meet Mr. Bryan's proposition that you have stolen his clothes and are only carrying out his policies. . . . The main differences between you and Bryan are, first, that when he proposes a thing it is merely to catch votes, and not with any sense of responsibility as to the possibility of carrying it out, or the effect of carrying it out; consequently, that he is always opposed to wealth, property, and its accumulation under the protection of a strong government. He is in favor of the punishment of the rich, but opposed to a strong government which shall punish both the poor and the rich. In other words, his tendency is toward the rule of the mob.

I, with deference, have never met a man more strongly in favor of a strong government than you are and more insistent that courts should not only have power to enforce the law, but should enforce the law. Bryan's attitude is that of one who would weaken the sanction of all government, would reduce the army and navy, would take away all power in the courts to increase their own orders; and would reduce the government to a mere town meeting by whom [sic] the laws should be enforced against the rich, but should be weakened as against the poor. . . . You haven't time to read and I haven't time to dictate an exact logical statement of the differences which I wish to elaborate, but I think this will give you some idea.[28]

On the speaking tour which followed this analysis, not wholly judicial, of the probable Democratic candidate, Taft told his audiences that Bryan would spend $14,000,000,000 of the taxpayers' money for the railroads and would— "Shades of Jefferson"— operate them "as a government institution." The Democratic party, he added, would never know how to govern because it consisted of

[27] Pringle, H. F., op. cit., p. 369. [28] Taft to Roosevelt, July 16, 1907.

a "combination of protestants . . . who only agree in the protest and don't agree in any other common policy." [29]

Bryan's unfortunate declaration for public ownership silenced the cries that Roosevelt was too radical and that Taft, as his heir, was disqualified on the same ground. Charles D. Hilles, by now giving most of his time to the preconvention campaign, reported that Wall Street would be "well-satisfied with Mr. Taft." [30]

Bryan's second error was to announce that tariff revision was not the fundamental issue of the campaign. He might have forced the fighting on that line and he would, in any event, have placed Taft on the defensive. Ultimately, the question was to be a major factor in splitting the party.[31]

On February 15, 1908, Assistant Postmaster General Frank H. Hitchcock resigned his post to assist in the Taft canvass. The hunt for delegates continued.[32] Taft viewed with distaste the scramble for adherents among the Negro Republicans of the South.

". . . the South has been the section of rotten boroughs in the Republican national politics," he admitted, "and it would delight me if no southern state were permitted to have a vote in the National Convention except in proportion to its Republican vote. . . . But when a man is running for the presidency, and I believe that is what I am now doing, he cannot afford to ignore the tremendous influence, however undue, that the southern vote has, and he must take the best way he can honorably to secure it. In the past it has been secured too frequently by pure purchase. Of course I would never stoop to that method." [33]

It is a safe assumption, however, that Taft was permitted to know as little as possible about the harvesting of southern delegates. On March 20, 1908, Hitchcock claimed 552 delegates out of a total of 980. The southern states, he said, had 194 votes and of these the secretary of war was already certain of 128.[34] Only 491 votes, a majority, were needed to ensure the nomination. When the convention assembled at Chicago, 125 of the delegates were federal officeholders and 97 of them were pledged to Taft.[35]

[29] *Addresses*, Vol. IV, pp. 66, 120. [30] Hilles to Vorys, July 24, 1907. [31] W. R. Nelson to Taft, Jan. 30, 1908. [32] *War Secretary Diaries*, p. 2644. [33] Taft to W. R. Nelson, Jan. 18, 1908. [34] *War Secretary Diaries*, p. 2837. [35] New York *World*, June 4, 1908.

—4—

On April 1, 1908, Taft left for a final speaking trip before the convention and journeyed as far west as Omaha. He hurried back to Washington to prepare for another visit to Panama where, according to custom, the elections had again been marked by fraud. On May 17, having effected a degree of peace, the secretary of war was back at his desk.[36] Cheerful news awaited him. Hitchcock reported that 563 delegates were pledged to his cause. Senator Knox, his closest rival, had only 68 and Hughes, who had once seemed so dangerous, was credited with but 54.[37] The secretary was, however, almost buried under the work which confronted him. War Department matters had to be settled. An unending stream of political petitioners thronged his waiting rooms.

"I have got to make a speech at the Grant monument . . . in New York next Saturday," he complained, "and I haven't written a line of it and I am under such pressure that I do not know when I am going to get time to do it." [38]

Time with its pronged fork began stabbing at him, and try as he might, Taft did not escape the stabbings until that happy day in March, 1913, when he abandoned forever the unpleasant duties of political life. One or two of his most disastrous mistakes were due to this inability to keep up with the work. "I do not know where I am going to get the time" was to be a frequent complaint. "I simply have not time to think," he might have added. Such was the case when he made this address, at Grant's Tomb on Memorial Day. The audience consisted mainly of Civil War veterans. Taft paid his tribute to the Union armies. The veterans smiled and puffed out beribboned chests. But their smiles faded when the secretary of war began a eulogy— so, at least, he had intended it— to General Grant. Taft said that the character of Grant was "as remarkable in its way, considering his previous history, as was that of Lincoln." He continued, and then the heroes of Bull Run listened with indignation:

[36] *War Secretary Diaries*, pp. 2874, 3087, 3142. [37] *Ibid.*, p. 3149. [38] Taft to Horace D. Taft, May 27, 1908.

". . . in 1854 he resigned from the army because he had to. He had yielded to the weakness of a taste for strong drink, and rather than be court-martialed, he left the army." [39]

It did not matter that Taft went on to describe the astonishing return of Grant to the army when war came after years of failure as a farmer, wood-seller and clerk. It did not matter that Taft was entirely accurate as to his facts. The old soldiers forgot, for the moment, their all-absorbing interest in pensions and jobs, and hurled anathema at this villain who had slurred their commander in chief.

"After your performance at Grant's Tomb," said a fairly typical letter, "I trust you will have the grace to go and hang yourself rather than attempt to belittle a nation by running for the presidency. I regret that no member of the Grant family had the sand to kick you off the premises. As an old soldier . . . said . . . when told of it, 'Was there no one there to kill the scoundrel?' There ought to have been." [40]

Taft resisted any impulse to hara-kiri. He was bewildered as well as worried over the possibility that he had sacrificed the soldier vote. "I said what I did only for the purpose of showing what a wonderful victory he had over his own weakness," he protested. "I might have been more tactful and diplomatic," he added.[41]

The cloud ultimately vanished, however, and otherwise the skies were blue. Only an unprecedented catastrophe could prevent Taft's nomination when the convention met at Chicago. It was not merely that the Roosevelt-Taft forces controlled the Republican machine. No concerted opposition to Taft existed. The strength of Hughes was nebulous; even his own state leaders were not sincerely behind him. Foraker was a political corpse. LaFollette stood for definite progressive principles but he could count on Wisconsin alone. Fairbanks of Indiana, like Uncle Joe Cannon, did not have the slightest chance of being nominated. Senator Knox of Pennsylvania was the only possible menace. He was able. The mantle of Roosevelt could logically be transferred to him. He could command the support of the large business interests. But even Knox could not be nominated unless for some reason Taft failed to win on the

[39] *War Secretary Diaries,* pp. 3236-3237. [40] F. H. Challis to Taft, June 2, 1908.
[41] Taft to W. M. Campbell, June 4, 1908; to D. D. Thompson, June 6, 1908.

first few ballots. President Roosevelt, of course, remained apprehensive that a stampede for a "second elective term," as it was now being called, would occur. Partly, he was sincere. Partly, no doubt, his ego required this peril. The facts do not show that it actually existed. Roosevelt, however, took every precaution against it. He insisted, in a letter to be circulated if a crisis arose, that the Taft delegates were to stand steadfast until the end.[42]

All national political conventions are an insane mixture of noise and synthetic enthusiasm. Nothing can really be accomplished in a gathering with almost a thousand participants. The work is done behind the scenes, more or less. At Chicago, in 1908, the nomination of Taft was made certain by preliminary sessions of the committee on credentials at which disputes in the various delegations were settled. These invariably occur in the selection of state representatives: one local faction will quarrel with a second and two batches of delegates thereupon march on the convention. In Chicago the committee on credentials ruled, as such committees always do, in behalf of the machine selections. That is, it ruled for Taft.[43]

One vital issue relating to labor disputes was, however, being debated in the rooms of the convention hotels. Taft was to surrender on it and to earn, thereby, the hostility of organized labor. The anti-injunction plank ultimately adopted was a compromise, and did not satisfy the foes of labor either. The candidate had already made his position clear in innumerable speeches. At first Taft was adamant, or nearly so, in insisting that the Republican platform go firmly on record against "this reckless use of ex parte injunctions" in labor disputes. To do so might mean the elimination of James S. Sherman, a probable vice-presidential nominee, but "I think he ought to be eliminated." [44] Taft wrote the original plank himself, after conference with Roosevelt. It was forthright and direct.[45] The convention would meet on June 16. On the previous day Taft telegraphed to Hitchcock, his chief strategist, that he would "rather cut my hand off" than take from the courts their power to protect property. On the other hand, the courts had "by hasty and ill-considered issue of injunctions, without notice or hear-

[42] Dunn, A. W., *From Harrison to Harding,* Vol. II, pp. 69-81. [43] New York *World,* June 17, 1908. [44] Taft to Roosevelt, June 15, 1908. [45] Wade Ellis to E. A. Mosely, Oct. 7, 1908.

ing, incurred the just criticism of laboring men engaged in a lawful strike."

"We can fight well when we are right," he added.[46]

On June 16, Taft appealed to Frank B. Kellogg of the Minnesota delegation to "stand by the injunction plank as proposed." He agreed that it would not satisfy the extremists of either side.[47] Protests had already reached Washington. James W. Van Cleave, president of the National Association of Manufacturers, had insisted that any references "to anti-injunction and labor amendments . . . will jeopardize party success." They should be eliminated.[48] In Chicago, meanwhile, Samuel Gompers of the American Federation of Labor was demanding a strong, affirmative repudiation of the injunction.[49]

Roosevelt agreed to a compromise plank which began with a pledge to "uphold the authority and integrity of the courts" and which protested against the injunction abuses in terms that were weak and guarded. This was drafted in Chicago and telegraphed to Washington.

"Have talked with the President," replied Taft, "and if the changes . . . suggested in the plank will effect an agreement, we are entirely willing to concur." [50]

Gompers declared that labor had been "thrown down, repudiated and relegated to the discard by the Republican party." The plank, he said, called for "legislation that will legalize what we have been trying to abolish." [51] Nor was Van Cleave of the National Association of Manufacturers happy, either. On June 30, he sent a pastoral letter to the members of his organization:

Although we got most of what we wanted at Chicago we did not get all. *The convention refused* to commit its party to make an *attack on the injunction.* . . . But the convention ought not to have mentioned the injunction at all. *The plank,* it is true, which deals with it, *takes pains to affirm* its support of *the present procedure of the courts.* But by mentioning the injunction the platform gives a chance to demagogues to construe this expression into a distrust, or pretended distrust, of the courts . . . and . . . some persons . . .

[46] Taft to Hitchcock, June 15, 1908. [47] Taft to F. B. Kellogg, June 16, 1908. [48] J. W. Van Cleave to Taft, June 15, 1908. [49] New York *World,* June 19, 1908. [50] Taft to Wade Ellis, June 17, 1908. [51] New York *World,* June 19, 1908.

who neglected to examine the words of the injunction plank closely may be deceived.[52]

Otherwise the convention did its work according to the orders from the White House. Herrick, Vorys, and Charles P. Taft were on hand, in addition to Hitchcock, to protect the interests of the secretary of war. At the opening hour on June 16, the Ohio delegation marched in with a portrait of Taft on a huge silk banner; this was the signal for the first cheers. Shortly after twelve o'clock Senator Burrows of Michigan began to drone through the reading of his speech as temporary chairman. Well-rounded sentences extolling the Republican party echoed to the far walls of the old Coliseum. The delegates stirred and yawned and twitched in the June heat. An explosion of cheers rang through the hall when Burrows mentioned Roosevelt's name. There was also applause, although not quite so loud, when he referred to Taft. A mention of Lincoln brought a polite patter of handclapping; after all, Lincoln no longer had jobs to dispense. After two hours of this, the convention recessed. The second day's session was, as it started, almost as colorless. The credentials committee reported, as everyone knew it would, the seating of all Taft delegates. Senator Lodge of Massachusetts, as permanent chairman, began his own, lengthy oration. But this time, for some reason which defies analysis, a reference to the President resulted in a demonstration which lasted for forty-nine minutes. "Four— four— four years more!" came from the galleries and the chant was caught up by the delegates. For some minutes it seemed possible that Roosevelt might, after all, be nominated.

"Anyone who attempts to use his name as a candidate for the presidency," warned Lodge, "impugns both his sincerity and his good faith."

The cheers died down. Before long, the convention had recessed again. The nomination speeches began on the morning of June 18. Eulogies were sounded for Uncle Joe Cannon, for Fairbanks, for Hughes. Then the clerk called for an expression from Ohio, and Senator Theodore E. Burton made his way to the front of the platform. The Ohio delegation, according to instructions,

[52] Taft papers, War Secretary files, Library of Congress.

leaped to its feet. The immemorial nonsense of flag-waving, parades, cheers and songs was repeated. After twenty-five minutes of it, Chairman Lodge pounded for order and the nominating speeches continued. Foraker was offered for the presidency. So was LaFollette. But their names meant nothing. The delegates were eager to get on with the balloting.

"Alabama!" called the clerk.

"Alabama casts her twenty-two votes for William Howard Taft!" screamed back the chairman of that delegation.

At 5:22 P.M. it was all over. The vote stood: Taft, 702; Knox, 68; Hughes, 67; Cannon, 58; Fairbanks, 40; LaFollette, 25; Foraker, 16. A motion was offered by Senator Penrose that the nomination be made unanimous. It was so ordered. The convention adjourned to debate, again behind the scenes, the choice of a vice-president.[53]

The secretary of war had listened to the returns at his office in Washington where Mrs. Taft was a nervous auditor as bulletins came over a long-distance telephone. A few close friends were present, but it was not an entirely happy occasion. Mrs. Taft, even now, could not purge herself of suspicion that Roosevelt was not a completely true friend of her husband. On the second day of the convention, June 17, she did not disguise her apprehensions or impatience when, during Lodge's speech, the long Roosevelt demonstration took place. But reassurance came from Hitchcock, who promised that it meant nothing. Taft was not in the office when the incident occurred; he had left to call on Secretary of State Root on some official matter.

June 18 brought additional tension to the little group of listeners. Word was flashed that Taft's name had been placed in nomination. Word was flashed that the cheering had started. Mrs. Taft, ever unable to find virtue in suppressing her thoughts, said that she had only one hope— that the cheering would last longer than for Roosevelt on the previous day. But it was briefer by twenty minutes. Another nervous moment came when a portrait of the

[53] New York *Tribune*, June 17, 18, 19, 1908.

President was lifted to the rostrum in Chicago. Mrs. Taft's face drained of color as new cheers were reported. Soon, however, it was over. The delegations began to cast their ballots for Taft. He had won the nomination. In all human probability he would be the next president of the United States. All the while, Taft had been rather silent. He had glanced up in distress as his wife had declared, once more, her jealousy of his friend in the White House. "Oh, my dear! my dear!" he had reproved. Beyond this he had said nothing to express either apprehension or joy. Was he pondering, until dusk on June 18, that the avenues of escape were fast being closed? Would he still have been elated had the nomination been denied him in the end? [54]

A detail remained to be settled at the convention; the trivial matter of selecting a candidate for vice-president and on this, too, Taft was to be thwarted.

"I am a great deal troubled about that," Taft had written two weeks before. "My own preference would be to have a man west of the Mississippi, like Senator Dolliver [Senator J. P. Dolliver] of Iowa, or some western senator who has shown himself conservative and at the same time represents the progressive movement." [55]

Taft declined, however, to take any part in the contest. He was deaf to pleas from Senator William E. Borah of Idaho, made on June 18, that some concession should be made to the progressives. Borah thought that Governor A. B. Cummins, also of Iowa, was the best possible selection. His nomination would go far toward convincing the LaFollette wing that the G.O.P. was not wholly conservative.[56] W. R. Nelson, publisher of the Kansas City *Star,* agreed that "a running mate to help lick Bryan, not one to please reactionaries" should be selected.

"Sherman would be a sinker in our section," Nelson telegraphed. "What about Beveridge?" [57]

Beveridge was urged to take it, but flatly refused. The senator from Indiana was unhappy over the platform adopted at Chicago. He deplored the rejection of LaFollette doctrines. Besides, he had no intention of wasting his own great talents in so obscure an

[54] Bishop, J. B., *Presidential Nominations and Elections,* pp. 73-74. [55] Taft to Charles Nagel, June 1, 1908. [56] W. E. Borah to Taft, June 18, 1908. [57] W. R. Nelson to Taft, June 17, 1908.

office.[58] So Sherman of New York, a conservative political hack distinguished chiefly for his nickname, "Sunny Jim," was nominated.

"I knew that you were just as much disappointed as I was," Taft told Nelson of the *Star*.[59]

The choice of a running mate on this occasion was, of course, a matter of supreme importance. But even Roosevelt had nodded and Taft nodded, too. They made no energetic fight. And when 1912 came, "Sunny Jim" was among the outspoken foes of Roosevelt while Beveridge was polishing and repolishing golden phrases to be used in Bull Moose orations. The reactionaries had captured many vital objectives at Chicago in the warm June of 1908. They had not yet captured William Howard Taft but they would do that, too, in the end.

The progressives may have been disappointed by the Republican convention. Others were pleased, however. "Good! good!" growled J. P. Morgan when he came down the plank of the S.S. *Mauretania* on June 19 and was asked for his comments on the results.[60] A telegram of congratulation arrived from John D. Rockefeller.[61] A contribution of $20,000 was promptly made by Andrew Carnegie.[62] But these felicitations did not, in themselves, constitute any proof that Taft had surrendered to conservative influences. Morgan, the Standard Oil Company, the railroads and the insurance companies had contributed heavily to Theodore Roosevelt's $2,195,-000 fund in 1904.[63] And this had been done when the Democratic candidate was the soundly conservative Alton B. Parker. Now Mr. Morgan and his associates faced their archenemy Bryan. The doctrine of the corporations, in all presidential elections, is that any Republican is better than any Democrat.

On June 30, Taft resigned as secretary of war to give all his time to the campaign. He determined to rest, for a little while, at Hot Springs, Virginia. Meanwhile, the nation knew that a vote for Taft was a vote for Roosevelt. This was the paramount issue. The President, in exuberance, had issued an extravagant statement im-

[58] Bowers, Claude, *Beveridge and the Progressive Era*, p. 288. [59] Taft to Nelson, July 30, 1908. [60] New York *World*, June 20, 1908. [61] J. D. Rockefeller to Taft, June 19, 1908. [62] G. R. Sheldon to Taft, July 21, 1908. [63] Pringle, H. F., *op. cit.*, pp. 356-357.

mediately upon receipt of the news from Chicago. He was to wish, not too far in the future, that he had toned it down:

> I feel that the country is indeed to be congratulated upon the nomination of Mr. Taft. I have known him intimately for many years and I have a peculiar feeling for him because throughout that time we have worked for the same object, with the same purposes and ideals. I do not believe there can be found in the whole country a man so well fitted to be President. He is not only absolutely fearless, absolutely disinterested and upright, but he has the widest acquaintance with the nation's needs without and within and the broadest sympathies with all our citizens. He would be as emphatically a President of the plain people as Lincoln, yet not Lincoln himself would be freer from the least taint of demagogy, the least tendency to arouse or appeal to any class hatred of any kind. He has a peculiar and intimate knowledge of and sympathy with the needs of all our people— of the farmer, of the wage worker, the business man, the property owner.[64]

So praise was heaped upon him and was sweet. Cabot Lodge transmitted the ultimate accolade. The aloof and normally pessimistic Henry Adams, he wrote, "said to me . . . that you were the best equipped man for the presidency who had been suggested by either party during his lifetime." [65] But Taft worried, as was his custom. Bryan had, of course, been nominated by the Democrats at Denver. The Democratic platform, Taft wrote from Virginia, embodied "most of his views except those in respect to government ownership, and we shall now try out the question whether the country is for those extreme views or is for progress without destruction. I am by no means overconfident, and I hope that my friends will strain every nerve . . .

"The next four months," he added, "are going to be a kind of nightmare for me." [66]

He shrank from the ordeal. Woe was already upon him. "I never get up now and look at the headlines in the newspapers that I do not do so with a fear that there is to be found something in their columns calling for denial or explanation," he complained.

[64] *War Secretary Diaries*, p. 3370. [65] Lodge to Taft, June 22, 1908. [66] Taft to C. E. Magoon, July 10, 1908.

"Those things that can be denied I do not fear. It is those things that have to be partly denied and partly explained that are trouble-some." [67] It was annoying, moreover, to be "in the limelight and to have oneself and one's family exposed to all sorts of criticism and curious inquisitiveness." [68]

Such were the handicaps of a sensitive man, a judicial man, in public life. But there was no escape now. It may be wondered, as the perplexities mounted at Hot Springs, whether Taft remembered the warning of that wise and able lady, his mother, who had pre-dicted, before she died, that "the malice of politics would make you miserable."

[67] Taft to Mabel Boardman, July 14, 1908. [68] Taft to Sir John Rodgers, July 19, 1908.

CHAPTER XXI

VICTORY, PERHAPS

POOR old boy!" sympathized Theodore Roosevelt from Oyster Bay. "Of course, you are not enjoying the campaign. I wish you had some of my bad temper! It is at times a real aid to enjoyment." [1]

But Roosevelt was not to enjoy the 1908 campaign very much, either. Inaction depressed him. During a fight, even more than at other times, the side lines were intolerable. Thus he had been unhappy during his brief service as vice-president. So bitterness would gnaw deeply into his heart when Woodrow Wilson, in 1917, was in command of a war peculiarly suited to Rooseveltian talents. The President had the best intentions as the 1908 canvass began, however.

"You are now the leader," he told Taft, "and there must be nothing that looks like self-depreciation or undue subordination of yourself. My name should be used only enough thoroughly to convince people of the identity and continuity of our policies." [2]

This was to be quite impossible. On the one hand, Taft appealed almost daily for guidance and assistance. On the other, Roosevelt soon reached a characteristic conclusion— that all was lost and that Bryan would win, unless Taft became, as far as possible, a replica of himself. He attempted, in effect, to insert his own flashing teeth in Taft's conciliatory jaws. He placed a big stick in his hands and commanded him to belabor the foes of righteousness. By letter, telegram and personal conference he beseeched Taft to suppress any lingering judicial weaknesses. At the same time he urged caution. It must have been confusing to the nominee in Hot Springs, Virginia.

"I believe you will be elected," the President said, at about the same time, *"if we can keep things as they are;* so be *very* careful to say nothing, not one sentence, that can be misconstrued. . . . I

[1] Roosevelt to Taft, July 15, 1908. [2] *Idem,* July 21, 1908.

have always had to exercise a lynx-eyed care over my own utterances!" [3]

Roosevelt's exhortations for pugnacity were based on apprehension that the voters did not fully appreciate his candidate's sterling qualities. Before the end of July he was fretting over an apparent apathy in Ohio and New York.[4] "I earnestly want your personality put into this campaign," he pleaded in August, "and I want us to choose our ground and make the fight aggressively." [5] "Do not *answer* Bryan; attack him!" he commanded. "Don't let *him* make the issues. . . . Hit them hard, old man!" [6] Taft agreed. He, too, used the metaphors of the prize ring.

"I am convinced," he answered Roosevelt, "that it is necessary for me in this fight to get up close to Bryan— within arm-hold— and if I don't do it before the end of the campaign it is because I can't." [7]

It was all more than a little unfair to Taft, who faded to relative insignificance under the bright illumination cast by the President. At the White House the Roosevelt court— the faithful worshipers who adored him and resented that so young and so vivid a chief executive must soon retire— spread stories that the President was carrying the whole burden of the campaign. These were published by similarly adoring newspaper correspondents. The Roosevelt court applauded, it may be assumed, when their energetic and talkative chief told them of his efforts to make a fighter out of Taft. Archie Butt noted the conversations carefully in his diaries.

"I told him [Taft] he simply had to stop saying what he had said in this or that decision; for the moment you begin to cite decisions people . . . begin to nod," said the President during one of his impromptu lectures on practical politics. "I told him that he must treat the political audience as one coming, not to see an etching, but a poster. He must, therefore, have streaks of blue, yellow and red to catch the eye, and eliminate all fine lines and soft colors." [8]

[3] *Idem*, July 17, 1908. [4] Abbott, Lawrence F., *The Letters of Archie Butt*, pp. 66, 90. [5] Roosevelt to Taft, Aug. 29, 1908. [6] *Idem*, Sept. 1, 11, 1908. [7] Taft to Roosevelt, Sept. 14, 1908. [8] Abbott, L. F., *op. cit.*, pp. 143-144.

Mrs. Taft was frankly annoyed by the constant interference from the White House. Early in September she was in New York. Her husband was off on a stumping tour when a request came for her to see Roosevelt in Washington as soon as possible.

"I can't imagine what Teddy wants," she wrote, "but probably only to complain about something." [9]

Taft's emotions were mixed. He was grateful for the assistance; he had no doubt that it was essential to the campaign. But he grew very much discouraged by the public clamor that he wear a Rough Rider hat. "I am sorry," he told one volunteer counselor, "but I cannot be more aggressive than my nature makes me. That is the advantage and the disadvantage of having been on the bench. I can't call names and I can't use adjectives when I don't think the case calls for them, so you will have to get along with that kind of a candidate. I realize what you say of the strength that the President has by reason of those qualities which are the antithesis of the judicial, but so it is with me, and if the people don't like that kind of a man, then they have got to take another." [10]

—2—

Taft was not nearly so lamentable a candidate as Roosevelt seemed to consider him or, for that matter, so bad as he believed himself. He arrived at a major decision during the first weeks of the campaign without consulting Roosevelt, and then he declined to reverse himself on advice of the President. Cromwell, the New York attorney who had been so deeply involved in the Panama revolution and whose testimony concerning it had been vague, to say the least, contributed $50,000 to the campaign chest in July. Taft reported this to the President and said that he had grave doubts about accepting. Without waiting for a reply he sent his secretary, Fred Carpenter, to Cromwell with a letter which said that the "size of the subscription will be misunderstood and the inferences drawn from it will not be just or kind either to you or to me." Although aware that "nothing but the purest friendship

[9] Helen H. Taft to Taft, Sept. 5, 1908. [10] Taft to E. N. Huggins, Aug. 11, 1908.

and interest in the campaign" had inspired the donation, he felt compelled to ask that its size be reduced.[11]

"You blessed old trump," was Roosevelt's answer. "I have always said you would be the greatest president, bar only Washington and Lincoln, and I feel mighty inclined to strike out the exceptions. My affection and respect for you are increased by your attitude about contributions. But really I think you are oversensitive." [12]

This was despite Roosevelt's doubts, four years earlier, regarding the "very unfortunate" reputation of Cromwell. But Taft had already acted when Roosevelt's letter urging acceptance arrived. The donation had been cut to $10,000.[13] The subject of campaign contributions was a troublesome one in 1908, but Taft preserved throughout a similar rigidity regarding the benefactions from representatives of the Standard Oil or other vested interests which might, at some future date, face prosecution by the government. The insurance investigation under Hughes had already revealed the interest of finance and industry in political campaigns and Taft, from the start, was convinced that corporation money, direct or indirect, should be barred.[14] A federal statute forbade contributions from corporations, as such, but said nothing about taking money from their officers or directors. Bryan carried the issue further by suggesting that Taft join him in asking Congress to require publication of all contributions prior to election.[15] This was in May and it was a clever political stroke because the Democratic party, as Bryan was well aware, would receive much less, if anything at all, from corporate sources. Taft declined to go quite that far, but he urged publication when the election was over.[16] The G.O.P. bosses at Chicago contrived to eliminate mention of this subject from the platform. But Taft remained deaf to suggestions that future publicity would dry up the sources of revenue.

"I would like to have an ample fund to spread the light of Republicanism," he told Roosevelt, "but I am willing to undergo the disadvantage to make certain that in the future we shall reduce the power of money in politics for unworthy purposes." [17]

[11] Taft to Roosevelt, Aug. 5, 1908; to Cromwell, Aug. 6, 1908. [12] Roosevelt to Taft, Aug. 7, 1908. [13] Taft to Roosevelt, Aug. 10, 1908. [14] Idem, March 31, 1908. [15] W. J. Bryan to Taft, May 25, 1908. [16] Taft to W. J. Bryan, May 26, 1908. [17] Taft to Roosevelt, July 9, 1908.

It was a new departure in national politics, although New York State had already decreed publicity. It was a source of great distress to friendly or yearning financiers and industrialists as well as to the campaign officials who had to find money for special trains, literature, advertising, posters, celluloid buttons and other more furtive costs of electing a president. In his acceptance speech on July 28 at Cincinnati, however, Taft amplified his party's platform by pledging full publicity. He pointed out that George R. Sheldon, who had been appointed treasurer of the Republican National Committee, was a resident of New York and therefore bound by the state law. If elected to the presidency, Taft promised, he would recommend the extension of this principle.[18]

On September 19, Taft was warned by Frank B. Kellogg that Sheldon, his treasurer, contemplated an appeal to John D. Archbold of the Standard Oil Company.[19]

"I cannot believe this to be true . . ." wrote Taft, in haste, to Sheldon, "because as long ago as August 4 I wrote you that I was very anxious that no money should be received from the Standard Oil Company or anyone connected with it, following in this respect the suggestion of the President."[20]

He told Roosevelt that he had directed Sheldon not "to take any money from either the trusts or the people closely identified with them." He was quite certain that funds could be obtained elsewhere if enough energy was used.[21] Sheldon's first reaction was one of indignant protest. He did not understand that "you did not want me to take money from men who were connected with the Standard Oil Company." Now he was being further instructed that contributions from officers or directors of the railroads or the United States Steel Corporation were similarly unwelcome to the newly purified G.O.P. Andrew Carnegie's $20,000 was acceptable, presumably, because he had retired from the steel business.

"If all these avenues are to be closed," Sheldon wrote, "will you please tell me, Mr. Secretary, where I am going to get the money? I want to be very frank with you and let you know that the question of getting money enough to run this campaign is today

[18] *War Secretary Diaries*, p. 3614. [19] F. B. Kellogg to Taft, Sept. 18, 1908. [20] Taft to Sheldon, Sept. 19, 1908. [21] Taft to Roosevelt, Sept. 21, 1908.

the vital question . . . if we don't get money enough . . . the Democrats will win." [22]

Regarding Taft's suggestion that the smaller businessmen of the country would contribute toward defeating Bryanism, Sheldon was skeptical. He said that he had been raising funds for public purposes for twenty years and that success was impossible "without going to the rich men who are directors or officers of the so-called trusts or railroad companies." [23]

"It is very difficult," lamented Taft, "to get it out of Sheldon's head that the place to get money is confined to a narrow strip of street in New York." [24]

Minor embarrassments continued. Henry W. Taft reported from New York that offers of funds were being made with the specification that the names of the donors should never be revealed; among others the banker, Speyer, had held out an anonymous $10,000.[25] On the whole, however, Nominee Taft was correct in his belief that the businessmen of the nation, the countless industrialists who were not tied up with the wicked trusts, would rally to reject Bryanism. Sheldon, by October, was able to give assurance that "subscriptions both large and small are coming in much better." [26] He promised the candidate two weeks later that the list could be published without the faintest apprehension; not a single donation was from an improper source.[27] The total receipts were about $1,600,000 as compared with more than $2,200,000 spent for Roosevelt in 1904.[28]

The businessmen of America had been subjected to convincing propaganda. It was their duty, Van Cleave of the National Association of Manufacturers thundered, "regardless of their party, to bury Bryan and Bryanism under such an avalanche of votes in 1908 that the work will not have to be done over again in 1912, or ever." Van Cleave said that he had not even bothered to send his lobbyists to the Democratic convention at Denver. This was because the nomination of Bryan had been certain. It had been equally certain that the platform would call for drastic limitation of injunction issuance in labor disputes and this, said Mr. Van Cleave, was "revo-

[22] Sheldon to Taft, Sept. 21, 1908. [23] Idem, Sept. 28, 1908. [24] Taft to Roosevelt, Oct. 3, 1908. [25] W. H. Taft to Taft, Oct. 9, 1908. [26] G. R. Sheldon to Taft, Oct. 7, 1908. [27] Idem, Oct. 16, 1908. [28] W. N. Cromwell to Taft, Nov. 23, 1908.

lutionary and anti-American." The platform called for jury trial in injunction cases which would "give a license to violence, would make industry and property insecure, would increase the number and the destructiveness of labor contests, and would assail legitimate trade of all sorts."

". . . we saw that we would fail in Denver if we went there, and so we kept out," he added.[29]

Van Cleave, who had a weakness for excessive talking, was a liability as well as an asset to the G.O.P. The Republican strategists had a bad few hours when he boasted at a banquet that his loyal cohorts had forced the party to back down on Taft's original injunction plank and that the tempered expression on this issue, so vital to organized labor, was really only an attempt to get their votes.[30] Taft hoped, nevertheless, that "the dinner pail rather than . . . the injunction" could be made the paramount issue.[31] Why not? It had been effectively offered by Mark Hanna in 1896 and 1900. It had been used again in 1904. The Republican party had so often proclaimed itself the guardian of prosperity that most of its leaders actually believed it.

The businessmen believed it, too, and they worked manfully to convince their employees. Encouraging reports reached Taft. W. C. Brown, vice-president of the New York Central Railroad, said he had addressed his engineers and firemen at a meeting in Syracuse, New York, and "your name was applauded to the echo." Mr. Brown did more than talk. He made arrangements for 2,500 freight and passenger cars to be repaired at once in shops now closed down. This would give jobs to a large number of men.[32] The president of a fire insurance company instructed 2,000 of his agents in the Middle West to proselyte for Taft as they made their rounds.[33] A Missouri steel company added 400 men to its payroll just before Election Day. Its president told Taft that the men were not actually needed, although they might be when business picked up as the result of a Republican victory.

"Then," he added, "men at work make better Republicans

---

[29] Taft papers, War Secretary files, Library of Congress. [30] City editor, St. Louis *Republic* to Taft, Sept. 22, 1908. [31] Taft to J. P. Nelson, July 15, 1908. [32] W. C. Brown to Taft, Aug. 31, Oct. 11, 1908. [33] D. E. Thompson to Taft, Sept. 19, 1908.

than men idle and I felt I could do this much for the Cause, at least." [34]

Such are the aspects of the American political system which do not reach the headlines. They are not corrupt. They are practical rather than vicious. Bryan was perfectly familiar with the influences at work against him; he ought to have been, for they had opposed him in two other presidential campaigns. Not all of the compromising in the campaign of 1908 was on Taft's side. Almost as soon as he had made it, Bryan started to back away from his declaration on behalf of government ownership. He still believed in it, he said, but the nation might not be ready. Meanwhile, the remedy lay in stricter regulation of the railroads. So the Denver platform was silent on government ownership. Bryan concluded to talk, instead, about publicity for campaign contributions.[35]

—3—

Taft, meanwhile, had evolved a real issue. He expounded it in his speech of acceptance. It was an echo of that editorial indicted by Cobb of the New York *World* in the summer of 1907 which demanded "a breathing spell to permit the restoration of confidence and credit." It implied no disloyalty whatever to the man in the White House; Roosevelt had read the speech and had pronounced it "admirable." [36] The promise was that a span of quiet was to follow the years of tumult. Taft said:

The chief function of the next administration, in my judgment, *is distinct from, and a progressive development of that which has been performed by President Roosevelt.* The chief function of the next administration is *to complete and perfect the machinery* . . . by which the lawbreakers may be promptly restrained and punished, but which shall operate with sufficient accuracy and dispatch to interfere with legitimate business as little as possible. Such machinery is not now adequate. . . . The practical, constructive and difficult work, therefore, of those who follow Mr. Roosevelt is to devise the ways and means by which the high level of business integrity and obedience to law which he has established may be

[34] C. H. Howard to Taft, Oct. 28, 1908. [35] Hibben, Paxton, *The Peerless Leader, William Jennings Bryan,* pp. 278-280. [36] Roosevelt to Taft, July 20, 1908.

maintained and departures from it restrained without undue interference with legitimate business.[37]

This was enthusiastically saluted by the *Wall Street Journal* as
proof that Taft was "avoiding alike the extreme of eastern conservatism and the extreme of western radicalism." The editorial
continued:

Mr. Taft notwithstanding his apparent subservience to Roosevelt . . . is really mapping out a policy of his own. . . . His task
will be to finish and complete the work already done by Roosevelt
rather than to start some new and, it might be, sensational policy of
his own. . . . It is evident from a careful reading of the speech that
it would be distinct from the Roosevelt administration in another
important respect. Most of the criticism of Roosevelt has been
directed not so much at what he has done or attempted to do, but
at the methods of speech and action he employed in doing them.
. . . The *Wall Street Journal* . . . welcomes Mr. Taft's speech as
evidence that he is neither a reactionary nor a revolutionist, neither
a Bourbon nor a Jacobin.[38]

Emphasis of this doctrine might, it is true, have cost Taft some
progressive support in the West. But it would have enabled him to
stand for the presidency in his own right to a far greater extent. In
any event, the issue was soon lost in the clamor over whether Bryan
or Taft was the better qualified to carry out Roosevelt's policies.
Bryan claimed superiority on the ground that many of them had
originated in the platforms of the Democratic party.

Taft was relatively forgotten in the campaign. The speeches
he made have been forgotten, too. At first he deluded himself with
an idea that he could remain, more or less, in Cincinnati. By
September, however, he had concluded that a stumping tour was
necessary.[39] The first trip took him through Indiana and Wisconsin
and as far west as Colorado. He started homeward with encouragement in his heart. The people had been warm and friendly. Great
crowds had thronged to the meetings. He told the President that
Bryan's claim "to be the heir of your policies is now the subject of

[37] *War Secretary Diaries*, pp. 3589-3590. (Italics mine.) [38] *Wall Street Journal*, July
29, 1908. [39] Taft to C. P. Taft, Aug. 31; to Roosevelt, Sept. 11, 1908.

laughter and ridicule." He discerned, as candidates nearly always do, a ground swell in his direction.[40]

Far worse campaigns have been made than this one by Taft in 1908. He had to read his speeches. Nearly all of them were far too lengthy. He developed no gift for oratory. Despite the urgings of Roosevelt, he found it impossible to paint gaudy posters for the edification of the voters. But his personality was definitely pleasing. Crowds warm to mannerisms as well as to rhetoric. A political asset of unquestioned worth lay in the subterranean chuckle which preceded Taft's frequent laughter. It was, by all odds, the most infectious chuckle in the history of politics. It started with a silent trembling of Taft's ample stomach. The next sign was a pause in the reading of his speech and the spread of a slow grin across his face. Then came a kind of gulp, which seemed to escape without his being aware that the climax was near. Laughter followed hard on the chuckle itself and the audience, invariably, joined in. They laughed even when the point which had amused Taft was vague to them. It might be some obscure legalism over which judges laugh in their robing room when court has adjourned. It might be some subtle joke of his days on the bench. The audience laughed, whether they understood the source or not.

The audiences liked Taft, too, because he was so patently honest. He may not have been a fighting man, but he said, by and large, what he thought. He talked endlessly about the injunctions he had issued as a judge, but never once did he admit that he had been wrong. He never intimated that he had changed his mind about the illegality of certain boycotts in labor disputes. He insisted that Eugene Debs was a Socialist "who would uproot existing institutions, destroy the right to private property and institute a new regime." [41] On October 28, he spoke at Cooper Union in New York, a stronghold of liberalism and labor sentiment, and reiterated his belief in the right of the workingman to strike and to organize his fellows into unions.

"But they may not injure the property or unlawfully injure the business of their employers," he warned, "and they may not institute a secondary boycott in such a dispute." [42]

[40] Taft to Roosevelt, Oct. 3, 1908. [41] New York *Tribune*, Oct. 14, 1908. [42] *Ibid.*, Oct. 29, 1908.

He was equally forthright on tariff reductions. On the troublesome subject of physical valuation of the railroads— valuation, naturally, was violently opposed by the corporations because of their watered stock— he was steadfast too. In July, he was warned by Senator LaFollette that a "declaration against valuation would . . . be fatal to your candidacy" and would bring about the loss of Wisconsin.[43] Taft answered that he had no intention of making any such declaration, that valuation was essential in fixing railroad rates because it was a factor in determining the actual worth of the lines.[44] He amplified this in his acceptance speech, saying that rates should depend on the "reasonable value of the company's property" and should be reduced when they were in excess of a fair return on that value.[45]

A third issue was pregnant with danger. The panic of 1907 had gone far toward undermining confidence in banks and Bryan had offered, in remedy, a plan roughly comparable to that adopted twenty-five years later by President Franklin D. Roosevelt. A tax was to be imposed on national banks, and upon such state institutions as desired it, whereby an insurance fund for the guaranty of bank deposits would be established. It met with wide public endorsement. Kansas had already created such a fund for its state banks. But Taft, as well as Theodore Roosevelt, believed it unsound and regarded it as a device through which strong financial institutions would be forced to support weak and recklessly managed ones. Taft said that the proposal was possible only if the banks were so closely supervised "as practically to create a government bank." Otherwise, it would "bring the whole banking system of the country down in ruin."

The Republican party offered, instead of this radical departure, a greater elasticity of the currency, to prevent panics, and a system of postal savings banks where the money of the small depositor would be entirely safe.[46] But Bryan's scheme was far more attractive to some of the voters and a good many loyal party workers protested to the White House against Taft's bullheaded policy of attacking it.

[43] LaFollette to Taft, July 17, 1908. [44] Taft to LaFollette, July 19, 1908. [45] *War Secretary Diaries*, p. 3591. [46] *Ibid.*, pp. 3606-3608.

"I am sorry," retorted the candidate to one such plea, "but I just can't help taking the matter up and going for it just as hard as I can. It is wrong, *wrong*, WRONG, and it is all the more wrong because it is so specious." [47]

—4—

It does not seem, in retrospect, that Roosevelt's impatience with Taft was justified. The nominee of his choice made no serious mistakes during the hazardous weeks of the campaign. The difficulties he faced were infinitely greater than those of the campaign of 1904 when Roosevelt, his campaign chest enriched by corporate gold, had emphasized how soundly conservative were his views. In political parties, as among nations, the shadows of conflict are often discernible before the conflict itself. The Grand Old Party which had ruled since it had saved the Union— except, of course, for the unfortunate two terms of Grover Cleveland— was torn by strife in 1908. This was a presidential campaign and harmony demanded that the boys profess their love. But underneath their honeyed speeches lay hatred, resentment and bitterness. The shadows had been very faint in 1904, if they existed at all. Now they were black.

There was, for instance, the shadow of Uncle Joe Cannon and his long, odorous cigars. Uncle Joe knew that his enemies in the House of Representatives were plotting his downfall. He knew that he might be defeated for re-election as speaker; at best, in all probability, his powers would be clipped. But Uncle Joe was arrogant and outspoken. He was proud of his conservatism, of his opposition to tariff reform and other plans so close to the hearts of the progressives.

"Confidentially," wrote Taft as the campaign got under way, "the great weight I have to carry in this campaign is Cannonism. . . . Of course, it would not do for me to express such a desire publicly, or to anybody but a very few friends. I should not be at all disappointed if a new speaker were elected in the next Republican House, if it is to be Republican." [48]

[47] Taft to William Loeb, Jr., Sept. 18, 1908. [48] Taft to D. D. Thompson, Aug. 27, 1908.

Uncle Joe was stubborn as well as arrogant. He was interested, primarily, in the Congressional campaign and it was announced that he would make a number of speeches in Kansas. Taft pointed out that it "would be a great mistake to send Cannon into Kansas, because he is not popular there."

But this, also, was a "delicate matter," Taft said, and must be handled with extreme care.[49] For one thing, he told the President, Cannon was too ardent a defender of high tariffs.

"I don't propose to be involved in a bunko game with the public," said the supposedly too-cautious Taft. ". . . The people are so insistent, as they ought to be, on a real revision, that we are not going to encounter the difficulties that we would have encountered in the last Congress had such a revision been proposed."[50]

It was the belligerent Roosevelt, this time, who pleaded for compromise. He agreed that Taft was right on the tariff, but said it would be very bad to give an impression of conflict with the Congressional campaign committee. The belligerent Roosevelt abandoned, for the moment, his cries for battle and offered a thesis in pragmatism:

Of course, this is merely another way of saying that you will have to act with great caution in every such matter of policy now, just as I had to do in 1904. . . . I am here giving you merely the advice on which I myself act, and the advice I am sure Root would give you. I do not wish you to do anything that would give the New York politicians, for instance, the feeling that your attitude toward party workers is that of Hughes. As far as I know I never either as police commissioner, governor or president yielded improperly to Platt [Republican boss of New York] . . . or anyone else; but I resolutely refused to be drawn into a fight with them. . . . Now and then the need comes for a smash, as in this case of Foraker. But the fight should never be gone into until it cannot possibly be avoided.[51]

The shadow of Foraker had appeared to lift after the convention in Chicago. The Ohio senator had opposed the Roosevelt program and had defended the Negroes of the Brownsville riot. But now, with Taft nominated, he sent a message of congratula-

[49] Taft to C. F. Brooker, Sept. 12, 1908. [50] Taft to Roosevelt, Sept. 21, 1908. [51] Roosevelt to Taft, Sept. 24, 1908.

tion even though it might be "unwelcome and probably misunderstood." Taft was touched. His mind went back across the long years.

"... your kindly note ... gave me the greatest pleasure and I thank you from the bottom of my heart," he wrote impulsively. "I have never ceased to remember that I owe to you my first substantial start in public life." [52]

Foraker's assistance, as Taft phrased it, was "of some moment in Ohio." In late August the candidate and the senator happened to meet at Toledo and both made friendly, innocuous speeches. The nominee hastened to assure Roosevelt that no deal had been made. [53] He said that he would take no part in the Ohio contest for senator. Foraker "can be useful with the colored vote and with the Grand Army vote ... but his doing so will not in the slightest degree affect my previous attitude with respect to the Roosevelt policies and my determination to carry them out." [54] The President offered no criticism, unless it was verbal. He did not mention Foraker in his early September letters to Taft. But he was unaware, as Taft was, of the bomb soon to be exploded under the gentleman from Ohio. This was ignited on the evening of September 17, 1908, by the puckish Mr. Hearst.

Hearst had deserted Bryan after the Commoner had turned his back on government ownership, and had thrown his support to two political nonentities who had been nominated by the Independence party which he controlled. The publisher was enjoying himself vastly. On September 17 he spoke at Columbus, Ohio, and began reading letters addressed to Foraker from 1900 to 1903 by Archbold of the Standard Oil. They concerned the necessity for defeating legislation obnoxious to the Rockefeller interests. Several mentioned payments of large sums to Foraker. They were searing, utterly damning indictments. [55] Immediately, of course, the best minds of the Republican party went into conference. Foraker had been scheduled to speak with Taft a few days later. But this was now impossible. Foraker withdrew from the meeting and notified the nominee that he would take no further part in the campaign. [56]

[52] Taft to Foraker, Aug. 24, 1908. [53] Taft to Roosevelt, Sept. 4, 1908. [54] Taft to W. R. Nelson, Sept. 4, 1908. [55] Winkler, J. K., Hearst, an American Phenomenon, pp. 224-228. [56] War Secretary Diaries, p. 3799.

372 THE LIFE AND TIMES OF WILLIAM HOWARD TAFT

Roosevelt seethed with wrath and excitement. He did not know that the Standard Oil had contributed heavily to his own war chest in 1904. On September 19 he telegraphed Taft that if he were running for president he would "decline to appear upon the platform with Foraker."

"I would have it understood in detail," he said, "what is the exact fact, namely, that Foraker's separation from you and from me has been due not in the least to a difference of opinion on the Negro question, which was merely a pretense, but to the fact that he was the attorney of the corporations, their hired representative in public life, and that therefore he naturally and inevitably opposed us in every way. . . . I think it is essential, if the bad effect upon the canvass of these disclosures is to be obviated, that we should show unmistakably how completely loose from us Mr. Foraker is. If this is not shown affirmatively there is danger that the people will not see it and will simply think that all Republicans are tarred with the same brush." [57]

The Ohio senator was to be "completely loose," that is, now that he had committed the sin of getting caught. Taft answered on the same day that he had "made up my mind from the first not to appear on the same platform with Foraker." He agreed fully with Roosevelt regarding Foraker's perfidy "although I never suspected his complicity with the Standard Oil." The nominee was confident that "it will be generally understood that he has constantly opposed you and me until it became essential in his desire to return to the Senate for him to support me. I did not solicit his support. He tendered it." [58] But this seemed too tame to Roosevelt. He told Nicholas Longworth that Taft should put "more energy and fight into the matter."

"He ought to throw Foraker over with a bump," the President said. "I have decided to put a little vim into the campaign by making a publication of my own." [59]

He did so. The President's heart was made joyous when Hearst also connected C. N. Haskell, treasurer of the Democratic National Committee, with the oil trust. He challenged Bryan to get rid of his own villain, and Haskell resigned. [60] The whole affair

---

[57] Roosevelt to Taft, Sept. 19, 1908. [58] Taft to Roosevelt, Sept. 19, 1908. [59] Pringle, H. F., *Theodore Roosevelt, a Biography,* p. 505. [60] Hibben, Paxton, *op. cit.,* p. 287.

SECRETARY TAFT IN HIS RESCUE ACT.

Cartoon by G. K. Berryman, Courtesy The Washington Post

See page 307]

Discharged Without Honor.

SERGT. MINGO SAUNDERS.

FROM A CONTEMPORARY CARTOON

[*See page 324*

proved what everybody half suspected; that both parties bowed, from time to time, to their masters of industry and finance.

A third shadow, more gray than black, was LaFollette of Wisconsin. Taft agreed, no doubt, with Roosevelt's grossly unfair analysis of LaFollette made in June, 1908. The President had written, privately, of course, that LaFollette's program was a "string of platitudes," that people listened to him "on the whole not getting any ideas at all." [61] There may have been a shade of jealousy in this. Having been governor of Wisconsin, LaFollette entered the Senate in January, 1906. He was the unquestioned champion of liberalism; no one accused him, as they did the more pragmatic Roosevelt, of trimming his sails before the storm. He was never elected, it might be parenthetically noted, to the presidency. During the campaign of 1908, however, he had remained faithful to the Republican party.

Taft had misgivings regarding LaFollette's fidelity. He asked him to "go out and speak for the ticket outside of Wisconsin as soon as possible," for his assistance would be highly valuable.[62] But expediency dictated this appeal. Taft felt, in his heart, that LaFollette and the other progressive leaders were "closely identified with Bryan and his policies, and LaFollette and Bryan are not very far apart." [63] This was true enough; Roosevelt and Bryan, on occasion, had been brothers too. The uncertain harmony between Taft and LaFollette was not shattered during 1908, however. This was despite a disquieting description received by Taft of a speech at La Crosse, Wisconsin, at which LaFollette had openly praised the Democratic candidate. Taft's informant wrote:

About four minutes before he finished his speech he had become very much worked up and took off his collar—for the purpose, some of the boys said, of enabling him better to get out the word "TAFT" which he had been unable to pronounce up to that time.[64]

Still another shadow took the form of attacks on Taft's religious beliefs. "I am a Unitarian. I believe in God. I do not believe in the Divinity of Christ," he had written a decade before when

[61] Pringle, H. F., *op. cit.,* p. 418. [62] Taft to LaFollette, Sept. 29, 1908. [63] Taft to E. J. Hill, Aug. 10, 1908. [64] E. A. Edmunds to Taft, Oct. 22, 1908.

the presidency of Yale had been tentatively offered to him. These perfidious statements were in a private letter to Henry Taft and they were not, of course, made public in 1908. But many good Christians among the voters needed no evidence to convince them that Taft, a Unitarian, was necessarily also an infidel. From the Middle West, in particular, came scores of letters demanding to know whether the Republican nominee rejected Christ.

"Think of the United States with a *President* who does not believe that Jesus Christ was the Son of God," shuddered the editor of one religious paper, "but looks upon our immaculate Savior as a common bastard and low, cunning impostor!" [65]

Concurrently, strangely enough, the nominee was accused of being a Roman Catholic and, therefore, a slave of the Pope. These charges were based on distorted accounts of his negotiations, as governor of the Philippines, for the sale of the friars' lands. Methodists whispered to Baptists, who passed on the rumor to Congregationalists, that Taft had unduly favored the Catholics in that dispute and had recommended the payment of unjustified millions for the church properties in the Philippines. Even in Cincinnati, where the most rabid Christians should have known better, Taft was attacked. The pastor of the Second Presbyterian Church urged his flock to vote for Bryan.

"As this is a church of which Charley [Charles P. Taft] is a trustee and Annie [Mrs. Charles P. Taft] is a member," wrote Taft, who could not quite decide whether it was all an outrage or humorous, "it makes it a pleasant family arrangement." [66]

Campaign strategists assured the public that Taft, although a Unitarian, was a good Protestant and no papist. It was pointed out that Mrs. Taft was an Episcopalian and that Helen, their daughter, had been confirmed in that faith.[67] But Taft flatly refused to inject himself into an open controversy.

"Of course, I am interested in the spread of Christian civilization," he told one supporter, "but to go into a dogmatic discussion of creed I will not do whether I am defeated or not. . . . If the American electorate is so narrow as not to elect a Unitarian, well and good. I can stand it." [68]

[65] *Pentecostal Herald*, July 15, 1908. [66] Taft to H. P. Lloyd, Sept. 12, 1908. [67] Washington *Post*, June 17, 1908. [68] Taft to J. W. Hill, Aug. 12, 1908.

A final annoyance of the campaign was the prohibition issue. On September 17, 1908, the militant Carry Nation called on Mr. Taft and demanded that he state his position on the menace of alcohol. He declined to answer her questions and she left, indignantly, to proclaim that he was a foe of temperance as well as an infidel.[69] Taft's views were sound, in view of the ultimate record of federal prohibition. He was opposed to any law "that is not enforced." Regarding his own habits, he wrote:

I venture to say that I am as temperate a man as there is anywhere. I am not a teetotaler, but I rarely drink anything. It does not agree with me and I know that I am better off without it. I am strongly in favor of local option, because I believe in giving to the members of a locality, either township or county, the opportunity to say whether liquor shall be sold within that jurisdiction.[70]

The prohibitionists, however, were beginning to feel their power and demanded much more than temperance. They insisted on mandatory legislation, state and federal. The President and Taft had agreed, prior to the national convention, that the party would take no stand with respect to the liquor question. This was, Taft told the Rev. D. D. Thompson, one of the ardent prohibition workers, "not a national, but . . . necessarily a state and local issue, and . . . one upon which Republicans differ as do Democrats."[71] But Thompson would not be quiet, and Taft asked Roosevelt whether he had been correct in declining to surrender to the drys.[72] The President answered:

Of course your position is absolutely sound. If ever there was a wicked attitude it is that of those fanatic extremists who advocate a law so drastic that it cannot be enforced, knowing perfectly well that lawlessness and contempt of the law follow. But as a mere matter of precaution I would be careful to put in your hearty sympathy with every effort to do away with the drink evil. . . . I favor the local option plan. . . . But to pass prohibitory laws to govern localities where the sentiment does not sustain them is simply equivalent to allowing free liquor, plus lawlessness, and is the very worst possible way of solving the problem. My experience with

[69] *War Secretary Diaries*, p. 3796. [70] Taft to H. E. Hinshaw, July 11, 1908. [71] Taft to D. D. Thompson, July 13, 14, 1908. [72] Taft to Roosevelt, July 13, 14, 1908.

prohibitionists, however, is that the best way to deal with them is to ignore them. I would not get drawn into any discussion with them under any circumstances.[73]

Taft must have grown more than a little weary before, at last, Election Day arrived, of the complaints and petitions which reached him. They referred, in addition to the Standard Oil and the Divinity of Christ, to the subject of golf, a game to which he was devoted. Golf, wrote a correspondent from Illinois, was regarded by "thousands and thousands of laboring people" as a "dude's game." Taft must be a plain man, rough-hewn, to convince the rugged voters that he was qualified for the White House. He should, this writer pleaded, "cast aside [sic] golf and take an ax and cut wood." [74] This time the President of the United States agreed.

"I have received literally hundreds of letters from the West protesting about it . . ." he told Taft. "It is just like my tennis; I never let a photograph of me in tennis costume appear." [75]

—5—

But all things ultimately end. The most sluggish political river winds somewhere to the sea. Election Day, November 3, 1908, dawned clear and cold. In the morning a reassuring telegram arrived at Cincinnati from Chief Willis L. Moore of the Weather Bureau at Washington. He said that "nature smiles her approval"; the weather was "perfect . . . for the getting out of the Republican country vote." [76] The voice of the people would not be stilled by Bryanesque rains or Democratic muddy roads. For the Democrats, to an extent, dwelt in cities and could get to the polls despite the elements. Taft did not return from his last speaking trip until eight o'clock that morning and he spent the day, going out to vote at four o'clock, at the pleasant mansion of Charles P. Taft on Pike Street. Toward dusk the returns began to arrive; the first were from New York and they gave indication of victory. By mid-

[73] Roosevelt to Taft, July 16, 1908. [74] S. L. Wallace to Taft, Aug. 12, 1908. [75] Roosevelt to Taft, Sept. 5, 1908. [76] W. L. Moore to Taft, Nov. 3, 1908.

night the result was fairly clear. New York had gone for Taft. So had Massachusetts, New Jersey, Connecticut and Michigan. The Republican party was showing surprising strength in Maryland and even in Tennessee. Wisconsin, by the grace of LaFollette, was safe. California, by the grace of the old-line conservatives, was safe too. Gus Karger, a Cincinnati newspaperman who had been a publicity aide during the campaign, read the press bulletins as Mr. and Mrs. Taft, Mr. and Mrs. Charles P. Taft, Alice Roosevelt Longworth and a few others listened. The reading was interrupted by the sound of a band outside the house and by the glare of red fire. The Citizens' Taft Club had assembled to pay its respects, to cheer the winner.[77]

Taft went out to acknowledge the greeting. His voice was hoarse and the lines of his face were deeply etched in the glare of the torches. He was utterly tired. His phrases of appreciation were conventional. He pledged that his administration would, so far as he was able, be "a worthy successor of that of Theodore Roosevelt." But he had been talking for forty days, he pleaded. He was worn out. At three o'clock he went to bed. In Oyster Bay a jubilant president was also listening to the chatter of telegraph instruments.

"We have them beaten to a frazzle!" he kept repeating.[78]

The electoral vote was 321 for Taft to 162 for Bryan. President-elect Taft told Roosevelt that the result had surprised him, that he had not expected such large popular majorities in New York, New Jersey and New England.[79] Roosevelt answered in much the same vein.[80] Clearly, the political judgment of both was blunted by the returns which had just come in. Had they studied these more closely, disquieting factors would have been apparent. Taft's lead over Bryan was 1,269,606 votes, but this was less than half the lead piled up by Roosevelt four years before. The statistics gave warning of the unrest which was to increase during the coming four years. Taft had lost Colorado, Nebraska and Nevada which Roosevelt had captured in 1904. Oklahoma, voting in a presidential election for the first time, was also a Bryan state. Democratic governors had been elected in Taft's own Ohio, in Indiana, Minnesota, North

[77] War Secretary Diaries, pp. 3899, 3901. [78] Abbott, L. F., The Letters of Archie Butt, p. 153. [79] Taft to Roosevelt, Nov. 7, 1908. [80] Roosevelt to Taft, Nov. 10, 1908.

Dakota and Montana. The tide was beginning to run against the Grand Old Party, as it had done in 1884 and 1892 and would do, at faster pace, in 1912.

A note of warning might have been found, too, in certain of the congratulatory messages which poured in on the President-elect. Most of them were fatuously routine. An obscure Indiana politician, Will H. Hays, offered a tribute, for instance, to Taft's "great personal victory." [81] Van Cleave of the National Association of Manufacturers said that "Americanism still reigns supreme in the United States." [82] "The people do rule," said Uncle Joe Cannon, possibly with satire.[83] But a few of the messages would have justified close attention by the President-elect. There was an ominous rumble behind the friendly phrases of the message from LaFollette.

"No man ever had a greater opportunity," he telegraphed. "The country confides in your constructive leadership *for the progressive legislation needed to secure equal opportunity for all in our industrial development.*" [84]

And now Taft was to be President of the United States. He was sentenced to four years— it might be eight!— in the madhouse of active political life. He would have to enter the madhouse doors even before inauguration in March. They were swinging open already, while for a few days he rested at Hot Springs, Virginia, and Taft cast one longing backward glance toward a quiet, dimly illuminated room in the Capitol at Washington.

"I pinch myself every little while to make myself realize that it is all true," he told a friend. "If I were now presiding in the Supreme Court of the United States as chief justice, I should feel entirely at home, but with the troubles of selecting a Cabinet and the difficulties in respect to the revision of the tariff, I feel just a bit like a fish out of water. However, as my wife is the politician and she will be able to meet all these issues, perhaps we can keep a stiff upper lip and overcome the obstacles that just at present seem formidable." [85]

---

[81] W. H. Hays to Taft, Nov. 4, 1908. [82] J. W. Van Cleave to Taft, Nov. 4, 1908. [83] J. G. Cannon to Taft, Nov. 3, 1908. [84] LaFollette to Taft, Nov. 3, 1908. (Italics mine.) [85] Taft to H. A. Morrill, Dec. 2, 1908.

CHAPTER XXII

A NEW KING RIDES

A MINOR flaw in the American system lies in the fact that the retiring king merely retires. He is dead, but decent burial is denied him and for the rest of his years he is a pathetic rather than a majestic figure. There are no further worlds to conquer.

This is not very important so far as most retiring presidents are concerned. They are, for the most part, old men and weary ones and the shelf of private life is not unpleasant. Theodore Roosevelt, however, was far too young for this. He had been only forty-three when McKinley fell under a madman's shots; he took office as the youngest president in history. And now, as 1908 ended, the close of the reign rushed on too swiftly. Roosevelt was only fifty. Tragedy for Taft and for Roosevelt, too, was to be born of this accident of Roosevelt's youth. A close, warm and sincere friendship was to be broken and a political party wrecked.

"When you see me quoted in the press as welcoming the rest I will have . . . ," Roosevelt had confessed earlier that year, "take no stock in it. I . . . like my job. The burdens . . . will be laid aside with a good deal of regret." [1]

No hint of jealousy or regret clouded the Roosevelt-Taft relationship at the close of 1908. The retiring king sent a greeting to the new one. On New Year's Day, President and Mrs. Roosevelt jointly telegraphed Taft, who was in Augusta, Georgia.

"We believe," they said, "that the coming years will be very happy for you and we know that through you they will be years of benefit to *our people.*" [2]

The "our people" may have been a phrase from the murky realm of the subconscious. More probably, it had no significance at all and cannot be offered in support of the theory, in due time

---

[1] Pringle, H. F., *Theodore Roosevelt, a Biography,* pp. 476-477. [2] Theodore and Edith Roosevelt to Taft, Jan. 1, 1909. (Italics mine.)

offered by fiery Marse Henry Watterson of the Louisville *Courier-Journal,* that Roosevelt aspired "to be an imitation Caesar." [3] Roosevelt had effectively explained away an incident earlier in 1908 which had been hailed as evidence of his royalist leanings. A routine telegram had gone to the President of Peru conveying good wishes from "me and my people" and had borne Roosevelt's name. But Roosevelt had not seen it. The signature had been affixed by Secretary of State Root and the President was not to blame, as he said privately with infinite amusement, for this supposed proof of "[my] marked imperialistic and megalomaniac tendencies." [4]

Roosevelt was, in fact, the soul of consideration in his desire to leave President-elect Taft free and unhampered in the administration about to start. Dr. Butler of Columbia University had suggested some time before that Roosevelt should become senator from New York in March, 1909, and the President gave passing thought to the proposal. Taft endorsed the plan. Roosevelt, however, concluded to remove himself from all possible political activity by going to Africa on a hunting trip. He told Taft that Root would undoubtedly be elected United States senator by the New York legislature "and will be a tower of strength for your administration." [5] Not a trace— not even the faintest, passing trace— of resentment is discernible in the letters addressed by Roosevelt to his successor. Pressed for time as he was, he agreed to write a biographical appreciation of this man who was still, beyond any doubt whatever, his trusted friend and the heir of his policies.

"Will you please send me at once," he requested, "the date of your birth and any salient fact in your past career (of a noncriminal type!) with which I am apt not to be acquainted." [6]

"Ha! Ha! *You* are making up your Cabinet," the President teased a few days later. "*I* in a lighthearted way have spent the morning testing the rifles for my African trip. Life has compensations!" [7]

Taft did not disguise his inner misgivings. It seemed almost as though he was afraid to predict that he would be a success for fear the gods might frown at such egotism. He propitiated them

---

[3] Louisville (Ky.) *Courier-Journal,* April 27, 1912. [4] Pringle, H. F., *op. cit.,* p. 489.
[5] *Ibid.,* p. 491; Taft to Roosevelt, Nov. 7, 1908; Roosevelt to Taft, Nov. 10, 1908. [6] Roosevelt to Taft, Dec. 21, 1908. [7] *Idem,* Dec. 31, 1908.

by frequent prophecies of failure; one of these, at least, was unpleasantly accurate.

"I thank those who were good enough to say something pleasant about the incoming administration," he told an audience in New York, "for I am glad to get it now. I have heard of the man who went into office with a majority and went out with unanimity." [8]

"I look forward to the future with much hesitation and doubt as to what is to happen," he admitted to Roosevelt, "but if we put our shoulder to the wheel and follow the course marked out by you . . . I am very hopeful that, while we may not accomplish all we have promised, we shall give evidence of an earnest and sincere attempt to do so." [9]

"It is a very different office from that of governor general of the Philippines," Taft said in another gloomy prediction, "and I don't know that I shall arise to the occasion or not." [10]

—2—

Thus the crows of defeat perched, from the start, on the banners of victory. Two roads stretched before Taft as he made plans for his administration. Boulders obstructed each of them, however. He could attempt to be a second Roosevelt and continue to agitate for righteousness in a series of swift attacks and strategic, carefully obscured, retreats. But this was impossible, as Taft realized all too well. Only a Roosevelt could successfully travel such a road. So he chose a second one which constituted an evolution of his speech of acceptance declaration; that the "chief function of the next administration is to complete and perfect the machinery" of reform. Taft amplified the doctrine on the eve of his inauguration:

I am going to be criticized for putting corporation lawyers into my Cabinet. I think I shall have in the Cabinet five as good lawyers as there are in the country, and being good, first-class lawyers, they have had a good deal of corporate employment.

[8] *War Secretary Diaries*, p. 4019. [9] Taft to Roosevelt, Jan. 2, 1909. [10] Taft to C. H. Brent, Dec. 22, 1908.

Mr. Roosevelt's function has been to preach a crusade against certain evils. He has aroused the people to demand reform. It becomes my business to put that reform into legal execution by the suggestion of certain amendments of the statute in the governmental machinery. . . . The people who are best fitted to do this, without injury to the business interests of the country, are those lawyers who understand corporate wealth, the present combination, its evils, and the method by which they can be properly restrained. I am hopeful, moreover, that the suggestions that we shall make to the first regular session of Congress will be received with respect and a desire to support them by those men— leaders in Congress— who would certainly oppose recommendations made by a Cabinet consisting of the *more radical members of the party*. What I am anxious to do is to do something, and not to make a pronunciamento, and then at the end of my administration have nothing to point to. . . .

I much prefer to be criticized now and charged with reactionary tendencies, than to give the right to those men interested in the progress of things to show that at the end of the administration I have done nothing.[11]

This was the very heart of Taft's policy. It was set forth, although less boldly, in his inaugural address. Roosevelt was familiar with all its aspects and its every significance. Roosevelt gave it his unstinted approval.

"I did not express to you what I had at heart after you had read my inaugural, and that was a renewed appreciation of your breadth of soul and mind and magnanimity," wrote Taft after a conference with the President.[12]

"How could I but be delighted . . . ?" the President answered. "It is simply fine in every way. I cannot imagine a better inaugural, and it marks just exactly what your administration will be." [13]

Perhaps no man, in 1909, could have seen the boulders. But Taft, of all men, should have had eyesight keen enough. For he knew his Roosevelt well. He knew that Roosevelt was easily led astray by appearances. He should have realized that Roosevelt, out of office and thus no longer bound by the evasions and compromises which had marked his own seven years, would soon grow sus-

[11] Taft to W. R. Nelson, Feb. 23, 1909. (Italics mine.) [12] Taft to Roosevelt, Feb. 25, 1909. [13] Roosevelt to Taft, Feb. 26, 1909.

picious of corporation lawyers serving as apostles of reform. Taft might, perhaps, have silenced the growing suspicions by a gesture or two. He might have excoriated Uncle Joe publicly and then, in a private letter, have assured the speaker, as Roosevelt did, that "you need never waste your time in thinking that I will give so much as a second thought to any kind of a story . . . reflecting on you." [14] He might have attacked the wealthy malefactors and then allowed them to settle, in their own way, a financial upheaval. Roosevelt did that too. But Taft could not make gestures.

—3—

It is unjust, I think, constantly to interrupt the story of the Taft years with accounts of his ultimate friction with his predecessor. The story can be told in full, with all its stupidities and heartaches, in its more fitting place: the campaign of 1912. But it seems logical, at this point, to examine the specific indictment that Taft betrayed Roosevelt in the formation of his Cabinet, that the friendship was already broken on the stormy day in March, 1909, when Taft took his oath as president of the United States. The biographer, groping toward exact truth in so inexact a realm as history, walks warily among the memoirs of men who do not remember clearly, among the ex post facto statements of other men who wish to justify themselves or condemn others.

"One of the things that a man has to . . . do . . . is to strain his heart strings . . . by declining to comply with the impulses of personal friendship," Taft wrote when, toward the close of February, 1909, his Cabinet had finally been chosen. [15]

Such was Taft's own version of the independent manner in which he had selected his official family and it was true, save in one vital detail. He did not strain his heart strings at the very start. His sin was a Rooseveltian sin. He was elated just after the victory at Chicago in June, 1908. The evidence is clear that he indulged at that time in some enthusiastic generality to the effect that he wished to keep in office the members of the Roosevelt Cabinet. Taft admitted as much, himself, in a conversation in October, 1910:

[14] Pringle, H. F., op. cit., p. 476. [15] Taft to H. M. Lurton, Feb. 25, 1909.

"One day, *just after I was nominated,* I told Roosevelt that, should I be elected, I did not see how I could do anything else but retain all the old members of the Cabinet who had been associated with me. I thought nothing more about it, but I learned later that Roosevelt had practically told every member of his Cabinet that he was going to be retained should I be elected." [16]

Roosevelt's own version, although it was not given until February, 1916, is substantially the same. Taft had expressed a wish, he said, that the President would "tell the boys I have been working with that I want to continue all of them." Roosevelt had demurred; why did not the nominee tell them himself? Taft said that he preferred not to do this. He wished to be able to say during the campaign that he was bound by no promises. However, he would like to have Roosevelt "tell them just how I feel and let them know that I want the Cabinet to stand just as it is." Thereupon Roosevelt said that Secretary of State Root, unless he became senator from New York, wished to resume his law practice. Secretary of the Navy Newberry also desired private life. He added that Secretary of the Treasury Cortelyou would not, in his judgment, work in harmony with Taft. Four Cabinet officers would be delighted to serve, however. With Taft's permission, Roosevelt said, he would gladly pass on the good news to Postmaster General Meyer, Secretary of Commerce and Labor Oscar Straus, Secretary of Agriculture Wilson and Secretary of the Interior Garfield.

"I wish you would," said Taft.

This, it will be noted, is far more specific than Taft's own recollection. But the quotations, dictated by Roosevelt nearly eight years after the conversation, cannot be taken too literally. In any event, the promises made were limited, after the eliminations suggested by the President, to four men: Meyer, Straus, Garfield and Wilson. But on a separate occasion, Roosevelt also insisted, Taft had promised to continue Luke E. Wright as secretary of war. Thus the total regarding whom pledges are supposed to have been given was five.[17] Of the five, it may be noted in passing, Taft did retain two: Meyer and Wilson. He also did his best to hold Root. And when Root declined, he asked Senator Lodge, who was Roosevelt's

[16] Butt, Archie, *Taft and Roosevelt,* Vol. II, p. 551. (Italics mine.) [17] Stoddard, Henry L., *As I Knew Them,* pp. 383-387.

closest friend, to become secretary of state. Lodge refused, on the ground that he could serve the Taft administration better in the Senate.[18]

Six months intervened between the time of these conversations and Taft's withdrawal to Hot Springs and to Augusta, Georgia, to begin the actual task of naming his aides. Probably a hundred letters passed between Roosevelt and Taft during the half year; scores of personal conferences were held. But there is not a single scrap of evidence to indicate that the promise to keep the Roosevelt aides was ever mentioned between them again. It must be borne in mind that Roosevelt's account of Taft's promises was made when the 1912 break was still fresh and bitter in his mind. But that Taft handled a delicate situation clumsily is not open to question.

Roosevelt said in 1916 that Henry and Charles P. Taft were the influences which persuaded the President-elect to reject his trusted advisers. There is nothing to support this. Both were house guests of the W. H. Tafts before the Cabinet was finally chosen. But the older man, the half brother, was in more than a little disfavor because of his ill-considered attempt to win election as senator from Ohio. Taft did not, it would seem, consult Henry Taft to any great extent. Indeed, one of the astonishing things about Taft's four years in the White House was the almost total lack of men, related or otherwise, upon whom he could lean. He had no Cabot Lodge. He had no Colonel House. For the most part he faced his troubles alone. In the months before March, 1909, he labored, virtually by himself, in choosing his Cabinet from the myriad suggestions which almost swamped him.

"I made up my own Cabinet and I did not confer with anybody except as to the secretary of the treasury and the secretary of state," he subsequently declared.[19]

Senator Knox of Pennsylvania accepted the most important portfolio, secretary of state, toward the middle of December, 1908.[20] He then became closer, perhaps, than almost anyone else to the President-elect and he was kept informed, from time to time, of the potential selections. In late December, Taft told Knox that he was thinking of retaining Wright in the War Department. He was

[18] H. C. Lodge to Taft, Dec. 9, 1908. [19] Taft to Horace D. Taft, Feb. 1, 1910. [20] E. F. Baldwin to Taft, Dec. 20, 1908.

considering a transfer of Meyer from the Post Office to the Navy. He would keep Wilson as secretary of agriculture and bring in Charles Nagel of Missouri, one of his ardent supporters in the campaign, as secretary of commerce and labor. On the other hand, he might keep Oscar Straus although he thought that "Straus has not been a very successful secretary." For secretary of the interior he might pick Richard A. Ballinger, whose reputation was that of a Roosevelt conservationist. He was inclined to ask George W. Wickersham to become his attorney general.[21] Taft did not even mention James R. Garfield, Roosevelt's secretary of the interior and his passionate admirer.

"The reason why I kept Garfield out of the Cabinet was because I knew him," was Taft's cryptic explanation fourteen months later.[22]

Certainly Taft had no recollection whatever of any pledge made to Roosevelt as he worried over the task which was so "like the making of a picture puzzle." [23] There are indications that Roosevelt had forgotten about it too. Taft was cooling toward Wright, whom he had known intimately on the Philippine Commission; he felt that Wright was less active than he might be and uncertain in his decisions.[24] The weeks passed. Taft erred gravely in that he did not inform Garfield and the others immediately that he required their services no longer. On the other hand, he was not sure, himself, that he did not. On January 4, 1909, President Roosevelt suggested that it would be wise "to write them all at once."

"They will be making their plans," Roosevelt said, "and less than two months remain, and I do not think they ought to be left in doubt." [25]

Taft thereupon explained to Cortelyou, Attorney General Charles J. Bonaparte, Garfield, Wright and the others that he would not need them. His reason was the same in each case; that the task which confronted him was different from that of the Roosevelt years and a "somewhat different personnel in the Cabinet" seemed necessary.[26]

    [21] Taft to Knox, Dec. 22, 1908. [22] Taft to Horace D. Taft, Feb. 1, 1910. [23] Taft to C. N. Bliss, Dec. 24, 1909. [24] Taft to Knox, Dec. 23, 1908. [25] Roosevelt to Taft, Jan. 4, 1909. [26] Taft to G. B. Cortelyou, Jan. 22, 1909.

"I feel very much torn in my feelings in respect to the Cabinet and the leaving out so many men for whom I have the highest respect and a strong feeling of comradeship," Taft told the President a month before Inauguration Day, "but I believe I am doing right. . . . I shall be attacked for having more lawyers in my Cabinet than I ought to have." [27]

Certainly there was an overabundance of legal talent in the group finally chosen. Knox (secretary of state), Wickersham (attorney general), Jacob Dickinson (secretary of war), Hitchcock (postmaster general), Nagel (secretary of commerce and labor), and Ballinger (secretary of the interior) all were lawyers. Secretary of Treasury Franklin MacVeagh, Secretary of Agriculture Wilson and Secretary of the Navy Meyer, alone, lacked the blessings of training at the Bar. Perhaps this surfeit of legal minds did as much as anything else to alienate Theodore Roosevelt. He had sampled a legal education, himself, many years before and had turned from it in distaste. He never had much respect for the law or lawyers, particularly when they got in his path. Yet Bonaparte, Garfield and Wright, whom Taft had replaced, were lawyers too.

—4—

Beyond any doubt, Roosevelt was puzzled and a degree hurt in the last days of his administration. He loyally suppressed, save on one or two occasions, any temptation to give expression to the first seeds of doubt regarding the man he had pushed into glory. Most of the time, perhaps, he did not admit, even to himself, that they existed. Roosevelt made but two personal requests of Taft and these were promptly granted. He asked that William W. Sewall— the Bill Sewall of Roosevelt's joyous ranching days in the West— be retained as a federal marshal in Maine.

"Of course," answered Taft, "that was understood long ago." [28]

The second request was less simple, but it was satisfactorily arranged. In December, 1908, Taft expressed embarrassment over "Loeb's [William Loeb, secretary to the President] urgency to become a member of the Cabinet." Roosevelt had suggested, Taft dis-

[27] Taft to Roosevelt, Feb. 1, 1909. [28] *Idem*, Dec. 28, 1909.

closed, that Loeb be named "for a few months . . . to give him the prestige of a cabinet position which would then secure him a good place in business." But this, the President-elect felt, partook of a "manipulation of a Cabinet place for personal reasons . . . that is hardly dignified." [29] The problem was solved by appointing Loeb as collector of the port of New York. The recipient of the favor expressed delight; for himself and on behalf of the President, as well. He told Taft that Roosevelt was "as happy as a clam at high tide, and thinks only of Africa." [30]

It was a shade too bright a picture. "Taft is going about this thing just as I would do," the President insisted stubbornly, "and while I retained McKinley's Cabinet the conditions were quite different. I cannot find any fault in Taft's attitude to me." [31] But favorites at the Roosevelt court, bitter and unhappy that the reign was nearly over, continued to ride from the court of the New King and to leap from their saddles with stories of perfidy. Cabot Lodge was one of these. That cold Bostonian was to betray even his friend, Theodore Roosevelt, when, after the friend was dead, he urged a payment of $25,000,000 to the republic of Colombia in atonement for the seizure of Panama. His attitude toward Taft in early 1909 was just as ungracious. The President-elect had invited Lodge to be secretary of state. He retained Meyer in his Cabinet at the instance of the Massachusetts senator; Meyer came from the same Congressional district as did Augustus P. Gardner, the senator's son-in-law, and was, therefore, a possible rival for the House of Representatives. [32]

Lodge had every reason for friendliness toward Taft. Instead, he helped to sow the first seeds of discord between Taft and Roosevelt. At the invitation of the President-elect, Lodge went to Augusta on January 2, 1909, and saw Taft that afternoon. Taft told Roosevelt that "we have enjoyed his visit very much." [33] But something, it appears, had annoyed the senator. He told the President when he returned that he had not been allowed to see Taft alone. He gave warning that Taft did not plan to retain any of the Cabinet, unless it was Meyer; moreover, he would get rid of everyone else who

[29] Taft to Knox, Dec. 23, 1908. [30] William Loeb to Taft, Jan. 5, 1909. [31] Abbott, L. F., *The Letters of Archie Butt*, pp. 307-308. [32] Hammond, J. H., *The Autobiography of John Hays Hammond*, Vol. II, p. 542. [33] *War Secretary Diaries*, p. 4077; Taft to Roosevelt, Jan. 4, 1909.

had been close to the throne. The indefatigable Archie Butt heard these reports from Mrs. Roosevelt herself.

"Lodge is so hopelessly selfish," Butt confided to his sister-in-law, "that if the Tafts did not kowtow to him he would delight in making trouble between them and the Roosevelts. . . . I suppose everybody from now on will be trying to carry tales and make bad feeling between the families."

Try as hard as he might, a character so volatile as Roosevelt inescapably had moments when black suspicions, thus nurtured, could not be exorcised. Two weeks before the end he saw Wright, by now informed that Taft did not want him as secretary of war.

"I am distressed, general," said the President; ". . . unfortunately, you have been too close to me, I fear." [34]

This was quite without foundation and Roosevelt, it is fairly certain, forgot the aspersion as soon as he had uttered it. The President, able politician that he was, knew perfectly well that Taft would have innumerable difficulties, quite apart from the selection of a Cabinet, when he entered the White House. Roosevelt was having difficulties himself. He had been at odds with Congress during most of 1908. His last annual message in December had been a vicious criticism of the legislative, and theoretically co-ordinate, branch of the government. In December, 1908, arrows of accusation flew down Pennsylvania Avenue from the Capitol toward the White House. The President, said Congress, had illegally used the secret service to spy upon its members. But Roosevelt caught the arrows, fitted them into his own bow and sent them speeding back. Congress was not doing its duty by the nation, he said in effect. [35]

Theodore Roosevelt had not quarreled with Congress on taking office in 1901 or on election in 1904, however, and he would have emphatically advised against it had Taft quarreled now. So he offered no objection— he distinctly approved— when the President-elect made his gestures to the old-line leaders. Roosevelt felt no resentment, even, when Taft indicated a point or two on which his policies would be different from those of his benefactor. The President-elect agreed to confer with Booker T. Washington regarding

[34] Abbott, L. F., *op cit.*, pp. 271-273, 338. [35] Pringle, H. F., *op. cit.*, pp. 482-485.

appointments from the members of his race.[36] But he did not think, and he was unquestionably correct, that Roosevelt had advanced the cause of the Negroes by appointing them in southern communities where their presence was bitterly resented. Roosevelt's most flagrant case had been Dr. W. D. Crum, a Negro whom he had named collector of the port at Charleston, South Carolina. The Senate refused for over a year to confirm the appointment, but Dr. Crum, at the President's insistence, had served nevertheless.

"I am going to take a decided step in respect to southern Negro appointments," Taft decided. "I am not going to put into places of such prominence in the South, where the race feeling is strong, Negroes whose appointment will only tend to increase that race feeling; but I shall look about and make appointments in the North and recognize the Negro as often as I can. . . . There is no constitutional right in anyone to hold office. The question is one of fitness. A one-legged man would hardly be selected for a mail carrier, and although we would deplore his misfortune, nevertheless we would not seek to neutralize it by giving him a place that he could not fill." [37]

So Dr. Crum was to be persuaded to resign. Taft was assured by Dr. Washington that he had taken the situation in "good spirit."

"This is first-rate," said Roosevelt, when he heard about it.[38]

—5—

One major duty remained, in addition to the drafting of the inaugural address. The work at Panama had been criticized on the ground that a satisfactory foundation could not be built for the Gatun Dam on which a lock-type canal depended. So Taft made another visit to the isthmus with a group of engineers toward the end of January. He was able to report, on February 1, that the work was progressing "in a most satisfactory way." The experts had examined the ditch in detail and were unanimously of the opinion that no change in the design should be made.[39] On February 7,

[36] B. T. Washington to Taft, Dec. 1, 1908. [37] Taft to W. R. Nelson, Feb. 23, 1909; to N. W. Aldrich, Jan. 31, 1909. [38] B. T. Washington to Taft, Feb. 28, 1909; Roosevelt to Taft, Feb. 26, 1909. [39] Taft to Roosevelt, Feb. 1, 1909.

the President-elect landed at New Orleans and proceeded homeward by rail through the South. He made several speeches on the way; his motivation was the hope, a hope with which Republican presidents so often delude themselves, that it would soon be possible to break the deathlike grip of the Democratic party below Mason and Dixon's line.

"I am greatly interested in the southern question and have only just begun," Taft had written after the election returns, on November 3, had shown a heavier Republican vote in certain sections of the South.[40]

Mrs. Taft, in the meanwhile, had been waiting for the consummation of her most fervid dream with energetic anticipation. Captain Archie Butt, as senior White House aide, went to Augusta to confer with Mrs. Taft on probable changes in the routine of the executive mansion. When he returned, his reports added further fuel to the resentment of Roosevelt court favorites. Butt's protests that every incoming First Lady made changes were futile.

"To hear them talk," Butt wrote, "one would think that Mr. Roosevelt was being driven from the White House by Mr. Taft and that Mrs. Taft was not even civil toward his wife."[41]

Irritation was expressed over Mrs. Taft's decision to have liveried Negroes at the front door instead of the customary frock-coated white ushers. She would replace the male steward with a woman housekeeper who, as Mrs. Taft explained in her memoirs, "could relieve me of the supervision of such details as no man . . . would ever recognize. . . .

"Perhaps I did make the process of adjusting the White House routine to my own conceptions a shade too strenuous, but I could not feel that I was mistress of any house if I did not take an active interest in all the details of running it. . . . I made very few changes, really."[42]

Nor did she. Mrs. Taft's mistake, if she made one, was to arrange for them before the Roosevelts had moved out and to have them effective on the first moment that the Tafts came in. This, to the court favorites, was lese majesty. Mrs. Roosevelt was made unhappy by the impending dismissal of the servants who had served

[40] Taft to H. W. Anderson, Nov. 4, 1908. [41] Abbott, L. F., *op. cit.*, p. 371. [42] *Ibid.*, p. 205; Taft, Mrs. W. H., *Recollections of Full Years*, pp. 347-349.

her so faithfully, but she was scrupulously careful, as always, to give no hint of this.

"I don't feel any resentment at all; only I hope he will take care of the men who have served me here," said Roosevelt stoutly. ". . . So tell Taft for me that all his changes will meet with my approval." [43]

Vague doubts probably troubled both men in the watches of their nights as Inauguration Day arrived; who can say? The President even put them into words, to one or two confidants. He said that Taft would do his best, "But he's weak." [44] The whispers of friction continued. Small men, with malice and purpose in their hearts, said that Roosevelt and Taft were no longer friends. Still, there was no outward sign. The President-elect and Mrs. Taft were to spend the night of March 3 at the White House.

"People have attempted to represent that you and I were in some way at odds during this last three months," wrote Taft, in accepting the invitation, "whereas you and I know that there has not been the slightest difference between us, and I welcome the opportunity to stay the last night of your administration under the White House roof to make as emphatic as possible the refutation of any such suggestion.

"With love and affection, *my dear Theodore.*" [45]

"Your letter," answered Roosevelt promptly, "is so very nice— nice isn't anything like a strong enough word, but at the moment to use words as strong as I feel would look sloppy— that I must send you this line of warm personal thanks and acknowledgment. . . . You put in the right way to address me at the end!" [46]

A short time before dinner on March 3, the President-elect and Mrs. Taft arrived at the White House and were escorted to a suite at the southeast side. This was to be their home, for good or evil, during at least four years and burning logs were part of a welcome which was warm and sincere. The Roosevelt children had already left; only the President and Mrs. Roosevelt remained for the final night. But the dinner was not a great success. Conversation was not easy, for the minds of all those present must have been a seething turmoil of private thoughts. It was a small dinner. In addition to

[43] Abbott, L. F., *op. cit.,* p. 253. [44] Sullivan, Mark, *Our Times,* Vol. IV, pp. 331-332. [45] Taft to Roosevelt, Feb. 25, 1909. (Italics mine.) [46] Roosevelt to Taft, Feb. 26, 1909.

the Tafts and the Roosevelts there were Admiral and Mrs. W. S. Cowles, the sister of the President; Nicholas and Alice Longworth; Mabel Boardman; Senator and Mrs. Root; Captain Butt. The senior aide, who worried about such things, dreaded the dinner but concluded, when it was over, that it had gone off better than he had anticipated. Mrs. Taft noticed that Mrs. Roosevelt was depressed and concluded that the approaching African hunt of her husband was worrying her.

"The President and Mr. Taft, seconded by other guests," she remembered, "did their best . . . to lighten the occasion, but their efforts were not entirely successful." [47]

The years passed. Election Day of 1912 came and with it came defeat. A suggestion was made that Woodrow Wilson should be invited to the White House, but President Taft hesitated.

"Nellie is dead set against it," he told Mabel Boardman, "because of her memory of the Roosevelt dinner to me. You were at that funeral." [48]

The evening was terminated at an early hour when Mrs. Roosevelt arose and said she would retire. She grasped the hand of Mrs. Taft as she did so. Might her first night in the White House, she said, be soothed by deep and pleasant slumber.[49] And so the lights were dimmed and the logs on the hearths burned down. Outside, the guards paced their posts. Inside, the secret-service men watched as always. They would serve a new individual after tomorrow but their master had not really changed; he was the President of the United States.

—6—

March 3, 1909, had been a stormy day, with rain and snow. But this did not daunt the enthusiasm of Weather Chief Moore who, on Election Day, had hailed the fine Republican sunshine which would bring out the G.O.P. vote. He telegraphed the President-elect, sometime on March 3, that a change would come before morning. It would be clear "with plenty of sunshine and invigorat-

[47] *Official Functions*, 1909, p. 1; Abbott, L. F., *op. cit.*, p. 378; Taft, Mrs. W. H., *op. cit.*, p. 326. [48] Taft to Mabel Boardman, Nov. 10, 1912. [49] Abbott, L. F., *op. cit.*, p. 390.

ing air." The temperature would vary between 35 and 40 degrees.[50]
But this time the weather chief was wrong. The storm had grown
worse through the night. The trees on the White House lawn hung
heavy with ice and the streets were coated. It seemed impossible that
the inauguration exercises could be held outdoors.

The President-elect was downstairs at an early hour for breakfast. He was joined in a few minutes by the President. They listened,
for a moment to the howl of the wind.

"Even the elements do protest," said Taft. There was no escape
for him now. In a few brief hours he would be president of the
United States.

"I knew there would be a blizzard when I went out," said
Roosevelt. He did not interpret the remark.[51] There was no time
for further conversation, for solemn men were soon arriving in cabs.
The Joint Committee of the Senate and House on Arrangements at
the Capitol appeared at nine-thirty, funereal in their long black
coats and silk hats. Roosevelt's Cabinet was presented. The vice-
president was presented. No time remained for further thinking;
no time for inner doubts. The procession toward the Capitol began.

All hope of the usual outdoor ceremony in front of the Capitol
had been abandoned before the official party left the White House at
ten o'clock. The President and the President-elect were in the first
carriage, with Senators Lodge and Knox as escort. The carriages
moved slowly on the ice-covered streets; the horses of Troop A,
Ohio National Guard, stepped gingerly. The party proceeded immediately to the Senate Chamber. Chief Justice Fuller stepped forward to give the oath of office and the new President began to
deliver his inaugural address. In front of him were Roosevelt and
his Cabinet. Jammed into the room were the members of the Supreme Court, the diplomatic corps, the members of the Senate and
the House and, in the galleries, the friends of Roosevelt and Taft
and a few other spectators.

The new President spoke slowly, clearly. The face so often
wreathed with smiles was solemn now. He mentioned, as he began,
the "heavy weight of responsibility" which was his. He said that it
had been his honor to have been "one of the advisers of my distinguished predecessor, and, as such, to hold up his hands in the reforms

[50] New York *Times,* March 4, 1909. [51] Fred W. Carpenter to author, Aug. 12, 1933.

he has initiated. I should be untrue to myself, to my promises, and to the declarations of the party platform on which I was elected to office if I did not make the maintenance and enforcement of those reforms a most important feature of my administration."

Taft amplified this. He dwelt on the lawlessness which had been suppressed through the legislation passed by Congress at Roosevelt's command. Then he turned to the keynote of his own policy.

"To render the reforms lasting . . . and to secure at the same time freedom from alarm on the part of those pursuing proper and progressive business methods, further legislative and executive action are needed," Taft said.

This was not a great inaugural address; few of the solemn speeches offered by incoming presidents are important state documents. They are, rather, expressions of hope made by men who may have been merely politicians, who may have achieved their eminence by chicanery and compromise, who may have been merely mediocre men upon whom chance has smiled in dazzling fashion. But no president, I suspect, has started the reading of his inaugural without an inner prayer that he was done with mediocrity. Taft, whatever his faults, could look back on the last three years and know that eminence had come to him without his active seeking. He could know that he was handicapped by no touch of dishonor.

The measured phrases of his brief address were Taft's hopes for the coming years. The antitrust laws and their enforcement needed attention, he said. Above all, the Dingley tariff must be revised downward. The nation's forests and other natural resources must be preserved. The army and navy must be built to a point where the United States, never the aggressor, could enforce her desires for peace. Additional protection against the abuses of industrial life should be given to the workingman. The nation's currency was too rigid; greater elasticity was needed. And Taft remembered, of course, his beloved Philippine Islands. Manifest destiny— he did not use the phrase, for it was ancient and shopworn now— had not brought complete prosperity to the archipelago. But the United States had, at last, lifted the tariff barriers between the islands and the mainland and the eastern skies were lightening. The President touched on other problems: the status of the Negro, the political situation in the South, the abuse of injunctions in labor disputes, the authority of the courts. So saying, he lifted his eyes from the small sheets of paper on which the address had been printed in large type, for easy reading, and asked for help from the Unitarian God who had been so severely criticized by the Methodist and Baptist voters in the campaign of 1908.

"I invoke the considerate sympathy and support of my fellow citizens and the aid of Almighty God in the discharge of my responsible duties," he said.[52]

A ripple of applause was drowned in the bustling of gold-braided aides who dashed into action as though a military objective were about to be taken. Ex-President Roosevelt lunged forward and seized the President's hand.

"God bless you, old man," he said. "It is a great state document." [53]

And Roosevelt, his eyes glistening behind their glasses, strode into the unsatisfactory corridors of private life. An intimate among the correspondents had asked him about his plans a fortnight earlier and had received an answer on condition that it should not be published until March 5. Did he intend to become a sage? The scorn in the answer must have been terrific.

"Certainly not!" he had answered. "By that term is meant a 'has-been.' I step back into the ranks, but I do not quit the army. I shall continue to fight for what I deem to be right." [54]

But Roosevelt had tact as well as an awareness of the dramatic; the two, after all, are often identical. Roosevelt had decided two years before, at a time when he did not know who would be his successor, that he would change the custom of riding back from the inaugural with the new Chief Executive. This was Taft's day. The stage was his. Besides, ego may have dictated that a retiring star does not linger in the wings. Mrs. Taft had been informed of this decision a few days earlier and announced at once that she would take this place of honor. She had her way, although the Congressional committee demurred on the ground that some of its members should make the ride.[55] This, too, was unfairly hailed as a mark of friction between the Roosevelts and the Tafts.

[52] Official Functions, 1909, pp. 1-19; Addresses, Vol. XIV, pp. 1-7. [53] Taft, Mrs. W. H., op. cit., p. 331. [54] St. Louis Post-Dispatch, March 5, 1909. [55] Abbott, L. F., op. cit., p. 362; Taft, Mrs. W. H., op. cit., pp. 329, 331.

The sun had emerged— it was hailed as a good omen, of course— when two carriages started in opposite directions from the Capitol. One turned toward the White House and the crowds which lined the streets bared their heads and applauded as it came by. The other, bearing Roosevelt, went directly to the railroad station; the cheers which greeted it were at least as friendly. He arrived in Oyster Bay that night. He really intended to be a private citizen.

"Gentlemen," he told the correspondents when they called at Sagamore Hill the following day, "I have nothing to say."

"What, never?" they asked.

"As long as I remain a private citizen," he answered.

"How long will that be, Mr. Roosevelt?"

"As long as I can make it. I have finished my talks with newspapermen. They stop right now." [56]

Meanwhile the Tafts had entered the White House. A hasty luncheon followed the ceremonies at the Capitol. At 2:45 p.m. the President had taken his place in the reviewing stand and was watching that strange American custom, the inaugural parade. This one was an anachronism; it would be interesting to know whether Taft was aware of its antiquity as he watched. It was the past rather than the present which marched by in salute. The future was not represented at all. Troops of the Spanish War and of the Philippine Insurrection came by. So did sailors, home from the voyage of the fleet around the world. In line, too, were veterans of the Civil War. It was, however, the political clubs which chiefly emphasized the past. Among them were the "Young Men's Blaine Republican Club" of Cincinnati— and who was James G. Blaine save a dim figure touched with dishonor? The "Conkling Unconditionals" of Utica strutted past— and who was Roscoe Conkling, dead from a blizzard these many years, save another sinister Republican boss? [57] The parade was significant for the gaps in its marching men. The farmer was not there. The pioneer of the western plains— by now he was beginning to wonder whether all the frontiers were gone— was not there, either. And where were the insurgents, who in a few days would start to clip the powers of Uncle Joe Cannon? Where were the progressives of Wisconsin?

[56] New York *Times*, March 6, 1909. [57] Sullivan, Mark, *op. cit.*, Vol. IV, pp. 333-337.

The parade was not over until almost six o'clock, but the program was far from finished. Immediately after it, a reception was held for Taft's classmates at Yale. Then came a dinner at the Metropolitan Club at which the class of 1878 was host. Then came the inaugural ball at the Pension Building. It was one o'clock before the presidential party drove home through a night which had grown warmer. Snow still lay in patches on the lawn, but the air was softened by a promise of spring and by the sweet smell of moist turf. The President was weary. He had been on his feet all day. Mrs. Taft was tired too. Throughout the day she had surged with energy. Her high moment had been the return from the Capitol shortly after noon when she had paused in the White House doorway.

"I stood for a moment," she remembered, "over the great brass seal, bearing the national coat of arms, which is sunk in the floor in the middle of the entrance hall. 'The Seal of the President of the United States,' I read around the border, and now— that meant my husband!" [58]

But Mrs. Taft did not have to be President, herself. That night, in scores of newspaper offices, the presses were spewing forth the morning editions and in them were editorials praising the inaugural address and praising Taft. The New York *World* said that an era of good feeling lay ahead. The nation was weary of the Rooseveltian battles. It wanted tranquillity. It yearned for "rest and peace and assurance."

"It is a task for which Mr. Taft is fitted by training and temperament," the editor had written. "There has been no time since Lincoln's death when the nation more sorely needed a man of his temperament, or when a President had greater opportunities for rendering public service of lasting benefit to the Republic." [59]

This was a surface analysis, and unsound. The farmers of Nebraska and the cattlemen of the plains would not be satisfied with mere tranquillity. Nor would the workingman, who saw the cost of living grow greater day by day.

[58] Taft, Mrs. W. H., *op. cit.*, p. 333. [59] New York *World*, March 5, 1909.

CHAPTER XXIII

THE LONELY HOUSE

THE first weeks after March 4, 1909, were particularly strange. He sat at a vast desk which was the desk of the President of the United States. He was told, very politely, that he must walk ahead of everyone else— even Mrs. Taft— when he entered a room. He must leave every gathering first, so that the others could depart. They called him Mr. President. "As I see it, Mr. President . . ." began the visitors who swarmed, in the main to get jobs. "Now in my judgment, Mr. President . . ." said the senators, who wanted many things in addition to jobs for their followers. "I have the honor, Mr. President, to report that My Government inclines to the position . . ." said, sonorously, the elaborately dressed ambassadors.

Toward the end of his first week in the White House, President Taft went horseback riding with Captain Butt, whom he had retained as chief aide. W. Bourke Cochran of New York was invited to join them. He asked the President, as their horses stepped out together, how he liked the awe-inspiring post which was now his.

"I hardly know, yet," said Taft. "When I hear someone say Mr. President, I look around expecting to see Roosevelt."

At dinner, a few nights later, he kept referring to Theodore Roosevelt as "the President," and this did not please Mrs. Taft. What he obviously meant to say, she pointed out, was "the ex-President."

"I suppose I do, dear," he answered, "but he will always be the President to me, and I can never think of him as anything else." [1]

Yet it was to be impossible ever again to lean on "my dear Theodore" for guidance and advice. Roosevelt was sailing for his African hunt on March 23 and when he returned in June, 1910, misunderstanding and doubt were chill auguries of the quarrel which would send Woodrow Wilson to the White House. President Taft delegated Archie Butt to present his departing friend with a

[1] Butt, Archie, *Taft and Roosevelt*, Vol. I, pp. 9, 14.

gift. He also sent a letter of farewell. It was a poignant communication, eloquent with the perplexities of the new President. If Roosevelt had only remembered this, too, he might have been more charitable in the years ahead. Taft wrote:

My dear Theodore:

If I followed my impulse, I should still say "My dear Mr. President." I cannot overcome the habit. When I am addressed as "Mr. President," I turn to see whether you are not at my elbow. When I read in the newspaper of a conference between the speaker and the President, or between Senator Aldrich and the President, I wonder what the subject of the conference was, and can hardly identify the report with the fact that I had had a talk with the two gentlemen.

I write to you to say "farewell," and to wish you as great pleasure and as much usefulness as possible in the trip you are about to undertake. I have had my qualms as to the result, but in thinking it over they disappear. You will undertake no foolhardy enterprise, I know, and will observe those ordinary precautions that generally bring a man through any experience unharmed and untouched. Of course Mrs. Roosevelt naturally has fears on the subject, but the truth is that we have learned as [sic] much about life in the tropics, whether it be in a wild country or one more civilized, that the dangers that used to exist are not longer present. The advance of medical science in this regard is marvelous.

Many questions have arisen since the inauguration with respect to which I should like to have consulted you, but I have forborne to interrupt your well-earned quiet and to take up your time when it must have been so much occupied with preparation for your long trip. . . .

I have no doubt that when you return you will find me very much under suspicion by our friends in the West. . . . I knew . . . I should make a capital error in the beginning of my administration in alienating the good will of those without whom I can do nothing to carry through the legislation to which the party and I are pledged. Cannon and Aldrich have promised to stand by the party platform and to follow my lead. They did so, I believe, for you in the first Congress of your administration and this is the first Congress of mine. Of course I have not the prestige which you had or the popular support in any such measure as you had to enable you to put through the legislation which was so remarkable in your first Congress; but I am not attempting quite as much as you did then, and I am hopeful that what I do offer will be accepted and put through. . . .

I want you to know that I do nothing in the Executive Office without considering what you would do under the same circumstances and without having in a sense a mental talk with you over the pros and cons of the situation. I have not the facility for educating the public as you had through talks with correspondents, and so I fear that a large part of the public will feel as if I had fallen away from your ideals; *but you know me better and will understand that I am still working away on the same old plan* and hope to realize in some measure the results that we both hold valuable and worth striving for. I can never forget that the power that I now exercise was a voluntary transfer from you to me, and that I am under obligation to you to see to it that your judgment in selecting me as your successor and in bringing about the succession shall be vindicated according to the standards which you and I in conversation have always formulated.

I send you this letter by Archie Butt to be delivered personally, that it may express to you what I would say to you if I were on the deck of the *Hamburg,* where I should be delighted to be and once again to clasp your hand and say the fond farewell, or rather to say "Auf wiedersehen. . . ." With love and best wishes, in which Mrs. Taft joins me, believe me as ever,

Affectionately yours . . .[2]

Roosevelt was besieged by a mob of well-wishers when Captain Butt delivered the letter on the deck of the S.S. *Hamburg.* It was utterly impossible for him to read it then. But he opened it as the vessel turned down the Hudson River and headed for the lower bay. He called for a steward and scribbled a telegram to be taken ashore with the pilot and dispatched to Washington by way of Sea Gate, New Jersey.

"Am deeply touched by your gift and even more by your letter," the message said. "Greatly appreciate it. Everything will turn out all right, old man. Give my love to Mrs. Taft."[3]

[2] Taft to Roosevelt, March 21, 1909. (Italics mine.) [3] Roosevelt to Taft, March 23, 1909.

—2—

On the first major issue of his administration, Taft had actually discussed the "pros and cons" with Roosevelt and had taken his advice. This was the revolt against Speaker Cannon, which Taft ultimately declined to support. It was an issue which did as much as anything else, perhaps, to subject Taft to "suspicion by our friends in the West." The opposition to Cannon had been a major reason for the diminished Republican vote in the West on Election Day, 1908. It was at this point, if ever, that Taft should have assumed the offensive against a politician who stood for conservatism. But he was advised by everyone, including Roosevelt, not to do so yet. Afterward, it was too late.

"Very early in the campaign," Taft said, "I thought of encouraging a movement to beat Cannon, but I found that he was so strongly entrenched . . . that it was impossible." [4]

Uncle Joe was a worthy foe of any president. He was partly a fraud and partly a genius. He had been a member of Congress since 1873, with the exception of a single term. A North Carolinian by birth, he had been taken to Illinois by his parents and this had been his native state ever since. He was the last of the great bucolics in American public life. It is impossible to say how much of Cannon was real and how much was affectation. On the surface he was a rough, crude countryman whose skill in tobacco expectoration was the equal of any cracker-barrel philosopher. He quoted the Bible in one breath. With the next he told stories with an outhouse odor. He could impress his stupid constituents by the use of complicated words. He could move them by the homely, homespun political doctrines which he offered. In short, he was an effective campaigner and a fraction of his auditors, no doubt, confused him with Abraham Lincoln. In appearance, although tall and erect, he was distinctly a dirty old man. This was caused by a habit inaccurately called "dry smoking"; that is, he rolled villainous black cigars between his lips. The cigars began to come apart as he continued to chew on them. Uncle Joe's lips became smeared with tobacco shreds.

On the stump, then, Cannon was a man of the people. The

[4] Taft to W. A. White, March 12, 1909.

crudities dropped from him, however, when he presided as speaker of the House of Representatives. Uncle Joe's fundamental political belief was party government and no doubt ever troubled his soul regarding the fitness of the Republican party to govern. Within the party, he believed in discipline and opposed change. Speaker Cannon actually had the powers of a czar, owing to the rules of the House. He appointed the majority members of the Committee on Rules as well as the majorities of all other committees. But the Rules Committee was the most important. Few congressmen, save those assigned to it, understood the purposely technical parliamentary methods by which the business of the House was carried on. It was a method designed to silence opposition and to accelerate the business at hand. And no change could be made without consent of the Committee on Rules, which Cannon dominated. This, then, was the struggle. The insurgents, for all their fuming, could not translate their protests into legislation. Their only possible course was to defeat Cannon or to strip him of his power.[5]

Cannon was a realist. He was cynical. He said what he thought. A day or two after the election he made a speech in Cleveland during which he dwelt upon Congress, political parties and the faults of both. He told of the instances where members of the House were instructed by lobbyists to vote for specific legislation and were threatened with defeat if they refused.

"I have been through it all," he said. "I have been scared almost out of my life by these people, when I was a younger man. But as I grew older and found that the rain don't always follow the thunder, I have put on the mask . . . of courage."

The Republican party, the speaker continued, now controlled the White House and both branches of Congress. It would redeem, he promised, the platform pledges made at Chicago and this would include a downward revision of the tariff.

". . . in my judgment," he said, "we will be able inside of a hundred days to put, not a perfect revenue law upon the statute books— because all legislation is a compromise. We have 90,000,000 people with varied interests [but] we will put on the statute books the *best revenue law ever written*. We will compromise. Our friends, the enemy, will kick and say it is wicked, that it is robbery. Once

[5] Sullivan, Mark, *Our Times*, Vol. IV, pp. 374-379.

in a while our friends will be disappointed and they will kick; but in the last analysis it will be the best that can be done by your representatives in Congress, with the approval of the President. . . . And under it we will march to further development of the great Republic."

Old Uncle Joe was perfectly aware, he disclosed, of the opposition to his re-election as speaker. Two years before, he said, he had been fought by the American Federation of Labor and by the Anti-Saloon League. He knew that he would be opposed again, this time the attacks would be "supplemented by people that misrepresent."

"I have had it a-comin' and a-gwine, as the nigger said," he concluded. "All's well that ends well. If I get my way about it, I will be elected speaker early in March next. If I am not re-elected, I am a representative, and I will be a member down on the floor, and a member of the whole House when the House resolves itself into a .Committee of the Whole, and I shall be perfectly content." [6]

This speech shocked the President-elect. If Roosevelt had said the word, Taft would in all probability have declared war on the speaker. He told the President, just after Election Day, of the "movement now in the East and among the strong protection interests to secure Cannon's nomination."

"Throughout the West, I am sure," Taft continued, "there will be a movement to defeat it, and if by helping it I could bring it about I would do so, but I want to take no false steps in the matter, because to attempt to defeat 'Joe' and not to succeed would be worse than to let him get in and deal with him as best I can." [7]

The President and the President-elect arranged to discuss the situation at the White House shortly after this. The President said that Secretary of State Root would take part in their conference and added:

It would, of course, be well if there was some first class man to put in his place as speaker; but we cannot think of putting in some cater-cornered creature like Burton [Theodore E. Burton of Ohio]; and, moreover, if it is evident that four-fifths of the Republicans want Cannon I do not believe it would be well to have him

[6] Taft papers, Library of Congress, War Secretary files. (Italics mine.) [7] Taft to Roosevelt, Nov. 7, 1908.

THE TAFT SMILE—FROM AN UNIDENTIFIED SKETCH. ABOUT 1908.

See page 336]

THE AGE OF PHOTOGRAPHY IN POLITICS; FROM A POSTCARD CIRCULATED IN THE 1908 CAMPAIGN

[*See page 356*

in the position of the sullen and hostile floor leader bound to bring your administration to grief, even though you were able to put someone else in as speaker.[8]

Root was even more emphatically opposed to a war with Uncle Joe. He pointed out that "it would be very unfortunate to have the idea get about that you wanted to beat Cannon and are not able to do it." With whom could he conceivably win? Burton was "respected, but not popular." Interference by the Chief Executive would surely result in an alignment by the House against this usurpation of legislative powers.

"I have treated all the newspaper talk about your going into a fight against Cannon as mere newspaper talk," Root said. ". . . I hope you will find some way to dispel the impression that it tends to create." [9]

Of the three, Taft was the most violent in his antagonism toward the speaker. He answered Root:

I think that the attitude of Cannon, the cynical references that he has made in some of his speeches about promises and compliance with them, are enough to damn the party if they are not protested against. I have not said anything for publication, but I am willing to have it understood that my attitude is one of hostility toward Cannon and the whole crowd unless they are coming in to do the square thing. If they don't do it, and I acquiesce, we are going to be beaten; and I had rather be beaten by not acquiescing than by acquiescing. You know me well enough to know that I do not hunt a fight just for the fun of it, but Cannon's speech at Cleveland was of a character that ought to disgust everybody who believes in honesty in politics and dealing with the people squarely, and just because he has a nest of standpatters in his House and is so ensconced there that we may not be able to move him is no reason why I should pursue the policy of harmony. I don't care how he feels or how they feel in the House. I am not going to be made the mouthpiece of a lie to the people without disclaiming my responsibility. If they will play fair I will play fair, but if they won't then I reserve all my rights to do anything I find myself able to do.[10]

[8] Roosevelt to Taft, Nov. 10, 1908. [9] Root to Taft, Nov. 23, 1908. [10] Taft to Roosevelt, Nov. 25, 1908.

These were fine, brave words; they referred, of course, to Cannon's probable fight against tariff revision rather than to the contest over his powers in the House. It was the normally pugnacious Roosevelt who, on this occasion, sought to soothe his normally pacific successor. The President informed Taft, who was still in Hot Springs, that Representative J. A. Tawney had called at the White House and was "very anxious to have an interview arranged between you and the speaker." It was, said Roosevelt, "extremely important that you should have this interview. . . . I should like to have a chance to see you and give you a full statement of the facts as they seem to me and also of the facts as Cannon and Tawney tell me *they* see them." [11]

Taft agreed, of course. But he fortified himself, before he saw Cannon, with all possible information regarding the probable strength of the speaker. He asked Arthur Capper, the publisher and future senator, how the Kansas delegation stood on Cannonism. He made the same inquiry of J. N. Dolley, also of Kansas. The replies were not encouraging to a president-elect who already suspected that the insurgent movement had not acquired sufficient strength. Capper reported that five out of the eight Kansas congressmen would be for the re-election of Cannon. Dolley substantiated this. Only three members, he said, were "heart and soul with you and against Cannon and a superficial revision of the tariff." [12] So Taft, by early December, 1908, abandoned his last hope that an effective onslaught on the speaker could be made. [13] He had conceded defeat when, at Roosevelt's request, he saw Uncle Joe. The speaker, it would seem, was smooth and plausible as well as co-operative.

"I had a most satisfactory talk with him," the President-elect noted, "in which he said that he was entirely in sympathy with my effort to carry out the pledges of the Chicago platform, and that he would assist me as loyally as possible. He asked me to see the Ways and Means Committee, which I did, and I explained to them my position, and they assured me that they were fully in sympathy with it and were going to do what they could." [14]

No sane president-elect could have taken a course different from

[11] Roosevelt to Taft, Nov. 28, 1908. [12] Arthur Capper to Taft, Nov. 27, 1908; J. N. Dolley to Taft, Nov. 28, 1908. [13] J. L. Bristow to Taft, Dec. 9, 1908. [14] Taft to Horace D. Taft, June 27, 1909.

this one by Taft. A more clever politician, or a less open and frank one, would have avoided, however, a mistake which he immediately made. This was to tell the newspaper correspondents that he had seen Cannon and was confident of the speaker's good faith.[15] These preliminary months were a time when guile and stealth were needed. The open announcement of a working arrangement— there was, in fact, nothing sinister whatever about it— sent a chill of discouragement over the valiant but futile band of House insurgents who still hoped that they might unhorse the speaker when the special session of Congress, summoned for tariff revision, opened in March. The insurgents seem to have believed, almost to the end of 1908, that Taft was their ally and might yet throw his weight, prestige and patronage powers behind them. They were to grow bitter and make unjust and untrue accusations when they finally learned that he had followed the counsel of Roosevelt and Root.

The struggle for democracy against autocracy in the House of Representatives between 1908 and 1910 has been slighted, to an extent, by the chroniclers of liberty. It was a decisive battle. It is unimportant whether Uncle Joe Cannon was really the archprotector of privilege; he was, by and large, a politician, and he bowed when the winds of revolt became too strong. The evil part of the system in the House was that it blocked the winds before they had a chance to grow strong. A little handful of twenty-five congressmen— possibly thirty— was leading the fight toward the end of 1908 and the extraordinary thing is that they had no leader who could command the ears of the nation. Roosevelt was deaf to them. LaFollette was busy with his own program; besides, a superior senator could not take too active a part in a mere House matter.

The insurgents had leaders, of course. From the plains of Nebraska had arrived a new representative in 1903; a man of forty-two, George William Norris had gone into Nebraska from Ohio in 1885 and had hung out a law shingle. He had been a prosecuting attorney and then a judge. He was elected to the Fifty-eighth Con-

[15] *War Secretary Diaries*, p. 4016.

gress in 1902 and for more than thirty years— in the House and then in the Senate— he was to be a passionate disciple of liberalism. Small, nervous and active, Norris received no acclaim for decades. At last it came to him. A Democratic president ordered that one of the greatest public works projects in history should bear the name of this Republican senator. In Norris's brief autobiography in *Who's Who in America,* however, continues to appear this line:

Led fight in Ho. of Rep. which overthrew "Cannonism." [16]

Norris was to command the final battle. There were other valiants, who dared openly to oppose the czar and risk, thereby, defeat when again they stood for election. On the night of December 11, 1908, they conferred at the office of Representative Peter Hepburn of Iowa. Twenty-five members attended the meeting. Among them was Representative Charles Augustus Lindbergh, from the Sixth Minnesota District; his son of the same name would one day inflame the world by a transatlantic flight and would then support Herbert Hoover for the presidency. There were four members from Wisconsin and four from Kansas. California, Michigan, Missouri, Vermont and Massachusetts were the other states represented. Two of the congressmen present had personal grievances. Henry Allen Cooper had been removed from the Committee on Insular Affairs because he had dared to oppose organization legislation. Victor Murdock of Kansas had been demoted, for similar reasons, from fifth to tenth place on the Committee on Post Offices and Post Roads.[17]

A report on the meeting was sent to President-elect Taft. This predicted that fifty or sixty members of the House would probably join the revolt— a far too optimistic statement. The following changes in the rules would be demanded when the extra session convened:

First—To abolish the arbitrary power of recognition by the speaker and restore the rule in force prior to 1879.
Second—A representative committee of seven or more on rules *to be elected by the House.*
Third—The compulsory calling of the committees on two or three days of each week, specified.[18]

[16] *Who's Who in America,* Vol. XVIII, p. 1784. [17] Sullivan, Mark, *op. cit.,* Vol. IV, pp. 378-379. [18] H. E. Hinshaw to Taft, Dec. 12, 1908.

"I am glad that you think it likely that the rules will be changed," Taft told a member of the conference. "I should think the first two amendments you suggest would be of very great benefit. The taking away of the committees from the speaker would reduce the speakership to an almost judicial position, and I am rather inclined to think that would be better. I doubt, however, whether the speaker would consent to it." [19]

Taft's expression of "doubt" was an understatement; Cannon had no intention whatever of being relegated to so ridiculous and impotent a role as that of a judicial officer. The insurgents failed in their attack in March, 1909. But they continued their agitation throughout the year. Norris emerged as their outstanding leader. He drafted a resolution which called for election of a Rules Committee by the House instead of by appointment of the speaker. A year later, March 17, 1910, he moved its adoption and after a long debate he won, through a combination of rebellious Republicans and co-operative Democrats, by 191 to 156. It looked like the end of Uncle Joe. He heard the vote silently; his cold eyes gave no indication of his inner turmoil. Then he proposed that the speaker's chair should be declared vacant. The czar would abdicate. Let the new order elect its own speaker. But this was too severe; the most bitter of the insurgents could find no such malice in their hearts. The emotional Champ Clark reached for his handkerchief and wept at the spectacle of a mighty monarch offering to give up his throne. So a vote to unseat the speaker was defeated. His powers were gone, however. He was now more of a judicial officer than any speaker since that day when Tom Reed, so many years before, had fashioned the post into one of arbitrary powers.[20]

President Taft, meanwhile, had sacrificed, utterly and completely the earlier confidence of the insurgents. But he did not, in private, change his mind about Cannon all that year, 1909:

There is only one feature of the situation that I look forward to with considerable concern, and that is the continuation in politics of Cannon. I think he has been sufficiently honored to justify him in now retiring and in announcing his retirement, at least from

---

[19] Taft to H. E. Pollard, Dec. 22, 1908. [20] Sullivan, Mark, *op. cit.*, Vol. IV, pp. 38-82; Pringle, H. F., *Theodore Roosevelt, a Biography*, p. 529.

the speakership contest, in advance of the next general election. The American people are a decent, clean, pure-minded people as a whole, and they do not approve vulgarity and blackguardism in daily conversation for publication of their public men; and Cannon has driven from him by this characteristic, many who would support his general policies, and has made many doubt his sincerity of purpose and his patriotic devotion to duty. . . .[21]

Walter I. Smith [Representative Smith of Iowa] is the man I would select for speaker if we can only get Uncle Joe out of the way— and I think we can. If he shall succeed in continuing at the top during the present Congress he owes it to the public to relieve those who are his warm friends from the incubus of his future candidacy; and I believe this to be the opinion of those who are closest to him.[22]

Taft's countrymen would have understood him better if these candid observations had reached the public; they were, of course, expressed in confidential letters. He had been in the White House for less than ten months before he learned that the middle of the road was an uncomfortable place. He had alienated the insurgents because he had declined to assist them in their battle against Cannon. The conservatives were also critical, although less vehemently so, because he fought long and stubbornly for genuine tariff cuts. Taft was not mild, pleasant and judicial under the attacks. He resented them deeply, but he continued to express himself only in private. The first whispered criticism of Theodore Roosevelt and his followers is to be found in the unhappy letters written by Taft in 1909. The criticism was implied, not spoken:

The strenuous supporters of Mr. Roosevelt [it will be noted that he is no longer the President or even Theodore in Taft's mind], that is, the extreme supporters, those who like to call themselves "progressives" are very suspicious of me, and they refer to my refusal to assist the insurgents in the House to defeat Cannon by refusing to go into the caucus and voting against him on the floor, as an instance of how I am departing from the Roosevelt policies; and they, secondly, refer to my not infrequent interviews with Cannon and with Aldrich as an indication that I am consorting with anti-Roosevelt and reactionary people. . . . What a fool I

[21] Taft to Knox, Oct. 24, 1909. [22] Taft to O. T. Bannard, Dec. 20, 1909.

would be if I joined, or permitted myself to countenance, the yelping and snarling at Cannon and Aldrich, which these so-called "progressives" and their amateur political newspaper correspondents are insisting upon as a mark of loyalty to the Roosevelt policies, and to the carrying out of which I am pledged. In other words, they do not look beyond their noses. They do not seem to understand the only possible way of effecting the reforms, or to make real progress.[23]

"I am not so constituted," he wrote in a profound moment of self-analysis, "that I can run with the hare and hunt with the hounds." [24]

—4—

But this, unhappily, was not the whole story. Taft allowed himself to be forced into a position where he was the proponent and defender of Aldrich and Cannon and it availed him, therefore, very little when he denied that an alliance had been formed. Too, his earlier low opinions of the Senate and House leaders began to change. Uncle Joe, he wrote, in February, 1910, "enjoyed a popularity at one time that was in excess of his deserts, and he is suffering now from a bitterness of attack that is in excess of his deserts." As for Senator Aldrich: "He is a much higher tariff man than I am, and his attitude in respect to the tariff is one with which, in many respects, I do not agree; but he is a man who has been subjected to a great deal of unfounded criticism." [25]

As time passed, Taft grew almost lyrical in praising Aldrich. Early in 1911 the senator was away from Washington because of ill-health.

"I long for your presence," the President wrote. "I feel about you as Scott said of Rhoderick Dhu. A blast upon your bugle horn were worth a thousand men." [26]

It was preposterous for Taft to suppose that the senator from Rhode Island could ever work for honest tariff cuts. The President's memory was short if he did not recall the part played by Aldrich

[23] Taft to Horace D. Taft, June 27, 1909. [24] Taft to L. B. Swift, Feb. 19, 1910. [25] Idem. [26] Taft to Aldrich, Jan. 28, 1911.

in 1894 when Grover Cleveland had gone to war against entrenched wealth and the senator had been vigorous in resisting any lowering of the protective levies. Aldrich, with his allies, had mangled a Democratic president's tariff bill, then.[27] Taft might have known that he would do the same to the bill of a Republican president. Moreover, Taft had had— as we have seen— opportunity to learn the views of Aldrich at closer range. In January, 1903, Luke E. Wright of the Philippine Commission was in Washington to urge a reduction in the rates between the islands and the United States. Civil Governor Taft watched his efforts closely.

"I suppose from your letter . . ." he wrote from Manila, "that you have found your real opposition to be in Aldrich. . . . He seems to be the guardian of the tobacco, sugar and silver trusts." [28]

Aldrich, too, was one of the last of his breed but it was— except in a mutual devotion to the old order— a very different breed from crude old Uncle Joe Cannon. Aldrich was sixty-eight years old in 1909 and the milestones of his life had been a series of cold, logical decisions which had increased, step by step, his wealth and power. He made his first money in the wholesale grocery business; a fact which must have appalled him a little in the days of his magnificence as the leader of the Senate. He served for a little while— four months— in the Union armies. But it was difficult to amass a fortune while in uniform and so, with the war still to be won, he returned to his grocery warehouse and did quite well. Two motives seem to have drawn Aldrich into politics; the first was a desire to dominate other men. The second was a practical realization that the link between politics and wealth was very close. Aldrich was never stupid. He knew that only stupid men indulged in corruption of the variety which transgressed the law. So scandal never touched him.

Aldrich was precocious too. He was speaker of the House of Representatives of Rhode Island, his native state, when he was thirty-five years old. In 1878 he came to Congress and three years later he was a member of the Senate. At first he was inconspicuous. But the Old Guard— they were not really old then— discovered that Aldrich had an excellent mind. They learned that he could find

---

[27] Nevins, Allan, *Grover Cleveland, A Study in Courage*, p. 576. [28] Taft to L. E. Wright, Jan. 24, 1903.

his way through the puzzles of a tariff measure and invariably come out on the side of high protection. William Boyd Allison, the senator from Iowa, was one of the first to appreciate his gifts. So did the steel manufacturers of Pittsburgh. So did the oil interests, the railroad interests and Mr. J. P. Morgan. In 1901, in vivid proof of his social, political and financial status, his daughter was married to John D. Rockefeller, Jr., the coming young son of the oil king.

The one-time wholesale grocer progressed along every line except in his political and economic beliefs. These remained fixed and inflexible. Aldrich would have silently approved— he would never have been foolish enough to express it publicly— the pious sentiment of George F. Baer of the Philadelphia and Reading Iron and Coal Company: that the "rights and interests of the laboring man will be protected and cared for— not by the labor agitators, but by the Christian men to whom God in his infinite wisdom has given the control of the property interests of this country." Aldrich was a faithful ally, almost an intimate, of this Republican god. In 1886 he fought the first attempt to enact an interstate commerce law. He opposed the liberalism of Cleveland. He attempted to thwart the efforts of Theodore Roosevelt to end rebates by the railroads. He led, in the Senate, the attacks on the Roosevelt administration in its closing months.[29]

Aldrich had the intolerance frequent among signally successful self-made men. He had small ability to look into the future and he was quite deaf to the sound of rumbling tumbrils. Roosevelt had heard these and had turned them back. Taft heard them too. But the United States, to Aldrich, was not a nation which stretched from sea to sea with troubled farmers, baffled cattlemen and poverty-stricken miners laboring for a pittance in the valleys or the mountains which lay between. New York City was on his map. So were the textile areas of New England. Marked on it, too, were the steel mills of western Pennsylvania, the oil fields and those dark and gloomy stretches of the middle northwest where iron ore waited to be mined for the United States Steel Corporation. The American dream, to Nelson W. Aldrich, was of factories which blackened the sky and workmen who did not complain. He was the spokesman

[29] Stephenson, N. W., *Nelson W. Aldrich*, pp. 61-68; Pringle, H. F., *op. cit.*, pp. 267, 422-425, 489.

for the owners of the factories. His allies in the Senate were Allison, Penrose, Quay and the rest. His bitter foes were LaFollette, the talented and gracious Jonathan Dolliver, Borah, Beveridge, Moses E. Clapp of Minnesota and a few others.

The essence of leadership was in Aldrich. He carried his years well; no one would have guessed that he was close to seventy. He had charm, of a sort. But this was reserved for the senators who agreed with him and who did his will. Those who dared to disagree found themselves treated as persons of inferior breeding, devoid of intelligence. They were beneath his contempt. But they were not beneath his notice. Dolliver, qualified in every way, was eligible for the Senate's Finance Committee when his conservative colleague, Allison, died. But Aldrich did not trust Dolliver, so he gave the post to Senator Reed Smoot, apostle of the Mormon Church and the beet-sugar interests. This was a grave mistake. It gave further ammunition to the foes who would one day win; before whose might Aldrich would finally retire and close his years in private life and bitterness.[30]

—5—

It was this man to whom Taft turned because he felt he had to do so. The insurgents, in the Senate as in the House, were too weak. But before long Taft had made the almost incredible mistake of endorsing Aldrich in a public address and he insisted, stubbornly, that this was right and proper.

"I am not afraid to refer to Senator Aldrich as a friend of mine," he insisted, "and as one of the most useful men in the Senate, a man with whom *I don't always agree,* but whose effectiveness, straightforwardness and clearheadedness, and whose command of men everybody . . . must recognize." [31]

Protests streamed into the White House regarding Taft's closeness to Aldrich, and to one of these Taft answered:

Suppose that in dealing with the leaders of the Senate you were to find that he [Aldrich] was helpful to you in carrying out your

[30] Sullivan, Mark, *op. cit.,* Vol. IV, pp. 354-361; Bowers, Claude, *Beveridge and the Progressive Era,* pp. 321-324. [31] Taft to W. L. Fisher, Sept. 25, 1909. (Italics mine.)

policies; that he never violated any promise that he had made to
you; that he was always *frank and above board* . . . that you never
knew him to be dishonest . . . would you feel it necessary to quarrel
with him or to welcome his assistance when the burden of doing
something affirmative in legislation was thrown on you?[32]

"The alliance between Mr. Cannon, Senator Aldrich and myself
is one of the easy accusations to make," the President continued to
insist.[33]

Aldrich was repeatedly at the White House; every visit made
another headline. By June, 1910, Taft was admitting frankly that
he was leaning upon Aldrich and Senator Eugene Hale of Maine
who was, if anything, more conservative than the Senate leader.

"When you and Senator Aldrich are both absent from the
Senate," the President told Hale, "I feel much anxiety as to whether
the measures in which I am so much interested will receive proper
consideration. In other words, I yearn for the presence of an old
parliamentary hand." [34]

When the headlines, that same summer, hinted of a break
between the President and Aldrich, Taft denied them. He told the
senator that "nothing could be more absurd." They were, he said,
inspired by some of the newspaper correspondents who wished "to
save the administration from itself." [35]

Taft's ultimate defeat was caused, in no small measure, by these
repeated, incessant headlines which, try as he might, he could not
guide or control. Taft was well aware of the flaw which made it
impossible for him to deal successfully with the newspaper correspondents; he had mentioned this, too, in his farewell letter to
Roosevelt. And it was this inability which caused to evaporate, in
an astonishingly brief time, the good will which had been his. His
predecessor, needless to say, had to an amazing degree the flair,
utterly essential to a successful chief executive, for molding public
opinion through newspapers. Roosevelt was not content with editorial comment, merely; he actually made news. He was the first
president to employ a stratagem which has been valuable to politicians ever since. It is known, in practical journalist circles, as the

---

[32] Taft to R. M. Wanamaker, Nov. 29, 1909. (Italics mine.) [33] Taft to W. D.
Foulke, Nov. 18, 1909. [34] Taft to Hale, June 22, 1910. [35] Taft to Aldrich, Aug. 15,
1910.

"trial balloon." The method was simple. Roosevelt would call in a favored correspondent or two— he held no general press conferences— and would divulge, on a pledge that he would not be quoted, some probable policy regarding the railroads, the Standard Oil or pure righteousness. The correspondents would then write articles setting forth that "the President, according to close intimates," proposed to take the action in question. Roosevelt, during the next fortnight, could sit back and watch the reaction to his scheme. If it was favorable, he would go ahead. If the hostility was too pronounced, the whole matter would be quietly forgotten. If some political foe declared that the President had shifted his policy, he was nominated for the Ananias Club.

But Taft did not feel that his judicial nature— he was just a shade smug about it— would permit him to indulge in these useful extravagances. He had been in the White House for less than a month before the correspondents at Washington, perhaps spoiled by the fruitful Roosevelt years when their work had been so easy, were complaining that the President was withholding the news. Archie Butt carried the complaint to Taft who said that he "could not talk to the newspapermen" as Roosevelt had done but that he would "try to accomplish just as much without any noise." Captain Butt continued to worry. He noted that neither the President nor his private secretary, Fred Carpenter, gave out any news. Thus the correspondents had to get it elsewhere and they interviewed, among others, the opponents of the administration.[36] The situation might have been remedied, to a degree at least, by the employment of some trained newspaperman in the White House. But nothing was done. In this, as with respect to other instances when things went badly, the President had, to quote a member of his Cabinet, "the stubbornness of an uncertain man." [37]

So if the newspapers criticized him, he concluded, the newspapers were wrong and it was useless to take any action. "Don't worry over what the newspapers say. I don't; why should anyone else?" he asked a friend in August of his first year.[38] Yet he worried, none the less. He resented the editorial criticisms during the tariff battle and suggested that his secretary should no longer show him

---

[36] Butt, Archie, *op. cit.*, Vol. I, pp. 29-31. [37] Charles Nagel to author, Oct. 25, 1934.
[38] Taft to Marion DeVries, Aug. 12, 1909.

clippings "from the New York *Times* which is in a state of free trade fury. I only read the headlines and the first sentence or two. . . . I don't think their reading will do me any particular good, and would only be provocative of . . . anger and contemptuous feeling." [39]

"I see very few newspapermen," the President wrote late in 1909.[40]

The pressure of work in the White House was incredible. "He cannot be hurried . . . and he does not mind breaking engagements," Mrs. Taft told Butt, who concluded that the President would "be about three years behind when the fourth of March, 1913, rolls around" unless he somehow accelerated his program.

"Archie, it seems to me I will never catch up with my work," said the President, himself; ". . . there is so much to be done and so little time to do it in that I feeel discouraged." [41]

Doubt and pessimism mounted. By the end of June, he admitted, it "seems likely in view of the complications" that he would be in the White House for but a single term.[42] It was noted that the President, when he returned to the private rooms of the White House at dusk, seemed tired. Weariness was heavy upon him and he would fall asleep almost as soon as he had settled into a chair. New, deep lines were visible in his face.[43]

[39] Taft to Fred W. Carpenter, Oct. 24, 1909. [40] Taft to W. D. Foulke, Nov. 29, 1909. [41] Butt, Archie, *op. cit.*, Vol. I, pp. 3, 5. [42] Taft to C. P. Taft, June 28, 1909. [43] Butt, Archie, *op. cit.*, Vol. I, p. 76.

CHAPTER XXIV

LEGACY OF DOOM

N O MATTER how great an improvement the new tariff may be," observed Uncle Joe Cannon during the Roosevelt years, "it almost always results in the party in power losing the election." [1]

"Of course," wrote Theodore Roosevelt to Cabot Lodge from Africa, where the lions were far less dangerous than sugar and lumber and wool schedules, "you are bound to have dissatisfaction with any tariff bill." [2]

They were entirely correct. They might have added that any president who attempted tariff revision was likely to suffer frustration and defeat. Such was the legacy bequeathed by Roosevelt to his friend and successor. The Dingley act, passed in 1897, had been in force for twelve years; its rates were higher than under any other tariff in the history of the country. William Howard Taft may have lacked many qualities essential to the presidency. But there is a fine, high courage— in marked contrast to the evasions of Theodore Roosevelt— in the way he accepted his legacy of doom. A man more skilled in politics would have waged a more successful battle against the high-tariff forces. A president with a different theory regarding the proper powers of the Chief Executive would have, to a greater degree, imposed his will on Congress. A less honest man might have convinced the nation that the Payne-Aldrich act of 1909 met, in every major aspect, the promises of the party and himself. But no president could have shown greater valor in baring his chest to the arrows of the tariff controversy. And what progress he actually made toward lowered levies was obscured by the partisan attacks which followed in its wake.

The history of tariff reform is a record of failure; let us go back over twenty years, to that historic day in December, 1887, when

---

[1] Busbey, L. White, *Uncle Joe Cannon*, p. 211. [2] Lodge, H. C., *Selections from the Correspondence of Theodore Roosevelt and Henry Cabot Lodge*, Vol. II, p. 335.

President Cleveland branded the tariff schedules "vicious, inequita-ble, and illegal sources of unnecessary taxation." [3] A bill with low-ered rates passed the House (not the Senate) the following summer, but Cleveland, although other issues contributed to his downfall, was defeated for re-election in 1888.[4] Then came the McKinley act of 1890 with still higher duties. Back in the White House in March, 1893, Cleveland returned to the fray. Again interminable tariff debates dragged on. The President was disgusted with the Wilson-Gorman act of 1894 but permitted it to become law without his signature. For a time, he had debated the wisdom of vetoing this compromise.[5]

The parallel between Cleveland's tariff woes and those of Taft is strangely exact. The agrarian interests were not satisfied with the revision in 1894 any more than they would be in 1909. The tariff struggle of 1894 split the Democratic party; after its defeat in 1896 it did not return to power until 1912. The dissension over the Payne-Aldrich act in 1909 contributed to the G.O.P. disaster in 1912, and the Republicans starved for eight years. But both Cleveland and Taft refused to flee from the almost certain peril of tariff reform— a parallel between the characters of the two men can be found too. Cleveland accomplished this much; the Wilson-Gorman act of 1894 marked the first halt in the upward tariff trend since 1861. Taft accomplished this much; the Payne-Aldrich act was the first Repub-lican tariff which was lower than the one it replaced. President McKinley, coming after Cleveland, said he favored schedules which were only moderately protective. As a Republican he faced, of course, the necessity of repealing the Wilson-Gorman act, a Demo-cratic measure. It had been clearly understood, however, that reason would rule. But when the Dingley act became law in 1897 its rates were, on the average, higher than those of the Republican measure passed seven years before.[6] McKinley had made no energetic fight. He had incited no strife. He was re-elected in 1900. On the day be-fore he was shot, however, the President had called for downward revision through reciprocity agreements with other nations.[7]

[3] McElroy, R. M., *Grover Cleveland*, Vol. I, pp. 271-272. [4] Nevins, Allan, *Grover Cleveland, A Study in Courage*, pp. 393, 440-442. [5] *Ibid.*, p. 587. [6] Rhodes, J. F., *The McKinley and Roosevelt Administrations, 1897-1909*, pp. 37-39. [7] New York *Times*, Sept. 6, 1901.

So Roosevelt fell heir, too, to a tariff revision legacy. He declined to accept the dangerous gift. He convinced himself that it was not a true Rooseveltian issue because it had no moral connotation, such as the onslaught on the trusts. He doubted, in the spring of 1903, whether it would be "wise to make a reduction in the year preceding a presidential election." [8] Uncle Joe Cannon was very much pleased. He remembered, as he dictated his memoirs, that Roosevelt had been "full of revision" when he had succeeded to the presidency.[9] But his ardor had cooled; after all, he was an extremely busy chief executive and the tariff was a dull as well as a dangerous subject.

"For the last two years," a complacent President told a gratified speaker of the House in February, 1907, "I have accepted your view as to just what we should say on the tariff— or rather as to what we should not say— and I am satisfied that it was wiser than the course I had intended to follow." [10]

Uncle Joe could not understand the continued demands for tariff changes, in the face of this joint perspicacity. "Whence comes this so-called demand for tariff tinkering?" he demanded. "Aren't all our fellows happy?" [11] The fellows who represented what Grover Cleveland had called the "communism of pelf" were doubtless happy enough. But the day had passed when the voters accepted, without question, the doctrine that big business and the average man traveled hand in hand on the same road toward Utopia. Resentment toward the trusts was growing. The trusts benefited from protective tariffs, and so the hostility toward high import duties was increasing too. It was all very well to tell the workingman that his wages— high compared with those of Europe— depended on maintenance of those duties. Suppose his wages were too low to meet the increasing cost of the things he bought, however? Suppose he was out of work and had no wages at all? The depression which followed the panic of 1907, brief as it was, had increased the discontent.

Taft was a more outspoken advocate of lowered levies than Roosevelt, possibly because of his continued agitation for a reciprocal arrangement between the Philippine Islands and the United States. He had made, as we have seen, his first formal declaration for down-

[8] Pringle, H. F., *Theodore Roosevelt, a Biography*, p. 342. [9] Busbey, L. W., *op. cit.*, pp. 209-210. [10] Pringle, H. F., *op. cit.*, p. 415. [11] Washington *Post*, Nov. 17, 1905.

ward revision during the Congressional campaign of 1906. This was on September 5 when, "speaking my individual opinion," Taft said that it was "wise and just to revise the schedules" of the Dingley act. A probable presidential nominee at the time, Taft was not blind to the political dangers.

"The readjustment of tariff schedules," he said with vision which equaled that of Speaker Cannon, "is a most difficult matter. . . . A proposition to change them, when carried to the point of actually formulating a bill, always creates division in the party proposing it." [12]

—2—

It is vital, in view of ultimate declarations by Aldrich and Cannon, to make clear the position of Taft on tariff reform. He sought the nomination as a moderate revisionist and declined to be "mealymouthed" on the subject.[13] He took the issue to the people and asked for election on precisely the same basis. Senators Aldrich, Hale and Lodge trifled with the truth when, the tariff debate under way in April, 1909, they said they were not pledged to lower schedules. On the other hand, the platform adopted at Chicago was evasive; such is the invariable goal of the men who draft these curious and useless documents. The tariff plank declared "unequivocally for the revision of the tariff by a special session of Congress immediately following the inauguration of the next president." It did not say, specifically, that this was to be "downward." It added that the "true principle of protection" was best maintained by the "imposition of such duties as will equal the difference between the cost of production at home and abroad, together with a reasonable profit to American industries." [14] The platform makers at Chicago told themselves that this gave the Republican party a right to increase the tariff if expediency so dictated after the election.

Taft did not sanction such nonsense; there is nothing to indicate that he thought, for a moment, that this interpretation could be placed on the tariff plank. In his acceptance speech he said:

[12] *Addresses*, Vol. IV, pp. 159-160. [13] Taft to Vorys, Aug. 2, 1907. [14] *War Secretary Diaries*, p. 3353.

In 1897 the Dingley Tariff bill was passed, under which we
have had . . . a period of enormous prosperity. . . . The consequent
material development *has greatly changed the conditions* under
which many articles described by the schedules of the tariff are now
produced. The tariff in a number of the schedules *exceeds the
difference between the cost of production of such articles abroad
and at home,* including a reasonable profit to the American pro-
ducer. The excess over that difference serves no useful purpose,
but offers a temptation to those who would monopolize the production and the sale of such articles in this country, to profit by
the excessive rate.[15]

The Republican candidate held to this position throughout the
presidential campaign, despite the opposition of Cannon and the
occasional alarm of Roosevelt. After the campaign, as the speaker
and his allies began to say soothingly that little, after all, might be
necessary in the way of tariff change, Taft's patience snapped.

"I am not . . . particularly averse to have Mr. Payne [Repre-
sentative Sereno E. Payne], and Mr. Dalzell [Representative John
Dalzell], and Mr. Cannon understand," he wrote Root, "that they
cannot go ahead and fool the public without a protest from somebody and that protest seems to fall to me. If they do not pass a bill
that is a genuine revision bill I will veto it, and if I find they are in
a spirit of recalcitrancy I would just as lief have them believe that
I am going in and fight." [16]

In January, 1909, Taft admitted that he would probably have a
"fight right through my administration" on tariff reform.

"I believe the people are with me," he said, "and before I get
through I think I will have downed Cannon, and Aldrich too, if
Aldrich gets in the way, or else will have broken up the party and
turned the matter over to the Democrats to make fools of themselves, as they doubtless would." [17]

These were brave words, even if privately spoken. They were
quite sincere. To an extent, Cannon and Aldrich really were
downed. Taft's mistake seems to have been that he gave too much
credence to pledges of support from the speaker and the Senate

[15] *Addresses,* Vol. XI, pp. 67-68. (Italics mine.) [16] Taft to Root, Nov. 25, 1908.
[17] Taft to W. R. Nelson, Jan. 5, 1909.

leader. He admitted that the revisions would probably not suit him, but the tariff bill to be enacted "will be a good deal better than it would have been if I had not made a fuss about it." [18] In his inaugural address the President-elect went further than any Republican predecessor when he declared that in "the making of a tariff bill the prime motive is taxation and the securing thereby of a revenue." [19] This was astonishingly close to recommending a tariff for revenue only, a doctrine hitherto limited to unsound members of the Democracy.

The need of the federal government for additional revenues was merely one of the complications which confronted the President in connection with the tariff. The fiscal year's deficit, Taft pointed out as he took office, would exceed $100,000,000, so "the framers of the tariff bill must, of course, have in mind the total revenues likely to be produced by it and arrange the duties so as to secure an adequate income." [20] Taft learned, in traveling through the South while he was still president-elect, that there was a new cross-current. He attended a banquet of the Chamber of Commerce at Augusta, Georgia, on January 20, 1909. He discovered that the Democrats of the South, while they might unite on the superiority of mint juleps and the continuing menace of the Negro, had varied views on tariff cuts. Judge Joseph R. Lamar spoke on "Augusta's Relation to Foreign Commerce" at the dinner.

"Until lately," said the judge, "our only interest in the tariff was in having it reduced. But the recent years— stimulating manufactures in wood and iron and cotton and witnessing the importation of Egyptian long-staple cotton— have raised up many men who take a view regarded as utterly heretical. Indeed, as interest in high tariff appears to wane at the North, it begins to grow in the South." [21]

Similar sentiments were echoed in February when Taft paused at Hattiesburg, Mississippi. He had finished his address when a voice in the audience called out: "We want to protect our lumber." Taft must have struggled between irritation and amusement as he answered:

[18] Taft to Horace D. Taft, Jan. 13, 1909. [19] *Addresses*, Vol. XIV, p. 2. [20] *Ibid.* [21] *War Secretary Diaries*, p. 4239.

That is the trouble about you. That is the trouble down in New Orleans. That is the trouble all over here [the South]. You wake up every morning to embrace a doctrine and are very strongly in favor of it, and then you find to your surprise that it is a Republican doctrine. However, it doesn't make any difference. We don't require you to be consistent. I have no doubt that the Republican party will adopt just as good a tariff as it can in the interest of all sections. We are not going to frame a sectional law. I say "we." I am not a member of the legislature, but such influence as I have will be thrown to the performance of a contract which we made at Chicago; to which I believe you were not a party, but we are going to bring you in— by which we shall revise the tariff so as not to injure, if possible, any part of the country.[22]

If Taft had really meant "we," he would, beyond any possible doubt, have been immeasurably more successful in the fight which he now faced. His administration was just starting. He enjoyed not only the prestige of popular good will; he had at hand the very practical power of controlling Congress through the thousands upon thousands of offices which depended upon the appointing power of the President. The struggle for universally lower rates might have been won if Taft had summoned recalcitrant senators and representatives and had told them, quietly but forcefully, that their pleasant streams of patronage would dry up unless they heeded his orders. Victory lay in the murky, sordid depths of practical politics— in the appointment or nonappointment of good Republicans to postmasterships, to the offices of revenue collectors, to myriad other government havens. But Taft would take no such course at the start, although he later threatened to use patronage to get what he wanted. Then it was too late.

It was not timidity which made the President decline. It was that he believed, in his innocence, that the executive could not properly, under the Constitution, adopt such a policy. He subsequently lectured on "The Presidency" at the University of Virginia — this was in January, 1915, when the days of struggle were over— and he held forth, then, on the limitations upon the presidential powers. He said that "our President has no initiative in respect to legislation given him by law except that of *mere recommendation,*

[22] *War Secretary Diaries,* p. 4216.

and *no legal or formal method* of entering into the argument and discussion of the proposed legislation while pending in Congress." The executive power, he said, was "limited, so far as it is possible to limit such a power consistent with that discretion and promptness of action that are essential to preserve the interests of the public in times of emergency or *legislative neglect or inaction.*" Mr. Taft could not ignore the radically different doctrine of Theodore Roosevelt whose *Notes for a Possible Autobiography* had recently appeared. He quoted Roosevelt's own belief that the "executive power was limited only by specific restrictions and prohibitions appearing in the Constitution. . . . Under this interpretation . . . I did and caused to be done many things not previously done by the President. . . . I did not usurp power, but I did greatly broaden the use of executive power."

Taft read the extract with disapproval. It was, he said, an "unsafe doctrine" which might "lead, under emergencies, to results of an arbitrary character."

"The mainspring of such a view," he concluded, "is that the executive is charged with responsibility for the welfare of all the people in a general way: that he is to play the part of a universal providence and set all things right." [23]

—3—

So Roosevelt, on advice of Uncle Joe Cannon, would not do battle for tariff cuts and Taft, because of his conceptions of the presidency, could not make effective war. The result was that the rates remained highly protective until Woodrow Wilson became president of the United States. Taft convened the special session of Congress on March 15, 1909, and transmitted a brief message on the following day. In his inaugural, the President pointed out, he had "stated in a summary way the principles upon which, in my judgment, the revision of the tariff should proceed. . . . It is not necessary for me to repeat what I then said." [24] Thus there was no specific recommendation for downward revision in the message itself and

[23] Taft, W. H., *The Presidency*, pp. 7, 125-126, 139. (Italics mine.) [24] *Addresses*, Vol. XIV, pp. 9-10.

parallel between Taft and Cleveland comes to an abrupt end. This was the first disappointment of the embattled low-tariff men in both houses. They clearly expected that the President would sound a stirring call for action. The message required, for its reading by the clerk, only a scant two minutes and the insurgents exchanged glances as they listened; had the President already deserted their crusade? [25] More reasonable men would have recalled the repeated declarations already made. But the insurgents were emotional, not reasonable men. They were fighting for a cause in which they believed passionately and the odds for victory were all against them.

Their new suspicion of Taft was groundless. But they had ample basis for distrusting the Congressional leaders in whose hands lay the framing of the tariff measure itself. Speaker Cannon, in the chair, had named all the committees of the House. Sereno E. Payne, author of the bill in the lower house, had collaborated with Nelson Dingley of Maine in drafting the 1897 law which was now to be replaced. Dalzell, also a House leader, had taken part, too, in that most generous protective levy. In the Senate, obviously, Aldrich would be in command. But a tariff law, under the Constitution, was initiated in the House of Representatives. It was there that the battle began. For nine months, more or less, experts of the Treasury Department had been conferring with the G.O.P. leaders regarding the doctrine, new in the drafting of a tariff, that protection was maintained by duties which equalized the cost of production at home, plus a fair profit, with the cost of competing industries abroad. This was a pleasing idea which rolled sonorously from the tongues of campaign orators. But nobody— the President or the legislative leaders or the insurgents or the experts themselves— had more than the vaguest idea of what this really meant.

How could they know what it meant? The doctrine was based on the fallacy that the costs behind the production of thousands of articles in the United States could be ascertained. It was based on the impossibility that any valid information whatever could be obtained on costs and wages abroad. Inevitably, when leaders of industry were called to testify before the Ways and Means Committee, they placed the highest credible figure on their manufacturing expenses. The manufacturer who was incompetent or ex-

[25] Bowers, Claude, *Beveridge and the Progressive Era*, p. 334.

travagant— or whose cost of raw materials for geographic or other reasons was excessive— claimed that *his* cost, not that of the efficient manufacturer, should be the basis of the tariff in which he was interested. In addition to these perplexities, no definition of manufacturing cost existed. It was permitted to include salaries and bonuses paid to executives. Undoubtedly, it was allowed to include return on capital, both bonds and stocks. But the public, bewitched by the speeches of the late campaign, believed that the doctrine, when translated into law, would mean lower prices. True, they would be a little higher than prices for the same goods in England and on the Continent. But they would be definitely below those of the past few years.[26] Disillusionment awaited the public and this would result in the anti-Republican votes which delivered the House of Representatives into Democratic hands in November, 1910.

It was not enough for Taft to face the issue with courage as he did. He needed, in addition, detailed knowledge of tariff matters. He did not have this.

"Taft wants a tariff that will strike the country favorably . . ." Cabot Lodge told Roosevelt, who should have been sympathetic to his successor's ignorance, "but he knows little of the questions and the arguments and the conditions which beset the various industries."

Lodge added, in this letter written in late April, that the "one thing which surprises me about Taft is that he does not know more about politics. With all his great experience . . . he does not seem to have got hold of the elements of politics which must enter into so many matters, especially appointments." [27]

Especially appointments. . . . On April 4, 1909, Taft went motoring with Vice-president Sherman, whose grasp of the elements of politics was excellent, and they discussed the tariff situation.

"You can't cajole these people," Sherman said, referring to the lawmakers who were beginning to evade downward revision. "My advice is to begin to hit. I would send for [Postmaster General] Hitchcock and shut off the appointments of postmasters until the bill is passed."

[26] Taussig, F. W., *The Tariff History of the United States*, pp. 361-366. [27] Lodge, H. C., *op. cit.*, Vol. II, p. 334.

"I have already sent for Hitchcock for this very purpose," Taft answered, "but I only want to use this lever on the members and senators who are recalcitrant."

"Shut them all off," said the practical Sherman, "so that the innocent can work on the guilty and it can all be done without any personal threat. Simply have it announced that the party is committed to this reform bill . . . and that any person who tries to defeat the party wishes must necessarily be considered hostile."

"I hate to use patronage as a club unless I have to," said the President.[28]

There is no evidence that he did so; certainly he held stubbornly to his theory of presidential noninterference for the first few weeks and contented himself with giving advice. But this was also partly due to Taft's conviction that the House bill, which was reported to the Senate on April 9, was a fairly accurate fulfillment of the party's pledges and his own. It came, he said, "as near complying with our promises as we can hope." [29] "I mean to make the tariff bill as near like the House bill as I can," he said later. "I don't know how I shall succeed, but I am going to make a great effort." [30] On a torrid day toward the end of June he still felt that the House measure had been satisfactory. He reviewed the tariff struggle at great length in a letter to Brother Horace:

It is a hot Sunday afternoon, and with drawers and a kimono, in the presence of Nellie, and looking like a Chinese idol, I am walking my room dictating to you. I am doing it for the purpose not alone of informing you, but of putting in permanent form, so to speak for my own use, my state of mind at the present moment as to the political situation. . . .

I am convinced that the House committee, with Payne at its head, went to work conscientiously to carry out the plank of the platform . . . and that the Payne bill was a genuine effort in the right direction, and that while the step was not as great as I would have been glad to take, it contains much of what I approve. They did insert an increase in hosiery and in gloves in order to establish industries here, which, while they might be justified on principles of protection, I thought were inappropriate at the present time. There-

[28] Butt, Archie, *Taft and Roosevelt,* Vol. I, p. 41. [29] Taft to J. B. Farwell, April 13, 1909. [30] Taft to T. J. Atkins, June 24, 1909.

fore, I should be glad to sign a bill like the Payne bill, with the hosiery and glove schedules left out.[31]

Aldrich and his colleagues in the Senate had not been in action very long, however, before Taft was debating the wisdom of vetoing the bill which would probably emerge as a result of their labors.[32]

"I am dealing with very acute and expert politicians," was the realization which dawned upon him, "and I am trusting a great many of them and I may be deceived."[33]

The President might have added another adjective— unscrupulous— to his description of the politicians without violation to his strict judicial leanings. For Aldrich, Lodge, Hale and also William B. Heyburn of Idaho had the arrogance to declare in open debate on the floor of the Senate that no obligation existed to slash the tariff. Aldrich was the first to betray his president. He was bland and unembarrassed when he asked, on April 22: "Where did we ever make the statement that we would revise the tariff downward?"[34] Nor was Lodge discomfited by twinges of conscience on May 8 when he insisted that nobody "ever pledged me to revision downward, any more than to revision upward."[35] Senator Heyburn grew poetic a month later, as the debate went on.

"This talk of being under obligations to revise the tariff downward," he said, "comes from somewhere, I do not know from where, from some political, I was going to say swamp, like a miasma. It was a concession, a sop, by those lacking confidence in the voters whose support they thought they had to have."[36] Hale echoed these untrue denials.[37] Even Root, who had been urging tariff revision since 1904, voted with Aldrich 104 times on the amended schedule and against him only 24 times.[38]

Aldrich was the spokesman of privilege; naturally he refused to concede an obligation for downward changes. Heyburn, who came from Idaho and should have known better, was merely stupid. "This talk" for tariff revision arose from no political swamp and it was no miasma. Behind it was the collective voice of a very

[31] Taft to Horace D. Taft, June 27, 1909. [32] Taft to Martin Egan, April 30, 1909. [33] Taft to Helen H. Taft, July 18, 1909. [34] *Congressional Record*, April 22, 1900, p. 1409. [35] *Ibid.*, May 8, 1909, p. 1911. [36] *Ibid.*, June 8, 1911, p. 2950. [37] *Ibid.*, May 9, p. 2275. [38] Jessup, P. C., *Elihu Root*, Vol. II, p. 217.

large segment of the United States. Even Taft, whose ears were never too keen, heard the voice. The insurgents had been hearing it for years. But Cabot Lodge did not and neither, it appears, did Theodore Roosevelt.

". . . as far as I can see," he wrote from the jungle, "there is no real ground for dissatisfaction . . . with the present tariff; so that what we have to meet is not an actual need, but a mental condition among our people."

Lodge was delighted with this analysis and showed it to Aldrich, who was also pleased.

"He put the whole situation in those few lines," affirmed the senator from Rhode Island. "We are dealing with a mental condition and that is the exact trouble with the situation."[39]

President Taft knew of the senatorial statements— he called them "most unfortunate"[40]— repudiating his policy. It would have been a simple matter for him to have called in the newspaper writers and challenged the disloyalty to the party and to himself. The period in April and May, 1909, as the Senate started to emasculate the tariff cuts offered by the House, was his moment to start an Ananias Club of his own. But this Taft could not do.

"Of course," he was to declare, regarding another issue, "Roosevelt would have come back at those preferring the charges and would . . . have them on the run, but I cannot do things that way. I will let them go on, and by and by the people will see who is right and who is wrong. There is no use trying to be William Howard Taft with Roosevelt's ways."[41]

Besides, to have assailed the Aldrich group would have meant an alignment with the insurgents. Taft was amazingly free of prejudice during the first weeks of his administration. But this did not last. The insurgents had windy enthusiasms which were alien to the President. Their enthusiasms, which were not unmarked by ego, caused Taft, in the end, to abandon fairness. He had lost his confidence in the insurgents by June, 1909. Soon his judgment was perverted by active hatred. Beveridge, although an "honest and able man" was a "selfish pig."[42] "He tires me awfully," Taft added. "He attitudinizes so much, and is so self-

[39] Lodge, H. C., *op. cit.*, pp. 335, 337. [40] Taft to W. H. Miller, July 13, 1909. [41] Butt, Archie, *op. cit.*, Vol. I, pp. 235-236. [42] *Ibid.*, Vol. I, p. 40.

centered and so self-absorbed." [43] At about the same time he lamented the fact that he would have to attend a cornerstone laying where Senator LaFollette and "somebody else equally objectionable" would speak.[44] Dolliver and Albert B. Cummins of Iowa were just as bad. Taft's retort was acid when an adviser suggested that it would be well to play golf and be seen in public with them instead of only with Aldrich or other conservatives.

"I have no objection to playing with a Democrat or with a Republican," the President snapped, "but I have better use for my time than spending it with such a blatant demagogue as either Dolliver or Cummins." [45]

—4—

Thus emotional angles were by no means absent from Taft's decision that he could not sacrifice the support of the Old Guard "because there are other things beside the tariff bill that I need during the coming administration." [46] Archie Butt, who adored being close to the Great so that he could ponder on their characters, had not watched Taft for a month before he concluded that the President was "persistent in his antipathies. . . . Mr. Roosevelt once said that Mr. Taft was one of the best haters he had ever known, and I have found this to be true." [47]

"He is easily influenced to do what he wants to do," was Archie's final characterization, "but he is stubborn as an ox when he gets set in the other direction." [48]

The insurgents deluded themselves in the spring and summer of 1909 if they believed that the President was to be their ally. But this does not mean that Taft surrendered to Aldrich, either. The insurgents were a gallant band, if tainted by an excess of self-esteem. They were well aware of the kind of bill which would emerge from the Senate Finance Committee. For two days, Aldrich worked behind closed doors and listened to the arguments of the industrialists and financiers. These keen gentlemen made short work of the reductions recommended by the House. Then Aldrich

[43] Taft to Helen H. Taft, July 14, 1909. [44] Idem, July 11, 1909. [45] Taft to F. H. Shaffer, March 26, 1910. [46] Taft to E. E. Colston, June 24, 1909. [47] Butt, Archie, op. cit., Vol. I, p. 38. [48] Ibid., Vol. II, p. 591.

arose, tall in his superiority, and presented the bill to his colleagues. He did not bother to offer a reason for increases on about
six hundred items. He asked for prompt consideration. Was not
American industry waiting for Congress to settle this troublesome
issue? Delay would retard business.[49]

Taft had been informed of what was coming. He told Secretary
of the Navy Meyer that he was "not very anxious for a second
term, as it is, and I certainly will not make any compromises
to secure one. I fear Aldrich is ready to sacrifice the party, and I
will not permit it." [50] The President appears to have encouraged
LaFollette, although the evidence on this point is not clear, to
offer amendments which would eliminate the Senate increases. The
Wisconsin leader recalled a conversation in which Taft declared
that he would watch the struggle closely and would disapprove the
measure unless it met the platform obligations.[51] A similar statement had been made to Beveridge and Dolliver.[52] With these three
senators were aligned, also, Borah, Clapp, Joseph L. Bristow of
Kansas and Cummins. They were to give Aldrich some very bad
hours in the chamber which he had ruled, almost without opposition, for so long.

The battle was well under way toward the end of April, 1909.
The Senate insurgents had more than enthusiasm; they had a
flair for hard, intelligent work. They divided the schedules among
themselves, so that each would become a master of the cotton or
metal or sugar or oil or other important rates. They made speeches
or attended committee meetings in the daytime. At night they
met at somebody's house— one feature was a case of beer supplied by the host— and pored over complicated statistics. This, to
Aldrich, was revolution. For decades, now, his decisions had not
been questioned. He grew crimson with wrath and stalked from
the Senate Chamber when the insurgents spoke. It was not only
revolution; it was impertinence as well. To a speech by Dolliver
he once deigned to reply. The insurgent attack, he said, was an
"assault on the very citadel of protection." [53] So the debate continued, from April 9 through Washington's brief spring into warm

[49] Bowers, Claude, op. cit., pp. 334-336. [50] Butt, Archie, Vol. I, p. 41. [51] LaFollette,
R. M., LaFollette's Autobiography, p. 440. [52] Bowers, Claude, op. cit., p. 337. [53] Ibid.,
pp. 337-339; Sullivan, Mark, Our Times, Vol. IV, pp. 365-367.

June and July. Meanwhile, Taft said nothing publicly. Privately, however, he was more active than his critics realized— and more effective.

"I did defeat both Aldrich and Cannon," [54] Taft boasted when the battle had ended, and he was, up to a point, correct.

An essential part of any tariff bill, necessarily, was some method for raising additional revenues in the event that the new duties were lower than the old; in this instance the $100,000,000 deficit, which had piled up under the existing act, made new taxes imperative. Even Cabot Lodge, who held so low an opinion of the President's abilities as a political strategist, must have given reluctant admiration to the manner in which Taft suddenly capitalized this situation to force through Congress a tariff bill in "substantial compliance" [55] with the Republican platform. The issue arose on April 1 when Senator Joseph Bailey of Texas announced that he would ask for a general income tax as an amendment to the Payne-Aldrich bill. He was joined by Senator Cummins; the amendment called for a three per cent tax on all incomes above $5,000.

The President had no basic objection to this form of taxation. In an address back in January, 1908, he had declared that the nation would, in all probability, some day resort to such a method for raising revenue.[56] But in 1895 the United States Supreme Court had declared the income tax unconstitutional. It had been an excessively unpopular decision and had been a factor in the rise of Bryan and Populism in the Middle West. But Taft opposed re-enactment of the tax in 1909.

"While I am generally in favor of the principle of the income tax and certainly in favor of the power of the government to levy such a tax," he explained, "the truth is that the Supreme Court has decided that such a tax is unconstitutional, and this bill proposes to resubmit the question to the Supreme Court. I am opposed to this method of securing an income tax or the power to pass one. I think it exposes the court to very severe criticism whatever it does, and the best thing to do is to accept the opinion of the court and submit to the people the question of a constitutional amendment." [57]

[54] Taft to Horace D. Taft, Aug. 11, 1909. [55] Taft to Beveridge, July 13, 1909. [56] *War Secretary Diaries,* pp. 2470-2471. [57] Taft to Therese McCagg, June 26, 1909.

Aldrich, too, was emphatically against another attempt to levy an income tax through Congress; anything which might undermine the Supreme Court naturally filled him with alarm. Taft saw his chance. In his inaugural address he had suggested a graduated inheritance tax as a fair source of revenue. The Senate rejected it, as Taft explained, "on the ground that the states— some thirty-six of them— had already adopted inheritance taxes and . . . this would be perhaps oppressive." Taft did not agree; he pointed out that the levies in England were far heavier. But he did not, for the moment, press the point. He had another card up his sleeve. He recommended to Aldrich a tax on the income of corporations. The Senate leader backed away from this too. Why pass any tax? A deficit might exist for the next two years, but after that the treasury, owing to revenues from the tariff, would be in excellent shape.[58]

The President was cognizant of the real basis of Aldrich's hostility to the corporation tax; it was, he pointed out privately, because it would "give a degree of publicity to the business of all corporations."[59] Senator Aldrich, however, was rapidly discovering that he had been maneuvered into an impossible position. Senators Borah and Cummins called at the White House and reiterated their intention to press for an income tax in the face of the Supreme Court decision. Taft repeated his opposition; he may or may not have concealed his inner elation. He described the situation to his brother:

They [Cummins and Borah] left me and went back to the Senate. Before they got through Cummins had made an agreement with the Democrats, especially with Bailey, to support an income tax, such as that he had said he was in favor of. They secured the assent of nineteen Republicans in addition to all of the Democrats to the proposition to pass a regular income tax exactly in the teeth of the decision of the Supreme Court in order to bring it up before the Supreme Court.

Thereupon Senators Aldrich, Lodge and Murray Crane "came to appeal to me to save them from that situation." Taft seems to have been suave. Aldrich, as gracefully as possible, said he was

[58] Taft to Horace D. Taft, June 27, 1909. [59] Taft to Therese McCagg, June 26, 1909.

aware that the President favored an excise on the earnings of the corporations. He also realized that Taft desired an amendment giving to Washington the power to levy against all incomes. He would agree to a constitutional amendment for the latter, he said. As for the former, he would consent on condition that a limit of two years was placed upon it. But Taft was enjoying the sweet sensation— it would be all too brief— of being in the saddle.

"I objected to the limitation," he wrote, "and said that I did not think I could break up the nineteen Republicans, or get support from the people from whom it was necessary to get support, if that limitation was in. Accordingly the next day . . . Aldrich withdrew his objection. . . . I have gone into this to show you that the situation is not one of my yielding to Aldrich, but of Aldrich yielding to me." [60]

On June 16, the President sent a message to Congress which set forth the dangers of enacting a law in the hope that the Supreme Court would reverse itself. He recommended, instead, a two per cent tax on the net incomes of all corporations except national banks, savings banks, and building and loan associations.

"This," he explained, "is an excise tax upon the privilege of doing business as an artificial entity and of freedom from general partnership liability by those who own the stock. I am informed that a two per cent tax of this character would bring into the treasury of the United States not less than $25,000,000."

The message also called for the "adoption of a joint resolution" for the submission to the states of a constitutional amendment permitting federal income taxes.[61]

"Gentlemen . . ." said Taft at a White House dinner at which the situation was discussed with the Senate Finance Committee, "either you take the bill and the proposed submission of the constitutional amendment to the people, as I have suggested, or else the alternative is the income tax law that the insurgent Republicans propose to pass in association with the Democrats."

"This is the very distressing and embarrassing alternative and there is no other," murmured Senator Hale.

"Yes," agreed Aldrich, "that is exactly it; I do not hesitate to say to you, Mr. President, that if it had not been so I should

[60] Taft to Horace D. Taft, June 27, 1909. [61] 61st Congress, 1st Session, Sen. Doc. 98.

never have come to make the proposition which I did for a message and the submission of the amendment." [62]

It meant, further, that no tariff bill at all would be passed unless it was in accordance with the pledges made by Taft. The distressing thing is that the President did not force the fighting further. The conservatives, undeniably thrown back, were not yet willing to admit complete defeat, but they might have been forced to do so. Despite the valiant and efficient work by Dolliver, Beveridge and their allies, the Senate rates were appreciably higher than those of the lower house. Now a Conference Committee would be appointed from the members of both houses by which, if possible, the differences would be reconciled. The final stand of the die-hards was on this committee; they proposed to dominate it, if they could.

—5—

It had been clear from the start that the differences between the House and Senate rates would have to be ironed out in conference, and Taft received his first warning in April that the committee would be packed with the friends of high rates. Representative E. J. Hill of Connecticut, one of the few well-informed tariff men in the House, told the President about "strange intimations . . . that I am not to be on the Conference Committee, but that some man who can be more successfully handled will be substituted for me. Let me say to you that *your* danger is right in that direction." [63] Precisely this happened. In addition to himself, Aldrich chose Hale, Boies Penrose and Julius C. Burrows, of Michigan, all extreme protectionists, for the majority. Cannon picked Payne, Boutelle, Dalzell and Fordney who were equally orthodox. The President was angry.

"I don't think that Cannon played square," he said. "He nominated a Conference Committee that had four high-tariff men on it . . . who would not fight for the low provisions of the House bill." [64]

But Taft was not unduly disturbed. He saw that Cannon's un-

[62] Taft to Horace D. Taft, June 27, 1909. [63] E. J. Hill to Taft, April 23, 1909.
[64] Taft to Horace D. Taft, Aug. 11, 1909.

"WHEN FIRST I PUT THIS UNIFORM ON
I SAID, AS I LOOKED IN THE GLASS,
IT'S ONE TO A MILLION IF ANY CIVILIAN
THIS FIGURE OR FACE CAN SURPASS."

Cartoon by C. G. Bush, May 26, 1905, Courtesy New York World

See page 358]

THE CHUCKLE EXPLODES

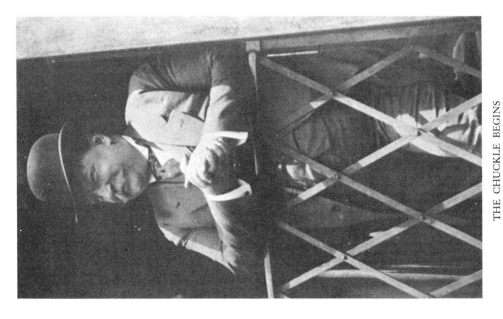

THE CHUCKLE BEGINS

See page 2671

fairness had aroused the "indignation of the House" and that the members were inclined to force concessions from the committee.[65] The committee was in session through all of July and its task was complicated in the extreme. Two enormously involved bills had to be reconciled and this was done, of course, by the immemorial method of making trades and bargains. The President, however, seems to have watched the proceedings with a new note of self-confidence; this was due to his knowledge that a combination of insurgent Republicans and Democrats might still insert an income tax into the bill and his conviction that Aldrich would back down in the face of a catastrophe which might undermine the prestige of the Supreme Court.

"I am not a high-tariff man, I am a low-tariff man," the President insisted while the Conference Committee perspired and toiled and cursed the Washington heat.[66]

The President no longer debated, even privately, the probable necessity of putting a veto on the bill which would emerge. A fortnight earlier the chance of this had tormented him; he had worried about it, in fact, since the beginning of the special session. Taft's high-minded reluctance to veto a bad tariff bill was faintly absurd.

"I could make a lot of cheap publicity for the time being by vetoing the bill," he admitted, "but it would leave the party in a bad shape— and it would leave us in a mess out of which I do not see how we could get, and the only person who would gain popularity would be your humble servant."

Taft was almost always suspicious of any action likely to send a wave of popularity rolling toward him; he felt, possibly, that this, per se, proved that the action was unsound and demagogic. In the case of the Payne-Aldrich tariff, moreover, a veto "would throw me out with the leaders in the Senate and the House, and would make me almost hopeless in respect to effecting my reforms of next year, so you see how much more hangs on the question than the mere subject of the rates in the tariff bill."

"Of course," he added— this was included in the lengthy letter to Horace Taft, "the position I have taken in respect to the tariff bill and the downward revision may open me to a charge of inconsistency, and not standing to my promise, if I were to

[65] Taft to Helen H. Taft, July 25, 1909. [66] Taft to W. D. Foulke, July 15, 1909.

sign a bill that was distinctly at variance with those promises, and that is the only thing that puts me in a position where I can contemplate a possibility of a veto." [67]

While the Conference Committee worked, Taft concluded that the Payne-Aldrich act, if imperfect, was adequate. He assured Beveridge on July 13 that he would "secure as far as possible a return to the free raw material feature of the Payne bill, which is its chief characteristic. . . . I am strongly convinced that both Payne and Aldrich are anxious to make such a bill as I desire." He would, in all probability, sign the measure. [68] The President denied with growing irritation the charge that tariff has been increased:

. . . the advances made in the Senate on the tariff . . . which will be adhered to by the Senate and will be acquiesced in by the House, cover only the highest priced cotton goods (which are luxuries), the highest priced silk goods (which are luxuries), and liquors and champagnes. The heavy cuts are made in the iron schedule, for instance, which according to Mr. LaFollette's method of calculation are not important because the cuts are not sufficient to increase the importations of iron and steel. Neither the Republican party nor I ever made a promise to reduce the tariff in such a way as to let in free trade in the articles that are to be protected. . . . My argument was that we ought not to have excessive rates. . . . The excessive rates were favored by the men interested in the preservation of monopolies, or by men who attempted behind such rates to make monopolies for the purpose of profit.

Now the reductions— as for instance in the iron schedule . . . are reductions exactly in the line of our promises on the most important articles of consumption by the common being, and are exactly in compliance with our promise even though they do not increase the importation of iron and steel in this country, which it was no part of the purpose of the platform or the party to effect. [69]

Taft's analysis was accurate enough. Even LaFollette, Beveridge and Dolliver had proclaimed their loyalty to the protective principle. On June 30 in an address at Yale, the President broke his silence: ". . . if the Republican party does not live up to what the people expect of it," he warned, and no one doubted that the

[67] Taft to Horace D. Taft, June 27, 1909. [68] Taft to Beveridge, July 13, 1909. [69] Taft to W. D. Foulke, July 15, 1909.

tariff was in his mind, "it will be relegated to 'His Majesty's opposition.' " [70] The end of the battle was approaching as July closed. Taft demanded the free admission of hides, lumber, coal, iron, newsprint paper, gloves and wool. In the end, he was forced to compromise, but he put through a surprisingly large part of his program. Taft compromised regarding rates in order to get a bill passed but he flatly rejected, when he knew about them, the shady deals which are so often part of the legislative processes. The villain of one of these was Lucius N. Littauer, a Republican from upstate New York. Uncle Joe Cannon stood behind Littauer's demand for protection of the glove industry.

"The speaker," complained Taft, "is engaged in trying to foist a high tariff on gloves in the interests of a friend named Littauer and he has been threatening Aldrich, and I believe he will threaten me, with defeating the bill unless this goes in. It is the greatest exhibition of tyranny that I have known of his attempting. . . . The glove schedule is a scandal and I wouldn't permit it for a minute to be thought that I acquiesced in such a pernicious piece of personal political robbery." [71]

So the glove schedule was thrown out and Cannon was thwarted in his benevolent purpose of aiding Littauer.[72] A more bitter struggle was fought over the tariff on lumber. Under the Dingley tariff the rate had been $2 per thousand feet. The House bill had cut this to $1, but the Senate had raised it to $2 again. On July 29, Taft outlined his final position to Aldrich:

I believe that $1.25 on undressed lumber is all that ought to be put in this tariff bill. . . . I regret exceedingly to differ with you upon this subject when you have worked so conscientiously to bring about an agreement in respect to the bill; but I am confident that any higher duty would not meet with the approval of many regular Republicans in the House, would not receive the approval of the party generally in the country, and would not be such a reduction as ought to be made.[73]

The climax came on July 28. Cannon blustered that he would adjourn the House without action unless his demands were met.[74]

[70] Addresses, Vol. XIV, p. 141. [71] Taft to Helen H. Taft, July 27, 29, 1909. [72] Taft to Horace D. Taft, Aug. 11, 1909. [73] Taft to Aldrich, July 29, 1909. [74] New York Times, July 28, 1909.

Aldrich was alarmed by this; he seems to have been losing his grip as a cold, hard dictator. He told Taft that it might be wiser to accept $1.50 on lumber, after all. But the President would not recede. He made his own threat now. He said that Congress would immediately be convened again unless a satisfactory tariff bill was passed at this session. Both Cannon and Aldrich paled at the thought; such a stratagem would place the blame on Congress.[75] As things now stood, dissatisfaction with the bill they enacted would rest on the shoulders of the President.

Doubt clouds the exact manner in which Taft presented his threat to reconvene Congress; the subject is not mentioned in his correspondence. On the following day he wrote to Aldrich in terms that were guarded:

I have no disposition to exert any other influence than that which it is my function under the Constitution to exercise; but I can say that while there are some other parts of the bill which are not as satisfactory to me as they could be made, it has so many virtues and accomplishes so much in the direction promised by the party, that if the conference report could follow my recommendations . . . in respect to lumber and gloves, I shall be glad to exert all the influence possible and proper to secure the adoption of the report in both Houses, and should give the bill my approval.

I write this with a full sense of the responsibility that the decision imposes on me, and with a full understanding that it may result in a report of a disagreement. This I should greatly regret; but after balancing the conflicting considerations, I am willing to face the disagreement and its consequences rather than to express concurrence in any higher duty on lumber . . . and in any increase on gloves for the purpose of establishing a new industry.[76]

The President was done with talking. On the following morning a further appeal for surrender came from Capitol Hill and was denied. Taft was to dine that night at the home of Beekman Winthrop. He worked at his desk until late afternoon and then left for the links.

"They have my last word," he said, "and now I want to show

[75] New York *Times*, July 29, 30, 1909; Stephenson, N. W., *Nelson W. Aldrich*, pp. 359-360. [76] Taft to Aldrich, July 29, 1909.

my scorn for further negotiations by spending the afternoon on the golf links."

He said he would dress at the golf club and go directly to the Winthrops'. He had been there for about ten minutes when word came from the White House that the Senate and House conferees had accepted the specifications for the tariff which the President had demanded. A smile spread across his face.

"Well, good friends, this makes me very happy," he said.[77]

Surely he was entitled to his brief moment of triumph. Next night he dined on the South Portico of the White House with Attorney General Wickersham and Secretary of the Treasury Mac-Veagh. They left at about eleven o'clock and the President turned to his aide.

"There is something about the atmosphere of this South Portico which challenges your thoughts for the past and brings to your mind the fact that every president, since Monroe at least, has come here when worried and from this spot has renewed his courage for the fight."[78]

The ghost of Lincoln could have told him he would need all his courage in the months ahead. The ghost of Cleveland could have echoed it as night breezes from the dark Potomac stirred the August heat. For that matter, Taft needed no warning.

"Your husband," he had written two days before, "will be damned heartily in many corners of the Capitol and elsewhere. It is most uncomfortable, but I believe I am right and that must be my solace."[79]

[77] Butt, Archie, *op. cit.*, Vol. I, pp. 163-164. [78] *Ibid.*, Vol. I, pp. 166-167. [79] Taft to Helen H. Taft, July 29, 1909.

CHAPTER XXV

DARKENING SKIES

Y OU CAN be very certain that I am fully aware of the opinion in the Middle West in favor of downward revision," the President wrote to a western adviser while the tariff struggle was going on. Taft had faith that the people, in the East as well as the West, would ultimately appreciate the truth about the Payne-Aldrich act. Eighteen months remained, he said, "in which the effects of the bill can be discussed and shown to the public, and the misrepresentations which have occurred in the press can be corrected by a clear statement of the facts." On the other hand, the President repeated, he was "not at all blind" to the general hostility; he felt it had been aroused, in part, "by the most unfortunate statements of Aldrich and Lodge that a downward revision was not promised." [1]

So Taft, like Woodrow Wilson and Herbert Hoover after him, believed that the people would approve if only they could be made to understand. But first he would rest for a little while and shed the warmth of his love and solicitude on Mrs. Taft, on whom great misfortune had fallen. The theory that a president should not leave his native soil made it impossible for the Tafts to find contentment at Murray Bay, as they had done for years. A cottage had been taken at Beverly on the North Shore of Massachusetts. It was a poor substitute, at best, for the old familiar haunts above the magic St. Lawrence River. But golf links were nearby. The air was cool. Mrs. Taft was established there in July and the President followed as soon as he had signed the tariff bill in August.

Worn down by the excitement of the past year and the exhaustion of her White House obligations, Mrs. Taft's health had given way in May and for a few days, until she began to improve, the President had looked into an abyss of utter tragedy. The collapse occurred on May 17, 1909. It appears to have been precipi-

[1] Taft to W. H. Miller, July 13, 1909.

tated by an adenoidal operation performed on eleven-year-old Charley Taft that day. Mrs. Taft had insisted on being present in the hospital. At 4 o'clock she joined the President on the *Sylph,* then being used as the official yacht, for a visit down the Potomac to Mt. Vernon. The vessel had barely pulled out into the stream when Attorney General Wickersham, who had been standing with Mrs. Taft, turned suddenly to Captain Butt.

"Mrs. Taft has fainted," he said. "See if there is any brandy aboard."

She was carried into the saloon where she revived but was unable to speak, as though stricken with paralysis. Butt summoned the President who "went deathly pale." The *Sylph* put back toward the wharf and a sad procession started for the White House.[2] The next day the President dictated a letter to his older son at Yale:

George Wickersham . . . said something which she did not answer. He said it again and she failed to answer and then he noticed that she looked as if she had fainted. She had not lost consciousness, but she did have a very severe nervous attack, in which for a time she lost all muscular control of her right arm and her right leg and of the vocal cords and the muscles governing her speech.

Her symptoms, the anxious husband and father added, were "very alarming because they indicate paralysis— that is, a lesion of the brain." But the doctors held out hope that it might be nervous hysteria and not actual paralysis. Mrs. Taft could hear; this was an encouraging sign.[3] The night of the stroke was, however, one of horror for the man who had married Nellie Herron of Cincinnati almost twenty-five years before and whose married life had been an unchanging light of happiness.

"The President," noted Archie Butt, "looked like a great stricken animal. I have never seen greater suffering or pain . . . on a man's face."[4]

The fates, so often kind to William Howard Taft, were not, however, to laugh in mockery at the very time when other troubles were beginning to darken the skies. Mrs. Taft had a stout consti-

[2] Butt, Archie, *Taft and Roosevelt,* Vol. I, pp. 87-88. [3] Taft to R. A. Taft, May 18, 1909. [4] Butt, Archie, *op. cit.,* Vol. I, p. 88.

tution. In all probability, she had a cerebral hemorrhage, but her health soon began to mend. Her speech was affected, though, and it was a long time before she could resume her place at the head of the presidential table. The President learned, when he reached Beverly in August, that she was greatly improved.[5]

Indeed, as the winds of probable defeat grew more threatening, the President found a degree of comfort in the fact that his wife, so zealous and so ambitious on his behalf, was protected from their violence by illness. A year later he told Roosevelt who was, consciously or not, causing the winds to blow, that Mrs. Taft was still unable to attend social affairs.

"I am glad to say," he told the returning hunter, "that she has not seemed to be bothered by the storm of abuse to which I have been subjected and that fact has reconciled me more than anything else." [6]

A more astute observer of the political skies than Taft, so rarely astute, might have been deceived by apparent stretches of sunshine and blue sky in the summer of 1909. He discounted the newspaper criticisms of the Payne-Aldrich act. He felt, in all sincerity, that he had met the demands of the insurgents with the corporation tax, the income tax amendment resolution and lowered tariffs in the major schedules. He had not seriously alienated the Aldrich group; their irritation over his last-minute domination would fade. So Taft forgot, for a moment, his earlier prediction of being widely damned.

"The close . . . was all very peaceful and sweet," he said. "I gave a dinner to both the committees, and I think everybody left with a good taste in his mouth, except possibly Cannon." [7]

Even Cabot Lodge saw no clouds. He told Roosevelt that Taft had "stood very firmly for what he demanded and forced a number of reductions which ought to have been made. I think his influence has been salutary in a high degree and his action has strengthened the party with the country, strengthened him." In due time a dark-skinned runner set out from Mt. Kenia through the African jungle with the answer. Roosevelt thought that the tariff had "come out

[5] Taft to Horace D. Taft, Aug. 11, 1909. [6] Taft to Roosevelt, May 26, 1910. [7] Taft to Horace D. Taft, Aug. 11, 1909.

as well as we could hope." He was not at all surprised, the ex-President said, to learn that Aldrich had been a stanch ally.

". . . my intercourse with Aldrich," said the exponent of right-eousness, "gave me a steadily higher opinion of him. Least of all am I surprised . . . at the unfairness of the newspapers. If, as I am confident, business steadily improves, the grumbling will have no permanent effect— unless, indeed, the spirit of unrest in the West grows strong." [8]

The President signed the Payne-Aldrich act on August 5 with appropriate ceremonies. It was not, he said, "a perfect bill or a complete compliance with the promises made, strictly interpreted"; none the less, it represented "a sincere effort on the part of the Republican party to make a downward revision." [9] And with such an analysis, if only Taft had held rigidly to it, small fault could be found. From that point he might have gone on to pledge his aid to further revisions. He might have carried the country with him. But Taft was on the verge of the first of a series of blunders which were to contribute to his political doom.

—2—

First, however, it is essential to examine the Payne-Aldrich act over which so much oratory was to be spent and concerning which infinite inaccuracies were to be spread. Taft ultimately insisted that the only fair method for calculating its effect was to compare the consumption of articles on which tariffs had been decreased with the consumption of articles on which higher duties had been levied. He pointed out that Representative Payne, joint author of the measure, had done this. Goods valued at $5,000,000,000 on which decreases had been effected were consumed in a year. The higher rates applied to only $600,000,000 in consumer goods for the same period, and half of this total represented luxuries.[10] The President was undoubtedly putting the best possible interpretation on the bill. Such abstractions, valid though they may have been, did not

[8] Lodge, H. C., *Selections from the Correspondence of Theodore Roosevelt and Henry Cabot Lodge,* Vol. II, pp. 343, 346. [9] New York *Times,* Aug. 6, 1909. [10] Taft to C. H. Grosvenor, March 9, 1910.

interest the public. The mythical "man in the street" had hoped that the cost of living would be reduced by the new law and in this he had been disappointed.

The Payne-Aldrich act, in the expert and impartial judgment of Dr. F. W. Taussig, "brought no essential change in our tariff system. It still left an extremely high scheme of rates, and still showed an extremely intolerant attitude on foreign trade." The abolition of duty on hides, for which Taft was responsible, was the "one change of appreciable importance" which came out of all the dreary wrangling in Congress. Dr. Taussig added:

Most disappointing was the mode in which the subject was dealt with. . . . In the House, under the leadership of Mr. Payne, there was an endeavor to maintain publicity. . . . In the Senate, things went in star-chamber fashion, and the familiar process of log-rolling and manipulation was once again to be seen. The act as finally passed brought no real breach in the tariff wall, and no downward revision of any serious consequence.

None the less, a somewhat different spirit from that of 1890 or 1897 was shown in 1909. Though the act as a whole brought no considerable downward revision, it was less aggressively protectionist than the previous Republican measures. The increases . . . were more furtive, the reductions more loudly proclaimed. The extreme advocates of protection were on the defensive. There was unmistakable evidence in Congress and in the community of opposition to a further upward movement. High-water mark apparently had been reached, and there was reason to expect that the tide, no longer moving upward, might thereafter begin to recede.[11]

This much may be stated dogmatically: LaFollette was completely in error when he said that the increases applied to over $10,000,000 of annual imports and the decreases to but $45,000. Champ Clark, the Democratic leader in the House, was wrong, too, when he insisted that the average tariff was increased 1.70 per cent by the Payne-Aldrich act.[12] The following analysis will give an idea, at least, of the extent to which the new law effected slashes as compared with the Dingley act of 1897:

[11] Taussig, F. W., *The Tariff History of the United States*, pp. 407-408. [12] Sullivan, Mark, *Our Times*, Vol. IV, pp. 369-370.

Dingley Bill 1897	Payne-Aldrich Bill 1909
1. *Hides* 15%	House bill .... free
	Senate bill 15%
	Conference and final bill free
a. Leather 20%	.... 5%
b. Shoes 25%	.... 10%
c. Harness ⎱ .... 35% Saddlery ⎰	.... 20%
2. *Coal* ....ton 67¢	House bill .... free
	Senate bill ....ton 60¢
	Conference and final bill ....ton 45¢
3. *Iron ore* ....ton 40¢	House bill .... free
	Senate bill ....ton 25¢
	Conference and final bill ....ton 15¢
4. *Lumber* ..per 1000 feet $2.00	House bill $1.00
	Senate bill 1.50
	Conference and final bill .... 1.25 [13]

Glaring faults were in the bill; political faults and economic faults as well. They illustrate the utter futility of applying political methods to so involved a subject as the tariff. There was, for instance, the ominous and mysterious "Schedule K" which dealt— or more accurately did not deal— with wool. Schedule K was to be an outstanding issue in the 1910 Congressional campaign and in the presidential contest two years later. It was to typify the perfidy of the standpat Senate leaders. Democratic orators were to declare that by means of it the President had forced on a suffering nation higher prices for clothing. That this was untrue made no difference at all. Even the formerly innocent letter— K— was fashioned into an evil ogre by the cartoonists. The fact is that the duties on wool were hardly changed at all in the Payne-Aldrich act.

[13] Powell, J. H., *President Taft and the Payne-Aldrich Tariff*, Swarthmore College, 1934, Appendix B.

No doubt they should have been. The President favored a cut. This time, however, the supposedly insurgent West opposed it.

". . . the union of the wool growers and the woolen manufacturers is so strong," Taft explained in July, "that though both Payne and Aldrich are quite willing to have a reduction . . . it seems impossible to effect it. . . . The press has given the impression that the Senate has increased the duty on woolens. This is altogether a mistake, for the schedule . . . is exactly the same as it was in the Dingley bill. . . . I wanted a reduction if I could get it; but the . . . wool men and the woolen manufacturers together control so many votes . . ." [14]

"It is the one important defect in the Payne tariff bill," the President admitted during his nation-wide tour in the fall of the year. ". . . I am quite willing to admit that allowing the woolen schedule to remain where it is, is not a compliance with the terms of the platform as I interpret it and as it is generally understood." [15]

Explanations were, of course, completely ineffective.

"Why, great Heavens!" exclaimed Mr. Payne in the House as the debate closed, "we have not altered the wool schedule except to reduce three paragraphs— not much, but reduce them— and yet I understand that all of the clothing merchants in the United States are advertising that because of the increase in the rates on wool . . . which did not exist anywhere, the price of clothing would go up 20 or 50 per cent after the bill was passed. Thank God . . . this bill . . . will be felt throughout all of this broad land for fifteen months before the next election, and the people will have a chance to see what it does and the relief it will bring, and know from their own experience what it has accomplished." [16]

Even more grave, from Taft's viewpoint, was the debate on newsprint. He felt, and probably with justice, that failure to give greater reductions was behind the newspaper hostility to the Payne-Aldrich act and to himself.

"The newspapers in the East are generally free-trade papers," he said, "and they have been personally interested in the reduction of the tariff on print paper, which, by the way, in the House was reduced from $6 a ton to $2 a ton, and has been increased in the

[14] Taft to Beveridge, Taft to W. H. Miller, July 13, 1909. [15] *Addresses*, Vol. XV, pp. 58-59. [16] *Congressional Record*, July 31, 1909.

Senate to $4 a ton. Payne told me that . . . the reduction to $2 a ton was unfair to the American manufacturers." [17]

The tariff on newsprint vitally affected the earnings of the large newspapers of the country. The great mills of Canada had been supplying a large proportion of their paper tonnage. The $6 rate of the Dingley act was too great protection for domestic mills; many of them were inefficient and made paper at high cost. The newspaper publishers had been led to expect a $2 rate because of an investigation conducted in the House. The American manufacturers offered violent protest to this.

"We did not want to shut up any paper mills in the United States," explained Payne in offering the final compromise. "We are not here for that purpose, no matter who demands it." [18]

The President believed that $3 was fair, that it would protect the American mills and not cut off Canadian importations. He said that LaFollette of Wisconsin had agreed; in fact, he had suggested $4.

"I merely mention this," Taft said, "to show you the motive of the press for misrepresenting everything that is done in the Senate." [19]

The ultimate compromise was $3.75 on the paper itself and no change in the rate on wood pulp, the raw material out of which newsprint is made. It was agreed, however, that pulp would be admitted free and the newsprint duties lowered if Canada would repeal her export tax on pulp. But the compromise did not satisfy that element among the newspaper publishers which sternly exposed the efforts of the coal or steel or sugar interests to influence Congress on behalf of low duties, but felt it entirely proper to use the same methods for free paper. Taft was to make the situation infinitely worse in his December, 1909, message to Congress when he demanded an increase in the second-class postal rates which, because they were so low, constituted a virtual government subsidy to the newspapers and magazines of the country.

"I am myself not particularly concerned about a Democratic majority in the House," said a discouraged Taft in the spring of 1910 as the criticisms continued. "I would like to have these news-

[17] Taft to Horace D. Taft, June 27, 1909. [18] *Congressional Record*, July 31, 1909. [19] Taft to W. H. Miller, July 13, 1909.

papers that are now seeing everything bad in the tariff get a little Democratic medicine." [20]

Certainly the attacks on the Payne-Aldrich law, whether sincere or influenced by business office needs, were virulent enough. The New York *World* published a "Roll of Honor" listing the ten Republican senators who had "voted for the people against privilege, plutocracy and the betrayal of the party faith." This was in the form of a cartoon and in front of the tablet setting forth their names was a representation of a haggard woman and her haggard child. On her arm was the "Market Basket." [21] The outcry was greatest in the West (whose representatives had held to their wool subsidies). The St. Paul *Pioneer-Press,* for example, insisted that the "western Republicans have made up their minds that they are not going to be ruled by New England and for New England." The Des Moines *News* cried: "Shades of Theodore Roosevelt! May ghosts of animals he has killed in Africa ever haunt him for having foisted on the country this man Taft." [22] The editor, needless to say, had not been privileged to read the correspondence between Roosevelt and Lodge in which each had praised the measure thus branded with infamy.

Against this emotional storm, Taft prepared to throw calm and logical reasoning. This, in itself, was certain to meet defeat. In addition, he handled a precarious political situation badly. Weariness may have been a factor in the ineptitude which marked the weeks he spent at Beverly and, to an even greater degree, his 13,000-mile swing through the country which started in September. The President did not reach his summer home until August 11, 1909. It was hardly a month before he was on the road, for all the world like a traveling salesman. In the meanwhile he had played golf and had found some relaxation in swift motoring over the Massachusetts roads. He made the rather fatal mistake of dining— of course, the newspapers published the fact— with Henry C. Frick, the steel magnate, who had a country place near by. Secretary of State Knox, a house guest at the Frick mansion, seems to have been responsible for this blunder. The occasion was hailed as further proof that Taft was no faithful follower of Roosevelt but

[20] Taft to W. H. Ellis, April 28, 1910. [21] New York *World*, July 10, 1909. [22] Sullivan, Mark, *op. cit.*, Vol. IV, p. 371.

a friend and intimate of the wealthy malefactors. The man was tired. He was suffering from a touch of lumbago, besides. He was aware that it was unwise to have his name linked with Frick. But it was easier, so much easier, to consent than to refuse.

"If it were not for the speeches," the President told his military aide, "I should look forward with the greatest pleasure to this trip."

—3—

But the purpose of the journey lay in making speeches. They concerned complicated subjects, the tariff among others. To be effective, they required careful preparation. And the President simply would not prepare them. Archie Butt, in some ways wiser than his chief, saw the possible danger although he did not anticipate how bad the result would actually be. At the end of August he predicted that not a single address would be written in full before the trip started. The President, he feared, would "spend the first two or three days on the train preparing speeches."

"I would give anything in the world if I had the ability to clear away work as Roosevelt did," the President replied to some mild warning from Butt. "I am putting off these speeches from day to day." [23]

Procrastination was to earn a bitter penalty when, at last, the presidential party reached Winona, a small town in Minnesota which would live in history only because a president of the United States made a serious mistake within its limits. Taft worried instead of working. On September 14, as the trip began, he told the Boston Chamber of Commerce that it would "involve much hard work and a great deal of mental effort to think of things to say, and to say them simply and clearly, so that they can be understood." His greatest apprehension, he repeated, was the "necessity for speaking every day on some subject or other to a listening multitude . . . It becomes a brain-racking performance."

Such things are ordered better now. A president can surround himself, and always does, with secretarial assistants who are trained in the mysteries of headlines and public reactions to them. Such an

[23] Butt, Archie, *op. cit.*, Vol. I, pp. 185-192.

adviser, had he known his trade, would have eliminated from this same Boston speech a tribute by Taft to Senator Aldrich; to his talents as one of the "ablest statesmen in financial matters in either House," to his "clear-cut ideas, and simple but effective style of speaking." Taft added a hope that Aldrich would tour, himself, through the West and explain his ideas on monetary and banking reform.[24] A publicity expert would have blue-penciled, too, a reference at Springfield, Massachusetts, to Senator Murray Crane, another veteran of the Old Guard whom Taft rashly proclaimed a worthy representative of the state.[25]

The presidential party traveled westward through New York, with the first major stop at Chicago where Taft outlined his attitude toward labor and spoke at length on the necessity for drastic reform of the American legal system.[26] On September 17, he entered Wisconsin, the home state of LaFollette and the proving ground for progressive ideas. At this point the publicity adviser, had Taft enjoyed the services of one, would have recommended an addition to the speeches made.

"Say something about LaFollette right away," he would surely have urged. "Pay tribute to his courage. Admit that you do not agree with all his views. But say that you are filled with admiration for the senator's ability as a fighter, for the manner in which he has upheld Roosevelt's program. Say that but for the work of LaFollette, Beveridge and the rest of the insurgents, you would not have obtained the tariff cuts that you did. Make it strong, Mr. President."

But Taft never mentioned LaFollette, although he made a half dozen speeches in Wisconsin. Perhaps it never occurred to him to do so. Perhaps his slowly mounting distaste for the Wisconsin leader caused the words to choke in his throat. Taft made an emphatic plea at Milwaukee for the postal savings bank system. On that same day he reached the village of Winona in Minnesota. The specific purpose of his appearance there was to make a speech on behalf of Representative James A. Tawney, chairman of the Appropriations Committee and a resident of the town, who was being criticized for advocacy of the Payne-Aldrich act. Taft had been considering, for almost a month, the advisability of using this occasion, also, for his defense of the new tariff; he so wrote on August 23.[27] But he did not prepare a speech.

"Tomorrow Milwaukee and Winona," he telegraphed in his almost daily report to Mrs. Taft. "Hope to be able to deliver a tariff speech at Winona but it will be a close shave." [28]

"Speech hastily prepared, but I hope it may do some good," was his telegram from Winona itself on the following day.[29]

The President apologized, again, to the audience which faced him that night in the Winona Opera House. He would have to read his address, he said, because the subject was one "that calls for some care in expression." It was not a very good manuscript, he added, because "I had to dictate it coming up from Chicago." The speech was really not so bad as all that. Taft outlined his consistent advocacy, since August, 1906, of tariff reductions and told in clear and simple language the story of the progress of the Payne-Aldrich act through the House and the Senate at the special session. He thought that the Senate bill had been overseverely criticized and that this, too, had effected reductions. He analyzed carefully the changes made in the various schedules and repeated his claim that the reductions related to $5,000,000,000 in articles consumed annually and the increases to but $600,000,000. Regarding the accusation that the tariff cuts were not low enough to reduce the cost of living he said:

Now the promise of the Republican platform was not to revise everything downward . . . and I did not promise that everything should go downward. What I promised was that there should be many decreases, and that in some few things increases would be found to be necessary; but that on the whole I conceived that the change of conditions would make the revision necessarily downward— and that, I contend . . . has been the result of the Payne bill. *I did not agree, nor did the Republican party agree, that we would reduce rates to such a point as to reduce prices by the introduction of foreign competition.* That is what the free traders desire. That is what the revenue tariff reformers desire; but it is not what the Republican party wished to bring about.

[27] Taft to F. B. Kellogg, Aug. 23, 1909. [28] Taft to Helen H. Taft, Sept. 16, 1909. [29] *Idem*, Sept. 17, 1909.

On that basis he defended the cotton, crockery, paper and lumber rates. As for Schedule K, he agreed again that the wool rates were too high and probably represented "considerably more than the difference between the cost of production abroad and the cost of production here." The President denied that the increases in living costs were due to the Dingley act, now replaced.

"The high cost of living, of which 50 per cent is consumed in food, 25 per cent in clothing, and 25 per cent in rent and fuel," he said, "has not been produced by the tariff, because the tariff has remained the same while the increases have gone on. It is due to the change of conditions the world over. Living has increased everywhere in cost— in countries where there is free trade and in countries where there is protection."

The Winona speech, if read as a whole, offered no claim that the Payne-Aldrich act was perfect. Taft specifically stated, in fact, that it did not accomplish "certain things in the revision of the tariff which I had hoped for." He had sacrificed these because the bill was a substantial improvement and "in order to maintain party solidarity, which I believe to be much more important than the reduction of rates in one or two schedules." But there were twenty-five words in the lengthy address which flared into the headlines and caused all the others to be forgotten; they were the most damaging twenty-five words ever uttered, perhaps, by a president of the United States.

"On the whole, however, I am bound to say that I think the Payne bill is the best bill that the Republican party ever passed," said Taft, utterly innocent of the effect of what he was saying.[30]

It is of no importance that these were true words, that the Payne-Aldrich act was the first downward revision in the history of the party. On the special train which bore the President on his journey were eight or nine newspaper correspondents who had one common purpose, whether or not their papers were friendly to the President. The correspondents wanted news. Headlines are rigid phenomena of American journalism, as many a publicist besides Taft has learned to his lasting sorrow. There is no space in headlines for honest, logical reasoning. There was no space, this time, for the President's intelligent analysis of the faults and

[30] *Addresses,* Vol. XV, pp. 53-61. (Italics mine.)

virtues of the new tariff. There was room, however, for some of the unfortunate twenty-five words in which Taft said that this was "the best bill that the Republican party ever passed." The correspondents hurried to telegraph instruments after the speech. They dashed off the opening paragraphs of their dispatches: "Speaking at Winona tonight," they wrote, in substance, "President Taft declared that the Payne-Aldrich tariff law was 'the best bill that the Republican party ever passed.'" The words clicked east, west, north and south; that night, in a thousand newspaper offices, copy readers seized their pencils and scrawled a headline for the dispatches sent by their correspondents or by a press association from Winona. They wrote, with minor variations:

PAYNE ACT BEST TARIFF
IN HISTORY, STATES TAFT

Underneath the headlines could be found, of course, the President's speech in full or extracts from it. The closely packed type was of no significance, however, compared with the headlines. The newspapers spewed from the presses. Next day, and for weeks thereafter, men discussed the headlines. "Did you see what Taft said about the tariff?" the farmer, disgruntled over the cost of farm machinery, would ask his neighbor. "I see where Taft says we never had a better tariff!" declared the white-collar worker, the laboring man, the tenement dweller. They, too, were disgruntled; because of the increasing cost of the necessities of life. And in due time Democratic orators, yearning for the day when their party would be returned to power and when soft government jobs would be theirs for the asking, repeated again and again the substance of the twenty-five words so carelessly spoken on a September day in 1909. Such is the evolution of public opinion, a process never understood by William Howard Taft.

He seems to have realized that criticism would follow the Winona address, although there is nothing to indicate that he appreciated the dangerous interpretation which would be placed on an isolated passage.

"However," he telegraphed Mrs. Taft three days after making the speech, "I said what I thought and there is that satisfaction." [31]

[31] Taft to Helen H. Taft, Sept. 20, 1909.

"There are four or five free-trade newspapers of Republican tendency," he said in October, "that are engaged in hammering me for my speech at Winona . . . but my impression is that the speech is the best thing I have done. It is a truthful statement of what I think and it is the only ground upon which the party can stand with anything like a united force and win victories." [32]

"I cannot . . . see that I have done anything to call for such severe criticism," he protested a fortnight later. "I meant every word of my Winona speech. . . . [It] is not properly quoted, but its purport is misrepresented and what I said is perverted." [33]

Realization of what had happened was long in dawning. In December, 1911, the President consented to be interviewed on the triumphs and failures of his administration. By then, the break with Roosevelt was complete and hope was almost gone. His mind went back to the railroad trip from Chicago to Winona in September, 1909, and the speech he had delivered.

"I dictated that speech to a stenographer on the cars between two stations," he said— the interview was to be published and this confession, too, would be used against him, "and glanced through it only enough to straighten out the grammar. . . . The comparative would have been a better description than the superlative." [34]

The Winona speech was additionally unfortunate because the criticism which it aroused obscured public appreciation of certain very definite forward steps taken in Payne-Aldrich act. "If I had more technical knowledge, I should feel more confident," the President had admitted during the tariff debate in Congress.[35] The attempt to change the schedules, he added, had been replete with "humiliation and groping in the dark." [36]

"Why, it is just like Choctaw to a man who is not an expert," the President protested during his western trip, "and you take an expert on part of it and he will find that a good deal of the rest that he is not an expert on is Choctaw to him." [37]

But all this had been changed, so Taft hoped, by a provision creating a tariff board consisting of experts who could actually

[32] Taft to R. A. Taft, Oct. 28, 1909. [33] Taft to Foulke, Nov. 18, 1909. [34] *Outlook*, Dec. 11, 1911. [35] Taft to Helen H. Taft, July 8, 1909. [36] Taft to E. F. Baldwin, Aug. 9, 1909. [37] *Addresses*, Vol. XV, p. 285.

bring forward accurate information on which future revisions would be based. Congress appropriated $75,000 for the purpose.[38] The President had supported this clause and had been opposed, obviously, by Uncle Joe Cannon, who saw the awful possibility that a low tariff man might be put on the commission. Would Taft pledge himself to name solid protectionists and not theoretical economists?

"I am not a damn fool and I am a protectionist . . ." snapped the President angrily when word to this effect was brought to him, "[but] if the bill is passed I will appoint the commission without his [the speaker's] assistance." [39] The men he selected were honest, impartial students: they were Alvin H. Saunders, J. B. Reynolds and Henry C. Emery. The immediate purpose of the commission was somewhat different from its ultimate one of furnishing information on tariffs in general. The Payne-Aldrich act contained a second provision, that the minimum rates set forth in its schedules could be increased in the event that foreign nations sought to discriminate against the United States. The increases permitted were large: 25 per cent of the actual value of the article imported from the offending country. So the tariff board appointed by Taft was to keep an alert eye on eventualities of this nature and recommend to the President, who had power under the law, changes where needed. Taft, in explaining it, expressed a hope that "very little use may be required of this clause." Nor was it, despite pressure from dissatisfied protectionists, applied.[40]

The tariff, postal savings banks, trust control, currency and banking reform, conservation, the development of inland waterways: these were among the subjects the President intended to discuss on his tour of the country. The chief of these, obviously, was the tariff itself. In the minds of certain Taft intimates, however, the trip had a larger significance; it was believed that his shining personality would dispel the increasing criticism of the administration. To this theory, he subscribed. He would, he promised, "get out and see the people and jolly them." [41] The jollying was accomplished with a master's touch, and this was in marked contrast to Taft's first weeks as president. He had declined to salute the

[38] *Ibid.*, Vol. XV, p. 60. [39] Butt, Archie, *op. cit.*, Vol. I, p. 155. [40] *Addresses*, Vol. XV, p. 60; Taussig, F. W., *op. cit.*, pp. 404-406. [41] Taft to F. H. Gillett, Sept. 13, 1909.

crowds which gathered on one or two brief trips. He paid slight
attention to their cheers when he was driven through the streets.[42]
But this time it was different. He made brief speeches from the rear
of his train. His good nature never faded under the idiocies of
the mobs which swarmed to see him.[43]

These would have strained the good nature of a saint. Dignity,
manners and restraint vanish when the great American public
has an opportunity to greet its chief executive. A presidential tour
is like the progress of a circus train. The President has no privacy.
He is stuffed with food and then made even more somnolent by
dreary, long-winded local orators. He has to walk cautiously
among conflicting claims of state and city politicians. He has to lay
cornerstones for churches, hospitals, fraternal organizations and
railroad terminals. He must visit an unending list of county fairs
if, as Taft was doing, the journey is in the fall of the year.

"I ought not to omit to mention as a useful result of my journeying," observed Taft as he began his trip, "that I am to visit a
great many expositions and fairs, and that the curiosity to see the
President will certainly increase the box receipts and tend to rescue
many commendable enterprises from financial disaster. This is an
innocent . . . but very useful, function of the presidential office." [44]

The ubiquitous Archie Butt accompanied the official party and
kept a diary, apparently for the eyes of the President alone as
it was not included among the daily posterity letters which he
penned. It is probably the best running description of a presidential
circus in existence. On September 23, 1909, for instance, the special
train pulled out of Pueblo, Colorado, in the early evening and
wound through the spectacular Royal Gorge. The President
watched the scenery until, at last, sheer exhaustion forced him to
take to his stateroom. Captain Butt noted:

The President retired early, thinking to get a continuous sleep,
but at Salida the whole train was awakened by a frightful cataclysm
[sic] of sounds from steam whistles, through which the citizens . . .
tried to express their welcome to the Chief Executive. One whistle
they put immediately under his car, and as it took about ten minutes

---

[42] Butt, Archie, op. cit., Vol. I, p. 18. [43] Official Functions, p. 175. [44] Addresses,
Vol. XV, p. 2.

to take on water, the reception was one that he will long remember. He had hardly got to sleep when apparently he had to be called again.

The train was scheduled to stop three-quarters of an hour at Glenwood Springs (it was about 5:30 o'clock) but no program had been arranged. However, as soon as the train stopped the greatest hubbub was heard around the car and upon inquiry it was found that Representative Taylor, the Episcopal Bishop of Western Colorado, Bishop Brewster, the Mayor, with a large committee of leading citizens had arisen early not only to welcome the President but to take him to the hotel to make a speech, and incidentally to take a bath in the pool supplied from the hot springs. . . .

As he stepped on the platform a committee of ladies of the W.C.T.U. presented him with a dish of trout. He threw the ladies into confusion by asking if there was anything intoxicating in the fish. They took his query most seriously and assured him that they were members of the total abstinence society. As the President got into his carriage, he remarked to the Bishop: "It is my experience . . . that the good women who head the temperance movement are usually totally devoid of humor."

The President made a speech at the hotel, but declined to take a bath in the pool when he learned that the program called for him to don a bathing suit and bathe in the presence of the entire populace.[45]

The journey continued through Utah where Taft alienated the left wing of his party further by praising the unusual abilities of Senator Reed Smoot, who also had voted for the tariff.[46] On September 29, the train reached Seattle where an exposition was in progress. Captain Butt's account is touched with acid:

The arrangements at Seattle had evidently been made with a view to keeping the President out of sight of the people as much as possible so as to increase the gate receipts at the exposition. The committee was told that such was not the President's desire nor was it the desire of the public men of Seattle, and they agreed to announce the route to the exposition so that the people on the streets would be able to welcome him as he passed. In spite of the agreement the President was hurriedly taken through streets which had not been announced . . . and he practically went through silent

[45] *Official Functions*, pp. 166-167. [46] *Addresses*, Vol. XV, p. 156.

avenues to the exposition grounds. The expectations of the management . . . were more than realized. . . . The gate receipts showed something like 80,000 people.[47]

San Francisco was more restrained. The President was capitalized only to boost the chances of the Republican candidate for mayor. A flashlight was unexpectedly exploded as he was shaking hands with that politician and it caused, if anything, widespread annoyance to an otherwise civilized community. Immediate apologies were offered.[48] Los Angeles, of course, staged a tremendous demonstration on October 11. A banquet was given at the Shriners' Auditorium where the dais faced an enormous map of the United States, outlined in electric lights, on which red and green lights shot back and forth to indicate the route across the continent which the President had followed. On the following day, Taft was escorted on a tour through the orange country to the south. Captain Butt wrote:

One of the unique features . . . was a committee of one hundred professional and business men from Los Angeles under the leadership of Joe Scott, who termed themselves the "Taft Boosters." Wherever his train would stop, they would line up and shout most lustily in chorus— "We are for Taft"— repeating it six times with a roar at the end.[49]

At every large city the reception committees arranged the most elaborate banquets, but the most astonishing feast of all was the one furnished at Savannah, Georgia, on November 4. To Butt, who was an expert in comparing such occasions, it was the most remarkable of the whole journey, "even eclipsing in brilliance the breakfast at Spokane and the dinner at Los Angeles." It began with "the release of twenty white pigeons, which fluttered like doves of peace over the immense banquet hall" and lasted until two o'clock in the morning. Captain Butt, at least, was not bored:

Nothing so novel in the souvenir line was possibly ever before developed at a banquet in the South. . . . Each course revealed some new souvenir until the guests became expectant with interest

[47] *Official Functions*, pp. 179-180. [48] *Ibid.*, p. 189. [49] *Ibid.*, pp. 203-204.

concerning what another round would bring forth. At each plate was found a Russian leather cigar case filled with cigars, and a rolled-gold scarf pin with the seal of the city of Savannah on its head. The almonds were placed in silver filigreed coasters, which were intended as souvenirs, and the caviar was served in china ash trays, on which were painted in gold the initials of the President. The punch was served in cut glass vases covered with silver-filigreed work . . . while the ices were served in jewel boxes, which represented the north pole, the polar bear and an arctic explorer standing at the summit. A graceful long-necked cut glass perfume bottle encased in silver filigree work contained the brandy, but the crowning achievement . . . was the individual chafing dishes with alcohol lamps containing the stewed terrapin.

The guests, Butt added, "could hardly believe they were intended as souvenirs," so shining and lovely was their copper luster. But as the terrapin disappeared, the dishes were gathered up and returned to each diner in a neat box. The President "gathered up his armful of souvenirs" and handed them to a secretary.

"I have never seen as much loot in my life before," he said.[50]

By far the most important official function on the 13,000 mile tour was an exchange of visits at El Paso, Texas, and Juarez, Mexico, with President Porfirio Diaz of Mexico, who had ruled the country with an iron hand since 1877 and who now trembled that his power was ending. This was Taft's first venture into the doubtful realms of dollar diplomacy and it was destined to fail. Diaz negotiated the meeting, which was conducted with pomp and ceremony, in the hope that thereby he might escape the downfall which the progressives and liberals of his country were plotting. But that hope was to fail too. He lasted for eighteen months after the cannons had boomed along the shores of the Rio Grande to mark his meeting with the powerful President of the powerful Republic on the north. Then revolution came. The dreamy Francisco I. Madero, whose idealistic conceptions of pure liberty were to be as futile as Diaz's stern capitalism, overthrew him in May, 1911, and was elected president in November.

American capitalists, like capitalists everywhere, find dictators

[50] *Ibid.*, pp. 267-270.

convenient, particularly in undeveloped countries. Diaz had permitted railroads to be built; and American capital had made profits in building them. He sponsored other material advancements too, such as roads and telegraph lines and ports. He established a degree of law and order. He neglected, however, to appreciate the strange paradox of capitalist development; that with material progress comes a degree of liberal thought. As Diaz grew older he became more and more intolerant of liberal thought. By 1909, as the friendly Taft prepared to meet him, he had been out of touch for years with all elements in Mexico except the wealthy businessmen who were the allies of the American capitalists. Two decades of Diaz rule had brought prosperity, of a sort, to Mexico. It was prosperity for the limited few. The peons were as wretched as ever and they listened, absorbed if only half understanding, when they heard from Madero that the poor man had rights as well as the rich man.[51]

That Taft had more than the most superficial knowledge of Mexico is doubtful. He does not appear even to have been certain of the sources which inspired the meeting on October 16, 1909. He told Mrs. Taft that he had "received a communication, perhaps directly from the old man, of an informal character, saying how glad he would be to have such a meeting brought about. He thinks, and I believe rightly, that the knowledge throughout his country of the friendship of the United States for him and his government will strengthen him with his own people, and tend to discourage revolutionists' efforts to establish a different government."[52] In another letter, the President was more specific:

The meeting with Diaz is to be a historical one. . . . I am glad to aid him . . . for the reason that we have two billions [of] American capital in Mexico that will be greatly endangered if Diaz were to die and his government go to pieces. It is questionable what will happen if he does die. He has designated a man to succeed him, but that is likely to lead to a revolution. I can only hope and pray that his demise does not come until I am out of office.[53]

[51] Hammond, J. H., *The Autobiography of John Hays Hammond*, Vol. II, pp. 569-570. [52] Taft to Helen H. Taft, Oct. 17, 1909. [53] *Idem*, Oct. 15, 1909.

Every detail of the meeting had been arranged by the State Department and the Foreign Office of Mexico; it was even specified that the President of the United States "will be attired in frock coat; the President of Mexico in uniform." But the searching of precedents had no bearing on the possibility that some friend of liberty might use the opportunity to kill two capitalistic presidents at one time. The most awful possibility, it appears, was that Diaz might be attacked in the United States or Taft in Mexico. The reverse, while to be deplored, would not cause a diplomatic incident.[54] So the functionaries on both sides of the river fretted and took precautions. The United States secret service moved in its men. Nothing happened.

"That the day did pass in such a way, with the exception of a fight between an American and a Mexican boy, which resulted in the death of the American," dictated a relieved Archie Butt as the presidential train steamed on that night, "was due to the vigilance of the trained secret service men of the United States and Mexico."[55]

Colonel Pablos Escandón, personal aide to President Diaz, was at the El Paso station when President Taft arrived. Thus began a day in which aides dashed back and forth presenting compliments from their principals and suggesting changes in the formal greetings, carefully prepared and approved at Washington and Mexico City weeks before, which the two chief executives would voice to each other without understanding each other's words; Diaz spoke no English and Taft's Spanish, never good, had grown decidedly rusty since his Philippine days. At ten-thirty a cavalry troop escorted President Taft to the El Paso Chamber of Commerce where— appropriately enough, in view of the $2,000,000,000 in American investments at stake— he would receive Diaz. The occasion did not disturb Taft's nerves. He retired to a conference room and lay down on a lounge. A few minutes later, when Butt scurried in for some decision, he found the President of the United States locked in slumber.

But soon trumpets were heard in the distance proclaiming the approach of El Presidente de Mejico and the President of the United States had to be awakened. He took his position in a large,

[54] *Official Functions*, p. 206. [55] *Ibid.*, p. 207.

center hall. Behind him were Postmaster General Hitchcock and two secretaries. Secretary of War Dickinson, who had also traveled to Texas for the occasion, entered the hallway with President Diaz, who was wearing, as Taft described it to Mrs. Taft on the following day, "a uniform with decorations emblazoning his appearance, which quite outshone your husband's civil garb." The ancient Mexican, he added, was "most remarkable in point of agility, quickness of perception and dignity of carriage."[56]

"The President of the United States— the President of Mexico!" announced Captain Butt at this point.

"I am very glad to welcome you, sir, here; I am very glad indeed," said Taft, in English.

"I am very happy to meet you and to have the honor of being one of the first foreigners to come over and to give you a hearty welcome," said Diaz, in Spanish.

A few more words of the same nature followed. Taft presented his Cabinet members and then the two presidents withdrew for a private conversation through an interpreter.[57] Captain Butt was in the small party which listened and he reported that during the twenty minutes before Diaz left further expressions of esteem had been exchanged. A toast was drunk in champagne just before the Mexican President departed. Taft prepared for the return call at Juarez. This took place at noon and the salutations differed only to the extent that Taft pointed out that no other President of the United States had "stepped beyond the border of the United States on the north or to the south." He predicted a closer union between Mexico and his own country.[58]

President Diaz gave a banquet in honor of President Taft at Juarez that night. Sixty guests were present at the magnificent function to which had been brought, from Mexico City, the silver and gold service dishes of the republic. Again, Captain Butt was permitted to overhear the dialogue. President Diaz asked about Mrs. Taft's health. President Taft inquired regarding Mrs. Diaz. He then suggested that Señora Diaz and Mrs. Taft both played, perhaps, an important part in the affairs of the public. No doubt, no doubt, said the President of Mexico, laughing. Mr. Taft told, also

[56] Taft to Helen H. Taft, Oct. 17, 1909. [57] *Official Functions,* pp. 208-213; *Addresses,* Vol. XVI, pp. 108-110. [58] *Ibid.,* Vol. XVI, pp. 111-112.

smiling, of the ambition he had abandoned, at Mrs. Taft's insistence, of going on the bench. Señor Diaz said that the señora had hardly been responsible for his election as president of Mexico, but she had probably assisted him in holding office.

"They enjoyed this sally, in which his young son joined," dictated Butt, "and President Diaz admonished him that he was at a state conference and should not betray any of its secrets to his mother." [59]

But at last it was over. Butt and John Hays Hammond, also with the party, returned to the special train with the President, who suggested that they seemed very nervous and that a highball might steady them.

"Thank God we're out of Mexico," Hammond said, as he drank one, "and the day's over. We've been half crazy for fear somebody'd take a shot at you."

"Oh, is that what's been bothering you?" the President replied. "Why should you have worried about that? If anyone wanted to get me, he couldn't very well have missed such an easy target." [60]

All the excitement and danger had been in vain. The $2,000,-000,000 of American investments were, none the less, to be placed in jeopardy and Taft was far from finished with the Mexican problem.

On the way to El Paso, the presidential train had passed through Arizona and New Mexico where the territorial inhabitants offered, again, their pleas for admission as states. On October 15, the Commercial Club of Albuquerque, New Mexico, entertained the President at a dinner and a principal speaker was Albert B. Fall who would one day be senator, then secretary of the interior in President Harding's Cabinet, then a convict in the state penitentiary at Santa Fe. Fall, whose ambitions in 1909 were limited to the Senate, told the diners that statehood was essential. He added, gratuitously, that it was unwise to place too much reliance in the promises made by presidents when they addressed local groups. On returning to Washington, they were likely to change their minds. Taft betrayed no anger when his own time came to speak. He said that Fall's remarks reminded him of a jurist he

[59] *Official Functions*, p. 217. [60] Hammond, J. H., *op. cit.*, Vol. II, p. 259.

had once known in whose court appeared an importunate and stupid attorney.

"I don't care to hear from you, I am with you," the judge said when the lawyer began to speak.

"It is my constitutional right to be heard on this motion and I propose to be heard," the lawyer answered.

"I have listened to you for an hour," said the court when he had finished, "and despite what you have said I am still with you." [61]

Taft described the incident, not without satisfaction, two days later. He thought that Fall was a "man who liked to cultivate notoriety by saying something rude and out of the ordinary rules of courtesy."

"I had to take him and spank him," the President observed, "which I think I did pretty successfully— at least everybody in the party seemed to think so, and it set him down where he ought to be politically. He has had aspirations for the Senate, upon the inauguration of statehood, but I don't think those aspirations are likely to be gratified." [62]

Unhappily for the Republican party— unhappily for Taft's own peace of mind— the chastisement was not thorough enough. If it had been, the oil scandals of the Harding regime might have been avoided. Fall might have been in no position to receive a satchel of cash from Edward L. Doheny in return for betraying his country.

One major part of the trip remained: a voyage down the Mississippi from St. Louis to New Orleans. The improvement of the inland waterways was a subject close to the hearts of the people who lived in the valleys of the Mississippi, Missouri and Ohio rivers. It was of vital importance to Chicago, where the industrialists dreamed of direct water transportation from the gulf. The subject was doubly important because of the increased costs of freight transportation and because the Panama Canal, before another decade had passed, would be open. About $600,000,000 had been invested in the river trade routes when Taft became president

[61] Hammond, J. H., *op. cit.*, Vol. II, p. 564; *Addresses*, Vol. XVI, p. 102. [62] Taft to Helen H. Taft, Oct. 17, 1909.

and the demand was incessant for the expenditure of additional funds.

"This improvement of waterways, the improvement by irrigation of arid and subarid lands, and all this conservation of resources," Taft said at St. Louis, "is not for the purpose of distributing 'pork' to every part of the country. Every measure that is to be taken up is to be adopted on the ground that it is to be useful to the country at large and not on the ground that it is going to send certain congressmen back to Congress. . . . The method I am in favor of is this: that we should take up every comprehensive project on its merits, and . . . determine whether the country in which that project is to be carried out is so far developed as to justify the expenditure of a large sum. . . . When you have determined that on the general principle of good to the entire country, then I am in favor of doing the work as rapidly as it can be done, and I am in favor of issuing bonds to do it. . . . Now there is a proposition that we issue $500,000,000 of bonds or a billion of bonds for waterways, and then that we just cut that up and apportion a part to the Pacific, a part to the Atlantic, a part to the Missouri and a part to the Ohio. I am opposed to it because it not only smells of the pork barrel, but it will be the pork barrel." [63]

The President was to be dissuaded from such heretical views, if possible, by his Mississippi trip. A flotilla of thirteen river steamers started the journey on October 25. A vast number of congressmen, state governors and other politicians were on board. Great crowds flocked to see the impressive junket which finally reached New Orleans. Taft did not compromise on his demand for a comprehensive improvement program. But among the politicians on the journey was, unfortunately, Speaker Cannon. Archie Butt was dismayed to watch Taft fraternizing with the man he honestly despised, permitting himself to be photographed with him, speaking on the same platform.

"I have never known a man to dislike discord as much as the President," the presidential aide wrote. "He wants every man's approval, and a row of any kind is repugnant to him." [64]

Butt was right. On October 28, the President and the speaker both attended a function at Vicksburg, Mississippi, and Taft referred in joking, almost affectionate, terms to Uncle Joe.[65] Only four days before, he had complained to Secretary Knox of the "vulgarity and blackguardism" of the man who now sat on the dais with him.[66] The President apparently left the banquet to dictate his daily letter to Mrs. Taft and to complain that Cannon would be the "incubus" of the 1910 Congressional campaign.[67] Only the public expressions of cordiality— these and the photographs of Taft and Cannon together— reached the voters, however. Only these reached the insurgent group of the House of Representatives which was busy plotting the downfall of Uncle Joe in the spring of 1910. No wonder they thought that Taft had bowed to their enemy.

The journey ended at Washington on November 10, 1909, after a pleasant processional through the South. Taft had come through the ordeal amazingly well. His health was good, although he had gained some weight. He had made 259 speeches. He had seen millions of his fellow citizens and he felt greatly encouraged regarding the status of himself and the party. The President had so concluded back in Texas:

I cannot be mistaken in finding that the people are very friendly to me. Whatever their judgment as to particular things I have done, I certainly up to this time have their good will. . . . The one note that I could hear everywhere was that of contentment and satisfaction with conditions, and such a note is inconsistent with the defeat of the party in power. I venture to think that our friends, the insurgents, will find this fact more and more apparent as the campaign for the next Congress comes on; and their sores and grievances will be of less interest to the public when the public are chiefly thinking of business profits and business prosperity than when they have complaints of their own to make. . . . Our friends, the insurgents, find themselves in such an attitude now that if they cannot create a division in the party they have lost all influence. They have become desperate, therefore, and their cry is heard above the quiet chant of contentment that exists everywhere in this country where I have been.[68]

[65] *Addresses*, Vol. XVI, pp. 207-208. [66] Taft to Knox, Oct. 24, 1909. [67] Taft to Helen H. Taft, Oct. 28, 1909. [68] Taft to Helen H. Taft, Oct. 24, 1909; to Knox, Oct. 24, 1909.

SHALL WE HAVE FOR PRESIDENT OF THIS NATION A MAN WHO REPUDIATES JESUS CHRIST?

Think of the United States with a *president* who does not believe that Jesus Christ was the Son of God, but looks upon our immaculate Savior as a common bastard and low, cunning impostor! What must Mr. Taft's feelings be toward our civilization, which is so permeated and interwoven with the religion of Jesus Christ? Take

---

Hon. W.H.Taft,

     cincinnati, Ohio,

Dear Sir:

     Some of my friends state that they will vote against you on the ground that you are an Infidel, and that you do not believe in our God. In order that I may answer this accusation, please let me know just how you stand on the subject.

Hon William Howard Taft,

     Cincinnati, Ohio.

Sir:—

     Beg to ask you "Do you believe in Jesus Christ as "your personal Saviour?"

     Hope I am worthy of a prompt reply,

Hon. W.H.Taft,

     Cincinnati,Ohio.

     Dear Sir: Objection is being urged to your election to the presidency on the ground that you deny the divinity of Jesus Christ.

     See inclosed leaflet of H.C.Morrison .

Please state whether you believe or disbelieve the statement of Peter: " Thou art the Christ the son of the living God" Matthew 16 16.

A FEW OF THE LETTERS ATTACKING TAFT BECAUSE HE WAS A UNITARIAN. CAMPAIGN OF 1908

See page 374]

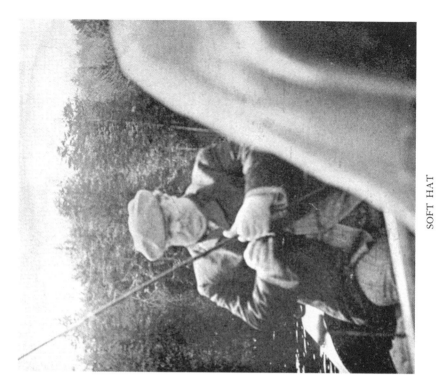

SOFT HAT

SILK HAT

The acoustics of a special train bearing the President of the United States are, however, notoriously bad. The President is told only good news by the politicians, yearning for favors, who crowd aboard. The voices of protest are drowned in the applause of those who swarm to see the circus. Nor are the darkening skies visible, either; the sundial of a president counts, all too often, none but the sunny hours. There was an additional fallacy in Taft's optimism. "I have seen millions of people, have been most cordially received," he wrote.[69] Of course, he had been cordially received. Of course, the people loved him. They always would; never more so than on the day three years ahead when he won the electoral votes of Utah and Vermont alone.

[69] Taft to Helen Taft (daughter), Oct. 28, 1909.

CHAPTER XXVI

THE INEVITABLE VILLAIN

THE PERSONS of the Pinchot-Ballinger drama were varied types, but they had certain traits in common. Each was certain that truth and justice lay on his side of the controversy. Each was somewhat impervious to facts which might cause him to alter his views. The principals in 1909 and 1910 were: a president of the United States, his secretary of the interior, an obscure government agent with a deeply suspicious nature, a passionately zealous conservationist whose title was "Chief of the United States Forest Service." Another principal did not actually tread the boards. He was in distant Africa and his voice was an off-stage voice of warning. Among the minor characters were coal operators, lobbyists, politicians, lawyers, newspaper correspondents and editors. The editors were the Cassandras of woe and they wrote blistering attacks based on inaccurate information.

In 1910, Louis R. Glavis, the suspicious government agent, testified before a Senate-House committee investigating the alleged Alaska land frauds. "So you wish to say to this committee that . . . you have observed nowhere a corrupt motive as to any of these officers; you state that, do you?" a member of the committee asked him.

"Well, yes, sir; there was no evidence of it," answered Glavis.

"There was no evidence *even to your mind* of any corrupt conduct on the part of any of them?"

"No, sir."

"You saw no corrupt conduct on the part of any of them . . . the most you wish to be understood as saying, the most you did say to the President . . . by your array of facts and what you did *mean to say to the country* in your array of facts in *Collier's Weekly,* was simply that you did not think the affairs of the government, that is, those conducted by the Interior Office, were in safe hands?"

"Yes, sir," said Glavis.[1]

". . . we are seeking," they asked Louis D. Brandeis, who was appearing as counsel for Glavis, "to ascertain specifically what the charges were. Do I understand now that they are, first, that upon certain occasions Mr. Ballinger acted improperly, but not entirely corruptly, and upon other occasions he designed and intended to act corruptly, but was prevented from doing so by Mr. Glavis?"

"I have not used the word 'corrupt' in any case . . . ," answered the future associate justice of the Supreme Court. "I have desired to bring, and I desire now to bring, without characterization, the facts before the committee." [2]

The testimony of Glavis and the explanation of Mr. Brandeis did not take place until January and February, 1910, however, and since early fall of the previous year the country had been assured that valuable Alaska coal lands were the objective of a larcenous conspiracy. Ballinger, it was declared, had aided the conspirators. The charge was as direct and specific as it was untrue. Certain of the editors of the United States had examined the evidence with gross carelessness. The worst offenders were Norman Hapgood of *Collier's Weekly* and Mark Sullivan, his associate, who in those remote days was a flaming liberal. Henry Watterson of Louisville also excoriated Secretary Ballinger more vigorously than accurately; but Marse Henry was, of course, a Democrat and a skilled exponent of the oratorical— as distinct from the factual— school of journalism.

The main attack in *Collier's Weekly* began on November 6, 1909, with an editorial which proclaimed that "the Cunninghams and Guggenheims are reaching out" for Alaska coal deposits "estimated as being worth three and a half billion dollars or more." An editorial spoke of the "reckless immorality with which the head of a great department is willing to work against the interests of the people whom he is supposed to represent." The President, "good-natured and trustful . . . has been outrageously misled." [3] This broadside was preliminary to publication in the next issue of an article by Glavis— on the witness stand, in February, 1910, the author protested that he had written only the text and was not responsible for the headings or the captions above the subdivisions.

[1] Sixty-first Congress, 3rd Session, Sen. Doc. 719, pp. 435-438. (Italics mine.) [2] *Ibid.*, pp. 24-71. [3] *Collier's Weekly*, Nov. 6, 1909.

Certain of these captions were inflammatory in the extreme: "The Whitewashing of Ballinger" . . . "Are the Guggenheims in Charge of the Department of the Interior?" . . . "The Alaska Coal Lands are in Danger in Ballinger's Hands." [4] Two weeks later, the weekly called Ballinger "tricky, furtive and menacing to the most far-reaching interests at present before the administration for consideration." [5] The following week, the secretary of the interior was accused of falsehood. Glavis, said *Collier's Weekly*, had "saved to the people natural resources estimated at perhaps three times the amount of our entire national debt." [6]

But Glavis, by then, had been dismissed by order of President Taft from his post as chief of the Field Division of the Interior Department. Gifford Pinchot, who supported and encouraged him, was soon to be dismissed, too, by a baffled and reluctant president who also was angry. Pinchot's dismissal brought the blast from the Louisville *Courier-Journal:*

For the first time in the history of the country a President of the United States has openly proclaimed himself the friend of thieves and the enemy of honest men. That, and that alone, is the issue precipitated by the executive order of Friday removing Gifford Pinchot from office. . . .

Many Republican Presidents have by indirection through the protective policy proclaimed themselves the friend of robbery under the forms of law; Mr. Taft becomes the first to depart from the process of licensed robbery, and to announce that the debts of his party are in future to be paid out of the people's domain. . . .

We shall have an investigation that will investigate. He who dallies becomes a dastard; he that doubts is sure to be damned. The black flag raised by the President floats at the masthead of the administration; let the Stars and Stripes float at the masthead of Congress! "No quarter" be the word, until the truth, the whole truth and nothing but the truth comes blazing from the crucible to put a blister upon the forehead of corruption, in vindication of true men, and all for the glory of God and the honor of the Republic! Amen! [7]

[4] *Collier's Weekly*, Nov. 13, 1909. [5] *Ibid.*, Nov. 26, 1909. [6] *Ibid.*, Dec. 3, 1909.
[7] Louisville *Courier-Journal*, Jan. 22, 1910.

"Great, great is flapdoodle," Marse Henry had remarked on another occasion. It would be difficult to find an editorial more replete with flapdoodle than this one. It would be equally difficult to find magazine articles or editorials more replete with inaccuracies than the ones which had appeared in *Collier's Weekly*. The Alaska coal lands as a whole were not worth even a sizable fraction of $3,500,000,000. The coal lands defended by Louis Glavis constituted one-fifteenth of one per cent of the total Alaska acreage. The Guggenheim interests had a remote connection with Alaska coal developments. Finally, as to Ballinger: Taft's secretary of the interior may have been less than forceful. He did a foolish thing when, in his private law practice, he accepted a retainer from one of the coal claimants. He handled this crisis— so grave that he was to die under a cloud— clumsily. He listened too readily, perhaps, to department bureaucrats and permitted delays fatal to his reputation and damaging to the Taft administration. But it is not true that he was dishonest. He was not furtive. He was a friend and not the enemy of conservation. An examination of thousands of pages of evidence can lead the impartial reader only to the conclusion that Ballinger was the victim of an attack fostered by fanaticism and nurtured by bad journalism. But Pinchot, Glavis, Hapgood, Sullivan, Marse Henry and the rest handed down their verdict against Ballinger in 1909 and 1910 and a large element of the public believed that they had spoken justly.

The President remained steadfast. He refused all importunities that to save himself he must dismiss his secretary of the interior. Never, he wrote, had there been "such an unjust conspiracy against a man as there has been against him. I am not in the habit of quitting, and I don't propose to go back on a man . . . when he has done nothing to deserve the opprobrium that is heaped on him." [8] To the specific suggestion that Ballinger was a serious political burden, which was true, Taft responded with splendid scorn and wrath:

If I were to turn Ballinger out, in view of his innocence and in view of the conspiracy against him, I should be a white-livered skunk. I don't care how it affects my administration . . . before

[8] Taft to Cyrus Northrop, June 24, 1910.

the people; if the people are so unjust as this I don't propose to be one of them. Mr. Ballinger has done nothing of any kind that should subject him to criticism. He has been made the object of a despicable conspiracy, in which unscrupulous methods have been used that ought to bring shame to the face of everyone connected with it.[9]

Taft's heart was heavy as the onslaughts against Ballinger grew more violent. Only the break with Roosevelt itself was to sadden him more during his four years, none of them wholly happy, in the White House. He pondered, at its height, "how long mere wind and declamation without definition of evil or remedy will pass as current coin— always with some people, I suppose, sometimes with all people, but not, I hope, always with all the people. . . . Will Pinchot remain the St. George and Ballinger the dragon?"[10] As always, though, he said these things privately and the people had no chance to realize that Ballinger was other than a dragon. This was Taft's failing and his personal tragedy as a public man. The fine, brave words he uttered were to lie covered with dust in locked files for decades. Only his mistakes— and his timid uncertainties— reached the headlines.

"I suppose," remarked the President another time, "the public has difficulty in getting at what it is all about."[11]

This was unquestionably the case. In its larger implications, the Ballinger-Pinchot row related to conservation. Theodore Roosevelt had made this a vibrant issue. The necessity for conservation of natural resources marked the first change in the American process. By the turn of the century a cherished phrase had become shopworn, even menacing: "opening up the country" no longer signified wagon trains pushing into the West. It was no longer an inalienable right of every American to go out past the frontiers, if he had the courage, and stake for himself rich claims in gold, silver, coal or timber lands. Other men, with less personal courage, in groups instead of by themselves, had followed in their paths and were opening up the country now. They had gathered the claims together, where the pioneers had failed, and had developed them under the

[9] Taft to P. A. Baker, May 21, 1910. [10] Taft to Horace D. Taft, Dec. 27, 1909. [11] Idem, March 5, 1910.

beneficent protection of the corporate form. Sometimes they owned gold mines, and this angered the advocates of soft money. Coal and timber had likewise found their way into the hands of a clever few. So had water-power sites. All this had been well enough while, so the people supposed, unending acres still waited for settlement. But the people reacted violently when the pinch came. Roosevelt, entering the White House in September, 1901, made conservation of remaining public lands a first duty. He found that the General Land Office and the other government agencies in charge of the public domain swarmed with incompetents or worse. The bona fide homeowner was not protected. The law was not enforced against the corporate interests which sought to accumulate natural resources for private profit.

Effective allies worked with President Roosevelt in his crusade. One of them was Senator Francis G. Newlands of Nevada, whose labors have been too little appreciated. Gifford Pinchot, Roosevelt wrote in his memoirs, "is the man to whom the nation owes most for what has been accomplished as regards the preservation of the natural resources of our country." [12]

"Gifford truly has an affection for me," Roosevelt once observed complacently. "It is almost fetish worship, and I have figured it out that Pinchot truly believes that in case of certain conditions I am perfectly capable of killing either himself or me. If conditions were such that only one could live he knows that I should possibly kill him as the weaker of the two, and he, therefore, worships this in me." [13] Unhappily for the Taft administration, the necessity for pleasing Pinchot in this sanguinary manner did not arise.

Pinchot's weakness for hero-worship was apparent in his appearance. His eyes, wrote the admiring Owen Wister, looked as "if they gazed upon a Cause." His face, during these youthful years, was "one of marked and particular beauty, in which enthusiasm and asceticism" were blended.[14] Pinchot had been a conservation enthusiast for years. A man of wealth, his luminous eyes had started to gaze on this cause soon after he graduated from Yale in 1889, so he studied forestry in Europe where, during three or four centuries, conservation had been practiced. He entered the government

[12] Roosevelt, Theodore, *Autobiography*, pp. 393-394. [13] Abbott, L. F., *The Letters of Archie Butt*, p. 147. [14] Wister, Owen, *Roosevelt, the Story of a Friendship*, p. 114.

service in 1898 to put in operation the theories and the knowledge he had accumulated. He unquestionably knew more about forestry than anyone else in the United States. Unquestionably, too, his enthusiasm burned with a brilliant light.

Roosevelt, as governor of New York, had consulted Pinchot on forestry matters. Soon after September, 1901, he became one of the White House intimates, a member of the Tennis Cabinet. For eight years he was very powerful. His domain included all the national forests in the country. He had wide regulatory authority regarding the use of these lands for grazing and their development for water power. The President's guiding doctrine, as expressed in terse Rooseveltian language, was that it was "better for the government to help a poor man to make a living for his family than to help a rich man make more profit for his company." [15] So the settler was favored in comparison with the large cattle, land, lumber or coal corporations. The acreage open to settlement by any one man was strictly limited and the passage of water-power rights out of government control was carefully restricted. Neither Roosevelt nor Pinchot, however, worried too greatly about the legality of their actions. The proponents of a cause rarely have time for such a trifle.

"If Roosevelt had taken a different way he would be further along in some of his reforms," observed President Taft after he had been in the White House for three months and had found time to examine certain aspects of the Roosevelt-Pinchot crusades.[16]

One of these was the withdrawal from public settlement of 16,000,000 acres of federal lands in the Northwest. By executive order, from time to time, President Roosevelt had set aside portions of the public domain and had ruled that no part of these lands would be delivered into private hands. Timber was on some of the land; minerals and water power had been located on others. But not all of the lands, by any means, had valuable natural resources. In September, 1907, the opponents of Roosevelt's policy, which was of doubtful legal standing, attached a rider to an agricultural appropriation bill which forbade the President to make further withdrawals in the six northwestern states. Roosevelt summoned Pinchot before signing the measure; he was forced to sign it because the main purpose of the bill was to provide money for the farmer. He

[15] Roosevelt, Theodore, *op. cit.*, p. 402. [16] Taft to Horace D. Taft, June 6, 1909.

instructed the forestry expert to prepare immediately plans for creating additional national forests in these states. Pinchot tabulated 16,000,000 acres. Roosevelt issued the order reserving this vast territory. Then he signed the agricultural bill which prohibited further action of the sort.

"The opponents of the forest service turned handsprings in their wrath," he noted.[17]

President Taft, in his veneration of the law, disagreed with such methods. He was in complete agreement, however, with the purpose itself.

". . . the preservation of our soil, and of our forests, the securing from private appropriation the power in navigable streams, the retention of the undisposed-of coal lands of the government from alienation, all will properly claim from the next administration earnest attention and appropriate legislation," Taft said in his acceptance speech in July, 1908.[18]

—3—

As president, he was faithful to his pledge. A troubled observer of the Ballinger controversy was Senator Newlands who, as an ardent champion of conservation, saw in it the possibility of a setback to the cause itself. In January, 1910, Newlands addressed his colleagues of the Senate on the question. He had been sorry that President Taft had not seen fit to retain Secretary of the Interior Garfield in his Cabinet, he said. But in the row in progress, he insisted, conservation was not an issue:

. . . we find that both sides have practically agreed as to the legislation which should be put upon the statute books. There is no real difference of opinion between those who believe with Mr. Ballinger and those who believe with Mr. Pinchot regarding the legislation which should be enacted as to the conservation of our natural resources. The difference which exists between them is as to the authority of law. Mr. Garfield . . . and Mr. Pinchot have both taken the view that the Executive Department, as the custodian of the great public domain, *can do anything that is necessary for the*

17 Roosevelt, Theodore, *op. cit.,* pp. 404-405. 18 *Addresses,* Vol. XI, pp. 98-99.

protection and conservation of that domain which is not forbidden by law. . . . I propose now to state the position of Mr. Ballinger—it is that in the protection and conservation of the public domain the Interior Department, or the Executive Department, *has only those powers expressly authorized by law.* As I remarked, before, all difference of opinion has practically disappeared as to what should be done with reference to the conservation of our natural resources, and the recommendations made by Mr. Ballinger *practically out-Pinchot the recommendations made by Mr. Pinchot.*

Senator Newlands added that on all such issues as coal land retention or fraudulent entry of public lands and its prevention, the views of Theodore Roosevelt were his too. He was confident that President Taft subscribed to them, also, and had put them into practice. He closed his speech with the assertion that he had been able to find "no trace of opposition to the conservation policy" in the secretary of the interior. On the contrary, Ballinger had vigorously rejected the theory that the public which owned the lands, was "legitimate prey for the unscrupulous." [19]

But Taft never imagined that the retention of Garfield was a vital part of the conservation program or that accusations of faithlessness to the cause would follow his rejection. Taft protested, as he was drawing up his own board of advisers in December, 1908, that his relations with all of Roosevelt's official family had been pleasant and that he felt particularly cordial toward "Jim Garfield, who is from my state." [20] But one reason he did not retain Garfield was because he believed his conservation policies had been, in certain aspects, illegal.[21] Political considerations played a part, but only a minor one, in the selection of Richard Achilles Ballinger for Garfield's place. It was important, Taft felt, for both the West and the South to be represented in his Cabinet. Ballinger, from Seattle, "would make an excellent Cabinet officer and would satisfy the west coast." [22] The President-elect had every possible reason to suppose, on the other hand, that Ballinger would energetically and faithfully carry on the Roosevelt program. He had, in fact, been appointed commissioner of the Land Office by President Roosevelt

[19] Darling, A. B., *The Public Papers of Francis G. Newlands,* Vol. I, pp. 112-113, 120-121. [20] Taft to Knox, Dec. 23, 1908. [21] Taft to Hulbert Taft, May 12, 1909. [22] Taft to Knox, Dec. 23, 1908.

in March, 1907, and had served, at personal sacrifice, for a year. Then, at his own request, he returned to his law practice. John Hays Hammond was delegated to see Ballinger late in 1908 and convey the President-elect's desire that he enter the Cabinet. At first the attorney said that he could not do so because of his limited means. Henry W. Taft was then pressed into service as an emissary. He overcame Ballinger's objections and soon the appointment was announced.[23] The selection met with general approval. The President-elect ignored a note of warning which reached him in January from Elbert F. Baldwin, an associate editor of the *Outlook:*

"I thought you might be interested in a comment made by Gifford Pinchot to me the other day concerning Dick Ballinger: 'I couldn't work with him as I have with Jim [Garfield]. Jim and I think alike concerning the matters in which the Forest Service and the Department of the Interior are closely related. Ballinger and I might clash.' " [24]

If this had any effect, it must have been to cement the President-elect's belief that he had chosen the right man. Taft respected the work Pinchot had done, but he had small respect for Pinchot himself. At about the same time a suggestion was made that the chief forester should be consulted regarding some legal appointment. Taft declined, and implied that Pinchot's advice would have some emotional basis.

"Gifford Pinchot . . ." he answered, "is quite likely to get some transcendentalist who hasn't any knowledge of the law, but who has commended himself in some way, because of some particular view that he has on a matter of sociology or political economy, either to Pinchot or the President." [25]

Taft had observed, when he was secretary of war, this lamentable tendency of Garfield and Pinchot to hold the law lightly. He had even protested to Roosevelt about it. One incident was typical. Pinchot had authority to license the passage of electric-power transmission lines through the national forests. This was purely a safety measure, to guard against fires. But Pinchot started to use his power as a club to force the companies to charge what he considered proper rates. If they did not do so, they were refused licenses. Roosevelt

[23] Hammond, J. H., *op. cit.,* Vol. II, pp. 542-543. [24] E. F. Baldwin to Taft, Jan. 13, 1909. [25] Taft to C. R. Edwards, Dec. 28, 1908.

took no action, however, and the question came up when Taft took office. The President immediately obtained an adverse ruling from Attorney General Wickersham, and Pinchot was instructed to abandon the practice.[26] Outer cordiality undoubtedly covered, early in 1909, a growing distrust and suspicion between the President and his emotional conservation expert.

"I do regard Gifford as a good deal of a radical and a good deal of a crank," the President admitted, "but I am glad to have him in the government."[27] He added:

It is not impossible, of course, after such an administration as Roosevelt's, and after the change of method that I could not but adopt in view of my different way of looking at things, that questions should arise as to whether I was going back on the principles of the Roosevelt administration. . . . We have a government of limited power under the Constitution, and we have got to work out our problems on the basis of law. Now, if that is reactionary, then I am a reactionary. I get very impatient at criticism by men who do not know what the law is, who have not looked it up and yet ascribe all sorts of motives to those who live within it. . . . Pinchot is not a lawyer and I am afraid he is quite willing to camp outside the law to accomplish his beneficent purposes. I have told him so to his face. . . . I do not undervalue the great benefit that he has worked out, but I do find it necessary to look into the legality of his plans.[28]

This was the issue which led to the inescapable conflict between Taft and Roosevelt. Conservation was merely the first important subject to which the basic disagreement applied. Yet Taft did not believe in a weak central government or fail to realize that changing conditions brought new problems which could not be handled by the states alone. Conservation, he said in December, 1908, "is going to put us to a new test of the practical character of our system of government." The Supreme Court, he felt, could be counted upon so to construe the Constitution "as to give the government of the United States power to carry out . . . those reforms that are necessary as the needs of our civilization advance."[29] But President Taft

[26] George W. Wickersham to author, Jan. 23, 1935. [27] Taft to Horace D. Taft, June 6, 1909. [28] Taft to William Kent, June 29, 1909. [29] *War Secretary Diaries*, pp. 4014, 4019.

would not act unless he was certain the law was on his side. Where Roosevelt's executives had done so, he nullified their actions.

The alarm of the conservationists, no less acute because it was really unjustified, began in March, 1909, and its basis was an erroneous belief that Taft and Ballinger were turning back into private hands certain lands which were valuable because of their water-power potentialities. During 1908 and the closing weeks of his administration, President Roosevelt had withdrawn from settlement large areas bordering rivers and streams in the Rocky Mountains and in the Pacific Coast states. Protest had been immediate. Included among the lands withdrawn were a good many thousand acres more or less suitable for farming. In any event, people were living on them. Secretary of the Interior Ballinger therefore ordered the restoration of all the lands withdrawn, but instructed the Geological Survey to investigate all the water-power sites so that these could be preserved for the future.[30]

The President fully endorsed Ballinger's course. Garfield, he said, had withdrawn the lands illegally. His action, it was true, had kept from occupation under the general homestead laws "a great amount of land which would be valuable near streams." But Taft felt that "it is more in accordance with the law and safer for me to find out through the Geological Survey the places where there are valuable power sites and then . . . set them aside out of harm's way." [31] The presidential temper was strained when this action was declared to be in violation of the conservation creed:

One of the propositions that I adhere to is that it is a very dangerous method of upholding reform to violate the law in so doing; *even on the ground of high moral principle,* or of saving the public. Congress has the power to dispose of lands; not the executive. It is the business of the executive to protect the public lands within the limitation of his authority. The power of the President to withdraw land appropriated to popular settlement by act of Congress is exceedingly limited under the decision of the courts. This power, I do not hesitate to say, was exercised far beyond legal limitation under Secretary Garfield—and, more than that, unnecessarily so.[32]

[30] Hibbard, B. H., *A History of the Public Lands*, p. 508. [31] Taft to Hulbert Taft, May 12, 1909. [32] Taft to William Kent, June 29, 1909. (Italics mine.)

Taft's policy, in contrast, was to accumulate reliable information and then obtain congressional authority for what was to be done. He told his secretary of the interior that the reclamation advocates, in their enthusiasm, would almost certainly lead the government "into enterprises . . . in advance of the possibility of profitable return. All I can say to you is that you must put the brakes down until Congress shall meet." [33] To this course the President held stubbornly. The United States Geological Survey busied itself with careful studies of actual or potential water-power lands. Congress acted in June, 1910. During the next two years, the President reserved all acreages demonstrated to be of value for the generations ahead.[34] On April 28, 1910, George Otis Smith, director of the Geological Survey testified before the Congressional committee regarding the attitude of Secretary Ballinger on conservation. Mr. Smith's devotion to preservation of the nation's resources was, like that of Senator Newlands, so steadfast and intelligent that it could not be impugned. But was it not true, they asked him, that Ballinger was not sincere? Had not Gifford Pinchot warned him during July that Ballinger, in his declarations of devotion to conservation, was attempting to deceive him? Smith agreed that the forester had thus cautioned him.

"The only reply that I could make to that," he said, "was that if Secretary Ballinger or any other secretary of the interior wished to withdraw coal and phosphate lands and power sites, and to approve our recommendation for higher valuation of the public coal lands, and in general, to support every recommendation of the survey with regard to survey work, and to do this simply for the purpose of fooling me, I would consider myself honored by such action." [35]

A decade passed. Wilson became president and went out of office. In March, 1921, Richard Ballinger received a letter from Alexander Vogelsang, who had been assistant secretary of the interior in the Wilson administration. Vogelsang wrote Ballinger that he had assumed office "with a very adverse opinion of yourself . . . based upon the public trials." However:

[33] Taft to Ballinger, Aug. 10, 1909. [34] Hibbard, B. H., op. cit., pp. 507-510. [35] Sen. Doc. 719, p. 3431.

Before my retirement I feel it due to myself to say that my experience here and the study and investigation I have made convince me that my impressions and my opinion were entirely wrong and unjust to you; that I now believe that you were an able administrator and as honest in impulse and action as any man who has ever held the office of secretary of the interior; and that in the history of the Republic the highwater mark of cruelty and injustice to a public officer was reached in the treatment accorded to you.[36]

—4—

But Taft's strict construction of the executive power, his disapproval of Garfield's and Pinchot's methods and, by inference, his disapproval of Roosevelt's as well— have no direct connection with the Alaska coal lands or the allegations of fraud which so seriously handicapped the administration. The Alaska controversy grew out of the problem of coal. By 1905 it had dawned on the people that they had been slowly robbed of the "black diamonds"— thus they were glowingly called, then, for the industrial use of petroleum had barely started— which lay under the jagged hills of the public domain. Shrewd men had sent their geologists out stealthily to investigate the possibility that coal might be found on some of the lands thrown open by a too-generous Uncle Sam for agriculture and homesteading. When the evidence was affirmative, they had often made application for the lands under the pretense that they were to be used for farming. Fortunes were thus fraudulently accumulated. Even worse, the deposits were mined with a shocking disregard for the future. Dire predictions were made— their inaccuracy was to be all too manifest after 1920— of a time in the near future when industrial America would come to a creaking halt because all of the black diamonds had been consumed.

To prevent this disaster, President Roosevelt during 1906 and 1907 withdrew from entry about 66,000,000 acres supposed to contain coal.[37] Very little of it, relatively speaking, had veins of commercial importance and much of the land was opened again to the

[36] Alexander Vogelsang to R. A. Ballinger, March 15, 1921. [37] Hibbard, B. H., *op. cit.*, pp. 473, 518-523.

homesteader. Of the total, 7,680,000 acres were in Alaska. The figures are large and deceptive. Less than one-tenth of this acreage actually contained workable coal. The portions under dispute were smaller still. But the public, in 1910, was still aroused over the diminishing supply of coal and was ready to listen when excited conservationists and careless journalists talked about billions of dollars being at stake. Little or no coal had ever come out of Alaska. An insignificant tonnage, in comparison with production in the United States, would be mined in the next quarter of a century. But gold had been found in the Klondike in 1896 and anything seemed possible in that remote and fantastic country.

The coal fields which became the subject of discussion were far off the railroad, inland from Seward and east of Cook Inlet in southern Alaska. Transportation would be an almost insuperable problem. A railroad had been started from Seward, but its promoters had gone into bankruptcy in 1907 after pushing about seventy miles toward the coal areas. The Matanuska beds lay somewhat west of the Katalla deposits. Both of these fields were declared to be the objective of the conspiracy which Ballinger was accused of assisting. The archconspirator was supposed to be Clarence Cunningham of Wallace, Idaho, who in October, 1902, had penetrated the desolate wastes of the Alaska coast. Between the Bering and Martin River glaciers he discovered coal deposits of which he had already heard. He agreed to pay $300 a claim to some squatters who actually had no legal title at all. Then he returned to Idaho with samples of the coal and started to interest his friends in what he fondly believed to be a great strike. Cunningham went back to the fields the following year and staked out thirty-three claims in all. He took them out for himself and on behalf of friends. He seems to have had no idea that within five years he would be portrayed as an opulent capitalist, comparable to the Guggenheims, and charged with attempting to steal the people's coal. In any event, whether he violated the law or not, he made no secret of what he had done. In fact, he bustled about among his acquaintances and tried to raise money with which to begin operations.

Cunningham was not familiar with the coal-land law. He supposed that coal mining was like any other prospecting. You staked your claim, filed the proper papers and were allowed to go ahead. But in 1904, Congress decreed that 160 acres was the maximum claim allowed any single coal prospector in the territory. A group of four or more persons could take up a total of 640 acres. It was specified that $10 an acre was to be paid for the land, that six months would intervene for the purpose of investigation and that then title would pass to the prospector. After that, he was free to sell the land or dispose of it in any other manner. But any plan to consolidate claims prior to six months, stated the act of 1904, was fraud. Cunningham prepared to obey this law. He returned to Alaska in the summer of 1904 and filed notices of location on thirty-three claims aggregating 5,280 acres. Less than three years later the Cunningham group paid $52,800 to the Treasury of the United States. Its leader supposed that the lands were owned by his associates and himself. Their development as coal areas was started. Technically, he was correct. Actually, Cunningham was already the subject of investigation by agents of the Interior Department and his good faith was being questioned. Meanwhile, the situation was further complicated in November, 1906, by Roosevelt's order withdrawing all Alaska coal lands from further acquisition. It was specifically stated that the ruling would not "impair any right acquired in good faith under the coal land laws existent at the date of such withdrawal." [38] So this ruling, assuming that the claims had been acquired "in good faith," did not affect the Cunningham 5,280 acres. It did, however, cloud the issue and it was the basis for further excitement when the whole tangle became a public matter.

Behind all the verbiage regarding conspiracies to mulct the public domain was a question which would have aroused no interest at all had it been clearly presented to the people. It was never so presented. This question, under the act of April 28, 1904, was whether Cunningham and his colleagues had effected an agreement to operate their 5,280 acres as a unit for their common good *prior to* approval of their claims by the United States Land Office at Juneau, Alaska. Such an agreement did not have to wait upon the final award of patents by the Interior Department at Washington. If it had been entered into *after* approval at Juneau, no fraud attached to such an agreement. Cunningham could sell his claims to John

[38] Sen. Doc. 719, pp. 490-495.

D. Rockefeller or William Jennings Bryan or Louis Glavis or anybody else he chose. Thus, reduced to the simplicity it really merited,
the question was one of fact and not of law. When, if at all, did
Clarence Cunningham and his friends decide that their coal mines
could best be operated by forming a company? It was universally
agreed, incidentally, that Alaska coal could not profitably be mined
in units of 160 or even of 640 acres.

If Cunningham at any time attempted evasion, there is small
evidence of it in the voluminous record of the case. All that Glavis
could find was a journal notation of 1903 in which plans for a stock
company were set forth. The Congressional committee decided
that this was merely a "hope" that such a company might be formed
and that it did not transgress the law.[39] Cunningham asked for
approval of his claims in July and August, 1904, at Juneau. In
October and November, 1905, H. K. Love, a land office agent stationed there, informed his Washington office that he was making a
routine investigation into their validity. On February 6, 1906,
Cunningham frankly told W. A. Richards, who was Ballinger's
predecessor as commissioner of the Land Office, what he proposed
to do with the 5,280 acres. He said that a large amount of money
had to be spent— among other things, a costly tunnel had to be
built— and asked whether it would be proper for his thirty-two
associates to form an organization whereby the benefits would be
jointly enjoyed. Richards answered merely that such an association
would be investigated. On August 2, 1907, Special Agent Love
reported a conversation with Cunningham. His claims, in the interim, had been approved at Juneau. Cunningham said it was now
his intention to form a company to which the separate holdings
would be transferred. In Love's opinion this was "allowable under
the law." [40]

Ballinger had become commissioner of the Land Office in
March, 1907, and thus was in general charge during these later
inquiries. They related, however, to 800 or 900 claims in Alaska.
While Love was looking into the Cunningham applications, specifically, Horace T. Jones, another special agent, was instructed to
examine the entire mass of tangled claims for the Alaska coal lands.
On August 10, 1907, Jones said that he had looked into 523 of the

[39] *Joint Committee Report,* p. 13. [40] Sen. Doc. 719, pp. 492-495.

petitions and that some of them had certainly been made under a misapprehension of the law. He suggested further investigation and said this was "particularly necessary" in regard to certain groups. But the Cunningham group was not one of those he named. On August 13, 1907, however, Jones brought the menacing name of Guggenheim into the situation with a suggestion that conversation with attorneys had led him to believe "that the disposal of the lands all tends toward one direction, and that is, the Guggenheim companies." [41]

It was this possibility which seems to have caught the suspicious eye of Louis Russell Glavis in the spring and summer of 1907— at a time when he was engaged in other investigations on the Pacific coast and had no connection with Alaska coal matters. Glavis was an exceedingly young man in 1907, only twenty-four years old, and he had for three years been a skilled and vigorous special agent in the General Land Office. The supposed Alaska land conspiracy was a subject of discussion in the newspapers of Seattle at this time. Glavis heard further details when Special Agent Jones called on him in that city. Toward the end of the year, Glavis concluded that the truth would best be served if the Alaska matters were transferred from the other agents into his own hands. He suggested this to H. H. Schwartz, chief of the field work and his immediate superior, on November 22, 1907. He was instructed to report in Washington a few days later and there, according to his subsequent testimony, he discussed the coal lands in general and the Cunningham claims in particular. Thereupon he was ordered to take charge of the investigation.[42]

At this point the complicated story, as unfolded before the joint committee, becomes cloudy with contradictions. Secretary Ballinger swore that Glavis had never declared, while in Washington, that all the claims were fraudulent. Glavis insisted he did so. In any event, the secretary of the interior assigned the further inquiry to his most suspicious and hostile subordinate; this, at the least, would seem to indicate honesty of intention and a willingness

[41] *Ibid.*, pp. 496-598. [42] *Ibid.*, pp. 6, 501.

488   THE LIFE AND TIMES OF WILLIAM HOWARD TAFT

to have corruption, if such existed, brought to light. But Ballinger, it is quite clear, did not believe the Cunningham group dishonest and neither did anyone else in the Interior Department. It was, all in all, a routine matter of no outstanding importance. Glavis, having been authorized to go ahead, returned to his home office at Portland, Oregon. He had been gone for but a few days when Miles C. Moore, one of the Cunningham claimants, arrived at the capital to ask for some action. The reports of Love and the other agents were studied by Ballinger and his subordinates. They agreed, after discussion, that the thirty-three Cunningham petitions were legal. Word was telegraphed to Glavis— additional evidence of high integrity on Ballinger's part— that final approval was to be given to the Cunningham group. This gave him an opportunity to protest.[43]

Glavis did so on January 22, 1908. Ballinger immediately consulted Secretary of the Interior Garfield and on the same day rescinded the order approving the claims.[44] They remained in that status for over a year, while the Cunningham group wondered whether value would ever be received for the $52,800 paid over to the United States. On March 4, 1908, Ballinger resigned as land commissioner to replenish his income, diminished by working for the government. From this point the matter dragged. Glavis worked on the Cunningham and other matters during the spring and early summer. In July, Glavis went to Alaska but did not visit the coal fields which, so he ultimately contended, were the subject of a Cunningham-Guggenheim plot.[45] This, of course, was the year of the presidential campaign. In due time, Ballinger became secretary of the interior in Taft's Cabinet. He had been in office for only a few days when a committee from the American Mining Congress asked that some action be taken on these long-delayed Alaska matters. So Glavis was instructed to send in without further delay his conclusions regarding the Cunningham and the other claims. But the agent again protested that further work was necessary. He said a field investigation was essential, although he had been in Alaska the previous summer and had not gone near the disputed areas. His superiors in Washington began to grow weary.

"Glavis has these coal cases on the brain" was the conclusion, in

43 *Joint Committee Report*, p. 15. 44 *Ibid.*, p. 27. 45 *Ibid.*

July, 1909, of Fred Dennett who had become commissioner of the General Land Office, "and he cannot see anything but just one line."[46]

That line was the probability of corruption. Things were to move faster after May, 1909. On May 17, Glavis was again in Washington and outlined his views to Ballinger. The secretary of the interior said he would get a ruling on the matter and assigned the subject to Frank Pierce, assistant secretary of the interior, who said that in his judgment no evidence of fraud existed.[47] Glavis wrote in *Collier's Weekly:*

> I was then in a very difficult position. I knew what the law was, and my superiors were against me. . . . Without consulting with my superiors, I went to Attorney General Wickersham and stated the matter to him. I understand that he asked Mr. Ballinger to refer the matter to him. . . . Ten days later, the Attorney General delivered an opinion on the subject. . . . it upheld my contention, and saved the Alaska coal cases.[48]

This was less than an entirely accurate interpretation of the Pierce and Wickersham legal rulings. Moore and the other Cunningham claimants were increasingly bitter over the fact that nothing was done, either for or against their claims. On June 29, 1909, Assistant Interior Secretary Pierce decided that justice required a prompt adjudication of the charges preferred by Glavis against Cunningham and his associates. But Glavis, who had returned to the coast, wired that "valuable evidence" was still being secured. He needed at least an additional sixty days. Schwartz, his superior, had now become convinced that Glavis was "overcautious . . . was simply jockeying," so he refused the request. The proposed action, this time, was not to validate the claims but merely to bring them to trial.[49]

Glavis made a final appeal. Secretary Ballinger was in Seattle, so the agent called on his chief on July 16, 1909, and said he was being forced into a hearing when he could offer a much stronger case if allowed additional time. Ballinger suggested that his reasons be stated in a telegram to Washington and that he would be allowed

---

[46] Sen. Doc. 719, pp. 192-199, 289. [47] *Ibid.*, pp. 533, 240-241. [48] *Collier's Weekly,* Nov. 13, 1909. [49] Sen. Doc. 719, pp. 541-543.

delay if it was really necessary. Again, it was granted. But Glavis, too, was growing impatient. He had also become exceedingly suspicious of the honesty of the Interior Department officials.[50] On this same day, July 16, he telegraphed A. C. Shaw, law officer of the Forest Service, that the Cunningham claims lay in the boundaries of the Chugach forest reserve in Alaska, that the property was "valued at millions," that they were in danger and that he needed the assistance of the department of which Gifford Pinchot was the head. So Shaw started to look into the matter.

Thus the matter came officially to the attention of the leading conservation enthusiast and a scandal of the first order was brewing. On August 2, the Forest Service officials were informed by Glavis that he had "damaging and conclusive evidence" showing "official misconduct" of Secretary Ballinger and Land Commissioner Dennett.[51]

---

[50] *Collier's Weekly*, pp. 543-544. [51] O. W. Price and A. C. Shaw to Pinchot, Jan 5, 1910.

CHAPTER XXVII

MY DEAR GIFFORD . . .

MY DEAR Gifford . . . I urge that you do not make Glavis's cause yours," the President begged in September, 1909. ". . . I write this letter in order to prevent hasty action on your part in taking up Glavis's cause, or in objecting to my sustaining Ballinger and his subordinates within the Interior Department, as a reason for your withdrawing from the public service. I should consider it one of the greatest losses that my administration could sustain if you were to leave it." [1]

This was sincere enough, but President Taft realized, too, the political dangers of a break with the chief of the United States Forest Service. Besides, he was sincerely behind Pinchot's conservation program and willingly conceded that he was its leading proponent. The accusations of Louis Glavis could undoubtedly be handled. This was particularly true because, Taft was utterly convinced, fraud had not marked the proposed development of the Alaska coal lands. But for Pinchot to sponsor the accusations was an entirely different matter. For him to resign in protest would be to brand the administration as opposed to conservation. Even more grave was the certainty that it would be regarded by the voters as the first definite break with Theodore Roosevelt.

By September, however, it was too late. The chief forester had already leaped into the thick of the fight and the President, who suspected that it was too late, pondered the reason for his doing so. Certain of Pinchot's views, of course, were "of a lunar character," Taft thought.[2] But the cause was deeper than that. The President's mind went back to the days when he had been secretary of war. Roosevelt had admitted, he said, that Pinchot was a "fanatic" but "he gave him great scope and introduced a lack of discipline into the Interior and Agricultural departments. . . . Pinchot was known

[1] Taft to Pinchot, Sept. 13, 1909. [2] Taft to Francis G. Newlands, Sept. 9, 1909.

to be the power behind the throne." [3] Pinchot's failing, continued Taft, "has been an inability to credit high and honorable motives to those who differ with him as to his method . . . when he is pursuing a worthy object with all the enthusiasm of his nature." [4] The more Taft thought about it, the more doubtful he became that it would be possible to work in harmony:

> I am convinced that Pinchot with his fanaticism and his disappointment at my decision in the Ballinger case plans a coup by which I shall be compelled to dismiss him and he will be able to make out a martyrdom and try to raise opposition to me on Ballinger's account. I am afraid that he has a good deal of the guile attributed to the Jesuits in his nature. . . . His trouble is that . . . he seizes shreds of evidence as conviction stronger than the Holy Writ.

The most unhappy aspect of the whole unpleasant situation was that Taft's mind, whether he was aware of it or not, was being slowly converted to a conviction that Theodore Roosevelt had, after all, been less than a perfect president of the United States. Already, with but seven months gone of his administration, he was convinced that his predecessor had made serious mistakes. Never again would the two men be as close as they had been before. Taft insisted that he liked Pinchot, but the chief forester "and Roosevelt sympathized much more than he and I can, for they both have more of a Socialist tendency. . . .

"The truth is," he added, "the whole administration under Roosevelt was demoralized by his system of dealing directly with subordinates. It was obviated in the State Department and the War Department, under Root and me, because we simply ignored the interference and went on as we chose. . . . The subordinate gained nothing by his assumption of authority, but it was not so in the other departments." [5]

Pinchot had injected himself in the Alaska coal matter, although unofficially, in early August, 1909. He was in Washington on August 2 when his legal aide, A. C. Shaw, was informed by wire that Glavis had gathered evidence relating to the Chugach Na-

---

[3] Taft to Horace D. Taft, Sept. 6, 1909. [4] Taft to Ballinger, Sept. 13, 1909. [5] Taft to Helen H. Taft, Oct. 3, 1909.

tional Forest in Alaska and that this involved Ballinger and Land Commissioner Dennett. He was shown the telegram. He left immediately to attend a conservation convention at Spokane and was not, it would appear, in active touch with the assistance given by Shaw to Glavis.[6] Behind the situation lay Pinchot's distrust of Ballinger. This had flared up during minor departmental matters from time to time. He told George Otis Smith of the United States Geological Survey in July that the new secretary of the interior had reversed the policies of former Secretary Garfield. This was contemptible, he added, and he then referred to Ballinger, said Smith in his testimony before the joint committee, as a "yellow dog."

Friction between Ballinger and Pinchot was manifest again at the Spokane gathering.[7] On February 26, 1910, the chief forester was called as a witness by the Congressional investigating committee and declared that Ballinger was "an enemy of the policy of conservation," that he had been unfaithful to his trust as a servant of the people and as the "guardian of public property of enormous value." Pinchot admitted that he had been consulting with former Secretary Garfield in the matter. Garfield, Glavis and he, Pinchot said, were the sincere friends of conservation and Ballinger was an obstacle in the path of their cause.[8]

On August 5, 1909, during the sessions of the conservation convention, Pinchot and Glavis conferred at Spokane. Glavis outlined the evidence he had accumulated in the Cunningham coal cases and expressed an intention of making it public. Pinchot suggested, however, that he call on President Taft, instead, and that he go east at once for this purpose. Shaw, meanwhile, was also in Spokane and assisted Glavis in preparing his facts for Taft's eyes. It may be assumed that until now the President knew little about the Alaska coal claims, Glavis, Cunningham or the other individuals involved. But he was aware of the deep antagonism between Pinchot and his secretary of the interior.

"I am sorry about this Pinchot-Ballinger business," he wrote that month. "I think they misunderstand each other. But if they go on hitting each other I shall have to decide something between them. . . . I shall have to knock some heads together when I get back to

[6] A. C. Shaw and O. W. Price to Pinchot, Jan. 5, 1910. [7] *Joint Committee Report*, pp. 79, 73; Sen. Doc. 719, pp. 1143-1144, 1320-1321. [8] *Ibid.*, p. 1414.

Washington, after my trip. There is too much of a disposition to charge people with bad faith, and to give encouragement to newspaper controversy." [9]

—2—

The trip was the 13,000 mile tour on which Taft hoped to convince the nation that the Payne-Aldrich act was honest downward revision. Already weary from the March to August special session of Congress, the President was attempting to find time to write some speeches when Glavis, loaded with documents and accusations, arrived out of the West. The President seems to have regarded the situation too lightly. The issue between Pinchot and Ballinger, he said, was not serious and "when the whole matter is investigated they will be seen working for the same end. . . .

"I think I can clean up the whole matter when I get back to Washington," he wrote.[10]

Glavis called at Beverly, Massachusetts, on August 18 and was received by the President. Attorney General Wickersham, also yearning for a vacation, chanced to be in the vicinity. He was familiar, in a general way, with the charges and now received from the President all the documents and exhibits offered by Glavis. Two or three days later, Taft conferred with his attorney general, Secretary of the Treasury MacVeagh and Secretary of the Navy Meyer. They went over the evidence and agreed, as Taft subsequently explained, that jealousy between bureaus of the Interior Department and the Forestry Service was behind the quarrel.[11]

None the less, Taft transmitted certain of the papers to Ballinger and to the other officials named by Glavis and asked for a statement which would be "as full as possible." [12] The secretary of the interior reached Beverly from Seattle on September 6; that evening the charges were discussed. On the following night, Taft "sat up until three o'clock . . . reading the answers [from the accused officials] and the exhibits; so that at my next conference I was advised of the contents of the entire record and had made up

[9] Taft to E. F. Baldwin, Aug. 13, 1909. [10] Taft to I. E. Bennett, Aug. 27, 1909; to L. F. Abbott, Aug. 31, 1909. [11] Taft to Ballinger, Aug. 22, 1909. [12] Taft to Ballinger et al., Aug. 21, 22, 1909.

my mind that there was nothing in the charges upon which Mr. Ballinger or the others . . . could be found guilty of either incompetency, inefficiency, disloyalty to the interests of the government or dishonesty. . . ." But the President studied the case further during the next three days. On September 11 he discussed it at length with Mr. Wickersham and on Sunday morning, September 12, he did so again. That night, having taken the papers away with him, the attorney general again conferred with the President. He drafted a report, the famous "predated" document of September 11, 1909, which was later brought to light and magnified into a major scandal. On the strength of Wickersham's views and his own study, Taft prepared a lengthy exoneration of his Cabinet member.[13]

Glavis's report, the President assured Ballinger on September 13, "does not formulate his charges against you and the others, but by insinuation and innuendo as well as by direct averment, he does charge that each one of you while a public officer has taken steps to aid the Cunningham claimants to secure patents based on claims that you know or have reason to believe to be fraudulent and unlawful." Taft then said that "the case attempted to be made by Mr. Glavis embraces only shreds of suspicion without any substantial evidence to sustain his attack. The whole record shows that Mr. Glavis was honestly convinced of the illegal character of the claims in the Cunningham group"; it also revealed, however, that Glavis had procrastinated in preparing the evidence on which to bring the claims to trial and that justice required more speedy action. The agent, said the President, had not submitted all the evidence in making his contentions. There was "no doubt that in his zeal to convict yourself, Assistant Secretary Pierce, Commissioner Dennett and Mr. Schwartz, he did not give me the benefit of information which he had that would have thrown light on the transactions, showing them to be consistent with an impartial attitude on your part toward the claims in question." The accusations were nullified by the fact that Glavis was allowed "during all the years of the pendency of these claims, to remain in charge of them as an agent of the department, when it would have been entirely easy . . . to remove him . . . and thus take the claims out of his jurisdiction."

The President also took occasion to refute the contention that

13 Taft to Knute Nelson, May 15, 1910.

Ballinger had turned back into private hands valuable water-power sites.

". . . it is learned," he said, "that under the withdrawals made by your department from time to time . . . there are now withheld from settlement awaiting the action of Congress, fifty per cent more water-power sites than under previous withdrawals, and that this has been effected by a withdrawal from settlement of only one-fifth of the amount of land."

As for the zealous, if inaccurate, Glavis: the President concurred in Ballinger's suggestion that he be discharged "from the service of the United States for disloyalty to his superior officers in making a false charge against them . . ."

When a subordinate in a government bureau or department has trustworthy evidence upon which to believe that his chief is dishonest . . . it is of course his duty to submit that evidence to higher authority than his chief. But when he makes a charge against his chief founded upon mere suspicions, and in his statement he fails to give his chief the benefit of circumstances within his knowledge that would explain his chief's action on proper grounds, he makes it impossible for him to continue in the service of the government.[14]

On the day following the dictation of this exoneration, the President entrained for the West. He hoped, but was far from certain, that this was the end of the altercation. It was not in his nature to create the impression, for political reasons, that he had not meant every word of his endorsement of Ballinger. When he reached Spokane he expressed gratitude to the State of Washington "for giving me such a competent official." He was glad, Taft said, "to testify to his efficiency and integrity." [15]

—3—

But back in the East, as the President thus reiterated his faith, machinery was grinding which would bring the Ballinger-Pinchot affair before the public with added emphasis. An able propaganda machine, which was part of the Forest Service, was disseminating

14 Taft to Ballinger, Sept. 13, 1909. 15 Ballinger to H. W. Mabie, Oct. 4, 1909.

to the newspapers portions of the material contained in Glavis's charges. This was done by A. C. Shaw, the departmental lawyer, and by Overton W. Price, a second Pinchot aide. They gave information to the correspondents and also to representatives of national magazines. Shaw assisted Glavis in assembling his material for publication in *Collier's Weekly*.[16]

Among other periodicals, *Collier's* had been criticizing the administration of the Interior Department and had been giving credence to the rumors of corruption. On September 29, 1909, Attorney General Wickersham encountered Norman Hapgood, the weekly's editor, on the street in New York and described the meeting to the President. Mr. Wickersham explained that he had known Hapgood "since he was a boy." The previous week, he added, a "very nasty editorial" relating to Ballinger had been published. Hapgood stopped the attorney general and began to discuss the case:

He asked me whether I had personally examined the record. I told him that I had read every line . . . and that I thought he had done Mr. Ballinger a very grave injustice. . . . He told me that the Glavis charges were being very carefully worked up by some people whom he was not at liberty to identify; that the matter was by no means dead . . . that . . . he felt that you had been misled and that there was much more in Secretary Ballinger's connection with the people interested in Alaska coal lands and in other lands, than appeared on the surface.

Attorney General Wickersham thereupon protested "very vigorously" and gave Hapgood "an outline of the real facts, after which he expressed great regret that it was too late to stop another editorial which he had written and which had gone to press . . . but he said that, before going into what he called 'the larger question,' he would look very carefully into the material which was furnished to them and would come and talk with me." There was no doubt in Wickersham's mind, as a result of this conversation, "that a campaign against Secretary Ballinger is being prepared by someone, and that the subject will be exploited first in the press and then in

16 A. C. Shaw and O. W. Price to Pinchot, Jan. 5, 1910.

Congress. . . . I am quite sure that much is going to be made of the subject by those unfriendly to the administration." [17]

Hapgood did not, however, abandon the attack. Shortly after the conversation with the attorney general, Glavis was brought to the editor's office by a journalist, John Bass.

"As Secretary Ballinger, Attorney General Wickersham, and President Taft have all turned down Glavis's report on the stealing of the public domain," Bass said, after presenting the youthful agent, "we have decided to go straight to the public."

He said that Glavis had written a version of his report to Taft. Another magazine had offered $3,000 for it, but Glavis was unwilling to benefit financially and would permit publication in *Collier's Weekly* on the stipulation that there should be no fee. Hapgood remembered that he "read the article that night and accepted it the next day." [18] In other words, Glavis's version was accepted without examination of the documents on which it was based. It was published in the issue of November 13, 1909. Subsequently, on the stand, Glavis disclaimed any intention of attributing corrupt motives to Ballinger or the other Interior Department officials involved. But there were accusations enough in the article. It was the article, not the subsequent testimony, which stirred public excitement and damaged Taft. It is fair, then, to examine the accuracy of the Glavis attack on the basis of the contents of the November 13, 1909, issue of *Collier's Weekly*. Glavis wrote:

1. The coal lands of Alaska constituted "the future coal supply of the nation, of almost inestimable value."
2. Of the 900 claims to Alaska coal lands— among them were the thirty-three Cunningham claims— "the majority are fraudulent."
3. The Land Office of the Interior Department ordered the Cunningham claims approved "without due investigation when Commissioner Ballinger [this was when he was commissioner of the Land Office] knew that they were under suspicion."
4. While holding the post of land commissioner, Ballinger "urged Congress to pass a law which would validate fraudulent Alaska claims."

---

[17] Wickersham to Taft, Sept. 30, 1909. [18] Hapgood, Norman, *The Changing Years, Reminiscences of Norman Hapgood*, pp. 182-183.

5. Shortly after resigning from office, Ballinger "became attorney for the Cunningham group and other Alaska claims."

6. Soon after Ballinger became secretary of the interior, "his office rendered a decision which would have validated all fraudulent Alaska claims. A reversal of that decision on every point was obtained from Attorney General Wickersham."

7. In May, 1908, by order of Acting Land Commissioner Dennett, Glavis was "taken off the Alaska case . . . and ordered on other work." [19]

The first specification by Glavis was a perfectly proper conviction that the Alaska deposits were valuable; that it proved, in the light of expert examination, to be a gross exaggeration does not diminish his right to believe it in 1909 or his sincerity in making the statement. The second specification is nowhere proved in any of the documents. Unquestionably, certain of the claims were fraudulent. As to the Cunningham claims, the evidence of fraud is far from conclusive.[20] Glavis's third specification is contradicted by the evidence. It is invalidated by Ballinger's willingness to notify Glavis that approval was pending. It is further invalidated, as the President pointed out, by the fact that he was allowed to continue in charge of the investigation and that approval was postponed after he had protested in January, 1908.[21]

The fourth specification was grossly unfair to Ballinger. The law to which Glavis referred was the act of May 28, 1908, which provided that individuals who had "in good faith" made locations of coal land in Alaska prior to the withdrawal order of November 12, 1906, would be allowed to consolidate their claims up to 2,560 acres. This could be done through a corporation if the claimants chose.[22] This law was an attempt to end the ridiculous limitation whereby an individual or a group could own only from 160 to 640 acres. Secretary of the Interior Garfield, whose character as a conservationist was universally called spotless, recommended strongly in his 1907 report that this be changed. In fields "containing the highest grade of coal," Mr. Garfield said, "it would be possible to develop a mine profitably on this small acreage, but in the very great majority of instances a much larger acreage is necessary. . . . The coal

[19] *Collier's Weekly*, Nov. 13, 1909. [20] See Chapter XXVI, pp. 487-489. [21] See Chapter XXVI, p. 488. [22] *Joint Committee Report*, p. 9.

remaining in the public domain should be so used as to induce its development in accordance with the needs of the country. . . . In order to accomplish these purposes the man *or the corporation* producing the coal must be given an area sufficiently large to warrant the expenditure of the money necessary to profitably [*sic*] develop and market the coal." Even President Roosevelt, the patron saint of the conservationists, called the limitations "absurd, excessive"; he said they "served no useful purpose and often render it necessary that there should be either fraud or else abandonment of the work of getting out the coal."

"The regulations," said President Roosevelt, "should permit coal lands to be worked in sufficient quantity by *the several corporations.*" [23]

More than this, Secretary Garfield admitted that the proposed curative legislation would probably legalize many claims filed in accordance with the immemorial practice of attempting to evade the 160 to 640 acre limitation. But even where the "culpability of such evasion is admitted . . . ," he wrote in a memorandum while Congress debated the law, "if those under charge of wrongful action should be willing to take their land with the very considerable penalty of assuming all the burdens and restrictions of the new law, it would seem proper to confirm" their right up to 2,560 acres.[24] This, with unimportant technical amendments, was the law ultimately approved by Congress. Garfield had urged its passage. Glavis's specification that Ballinger had "urged Congress to pass a law which would validate fraudulent claims" was, by its inference if not by its facts, a mendacious charge. Ballinger was following in the path of Roosevelt and Garfield.

But this charge, naturally judged by the public in connection with Glavis's fifth specification, was damning. Among all the accusations hurled against the too-simple Ballinger, the most serious was that he had acted as attorney for Clarence Cunningham and other coal promoters in the interval between resigning as land commissioner and his elevation, in March, 1909, to Taft's Cabinet. It was the most damaging because a categorical denial could not be made. A fee of $250 which he received from the Cunningham claimants was undoubtedly among the most costly ever accepted

---

[23] Sen. Doc. 719, pp. 510-513. (Italics mine.)   [24] *Ibid.*, p. 514.

Photo by Leonard O. Philbrick

SENATOR HENRY CABOT LODGE AND PRESIDENT TAFT

See page 430]

Photo by Harris & Ewing

THE FIRST LADY

[*See page 443*

by an honest lawyer. Ballinger's assertions that there was nothing improper about the fee were, although true, completely futile.

"I deny," testified Ballinger before the Congressional committee, "that I was retained as 'legal representative' for the Cunningham group and that I represented such claimants until I became secretary." [25]

A year passed between the time of Ballinger's resignation from the General Land Office and his appointment as secretary of the interior. On September 4, 1908, he drafted an affidavit for Cunningham in which the legality of the coal claims was set forth. This represented Cunningham's, not Ballinger's, views on the situation. At various times during that summer, Ballinger testified, he had warned Cunningham and his associates that their petitions would not be granted unless they met all the specifications of the new act of May 28, 1908, particularly the limitations regarding monopolies in restraint of trade. But he consented to make a trip to West Mentor, Ohio, where Secretary of the Interior Garfield was on vacation, and advance the contentions of Cunningham. Garfield, however, insisted that the requirements of the law were applicable to the claims. Ballinger declined to press the matter, returned to Seattle and so informed Cunningham and his associate, Charles J. Smith. Even Garfield agreed, when called upon to give his version of the conference, that Ballinger "left with me the impression that it was in the nature of a casual matter of filing this affidavit with me for the persons he knew in Seattle, and was representing them in that casual way." [26] The fee of $250 hardly covered the expenses of the journey to Ohio.

President Taft, in upholding Ballinger, pointed out that as land commissioner he had acquired no knowledge of the claims "except that of the most formal character." This was true. The President pointed out, further, that from the day of Ballinger's incumbency as secretary of the interior, he had "studiously declined to have any connection whatever with the Cunningham claims, or to exercise any control over the course of the department in respect to those claims." [27] This, too, is overwhelmingly supported by the testimony. From March 5, 1909, on, Ballinger insisted that First

[25] Ibid., p. 509. [26] Ibid., pp. 509-510; Joint Committee Report, p. 26. [27] Taft to Ballinger, Sept. 13, 1909.

Assistant Secretary Pierce handle all aspects of the Cunningham claims.

"I cannot undertake to issue any order or make any ruling in the matter," Ballinger protested when the Cunningham claimants appealed to him for action in May, 1909, "because of the embarrassment which would result from the fact that I was, while not holding an official position, called upon to advise in the matter." [28]

The protests were, however, completely lost during the heated allegations that the secretary of the interior had been willing to deliver to former clients the fabulously rich coal deposits of the frozen north.

In his sixth major specification against the secretary of the interior, Glavis was confused. He did not understand the complicated land laws or the decisions which related to them. He wrote in *Collier's Weekly* that on May 19, 1909, Assistant Secretary of the Interior Pierce submitted an opinion on the Alaska coal lands which meant their loss "with no hope of recovery"; thereupon Glavis had gone to Attorney General Wickersham for a ruling. He contended that this "overruled the Pierce decision on every point, upheld my contention, and saved the Alaska coal lands." Wickersham, himself, demolished this contention in a lengthy memorandum dated— although not then written, as we shall see— September 11, 1909. The Pierce decision, he pointed out, did not relate to the Cunningham claims. This was proved by the fact that the letter submitting the question, which was drafted with the assistance of Glavis, referred to claims "in which payment had not been made and cash certificates had not been issued." The Cunningham group had, of course, deposited $52,800 with the Treasury of the United States and had received their certificates. Pierce was ruling on the other cases and their status under the law of May 28, 1908, which Roosevelt and Garfield had both favored. The assistant secretary wrote that this was a "curative act and should be liberally construed." This was precisely what Roosevelt and Garfield had desired. But the shadow on the Cunningham locations was whether, prior to payment and filing at Juneau, Alaska, an agreement had been made to create a corporation. The attorney general ruled on this

[28] Sen. Doc. 719, pp. 526, 534.

point. He said, in effect, that if such was the case they were fraudulent.[29]

The seventh specification by Glavis, that he had been "taken off the Alaska case" in May, 1908, was unfair. President Taft ordered Glavis discharged because, among other offenses, "he did not give me the benefit of information which he had" which would have cleared up this and other points.[30] Glavis, in *Collier's Weekly*, pointed out that the "reason given for this action was lack of funds" and the implication is clear that some other, more sinister, motive was really behind it. But such was, in fact, the reason. Glavis was notified by Land Commissioner Dennett— Ballinger was now out of office— on April 28, 1908, that the operation of the office required economies unless a sundry civil service bill, before the House of Representatives, became law. Meanwhile government suits regarding timber holdings in Oregon demanded immediate action. The Alaska coal cases were in a state of suspension and their status could not change. On May 2, Glavis was instructed by telegram to discontinue the coal investigation and to assign his agents "to Oregon matters." On May 28, however, Congress appropriated $500,000 for further work of the Land Office. Dennett immediately wired Glavis that the "limitation of April 28" was revoked.

"Push work," he ordered.[31]

This telegraphic license to go ahead was not included, according to Wickersham, in the documents and papers submitted to the President. It was not mentioned in *Collier's Weekly*. The attorney general told Taft that Glavis's reports "omit to a degree that amounts to suppression letters, telegrams, and other documents, some of which were in his possession, and others which were available to him . . . which completely rebut inferences he seeks to have drawn from those which he did submit." [32] Glavis's viewpoint was that of a prosecutor; he refrained from mentioning aspects of the situation which were to the credit of Ballinger and the other officials whom he was accusing of misconduct and betrayal of trust.

[29] *Ibid.*, pp. 535-536, 561-562. [30] Taft to Ballinger, Sept. 13, 1909. [31] Sen. Doc. 719, pp. 561-562. [32] *Ibid.*

—4—

Glavis was not primarily responsible for a further misunderstanding which poisoned the public mind. He mentioned only in passing the possibility that the Guggenheim interests had cast an avaricious eye on Alaska. "Are the Guggenheims in Charge of the Department of the Interior?"— the headline over Glavis's article in *Collier's Weekly*— was a gross distortion and untrue. Glavis, however, did not write it. Cunningham specifically denied that the Guggenheim syndicate was "directly or indirectly interested" in the coal lands; he said it had contributed no part of the $52,800 paid to the government for them. In substance this was the fact, but it was not quite true that a group of financiers usually called the Morgan-Guggenheim syndicate had no indirect connection with the Cunningham coal locations. Between 1903 and 1905 the syndicate acquired large copper interests in Alaska and started to construct a railroad from Katalla Bay for the purpose of developing the mines. This road would have tapped the Cunningham coal fields, also. In 1907, as work on the railroad started, an agreement was executed whereby a half interest in the 5,280 acres would have been transferred to the Guggenheim group upon construction of the railroad. It was also specified that coal would be purchased from the Cunningham group. The railroad was never finished, however. The agreement was probably not binding because not all of Cunningham's associates signed it. No evidence exists to show that the Guggenheim-Morgan syndicate had sought further holdings in the 8,000,000 coal acres of Alaska.[33]

It was the accusations of evil which remained in the public mind, of course; the truth had a fatal flavor of the defensive and was ignored. Characteristically, President Taft took no drastic action until it was too late. It is conceivable that public opinion would have swung sharply to him if, at the start, he had branded Pinchot insubordinate, if he had said that the chief forester had sponsored accusations that were flimsy at the best. Surely many a voice in the nation would have agreed if the President had declared publicly, as he did in private, that to desert Ballinger, who was innocent of

[33] *Joint Committee Report*, pp. 54-55.

wrong, would be the craven act of a "white-livered skunk." Voices are invariably lifted in praise of loyalty, in praise of the man who will not desert a faithful aide merely because political storms darken the sky. "Roosevelt would have come back at those preferring the charges and would by now have them on the run," the President admitted, "but I cannot do things that way. I will let them go on, and by and by the people will see who is right." [34] Thus Taft took an exactly opposite course. The President based his letters of exoneration on September 13, 1909, partly on an opinion drafted by Assistant Attorney General Oscar Lawler. But he rejected Lawler's criticism of Pinchot, which was set forth in this opinion.[35] He did his utmost, instead, to conciliate the fiery conservationist. He wrote a private letter to Ballinger which accompanied the public one:

Please . . . advise your subordinates to be very particular not to involve Mr. Pinchot in this matter and to rest silent in view of the complete acquittal they receive from my letter.

Should it be necessary, as is not unlikely, to submit all this record and evidence to Congress, I shall be glad *to have your authority and that of your subordinates to leave out of your answers any reference to Pinchot* or the part he took in bringing Glavis's report to my attention.

Can Taft have meant that he might go so far as to distort, by such omissions, the evidence to be passed on to Congress? He closed by assuring Ballinger that he had "every confidence in both you and Pinchot . . . you are a lawyer like me and insist on the legal way; while Pinchot is impatient of such restraint." [36] The President did not, in any event, protect his forester by sending censored letters to the joint committee. He told "My dear Gifford" that his name had not been mentioned in the exoneration of Ballinger "because I do not wish to bring you into the controversy at all." The President pledged again his sympathy with the conservation cause.

"I must bring public discussion between departments and bureaus to an end," said Taft, almost pathetically. "It is most demoralizing and subversive of governmental discipline and effi-

---

[34] Butt, Archie, *Taft and Roosevelt*, Vol. I, pp. 235-236. [35] Taft to Knute Nelson, May 15, 1910. [36] Taft to Ballinger, Sept. 13, 1909. (Italics mine.)

ciency. I want you to help me in this. I can enforce teamwork if I can keep public opinion out of newspaper discussion." [37]

Hope that Pinchot might subside grew less bright during the President's tour through the country. He saw the chief forester at Salt Lake City on September 25, 1909; after this, hope began to die out entirely. "I don't know how long I shall be able to get on with him," he telegraphed, that night, to Mrs. Taft.[38] Pinchot was "in a state of mind that I fear will ultimately lead to a break." [39] The President did not act against Pinchot even when he was informed by Wickersham of the impending attacks in *Collier's Weekly*. He felt that "we may exaggerate the importance of the paper's attitude." But he was confident that Pinchot was "at the bottom" of the criticism. He was afraid that "the action that I fear we must take in time." [40] This, of course, was the dismissal of the forester.

On returning to Washington on November 10, Taft found his supporters filled with gloom. They were, he told Archie Butt, "predicting all sorts of evil. One member of the Cabinet tells me that there is a cabal of Roosevelt's friends to force an issue between us and another that Pinchot has got to be dismissed." [41] The President still thought it possible that this drastic and politically perilous step could be avoided. He was annoyed when it was intimated that he did not have the courage to exterminate the troublemaker.

"The fact is, that whether it takes courage or the opposite trait of character," he said in late November, "I do not expect to ask for his resignation." [42]

A final letter of conciliation, again to "My dear Gifford," was dispatched a few days later; the President said that "with some self-restraint we can come out all right in this business." [43] But if Taft possessed this quality to excess, Pinchot had little or none of it.

"Gifford Pinchot is out again defying the lightning and the storm and championing the cause of the oppressed and downtrodden and harassing the wealthy and the greedy and the dishonest," Taft told his brother as 1909, the first of his troubled years, drew to its close.[44]

[37] Taft to Pinchot, Sept. 13, 1909. [38] Taft to Helen H. Taft, Sept. 25, 1909. [39] Taft to Charles Nagel, Sept. 25, 1909. [40] Taft to Wickersham, Oct. 7, 1909. [41] Butt, Archie, *op. cit.*, Vol. I, p. 208. [42] Taft to A. P. Stokes, Nov. 21, 1909. [43] Taft to Pinchot, Nov. 27, 1909. [44] Taft to Horace D. Taft, Dec. 27, 1909.

—5—

The President concluded, not without reason, that Pinchot was more than willing to be dismissed and he would not, he insisted, fall into the trap. He saw a well-planned conspiracy to drive a wedge between himself and Roosevelt and to discharge the chief forester "would only bring about what they are trying to do, an open rupture between Roosevelt and myself. . . .

"I am determined," he told Brother Charles, "if such a rupture is ever to be brought about that it shall not be brought through any action of mine. Theodore may not approve of all I have done and I don't expect him to do so, but I shall try not to do anything which he might regard as a challenge. . . . No . . . I am going to give Pinchot as much rope as he wants and I think you will find that he will hang himself." [45]

Taft was confident that he was in the right. He welcomed the proposal for a Congressional inquiry because he was certain that this would demonstrate the leniency accorded Pinchot.[46] Outward cordiality between Taft and Pinchot lasted for a time. On November 4, 1909, as a result of their conversation at Salt Lake City, Pinchot sent a long letter to Taft. He expressed appreciation of the President's desire that he continue in office. For the moment he would do so. But he did not doubt that Taft had been misinformed regarding the relations of the Interior Department to the conservation cause; Pinchot said he might "find it necessary to make public my opinion as to these relations, even if it should involve separation from my official position." The conservationist then reviewed the coal cases at length. He attacked the position of Ballinger on co-operation with the Forest Service, on water-power sites, on reclamation. The issue, said Pinchot, was the "most critical and far-reaching problem this nation has faced since the Civil War" and Ballinger was the "most effective opponent the conservation policies have yet had." [47]

The ultimate explosion was delayed until the new year. Then Pinchot wrote to Senator Dolliver of Iowa regarding the activities

[45] Butt, Archie, *op. cit.*, Vol. I, p. 245. [46] *Ibid.*, Vol. I, p. 235. [47] Pinchot to Taft, Nov. 4, 1909.

of his aides, Shaw and Oliver, in assisting Louis Glavis. He re-counted their co-operation with the special agent in obtaining publication for his accusations against Ballinger. But this was done only after action "through the usual official channels, and finally even an appeal to the President, had resulted (because of what I believe to have been a mistaken impression of the facts) in eliminat-ing from the government service, in the person of Glavis, the most vigorous defender of the people's interests." Pinchot had no doubt that Shaw and Oliver had "acted from a high and unselfish sense of public duty . . . they deliberately chose to risk their official posi-tions rather than permit what they believed to be the wrongful loss of public property." It was true, he admitted, that they "trans-gressed propriety." It might even be that "they appealed too readily to public opinion." For this, said the chief forester, they "deserved a reprimand" and such had been administered. It was undoubtedly the lightest of chastisements. Pinchot said they deserved no further punishment for the "rules of official decorum exist in the interest of efficient administration and of that alone. When they are used to prevent an honest and vigilant public officer from saving property of the public, their purpose is violated and they have become worse than useless." [48]

This marked the end of all hope. The letter was made public. It was an utterly improper appeal from an executive subordinate to the legislative branch of the government and an unhappy presi-dent prepared to separate Pinchot from public office. Archie Butt was unhappy too. The President looked "haggard and careworn . . . he looked like a man almost ill." No one failed to see the real consequences. Meanwhile Elihu Root had gone through the records of the case.

"There is only one thing for you to do now," he told the President, "and that you must do at once." [49]

The dismissal letter, of course, was calm and judicial. No stirring phrases leaped from it to confound the Pinchot cohorts. But the "My dear Gifford" of previous communications was replaced by an austere "Sir." The "plain intimations in your letter," said the President, "are, first, that I had reached a wrong conclusion as to the good faith of Secretary Ballinger and the officers of the Land

[48] Sen. Doc. 719, pp. 1283-1285. [49] Butt, Archie, op. cit., Vol. I, pp. 253-256.

Office, although you and your subordinates had only seen the evidence of Glavis, the accuser, and had never seen or read the evidence of those accused or the records that they disclosed which were submitted to me." Pinchot's letter, he went on, constituted an accusation that the President and his assistants "would have allowed certain fraudulent claims to be patented on coal lands in Alaska" had it not been for activities of Shaw and Oliver. Taft concluded:

Your letter was in effect an improper appeal to Congress and the public to excuse in advance the guilt of your subordinates before I could act, and against my decision in the Glavis case before the whole evidence on which that was based could be considered. I should be glad to regard what has happened only as a personal reflection, so that I could pass it over and take no official cognizance of it. But other and higher considerations must govern me. When the people . . . elected me president, they placed me in an office of the highest dignity and charged me with the duty of maintaining that dignity and proper respect for the office on the part of my subordinates. Moreover, if I were to pass over this matter in silence, it would be most demoralizing to the discipline of the executive branch of the government.

By your own conduct you have destroyed your usefulness as a helpful subordinate of the government, and it therefore now becomes my duty to direct the secretary of agriculture to remove you from your office as the forester.[50]

"I would not have removed Pinchot if I could have helped it," observed the President, sadly, two or three days later.[51]

—6—

Ballinger demanded a Congressional investigation to pass on the accusations of misconduct and this was authorized on January 19, 1910. Senator Knute Nelson of Minnesota was chairman of the joint committee of six senators and six representatives and the hearings lasted from the end of January until May 20, 1910. Not much light was thrown on the complicated issues although the majority

[50] Taft to Pinchot, Jan. 7, 1910. [51] Taft to C. H. Kelsey, Jan. 10, 1910.

members— who included Root— ultimately ruled on behalf of the Taft administration and Ballinger. One incident occurred, however, which further discredited the President. It grew out of one of the major errors of his incumbency. As in the case of the others, ineptitude was behind it and this was distorted, as ineptitude in public life so often is, into a semblance of evil.

The editors of *Collier's Weekly* were disturbed, as the Congressional investigation started, by a report from Washington that the committee would probably exonerate Ballinger and that a libel suit for $1,000,000 would then be started against the magazine. So a meeting was held at the law office of Henry L. Stimson in New York at which Pinchot, Garfield, Hapgood and several others discussed the peril and concluded to engage Louis D. Brandeis of Boston as attorney for Louis Glavis who would, naturally, be the most important witness for the prosecution. Brandeis's unusual mental gifts enabled him to acquire a detailed working knowledge of the Interior Department, conservation and the other issues involved. He appeared as the attorney for Glavis; nothing was said of his engagement by *Collier's Weekly* at a fee of $25,000 although it is inconceivable that it was not generally known among the members of the committee. Glavis had no funds with which to hire so distinguished an attorney.[52]

The only real sensation of the Congressional inquiry— which otherwise merely passed on evidence already spread before the public— was developed by Brandeis. His sincerity in what he did is not open to question. His fairness, however, was less than complete. On a night while the hearings were in progress, Brandeis told Norman Hapgood that he had made an exciting discovery. This, in substance, was that Attorney General Wickersham had predated the report of September 11, 1909, on which the President had acted, two days later, in upholding Ballinger and dismissing Glavis. This, Brandeis said, was obvious. The report was based on hundreds of pages of technical documents. It seemed impossible that Wickersham could have mastered, in the brief time between the receipt of the documents and September 11, the ostensible date of his report,

[52] Hapgood, Norman, *op. cit.*, pp. 183-186; *Hearings,* Subcommittee of the Judiciary Committee, United States Senate, on Nomination of Louis D. Brandeis to be Associate Justice of the Supreme Court, Part 7, pp. 388-389.

so heavy a mass of evidence. Brandeis told Hapgood that he had calculated the time necessary for a document as lengthy as Mr. Wickersham's summary of the evidence. The attorney general could not have done it in a single week, which was the approximate time allowed him, unless he had given every single working moment to it. But, in fact, he had been pressed with other duties during that week.

To Hapgood and to Brandeis, as the former summarized it in his memoirs, the inference to be drawn was that Taft and Wickersham were trying "to make the public think that, in supporting Ballinger, the Attorney General and the President, instead of a political white-wash, had given to the case an attention which at that time they actually had not given it." But as yet the predating was not proved. Hapgood and Brandeis thought it probable that Wickersham's report had been "prepared in Ballinger's own office, ready for the Attorney General and the President to rubber-stamp." But at this point, Mr. Hapgood recalled, "fate intervened."[53] It took the shape of a stenographer, Frederick M. Kerby, employed in the office of the secretary of the interior. One night in February, 1910, Kerby was brought to Gifford Pinchot's house in Washington and there found Garfield and Brandeis. He said that Assistant Attorney General Lawler had dictated to him a preliminary report for the use of the President. Since Lawler was assigned to the Interior Department and therefore was in close touch with Ballinger, the prosecution then assumed that their charge was proved. Taft had not leaned on Wickersham's analysis. He had used this biased Lawler analysis. To convey this idea to the public, the innocent and apprehensive Kerby was persuaded to talk with a newspaper syndicate. When he protested that he would lose his post as stenographer, as a result, he was promised another position by the syndicate.[54]

"Then," recalled Norman Hapgood, "began in the committee the assault on the administration-defenders that was to be their ultimate destruction."[55] The headlines which charged conspiracy and a predated document coated with whitewash were ugly and, to a public which did not understand the issues, convincing. As always, Taft delayed too long. When he offered his explanation no one

[53] *Ibid.*, pp. 188-189. [54] *Joint Committee Report*, pp. 57-59; Wickersham to author, Jan. 23, 1935. [55] Hapgood, Norman, *op. cit.*, p. 189.

listened. But the explanation, although it reveals that Taft and Wickersham had made a mistake, clearly proves innocence of wrongdoing. The President explained that Lawler had accompanied Ballinger when the secretary of the interior came to Beverly, Massachusetts, on September 6, 1909. The Glavis charges were discussed again on the next night. Taft, pressed for time because of his forthcoming trip, instructed the assistant attorney general "to prepare an opinion as if he were president." During the next three days the President examined the evidence further. On September 12, Attorny General Wickersham arrived at Beverly for the final consultation and brought with him Lawler's opinion:

> During the day I examined the draft opinion of Mr. Lawler, but its thirty pages did not state the case in the way I wished it stated. It contained references to the evidence which were useful, but its criticism of Mr. Pinchot and Mr. Glavis, I did not think it proper or wise to adopt. I only used a few paragraphs from it containing merely general statements.

All that day, September 12, Wickersham had been studying the documents. That night he "reported the conclusions which he had reached," Taft explained, "which were in substantial accord with my own." Thereupon, the President drafted his letter of September 13, upholding Ballinger. Explaining all this, Taft continued:

> The conclusions which I reached were based upon my reading of the record, and were fortified by the oral analysis of the evidence and the conclusions which the attorney general gave me, using the notes which he had made during his reading of the record. I was very sorry not to be able to embody this analysis in my opinion, but time did not permit. I therefore directed him to embody *in a written statement such analysis and conclusions as he had given me, file it with the record, and date it prior to the date of my opinion, so as to show that my decision was fortified by his summary of the evidence and his conclusions therefrom.*[56]

This was a grave error; the appearance of evil, in public life, is often worse than evil itself and explanations are invariably futile.

[56] Taft to Nelson, May 15, 1910.

On October 28, 1909— pausing in Vicksburg, Mississippi— the President acknowledged receipt of the report which Wickersham had meanwhile prepared, had dated September 11, 1909, and had filed with the Ballinger dossier.[57] The incident remained, an unfair cloud on Taft's record, through all the years. In March, 1916, the *New Republic* published a hasty editorial in which was repeated the slur that former President Taft had "antedated a public document in the Ballinger case" and then had deceived the public. Taft, teaching law at Yale, considered the advisability of suing for libel. But Wickersham, whom he consulted, thought it was unwise thus to dignify a weekly with but four or five thousand circulation.

"Certainly neither you nor I thought we were doing anything wrong in formulating the facts we had found in the documents we had before us on September 11, 1909, and the conclusions we reached," he recalled to Taft, "in the form of a memorandum and recommendations actually written after that date, but having dated [*sic*] on the day you promulgated your decision. It remained for the sophistry of a Brandeis to put an immoral construction upon it. I was pilloried in *Collier's,* the New York *Sun* and a large variety of other publications at the time for my share in it, and called by every vituperative epithet applicable to a liar and a forger." [58]

Taft never deceived himself, in 1910, on the real issue. This was the possibility that Theodore Roosevelt, emerging from Africa, would uphold his passionate conservationist. Pinchot made this his main objective. He hurried abroad to lay the facts before his former chief. Hapgood of *Collier's Weekly* sailed for the same purpose.[59] The charge against the President was to be far more sweeping than the Glavis accusations. It was to be that he had turned his back on conservation, so vital a part of the Roosevelt program. At first, however, Roosevelt struggled to be fair. He heard Pinchot's indictment. He was "not yet sure whether Taft could . . . have followed any course save the one he did," he told Lodge in April.[60]

"The Garfield-Pinchot-Ballinger controversy," the President wrote in a letter which reached Roosevelt as he was about to sail from Southampton in June, 1910, "has given me a great deal of

[57] Taft to Wickersham, Oct. 28, 1909. [58] Wickersham to Taft, March 26, 1910; Wickersham to *New Republic,* March 27, 1910. [59] Hapgood, Norman, *op. cit.,* p. 216. [60] Lodge, H. C., *Selections from the Correspondence of Theodore Roosevelt and Henry Cabot Lodge,* Vol. II, p. 237.

personal pain and suffering, but I am not going to say a word to you on that subject. You will have to look into that wholly for yourself without influence by the parties, if you would find the truth." [61]

[61] Taft to Roosevelt, May 26, 1910.

CHAPTER XXVIII

FORGOTTEN CREDITS

W HAT I am anxious now to do," the President wrote in March, 1910, "is to secure my legislation. . . . What I want to do is to get that through, and if I can point to a record of usefulness of that kind, I am entirely willing to quit office."

Taft realized, however, that this was not going to be easy. He had never known a political situation, he continued, "where there has been so much hypocrisy, so much hysteria, so much misrepresentation by the press growing out of their own personal interest in legislation as within the last year." [1] The voters "have a yearning for something startling and radical that we are not likely to furnish them, and they have a degree of suspicion of public men, prompted by muckraking newspapers and magazines." [2]

"I do not know much about politics," was his wistful apology, "but I am trying to do the best I can with this administration until the time shall come for me to turn it over to somebody else." [3]

Taft apologized too much, but his pessimism had basis. The political sky did not grow lighter during the first half of 1910. Theodore Roosevelt was increasingly a source of party confusion. The insurgents were growing stronger. Ominously, in March, a Democrat came out ahead in a special Congressional election in Massachusetts although the district was normally heavily Republican. [4] The President admitted the probability that his party would lose control of the House that fall.

"You describe the feeling among the Republicans as a 'don't care a damn' feeling," he told H. H. Kohlsaat, the Chicago editor. "I have that myself. It is exactly that feeling that I have with reference to the views of the press and of those people who think that they are going to have a better government by defeating the Re-

[1] Taft to H. H. Kohlsaat, March 14, 1910. [2] Taft to Whitelaw Reid, April 7, 1910. [3] Taft to D. K. Watson, May 16, 1910. [4] Taft to J. L. Waite, March 24, 1910.

publican party." [5] Again and again in private letters he expressed his conviction that defeat was certain in 1912, if not sooner. "I can afford to get along on one term . . ." [6] became, in his correspondence, a wearisome and repetitious phrase.

Taft apologized too much. He might, far better, have allowed his mind to dwell on the achievements of his administration. They were to be forgotten in the years immediately ahead. The President never received due credit for the things that he did. But this is not remarkable because it seemed, at times, as though he had forgotten them himself. Among the important items on the credit side of the presidential ledger was the creation of a postal savings system.

It was an old reform. Victor F. Lawson of the Chicago *Herald* pioneered on its behalf in 1897, and it had been recommended by President Roosevelt from time to time. Like all measures relating to finance, however, it had not been a subject of prime interest to Roosevelt. In his message to Congress on December 3, 1907, he said that a postal savings system would "encourage among our people economy and thrift and . . . give them an opportunity to husband their resources." More important still, it would afford a depositary in which confidence would not lapse even in times of financial upheaval; hoarding would thereby largely be eliminated. A year later, Roosevelt again urged passage of the bill. He pointed out that banking facilities were decidedly inadequate in so far as citizens of small means were concerned. Over $3,500,000,000, or 98.4 per cent of the total savings bank funds, were on deposit in only fourteen states. In all the remaining thirty-two states the total was only a little more than $70,000,000, or 1.6 per cent. The result, Roosevelt said, was that people hoarded their money in many communities.[7] The President's statistics were promptly challenged as inaccurate, but they gave an approximate picture of the situation.

[5] Taft to Kohlsaat, March 14, 1910. [6] Taft to G. W. Mallon, Jan. 13, 1910. [7] Roosevelt, Theodore, *Presidential Addresses,* Vols. VII, VIII, pp. 1550, 1947.

—2—

No action was taken during the Roosevelt years. Postal savings banks were endorsed in the 1908 Republican platform. President Taft, in his inaugural address, expressed a hope that Congress would promptly fulfill this pledge.

"It will not," he said, "be unwise or excessive paternalism. The promise to repay by the government will furnish an inducement to savings which private enterprise cannot supply and at such a low rate of interest as not to withdraw custom from existing banks. It will substantially increase the funds available for investment as capital in useful enterprises." [8]

The President's reassurance was for the benefit of the nation's bankers. But those gentlemen did not violate their tradition of opposing with energy nearly all progressive legislation. The Savings Bank Section of the American Bankers Association organized a Committee on Postal Savings Banks and circulated, toward the end of 1909, a broadside assailing the plan. The alarm of the bankers was extreme. Their committee declared that an investigation "by competent businessmen and publicists" had demonstrated that the demand for a postal savings system was a "political creation" which grew out of the panic of 1907. No actual need for it existed. The bankers could find no redeeming feature whatever in the plan. Thrift, they said, would not be encouraged, because the private banks were already doing everything possible to stimulate it. The system was not necessary, even in rural districts, because "banks are being established in all sections practically as fast as there is need for them."

The committee also pointed to the inevitable dangers of postal savings banks. They would "draw funds to large commercial centers, thereby interfering with local development." In periods of financial stress, "timorous depositors would withdraw their funds from regular banks . . . and by so doing would add materially to the crisis; . . . the South, Southwest, Middle and Northwest and West would be overrun with bandits," because post offices "are probably the most fertile field for robbery." To safeguard against

[8] *Addresses*, Vol. XIV, p. 4.

this the government would have to put burglarproof safes in 40,000 post offices which "would in itself cost millions." Besides, there would be "innumerable opportunities for theft among the thousands of clerks whom it would be necessary to employ at Washington in order to make the entries of deposits, withdrawals and corrections." Finally, the banks would be a haven for debtors and tax dodgers. The former could put their money in the post-office banks with assurance that it would be "beyond legal process." The latter could withdraw their money from regular banks at tax time and hide it in postal banks where it could not be taxed, "thus raising the tax rate on real estate in every locality." It was "beyond human credulity," concluded the warning, "to suppose that politicians," thus entrusted with millions of dollars of the people's money, would not speculate with the funds.[9]

President Taft declined to share the consternation of the financiers. "I am sorry to oppose the bankers in this matter," he said in September, 1909, "but I really think it would be wiser for them to come in." [10] At Milwaukee, on September 17, he denied the contention that postal savings marked the death of individualism:

. . . it is said that the postal savings bank is a very paternalistic institution; that it has a leaning toward state socialism. . . . Now I am not a paternalist, and I am not a socialist, and I am not in favor of having the government do anything that private citizens can do as well or better, . . . [But] we have passed beyond the time of . . . the laissez-faire school which believes that the government ought to do nothing but run a police force. We do recognize the interference of the government because it has great capital and great resources behind it.

The President's case was convincing. He pointed out that some $8,000,000 in money orders had been purchased at post offices the previous year by men who did not know what else to do with their hard-earned dollars. On this money, of course, no interest had been paid; the purchasers had actually paid a fee so that the government would guard their savings. Newly arrived aliens, moreover, had sent abroad in the same period about $90,000,000 to be deposited in

[9] Committee on Postal Savings Banks, American Bankers Association, Dec. 27, 1909.
[10] Taft to Pierre Jay, Sept. 19, 1909.

the postal savings systems of European nations; all this capital had been lost to the United States. Taft denied that the proposed interest rate of two per cent would draw funds from the private banks. On the contrary, the man who learned how to save at the post office would, in due time, withdraw his money and obtain the three per cent or more paid by the established savings institutions.[11]

The special session called for tariff reform did not take up the matter. President Taft again urged enactment in his December, 1909, message to the Sixty-first Congress [12] and it was made a subject for immediate consideration. More lay behind Taft's support than mere belief that such a system would help the poor man to save. Distrust of the nation's banks had led to laws in Oklahoma, Kansas, Nebraska and South Dakota whereby those states guaranteed bank deposits. This was universally criticized as unsound in that it would encourage careless banking. The fact that it had been recommended by William Jennings Bryan in the campaign of 1908 must have been enough to condemn it in Taft's mind. Postal savings, he felt, might halt the spread of such heresy.

Argument in Congress centered largely on the investment of the funds deposited in the post-office banks. Senators Bristow, Cummins, LaFollette and others among the insurgents fought for a provision that the money could be redeposited by the government in local banks only. The President, annoyed, threatened a veto. "The insurgents," he said, "were utterly oblivious to the importance of maintaining the credit of the government, or of doing anything except filling the coffers of the country banks with these collections." [13] In its final form the bill created a Board of Trustees— the postmaster general, the secretary of the treasury and the attorney general— with wide discretionary powers. As a working policy, the money deposited in the postal banks was, however, largely turned over to financial institutions in the vicinity.[14]

President Taft signed the measure on June 25, 1910. "I am as pleased as Punch," he exulted when the bill, in an approved form, emerged from the Congressional mill.[15] "It is one of the great Congressional enactments. It creates an epoch," he boasted.[16] This was

[11] *Addresses,* Vol. XV, pp. 37-44. [12] *Ibid.,* Vol. XVII, p. 35. [13] Taft to Longworth, July 15, 1910. [14] Kemmerer, E. W., *Postal Savings,* pp. 19-35, 40-41. [15] Taft to Bannard, June 11, 1910. [16] Taft to W. B. McKinley, Aug. 20, 1910.

true. The postal savings bill was a first-class piece of constructive legislation. Taft's victory marked the termination of a forty-year struggle for such a system. Eight postmasters general had recommended it. Similar plans had been in operation for decades in nearly every other civilized country. But the American Bankers Association, until now, had been able to block it.

The dire predictions of the bankers failed, with one exception, to materialize. The country was not subjected to a crime wave. The postal savings accounts, limited at that time to $500 and bearing but two per cent, served as feeders to private banks and did not compete with them.[17] Deposits grew rapidly, from $43,000,000 in 1914 to $1,180,000,000 in 1933. It appears to be true, however, that savings did flow into the federal system when the banking structure gave signs of collapsing after 1929. The deposits in 1931 were less than $350,000,000. They more than doubled the following year. Then they soared to over a billion dollars. On the other hand, most of this money would doubtless have been hoarded during the panic years.

—3—

Taft was consistent in the method by which he advanced his program in 1909 and 1910. ". . . with the assistance of my wicked partners, Cannon and Aldrich," he confided to Horace Taft in March, 1910, "I am hopeful that I can pull off the legislation that I have most at heart." He continued, too, his hostility toward the progressives. "Cummins, LaFollette, Dolliver, Clapp and Bristow," he added, "are five senators who are determined to be as bitter as they can against the administration, and to defeat everything that the administration seeks. Their method of defeat is to attempt to load down the legislation with measures so extremely radical that the sensible members of Congress won't vote for them, or that I shall have to veto if they come to me." [18]

The President felt that his own method was an effective compromise between conservative inaction and progressive unreliability. It had brought forth, in addition to postal savings, a tax on corpo-

[17] Kemmerer, E. W., op. cit., p. 77. [18] Taft to Horace D. Taft, March 5, 1910.

rate incomes. This, it will be recalled, had been reluctantly approved by Aldrich and Cannon during the debate on the Payne-Aldrich tariff bill in the summer of 1909. Actually, it developed, additional sources of government revenue were not necessary.[19] Taft was heartily in favor of the corporation tax. "I had Wickersham draft a bill," he remembered. "The things that were required in the bill were two: first, the tax as an excise tax upon corporations, and, second, a certain degree of publicity with reference to the returns. That publicity gives a kind of federal supervision over corporations, which is quite a step in the direction of similar reforms I am going to recommend at the next session of Congress, and with which Senator Aldrich has pledged himself to help me." [20] The President found no merit in the contention that a tax on corporations was discriminatory as compared with partnerships or single individuals. "The justification for the distinction," he said, "arises from the advantages which the business enjoys under a corporate form." Chief among these advantages were the limited liability of share owners and the fact that a corporation went on after the death of the current owners. Most of all, the President approved of the corporation tax because ". . . it . . . incidentally will give the federal government an opportunity to secure most valuable information in respect to the conduct of corporations, their actual financial condition." Such matters were now cloaked in secrecy, he pointed out; even stockholders found it difficult to get information to which they were entitled. The evidence accumulated by the tax collectors was to be kept secret unless otherwise ordered by the President.[21]

To the nation's industrialists, obviously, this was another long step toward socialism, and their protests were vehement. Taft denied that they were justified.

"So far as the feeling of the corporation men against me in that connection is concerned," he observed, "I will have to stand it." [22]

Suspicion on the part of the progressives that Taft had advanced the corporation tax to block a new income tax was without foundation. On this, too, he had made his views clear during the

[19] *Addresses,* Vol. XV, p. 115. [20] Taft to Horace D. Taft, June 27, 1910. [21] *Addresses,* Vol. XV, pp. 121, 126. [22] Taft to Tawney, Feb. 15, 1910.

closing days of the tariff fight in 1909.[23] The corporation tax was significant because it marked another victory in the slow march of government against entrenched privilege. The President had been badly informed when he was told that probable deficits required new taxes. Business was getting better. A deficit of $58,000,000 for the fiscal year ending June 30, 1909, had become a surplus of $28,000,000 in hardly more than twelve months. To this, also, Taft pointed with pride. It proved, he said, not only that the corporation tax was an efficient method of raising money; it also demonstrated that imports under the Payne-Aldrich tariff were increasing.[24]

—4—

Pioneers in reform win public applause; the less spectacular men who follow in their footsteps and consolidate those reforms are comparatively unknown. This was another basic reason why the accomplishments of President Taft have been forgotten. He chose his role deliberately. In his acceptance speech in the summer of 1908 he said that the "chief function of the next administration . . . is to complete and perfect the machinery by which the lawbreakers may be promptly restrained and punished." The machinery, he added, "is not now adequate." It was not adequate, for instance, with respect to the railroads of the nation and their operators.

Theodore Roosevelt had pointed with pride to the Hepburn act of 1906 as an important victory in his warfare on corporate evil. But Roosevelt, as he so often did, had compromised with true righteousness in permitting Congress to pass a bill far less strong than the legislation he had urged in his December, 1905, message. At that time he had favored a law which would "summarily and effectively prevent the imposition of unjust or unreasonable rates" by the carriers.

"It's only a railroad law you want," accused Lincoln Steffens, "not to cut the railroads out of the government." For once, Roosevelt had no reply.[25]

The Hepburn act was, however, a step forward. It gave juris-

[23] Addresses, Vol. XV, pp. 126-127. [24] Taft to McKinley, Aug. 20, 1910. [25] Pringle, H. F., Theodore Roosevelt, a Biography, p. 424.

diction over railroad rates and other aspects of transportation to the Interstate Commerce Commission. But Roosevelt had bowed to conservative pressure which eliminated wholly his original demand for summary power to bar unreasonable rates. The law permitted the courts to issue injunctions against the rulings of the commission; the result, of course, was long-drawn-out litigation and small relief for the public.

This, then, was one of the Roosevelt reforms to be completed and made more effective by President Taft. On August 20, 1909, Attorney General Wickersham began a three-day conference in New York with Chairman Martin A. Knapp of the I.C.C., Representative Townsend and Secretary of Commerce Nagel.

"We all recognized the fact," Mr. Wickersham reported to the President, "that, under the present workings of the law, many of the important orders of the commission which pecuniarily affect the railroads, or which they *think* will pecuniarily affect them, are suspended by injunctions . . . and there is a consequent prolonged delay; so that the benefits anticipated from the passage of the Hepburn act have not yet been realized."

The attorney general recommended, in substance, enactment of the bill which had originally passed the House of Representatives in Roosevelt's administration and which, prior to its emasculation, minimized what he termed "improvident injunctions." Mr. Wickersham urged also: giving power to the I.C.C. to act on its own initiative in rate cases instead of only on the complaint of shippers; that it have authority to postpone the date on which new rates went into effect; that the commission be given general supervision over the issuance of railroad bonds and stocks. As an even more essential change, he suggested that a special tribunal, perhaps to be called the Commerce Court, be established with jurisdiction to review and enforce the orders of the I.C.C.; this power was now in the hands of the district and circuit courts. The only appeal from the Commerce Court would be directly to the Supreme Court of the United States.[26]

This was to be the Taft program on railroad regulation. Interest in it was heightened by an announced intention of the carriers to increase their tariffs.[27] Bills were introduced after the President, on

[26] Wickersham to Taft, Sept. 2, 1909. [27] S. M. Felton to Taft, Jan. 4, 1910.

524 THE LIFE AND TIMES OF WILLIAM HOWARD TAFT

January 7, 1910, sent a special message to Congress in which he reviewed at length the operations of the Interstate Commerce Commission laws. The message went somewhat further than the Wickersham proposals. The President recommended that the I.C.C. supervise the construction of ladders, running boards, hand brakes and other devices to ensure the safety of railroad workers. He also suggested, "in view of the complete control over rate making" given by the proposed legislation to the federal government, that the railroads be permitted to make tariff agreements among themselves. This had been forbidden by the Sherman act.[28]

The protests against the reform were prompt. The ubiquitous National Association of Manufacturers was, of course, immediately recorded in opposition. It was unkind enough to quote a speech made by Circuit Judge Taft in 1895 in which he had deplored the attempts "to cut down their [the federal courts'] jurisdiction and cripple their efficiency." [29] President Taft denied, however, that he was overruling Circuit Judge Taft. The bill merely embodied, he said, "what is the best practice pursued by the best chancellors of experience and actually adopted by some of the federal courts." [30]

The railroads of the west then announced increases in freight rates. While Congress debated the administration bill, the President and his attorney general considered plans for blocking them. They would go into effect on midnight, May 31. Taft and Wickersham conferred on the afternoon of that day. Thereupon, with only a few hours to spare, an injunction was obtained at Hannibal, Missouri, on the ground that the western roads had combined in the framing of the schedules and had thereby violated the Sherman act.[31] The railroad heads announced loudly that they would fight the suit. On June 6, however, they agreed to compromise. They promised not to raise rates until the new legislation had been passed and the Interstate Commerce Commission possessed authority to pass on the reasonableness of the increases. In return, the government would not press for prosecution under the antitrust laws. Taft won a temporary victory and for a time even the insurgents in Congress praised him.[32]

---

[28] *Addresses*, Vol. XVII, pp. 81-85. [29] J. T. Hoile to Taft, March 9, 1910. [30] Taft to R. H. Moon, March 8, 1910. [31] New York *Times*, June 1, 1910. [32] *Ibid.*, June 2, 7, 1910.

The President was not dismayed by criticism which also resulted. He agreed, he said in answer to one critic, that the provision for supervision of railroad securities "will interfere with the building of railroads in the West, in so far as the building of railroads is dependent on the issuing of stock for nothing or for less than its par value. . . .

"But I wish to call your attention," he added, "to what is the fact, that this was the principle that carried in the Republican platform, and I must assume that the party thought it out well. It is one which I personally approve. I think we have reached a time now in the development of this country when we can afford to be more conservative, and not permit such conditions, even at the risk of slower development in railroad construction, as were shown in the . . . transactions of Mr. E. H. Harriman." [33]

But Taft, too, was forced to compromise. It was apparent, by the end of June, that the voice of the railroad magnate was still mighty in the halls of Congress. The bill which resulted, the President reported, "does not contain what I should like to have it contain, to wit, the clauses restricting the issue of stocks and bonds by interstate railroads, and making it subject to the supervision of the Interstate Commerce Commission." The insurgents were powerful in Congress too. The section which seemed sensible to the President— permission for strictly regulated roads to make rate agreements— had been eliminated at their demand. On the other hand, the I.C.C. now had the power to undertake physical valuation of the lines. This was essential, naturally, to any intelligent fixing of rates, and it was a cause for which Senator LaFollette, so often accused of demagogy by Taft, had been contending for years.[34] All that was needed was an appropriation by Congress.

Best of all, the new law authorized the appointment of a Commerce Court. President Taft realized that this would accelerate the adjudication of disputes between shippers and the carriers. Its members, he remarked, would be "especially versed in the principles and precedents controlling the application of the interstate commerce law.

"Expedition in the settlement of suits is what we need, and we

[33] Taft to V. L. Mason, March 26, 1910. [34] Taft to Wharton Baker, June 11; to J. A. Sleicher, June 21, 1910.

are woefully behind in it in the administration of justice generally; but I believe this Commerce Court is going to make the work of the Interstate Commerce Commission much more effective than ever before." The President reviewed, with satisfaction, other progressive aspects of the new law. The I.C.C. could investigate rates on its own motion. It could fix reasonable ones. It could change freight classifications, a favorite device of the railroads for hiding increases. It could suspend the operation of higher rates until their fairness had been determined.[35] Amendment of the Interstate Commerce law was, according to the President, second only to the corporation tax among the accomplishments of the Sixty-first Congress. As an afterthought he noted that telephone and telegraph lines were now under supervision of the I.C.C.; these, however, were still relatively unimportant in 1910. The general public used them rather little.[36]

The President of the United States presented a bill of particulars on his own behalf in the summer of 1910. He described to Representative William B. McKinley, chairman of the Republican Congressional Committee, the accomplishments which entitled the administration to a vote of confidence that fall. He had been faithful, for instance, to the Roosevelt program of two additional battleships.[37] He had followed, too, his predecessor's policy of maintaining the fleet as a unit. This had been the cornerstone of Admiral A. T. Mahan's naval strategy. Mahan had been Roosevelt's mentor on naval affairs; back in 1901 he had voiced warning that division of the fleet was folly.[38]

". . . my judgment," echoed Taft in 1909, "is that the strength of our navy is the union of all the fighting material at one point, and that when we need it in the East, we will need it all there. The construction of the Panama Canal in this light is of the highest importance."[39]

His administration, the President also pointed out, was entitled

---

[35] Taft to Longworth, July 15, 1910. [36] Taft to McKinley, Aug. 20, 1910. [37] *Idem*, Aug. 10, 1910. [38] Pringle, H. F., *op. cit.*, p. 409. [39] Taft to H. S. Brown, April 1, 1909.

to the support of labor because "all classes of employees, especially those engaged in occupations more or less hazardous, are the beneficiaries of laws which should operate to lighten the burdens which naturally fall on the shoulders of man." One of these laws had created a Bureau of Mines which would cut down the "awful losses of life in the operation of mines." The "most forward step" taken by Congress in social legislation, Taft said, had been the "creation of a Congressional commission to report a practical bill for the fixing of compensation for injuries received in the employment of interstate railways." This, he was confident, would terminate the endless litigation whereby an injured worker was so often denied justice.

The President did not mention the Ballinger-Pinchot controversy in his plea for a vote of confidence. He did, however, declare that he had been true to the principles of conservation; that is, the preservation of forests, the reclamation of arid lands, the proper treatment and disposition of coal, oil and other natural resources. He said that during the Roosevelt years— this was the first public criticism of Theodore Roosevelt and it was faint, indeed— "millions of acres of lands . . . were withdrawn in the United States proper and in Alaska, in order to await proper legislation." But doubt had arisen "as to the executive power to make these withdrawals." So Taft, the man of law, had requested and received from Congress authority to continue, but with unclouded legal right, the same policy. The administration had done even more than this to remedy dubious execution of a worthy cause. It had obtained authorization for a $20,000,000 bond issue for irrigation projects. Steps had also been taken to complete a survey of the public domain.

Taft claimed credit for progress toward the admission of New Mexico and Arizona as states. A law had been passed, too, requiring Congressional committees to account for their election expenditures. The President concluded his summation by describing "one of the most important parts of the administration's policy." This was an attempt to cut down the "national expenditures by the adoption of modern economic methods in doing the business of the government." [40]

". . . the main features of each bill," boasted the President as

[40] Taft to McKinley, Aug. 10, 1910.

he looked back on his accomplishments, "were foreshadowed in my annual message, in speeches I had made before Congress met, and in the bills which were especially prepared by my direction for the consideration of Congress." [41]

To a degree, the President received recognition for what he had done. It was, however, of brief duration. Charles Willis Thompson, who was one of the Roosevelt favorites among the Washington correspondents, informed his newspaper that the President had "somehow managed to produce more results than anybody else who has sat in his chair since the Civil War." Thompson said that a "fighting Taft" was ruling. Sometimes his "jaw . . . sets in grimness and his blue eye . . . flashes fire." Furthermore, he declared, no truth lay in the accusation that Taft had been subservient to Aldrich and Cannon.[42]

President Taft had included, in his letter to Representative McKinley, the Rivers and Harbors bill as a credit item. He was, though, less confident that this measure was wholly good. The bill would cost the taxpayers $52,000,000. Taft realized, he told McKinley, that it had been drawn up under the "old piecemeal system and appropriated something for nearly every project recommended by the army engineers." [43] The bill had, in the early spring of 1910, aroused wide condemnation. The Springfield *Republican* was among the journals which urged a veto of this pork-flavored act; it remarked that "so strong an exercise of executive power would do more than anything Mr. Taft has done . . . to impress the public imagination." [44] William L. Ward, the New York Republican leader, wrote virtuously that among the details in the act was the improvement of a river which would add $200,000 to some property he owned; none the less, the bill should be vetoed.

"You added wonderfully to your prestige when you fixed up the railroad situation," Boss Ward said. "You made another ten stroke [*sic*] when you took the stand you did relative to labor . . . but the vetoing of the river and harbor bill will put the party in such a position that I can confidently promise you a Republican House this fall." [45]

[41] Taft to Longworth, July 15, 1910. [42] New York *Times,* June 26, 1910. [43] Taft to McKinley, Aug. 10, 1910. [44] C. H. Poe to Taft, May (?), 1910. [45] W. L. Ward to Taft, June 24, 1910.

President Taft debated for ten days the wisdom of rejecting the bill.

"It will make me very unpopular with many congressmen," he wrote, "and a good many of them will think me ungrateful when they have stood by my legislation, in not signing a bill which gives each district a bit of pork and will help the congressman to return. . . . I am very much troubled about it. I am not sure what I ought to do." [46] He decided to pass out the pork, and signed the bill.

The President transmitted to Congress a message explaining why he had done so. It was because many improvements, seriously needed, were included. But he warned Congress that the "uneconomical method of carrying on these projects" should be remedied before another such bill was presented. Yet the defects in the measure at hand did not justify postponement of all this work.[47] Such a postponement, he told Boss Ward, "would greatly injure the public interest." [48] Among the telegrams of approval was one from the organizers of the Ohio Valley Exposition, whose headquarters were in Taft's beloved Cincinnati. To them, it was the "best bill ever framed." [49]

Some of these problems must have bored Taft profoundly; he was, after all, not much interested in tariffs or taxation or, despite Cincinnati, in the improvement of the Ohio River. But his absorption in the federal judiciary in general, and in the Supreme Court in particular, was complete. On the credit side of the Taft ledger belongs, too, his sincere attempt to elevate the quality of judicial appointments. He can be criticized, perhaps, for the ultimate conservatism which some of them revealed. But Taft's industry in searching for the best men is beyond dispute. He did not hesitate, either, to express criticism of existing jurists. President Taft, as his term in the White House started, had an opinion of the Supreme Court beside which the epithets of Andrew Jackson seem complimentary.

"The condition of the Supreme Court is pitiable, and yet those old fools hold on with a tenacity that is most discouraging," he confided to his old associate, Circuit Judge Lurton. "Really the Chief Justice [Melville W. Fuller, who was seventy-six] is almost senile;

---

[46] Taft to Helen H. Taft, June 24, 1910. [47] *Addresses,* Vol. XIX, pp. 71-75. [48] Taft to Ward, June 27, 1910. [49] M. C. Graber *et al.* to Taft, June 27, 1910.

Harlan [Associate Justice John M. Harlan] does no work; Brewer [Associate Justice David J. Brewer, who was seventy-two] is so deaf that he cannot hear and has got beyond the point of the commonest accuracy in writing his opinions; Brewer and Harlan sleep almost through all the arguments. I don't know what can be done. It is most discouraging to the active men on the bench." [50]

"It is an outrage," he told Cabot Lodge in September of the same year, "that the four men on the bench who are over seventy should continue there and thus throw the work and responsibility on the other five. This is the occasion of Moody's illness [William H. Moody, a stripling of only fifty-six who had been appointed by Roosevelt]. It is with difficulty that I can restrain myself from making such a statement in my annual message." [51]

President Taft had personal as well as official reasons for his irritation. Chief Justice Fuller, by his unreasonable longevity and his refusal to retire, had kept Taft, himself, from appointment to the highest judicial office in the summer of 1905. But the President refrained from presenting the issue to Congress. Had he done so he might— this is mere speculation— have ensured a Republican Congress in 1910 and his own re-election in 1912. For in the uproar which would surely have resulted the issues between the insurgents and the die-hard Republicans might have been forgotten. The evils of the Payne-Aldrich act might have been ignored.

Taft heard in October, 1909, that Associate Justice Rufus W. Peckham was suffering from an acute heart ailment and might die at any time. Associate Justice Edward D. White sent word that the "condition of the court is such that any vacancy which occurs ought to be filled at the earliest possible moment." [52] Peckham died on October 24, 1909. Thereupon the President, having deplored the senility of the highest court less than four months earlier, illogically proceeded to appoint a rather elderly judge, Lurton of the Federal Circuit Court. Taft had great respect for Judge Lurton's legal talents. But it seems probable that affection born of years of association on the circuit bench was also a motivating influence. Attorney General Wickersham protested. He told the President that opposi-

---

[50] Taft to Lurton, May 22, 1909. [51] Taft to Lodge, Sept. 2, 1909. [52] Wickersham to Taft, Oct. 13, 1909.

tion had developed on the court itself and among members of the bar.

"He says," the President noted, "I was elected by the people for a number of reasons, but one of the chief reasons that led to the support of the bar . . . was that I would be conscientious in the selection of judges to build up that great court to the place that it formerly occupied and that if I appoint Lurton, so soon to be seventy years of age, I shall sacrifice the needs of the country and the needs of the court to a personal feeling."

It was all "very distressing." The attorney general said that the appointment should go to a man not older than fifty-five who could give fifteen years of service before he, too, might be unable to keep awake. Taft answered that these suggestions "tore my heart strings . . . there was nothing that I had so much at heart in my whole administration as Lurton's appointment." [53]

Less serious, in Taft's mind, were objections from Samuel Gompers and other labor leaders who called Lurton a narrow conservative. His answer was that he had been eight years on the bench with Lurton and knew there was "no more liberal-minded man . . . that he would no more do injustice to the laboring man than he would to anybody else." [54] Taft hesitated for a fortnight in an attempt to decide whether Lurton's years were a basic disqualification. By the end of December he decided they were not. He would appoint Lurton. It was the "chief pleasure of my administration" to do so.

"I never had any other purpose," he told the judge, "and was never shaken in it until there was presented to me the challenge whether I was not gratifying my personal desires at the expense of public interests. . . . For this reason I took back my determination to appoint you . . . and gave two or three days to the introspective process to know whether I was yielding to personal preference and affection. I became convinced that I was not." [55]

In 1910 death did its duty, although tardily, in rejuvenating the Supreme Court. Associate Justice David J. Brewer— "so deaf that he cannot hear" had been Taft's indictment of him— was the first to go. The President, in April, offered the post to Governor

[53] Taft to J. M. Dickinson, Dec. 6, 1909. [54] Taft to W. S. Carter, Dec. 16, 1909. [55] Taft to Lurton, Dec. 26, 1909.

Hughes of New York. He was aware that reasons "would suggest themselves against your acceptance and I do not minimize them. I believe as strongly as possible that you are likely to be nominated and elected President sometime in the future unless you go upon the bench." Moreover, as Governor, Hughes had policies to be carried to completion. Finally, Mr. Hughes was certain, in private practice, of an "income which will make you independent in ten years":

1. To these suggestions, I would reply that if you prefer a judicial to a political life, you might as well take the step now.
2. If you accept, you need not qualify as justice or resign the governorship until the second week of October which would leave but two months and a half of your term remaining.
3. The position is for life. The salary is $12,500 and will in all probability be increased to $17,500. The chief justiceship is soon likely to be vacant and I should never regard the practice of never promoting associate justices as one to be followed. Though, of course, this suggestion is only that by accepting the present position you do not bar yourself from the other, should it fall vacant in my term.

Let me hear from you. I make this offer first because I know you will strengthen the bench as a lawyer and a jurist with a great power of application and second because you will strengthen the bench in the confidence of the people.

The President apparently decided, before sending this letter, that he had been a shade unwise in intimating that Hughes would become chief justice when Fuller died: "Don't misunderstand me as to the chief justiceship," he added in a postscript, "I mean that if the office were now open, I should offer it to you and it is probable that if it were to become vacant during my term, I should promote you to it; but, of course, conditions change so that it would not be right for me to say by way of promise what I would do in the future. Nor, on the other hand, would I have you think that your declination now would prevent my offering you the higher post, should conditions remain as they are." [56]

Governor Hughes promptly accepted the appointment. He told

[56] Taft to Hughes, April 22, 1910.

MRS. TAFT AND THE PRESIDENT; SHORTLY AFTER HIS INAUGURATION

TAFT THE SPORTSMAN

[*See page 450*

the President that his tastes were judicial, that the Supreme Court offered the greatest opportunity for expressing them, that in contrast the mere acquisition of wealth at the bar had no attraction whatever. As for the presidency, the governor brushed this possibility aside with the observation that the future was ever conjectural. Regarding the chief justiceship, Hughes was as tactful as he was suave. He fully realized that the President must reserve entire freedom. He must make his decision when the time came; without embarrassment and in accordance with his best judgment.[57]

—6—

Chief Justice Fuller died on July 4, 1910, but Hughes, who had not yet taken his seat on the bench, did not become chief justice until two decades had passed and he then succeeded Taft, himself. The influences which caused President Taft to change his original intention of selecting Hughes are not clear. It may be that his 1907 judgment of the New York governor as a "man without magnetism" was a factor. Theodore Roosevelt, who had branded Hughes a "very, very self-centered man," [58] was among those who opposed his elevation and brought about, instead, the promotion of Associate Justice Edward D. White.

The President gave "prayerful consideration" to the matter for months.[59] First, however, Associate Justice Moody was forced, by ill-health, to resign from the bench. He was one of the younger, more active members and Taft called this a "heavy loss to the nation." [60] In Moody's place, the President put Willis Van Devanter who became, in due time, one of the most bitter foes of President Franklin D. Roosevelt's New Deal policies. Meanwhile, the search for a chief justice went on. The possible selections, in addition to Hughes and White, included Senator Root and Secretary of State Knox. Knox, it would appear, did not receive very serious consideration.[61] But Elihu Root, under whom Taft had labored as governor general of the Philippines and who had been a fellow member of

---

[57] Hughes to Taft, April 24, 1910. [58] Leary, J. J., Jr., *Talks with T. R.,* pp. 52-53. [59] Taft to L. S. Overman, Oct. 12, 1910. [60] Taft to Moody, Oct. 4, 1910. [61] Max Pam to Taft, Oct. 31, 1910.

Roosevelt's Cabinet, seemed eminently qualified, save for his age. The President could not know, of course, that Root would live for more than a quarter of a century and that the edge of his keen intelligence would not be dulled through all the years. Root, in 1910, was sixty-five years old.

"I don't hesitate to say to you confidentially," Taft told Chauncey Depew, "that if Mr. Root were five years younger I should not hesitate a moment about whom to make chief justice . . . but I doubt if he has in him that length of hard, routine work and constant attention to the business of the court and to the reform of its methods which a chief justice ought to have. This is my chief . . . reason for not deciding to appoint him." [62]

These were arduous duties which faced the President. "I am having more of a burden of responsibility in respect to the selection of judges than any president since Washington," he pointed out. "I may say in passing that it has come to be the fashion to institute comparisons with Washington, so you will pardon me this little reference." [63]

The Supreme Court, itself, was not silent regarding this appointment of first importance. On a July afternoon soon after Chief Justice Fuller's death, the President summoned the members of his Cabinet who were lawyers. The court, he told them, appeared to favor the promotion of an associate justice. Word had reached the White House that Associate Justice Harlan— the one who "does no work," according to Taft's earlier attack on the older members— thought he should receive the elevation as a final ornament to his judicial career. His retirement would soon come. But the suggestion angered the President.

"I'll do no such damned thing," he exploded to Knox, Wickersham and the other advisers who were present. "I won't make the position of chief justice a blue ribbon for the final years of any member of the court. I want someone who will co-ordinate the activities of the court and who has a reasonable expectation of serving ten or twenty years on the bench."

Attorney General Wickersham was then delegated by the President to inquire among the justices of the Supreme Court and determine their preferences. He reported that Associate Justice White

[62] Taft to Depew, Oct. 15, 1910. [63] Taft to J. B. Cumming, Nov. 1, 1910.

was the court's first choice. He pointed out that White, in addition to being a Democrat and a Confederate veteran, was a Roman Catholic. Mr. Wickersham said that he did not, himself, consider either allegiance a reason against White's appointment. A degree of criticism was certain to follow, however. Taft replied that he would not take bigotry into account at all.[64] Besides, his admiration for White went back to his own days as a judge. In 1894, receiving word that White had been appointed to the federal bench, Circuit Judge Taft had written that he was a "very good man and will make a first-class judge . . . he is a man of high courage and ability." [65]

The exalted prize was slowly slipping from Hughes. Taft gave no sign that he remembered the praise he had voiced the previous April. The President received word that Roosevelt, interviewed in New York, had declared that the "promotion of Justice White would be the best possible thing." The President was also informed that the colonel would be distinctly displeased if the appointment went to Hughes.[66]

Taft had made up his mind by early December, 1910. "I have decided whom I will appoint chief justice," he told Assistant Secretary of the Treasury Charles D. Hilles, "and in doing so I have driven another nail in my political coffin." [67]

Actually, it was a very popular appointment. "If Taft were pope," growled Uncle Joe Cannon, "he'd want to appoint some Protestants to the College of Cardinals." [68] But the Bar was virtually unanimous in its approval. No one was in the least disturbed by this precedent of "moving over" an associate justice to the center of the bench. The Senate confirmed the nomination of Chief Justice White on December 12, 1910. Later that day Attorney General Wickersham sat with the President as the commission came to him for his signature. Taft picked up a pen.

"There is nothing I would have loved more than being chief justice of the United States," he mourned. "I cannot help seeing the irony in the fact that I, who desired that office so much, should now be signing the commission of another man." [69]

Taft's regret must have been heightened by the difficulties and

[64] George W. Wickersham to author, Jan. 23, 1935. [65] Taft to Helen H. Taft, Feb. 21, 1894. [66] Amassa Thornton to Taft, Nov. 25, Dec. 1, 1910. [67] Memorandum by Hilles for United States History Association. [68] Horace D. Taft to author, July 12, 1935. [69] Wickersham to author, Jan. 23, 1935.

disappointments he had already experienced. He no longer pretended that more than formal harmony, based on expediency, was possible with Roosevelt. From Beverly, Massachusetts, in September, 1910, the President outlined his troubles in a long letter to Charles P. Taft. He was not optimistic as to the future. But there was one thing, he said, that "neither the insurgents nor the active statesman of Oyster Bay, nor anyone else, can prevent." This was the thirty months of his term which remained.

"I shall have the appointment of probably a majority of the Supreme Court before the end of my term, which, in view of the present agitation in respect to the Constitution, is very important," he noted, with satisfaction.[70]

Lurton, Hughes, Van Devanter and White in 1910; Joseph R. Lamar in 1911 and Mahlon Pitney in 1912: these were Taft's appointments to the Supreme Court. They constituted, as he had hoped, a majority of the court. It was consoling, in the turbulent days of the 1912 campaign, for him to realize that the six stanch jurists would protect the Constitution from attacks by Roosevelt and other progressives. They would, he knew, be a bulwark even if Roosevelt, by some unhappy chance, was the victor in the campaign. Among the first duties of a Supreme Court jurist, Taft had said in 1910, was to "preserve the fundamental structure of our government as our fathers gave it to us." [71]

President Taft may have weighed conservatism too heavily in his judicial appointments. But he did not allow the stain of political expediency to discolor any that he made. This never failed to be a source of satisfaction to him. He looked back on it, with pleasure, when the joyous day of his own appointment as chief justice arrived. He was walking soon afterward toward the Capitol from his home and was joined by Josephus Daniels, secretary of the navy under Woodrow Wilson. Their conversation turned to the Taft years.

"Did you keep up with my appointments to the federal bench during my term as president?" Taft asked.

Mr. Daniels replied that these had been particularly appreciated in the South. Taft answered that he had chosen so many Democrats because they were the "outstanding lawyers in their states." Mr. Daniels repeated that Mr. Taft's action had been appreciated. He

[70] Taft to C. P. Taft, Sept. 10, 1910. [71] Taft to Moody, Oct. 4, 1910.

was, he said, highly esteemed by the Democrats of the South. The Taft chuckle began to bubble at this point.

"Yes," he said. "I am sure the southern people like me. They would do anything except vote for me." [72]

[72] Josephus Daniels to author, Dec. 17, 1934.

CHAPTER XXIX

THE HUNTER RETURNS

EVERYTHING is on the *qui vive* for the return of the Hunter,"
wrote the adoring and yet troubled Archie Butt on Easter
Sunday in 1910.[1] For Theodore Roosevelt would soon be
back from his triumphs in Africa and from his even greater
triumphs among the crowned heads of Europe. He was coming
home to learn at first hand whether the President he had created
was the foe of conservation, of the insurgents who stood for liberalism and of "my policies"; in short, a foe of righteousness
itself.

The President's chief aide was a very distressed young officer
as the arrival of Roosevelt grew closer in the spring of 1910.
He almost worshiped Theodore Roosevelt. But William Howard
Taft was now his president. His loyalty was complete. And for
Taft he felt, too, both admiration and warm affection. So Butt
was in a fretful mind on this Easter Sunday. The President "looks
very badly," he told his sister-in-law. "He is white-looking and
his pallor does not seem healthy. . . . I wish he would not tie
himself to his desk as he does. . . . It is hard on any man to
see the eyes of everyone turn to another person as the eyes of the
entire country are turning to Roosevelt." [2]

If possible, the President was even unhappier than his anxious
subordinate. He knew that Gifford Pinchot would be pouring a
tale of woe into Roosevelt's ears. Yet, how, when Pinchot had
been deliberately and flagrantly insubordinate in the Ballinger
row, could he have done otherwise than dismiss him? Taft knew,
also, that Roosevelt would hardly have landed in New York
before the insurgents of Congress would be complaining that the
President had supported Cannon, Aldrich and others of the Old
Guard. Yet had not Roosevelt specifically advised him to keep

[1] Butt, Archie, *Taft and Roosevelt,* Vol. I, p. 313. [2] *Ibid.*

the peace with Uncle Joe? Had not Roosevelt, too, used the senatorial strength of Aldrich to advance his causes?

Sometimes the presidential temper was strained as he pondered on these injustices. Criticism of Roosevelt was not absent from his private letters. ". . . no demoniac shrieks of Rooseveltphobia . . . will have the slightest influence upon what I do or say," he had declared as far back as November, 1909.[3] Stubbornness was growing within Taft, too. He returned from his transcontinental tour at this same time to find "everybody full of despair and predicting all sorts of evil." He was told that a cabal of Rooseveltians was conspiring to wreck his administration.

"But I have done nothing," the President insisted, "that I would not do over again, and therefore I must feel that their troubles are either imaginary or else someone else is to blame." [4]

During the next four months Taft's bitterness increased. So did this vein of stubbornness. He deplored the situation but had "given up hope of changing it."

I am going to do what I think is best for the country, within my jurisdiction and power, and then let the rest take care of itself. The misrepresentations which are made by the muckraking correspondents I cannot neutralize, and I don't intend to. . . . It may be — it probably is so— that we are living in a period of hysteria in which it is easy to make the better appear the worse, and, if so, I shall have to stand the result. It is sufficient honor to have been once president of the United States . . . even though the things done are not appreciated. . . . I am schooling myself to bear the shafts of criticism, whether proceeding from a hostile feeling, contemptuous indifference or patronizing friendship.[5]

Nor did Taft absolve Roosevelt, whom he had so greatly loved, of responsibility. The times, he wrote, "are a little out of joint at present, and there is a hysteria that is the aftermath of the crusade that Mr. Roosevelt preached. . . . That hysteria forms an atmosphere in which anything asseverated with sufficient emphasis, without proof, will be believed about any man, no matter how disinterested or high his character." [6]

[3] Taft to Loeb, Nov. 15, 1909. [4] Butt, Archie, *op. cit.,* Vol. I, p. 208. [5] Taft to J. H. Cosgrave, Feb. 23, 1910. [6] Taft to G. A. Copeland, Feb. 9, 1910.

—2—

Still, no martyr complex took root in Taft's heart. His criticisms of Roosevelt nearly always gave way, before long, to a conviction that his friend and benefactor would surely see the truth in time. On an evening in April some old Cincinnati friends were at the White House. The President talked frankly. He did not believe that Roosevelt would seek the nomination in 1912 but he would "most certainly be elected" if he did:

If he comes to Washington I shall discuss with him most frankly every act of the administration, and even should he have committed himself to Pinchot, I have no doubt but that he will change his mind after he learns the facts from me or Root in conversation.

It is a strange contradiction in Roosevelt's nature, but he has no pride of opinion at all. He does not mind how often he changes his mind if he thinks there is some reason for doing so. I have known him to commit himself to some proposition in the morning and reverse himself five times before evening. But each change was the result of some new information rather than the result of indecision.[7]

The President had sympathy, too, for the perplexities which would confront Roosevelt when he returned. He saw them more clearly than did most men; more clearly, indeed, than did Roosevelt himself. "I really feel sorry for him," Taft said. "His role is even more difficult than the one I have to play. Every man with an ambition, every new movement, will try to drag to him . . . and whether he will be able to keep out of it all I don't know."[8] Roosevelt did not know, either, how to keep out of it all when, on a morning in June, he stepped ashore and heard the applauding thousands.

Resentment against Roosevelt may have been increasing, but Taft did not cease to hope that all might yet be well. He made gestures of amity and good will— perhaps too many gestures for a man in his high place— as though to prove that all the talk of friction was but malicious gossip. Thus, toward the end of 1909,

[7] Butt, Archie, *op. cit.*, Vol. I, pp. 327-328. [8] *Ibid.*, Vol. I, p. 335.

he appointed Major General Wood to the highest command in the army. "I have decided to make Wood chief of staff," he admitted, "simply because I know that Roosevelt was anxious to have it done. With Loeb at the head of the customs in New York and Meyer at the head of the navy, and with Wood at the head of the army, I do not see that I am open to the charge that I am anti-Roosevelt." [9]

"I am glad," the President told Wood, "to feel that in making this order I am doing that which will gratify not only myself but President [*sic*] Roosevelt." [10]

Some of the gestures were trivial. Before leaving the White House, Roosevelt had filed with Taft a memorandum of the men who had been "stanch adherents" in the campaign of 1908. Among these was Seth Bullock, a frontiersman, whom Roosevelt had met on one of his western jaunts. The President retained Bullock as a federal marshal in South Dakota "in view of my obligation to President [*sic*] Roosevelt." [11] In April, 1910, Taft was informed by President Pagliano of the port of Maurizio, in Italy, that Roosevelt had arrived there en route from the jungle and had been received with due honors.

"I beg to assure you and all your countrymen," Taft cabled, "that the American people are very grateful for the reception . . . accorded to our most distinguished citizen." [12]

Taft's expressions of warmth toward Roosevelt were frequent; it is impossible to doubt their sincerity. On February 15, 1910, Mrs. Roosevelt sailed to join her husband in Europe and Taft telegraphed an expression of good will.

"Please convey to President [*sic*] Roosevelt my congratulations on the wonderful success of his African trip," he said. "His articles and book will lighten up the Dark Continent."

In all these communications, it will be noted, Roosevelt was still "the President" to Taft. Archie Butt saw this and was worried by it. "A man of tremendous personality himself," the chief aide said in one of his letters, "he still lives in the shadow of that other personality. . . . He is so broad as to show no resentment

---

[9] *Ibid.*, Vol. I, p. 236. [10] Taft to Wood, Dec. 20, 1909. [11] Taft to R. J. Gamble, Jan. 14, 1910. [12] Taft to Pagliano, April 10, 1910.

even if he feels it, and I am inclined to think he feels none whatever." [13]

—3—

The day of Roosevelt's arrival grew closer. Taft extended still
another olive branch on May 10 when he requested Roosevelt to
serve as "special ambassador to represent the United States at the
funeral of King Edward VII." He said that the "English people
will be highly gratified at your presence in this capacity, and . . .
our own people will strongly approve it." [14] Meanwhile, too, the
President was preparing a tribute to be published in the *Outlook* in
June. The return of the hunter, this said, "ought to arouse and
will arouse as great a demonstration of welcome as any American
ever received." Taft pointed out that Roosevelt had expected to
tour Europe as a private citizen; instead, "his path from the time
he landed . . . has been a royal progress, and the courtesy and
attention . . . shown him . . . have not been equaled since Grant
made his tour about the world." Roosevelt's association with the
rulers of Europe, the President suggested, "has given him an in-
sight into world politics that will make him still more valuable
to his country as a statesman." [15]

During February, Taft had considered a gesture more extreme
than all the rest. A committee in charge of the reception to Roosevelt had suggested that he go to New York and extend a welcome
in person. Butt noted, with disapproval, that "he is inclined to
do so" and was hesitating only because this gesture might lower
the dignity of his office. The President was also apprehensive that
it might be regarded as an attempt to placate Roosevelt. William
Loeb, who had been Roosevelt's private secretary, finally dissuaded
Taft. He warned that "it will be a T.R. day and there will be
no other note sounded." So Archie Butt would go in his place and
would carry with him a letter of welcome. [16]

An earlier letter had already started on its way to Roosevelt;
the most poignant letter, perhaps, among all the untold millions

[13] Butt, Archie, *op. cit.,* Vol. I, p. 278. [14] Taft to Roosevelt, May 10, 1910. [15] Taft
to Lyman Abbott, June 7, 1910. [16] Butt, Archie, *op. cit.,* Vol. I, pp. 278, 281.

that presidents of the United States— so often bothered and troubled men— have written. Taft drafted it in his own hand on May 26, 1910. It constituted, in effect, a report on the victories and the defeats of his administration. But behind the words was a plea— more eloquent because it was scarcely expressed— for understanding, sympathy and appreciation. To the "ifs" of history must be added still another: if Roosevelt had been capable of just a little more patience, if Roosevelt had been able realistically to view the difficulties of another man, if Roosevelt's loyalty had been a more rugged loyalty— if all these things had been true, a vast amount of heartbreak for one man and ultimate failure for a second might have been avoided.

"It is now a year and three months since I assumed office and I have had a hard time," declared Taft in one paragraph of his letter. "I do not know that I have had harder luck than other presidents but I do know that thus far I have succeeded far less than have others. I have been conscientiously trying to carry out your policies, but my method of doing so has not worked smoothly. . . . My year and two [*sic*] months have been heavier for me to bear because of Mrs. Taft's condition. A nervous collapse, with apparent symptoms of paralysis that soon disappeared, but with an aphasia that for a long time was nearly complete, made it necessary for me to be as careful as possible to prevent another attack. Mrs. Taft is not an easy patient and an attempt to control her only increased the nervous strain. Gradually she has gained in strength and she has taken part in receptions where she could speak a formula of greeting, but dinners and social reunions where she has had to talk she has avoided."

This was a curious document. At other times and to other men, the President had been satisfied enough with the progress of his administration and had specified its accomplishments. It was only now, as he addressed his former chief, that defeatism overcame him. The letter began with an explanation that he had not written since Roosevelt had sailed for the jungles "for the reason that I did not wish to invite your judgment on matters at long range or to commit you in respect to issues that you ought perhaps only to reach a decision upon, after your return to the United States."

Then the President cited the things he had done and which he yet hoped to do.

The Payne-Aldrich tariff act, for instance, while "not as radical a change as I favored," was "a good bill and a real downward revision." Its revenues had been "remarkable." However, "it did not cut low enough the rate on print paper and so we have had a hostile press, and this whether Republican or Democratic." But Taft insisted that it was an excellent law, doubly useful because it gave the government added control over the nation's large industries. Continuing his report, the President remarked that Congress was still debating the issue of railroad regulation. He predicted, however, that the administration's bill would pass. The postal savings bank measure would be approved. The chief conservation bill was also due for enactment. Statehood for New Mexico and Arizona would be granted. Salutary legislation for the protection of railroad workers had already gone through both houses. Yet the gloomy aspects of the picture, more than these bright spots, lingered in Taft's mind as he wrote.

"We have had a period of high prices, not produced by the tariff because the increases occur only where the tariff has been decreased or not changed," he wrote. "But the argument *post hoc propter hoc* is as formidable in a political controversy as ever. It is likely to lose us the next House which will not be an unmixed evil. . . .

"The fight for a year to move on and comply with our party promises has been a hard one. LaFollette, Cummins, Dolliver, Bristow, Clapp and Beveridge, and I must add Borah, have done all in their power to defeat us. They have probably furnished ammunition enough to the press and the public to make a Democratic House. Whether they will bring on a Democratic administration in three years remains to be seen."

This, of course, was a warning. More accurately, it was an appeal that Roosevelt turn a deaf ear, when he arrived, to the arguments of all these insurgents who would surely declare that Taft had betrayed their hopes. If only Roosevelt would lean on Nicholas Longworth, his son-in-law, and Elihu Root instead! Longworth was sound. He was complacently untouched by the trend toward insurgency.

Shortly before Roosevelt returned, Longworth gave a degree of reassurance to Archie Butt. His father-in-law had promised him the "first twenty-four hours of his return to America," Nick said. Roosevelt would "get an unbiased statement of the political situation as it appears to me."

"Nick," asked Archie, "can you reconcile all the things which Pinchot is now doing with the Pinchot we knew during the last administration? I can't."

"That," the Ohio congressman answered, "is one of the things I want to steer the President [sic] right on." [17]

Taft was aware of Longworth's support. Nick had, wrote the President in his long letter to Roosevelt, "been doing yeoman service in the House. His speeches on the tariff have been far and away the best." Furthermore, "Root has gone abroad and will doubtless see you. He has been of great assistance to me in the hard trials I have had and I hated to let him go."

The appeal closed with an invitation to come to Washington and stay at the White House, an invitation which Roosevelt would decline.

By this time— May, 1910— Root had already conferred with Roosevelt. He had, even before then, written the colonel at some length. It was an objective letter, dated February 11, 1910. "The change," he said, comparing the two administrations, "has been a good deal like that from an automobile to a cab. Taft is big and good natured and easy going. . . . He is making a good President . . . but he has not yet altogether arrived. . . . Altogether the administration has had anything but a smooth path. A good many of the so-called insurgents are talking Roosevelt against Taft and you will have to be pretty careful when you get here . . . not to say things that have meanings ascribed to them that you have never thought of."

This was supplemented in early June by a personal interview with Roosevelt in which the colonel, it appears, promised to be good. Years later Root walked past the hotel where it had taken place and remembered the conversation.

". . . if he had done as he promised me— kept out of things

[17] Butt, Archie, op. cit., Vol. I, pp. 383-384.

political— we would have been spared much of our past trouble," he recalled.[18]

—4—

Taft's letter reached Roosevelt just before he sailed. On June 8, 1910, in London, he dictated a hasty reply. It was not in Roosevelt's nature to be unmoved by an appeal. It was true, too true, he replied, that Taft had had a hard time in the White House.

"I saw Root the other day," he wrote, "and had with him an hour's talk, altogether too short and yet very satisfactory— as a talk with Root almost always is. I do not know the situation at home. *I am, of course, much concerned* about some of the things I see and am told; but what I have felt it best to do was to say absolutely nothing— and indeed to keep my mind as open as I kept my mouth shut! Fortunately, here in Europe, there has been ample on which I could think and talk."

Mrs. Roosevelt and himself, he added, were aware that the "sickness of the one whom you love most has added immeasurably to your burden. We have followed with the greatest concern the news of her trouble, and feel very genuine pleasure at learning how much better she is. Will you give her our warmest regards."

It was a friendly enough reply which Roosevelt sent to Taft. But underneath the apparent warmth, none the less, the President must have discerned a faint frigidity. "My dear Mr. President" was the salutation— but this could be explained by Roosevelt's high respect for the office and by his devotion to etiquette in White House matters. The signature, however, was "Most sincerely yours"— this from the man who for years had signed himself "affectionately," who had called Taft "dear old fellow." [19]

And yet this exchange of letters must have done at least something to clear away the clouds of misunderstanding which kept each of these well-intentioned men from appreciating the viewpoint of the other. Each had felt hurt at supposed neglect, nearly wholly imaginary, on the part of the other. Taft protested, for instance, to Chief Aide Butt that Roosevelt had not written him

[18] Root to Roosevelt, Feb. 11, 1910; Jessup, P. C., *Elihu Root*, Vol. II, p. 160.
[19] Roosevelt to Taft, June 8, 1910. (Italics mine.)

while abroad. He said that the colonel had not replied to the letter sent to the S.S. *Hamburg* in March, 1909, nor had even acknowledged the bon voyage gift which had accompanied it. Here Taft was in error. Roosevelt had sent two telegrams from the steamer, via the pilot, in which he had expressed his appreciation and a conviction that the administration would be a success. On his part, Roosevelt brooded that no word from Taft had greeted him when he emerged at Khartoum from his conquest of the African fauna. Further, a newspaper correspondent had encountered Roosevelt at Rome. He said he had called on Taft in Washington. But the President had not even inquired concerning Roosevelt's health.[20]

Another source of Taft-Roosevelt friction was the President's failure to retain Henry White as American ambassador at Paris. White had been one of Roosevelt's particular enthusiasms. "Of all the people in Europe you are the man in whom I have the most implicit trust," he had written in October, 1908. It had been assumed that he would be continued at Paris or transferred to London when Taft was elected. The termination of his services was one of the matters clumsily handled by the new President. On March 4, 1909, Taft instructed Secretary of State Knox to request White's resignation. But prior to that time he had told both Roosevelt and Cabot Lodge that White would be kept in office. Roosevelt so informed White in the summer of 1909.

"It was not, of course, a promise any more than my statement that I would not run for president again," he added, a shade ominously.[21]

That Taft blundered is beyond doubt. That he banished White because of an ancient grudge— this was the version widely circulated in 1909 and certainly believed by Roosevelt— is far less clear. The story, in brief, is that White was an attaché at the London embassy when, in 1886, Mr. and Mrs. Taft arrived there on their honeymoon. Taft asked White to obtain seats for a Parliament debate. The attaché could not do so for some reason and sent, instead, tickets to inspect the royal mews.

[20] Butt, Archie, *op. cit.,* Vol. I, pp. 364, 366-367. [21] Nevins, Allan, *Henry White,* pp. 290, 299.

"The Tafts never forgot the incident," wrote Allan Nevins in his life of White.[22]

This is possibly true. Taft told Butt a somewhat different version. He recalled that he had requested certain favors of White when, as secretary of war, he was in London with Mrs. Taft. They had been granted in a most grudging manner, the President said.[23] The Tafts, in any event, did not have a high opinion of White. During his mission to Rome in 1902, Governor General Taft heard that White was seeking promotion. He would not object if the aspiration was thwarted, he wrote his wife, because White "is such an infernal snob and toady."[24] Similarly, Charles P. Taft wrote from London in 1903 that he had not even bothered to call at the embassy because of his dislike.[25] It is not wholly credible, however, that a minor incident of years before was the sole motivation for Taft's action as president. It is mentioned in none of his letters. Taft appears to have had no idea that White regarded the request for resignation as anything but a routine change in the foreign staff.

Nor did White give indication of pique, either. In a friendly exchange of letters in May, 1909, the President expressed warm regard and said he was sending, as the ambassador had requested, a photograph of himself.[26] Taft was astonished when he heard that White was another reason for Roosevelt's growing hostility.

"I had no idea that his heart was set on Harry White," he protested. "If I had known it I would not have relieved White, but I supposed I was doing exactly what he approved when I put Bacon [Robert Bacon, a classmate of Roosevelt and assistant secretary of state under him] in White's place, because Bacon is one of the men whom he has always praised to the skies."[27]

—5—

The hostility faded momentarily into the noisy background of the official welcome for Roosevelt. A logical explanation for the

[22] Nevins, Allan, *op. cit.,* p. 299. [23] Butt, Archie, *op. cit.,* Vol. I, p. 285. [24] Taft to Helen H. Taft, June 7, 1902. [25] C. P. Taft to Taft, July 12, 1903. [26] Taft to White, May 13, 1909. [27] Taft to C. P. Taft, Sept. 10, 1910.

magnitude of the celebration is that it was planned by enemies of Taft. But no evidence exists to support the theory. The plans had been formulated by May 25, 1910, although Roosevelt would not arrive until June 18 on the *Kaiserin Augusta Victoria*. Grandstands had been erected at the Battery. A naval parade would go down the bay to meet the steamer. A medal had been struck to commemorate the occasion. Twelve vice-commodores would be in command of the flotilla which would greet the hero who had escaped the lions of Africa.[28]

Behind the noisy background, behind the bands and banners and solemn fat men in silk hats, were forces and influences still only half felt. The world had moved on a little since 1870, when clever men had pushed their railroads across the prairies and then, by their speculations, had helped to bring on a panic three years later. Men were out of work in 1910. They were out of work or, too often, they slaved until exhausted for inadequate wages. But they were not quite so desperate as they had been in 1894 and had listened to the cure-alls of General Jacob S. Coxey or William "Coin" Harvey and had cheered, two years later, for William Jennings Bryan. The world had moved on a little— but it was only a little.

So discontent lay behind the noisy background and would inspire, to a marked degree, the enthusiasm for Theodore Roosevelt. The unrest was different, though, from the unrest of 1873 or 1893 or 1896. Now it was political rather than economic. The people had been ruled by the educated few. They had been ruled by the greedy corrupt. They had been ruled by the banks and by the industrialists. Now they were groping for the right to rule themselves. Vast numbers of them would turn to Roosevelt, who had declared that big business and even the courts must not interfere. And in many a city shrewd politicians were watching to see whether it would be wise to cast their fortunes with him.

Having concluded that he could not go to New York, himself, President Taft delegated Archie Butt as his representative. He also instructed Secretary of the Navy Meyer and Secretary of Agriculture Wilson, both of whom had served under Roosevelt, to meet the *Kaiserin Augusta Victoria*. The S.S. *Dolphin* was assigned to

[28] New York *Times*, May 25, 27, 1910.

the official party by the Navy Department. On June 14, as though he had not already done enough, the President wrote a second letter, to be delivered by Captain Butt. In this he renewed his plea for Colonel and Mrs. Roosevelt to visit the White House. He expressed apprehension that the "pressure on you for some time to appear in public will be so great as to be a burden, and I judge from what I see that you may have accepted invitations which you would be glad now to be rid of." Again, he reported on the progress of administration measures in Congress.

". . . we shall have redeemed all of our pledges except the injunction bill," he pointed out, "which I am sure we can pass at the next session."

The President was now somewhat more optimistic concerning the November elections. Conditions had changed since his last letter and he would not "now be surprised if the vote were very close." The letter ended with expressions of cordial welcome and the "earnest hope that you may soon gain your hoped-for rest and quiet." The hope was even more earnest on Taft's part, perhaps, than on Roosevelt's. Mrs. Taft, at Captain Butt's suggestion, wrote a note to Mrs. Roosevelt. The chief aide was extraordinarily busy as a peacemaker on the eve of Roosevelt's arrival.[29]

The *Kaiserin Augusta Victoria* moved to the anchorage at Quarantine on the morning of June 18 while harbor whistles tore the air. Butt and the other members of the official party clambered aboard.

"Mr. President, I have a letter from the President," said Archie, saluting stiffly, "which I am charged to deliver at once."

Roosevelt ripped it open, read it hastily. "Please say to the President," he answered punctiliously, "that I greatly appreciate this letter and that I shall answer it later; also say to him that I am deeply touched that he has chosen to send it by you."

So the hunter returned. But for once it was a noncommunicative Roosevelt. Nicholas Longworth, who also came on board the steamer, was able to learn little or nothing. Cabot Lodge, very much worried over his senatorial prospects, gained no hint of what to expect. Secretary of Agriculture Wilson— he was privileged because he was an old man and had been in Roosevelt's Cabinet

29 Butt, Archie, *op. cit.,* Vol. I, p. 393.

for seven years— had a lengthy conversation with the colonel. He told Roosevelt that the administration was in complete harmony with his own. He pointed out that President Taft had carried into execution nearly every policy which Roosevelt had advocated. But the hunter remained a sphinx.

"Wilson," he said, "you must expect no comment from me. These things may be so, but I will make no comment or criticism for at least two months."

So there was little, of either cheer or discouragement, which Butt could carry back to the White House. On the following day he wrote an account of the historic occasion. It was a typical Butt description; wordy, overenthusiastic, faintly ridiculous in spots. But it contained one brief sentence concerning Roosevelt which was wiser, by far, than the military aide knew.

"He is bigger, broader, capable of greater good or greater evil, I don't know which," he noted.[30]

Roosevelt answered Taft's second letter promptly. This, too, shed very little light. He did not think it wise for an ex-president to come to the White House or even to go to Washington. He greatly appreciated the welcome in New York. He was being deluged with invitations to appear in public and was trying to avoid them.[31] Captain Butt, worrying again when he was shown this communication, concluded that Roosevelt was not going to the capital "for some ulterior reason that does not show in the letter itself." He knew, as everyone knew, that ex-presidents were constantly in Washington.[32]

—6—

Within four days after landing at New York, Roosevelt had broken his pledge that he would be silent for sixty days; at that, the four days probably constituted a record for taciturnity. He had asked that the newspaper correspondents remain away from Sagamore Hill. But when they came he talked, of course. He said, among other things, that no truth lay in the assertion that

[30] *Ibid.*, Vol. I, pp. 393-405. [31] Roosevelt to Taft, June 20, 1910. [32] Butt, Archie, *op. cit.*, Vol. I, p. 411.

he was opposed to the direct primary, a subject of current discussion in New York political circles. Anybody who attributed hostility to him was, he swore, a fit candidate for the Ananias Club, that fraternity of blessed memory to which liars had been consigned.[33] Before ten days had passed he had conferred with Gifford Pinchot and Senator LaFollette, whose opposition to the Taft administration was the ultimate in bitterness. LaFollette, leaving Oyster Bay, had declared his pleasure over the meeting. He had found the colonel "in fighting trim." Beyond question, he was the "greatest living American." [34]

Perhaps Roosevelt did not know it; more probably, he knew and could not help it. But in those ten days he had taken fatal steps down a path from which there was no turning. It would lead to friction in the Republican convention of 1912, to the break with his party when Taft was nominated, to the Bull Moose campaign and to ultimate defeat. Had Roosevelt refrained from the fatal steps he would almost surely have been nominated for president in 1916. He would, in all human probability, have made a far better campaign than Charles Evans Hughes, and would have been elected. But Taft, who was also to be defeated in 1912, had the last laugh. In 1917 Roosevelt's health was bad. The United States had entered the war. Woodrow Wilson, whom he detested, was in that place of high command which he might, himself, have occupied. At about this time, Taft was asked whether he would not again make overtures of peace.

"I have no hard feeling toward Theodore," he answered. "And if I had— I certainly could wish him no worse luck than to be sick in bed while Woodrow runs his war." [35]

For once the Taft chuckle was sardonic. That was years later, when a large measure of peace had come to him and the troubles of the presidency were hardly more than a vanishing bad dream. In June and July, 1910, as he read the dispatches from Oyster Bay, Taft was troubled and resentful. "The sage at Oyster Bay," he said impatiently, "is keeping the people in doubt as to just what he proposes to do." [36] He was anxious that Washington should not

[33] New York *Times*, June 23, 1910. [34] *Ibid.*, June 26, 28, 1910. [35] Pringle, H. F., *op. cit.*, p. 596. [36] Taft to Clarence Edwards, July 27, 1910.

also become a source of excited rumors and denials. He asked his official family to be careful in what they said.

"You may have noted," he wrote in a cautionary letter to Dickinson, Wickersham, Meyer and the others, "that there are a good many interviews being held at Oyster Bay with the insurgents and others and that sometimes authentic statements are made and sometimes statements that are not authentic— or at least statements made one day are denied he next. I think it is very important that nothing should be said on the subject one way or the other by either myself or any member of the Cabinet for the present. It is just as well to wait until the situation shall *open* itself; at least, we do not desire to create any situation. We may very well content ourselves with standing upon our record until circumstances arise calling for further action." [37]

Congress adjourned on June 25 and the President, believing himself entitled to satisfaction over its accomplishments, went to the Capitol to sign the final bills. Solicitor General Lloyd Bowers accompanied him. Members of Congress, preparing to hurry to their homes, paused to say farewell. But Taft was disturbed that none of the insurgent senators had bothered to do so. Beveridge, LaFollette, Dolliver and the rest did not appear. Borah of Idaho was in the room, but he did not speak to the President.

"Bowers," said Taft as they drove away, "did you notice the utter absence of the insurgent senators . . . ? I don't give a damn. If they can get along without me, I presume I can do the same without them." [38]

The time had not arrived, though, for a break with the insurgents or with Roosevelt, toward whom they looked as prophet. Outward harmony, at the least, was essential. A congressional campaign was about to start and things were bad enough. So Taft, resting at Beverly from the heat of Washington, agreed to receive Roosevelt on June 30, 1910. He must have dreaded the meeting, but he strove to be fair. That morning the President pointed out that Roosevelt "has some friends who are enemies of mine and expect him therefore to initiate an attack on my administration. I have no reason to suppose that he is going to do so." [39] Nor did the

[37] Taft to Dickinson *et al.*, July 7, 1910. [38] Butt, Archie, *op. cit.*, Vol. I, p. 414. [39] Taft to Hulbert Taft, June 30, 1910.

attack come at this time. A truce was arranged so that the G.O.P. might have some chance of victory in the fall.

No chronicle except that by Archie Butt is available for a description of the meeting between Roosevelt and Taft on June 30. But the one written by the White House Boswell is, as always, detailed and complete. Butt tried to be optimistic as he waited on the porch at Beverly for Roosevelt. He stood there with Jimmy Sloan of the secret service. The meeting, he said, would end all the stories of enmity. But Sloan, who prided himself on his realism, dissented.

"It does not mean anything," he said. "I know this man [Roosevelt] better than you do. He will come to see the President today and bite his leg off tomorrow."

The ex-President did not come to the meeting alone. He brought with him Cabot Lodge, who for personal reasons was urging a return to active politics. Butt notified Taft as their motor turned into the driveway. The President hurried out, with that paradoxically quick, light step with which so many stout men seem to defy gravity. He stretched out both hands.

"Ah, Theodore, it is good to see you," he said.

"How are you, Mr. President? This is simply bully," said Roosevelt.

They strove manfully to carry it through with a light touch. The President struck Roosevelt on the shoulder: "See here, now, drop the 'Mr. President.'"

"Not at all," answered Roosevelt. "You must be the President and I am Theodore. It must be that way."

Even now, however, Taft could not quite achieve this. The atmosphere chilled a little. He did not call Roosevelt "Theodore" again. When Roosevelt complained once more— it was almost as though he was rebuking a child for forgetting the rules of a game being played— Taft gestured helplessly.

"The force of habit is very strong in me," he said. "I can never think of you save as Mr. President."

The interview was less than successful because neither of the two men could quite face the ordeal of being left alone with the other. Lodge informed Captain Butt that such was Roosevelt's wish. Taft felt the same way. So Lodge, Butt and the President's secretary conversed together. The political situation in New York was touched upon. Conversation lagged until Taft suggested that Roosevelt recount his experiences in Europe. Then the colonel launched into a graphic account of his adventures with the Kaiser, King George of England, the King of Italy and other crowned heads. He held forth on his low opinion of their abilities. He told his stories well, of course, and Taft's laughter boomed. Finally Roosevelt arose to go. It was agreed that the waiting newspaper correspondents should be told that it had been merely a social occasion, that it had been wholly delightful.

"Which is true as far as I am concerned," Roosevelt said.

"And more than true as far as I am concerned," said Taft. "This has taken me back to some of those dear old afternoons when I was Will and you were Mr. President."

He could never return to those days of tranquil security. They were as remote and impossible to recapture as are the comfortable days of infancy in troubled adult years.

"Well, Archie," said the President after Roosevelt left, "that is another corner turned. I think he felt just as I did . . . that it was best not [to] give any opportunity for confidences which might be embarrassing." [40]

40 Butt, Archie, *op. cit.,* Vol. I, pp. 414-431.